Tolley's Equal Opportunities Handbook

by

Martin Edwards and Michael Malone

Tolley

A member of the Reed Elsevier plc group

Published by
Tolley
2 Addiscombe Road
Croydon Surrey CR9 5AF England
020 8686 9141

Typeset in Great Britain by
Phoenix Photosetting, Chatham, Kent

Printed in Great Britain by
Redwood Books, Trowbridge, Wiltshire

ISBN 075450 238–4

Contents

Contents

Contents

Table of Statutes

Table of Statutory Instruments

Table of Cases

Table of Cases

1 Acts of Discrimination

1.1 THE STATUTORY PROVISIONS

The *Sex Discrimination Act 1975* (*SDA 1975*), the *Race Relations Act 1976* (*RRA 1976*) and the *Disability Discrimination Act 1995* (*DDA 1995*) each define the acts and omissions which fall within the definition of discrimination and then state the respects in which it is unlawful for employers and others to discriminate.

Each of the three statutes imposes obligations on:

(*a*) employers;

(*b*) trade unions;

(*c*) employers' organisations; and

(*d*) trade and professional associations.

The great majority of discrimination cases are brought against employers and it is such cases which will be used for the purpose of most of the definitions and examples in this book. Rights against employers are given to:

(*a*) job applicants and other potential employees;

(*b*) employees; and

(*c*) contract workers.

The *DDA 1995* differs in the following respects from the *SDA 1975* and the *RRA 1976*:

(*a*) a different definition of discrimination;

(*b*) the additional duty to make *Reasonable Adjustments*;

(*c*) the exemption for employers with fewer than 15 employees.

The *SDA 1975* and the *RRA 1976* also go further than the *DDA 1995* in that they apply to:

(*a*) the armed forces;

(*b*) employment on some ships and aircraft; and

(*c*) police, prison and firefighting services.

The *SDA 1975* and the *RRA 1976* also give rights to partners and those who wish to become partners, so long (in the case of the *RRA 1976*) as the firm consists of six or more partners.

Employers must not discriminate against job applicants (whether under the *SDA 1975*, the *RRA 1976* or the *DDA 1995*) in any of the following respects:

(*a*) in the arrangements for deciding who should be offered employment;

(*b*) in the terms on which employment is offered; or

(*c*) by refusing or deliberately omitting to offer employment.

Employers must also, in all these respects, have regard to the duty to make *Reasonable Adjustments*.

The rights given to job applicants and the corresponding obligations placed on employers are dealt with under *Recruitment, Selection* and *Job Interviews*.

1.1 Acts of Discrimination

Selection and *Job Interviews* are also relevant to the rights which are given to existing employees. Employers must not discriminate against them in the way in which they are afforded access to opportunities for promotion, transfer or training.

There must also be no discrimination by employers in relation to:

(*a*) pay;

(*b*) other terms of employment; or

(*c*) other benefits, facilities or services.

Claims about pay and other contractual terms generally fall under the *Equal Pay Act 1970* (*EPA 1970*) rather than the *SDA 1975*. The demarcation between the two Acts, and the way in which the *EPA 1970* operates, are explained under *Pay, Equal Pay* and *Terms of Employment*.

There must also be no discrimination against an employee by:

(*a*) dismissing him or her; or

(*b*) subjecting him or her to any other detriment.

The duties of employers, in relation to all the above matters, include the duty to make *Reasonable Adjustments* under the *DDA 1995*, as well as the duty not to discriminate.

Please also see the particular provisions referred to in relation to *Employment Agencies*, *Qualifying Bodies* and *Training Bodies*.

2 Acts of Parliament

2.1 THE LEGISLATION

The principal current laws relating to discrimination and equal pay in England, Scotland and Wales are contained in the following Acts of Parliament:

(*a*) The *Equal Pay Act 1970* (the *EPA 1970*);

(*b*) The *Sex Discrimination Act 1975* (the *SDA 1975*);

(*c*) The *Race Relations Act 1976* (the *RRA 1976*);

(*d*) The *Disability Discrimination Act 1995* (the *DDA 1995*).

Each of these Acts (even the relatively recent *DDA 1995*) has been amended by subsequent legislation or regulations and all references in this book to a particular Act are to that Act as amended.

It is impossible to consider only the domestic legislation, particularly in relation to sex discrimination and equal pay, because there are provisions of Community, or European, law which have an overriding effect – see *Community Law*.

2.2 DEFINITIONS OF DISCRIMINATION

The *EPA 1970* works quite differently from the *SDA 1975*, the *RRA 1976* and the *DDA 1995*, each of which:

(*a*) contains a comprehensive definition of what is meant by the verb 'discriminate';

(*b*) imposes obligations on employers and others; and

(*c*) specifies the circumstances and ways in which it is unlawful to discriminate.

The scope of the legislation, in terms of the parties who are subject to obligations and the ways in which they must not discriminate, are explained under *Acts of Discrimination*.

The structure of the *SDA 1975* and the *RRA 1976* is broadly the same, to the extent that case law relating to either of these Acts is also relevant to the other. Each of the two Acts include *Direct Discrimination*, *Indirect Discrimination* and *Victimisation* in the definition of discrimination.

The *DDA 1995* defines discrimination in a different way – see *Disability Discrimination*. The *DDA 1995* also includes the duty to make *Reasonable Adjustments*.

2.3 OTHER PROVISIONS

All four Acts also contain *Exceptions* from the general obligations placed on employers and others. They also contain the machinery for Enforcement of the rights and obligations which they have created.

3 Advertisements

3.1 DEFINITIONS

The provisions in the *SDA 1975* and the *RRA 1976* relating to advertisements are quite different from those in the *DDA 1995*. The wording of the definition is also different, but in all three Acts the definition is a very broad one. It takes in every form of advertisement, whether to the public or not. Examples include:

(*a*) a job advertisement in a local, national or specialist newspaper;

(*b*) a vacancy notice on the factory or office notice board;

(*c*) job details in a bulletin to staff; and

(*d*) a vacancy notice at a factory gate or in a shop window.

3.2 THE SDA 1975 AND THE RRA 1976

Under both the *SDA 1975* and the *RRA 1976*, it is unlawful to 'publish or cause to be published' an advertisement which indicates, or might reasonably be understood as indicating, an intention by any person to discriminate unlawfully.

There are two particularly notable features of these provisions:

(*a*) When an employer advertises a vacancy in a staff bulletin or on a notice board, it is the employer who publishes the advertisement. When the employer arranges for a vacancy to be advertised in a newspaper, it is the newspaper publisher who publishes the advertisement and the employer who causes it to be published. The wording quoted above means that both the employer and the newspaper publisher are at risk of acting unlawfully.

(*b*) Even where an employer has no intention of discriminating in filling a vacancy, a clumsy use of language could mean that the employer is acting unlawfully in advertising the vacancy or placing an advertisement.

For the most part, the question whether an advertisement might reasonably be understood as indicating an intention to discriminate unlawfully is a question of fact for the employment tribunal. However, there is one specific provision in the *SDA 1975*. The use of a job description with a sexual connotation is to be taken as indicating an intention to discriminate, unless the advertisement contains an indication to the contrary. The Act gives two examples of job descriptions which would indicate an intention to discriminate against women ('waiter' and 'postman') and two which would be taken to indicate an intention to discriminate against men ('salesgirl' and 'stewardess').

Accordingly, when the job description which comes to mind is one which has a sexual connotation, the employer should take one of the following steps:

(*a*) find an alternative term which has no sexual connotation (such as salesperson instead of salesgirl), so long as it is possible to think of one which describes the job accurately and is not too ponderous;

(*b*) use the terms applicable to both sexes (such as 'waiter or waitress'); or

(*c*) expressly state that the job is open to both sexes.

The third option is probably the least satisfactory.

3.3 LAWFUL DISCRIMINATION BUT UNLAWFUL ADVERTISEMENT

The *RRA 1976* goes much further than the *SDA 1975*. Even if the discrimination suggested in the advertisement would be lawful, publishing or placing the advertisement may still be *unlawful*. The reason is obvious and was stated in the White Paper which preceded the enactment of the *RRA 1976*:

> 'The public display of racial prejudices and preferences is inherently offensive and likely to encourage the spread of discriminatory attitudes and practices'.

In practice, this provision operates only in the following two cases:

(*a*) Direct and indirect racial discrimination are not unlawful in relation to employment for the purposes of a *Private Household*, but it is unlawful to publish or place an advertisement which indicates (or might reasonably be understood as indicating) an intention to discriminate in recruitment for or in any other way in relation to a post in a private household.

(*b*) The *RRA 1976* does not apply to employment which is wholly overseas, but it is generally unlawful to publish (or cause to be published) in Great Britain an advertisement which indicates (or might reasonably be understood as indicating) an intention to discriminate in relation to a post overseas. The only exception is where the work is to be done entirely outside Great Britain and where the persons required for the post are defined otherwise than by reference to colour, race or ethnic or national origins. Effectively, therefore, the advertisement is lawful only if all the work is to be done overseas and the advertised intention is to discriminate directly on grounds of nationality or indirectly on residential grounds.

The provisions in the *RRA 1976* relating to advertisements are somewhat convoluted. The Act states the general principle that publishing or causing the advertisement to be published is unlawful, whether or not the act of discrimination would be lawful. There is then a long list of exceptions to this general principle, leaving only the *Private Household* and *Overseas* cases mentioned above. The various circumstances in which both the racial discrimination and the advertisement would be lawful are considered in relation to:

(*a*) *Genuine Occupational Qualifications*;

(*b*) *Positive Discrimination*; and

(*c*) *Statutory Authority*.

3.4 DEFENCES AND OFFENCES

Under both the *SDA 1975* and the *RRA 1976*, the publisher of an advertisement (usually a newspaper publisher) can have a defence if he has relied on a false statement made by the person (such as an employer) who has caused the advertisement to be published. Under the *RRA 1976*, the false statement is to the effect that one of the above-mentioned exceptions applies. Under the *SDA 1975*, the false statement is that the discrimination suggested by the advertisement would be lawful. In both cases, however, the defence is available only if it was reasonable for the publisher to rely on the statement made to him.

An offence is committed when a person (such as an employer) knowingly or recklessly makes a false or misleading statement, as mentioned above, to the publisher of an advertisement. The person making the false or misleading statement can be ordered to pay a fine, on summary conviction.

No criminal offence is committed, however, when a person acts unlawfully in publishing an advertisement or causing it to be published. The unlawful act has only civil consequences. Furthermore, the law gives no right of action to individuals on the ground that they are offended by the publication of the intention or apparent intention to discriminate.

It is the Equal Opportunities Commission which can take action where a person has acted unlawfully under the *SDA 1975* in publishing or causing the publication of an advertisement. If the unlawful act is under the *RRA 1976*, then action can be taken by the Commission for Racial Equality. In each case, the Commission can apply to an employment tribunal for a decision that the alleged contravention of the law has occurred. If a finding is obtained, the next step could be an application to a county court for an injunction to prevent a further contravention – see *Enforcement*.

3.5 THE DDA 1995

The *DDA 1995* does not make it unlawful to publish (or cause to be published) a discriminatory advertisement.

Instead, the *DDA 1995* contains a quite different provision to assist a disabled person who complains of disability discrimination, in not offering him or her a post for which he or she has applied.

The tribunal hearing, the complainant is required to assume in certain circumstances, unless the contrary is shown, that the employer's reason for the refusal or deliberate failure to offer the post to the complainant was related to the complainant's disability. This assumption is to be made when an advertisement for the post (of whatever kind) has indicated (or might reasonably be understood to have indicated) that any application for the post would (or might) be determined to any extent by reference to any of the following:

(*a*) the successful applicant for the post not having any disability at all;

(*b*) the successful applicant not having any category of disability which includes the complainant's disability; or

(*c*) the employer's reluctance to make a *Reasonable Adjustment*.

A possible example could be an advertisement which uses an expression such as 'active and dynamic' in relation to the candidate required for a post which involves sitting at a desk all day, where the complainant has a physical disability which limits his or her mobility and hence physical activity.

The presumption can arise whether or not the complainant has actually seen the advertisement and even if the advertisement has been published after the complainant has applied for the post.

3.6 RECRUITMENT ARRANGEMENTS

The *SDA 1975* and the *RRA 1976* do not contain any provisions corresponding to the above-mentioned provision in the *DDA 1995*. A tribunal hearing a complaint under either Act is not required to make any assumptions, but can of course treat the wording of an advertisement as relevant evidence.

It is, however, open to a tribunal to have regard to the wording of an advertisement when deciding whether there has been direct or indirect discrimination in *Recruitment* or *Selection*.

Furthermore, a job advertisement is part of the employer's arrangements for filling the post. If an advertisement does in fact indicate an intention to discriminate unlawfully (whether directly or indirectly), as opposed to giving rise to a mistaken understanding that there is such an intention, then the act of the employer in publishing the advertisement or causing it to be published could in itself be an act of unlawful discrimination in *Recruitment*. The relevant Commission could take Enforcement action in relation to that discrimination as well as or instead of action in relation to the advertisement section in the *SDA 1975* or the *RRA 1976*.

In principle, an individual should also be able to complain (whether under the *SDA 1975*, the *RRA 1976* or the *DDA 1995*) about discrimination in the arrangements for filling a post, if he or she has been put off from applying for the post because an advertisement indicates an intention to discriminate. An obvious example would be that of an advertisement which contains a requirement or condition for the post where:

(*a*) the complainant cannot comply with it; and

(*b*) it is indirectly discriminatory under the *SDA 1975* or the *RRA 1976*.

In 1994, the EAT, in *Cardiff Women's Aid v Hartup* [*1994*] *IRLR 390*, ruled that placing a discriminatory advertisement is not an act of discrimination in the arrangements for filling a post. On the face of it, this decision invalidates the comments made above, to the effect that an advertisement could be the sole basis for a complaint of discrimination by an individual or for Enforcement action relating to discrimination in recruitment. The principles underlying the decision may, however, require to be reconsidered in the light of the House of Lords decision in *Nagarajan v London Regional Transport* [*1999*] *IRLR 572* – see *Recruitment*.

The questions of how and where posts should be advertised (as opposed to the content of the advertisement) are considered in relation to *Positive Discrimination* and *Recruitment*.

3.7 ADVICE ON WORDING OF ADVERTISEMENTS

Employers need to take great care in the way in which jobs are advertised, whether formally in a newspaper or, for example, in a staff bulletin or on a notice board. The employer must not:

(*a*) describe the job using a term which has a sexual connotation, unless the advertisement clearly indicates that the post is open to candidates of both sexes;

(*b*) use any other language which indicates or suggests an intention to discriminate directly;

(*c*) include requirements or conditions which have an indirectly discriminatory effect under the *SDA 1975* or the *RRA 1976* and which cannot be justified;

(*d*) use language which suggests that a disabled person, or a candidate with a particular disability, would not be appointed; or

(*e*) use language which suggests that any disabled person who applies will have to take the job as he or she finds it and that no *Reasonable Adjustment* will be made.

4 Affirmative Action

4.1 THE SDA 1975 AND THE RRA 1976

Unlawful discrimination cannot be legitimised by a worthy motive. Under the *SDA 1975* and the *RRA 1976*, it is unlawful to discriminate against women or racial minorities in relation to employment at an establishment in Great Britain, unless the case is covered by one of the express exceptions in the relevant Act; it is equally unlawful to discriminate against men or in favour of racial minorities, even if the object is to correct a perceived imbalance or compensate for previous discrimination.

There are limited provisions which permit *Positive Discrimination*, in certain circumstances, in offering encouragement or providing training; it is never lawful to discriminate at the point of selection by rejecting, on racial grounds or on grounds of sex, a candidate who would otherwise have been appointed.

In *Application by Badeck [2000] IRLR 432* the ECJ ruled on questions which had been referred to it as a result of an equal rights law enacted by a regional authority in Germany. This law required that in the public service, where targets for women's advancement had not been achieved, there should be discrimination in favour of female candidates, where those candidates and male candidates had equal qualifications. Furthermore the German law required that in the assessment of qualifications, capabilities and experience acquired by looking after children or persons requiring care in the domestic sector should be taken into account, insofar as they are of importance for the suitability, performance and capability of applicants. The ECJ held that this national law was not precluded by the *Equal Treatment Directive*.

This decision by the ECJ suggests that it would be open to Parliament to adopt measures of affirmative action or positive discrimination which go further than the current very limited provisions in the *SDA 1975* and the *RRA 1976*. There is, however, no obligation for Parliament to do so. Furthermore, although in the public sector the Equal Treatment Directive can, in certain circumstances, be relied upon in cases where discrimination contrary to the Directive is permitted by domestic legislation, there is no authority for the converse proposition that a discriminating employer can rely on the Directive to justify discrimination which is prohibited by domestic legislation.

There has been a further move in favour of affirmative action at the European level. The Treaty of Amsterdam has amended Article 141 of the European Treaty to add the following proviso:

> '*. . . the principle of equal treatment shall not prevent any Member State from maintaining or adopting measures providing for specific advantages in order to make it easier for the under-represented sex to pursue a vocational activity or to prevent or compensate for disadvantages in professional careers.*'

Again, however, this amendment is permissive, not mandatory. It does not require any measures of affirmative action or positive discrimination to be adopted under domestic legislation.

4.2 THE DDA 1995

There is nothing in the *DDA 1995* to prevent affirmative action or positive discrimination in favour generally of disabled employees or job applicants. It would, however, be unlawful to discriminate in favour of disabled workers with one kind of disability if this meant discriminating against workers with different kinds of disability, unless the case is covered by a specific provision in the *DDA 1995* (for example that relating to *Supported Employment*).

5 Age Discrimination

5.1 SHOULD AGE DISCRIMINATION BE OUTLAWED?

There is at present no general statutory prohibition of age discrimination in employment within England and Wales. Yet it has been recognised increasingly in recent years that discrimination at work on the ground of age does exist. A strong consensus has emerged that steps should be taken to eliminate such discrimination in the UK; legislation prohibiting age discrimination exists in several overseas jurisdictions. But views remain divided as to the best way in which to achieve the goal. In opposition, the Labour Party favoured legislation, but following its election in 1997, its enthusiasm for statutory reform seemed to cool. The Government did, however, introduce in 1999 a non-statutory *Age Diversity Code of Practice*, and in 2000 its own Performance and Innovation Unit produced a report, *Winning the Generation Game*, which said that legislation should come in if the Code is unsuccessful. It is also worth noting that age discrimination can prejudice the young as well as the old.

5.2 UNFAIR DISMISSAL AND REDUNDANCY

A tribunal has no jurisdiction to hear a claim of unfair dismissal if there is no 'normal retiring age' or an employee is holding the position which the applicant held and the employee is over 65. In *Nash v Mash/Rowe Group Ltd (1998) IRLR 168*, an employment tribunal held that the upper age limit is unlawful indirect sex discrimination which breaches *Article 141* (formerly *Article 119*) of the Treaty of Rome, and therefore must be disapplied. An appeal to the EAT against this surprising and dubious decision was pending at the time of writing. Similarly, a tribunal has referred the question of whether the maximum age limit of 65 for entitlement to a statutory redundancy payment contravenes *Article 141* to the European Court of Justice.

Redundancy pay and unfair dismissal compensation are 'pay' for the purposes of *Article 141* and, if the decision in *Nash* is upheld, it would provide a valuable remedy against arbitrary discrimination on the ground of age.

5.3 AGE DISCRIMINATION AND SEX DISCRIMINATION

Section 6(4) of the *Sex Discrimination Act 1975* (*SDA 1975*) no longer provides that it is lawful to specify separate retirement ages for men and women. A fundamental aspect of the *Pensions Act 1995* is equalisation of the state pension ages for men and women at 65. This very significant provision will have effect from the year 2020, although it will be phased in during the preceding ten years.

Different treatment of men and women over the age of 60 will be unlawful even where the intention is to deal with apparent inconsistencies created by the fact that women are entitled to the state pension at 60, whereas men are entitled to the state pension at 65. *James v Eastleigh Borough Council* (*1990*) *ICR 554*, concerned a local authority's discount for pensioners seeking admission to its swimming pools, which was related to the pensionable age of 60 for women and 65 for men. A man's complaint of sex discrimination was upheld because entitlement to discount was determined by sex. Provided that there is no direct or indirect discrimination based on gender, it is possible for an employer to have a variety of retiring ages for different jobs. In *Bullock v Alice Ottley School* (*1992*) *IRLR 564*, the employer operated a retirement age of 60 for administrative and domestic staff and of 65 for maintenance and ground staff. All the latter were male and the vast majority of the administrative and domestic staff were female. A female employee complained of sex discrimination when her employment terminated at the age of 61. Overturning a decision of the EAT, the Court of Appeal ruled that there was no evidence of discrimination. The reason for the differential retirement ages was objectively justified on a ground unrelated to sex, i.e. the difficulty in recruiting skilled maintenance workers.

In *Jones v University of Manchester (1993) IRLR 218*, the tribunal had found that a preference stated in a job advertisement for someone aged between 27 and 35 had in practice become a 'requirement' within the meaning of *section 1(1)(b)* of the *SDA 1975*. However, the Court of Appeal held that because of the way in which the *Pool* had been defined, *Disparate Impact* had not been proved. Furthermore the employer was able to justify the age requirement objectively without reference to the sex of the complainant. In *Price v Civil Service Commission and the Society of Civil and Public Servants (1977) IRLR 291*, the EAT held that a maximum age limit of 35 for appointment as an executive officer in the Civil Service was, in practice, harder for women to comply with as they were more likely to have interrupted their careers to start or look after a family. The complaint of indirect sex discrimination was successful in that case.

5.4 AGE DISCRIMINATION AND RACE DISCRIMINATION

Age discrimination may overlap with unlawful discrimination on the ground of race, as in *Perera v Civil Service Commission and another (No 2) (1982) ICR 350*. A 39 year old VAT officer who came from Sri Lanka wished to become an administrative trainee. However, there was an upper age limit for trainees of 32. At the office where he worked there were 34 white officers, of whom 22 were under the age of 32. There were 13 ethnic minority officers, none of whom were under 32. The EAT ruled that the evidence justified a finding of indirect racial discrimination.

5.5 CONTRACTUAL BAR ON AGE DISCRIMINATION

Even in the absence of general legislation, contractual equal opportunities policies may provide employees with protection. It is possible for an employer to undertake a contractual obligation not to discriminate against an employee on the ground of age. In *Secretary of State for Scotland v Taylor [1997] IRLR 608*, the EAT upheld a finding that the terms of the Scottish Prison Service's equal opportunities policy, which stated that employees would be afforded opportunities on an equal basis 'regardless of gender, race, religion, sexual preference, disability or age', were incorporated into a prison officer's contractual terms of employment. The employer's argument that the policy should be regarded as a 'mission statement' which was not legally binding was rejected. The Court of Session, however, subsequently confirmed, at *[1999] IRLR 363*, that the decision compulsorily to retire the prison officer before he reached the age of 60 was not in breach of his contract, notwithstanding the contractual prohibition on age discrimination. Even if the operation of a contract involves factors dependent on age, that does not necessarily signify that there has been a breach of an equal opportunities policy which prohibits age discrimination. The Court of Session pointed out that it would be impossible to deprive a retirement age policy of all age discrimination content, since any retirement policy almost inevitably results in the retiring person being replaced by someone younger. It was only if the discretion to impose retirement before 60 was operated in an inappropriate discriminatory manner that a breach of contract would result. The employers had retained a discretion with regard to retirement which, the Court of Session concluded, could not have been intended by the parties to be fettered by age considerations. The House of Lords, at *(2000) IRLR 507*, rejected a further appeal; the introduction of the equal opportunities policy did not remove the contractual provisions about the minimum retirement age. The conditions for continued service were not discriminatory and there was no indication that the officer had been singled out because of his age.

5.6 PROPOSED EUROPEAN FRAMEWORK DIRECTIVE

In November 1999, the European Commission published a proposal for a Framework Directive to combat discrimination in employment on all grounds other than sex, referred to in *Article 13* of the Treaty of Rome. That Article was inserted by the Treaty of Amsterdam and empowers the Council of Ministers to 'take appropriate action to combat discrimination based on sex, racial or ethnic origin, religion or belief, disability, age or sexual orientation'. The proposal recognised that the establishment of maximum recruitment ages, the limitation of older workers' training rights concerning new technologies and the right to promotion, or dismissals of old workers within the context of restructuring, are all examples of discriminatory measures in employment which particularly affect older people. *Article 5* of the proposed Framework Directive provides a non-exhaustive list of differences in treatment on the ground of age which shall *not* constitute direct discrimination provided that they are objectively justified. It is intended both to limit the scope for claiming justification in cases of direct discrimination to exceptional circumstances, and to ensure that the limited range of exceptions respects the principles of necessity, proportionality and legitimacy laid down by the European Court of Justice in relation to the concept of indirect discrimination. Thus, member states may allow differences of treatment on the ground of age other than those listed in *Article 5*, in accordance with their legal traditions and political priorities, provided that they are appropriate and necessary to attain a legitimate aim. *Article 5* does not exclude the possibility of justifying discriminatory treatment by reference to a *Genuine Occupational Qualification*. The exceptions to the general principle of discrimination are:

(*a*) prohibiting access to employment or the provision of special working conditions to ensure the protection of young people and older workers;

(*b*) fixing a minimum age as a condition of eligibility for retirement or invalidity benefits;

(*c*) fixing different ages for employees or groups or categories of employees for entitlement to retirement or invalidity benefits on grounds of physical or mental occupational requirements;

(*d*) fixing a maximum age for recruitment which is based on the training requirements of the post in question or the need for a reasonable period of employment before retirement;

(*e*) establishing requirements concerning the length of professional experience;

(*f*) establishing of age limits which are appropriate and necessary for the pursuit of legitimate labour market objectives.

The UK Government welcomed the proposed Framework Directive. It will have two years from the date the Directive is adopted to implement legislation bringing it into force.

6 Age Diversity Code of Practice

6.1 BACKGROUND

In 1998, the Government published a report, *Action On Age*, on its consultation about employment and age discrimination. A key finding was the need to change outmoded attitudes and practices that are a factor in age discrimination. The Government took the view that a non-statutory Code of Practice would be a 'valuable tool' for achieving this. The outcome was *Age Diversity in Employment: A Code of Practice*, which is advisory in nature. It is accompanied by guidance illustrated with case studies on good and bad practice.

6.2 THE CODE'S RECOMMENDATIONS

Action to eradicate age discrimination should be taken as part of a wider personnel and equal opportunities strategy, to create a flexible and motivated workforce. An effective strategy will begin by reviewing the current position, to clarify what needs to be done and how to monitor progress.

The code covers six phases of the employment cycle.

6.3 Recruitment

To ensure that the best candidates apply, employers should:

(*a*) avoid using age limits or age ranges in job advertisements;

(*b*) place job advertisements specifying the skills and abilities required for the post;

(*c*) think carefully about the language used and avoid using phrases which imply age restrictions such as 'young graduates' or 'mature person'; and

(*d*) think strategically about where jobs are advertised. Different magazines and periodicals are aimed at different sectors of the market.

6.4 Selection

To select the best candidate for the job, employers should:

(*a*) focus on the skills, abilities and potential of the candidates when sifting applications;

(*b*) make sure that interviewers are aware of the need to ask job-related questions;

(*c*) use, where possible, a mixed aged interviewing panel;

(*d*) ensure all interviewers are trained to avoid basing decisions on prejudices and stereotypes;

(*e*) avoid making age an integral part of the application process; and

(*f*) select on merit, based on the application form information and the performance at interview.

6.5 Promotion

Employers should:

(*a*) ensure that promotion opportunities are advertised through open competition;

(*b*) make sure that promotion opportunities are made available to all staff who have demonstrated the ability or the potential to do the job;

(*c*) focus on the skills, abilities and potential of the candidates when sifting applications;

(*d*) make sure that interviewers are aware of the need to ask job-related questions;

(*e*) use, where possible, a mixed age interviewing panel;

(*f*) ensure that interviewers are trained to avoid basing decisions on prejudices and stereotypes;

(*g*) select on merit.

6.6 **Training and development**

Employers should:

(*a*) ensure the training and development needs of all staff are regularly reviewed and that age is not a barrier to training;

(*b*) make sure that all employees are aware of the training and development opportunities that are available and are encouraged to use them;

(*c*) focus on the individual's and the organisation's needs when providing training and development opportunities; and

(*d*) look at how training is delivered and ensure that different learning styles and needs are addressed.

6.7 **Redundancy**

Employers should:

(*a*) use objective, job-related criteria when considering candidates for redundancy;

(*b*) make sure the business retains the staff it needs to remain competitive;

(*c*) make sure age is not a criterion – and publicise this fact; and

(*d*) look at flexible options, such as part-time working, job-share or career breaks and short-term contracts when considering alternatives to redundancy.

6.8 **Retirement**

Employers should:

(*a*) base retirement policy on business needs, while also giving individuals as much choice as possible;

(*b*) make sure the loss to the organisation of skills and abilities is fully evaluated when operating early retirement schemes;

(*c*) consider alternatives to early retirement for those whose skills and abilities may be lost;

(*d*) not see age as the sole criterion when operating early retirement schemes (subject to pension rules);

(*e*) use flexible retirement schemes, where this is possible;

(*f*) use phased retirement, where possible, to allow employees to alter the balance of their working and personal lives and to prepare for full retirement. This can also help the business to prepare for the loss of the employee's skills; and

(*g*) make pre-retirement support available for employees.

7 Agency Workers

There are many workers, particularly in certain sectors of the economy, who are employed by agencies which then provide the worker's services either to one particular client or to a succession of different clients. These arrangements are particularly common in construction and related industries and also now in information technology (IT). In some cases an agency worker may be placed with a particular client for a period of years.

Under any such arrangement, the worker has rights against the client as well as against the agency and the client owes the worker a duty not to discriminate (whether under the *SDA 1975*, the *RRA 1976* or the *DDA 1995*) – see *Contract Workers*.

It should be noted that by reason of the extended definition of *Employment* which is contained in the *SDA 1975*, the *RRA 1976* and the *DDA 1995,* an agency worker could have rights as an 'employee' against the agency and rights as a contract worker against the client, even though the agency worker is not employed in the conventional sense by either the agency or the client.

8 Agents

Employers use outside agents or consultants in a wide variety of ways. The one obvious example is in relation to recruitment. An employer looking for a candidate for a post may:

(*a*) approach a private employment agency;

(*b*) ask for the vacancy to be advertised in a Jobcentre; or

(*c*) use 'head hunters' particularly if the post is a senior one.

Employers also use agents or consultants in order, for example, to:

(*a*) train and instruct employees;

(*b*) carry out medical examinations; and

(*c*) undertake *Psychometric Testing*.

An *Agency Worker* or *Contract Worker* can also be an employer's agent, where he or she is given responsibility for supervising employees.

The general rule is that employers and others who have obligations under the *SDA 1975*, the *RRA 1976* or the *DDA 1995* cannot escape their responsibilities by using agents. Anything done by the agent with the authority of the principal is also deemed to be done by the principal. The latter cannot escape responsibility by giving a nod and a wink or turning a blind eye. The authority may be express or implied and may be given before or after the event. The agent is also liable, because he is treated as having aided the principal in doing an unlawful act.

The following are examples of cases in which both an employer and an agent could incur liability:

(*a*) An employer adopts a requirement or condition which is indirectly discriminatory and which appears in an advertisement placed by a recruitment agency on the employer's behalf.

(*b*) On the employer's instructions, an employment agency tells a disabled candidate that it is not possible to consider making modest adjustments which the candidate has requested should be made to the duties of the post in order to accommodate his or her disability.

(*c*) An employer who uses an agency worker to supervise employees is aware that the agency worker is sexually harassing female employees and implicitly authorises this discrimination by choosing to take no action.

Sometimes it is the employer alone, and not the agent, who is legally liable for an unlawful act. The agent has a defence if he has reasonably relied on a statement made by the principal that a particular action would not be unlawful by reason of some provision contained in the Act concerned. This defence could apply, for example, to a recruitment agency which has placed an advertisement, if the employer has falsely but convincingly told the agency that the post being advertised is covered by one of the *Genuine Occupational Qualification* (GOQ) exceptions. In such a case, the principal who knowingly or recklessly makes the false or misleading statement to the agent is guilty of an offence and is liable to a fine on summary conviction.

Employers and others who use agents to recruit or manage staff or for any other purpose should bear in mind that:

8 Agents

(*a*) A principal cannot avoid liability for discrimination by acting through an agent.

(*b*) Clear instructions should be given to the agent, to ensure compliance with the law.

(*c*) The activities of agents should be monitored and reviewed, bearing in mind that authority for an unlawful act can be implicit and retrospective.

It is particularly important to take these steps, because at the time of writing there appear to be no appeal decisions giving guidance on the circumstances in which an agent would be held to have implied authority to discriminate on behalf of a principal. It is arguable that liability would attach to the employer in the following circumstances:

(*a*) an employer places a job vacancy in the hands of a recruitment agency;

(*b*) the employer does not intend the agent to discriminate unlawfully but fails to give any instructions on that issue, one way or the other;

(*c*) the agent does in fact discriminate unlawfully.

If it can be shown that clear instructions were given to the agent not to discriminate unlawfully, then the risk of a finding of implied authority will be considerably reduced.

It should also be noted that a person using an agent should take prompt and effective action to investigate and deal with a complaint that the agent has discriminated unlawfully. Otherwise, it could be argued that inaction by the principal amounts to retrospective authority for the discrimination.

9 Agreements

The *SDA 1975*, the *RRA 1976* and the *DDA 1995* each contain provisions to make certain contractual terms void or unenforceable if they are in furtherance of or provide for unlawful discrimination or purport to take away a person's rights under any of these laws. For example *section 77* of the *SDA 1975* includes the following provisions:

(*a*) a term in a contract which purports to exclude or limit any provision of the *SDA 1975* or the *EPA 1970* is unenforceable;

(*b*) any contractual term which provides for unlawful discrimination against a third party is void; and

(*c*) a contractual term which provides for unlawful discrimination against a party to the contract is unenforceable against that party.

There are similar provisions in the *RRA 1976* and the *DDA 1995*. The only exceptions to the rule against contracting out are the normal exceptions relating to *Conciliation* and compromise agreements. Where there is a particular complaint under the *EPA 1970*, the *SDA 1975*, the *RRA 1976* or the *DDA 1995*, the parties may settle that complaint and exclude the jurisdiction of the employment tribunal, so long as the prescribed conditions for compromise agreements are satisfied, including the requirement for the complainant to have independent advice.

The *SDA 1975* and the *RRA 1976* make provision for a party to a contract to apply to a county court (or sheriff court in Scotland) for an order removing or modifying a term of a contract, where that term, for example, provides for unlawful discrimination against the party making the application. The case of *Meade-Hill v British Council* [*1995*] *IRLR 478*, referred to under *Mobility*, was an example of such an application.

There is a similar provision in the *DDA 1995* (*section 26*), but it applies only to non-employment cases.

The provisions in the *SDA 1975* go further than those in the *RRA 1976*. An application may also be made under the *SDA 1975* to remove or modify a term contained in a collective agreement, works rules or the rules of professional bodies. Furthermore, there are provisions in the *Sex Discrimination Act 1986* under which such an application may be made to an employment tribunal instead of to a county court or sheriff court.

Where a binding agreement is reached, questions sometimes arise if the respondent wishes to keep the terms of the agreement confidential – a so-called 'gagging clause'. Whether such a clause is appropriate – or, in practice, even enforceable – will need careful consideration in each case.

10 Aircraft and Hovercraft

10.1 THE ISSUE

What is the position regarding employment on aircraft, whether as flight crew or cabin crew? Do the discrimination laws cover employment on internal flights, or on overseas flights, where some of them are to and from British bases?

The *SDA 1975* (for the purposes of the *EPA 1970* and the *SDA 1975* itself) the *RRA 1976* and the *DDA 1995* each deal with the issue in a different way. The provisions in each Act relating to aircraft also apply to hovercraft.

10.2 THE SDA 1975

Employment on an aircraft or hovercraft is covered, unless the work is done wholly outside Great Britain (i.e. in the case of aircraft, on flights which do not depart from or return to British airfields and do not cross British airspace) if the following conditions are satisfied:

(*a*) The aircraft or hovercraft is registered in the United Kingdom.

(*b*) The principal place of business or ordinary residence of the operator is in Great Britain.

10.3 THE RRA 1976

There is no specific reference to aircraft and hovercraft in the relevant section (*section 8*) of the *RRA 1976*. This means that, wherever the aircraft or hovercraft is registered, and wherever the operator is mainly based, the Act applies as long as:

(*a*) The work is not done wholly outside Great Britain.

(*b*) There is an establishment in Great Britain from which the work is done or with which it has the closest connection, such as the base from which the employee flies or the office to which he or she reports.

10.4 THE DDA 1995

Employment on board an aircraft or hovercraft is expressly excluded.

11 Alternative Dispute Resolution

11.1 THE EMPLOYMENT CONTEXT

An employment dispute with a legal element can be resolved in various ways. The traditional formal method of resolving a dispute concerning an alleged wrongful dismissal, for instance, was by way of litigation in the civil courts. The judicial system provides established court procedures, rules of evidence, and the application of substantive law and precedents. With the emergence of statutory employment rights, and the establishment of industrial tribunals (now known as employment tribunals) came alternative possibilities, intended to be more appropriate to the modern employment context. In particular, the Advisory, Conciliation and Arbitration Service (ACAS) was established in 1975. ACAS exists to improve industrial relations and employment practice, as well as to minimise conflict. Although financed by Government, it is independent in the sense that its operations are not directed by Government. ACAS prizes its unique and impartial role and, although its functions are regulated by statute, it prefers to operate by using voluntary methods. Its principal functions have included conciliation in trade disputes, arbitration, conciliation in cases of individual complaints to tribunals, giving advice and producing Codes of Practice.

In recent years, pressure for fresh options has grown. There has been increasing concern that tribunals have departed from their original aims of providing a readily accessible and cost-effective means of redress with the minimum of formality and delay. The case-loads of tribunals have risen dramatically, reflecting the tribunal's extending jurisdiction and a growing propensity to litigation in defence of employment rights. At the same time, developing case law, both at home and in Europe, has added to the complexity of cases coming before tribunals. The result has been perceived as increasing 'legalism' in tribunal proceedings. A range of possibilities were canvassed in a Green Paper published in 1994, *Resolving Employment Rights Disputes: Options For Reform*. One of the more intriguing outcomes of the reform process initiated by that Green Paper is a scheme set up by ACAS to provide arbitration of unfair dismissal cases as an alternative to the tribunal system.

Meanwhile, general awareness has arisen of the potential value of different forms of alternative dispute resolution (ADR). Mediation, in particular, is likely to become ever more important as a means of addressing disputes in respect of equal opportunities issues.

11.2 LITIGATION

Typical features of litigation include the following:

(*a*) in litigation, as in arbitration, the parties delegate to a third party adjudicator the function of resolving the dispute. In mediation, the parties take control themselves;

(*b*) litigation is ordinarily a public process, whereas arbitration and mediation are private and confidential;

(*c*) litigation often involves elements of delay, whereas mediation in particular can proceed at whatever pace the parties require;

(*d*) litigation costs are generally much higher than those of mediation, although if mediation does not result in a solution, mediation costs will be additional to the adjudication costs even though the mediation may have provided certain benefits;

(*e*) litigation and arbitration, are binding on the parties and carry a consequent risk of adverse decision. Mediation is relatively risk-free, because it depends upon agreement to become binding;

(*f*) litigation tends to escalate antagonism, whereas mediation may minimise it;

(*g*) litigation and arbitration offer enforcement of judgements and orders, whereas an agreement reached through mediation will usually be binding in contract; and

(*h*) in litigation, the adjudicator is a qualified lawyer who follows known or ascertainable rules of law and procedure. In mediation, non-lawyer professionals are less likely to be engaged in a partisan capacity and may act as mediators or consultants to the mediation.

11.3 CHOICE OF PROCESS

Litigation through the courts (or, where appropriate, binding arbitration) may be preferable or even essential in certain cases. For example:

(*a*) ADR cannot be used unless all the parties so agree;

(*b*) where an issue of fundamental principle is involved which necessitates a binding and public precedent, for example a civil rights issue, litigation is appropriate;

(*c*) sometimes, a substantial and serious power imbalance between the parties may be a contra-indication to ADR;

(*d*) if a case turns solely on legal issues which need to be decided, or if credibility plays a pivotal role, litigation may be indicated; and

(*e*) in cases where the immediate enforcement of a court order is essential, litigation is appropriate.

Conversely, ADR may be indicated in some or all of the following circumstances:

(*a*) where the parties have a continuing employment relationship;

(*b*) where the issues in dispute arise from a breakdown in communications or differences of respective perceptions of fairness;

(*c*) where the outcome could possibly be enhanced by a creative business-like solution between the parties;

(*d*) where the standards and criteria to be applied to the dispute are unclear and elements of judgement, discretion and perhaps even personal preferences are required;

(*e*) where confidentiality is required; and

(*f*) where, as is often the case, possible escalation of costs is a matter of concern.

The most economical way of resolving a dispute is likely to be negotiation, but negotiations may fail for reasons such as:

(*a*) personal antagonism between the parties;

(*b*) distrust of the other party;

(*c*) poor communications;

(*d*) unrealistic expectations; or

(*e*) tactical naivete.

11.4 MEDIATION

Mediation is a non-adjudicatory process, in which the parties engage a neutral mediator to help them to resolve a dispute themselves. The mediator is a facilitator who has no authority to make any decision binding on the parties. The broad objectives of mediation are:

(*a*) to allow the parties to be directly involved in the dispute resolution process;

(*b*) to avoid the risks and costs of litigation;

(*c*) to provide a private forum for testing the strengths and weaknesses of the parties' cases, with input from a neutral expert who may help to bring a sense of realism into the matter; and

(*d*) to enhance rather than damage the possibility of the continuing employment relationship.

11.5 MEDIATION OF EQUAL OPPORTUNITIES DISPUTES

Mediation may be particularly valuable in cases of alleged harassment and bullying or other forms of discrimination. It is a flexible tool which can be used when formal legal proceedings have not been issued. In the United States, many employers require employees, in their contracts, to engage in mediation, especially in relation to disputes arising from relationships at work (see *Relationships at Work*) prior to issuing court proceedings. This is not, however, appropriate in England, Wales and Scotland because of the statutory bar on contracting out of statutory employment protection rights.

If the parties decide to mediate, they will need to appoint an appropriately trained mediator. Various organisations provide training, including the Centre for Dispute Resolution (CEDR), which is an independent non-profit making organisation promoting ADR.

The form taken by mediation is highly variable. Typically, parties deliver their statement of events and relevant documents to the mediator and to each other. Confidential matters are sometimes submitted to the mediator by way of a private side letter. Often, the mediator will introduce the process and, after opening statements are presented by the parties, the mediator will meet privately with each party. Those discussions should be frank and confidential. The mediator will seek to identify the key issues and the true interests of the parties. Bargaining will follow, with the mediator acting as a channel of communication between the parties. The individual personality, style and approach of the mediator often shapes the course of the process. The aim is to secure a solution agreed by the parties which will then become binding upon them.

12 Amendments

12.1 ADDING NEW PARTIES

Employment Tribunals have the express power, under *rule 17* of the *Rules of Procedure*, to give directions for new parties to be added or existing parties to be dismissed from the proceedings.

The question of adding or substituting respondents can arise, for example:

(*a*) if the wrong company in a group of companies has been mistakenly named as the employer;

(*b*) if there has been a change in the identity of the employer, by reason of a transfer under the *Transfer of Undertakings (Protection of Employment) Regulations 1981 (SI 1981, No 1794)*, (*TUPE*);

(*c*) if only the employer has been named as respondent in a harassment case and the applicant wishes to add the names of the employee(s) responsible for the harassment.

Guidance on the approach to be adopted by employment tribunals when considering applications for a party to be added (and also when considering applications for amendments generally) was given in *Cocking v Sandhurst (Stationers) Limited* [*1974*] *ICR 650* and in *Selkent Bus Co. Limited v Moore* [*1996*] *ICR 836*. A new respondent can be added even though the (usually three month) time limit for an originating application against that party has expired. Tribunals have a wide discretion. The approach which they should adopt in exercising that discretion is briefly considered below.

12.2 OTHER AMENDMENTS

Rule 13(1) of the *Rules of Procedure* gives employment tribunals the power to regulate their own procedure. A tribunal has a discretion under that rule to grant leave to amend the originating application or the notice of appearance.

Usually the most contentious applications for leave to amend are those to amend the originating application by adding a new head of claim, where the time limit for a new originating application has expired.

Leave to amend is most likely to be granted in a case where the relevant facts are already set out in the originating application and the applicant seeks only to add a new label to the claim. An example is a complaint alleging a discriminatory dismissal where the same facts can be relied on in support of a complaint of unfair dismissal. In *Jesuthasan v Hammersmith and Fulham London Borough Council* [*1998*] *IRLR 372*, the Court of Appeal allowed an amendment of this kind even though the dismissal had been nearly two years earlier.

Leave to amend is much less likely in a case where an applicant seeks to raise an entirely new claim, on new facts, and that claim is out of time. An example is the case of *Harvey v Port of Tilbury (London) Limited* [*1999*] *IRLR 693*. The applicant, who had been dismissed on the ground of redundancy, presented a complaint of unfair dismissal, in which there was no suggestion that disability had been a factor in the selection for redundancy. The applicant applied for leave to add a complaint of disability discrimination. The time for a new originating application had expired and the application for leave to amend was refused.

12.3 RELEVANT PRINCIPLES

Guidance on the principles to be adopted in considering applications for leave to amend was given in the cases of *Cocking v Sandhurst (Stationers) Limited* [*1974*] *ICR 650* and *Selkent Bus Co. Limited v Moore* [*1996*] *ICR 836*. A key issue, when a tribunal is considering an application for leave to amend, is that of injustice or hardship. Would the injustice or hardship caused to the applicant if leave were to be refused exceed that caused to the respondent if leave were to be granted? Where the application is one for leave to add a new party, the question of injustice or hardship to that party must also be considered.

13 Appeals

Complaints of discrimination in the employment field (whether under the *SDA 1975*, the *RRA 1976* or the *DDA 1995*) are heard by employment tribunals.

The tribunal's findings of fact are final (except in the extreme case where a decision can properly be said to be perverse), but there is an appeal on a point of law to the Employment Appeal Tribunal (the EAT).

There is a time limit of 42 days for appeal to the EAT. This time runs from the date on which the decision of the tribunal is sent to the parties (not the date when it is actually received).

An unsuccessful party (whether the complainant or the respondent) who wishes to appeal to the EAT does not need leave, or consent, to do so. There is, however, a sifting process, under which the EAT holds a preliminary hearing in most cases at which only the appellant is present or represented. The purpose of this preliminary hearing is to identify arguable appeals and weed out the unarguable cases.

Any appeal from the decision of the EAT goes to the Court of Appeal (or Court of Session in Scotland), but there is no automatic right of appeal. The leave of the EAT or the Court of Appeal (or Court of Session) is required.

The final court of appeal is the House of Lords, but, again, leave to appeal is required. Leave is given in only a small number of cases.

There is no right of appeal at any stage to the European Court of Justice (the ECJ), but an employment tribunal or (more commonly) the EAT, the Court of Appeal, the Court of Session or the House of Lords may refer to the ECJ a question or questions on the interpretation and application of European (or *Community*) law.

14 Appearance, Notice of

The employer or other person who is the respondent to a complaint of discrimination or equal pay claim must enter an appearance to the complaint within 21 days after receiving the notice of the complaint. This is done by completing and returning the form of Notice of Appearance which is received from the tribunal office.

The time for entering appearance was formerly 14 days, but that time was readily (indeed virtually automatically) extended. The current time limit of 21 days is a much stricter one. The time can be extended, but there must be a good reason for the extension. Furthermore, even where an extension is granted, a respondent can be ordered to pay any additional costs which are incurred by the complainant as a result of the extension.

Accordingly an employer or other respondent who receives notice of a complaint to a tribunal should take the following steps immediately:

(*a*) The complaint should be investigated as a matter of urgency, if the respondent is not already familiar with the circumstances leading to the complaint.

(*b*) If a solicitor is to be instructed, this should be done at the outset and not just before (or even after) the 21 day time limit expires.

(*c*) If further details of the complaint are needed in order to respond fully to the complaint, then a prompt request should be made (with a copy to the tribunal) for further and better particulars of the complaint.

(*d*) Even if investigations are incomplete, appearance should be entered within the 21 day period, but with a note that it may be necessary to seek leave to amend at a later date in the light of the further investigations.

(*e*) If it is impossible to comply with the 21 day time limit, an application for an extension should be made well before the 21 days expire and should be supported by full reasons. These could, for example, be that it is impossible to respond to the complaint until the further and better particulars which have been requested are provided or because the only manager who knows about the case is out of the country.

Care should be taken to check any factual statements in the notice of appearance against the known facts, as contained in relevant documents or revealed by the investigation which is carried out. It rather undermines the credibility of a defence if the factual statements on which the defence is based are later shown to be wrong.

It is important to avoid a knee-jerk reaction to a complaint. If, for example, the complaint is one of racial or sexual harassment, which has not been raised previously, the employers should fully investigate the complaint, not simply assume that it must be false or mistaken. It will make matters worse to put in an automatic denial, if the complaint subsequently turns out to be well founded.

The response to the complaint which is set out in the notice of appearance should be clear and concise, not long and rambling. All the relevant issues should be addressed. It is particularly important, in an *Equal Pay* case, to raise any *Material Factor* defence.

The tribunal, as well as the parties, has a responsibility to be alert to any matters which are relevant to the jurisdiction of the tribunal. The respondent should, however, raise any such matters as soon as he becomes aware of them, particularly in view of the possibility that a *Preliminary Hearing* may be required. There could be an issue as to jurisdiction because:

14 Appearance, Notice of

(*a*) The *Time Limit* for presenting the complaint has not been complied with.

(*b*) The complainant works wholly *Overseas*.

(*c*) The complainant claims to have been an employee but does not fall within the statutory definition. (See *Employment*.)

15 Applicants

The term 'applicant' can be used in the context both of job applications and applications to an employment tribunal. In most of the examples given in this book, job applicants will be referred to as candidates and applicants to tribunals will be referred to as complainants.

Most complaints to tribunal are presented by employees or job applicants. So far as employees are concerned, the wide definition of *Employment* should be noted.

Complaints can also be presented by *Contract Workers* and, under the *SDA 1975* and the *RRA 1976*, *Partners* or candidates for partnerships.

Workers, whether or not currently in employment, or applying for a specific job, can present complaints against:

(*a*) *Trade Unions*;

(*b*) *Qualifying Bodies*;

(*c*) *Employment Agencies*; and

(*d*) *Training Bodies* (but not under the *DDA 1995*).

Employers themselves can be applicants as well as the respondent, for example in complaints against:

(*a*) *Employers Associations*;

(*b*) *Trade Associations*;

(*c*) *Professional Bodies*;

(*d*) *Qualifying Bodies*; and

(*e*) *Employment Agencies* (but not under the *DDA 1995*).

16 Applications to Tribunal

16.1 RULES OF PROCEDURE

A complaint of discrimination (including victimisation) in the employment field or a claim under the *EPA 1970* is instituted by making an application to an employment tribunal. There are rules of procedure for employment tribunals. The rules cover not only the procedure at the hearing but also all preliminary matters, including the requirements for presenting an application. The rules which apply in England and Wales are the *Employment Tribunals (Constitution and Rules of Procedure) Regulations 1993* (*SI 1993 No 2687*, as amended by *SI 1994 No 536*). There are similar rules for Scotland.

The starting point is for the complainant, or applicant, to set out the application in writing. There is a form of originating application, which is still known as the IT1, but it is not compulsory to use the form. An application may be made by letter or by using a home made form. The application, in whatever form, must be in writing and must include the following information:

(*a*) the name and address of the applicant (including an address for service in the UK if the applicant's own address is outside the UK);

(*b*) the name and address of any person (the respondent) against whom relief is sought; and

(*c*) the grounds on which relief is sought, with particulars.

The application should then be signed and sent or delivered to the appropriate office. In England and Wales, this is the office for the place where the applicant works or worked or (in the case of a complaint by a job applicant) the place where the alleged discrimination took place. In Scotland, originating applications must be sent or delivered to the central office in Glasgow. An application is not presented until it is actually received.

There are *Time Limits* in all cases:

(*a*) three months for complaints of discrimination; and

(*b*) six months for a claim under the *EPA 1970*.

In order to ascertain the date from which time runs, see *Time Limits* and *Continuing Discrimination*.

16.2 PRACTICAL ADVICE

A prospective complainant should at all times keep in mind the need to comply with the appropriate time limit. If an application to tribunal is not presented in time, the right to pursue the complaint could be lost.

So long as the time limit is not overlooked, consideration should be given at the outset to the following preliminary matters:

(*a*) pursuing an internal *Grievance* or appeal, if the complainant is employed by the respondent;

(*b*) the possibility of applying for *Assistance* or seeking advice, particularly from the appropriate Commission; and

(*c*) using the statutory *Questionnaire* procedure.

The appropriate Commission is:

(*a*) the *Equal Opportunities Commission* (EOC), if the complaint is under the *EPA 1970* or the *SDA 1975*;

(*b*) the *Commission For Racial Equality* (CRE) if the complaint is under the *RRA 1976*; and

(*c*) the *Disability Rights Commission* (DRC) if the complaint is under the *DDA 1995*.

It is not necessary for the application to tribunal to contain a detailed statement running into several pages. The application should contain sufficient information to make it clear what the complaint is about. All possible heads of claim should be listed, bearing in mind that the same facts or events (such as the termination of the complainant's employment) may give rise to more than one head of complaint, such as unfair dismissal and sex discrimination. In many cases relating to discrimination as between men and women it is unclear whether the complaint falls under the *EPA 1970* or the *SDA 1975*. Both Acts should be referred to. It is better for a complaint to have too many labels attached to it than too few.

In most cases there is no difficulty in identifying the person to be named in the application as the respondent against whom relief is sought. It will usually be the applicant's employer, former employer or prospective employer. The following points should, however, be noted:

(*a*) Consideration should be given to the possibility of naming one or more additional respondents, particularly, in a complaint of *Harassment*, the fellow employee(s) responsible for the harassment. The reason is that the employer may be successful in making out the defence that all *Reasonably Practicable Steps* to prevent the discrimination have been taken, leaving the individual harasser(s) as the only person(s) against whom relief may be claimed.

(*b*) Where, after a complaint has arisen, there is a change in the identity of the applicant's employer, because of a transfer covered by the *Transfer of Undertakings (Protection of Employment) Regulations 1981* (*SI 1981 No 1794*, as amended by *SI 1987 No 442*), the complaint should normally be presented against the new employer, not the old employer. In cases of doubt, both the new employer and the old employer should be named as respondents. The position can be clarified later.

17 Appraisals

Regular (usually annual) appraisals form an important part of the employment arrangements in many organisations; see also *Assessments*.

Often they are carried out by comparatively junior employees who have received no adequate guidance or training. Giving untrained employees responsibility for carrying out appraisals can lead to complaints of direct discrimination, because of the risk that appraisals will be subjective and inconsistent. Clearly an employee who receives a poor appraisal will be able to complain that he or she has been subjected to a detriment or denied access to a benefit or facility, because appraisals can play an important part in career development and can also be taken into account in decisions relating to:

(*a*) pay increases;

(*b*) promotion; and

(*c*) selection for redundancy.

Ideally, employers should limit responsibility for appraisals to those managers who have received guidance and training on how to carry out appraisals objectively and consistently. As a minimum, guidance should be given to all appraisers and appraisals should be subject to spot checks to identify those who are not competent to carry them out.

Where the performance of job duties is adversely affected by a disability, consideration should be given to a *Reasonable Adjustment* both of the appraisal and of the job duties themselves.

18 Aptitude Tests

Where work requires a particular skill or aptitude, there is no objection in principle to the use of tests to measure a job applicant's or employee's aptitude for the work. If the test is properly designed and carried out, that would usually be an objective and non-discriminatory way of selecting for the post.

Care should be taken, however, and if necessary specialist advice should be obtained, to ensure that the test does not incorporate requirements or conditions which would tend to disqualify candidates of either sex or of any particular *Racial Group*. For example, if candidates taking a test are required to read written instructions, this requirement could exclude candidates from particular racial groups (such as candidates from other European Union or Eastern European countries) for whom English is not their first language.

Employers must also be alert to the need to carry out *Reasonable Adjustments* in order to modify any test which places a disabled candidate at a disadvantage. Depending on the kind of test and the nature of the disability, the adjustments required could include:

(*a*) modifying the test itself;

(*b*) allowing the candidate more time;

(*c*) providing special equipment; or

(*d*) permitting assistance with certain aspects of the test.

19 Armed Forces

19.1 GENERAL

Members of the armed forces are in the service of the Crown. They are not conventional employees.

Legislation may nevertheless provide for members of the armed forces to be treated as employees and to be given the right to present complaints of discrimination and equal pay claims. Each Act deals with the matter in a different way and needs to be looked at separately.

19.2 THE SDA 1975

Until 1 February 1995 the *SDA 1975* contained a general exception for service in the armed forces. This exception was, however, overridden by the *Equal Treatment Directive*. It will be recalled that many service women who had been required to resign on becoming pregnant were able to pursue claims for compensation, based on the Directive.

The position now, following the amendment of the *SDA 1975*, is that, subject to three exceptions or special provisions, members of the armed forces, or those who wish to join, have the same rights under the *SDA 1975* as the rights given to conventional employees and job applicants.

The exceptions and special provisions are as follows:

(*a*) No complaint of sex discrimination may be made about any act done for the purpose of ensuring the combat effectiveness of the armed forces.

(*b*) Discrimination is permitted in admission to any cadet training corps for the time being administered by the Ministry of Defence, including the Army Cadet Force, Air Training Corps, Sea Cadet Corps and Combined Cadet Force.

(*c*) A person who has applied unsuccessfully to join the Armed Forces (apart from one of the cadet corps mentioned above) may present a complaint of sex discrimination just like any conventional job applicant, but there are special provisions relating to alleged acts of discrimination against serving members of the armed forces. A complaint cannot be presented to an employment tribunal unless the complainant has first made a complaint to an officer under the relevant service redress procedures and submitted that complaint to the Defence Council. A complaint may then be presented to an employment tribunal if the complaint to the Defence Council has been submitted and not withdrawn or if the Defence Council have made a determination with respect to the complaint.

Because of the requirement to make a complaint under the internal procedures, before presenting a complaint to an employment tribunal, the normal time limit of three months for employment tribunal complaints is extended to six months. It should be noted, however, that the ordinary time limit of three months applies where the complainant has not been obliged to use the internal procedures (for example where the complaint is by a person who has applied unsuccessfully to join the armed forces).

19.3 THE EPA

It has been possible since 1 October 1997 for members of the armed forces to submit complaints under the *EPA 1970*. Until that date, it was necessary for complainants to rely on *Article 141* (then *Article 119*) and the *Equal Pay Directive*.

Subject to one proviso, a member of the armed forces can make an equal pay claim as if he or she were an ordinary employee. The one proviso is that there is a similar requirement to that under the *SDA 1975* to make a complaint to an officer under the relevant service redress procedures and submit a complaint to the Defence Council under those procedures, before presenting a complaint to an employment tribunal.

Because of this requirement to use the internal procedures as a first step, the normal time limit of six months for a tribunal complaint is extended to nine months from the end of the period of service during which the claim arose.

19.4 THE RRA 1976

The general principle is that service in the armed forces is treated in the same way as employment by a private employer. Accordingly members of the armed forces and those who apply to join the armed forces have rights under the *RRA 1976*.

The *RRA 1976* contains similar provisions to those in the *SDA 1975* and the *EPA 1970* relating to the need to use the service redress procedures, and submit a complaint first to an officer and then to the Defence Council, before presenting a complaint to an employment tribunal. As under the *SDA 1975*, the time limit for complaints is, because of this requirement, increased from three months to six months. It should be noted, however, that, as under the *SDA 1975*, the ordinary time limit of three months applies where the complainant has not been obliged to use the internal procedures (for example where the complaint is by a person who has applied unsuccessfully to join the armed forces).

Although in principle there must be no racial discrimination either in admission to the armed forces or in the treatment of service personnel, these provisions are subject to the general exception relating to acts done under *Statutory Authority* and *National Security*. In particular, it is lawful for admission to the armed forces to be restricted by regulation on grounds of nationality or national origin.

19.5 THE DDA 1995

It is expressly provided in the *DDA 1995* that the employment provisions do not apply to service in any of the naval, military or air forces of the Crown.

20 Article 141

Article 141 is the re-numbered *Article 119* of the Treaty setting up what is now the European Union (before that the European Community and before that various other names).

Article 141 establishes the principle of equal pay for equal work as between men and women. It is particularly important because it has direct effect, so that it can be relied on by individuals who have taken their cases to employment tribunals. That direct effect is achieved by extending the relevant domestic legislation and disapplying provisions in that legislation which are inconsistent with *Article 141*. In Great Britain, the relevant domestic legislation is the *EPA 1970* in relation to contractual terms relating to pay and the *SDA 1975* in relation to non-contractual arrangements for pay. In each case, 'pay' is given a wide meaning – see *Equal Pay*.

An early example of the use of what was then *Article 119* was to override the requirement in the *EPA 1970* that a complainant and comparator must be in the *Same Employment* contemporaneously. It was held in the case of *Macarthys Limited v Smith* [*1980*] *IRLR 210* that a woman could base her claim on the pay received by her male predecessor. More recently, *Article 119* has been of considerable importance in relation to *Pensions*.

21 Assessments

The way in which workers are assessed is a key concern of the discrimination laws, particularly – but by no means only – the assessment of job applicants and candidates for promotion. Many employers give (and all should give) training to interviewers and others concerned in the selection process or in performance appraisals, to help them to avoid discriminating unlawfully or giving the impression of so doing.

Many employers overlook, however, the need to instruct and train managers in carrying out assessments for other purposes. A particularly important issue is that of redundancy selection. Increasingly, employers have moved away from exclusive reliance on length of service and other objective criteria and instead place the greatest weight on subjective criteria such as capability and motivation.

The use of these subjective criteria increases the risk of unfair selection and hence of unfair dismissal claims. It also increases the risk of direct sex or racial discrimination or disability discrimination.

Employers should give careful consideration to the arrangements for assessments, including *Appraisals*, to be carried out. The following are key elements:

(*a*) Assessments should be carried out by more than one person, to minimise the risk of favouritism or prejudice.

(*b*) Alternatively, all assessments should be checked by a senior person who has some knowledge of the employees being assessed.

(*c*) Consultation with the employees must take place as part of the assessment process.

(*d*) Guidance and training should be given to the assessors.

The training for assessors should include at least the need:

(*a*) for consistency;

(*b*) for impartiality;

(*c*) to rely on verifiable facts and not on instinct;

(*d*) to carry out assessments which can be explained and defended; and

(*e*) to give special consideration to and take advice on the assessment of disabled employees.

22 Assistance

A complainant or prospective complainant can apply for assistance to the relevant Commission, being:

(*a*) the EOC, if the complaint is under the *EPA 1970* or the *SDA 1975*;

(*b*) the CRE, if the complaint is under the *RRA 1976*; or

(*c*) the Disability Rights Commission (DRC) if the complaint is one of disability discrimination.

The assistance granted can include:

(*a*) advice at any stage;

(*b*) assistance in settling the claim; or

(*c*) representation at the hearing.

Complainants or prospective complainants should apply for assistance as soon as possible. There are two reasons:

(*a*) Advice may be needed at an early stage to set the case off on the right footing and, for example, to make effective use of the *Questionnaire* procedure.

(*b*) Applications for representation need to be investigated and reported on and considered by a committee, which can all take some considerable time.

It is expressly provided in the *Disability Rights Commission Act 1999*, the *SDA 1975* and the *RRA 1976* that when the Commission has incurred expenses in providing assistance to a complainant or a prospective complainant, the Commission has a first charge on any costs or expenses which become payable to the assisted person. This provision would be relevant in one of the rare cases where *Costs* are awarded against a respondent and would also apply if costs were to be payable by a respondent as part of a settlement.

There are many cases which the Commissions are unable to assist because of financial constraints. The cases which are most likely to receive assistance are those which raise a question of principle. Another factor which the Commission is required to take into account is that it is unreasonable to expect the complainant or proposed complainant to deal with the case unaided (for example because of its complexity or because the complainant is in a weak position in relation to the respondent).

Where the relevant Commission is unable or unwilling to provide representation, other possible sources include:

(*a*) any trade union to which the complainant belongs;

(*b*) a Law Centre, if there is one available;

(*c*) a CAB; or

(*d*) the Bar's Free Representation Unit and solicitors' firms.

Legal Aid for representation at tribunal hearings has never been available.

The Commissions do not have the power to assist respondents with representation, although respondents, like any other member of the public, can make enquiries about the legislation and its implications.

23 Associated Employers

It can be relevant to ascertain whether two employers are associated, because in an *Equal Pay* claim the comparator of the opposite sex who is named by the complainant need not have the same employer as the complainant, provided that the two employers are associated. The complainant and the comparator are regarded as being in the *Same Employment* for the purposes of the *EPA 1970* if they work for associated employers either:

(*a*) at the same establishment; or

(*b*) at two establishments at which *Common Terms and Conditions* are observed.

Two employers are associated if:

(*a*) one is a company of which the other (directly or indirectly) has control; or

(*b*) both are companies of which a third person (directly or indirectly) has control.

In both the above cases, the person having control could be, for example, one or more individuals or another company. If John Smith has control of both X Limited and Y Limited, then they are all three associated employers for the purposes of the *EPA 1970*.

24 Assumptions

Acts of direct discrimination or disability discrimination frequently occur because employers, managers or interviewers base selection and other decisions on lazy assumptions, without taking the trouble to investigate the true position.

Married women, for example, are turned down for jobs or promotion because it is assumed, without enquiry, that their childcare and other family responsibilities will prevent them from accepting jobs, promotions or transfers which will involve:

(*a*) working unsocial hours;

(*b*) relocating; or

(*c*) travelling overseas.

If a decision to turn down a woman's application or ignore her claims is based on any such assumption, that is a clear case of sex and marriage discrimination.

An example of direct discrimination under the *RRA 1976* would be turning down an application from a job applicant with a foreign sounding name on the assumption that he or she would be unable to meet the standards of written or spoken English required for the post.

The danger of basing employment decisions on uninformed assumptions is perhaps greatest in relation to disability discrimination. Many employers and managers are ignorant of the wide range of jobs which can be undertaken, with or without *Reasonable Adjustments*, by workers who have most severe disabilities. Where a disabled candidate would meet the required standard to be shortlisted and interviewed if the disability were to be disregarded, then that candidate should always be offered an interview. The questions whether the disability will make it difficult for the candidate to carry out the job, and if so whether a *Reasonable Adjustment* could help the candidate to overcome the difficulties, can then be explored positively and constructively at the interview.

25 Back Pay

Equal Pay claims are usually about pay (including not only hourly pay or salary but also, for example, contractual bonus schemes and contractual terms for the payment of commission), although they can also be about other contract terms.

When a claim is about pay, the purpose is normally twofold:

(*a*) to obtain increased pay for the future; and

(*b*) to obtain back pay at the higher rate.

Under the *EPA 1970*, the period for which back pay can be awarded is limited to the period starting two years before the application to tribunal is presented.

That limitation has now been overridden as a result of the decision of the ECJ in *Levez v T H Jenning (Harlow Pools) Limited [1999] IRLR 36*. It was held by the ECJ that the two year limitation was contrary to the principle of equal pay under *Article 141* (formerly 119) of the Treaty establishing the European Community. The reason for the decision was that the two year limitation was not a general one applying to equal pay claims and to other claims, unrelated to equal pay or sex discrimination – it was peculiar to the *EPA 1970*.

The EAT had to consider the practical implications of this decision when the case of *Levez* came back to the EAT together with another appeal which was heard at the same time, in the case of *Hicking v Basford Group Limited [1999] IRLR 764*. The EAT had to consider, in the light of the ECJ decision, whether it makes a difference, in claims for back pay going back more than two years, whether the employee has been misled by the employer. Mrs Levez could have been awarded the extra back pay on that narrower ground; Mrs Hicking's claim for the extra back pay could succeed only if the two year limit were to be struck down altogether.

The EAT allowed both appeals. Equal pay claims were compared with claims for moneys due under a contract, claims for unlawful deduction from wages and claims of unlawful discrimination in terms of employment on grounds of race or disability. It was held that *section 2(5)* of the *EPA 1970* (restricting claims for back pay to a period of two years)

> 'represents a unique limitation on compensation which applies only when the applicant is relying upon an equality clause. There are no compensating advantages . . . *s 2(5)* is a restriction on the right to have a full and effective remedy for breach of *Article 119* and the *Equal Pay Directive*. It is a breach of the principle of equivalence.' Accordingly '*s 2(5)* is no bar to the recovery of monies held to be due for a period of six years from the date of the commencement of proceedings.'

It had been suggested by Counsel that the six-year period might, arguably, not apply and that it was possible to look back over an unlimited period. The point was not developed in argument and the EAT saw no merit in it.

The position is different, however, in relation to *Pensions*, where there has been past discrimination (notably against part-time workers) in relation to access to pension schemes.

26 Beards

At face value (if the use of that expression can be forgiven), a requirement by an employer that job applicants, or existing employees, should be beardless is both an eccentric requirement and one which has nothing to do with discrimination.

There have, however, been cases about such requirements, not where the employer has prohibited beards for aesthetic reasons, but where there are concerns about hygiene, in chocolate and other food factories.

A requirement to shave off a beard, if employment is to be granted or retained, has a discriminatory effect against at least one ethnic group, the Sikhs. The requirement is not unlawful if it can be justified, but it is important that any employer minded to impose the requirement should in the first instance fully explore alternative methods which would not have a discriminatory effect (such as the use of some kind of protective covering). Unless this has been done, it will be difficult if not impossible to justify the requirement.

It is also arguable, at least in theory, that it is direct sex discrimination for an employer to require that job applicants or employees should not have beards. The argument would be that this is a gender based criterion and the use of it is direct sex discrimination against men, in the same way that pregnancy discrimination is direct discrimination against women. A complaint could perhaps be resisted on the ground that the concept of the bearded lady is not a fictitious one, even outside fairgrounds. Perhaps also this is one of the rare cases where (if there is no question of indirect racial discrimination in relation to the actual complainant) the concept of *De Minimis* may be taken out and dusted down. See also *Gender Based Criteria*.

27 Benefits

27.1 THE STATUTORY PROVISIONS

Most complaints of discrimination are brought because the complainant has applied unsuccessfully for a job (whether as an outside candidate or for an internal vacancy) or because the complainant has been dismissed or subjected to some other detriment, such as racial or sexual harassment.

Although opportunities for promotion and training are perhaps the most important benefits which can be afforded to employees, the *SDA 1975*, the *RRA 1976* and the *DDA 1995* also make it unlawful for employers to discriminate in relation to any other benefits, facilities or services. There must be no discrimination:

(*a*) by refusing access to benefits, facilities or services;

(*b*) by deliberately omitting to afford an employee access to them; or

(*c*) in the way in which an employee is afforded access to them.

It is not necessary to distinguish benefits from facilities or either of them from services. Usually a complaint will be about a benefit or facility rather than a service, since there are not many circumstances in which an employer can be said to be providing a service to employees.

Both the *RRA 1976* and the *DDA 1995* impose separate obligations on employers not to discriminate in the terms of employment afforded to employees. Accordingly a claim about discrimination in relation to other benefits, facilities or services will relate to non-contractual or discretionary matters.

27.2 CONTRACTUAL TERMS – THE *SDA 1975* AND THE *EPA 1970*

The position under the *SDA 1975* is more complicated. In the normal way, any complaint about pay or other contractual terms would be brought under the *EPA 1970*, not the *SDA 1975*. Any complaint about any contractual terms for the payment of money (including, for example, a claim under a contractual bonus scheme) must be brought under the *EPA 1970* and is dependent on identifying a suitable comparator of the opposite sex (see *Equal Pay*).

The position is less straightforward where the complaint is about a contractual term other than one for the payment of money. Suppose, for example, that a female employee contends that she should have a contractual right to be provided with a fully expensed company car. The first question in such a case is whether there is a suitable male comparator in the *Same Employment* (e.g. one employed on work of *Equal Value* – see *Equal Pay*). If there is, then she must bring a claim under the *EPA 1970*, which will fail if the employer is able to make out a *Material Factor* defence.

If, however, it is not possible to identify a male comparator, then the employee can present her complaint under the *SDA 1975*. Her case will be based on a hypothetical comparison, i.e. that if a man with her qualifications and experience had been employed to do her job then that man would have been given a contractual right to a fully expensed company car. Such a case could be hard to prove, based as it must be on a hypothetical comparison.

27.3 CONCESSIONARY GOODS AND SERVICES

Many employees are also customers of their employers. Stores sell goods to their employees, bus and rail companies and airlines transport their employees from place to place, hotels provide accommodation for their employees and banks and insurance companies lend money to their staff.

If an employee purchases goods and services on the terms which are available to any member of the public, then any complaint of discrimination in relation to the provision of those goods and services must be brought in the county court under the non-employment provisions of the relevant legislation.

Frequently, however, employers give concessionary terms to their staff. Any complaint of discrimination in relation to the concessionary terms offered (or in the refusal of concessionary terms) must be presented to an employment tribunal like any other complaint of discrimination in the employment field. For example, there have in the past been cases under the *SDA 1975* of discrimination against women:

(*a*) by banks and building societies in relation to eligibility for mortgage advances at preferential rates; and

(*b*) by rail companies in continuing concessionary travel arrangements for the families of former male employees but not for those of former female employees.

27.4 EXAMPLES OF NON-CONTRACTUAL BENEFITS AND FACILITIES

Employers provide a wide range of benefits which are sometimes contractual but frequently discretionary. These include concessionary goods, services and facilities of the kind already mentioned. They also include:

(*a*) discretionary bonus schemes;

(*b*) luncheon vouchers;

(*c*) membership of sporting or social clubs; or

(*d*) private health insurance.

Complaints may also relate to access to or the detailed operation of benefits or facilities such as:

(*a*) voluntary overtime;

(*b*) a grievance procedure; or

(*c*) voluntary redundancy.

For example, there would be a *prima facie* case of direct sex discrimination if an employer invites applications for voluntary redundancy on generous terms, accepts applications from male employees but turns down an application from a female employee. The employer would have a defence, however, if it could be shown that the application by the woman was turned down because she, unlike the men, was a key employee and there was a business need to retain her. She would not then have been refused voluntary redundancy because of her gender and the relevant circumstances of her case and those of her male colleagues would be different.

A complaint about the amount of a redundancy payment (as opposed to access to voluntary redundancy) would normally fall under the *EPA 1970* (read with *Article 141*), rather than the *SDA 1975*, whether the redundancy is compulsory or voluntary and whether the payment is statutory or contractual (but probably not if it is discretionary).

It is good practice, however, when acting for a complainant, to refer both to the *SDA 1975* and the *EPA 1970*, because the boundary between the two Acts is sometimes unclear.

27.5 SERVICE AND SENIORITY

In most organisations, the benefits and facilities, whether contractual or non-contractual, enjoyed by employees are more generous for senior employees than for junior employees. For example, where neither a senior employee nor a junior colleague need a car for the performance of their duties, the senior person is more likely to be provided with a car as a fringe benefit.

If most of an organisation's senior employees are white males, with much higher percentages of women and black employees in the lower ranks, then there could in theory be complaints of direct or indirect racial or sex discrimination about the benefits and facilities enjoyed by the senior employees (or complaints under the *EPA 1970* about contractual benefits enjoyed by the senior male employees). It is difficult to see how complaints of direct discrimination could succeed if superior benefits were enjoyed by senior employees, not because of their gender or colour, but because of their senior status. It would be possible to formulate complaints of indirect discrimination, but it is likely that a tribunal would find that employers have a reasonable business need to give senior employees more generous packages (in relation to fringe benefits as well as to pay).

It is of course important to distinguish complaints about access to benefits or facilities from complaints about access to promotion. If an employee complains that he or she would have a better job, and the pay and fringe benefits that go with that job, but for discrimination against him or her, then the complaint is about discrimination in access to opportunities for promotion.

Benefits and facilities are also sometimes linked to length of service. Sometimes employees receive improved benefits after a specified period of employment; in some organisations certain benefits are denied to employees altogether until they have completed a minimum period of employment such as one year.

There is no direct discrimination in such cases, if the rules are applied without regard to gender, marital status, disability or any racial factor. It is impossible to rule out the possibility of a successful complaint of indirect discrimination, however, where the employees who have not completed the qualifying period contain a high proportion of, for example, women in relation to the proportion of women in the organisation as a whole. If the justification for denying fringe benefits to employees in their first year is simply administrative convenience, that might not be accepted as being a reasonable business need.

27.6 REASONABLE ADJUSTMENTS

There are circumstances in which a disabled employee may be placed at a substantial disadvantage in comparison with employees who are not disabled, because the employee's disability prevents him or her from enjoying a particular benefit or facility. In such circumstances, the employer must consider making reasonable adjustments. The following are possible examples:

(*a*) An employee is entitled to be provided with a *Company Car*, but a disability prevents the employee from driving.

(*b*) An employee would normally be provided with private medical insurance, but the employee's disability makes the cost prohibitively expensive.

27.6 Benefits

(*c*) The employer would pay for the employee to join a golf club, but the employee is unable to play golf, and therefore unable or unwilling to join a club, because of a disability.

In all these examples, one possible adjustment would be for the employer to make payments to the employee, equivalent to the cost which would have been incurred by the employer in providing the benefit. In the first case, consideration should also be given to assistance with alternative transport arrangements, particularly where the disability makes it difficult for the employee either to perform certain duties or to travel between home and work.

28 Burden of Proof

The starting point, whether a complaint is under the *EPA 1970*, the *SDA 1975*, the *RRA 1976* or the *DDA 1995*, is that it is for the complainant to prove his or her case, but only on a balance of probabilities. For example, in a complaint of *Sexual Harassment*, where the facts are in dispute, it is for the complainant to satisfy the tribunal that it is more likely than not that the incidents complained of did take place and amounted to sexual harassment.

It is, on the other hand, up to the respondent to make out a defence which is available under the relevant Act, again on a balance of probabilities. For example:

(*a*) There is no discrimination under the *DDA 1995* if the employer can show that the treatment complained of is justified.

(*b*) There is no indirect discrimination for the purposes of the *SDA 1975* or the *RRA 1976* if the respondent can show the requirement or condition complained of to be justifiable irrespective of, e.g. the colour of the person to whom it is applied.

(*c*) An employer defending an equal pay case can put forward the *Material Factor* defence.

At the time of writing, there will shortly be a need to amend the *EPA 1970* and the *SDA 1975* in order to comply with the Council Directive (No 97/80/EC) on the burden of proof in cases of discrimination based on sex. The Directive is due to be implemented by 1 January 2001.

The Directive requires Member States to take the necessary measures, to ensure that in certain circumstances it shall be for the respondent to prove that there has been no breach of the principle of equal treatment. In other words, the burden of proof must in those circumstances lie on the respondent, not on the complainant.

It is possible that the *RRA 1976* and the *DDA 1995* will also be amended. It has happened previously (although not invariably) that changes to the *SDA 1975* which have been required under *Community Law* have also been reflected in the other discrimination legislation, for example the removal of the limit on compensation.

The implementation of the Directive is unlikely, however, to have any revolutionary effect on cases in Great Britain. This is because the burden of proof will be on the respondent only once the complainant has established facts from which it may be presumed that there has been direct or indirect discrimination. Once such facts have been established, the burden of proof already tends in practice to shift to the respondent.

So far as *Indirect Discrimination* is concerned, the requirements of the Directive appear to reflect exactly the current provisions of the *SDA 1975* and the *RRA 1976*. If the complainant can show that he or she has suffered detriment through being unable to comply with a requirement or condition which has been applied to him or her, and if the complainant can also show *Disparate Impact* in accordance with the formula set out in the *SDA 1975* or the *RRA 1976*, then the complainant will have established facts from which it may be presumed that there has been indirect discrimination. The Act then requires the respondent to justify the requirement or condition on grounds which are (in a case under the *SDA 1975*) unrelated to the gender of the person to whom it is applied or, in the words of the Directive, to prove that there has been no breach of the principle of equal treatment.

There are no correspondingly explicit provisions in the statutory definitions of *Direct Discrimination*, but case law has established a similar principle. The leading case of

King v The Great Britain – China Centre [1991] IRLR 513 is considered under *Evidence of Discrimination*. The case establishes the principle that a finding of difference in treatment and a difference in race or gender will often point to the possibility of direct discrimination and in such circumstances the tribunal will look to the employer for an explanation. If none is given, or the only explanation put forward is inadequate or unsatisfactory, then it is legitimate for the tribunal to draw an inference of discrimination. The need for the employer to give an explanation is effectively a shift in the burden of proof, even though the Court of Appeal stated in the above decision that the concept of a shifting burden of proof is unnecessary and unhelpful.

The likelihood is, therefore, that the implementation of the Directive will make little difference, except for making explicit in direct discrimination cases what now normally take place implicitly. Obviously, however, it will be necessary to look closely at the wording of the amending legislation.

29 'But For' Test

This is a helpful but not conclusive test for identifying cases of *Direct Discrimination*. For example, would the complainant have received the treatment complained of from the respondent:

(*a*) but for his colour;

(*b*) but for her national origin;

(*c*) but for being a woman;

(*d*) but for being a man; or

(*e*) but for her marital status?

The test was adopted by the House of Lords in the non-employment case of *James v Eastleigh Borough Council [1990] IRLR 288*. This was the case in which a man complained about having to pay for admission to a local authority swimming pool, while his wife, who was the same age but in receipt of a state pension, was allowed in free.

The 'but for' test is helpful in emphasising that the question to be considered is the reason for the treatment complained of, not the motive or intention of the person responsible for that treatment. It also covers cases where the complaint is about the application of a gender based criterion. In the above-mentioned case, the criterion adopted, as a qualification for benefits, was the eligibility for the state pension, notwithstanding the different qualifying ages of 60 and 65 for women and men. In other cases, the gender based criterion has been *Pregnancy* as a reason for dismissing female employees or turning down female job applicants.

The 'but for' test does not give the answer in all cases, however, because it suggests that the race, gender or marital status, as the case may be, of the complainant must be the only reason for the treatment complained of. That is not the case. It need only be an important or significant reason (see *Direct Discrimination*).

The automatic use of the 'but for' test may also suggest, perhaps misleadingly, that there is liability in a case where *Less Favourable Treatment* is not in any sense intended – see *Unintentional Discrimination*.

30 Can Comply

This term is a key part of the definition of *Indirect Discrimination*. A complaint can be made only by a person who is unable to comply with a requirement or condition, commonly (but by no means always) one which is attached to a job for which he or she is applying.

The term is also relevant to a further part of the definition, because in order to establish *Disparate Impact* it is necessary to show that the proportion of the members of the relevant group (such as women) who can comply with the requirement or condition is considerably smaller than the proportion of non-members (in this case men) who can comply with it.

Case law has established that 'can comply' means 'can in practice comply', having regard, for example, to family responsibilities and cultural traditions, so that there is inability to comply for the purpose of the definition even where compliance is physically or technically possible – see *Indirect Discrimination*.

A question which does not appear to have been decided yet is whether the reason for the complainant's inability to comply with a requirement or condition must be the same as the cause of the disparate impact. For example, could an unmarried and childless part-time employee complain about a requirement to work different, unsocial, hours if her inability to comply is because the new hours would clash with those of a second part-time job which she has? In principle, a complaint of indirect sex discrimination should not be upheld in these circumstances, but her case would appear to be covered on a literal construction of *section 1(1)(b)* of the *SDA 1975*. Possibly the answer is that the tribunal would in such circumstances expect very little by way of justification of the requirement.

31 Capability Dismissals

A reason relating to the capability of the employee is one of the substantial reasons for which an employee may be fairly dismissed under *section 98* of the *Employment Rights Act 1996*. In this context, there may be a lack of capability because of inability to perform the job to a satisfactory standard or because of sickness, leading to an unacceptable level of absence (whether a long term absence or repeated short term absences).

It is of course essential that employers dismissing for capability, as for any other reason, should avoid any sex, racial or disability discrimination. If a dismissal is discriminatory, then whether or not it is also unfair there will be no limit on the compensation, which can include a figure for injury to feelings.

So far as disabled employees are concerned, see *Disciplining* and *Dismissing Disabled Employees*.

Many employers include in the contract of employment, a term under which the disciplinary procedure does not apply during the probationary period of employment or for the first year of the employment, so that employees can be dismissed without formality for poor performance before they have acquired unfair dismissal rights. There is, however, no qualifying period for rights under the discrimination legislation and there is an enhanced danger of discrimination whenever an employee is dismissed without formality. In particular:

(*a*) Employers will live to regret hasty dismissals in cases where performance or attendance has been or could have been adversely affected by a disability.

(*b*) A consistent approach is essential in order to minimise complaints of direct discrimination.

(*c*) A dismissal for absences which are wholly or partly pregnancy related is an act of direct sex discrimination and is also an automatically unfair dismissal, there being no qualifying period in such cases.

32 Career Breaks

The availability of career breaks can be an important benefit or facility for employees, particularly those who have childcare responsibilities. Under the best schemes, the employer maintains links with the employee by, for example, sending him or her copies of newsletters and bulletins and inviting the employee to social events and even team meetings.

It must not be forgotten, however, that it is not only women who have childcare and other family responsibilities (such as caring for sick or elderly relatives). It is direct sex discrimination for an employer to refuse or fail to offer a career break to a man in circumstances in which it would be offered to a woman.

33 Case Law

All the discrimination laws give rise to difficult questions of interpretation.

In relation to the *EPA 1970*, the *SDA 1975* and the *RRA 1976*, we have the advantage of nearly a quarter of a century of appeal decisions (together with rulings of the ECJ on relevant principles of *Community Law*). The employment provisions of the *DDA 1995* did not come into force until 2 December 1996. There have been important appeal decisions on some issues, including the definition of disability, but there are important questions still to be answered.

Any party or advocate presenting or defending a case needs to select the decided cases on which reliance will be placed in support of legal submissions. The following are some suggested guidelines:

(*a*) Where there are conflicting appeal decisions, Court of Appeal decisions outrank EAT decisions and they must both bow to House of Lords decisions.

(*b*) The ECJ has the last word on questions of *Community Law* (but sometimes gives the last word more than once in different terms) but it is then necessary to consider how the ECJ ruling is applied when the case comes back to the EAT, the Court of Appeal or the House of Lords.

(*c*) It is not usually necessary or helpful to cite several authorities in support of the same proposition, especially where one particular appeal decision has become the established authority.

(*d*) Decisions on the interpretation of one of the discrimination laws are generally recognised as authoritative on corresponding provisions in the other Acts, but it should be noted that the definition of discrimination which is contained in the *DDA 1995* is quite different from that contained in the *SDA 1975* and the *RRA 1976*.

There is an understandable and sensible tendency to rely, where possible, on a recent appeal decision, particularly where the House of Lords or the Court of Appeal has considered earlier authorities and summarised the state of the law on a particular issue. There are, however, early cases which are still regularly referred to as leading authorities, such as:

(*a*) the EAT decision in *Capper Pass Limited v Lawton* [*1976*] *IRLR 366* (*Like Work*);

(*b*) the Court of Appeal decision *in Perera v Civil Service Commission* [*1983*] *IRLR 166* (*Indirect Discrimination*); and

(*c*) the House of Lords decision in *Nassé v Science Research Council* [*1979*] *IRLR 465* (*Documents*).

There are also many early appeal decisions on which reliance can no longer be placed, even where they have not been expressly overruled in later cases. An appeal decision can become unreliable for many reasons:

(*a*) Sometimes an appeal decision breaks new ground, so that all the earlier decisions on the same point must be either disregarded or treated with great caution. Examples are the House of Lords decisions in *Webb v EMO Air Cargo (UK) Limited* [*1993*] *IRLR 27* (*Pregnancy*) and *Nagarajan v London Regional Transport* [*1999*] *IRLR 572* (*Victimisation* and *Direct Discrimination*).

(*b*) Some appeal decisions, particularly at the EAT level, are plainly wrong and although not formally overruled are either ignored or distinguished (found to be inapplicable because of different facts) in future cases. An example is the case of *Kidd v DRG (UK) Limited* [*1985*] *IRLR 190* (defining the *Pool*).

(*c*) Sometimes an appeal decision reflecting particular attitudes becomes outdated (and is quietly ignored) because of changed social attitudes and employment practices. An example is the EAT decision in *Clymo v London Borough of Wandsworth* [*1989*] *IRLR 241* (*Job Share*).

34 Charities

34.1 THE GENERAL PRINCIPLE

The general principle is that persons employed by charities have the same rights as any other employees.

The *SDA 1975*, the *RRA 1976* and the *DDA 1995* each contain, however, an exception to cover the following cases, where:

(*a*) employment is provided pursuant to the provisions of a charitable instrument; and

(*b*) there are provisions in that instrument which provide for discrimination in the benefits to be conferred.

A charitable instrument is an enactment or other instrument passed or made for charitable purposes.

34.2 THE SDA 1975

The exception in the *SDA 1975* applies when a charitable instrument contains a provision for conferring benefits:

(*a*) exclusively on persons of one sex; or

(*b*) mainly on persons of one sex, benefits to persons of the opposite sex being exceptional or relatively insignificant.

In *Hugh-Jones v St John's College Cambridge [1979] ICR 848,* this exception was successfully relied upon to permit sex discrimination against a woman in an appointment to a research fellowship under the college statutes (those statutes being for the charitable purpose of advancing learning).

Exceptions of this kind do not sit very easily with the provisions of the *Equal Treatment Directive*, although the latter has direct effect only in the public sector.

34.3 THE RRA 1976

The exception in the *RRA 1976* applies where the charitable instrument provides for conferring benefits on persons of a class defined otherwise than by colour. Where a provision in an instrument restricts benefits by reference to colour, the instrument takes effect with that restriction removed.

The exception would, for example, permit direct or indirect racial discrimination in the following examples:

(*a*) Employment in a sheltered workshop is limited to persons born in Scotland.

(*b*) A university scholarship under a charitable trust is available only for the children of employees of a particular company, who happen to be all white.

The direct racial discrimination in the first case and the indirect discrimination in the second case are both permitted, but if the trust in either case had expressly restricted benefits to white persons then that restriction would have been struck out.

34.4 **THE DDA 1995**

The *DDA 1995* does not prohibit *Positive Discrimination* in favour of disabled persons, but it would normally be unlawful to discriminate in favour of one particular category and against other categories.

Discrimination of that kind is permitted if a charitable instrument provides for conferring benefits on one or more categories of person determined by reference to any physical or mental capacity. The exception would apply, for example, if a charity which exists to provide benefits for persons who have lost a limb, sets up a workshop to provide employment for such persons, using specially adapted equipment where necessary.

35 Childcare

There are some households in which the male partner has an equal or even the main responsibility for childcare. There are also some lone parent households which consist of a father and children.

These cases are, however, a minority. In society as a whole, it is still women who have the main responsibilities for childcare. In some households (and not only lone parent households) it is a responsibility which they undertake without any support at all from a male partner.

The main practical implication, in the employment context, is that many women are able to undertake only part-time work. Childcare responsibilities also make it impossible for some women to comply with requirements to:

(*a*) work unsociable hours;

(*b*) attend residential courses in order to receive training; or

(*c*) go on overnight business trips.

Employers need to be able to justify a requirement of full-time working and these other requirements in order to defeat complaints of *Indirect Discrimination*. Employers must be as flexible as business needs permit in relation to all these matters.

There are at least three respects in which employers can also stumble into acts of *Direct Discrimination* as a result of taking a superficial approach to questions of childcare. For example:

(*a*) It is generally good practice (and may even be necessary, to avoid indirect discrimination) for employers to allow female employees to switch to part-time working, to enable them to combine their work with their childcare responsibilities. The same facility must, however, be afforded in similar circumstances to male employees who have childcare responsibilities.

(*b*) Similarly, where employers provide financial assistance for childcare, or creches, or *Career Breaks*, male employees with childcare responsibilities must be given the same access as their female colleagues to all these facilities.

(*c*) In selecting job applicants for employment or employees for promotion or training, employers must not act on assumptions about the childcare and other family responsibilities of women. It would, for example, be a clear case of direct sex discrimination, if an employer were to refuse to appoint a woman to a post involving travel, simply because he assumes, without investigation, that her childcare responsibilities will prevent her from undertaking that travel.

36 Chivalry

It would be surprising if the law were to penalise the display of chivalrous attitudes and good manners in dealings between the sexes. If a male manager holds a door open for a junior female employee, or allows her to precede him into the lift, it is likely that an employment tribunal would give short shrift to a complaint by a male employee that he had been denied similar benefits. It is more likely that a complaint would be presented by the female employee herself, objecting to being singled out in either of the above respects, but her complaint could not be expected to succeed either.

The reason why findings of discrimination are implausible in the above examples is that the circumstances are so trivial that neither employee has been subjected to a detriment in any real sense. It is a very different matter, however, if notions of chivalry are allowed to influence employment decisions, for example in appointments to a particular post or in allocation of work. There is almost certain to be unlawful direct discrimination if employers decide these matters on the assumption that women are unsuitable for, or should be protected from, dangerous or unpleasant work (see *Detriment*). Suggestions to the contrary in an early Court of Appeal decision, *Peake v Automotive Products* [*1978*] *1 All ER 106*, should be disregarded.

37 Civil Service

Civil servants are not employees in the conventional sense, but the provisions of the *EPA 1970*, *SDA 1975*, *RRA 1976* and *DDA 1995* are expressly applied to servants of the Crown as if they were in private employment (subject to specific provisions relating to the *Armed Forces* and *Statutory Officers*).

Accordingly, a civil servant may present a complaint under the *EPA 1970* or a complaint of sex discrimination, racial discrimination or disability discrimination.

Complaints of discrimination may also be made in relation to arrangements for and applications for appointment to the Civil Service. The effect of the provisions in the *RRA 1976* in relation to acts done under *Statutory Authority*, however, is that rules made by a Minister of the Crown may lawfully restrict employment in the service of the Crown (or by some public bodies) on grounds of nationality, descent or residence (but not colour).

38 Codes of Practice

38.1 LEGAL STATUS

The *SDA 1975* and the *RRA 1976* each contain similar provisions relating to Codes of Practice.

The Equal Opportunities Commission (EOC) or the Commission for Racial Equality (CRE) (as the case may be) may issue Codes of Practice containing practical guidance for either or both of the following purposes:

(*a*) the elimination of discrimination; and

(*b*) the promotion of equality of opportunity.

Under the *RRA 1976*, the equality of opportunity to be promoted is that between persons of different racial groups. Under the *SDA 1975*, equality of opportunity is to be promoted between men and women and/or for persons who intend to undergo, are undergoing or have undergone *Gender Reassignment*.

A Code cannot be issued by either of the Commissions under the relevant Act until it has been through the following process:

(*a*) The Commission prepares the Code in draft and in the course of doing so consults with various bodies, such as unions and employers' organisations.

(*b*) The Commission then publishes the draft Code, considers any representations and may modify the draft.

(*c*) The draft is then submitted to the Secretary of State for approval.

(*d*) If the Secretary of State approves the Code, he or she then lays it before both Houses of Parliament.

(*e*) Either House may within 40 days resolve to reject the draft.

(*f*) If there is no such resolution, the Code is then issued by the Commission and comes into force on a day to be appointed by the Secretary of State.

Codes which have been through this lengthy process do not then create any binding obligations, but employment tribunals must take into account any relevant provision when dealing with cases:

(*a*) under the *EPA 1970* or the *SDA 1975*, in the case of a Code issued under the *SDA 1975*; and

(*b*) under the *RRA 1976*, in the case of a Code issued under that Act.

There are similar (but not identical) provisions for Codes of Practice to be issued by the *Disability Rights Commission* under the *Disability Rights Commission Act 1999*. Codes of Practice under that Act may be issued to give practical guidance to employers and others:

(*a*) on how to avoid discrimination;

(*b*) to promote the equalisation of opportunities for persons who have or have had a disability; and

(*c*) to encourage good practice regarding the treatment of such persons.

The *DDA 1995* contains provision for the Secretary of State to issue Codes of Practice and such Codes have been issued by the Secretary of State, as mentioned below. This power for the Secretary of State to issue codes is replaced by the new provisions outlined above.

The *DDA 1995* also gives the Secretary of State power to issue statutory guidance to assist tribunals in deciding whether a person has a disability. Guidance has been given and must be taken into account by employment tribunals considering this question.

38.2 RACIAL AND SEX DISCRIMINATION

The Code of Practice under the *RRA 1976* came into force many years ago, on 1 April 1984. One of the Codes of Practice issued by the EOC is nearly as old. This is the Code of Practice for the elimination of discrimination on the grounds of sex and marriage and the promotion of equality of opportunity in employment. This Code came into effect on 3 April 1985. The other code issued by the EOC, in relation to equal pay, is much more recent and is considered below.

The *SDA 1975* and the *RRA 1976* each expressly specify one of the important matters on which a Code of Practice may give practical guidance. This is the question of the steps which it is reasonably practicable for employers to take for the purpose of preventing their employees from discriminating unlawfully.

The two Codes are of limited value, because of the failure to update them in the light of the many developments in the discrimination laws since 1985. For example the code under the *RRA 1976* contains no express guidance at all on the prevention of racial harassment and the code under the *SDA 1975* deals with sexual harassment only in very general terms.

Nevertheless, the two Codes do contain some useful guidance on a number of matters, including *Recruitment*, *Advertising*, *Interviews*, *Selection*, *Positive Discrimination*, *Monitoring* and *Requirements and Conditions* which could be indirectly discriminatory.

Both Codes also emphasise the following key points:

(*a*) the need to avoid basing decisions on discriminatory *Assumptions*;

(*b*) the importance of *Consistency* in *Selection* and other employment decisions; and

(*c*) the need for *Training* as one of the *Reasonably Practicable* steps to be taken to prevent discrimination by employees.

38.3 THE DDA 1995

The Secretary of State has issued two Codes of Practice as well as the statutory guidance on the definition of disability. One of the Codes is a general code for the elimination of discrimination in the employment field. The other Code is on the duties of *Trade Organisations* to their disabled members and applicants. These two Codes came into force respectively on 2 December 1996 and 1 October 1999.

The earlier Code in particular is extremely user friendly and should be carefully studied by employers. It deals with the issues of *Justification* and *Reasonable Adjustments* by reference to practical examples.

Like the Codes on racial and sex discrimination, the Code warns strongly against basing decisions on assumptions. It reminds employers that there are circumstances in which they need to enquire about the possibility of a disability; they cannot safely adopt a policy of doing nothing until an employee discloses that he or she has a disability. The Code also points out that employers will from time to time need expert advice, for example on the extent of a particular individual's capabilities or on the *Reasonable Adjustments* to be considered.

38.4 EQUAL PAY

The EOC has issued a Code of Practice on equal pay which came into force on 26 March 1997.

The Code includes detailed advice for employers on adopting an equal pay policy and carrying out a pay systems review. There is no legal obligation for an employer to take either of these steps, but they are recommended as good practice by the EOC. Employers should become less vulnerable to equal pay claims if they carry out an effective pay systems review, which includes a thorough analysis of all pay systems and the development of a plan to correct any problems.

38.5 SEXUAL HARASSMENT

There is no statutory Code specifically on *Harassment*, but there is an EU Code, *Protecting the Dignity of Women and Men at Work*, which was adopted in 1991. This Code is frequently referred to in employment tribunal decisions and has also on occasion been endorsed by the EAT. The Code is now so well established that an employer who disregarded the guidance contained in it would have great difficulty persuading an employment tribunal that he had taken all *Reasonably Practicable Steps* to prevent *Sexual Harassment*. The recommendations in the Code are considered in some detail under *Harassment*.

38.6 AGE DISCRIMINATION

There is a non-statutory Code of Practice on *Age Diversity* in employment. The purpose of the Code is to set a standard, but the law does not prescribe any penalties for failing to meet that standard, except in those cases where *Indirect Discrimination* can be proved – see *Age Discrimination*.

39 Collective Bargaining

39.1 EQUAL PAY

The employers in an *Equal Pay* case may claim, as a *Material Factor* defence, that the pay or other contract terms of the complainant and the comparator have been negotiated through different collective bargaining arrangements, particularly where the two jobs are covered by different recognition agreements, involving different unions, and there are different negotiating committees.

This defence may be successful, in a case where there is no considerable difference in the proportions of men and women in the groups of employees to which the complainant and the comparator respectively belong, and where there is no other element of sex discrimination.

The fact of the separate and distinct collective bargaining processes is not sufficient defence, however, in a case where there is a considerable disparity in the relevant percentages of men and women. In the leading case of *Enderby v Frenchay Health Authority and Secretary of State for Health* [*1993*] *IRLR 591*, speech therapists, who were almost exclusively women, claimed the same rate of pay as pharmacists and clinical psychologists, who were almost exclusively men. The defence of separate collective bargaining was rejected by the ECJ.

This approach was followed by the Northern Ireland Court of Appeal in *British Road Services Limited v Loughran* [*1997*] *IRLR 92*. It was also held in that case that it was not necessary for the complainant's group to be almost exclusively women and the comparator's group to be almost exclusively men (or vice versa). Mere reliance on the separate collective bargaining arrangements was insufficient if the difference in the percentages was significant.

Where the significant or considerable difference in percentages exists, this does not mean that the complaint must succeed. What it does mean is that, in order to make out the defence, the employer cannot rely simply on the separate collective bargaining arrangements, but must go more deeply into the reasons for the difference in pay (or other contract terms), in order to show that the difference is objectively justified.

39.2 DISCRIMINATION

Access to collective bargaining may also be regarded as a benefit or facility for the purposes of the *SDA 1975*, the *RRA 1976* or the *DDA 1995*.

A complaint could arise, for example, if a predominantly male group of workers is covered by collective bargaining arrangements but there is no recognition agreement in respect of a group of predominantly female workers. There could also be complaints if the groups who are not covered are predominantly ethnic minority employees or contain a significant number of disabled employees.

There could also be a complaint about inequality in the *operation* of collective bargaining arrangements. In the following example, both the employer and the union could be liable:

(*a*) a factory has approximately equal numbers of male and female employees, each performing a wide range of duties;

(*b*) under the collective agreement, there are five elected shop stewards for the men, reflecting the range of duties;

(*c*) under the same agreement, all the women are lumped together, with one shop steward; and

(*d*) on the factory negotiating committee, each steward has one vote.

Under arrangements such as this (which are certainly not unknown in practice), the women are placed at a significant disadvantage in negotiations relating to pay, other contract terms and working conditions, wherever their interests are not identical to those of the men.

39.3 AMENDING COLLECTIVE AGREEMENTS

Under *section 77* of the *SDA 1975*, a person interested in a contract can apply to a county court (or sheriff court in Scotland) for a term in that contract to be removed or modified if, for example, it provides for the doing of an act of unlawful sex discrimination – see *Agreements*.

By *section 6* of the *Sex Discrimination Act 1986* the above right is extended, so that an application can be made for the removal or modification of a term in a collective agreement and also such an application can be made to an employment tribunal. If, therefore, a collective agreement provides for unlawful discrimination against women, who are affected employees (and therefore interested in the agreement), one of those women could apply to a court or employment tribunal for an order to remove or modify the offending term.

40 Colour

There is direct racial discrimination when less favourable treatment is on *Racial Grounds*. Colour is only one of those grounds, but it is perhaps the crudest and most offensive.

Colour is also one of the factors by which a *Racial Group* can be defined for purposes of indirect racial discrimination, but it is more usual for a racial group to be defined by reference to ethnic or national origins.

The definition of direct racial discrimination includes discrimination against white employees and job applicants and such cases do occur (normally as part of misconceived attempts to redress perceived imbalances or achieve targets – see *Affirmative Action*).

41 Comparators

Making comparisons is a key feature of discrimination law. The strongest cases of direct discrimination are those where the complainant can point to an individual, whether a fellow employee or another job applicant, who has been treated more favourably than the complainant, apparently for no better reason than his or her gender, marital status, colour or some other racial factor.

It is only in equal pay cases, however, that there is an explicit requirement to name a comparator of the opposite sex. As the law currently stands, it is impossible for a woman to complain that she receives or has received too little pay, if her predecessor and (if she has left) her successor were both female and she cannot point to any man in the *Same Employment* who is employed on *Like Work*, work of *Equal Value* or work rated as equivalent to her work.

There is no corresponding requirement in the *SDA 1975* or the *RRA 1976* to identify a named comparator. A complaint of direct discrimination can be based on a hypothetical comparator. A woman, for example, can complain that she has been treated less favourably than a man has been or *would have been* in similar circumstances. It is even possible for a woman to present a complaint of direct sex discrimination when the only person to have been treated more favourably is another woman (the two having the same marital status and there being no question of gender re-assignment). The following case would be an example:

> The best qualified candidate for a job is a pregnant woman. Because of her pregnancy, she is not appointed. Instead the job goes to the second best qualified candidate, another woman. This would be a clear case of direct sex discrimination. If a man, with the same qualifications as the pregnant woman, had applied for the post, then he would have been appointed. The best qualified candidate has been turned down because of her pregnancy, which is a gender related criterion.

Complaints of disability discrimination, also, may be but need not be based on the treatment of a named comparator. Care is needed in identifying an actual comparator or defining a hypothetical comparator, because of the way in which disability discrimination itself is defined. If, for example, an employee is dismissed for an absence which is caused wholly or partly by a disability, the first question to be considered is whether the dismissal would have taken place if the part of the absence caused by the disability had been discounted. It is well established that the appropriate comparator is *not* an employee who has had a similar absence but for reasons unrelated to any disability. Where the absence has been caused wholly by the disability, the proper comparison is with an actual or hypothetical employee who has not been absent at all. If part of the absence is unrelated to the disability, then the comparator is an actual or hypothetical employee who has been off for a period corresponding with that part of the absence.

42 Commission for Racial Equality

The Commission for Racial Equality, or CRE, is the statutory body which was set up under the *RRA 1976*.

The CRE has powers and responsibilities relating to the *Enforcement* of the *RRA 1976*. In particular, under the *RRA 1976*, it is only the CRE which can:

(*a*) carry out *Formal Investigations*;

(*b*) issue *Non-discrimination Notices*; and

(*c*) take steps to prevent *Persistent Discrimination*.

It is also only the CRE which can present a complaint to an employment tribunal on the ground that there has been a breach of the provisions of the *RRA 1976* relating to:

(*a*) *Discriminatory Practices*;

(*b*) discriminatory *Advertisements*;

(*c*) *Instructions to Discriminate*; or

(*d*) *Pressure to Discriminate*.

The CRE also has more general duties:

(*a*) to work towards the elimination of racial discrimination;

(*b*) to promote equality of opportunity and good race relations; and

(*c*) to keep the working of the *RRA 1976* under review and submit proposals to amend it.

One of the important functions of the CRE is to draw up, issue and consult on a Code of Practice.

Another, particularly important, function of the CRE is to give *Assistance* to actual or prospective complainants. There is no power to give assistance to respondents.

43 Common Terms and Conditions

The *EPA 1970* states that a complainant and comparator must be in the *Same Employment*. It is not essential, however, for them to be employed at the same establishment. It suffices if they have the same employer (or associated employers) and are employed either:

(*a*) at the same establishment; or

(*b*) at different establishments in Great Britain at which common terms and conditions of employment are observed either generally or for employees of the relevant classes.

The test for common terms and conditions is a broad test which is easily satisfied. The leading authority is the House of Lords decision in *Leverton v Clwyd County Council [1989] IRLR 28*. In that case a nursery nurse claimed the same rate of pay as male clerical staff employed by the council at different establishments. The employees at the relevant establishments were covered by the same collective agreement, set out in a document known as the 'purple book'. The nursery nurse worked $32^1/_2$ hours per week and had 70 days' annual holiday; the male comparators worked 37 hours a week and had 20 days' annual holiday.

It was ruled that the complainant and the comparators were *in the same employment*. It was immaterial for this purpose that the comparators worked longer hours than the complainant did and had less holiday. Lord Bridge said:

> 'The concept of common terms and conditions of employment observed generally at different establishments necessarily contemplates terms and conditions applicable to a wide range of employees whose individual terms vary greatly.'

This finding did not mean that the equal pay claim was upheld. The employees in the case were salaried employees. The nursery nurse was claiming the same annual salary as the male clerical workers. Their longer hours and shorter holidays were not relevant to the 'same employment' issue, but they were relevant in terms of explaining the difference in salary. Accordingly a *Material Factor* defence was upheld.

44 Communal Accommodation

The *SDA 1975* contains (in *section 46*) a general provision, which in certain circumstances authorises sex discrimination in the admission of persons to communal accommodation.

Communal accommodation is defined as residential accommodation:

(*a*) which includes dormitories or other shared sleeping accommodation which for reasons of privacy or decency should be used only by men (or only by women); or

(*b*) all or part of which should be used only by men, or only by women, because of the nature of the sanitary facilities serving the accommodation.

Sex discrimination in the admission of persons to communal accommodation is permitted if the accommodation is managed in a way which, given the exigencies of the situation, comes as near as may be to fair and equitable treatment of men and women.

There are three specific questions to be considered:

(*a*) Is it reasonable to expect the accommodation to be altered or extended?

(*b*) Is it reasonable to expect that further, alternative accommodation should be provided?

(*c*) How frequently do men as compared with women demand or need to use the accommodation?

Where this exception applies, there can be discrimination in relation either to:

(*a*) the use of the accommodation; or

(*b*) any benefit, facility or service which cannot properly and effectively be provided except for those using communal accommodation.

The general exception relating to communal accommodation applies both in the field of employment and in other areas covered by the *SDA 1975*. Some employers provide free or subsidised accommodation for employees (for example in hostels), but in most such cases there should be a reasonable expectation that suitable accommodation for both sexes can be provided. Another possible case is that of residential training, where the sleeping quarters consist of one dormitory and nothing more.

Where an employer relies on the communal accommodation exception, such arrangements as are reasonably practicable must be made to compensate for the detriment caused by the discrimination. For example, if an employee is refused training because he or she cannot be admitted to the residential accommodation in which the training is to be provided, then the employer must provide the training in some other way if it is reasonably practicable to do so.

45 Community Law

The European Community has had an important effect on individual complaints about equal pay and sex discrimination and on the development of the *EPA 1970* and the *SDA 1975*.

Community law prevails in any conflict with domestic legislation. Several of the original provisions of the *EPA 1970* and the *SDA 1975* have been removed or amended in the light of relevant decisions on Community Law by the ECJ. Furthermore *Article 141* has direct effect, as have *Directives* in the *Public Sector* so that individual complainants can rely on them even before the relevant domestic legislation has been amended.

Community law has also had some influence on the *RRA 1976* and the *DDA 1995*. In particular, after the limit on compensation under the *SDA 1975* was removed, because of a decision by the ECJ, a similar amendment was subsequently made to the *RRA 1976*. When the *DDA 1995* was enacted, there was from the outset no limit on compensation.

Although what was the European Community is now the European Union, it is still customary to refer to Community law rather than Union law.

46 Company Cars

Many employees are provided by their employers with the use of a company car and sometimes also with free petrol, either:

(*a*) to enable them to carry out the travelling which is required for the performance of their duties; or

(*b*) as a perk.

In the latter case, the company car and free petrol are benefits in kind which are increasingly under attack from the Inland Revenue.

Sometimes the arrangements are contractual and sometimes they are discretionary. In either case, there must be no discrimination under the *SDA 1975*, the *RRA 1976* or the *DDA 1995*. Any complaint relating to sex discrimination in the provision of company cars would normally be brought under the *EPA 1970* if the benefit is contractual and if a *Comparator* in the *Same Employment* can be identified; in other cases the complaint will be brought under the *SDA 1975*. It is good practice to make alternative claims by referring to both Acts.

Where a female employee has a contractual right to a company car before going on *Maternity Leave*, she will be entitled to retain that benefit during her 18 week ordinary maternity leave period.

Employers should consider *Reasonable Adjustments* for disabled employees who would normally be provided with a company car but whose disability prevents them from driving.

47 Company Directors

There is no express provision in the *SDA 1975*, the *RRA 1976* or the *DDA 1995* relating to company directors.

An executive director, who carries out work for the company under a contract of employment (written or unwritten) and receives payment for that work would normally fall within the definition of employee and have the same rights as any other employee.

A director who is a non-executive director and whose role is limited to attendance at board meetings would not normally be regarded as an employee. *Employment*, as defined in each of the discrimination laws, requires that there should be a contract (written or unwritten) with the individual concerned, whether a contract of service or apprenticeship or a contract to execute any work or labour personally. The statutory and other responsibilities of a non-executive director arise from his or her status as a director and sometimes not from any contract.

A company could nevertheless incur liability for any unlawful discrimination by a non-executive director if he or she was acting as an agent for the company with the authority (whether express or implied and whether precedent or subsequent) of the company.

48 Compensation

48.1 GENERAL PRINCIPLES

Compensation under the *EPA 1970* is considered under *Back Pay*.

An award of compensation is not automatic where a complaint of *Indirect Discrimination* is upheld, particularly if the complaint is under the *RRA 1976* rather than the *SDA 1975*.

The *Industrial Tribunals (Interest on Awards in Discrimination Cases) Regulations 1996 (SI 1999 No 2803)* came into force on 2 December 1996 (at the same time as the employment provisions of the *DDA 1995*). Under these Regulations, an employment tribunal may award interest (and must consider whether to do so) when making an award under the *EPA 1970*, the *SDA 1975*, the *RRA 1976* or the *DDA 1995*.

When an employment tribunal is assessing compensation under the *SDA 1975*, *RRA 1976* or *DDA 1995*:

(*a*) there is no statutory limit on the amount of compensation which may be ordered;

(*b*) compensation may be awarded for injury to feelings;

(*c*) aggravated damages can be awarded in an appropriate case; and

(*d*) the award can include damages for personal injuries caused to the applicant by the discrimination complained of.

48.2 UNLIMITED COMPENSATION

The fact that compensation is unlimited does not of course mean that a figure can simply be plucked from the air. When assessing compensation for actual and prospective loss of earnings, employment tribunals must adopt the usual approach of:

(*a*) calculating the losses up to the date of the hearing;

(*b*) deciding on an appropriate and realistic period for future losses; and

(*c*) in relation to both past and future losses, considering whether the applicant has or could have mitigated his or her losses.

Guidance has been given in appeal cases, such as *Abbey National plc v Formoso [1999] IRLR 222*, on the need to consider, in percentage terms, the chance that the applicant's losses would have been incurred even if there had been no discrimination against the applicant. In that case the applicant was dismissed for misconduct after having indicated that she would be unable to attend a disciplinary hearing because she was pregnant. It was necessary to consider how likely it was, in percentage terms, that she would have been dismissed if a fair disciplinary hearing had been held.

48.3 INJURY TO FEELINGS

There is an express statutory power in the *SDA 1975*, the *RRA 1976* and the *DDA 1995* to award compensation for injury to feelings. Such an award is made in nearly all cases where the complaint is upheld, but the amount can vary from a few hundred pounds to several thousand pounds. In the *Victimisation* case of *Chief Constable of West Yorkshire Police v Khan* [*2000*] *IRLR 324*, the Court of Appeal suggested that an award of £1,500 seemed surprisingly high, in comparison with damages awarded in personal injury cases, but the Court did not interfere with the award. In contrast, in *Armitage, Marsden and H M Prison Service v Johnson* [*1997*] *IRL 162*, the EAT upheld an award of £21,000 for injury to feelings. This was a case of serious racial harassment over a period of more than 18 months.

48.4 AGGRAVATED DAMAGES

Even in a serious case, an award of aggravated damages is not automatic and indeed is comparatively rare.

In *Alexander v the Home Office* [*1988*] *IRLR 190,* the Court of Appeal stated that aggravated damages may be awarded where the respondent has behaved in a high-handed, malicious, insulting or oppressive manner.

48.5 PERSONAL INJURY

Where the discrimination complained of has caused the applicant to suffer personal injury (whether physical, mental or psychiatric), that injury should be pleaded and compensation should be claimed.

In *Sheriff v Klyne Tugs (Lowestoft) Limited* [*1999*] *IRLR 481,* the Court of Appeal considered the question of damages for personal injury arising from racial discrimination. Mr Sheriff had brought a claim of racial harassment which had been settled with no admission of liability. He subsequently brought a claim in the county court for damages for personal injury, alleging the abusive and detrimental treatment which he had complained of in the racial discrimination case. His action was struck out as an abuse of process and he appealed.

The appeal was dismissed by the Court of Appeal on two grounds. The first ground, which is one of considerable general importance, was that the employment tribunal had 'jurisdiction to award damages for the tort of racial discrimination, including damages for personal injury caused by the tort.' It followed that his present claim fell within the terms of the earlier settlement. The principle that damages can be awarded for personal injuries caused by the discrimination will presumably apply also to complaints of sex and disability discrimination.

The second ground of the Court of Appeal's decision was that it is contrary to a well-established public policy principle for claims that have been or could have been litigated in one tribunal to be allowed to be litigated in another. The same factual issues lay at the heart of both the earlier employment tribunal proceedings and the later county court action and Mr Sheriff 'could have brought forward his whole claim for compensation in the tribunal'.

49 Conciliation

Once a complaint has been presented to an employment tribunal (and sometimes earlier), the services of an ACAS conciliation officer are made available, so that the parties can negotiate confidentially with a view to reaching a binding settlement.

Where the complainant is being assisted by the EOC or the CRE, it is commonly a term of any settlement that the respondent should take agreed measures to prevent further acts of discrimination. Such measures can of course be in the interest of the respondent, as well as in the public interest, if future discrimination and hence future complaints are successfully prevented.

Where the services of ACAS are not used, a binding settlement can be entered into only through a consent order of the tribunal or by entering into a valid compromise agreement – see *Agreements*.

50 Conditions

The word 'conditions' can be used in several different senses, as follows:

(*a*) terms and conditions of employment are relevant to rights under the *EPA 1970* (and also sometimes the *SDA 1975* if the term is not one for the payment of money), the *RRA 1976* and the *DDA 1995* – see *Terms of Employment*;

(*b*) terms and conditions of employment are also relevant to the definition of *Same Employment* under the *EPA 1970* – see *Common Terms and Conditions*;

(*c*) conditions in the sense of *Requirements and Conditions* are part of the definition of *Indirect Discrimination*;

(*d*) *Working Conditions* can be the subject of complaints about *Detriment* under any of the discrimination laws;

(*e*) *Working Conditions* can also be relevant in equal pay cases, as one of the demand factors in relation to *Equal Value* and also in relation to the *Material Factor* defence.

51 Conduct Dismissals

It is very important that employers should be consistent in disciplinary decisions, particularly decisions to dismiss an employee for misconduct. Differences in the treatment of different cases, where the employees concerned belong to different *Racial Groups* or are of different sexes, are likely to lead to findings of direct discrimination, if no credible and non-discriminatory reason can be given.

The danger of subjective and potentially discriminatory decisions is particularly great during the qualifying period of one year for full unfair dismissal rights, especially where any right to a formal disciplinary procedure has been excluded for the whole or part of that year. Ideally employers should follow a formal procedure even where there is no statutory or contractual obligation to do so, in order to ensure that decisions are made consistently and objectively and that explanations can be given for any apparent difference in treatment. As a minimum, the facts of any case should be considered by a senior person and by a member of the HR department (if there is one).

There may also be a need for *Reasonable Adjustment* where a disability has contributed to a disciplinary offence, for example if a mental illness has caused an employee to react violently to provocation.

52 Considerably Smaller

The expression 'considerably smaller' is an important part of the definition of *Indirect Discrimination* in both the *SDA 1975* and the *RRA 1976*.

For a complaint of indirect discrimination to succeed, it is not enough for the complainant to show that he or she cannot comply with a requirement or condition which has been applied to the complainant. It is also necessary to prove *Disparate Impact* (the expression which is commonly used, although not in the legislation). For example, if a woman complains of indirect discrimination against her as a woman, she must be able to satisfy the tribunal that the proportion of women who can comply with the requirement or condition which has been applied to her is considerably smaller than the proportion of men who can comply with it.

Ascertaining whether one proportion is considerably smaller than the other is not a simple question of arithmetic – *Indirect Discrimination*.

53 Consistency

One of the most important qualities which employers and managers need, in order to comply with the discrimination laws, is consistency. Dealing with similar cases in different ways leaves an employer wide open to tribunal complaints, if the employees concerned are, for example, of different gender or colour – see *Direct Discrimination*. The *EPA 1970*, the *SDA 1975* and the *RRA 1976* (and to a smaller extent the *DDA 1995*) are all about comparative treatment, although in some cases (except under the *EPA 1970*) the comparator can be a hypothetical one.

The importance of consistency is emphasised in the *Codes of Practice* under both the *SDA 1975* and the *RRA 1976*.

54 Constructive Dismissal

The general interpretation provisions in the *SDA 1975* (as amended) contain a provision that references to dismissal include the termination of the employment by the employee (with or without notice), in circumstances such that the employee is entitled to terminate the employment without notice by reason of the conduct of the employer. There are similar provisions to cover the case of a partner who resigns from a partnership, with or without notice, and would have been entitled by reason of the conduct of the other partners to resign without notice.

There are no corresponding provisions in the *RRA 1976* or the *DDA 1995*. The above provisions in the *SDA 1975* were inserted by the *Sex Discrimination Act 1986*.

Arguably, even without the express statutory provision, an employment tribunal could apply general principles to make a finding of constructive dismissal in a case of racial or disability discrimination. There appears, however, to be no direct authority on the point.

The circumstances in which an employee is or is not entitled under the *SDA 1975* to resign and treat himself or herself as dismissed are illustrated by two cases which are considered under *Dismissal* (section 8). Shortly stated, the relevant principles are as follows:

(*a*) There is no general rule that a single act, or series of acts, of sex discrimination justify an employee in resigning and claiming to have been constructively dismissed.

(*b*) This does not mean, however, that there cannot be exceptional cases where mutual trust and confidence is irretrievably lost by reason of the discrimination. One possible example could be a case of very serious discrimination by the employer personally or probably a senior fellow employee.

(*c*) A constructive dismissal is far more likely where the management know or should know that discrimination has or may have occurred and fail to take appropriate action.

The following are examples of cases where inaction or ineffective action by management could lead to a resignation and a finding of constructive dismissal:

(*a*) The management are aware of evidence which points towards sexual harassment but fail to investigate.

(*b*) The employer refuses to listen to a complaint of discrimination.

(*c*) The employer receives a grievance but fails to take it seriously or investigate it thoroughly.

(*d*) Allegations are made to senior management in confidence but that confidence is broken and the workforce are made aware that the employee has complained.

In all these cases there could be a finding of discriminatory dismissal as well as unfair dismissal. This can be important where the employee has not yet completed the qualifying period of employment for complaints of unfair dismissal. The case of *Reed and Bull Information Systems Limited v Stedman* [*1999*] *IRLR 299* (referred to under *Dismissal*) is an example of such a case.

55 Continuing Discrimination

The *SDA 1975*, *RRA 1976* and *DDA 1995* each expressly state that any act extending over a period shall be treated as done at the end of that period.

This provision is important in relation to *Time Limits* because time starts to run at the end of the period of continuing discrimination.

There is a discriminatory act extending over a period where a discriminatory rule, policy or regime is operated pursuant to which decisions may be taken from time to time. In *Cast v Croydon College [1998] IRLR 318,* the complainant was an information centre manager who worked full time. She became pregnant. Both before and after taking maternity leave, she asked if she could work part-time or job share when she returned to work. Each time her request was refused. She presented a complaint of indirect sex discrimination within three months after the last refusal, but it was held by the employment tribunal and the EAT that she was too late, because time ran from the date of the refusal of the request which she had made before going on maternity leave. She successfully appealed to the Court of Appeal. It was held that the tribunal's findings of fact clearly indicated the existence of a discriminatory policy in relation to her post, so that this was a case of an act of discrimination extending over a period.

In contrast, in the case of *Sougrin v Haringey Health Authority [1992] IRLR 416,* a nurse complained of the amount of pay which she received following a grading decision. She presented her complaint more than three months after the date of the grading decision, but argued that there was an act extending over the period during which her pay was affected by her decision. This was held not to be a case of continuing discrimination. There had been a single act, the grading decision, which then had continuing consequences.

It is frequently necessary for employment tribunals to consider in *Harassment* cases whether a series of separate incidents constitute separate acts of discrimination (in which case the complaint could be out of time in relation to the earlier acts) or a single act extending over a period. This is a question which can be decided only by looking closely at the circumstances of any particular case. If the acts complained of have occurred with some regularity, a tribunal would be likely to find that there has been a campaign of harassment, constituting a single act extending over a period. A different finding would be likely if there have been two or more unconnected acts with a long interval or intervals between them.

56 Contract Workers

56.1 TRIANGULAR CONTRACT RELATIONSHIPS

Where a person (who may be in business on his own account and performing work personally on a self-employed basis) is provided, by one contracting party to perform duties for the other contracting party, a triangular relationship arises between:

(*a*) worker;

(*b*) labour-supplier; and

(*c*) labour-user.

Typically, the labour-supplier is an employment agency. The labour-supplier must observe applicable parts of the *SDA 1975*, *RRA 1976* and *DDA 1995*, but on traditional principles the labour-user might fall outside the net of liability. The *SDA 1975*, *RRA 1976* and *DDA 1995* make specific provision to address this issue.

56.2 LIABILITY OF PRINCIPALS

Each of the three Acts make it unlawful for a principal, in relation to contract work, to discriminate against a person:

(*a*) in the terms on which he allows that person to do that work;

(*b*) by not allowing that person to do it or continue to do it;

(*c*) in the way he affords that person access to any benefits or by refusing or deliberately omitting to afford him access to them; or

(*d*) by subjecting that person to any other detriment.

For these purposes:

(*a*) 'principal' means a person ('A') who makes work available for doing by individuals who are employed by another person who supplies them under a contract made with A;

(*b*) 'contract work' means work so made available; and

(*c*) 'contract worker' means any individual who is supplied to the principal under such a contract.

A principal is placed under obligation akin to those of an employer and so the duty to make *Reasonable Adjustments* applies, although what is 'reasonable' in the case of a principal will presumably in practice often reflect the fact that the relationship between the principal and the contract worker may be short-term only.

56.3 PURPOSIVE INTERPRETATION

These provisions were considered by the EAT in *MHC Consulting Services Ltd v Tansell* [*1999*] *IRLR 677*. The EAT ruled that, where there is an unbroken chain of contracts between an individual and the end-user, the latter is the 'principal'. This interpretation gives effect, the EAT said, 'to the general principle which applies in social legislation of this kind, namely that the statute should be construed purposively, and with a bias towards conferring statutory protection rather than excluding it.' The case concerned a disabled person who was on the books of an employment agency which arranged for him to be interviewed by a company interested in his services. That company rejected his services (which he was to provide via his own company) because he was disabled. A tribunal had taken the view the disabled person was a contract worker for the agency, but not for the end-user. However, that was a misunderstanding of *section 12*. The end user's appeal to the Court of Appeal failed: *Abbey Life Assurance Co Ltd v Tansell* [*2000*] *IRLR 387*. In accordance with the assumed intention of Parliament to confer rather than deny protection to contract workers in all the discrimination Acts, the language of *section 12* was reasonably capable of applying not only where a principal made work available for an individual employed by an agency, but also where an extra contract was inserted, so that there was no direct contract between the principal and the employer of the worker.

57 Contractual Equal Opportunities Policies

57.1 SIGNIFICANCE OF CONTRACTUAL STATUS

Employers are increasingly issuing a wide variety of employment-related policies, including *Equal Opportunities Policies*. As policies proliferate, it is foreseeable that questions are more and more likely to arise as to the precise legal status, if any, of such policies. This is an important issue, because quite apart from any other consideration, if an equal opportunities policy forms part of an employee's terms and conditions of employment, then a breach by the employer of its own policy may mean that the employee has a legal right of redress in respect of breach of contract. Detailed discussion of the law of contract falls outside the scope of this Handbook but briefly, a claim in respect of an alleged breach of an employment contract traditionally had to be brought in the civil courts. This is no longer the case; such a claim may now, subject to certain conditions (most importantly, that the employment has ended), be brought in the employment tribunal, which currently has the power to award compensation of up to £25,000, (a limit which means that contractual disputes involving highly paid senior executives are still likely to be litigated in the civil courts).

57.2 IDEALISTIC POLICY STATEMENTS

Equal opportunities policies may cover matters which are not dealt with by legislation. If an employee's contract of employment includes a binding legal obligation upon the employer to comply with such a policy, then the employee's entitlements may be extensive. But there are limits, as the decision of the High Court in *Grant v South West Trains Ltd [1998] IRLR 188*, shows. The employer's equal opportunities policy proclaimed that it was 'committed to ensuring that all individuals are treated fairly and are valued irrespective of . . . sexual preference . . . No one is to receive less favourable treatment on any of the above grounds or is to be disadvantaged by requirements or conditions which cannot be shown to be justifiable. Our aim is to eliminate unfair discrimination'. The employee was contractually entitled to travel concessions which extended to a partner of the opposite sex. She was refused a travel pass for her female partner, with whom she had been living in a stable relationship. She brought civil proceedings, claiming that the policy was incorporated into her contract and that, on that basis, she was entitled to require her employer to extend the contractual travel concessions to her partner. The High Court rejected her application. Crucially, the judge found that the policy had not been incorporated into her contract: 'It is a statement of policy and not of contractual obligation. The policy is in very general, even idealistic, terms. It also covers such matters as "health and social class" which would be alien to employment contractual law.' The judge also considered that, on the facts, the way in which the policy was brought into being was indicative that no contractual rights were in the mind of the employer or the employees' representatives. No obligations were put by the policy upon the employer and the obligation on the employee was 'of the vaguest kind', i.e. to act 'in the spirit of the policy'. There was no evidence of any contractual intention on the part of the employer or employee, either from the documents or by inference from the whole of the evidence. There was no legal basis for implying the contractual terms on the basis of the policy. Further, since the contract specifically provided that concessions were granted for a partner of the 'opposite' sex, the policy could not be incorporated into the contractual terms so as to override that express provision. The employee's argument, the judge considered, effectively entailed that the incorporation of the policy into the contract had the effect of binding the employer to increase the employee's emoluments. The judge thought that could not be right.

57.3 LEGALLY BINDING POLICIES

There was a different outcome at one stage of the proceedings in *Secretary of State for Scotland v Taylor* [*1997*] *IRLR 608*. The employers issued a circular setting out an equal opportunities policy which included an undertaking 'to offer opportunities on an equal basis to all staff regardless of gender, race, religion, sexual preference, disability or age'. The employers introduced changes to their retirement policy, under which the normal retiring age was set at 55 in order to achieve a younger workforce. When the employee reached that age, he was given notice of dismissal. He claimed that this amounted to discrimination on the grounds of age, in breach of the equal opportunities provisions in his contract. The tribunal upheld his claim, having satisfied itself that the equal opportunities policy was incorporated into his contract. Changes to contracts were notified by circulars such as that setting out the policy; the change in the retirement policy had been notified in the same way. The EAT upheld the decision that the terms of the equal opportunities policy, including the undertaking not to discriminate on the ground of age, was part of the employee's contractual rights. The employers contended for a less strict interpretation, referring to the policy as 'a mission statement', but the EAT rejected that argument. The policy was binding in law upon the employer. On the facts, however, the EAT ruled that the tribunal had been wrong to find that the employee's dismissal was discrimination on grounds of age in breach of contract because the motive was to replace him with a younger person. As a matter of interpretation, parties to the contract would not, the EAT said, have contemplated that the provision relating to discrimination on grounds of age would apply once the contractual retirement age had passed and continuation of employment was entirely at the discretion of the employer. Age and retirement, the EAT said, are inextricably intertwined. The employee's protection in respect of age discrimination continued in the contract only as long as he was working in the currency of the contract up to normal retirement age. Put another way, since retirement age policy entirely depends on age, it could not reasonably have been intended that implementation of the policy on that basis alone should be capable of being described as 'discriminatory'. The Court of Session, took a similar view: [*1999*] *IRLR 363*. The employers had retained a discretion as regards retirement which the parties could not have intended to fetter by considerations of age. The House of Lords, at [*2000*] *IRLR 502*, took the same view; there was no evidence that the employee had been singled out on the ground of age. Nevertheless, the fact that the EAT, albeit mistakenly, ruled in favour of the employee, serves as a warning to employers that policy documents should neither be conceived nor implemented casually or without care. Their implications need to be thought through, especially as the House of Lords was quite prepared to accept that a policy of the kind in question could have legally binding status.

58 Contracts of Employment

There is a fairly common misunderstanding that acts of discrimination can be legitimised if they are pursuant to a contract of employment which the complainant has freely entered into. The discrimination laws are about difference in treatment (or *Disparate Impact* in cases of indirect discrimination). If an act of discrimination, as defined by the relevant legislation, has taken place, it is no defence to any complaint to show that the act is authorised by the contract of employment.

Indeed, the express purpose of the *EPA 1970* is to modify contractual terms which have been agreed by the operation of the *Equality Clause*.

59 Costs

Costs are rarely awarded against the unsuccessful party to tribunal proceedings. The ordinary rules of procedure apply. Under *rule 12*, costs may be awarded only against a party who in bringing or conducting the proceedings has acted frivolously, vexatiously, abusively, disruptively or otherwise unreasonably.

The cases where costs are most likely to be awarded are:

(*a*) the rare cases where a party has been ordered to pay a deposit as a result of a *Pre-hearing Review*; and

(*b*) cases where a party has acted unreasonably in the conduct of the proceedings, for example by causing an unnecessary postponement or by failing to comply with an order of the tribunal.

60 Course of Employment

The *SDA 1975*, *RRA 1976* and *DDA 1995* each provide that anything done by a person in the course of his or her employment shall be treated as also done by his or her employer, whether or not it was done with the employer's knowledge or approval. In order to ascertain whether the employer (or indeed the individual who has done the act) is liable for any particular act of discrimination, it is accordingly necessary to consider whether the act was done in the course of the individual's employment.

A broader approach is adopted than in the common law cases where damages are claimed for the negligent acts of employees, applying the principles of vicarious liability. Relevant authorities are considered under *Harassment*, this being the context in which issues relating to the course of employment most commonly arise.

The extended definition of *Employment* in the *EPA 1970*, the *SDA 1975*, the *RRA 1976* and the *DDA 1995* should also be noted.

61 Crown Employment

Servants of the Crown are treated as employees for the purposes of the *EPA 1970*, the *SDA 1975*, the *RRA 1976* and the *DDA 1995*, subject to specific provisions relating to:

(*a*) *Statutory Officers*;

(*b*) the *Armed Forces*; and

(*c*) (under the *DDA 1995*) police and prison officers.

62 Dangerous Work

The fact that work is dangerous is not a legal justification for discrimination against women in *Recruitment* or *Selection* for the work. There must also be no sex discrimination against existing employees in deciding who should be required to do such work – see *Detriment*.

Dangerous working conditions may require *Reasonable Adjustment* where the person who is or will be expected to do the work is disabled. The fact that working conditions are dangerous can also be relevant in an *Equal Pay* case – see *Working Conditions* – and, of course, to *Health and Safety*.

63 Defamation of Character

It is fundamental to equal opportunities in employment that a person making a complaint about (for example) a breach by a colleague or a superior of good practice should not suffer because of the making of that allegation. The legislation on sex, race and disability discrimination prohibits *Victimisation*, and for good reason. Moreover, even where (as is often the case) those against whom the allegation is made protest their innocence and seek to take legal steps to restore the damage that may have been done to their reputation, their options are apt to be limited. This is because, usually, it will not be possible to sue the person who has made the allegations for libel or slander since the allegation is likely to be protected by 'qualified privilege' under defamation law. However, it is possible for an accused person to sue for defamation if he or she can prove that the person making the allegation was motivated by malice. It is rarely easy to prove malice, but it is not always impossible. In an exceptional case that was widely reported in the press in 2000, a pharmacist was ordered to pay £400,000 in damages for defamation plus substantial legal costs to her former supervisor, after she had falsely complained to management that he had sexually assaulted and then raped her at work. Because the facts were extreme, the jury seems to have accepted the supervisor's argument that there was no scope to conclude that the accusation had arisen from a misunderstanding. Once it was found that the accusations were false, it was a short step to conclude that they were malicious. The position of the individual falsely accused of harassment is thus, whilst unenviable, not always legally hopeless.

64 De Minimis

It is increasingly unfashionable in the law to use Latin terms. In this particular case, the concept as well as the language is an endangered species.

It is all very well in theory to say that the law does not concern itself with trivial matters, but in the workplace even apparently minor decisions, which are based on gender or ethnic differences, can be significant in themselves or as part of a larger problem.

Take the not uncommon case of a company which invites customers to a sporting event, such as a football match or a golf tournament, and includes male but not female members of the sales team. A female sales executive, even if she is not interested in the sport in question, could reasonably feel that she has been sidelined or marginalised and excluded from contact with customers and thereby subjected to a detriment.

There are no doubt exceptional cases where the treatment complained of is so trivial that the complainant cannot be said to have been subjected to any real detriment or excluded from any real benefit. Any defence based on the doctrine of *de minimis* should, however, be approached with great caution; see also *Chivalry*.

65 Demotions

Demoting an employee could give rise to a complaint of wrongful or unfair dismissal, where the employee resigns and claims to have been constructively dismissed. Even if the employee has not yet completed the qualifying period for complaints of unfair dismissal and/or the demotion is authorised by a contractual term, the demotion will be a *Detriment* for the purpose of a complaint under the *SDA 1975*, *RRA 1976* or *DDA 1995*.

Furthermore, whenever a disabled employee is demoted, or subjected to any other detriment, because the performance of his or her work has been unsatisfactory, there will normally be a breach of the *DDA 1995* if the unsatisfactory job performance is for a reason wholly or partly related to the disability and the employer has not as a first step considered the question of *Reasonable Adjustment* to the job duties or working conditions.

66 Dependants, Benefits For

Some employers provide contractual or discretionary benefits for the dependants of their employees as well as the employees themselves. Such benefits can include:

(*a*) life insurance;

(*b*) private medical cover;

(*c*) free or concessionary travel (where the employer is in the travel or passenger transport business); or

(*d*) use of social or sports club facilities.

There must be no discrimination under any of the discrimination laws in relation to any such benefits or facilities. It would, for example, be a clear case of direct sex discrimination if benefits were provided for the dependants of male employees but not for those of female employees.

So far as benefits or facilities for ex-employees or their dependants are concerned, see *Post-employment Discrimination*.

67 Detriment

67.1 LEGAL PRINCIPLES

The *SDA 1975*, *RRA 1976* and *DDA 1995* all prohibit discrimination against employees by dismissing them or subjecting them to any other detriment. *Dismissal* is considered separately.

The meaning of 'detriment' was considered by the Court of Appeal in *Jeremiah v Ministry of Defence [1979] IRLR 436*. In that case, male inspectors at an ordnance factory were required to carry out particularly unpleasant work, inspecting colour bursting shells. Female inspectors objected to doing the work, and were excused. One factor was that having to take a shower afterwards was a greater inconvenience for women, with their long hair, than for men. The work carried a slightly higher rate than other work in the factory.

This bare recitation of the facts indicates that the case was one of the early cases under the discrimination laws, decided more than two decades ago. It would be difficult (one hopes) to find a case with similar facts today.

The case established the following principles:

(*a*) subjecting an employee to a detriment means no more than putting the employee under a disadvantage;

(*b*) the test is objective – would or might a reasonable employee take the view that he or she had been put under a disadvantage?

(*c*) subjecting an employee to a detriment cannot generally be excused on grounds of *Chivalry* or administrative convenience;

(*d*) an employer cannot buy a right to discriminate by making an extra payment to an employee who is subjected to a detriment.

The second and third of these principles effectively nullify the importance of an earlier case, *Automotive Products Limited v Peake [1977] IRLR 365*, in which a man complained unsuccessfully about a rule under which women were allowed to leave work five minutes early so that they would not be trampled in the rush through the factory gates. In that case it was said to be relevant that the rule had been introduced for reasons of *Chivalry* and the claim failed under the principle that the law does not concern itself with trivial matters. The question to be considered in any similar case now would be not the reason for the rule, or the degree of triviality, but whether a man subjected to the rule (or indeed one of the women ostensibly benefiting from the rule) would or might reasonably object to the difference in treatment.

67.2 EXAMPLES OF DETRIMENT

One of the most important examples of detriment is *Harassment*. The word 'harassment' does not appear in the *SDA 1975*, the *RRA 1976* or the *DDA 1995*. A complaint that an employee has been subjected to sexual or racial harassment, or harassment on grounds of disability, will succeed if it can be shown that in the circumstances complained of an employee would or might reasonably regard herself or himself as having been placed at a disadvantage.

67.3 Detriment

Subjecting an employee or job applicant to a detriment can also occur in the context of:

(*a*) allocation of work;

(*b*) searches;

(*c*) segregation from other workers;

(*d*) disciplinary matters;

(*e*) demotions;

(*f*) unfavourable appraisals;

(*g*) overtime requirements;

(*h*) mobility requirements; and

(*i*) interview arrangements.

Mobility, *Demotions* and *Job Interviews* are dealt with elsewhere, as is *Post-employment Discrimination*.

67.3 ALLOCATION OF WORK

Jeremiah v Ministry of Defence (1979) IRLR 436 was a case of discrimination in requiring an employee to carry out dirty and unpleasant work. Another example would be discrimination in requiring an employee to carry out *Dangerous Work*. In this context, a difference in the treatment of two employees may amount to unlawful discrimination against both of them. Where both men and women are employed on police, security or similar work, employers, superior officers or managers sometimes make well-meaning attempts to shield the women by allocating the more dangerous duties to the men. In such circumstances, the latter could claim that they have been subjected to a detriment, having been required on grounds of sex to undertake the more dangerous work. The women could also complain, on the ground that protecting and sidelining them is effectively reducing their status and holding back their career development.

67.4 SEARCHES

In the context of race relations, where particular sensitivity is required, a detriment can take an intangible form. In *BL Cars Limited v Brown* [*1985*] *IRLR 193*, a series of thefts had occurred and there was evidence that the offender was black. A written instruction was issued, under which black employees (but not white employees) were to be searched on entering their place of work. It was held that the issue of the instruction (which had not yet been implemented) was to subject the employees to a detriment on racial grounds.

67.5 SEGREGATION

In the *RRA 1976* the definition of racial discrimination expressly includes *Segregation* on racial grounds. It is likely that any employee segregated on racial grounds would be able to satisfy a tribunal that he or she had been subjected to a detriment, even if there was a good practical reason for the segregation, for example where a workforce includes two groups of workers whose countries of origin are at war.

Segregation from other workers is not expressly included in the definition of direct discrimination in the *SDA 1975* or the *DDA 1995*, but there are circumstances in which a segregated employee could be said to have been subjected to a detriment. An example under the *DDA 1995* would be that of an employee who is HIV positive and who is required to sit at a separate table in the factory canteen. The detriment would consist of the sense of isolation and embarrassment caused to the employee.

67.6 DISCIPLINARY MATTERS

Employers also need to take care to be consistent in their approach to disciplinary action, even where the action falls short of dismissal. If, for example, an employee is given a written warning, and an employee of a different gender or ethnic origin has been given only an oral warning for the same offence, then the employer will need to be able to give an explanation for the difference in treatment which is unrelated to the difference in gender or ethnic origin.

The same principle applies in relation to suspensions, even where the suspension is to enable an investigation to be carried out, is on full pay and is not a disciplinary action. An employee who has been suspended may reasonably take the view that he or she has thereby been placed at a disadvantage, even though no pay has been lost, and the employer will be at risk of a finding of unlawful discrimination if a consistent approach cannot be demonstrated.

The requirement to be even-handed does not, however, mean that, when considering the background to an alleged offence, an employer must disregard all aspects relating to the employee's race, gender or disability. On the contrary, if an offence, such as an assault, is a response to sexual harassment, racial abuse or insulting remarks about the offender's disability, that mitigating factor must be taken into account. Otherwise, if an unjustified warning is given, the employee could resign and claim to have been constructively and unfairly dismissed. The case of *Sidhu v Aerospace Composite Technology Limited* [*2000*] *IRLR 683* is dealt with under *Dismissal*, but the principle established by that case applies equally where disciplinary action short of dismissal is contemplated.

67.7 UNFAVOURABLE APPRAISALS

Many employers require their managers to carry out annual *Appraisals* of the employees for whom they are responsible. Even though appraisals are designed mainly to motivate employees or identify areas for improvement, they can also be taken into account when selecting employees for promotion or redundancy or when awarding pay increases.

There would clearly be grounds for a complaint of direct discrimination or victimisation in any of the following circumstances:

(*a*) An appraisal is adversely influenced by the gender or ethnic origin of the employee who is being appraised.

(*b*) A manager gives a hostile appraisal because the employee has brought a complaint of discrimination or an equal pay claim.

(*c*) The appraisal is cancelled or postponed because the employee has a pending discrimination case against the company.

Where the performance of a disabled employee has been detrimentally affected by the disability, but the appraiser does not record this fact, then consideration must be given to the amendment of the appraisal as a *Reasonable Adjustment*. This is particularly the case where the poor performance was atypical, either because the consequences of the disability were unusually severe in the year in question or because a reasonable adjustment to job duties or working conditions has subsequently mitigated the adverse effect of the disability.

67.8 **OVERTIME REQUIREMENTS**

Access to overtime can be an important *Benefit*. Overtime pay forms an important part of the income of many employees.

There are some employees, however, who are under a contractual obligation to work overtime when required, but who dislike having to work unsocial hours. Singling out an employee for excessive overtime, or requiring the employee to work at particularly unpopular times, could lead to a tribunal complaint if a selection is influenced by:

(*a*) the employee's gender;

(*b*) his or her ethnic origin; or

(*c*) the fact that he or she has previously complained of discrimination or made an equal pay claim.

68 Direct Discrimination

68.1 THE STATUTORY DEFINITIONS – GENERAL

There are two principal elements to the statutory definitions of direct discrimination, which are contained in the *SDA 1975* and the *RRA 1976*.

The first is *Less Favourable Treatment*. The complainant is treated less favourably than another person is or would be treated.

Second, the reason for that less favourable treatment is one of those specified in the relevant Act.

There has been direct racial discrimination when it is on *Racial Grounds* that the complainant has been treated less favourably than other persons have been treated or would have been treated. The expression '*Racial Grounds*' covers colour, race, nationality and ethnic or national origins.

The definition of direct discrimination in the *SDA 1975* involves one of five possible comparisons. There is direct discrimination for the purposes of the *SDA 1975* if:

(*a*) a woman is, on the ground of her sex, treated less favourably than a man is treated or would be treated;

(*b*) a man, on the ground of his sex, is treated less favourably than a woman is treated or would be treated;

(*c*) a person is treated less favourably than other persons are or would be treated, on the ground that that person intends to undergo, is undergoing or has undergone *Gender Reassignment*;

(*d*) a married woman is, on the ground of her marital status, treated less favourably than an unmarried woman is or would be treated; and

(*e*) a married man is, on the ground of his marital status, treated less favourably than an unmarried man is or would be treated.

It will be noted from the above definitions that, in spite of its title, the *SDA 1975* covers not only sex discrimination but also marriage discrimination and (since 1 May 1999) direct discrimination against transsexuals (as defined above).

There is a third element to the definition which somewhat overlaps with the second. When the treatment received by the complainant is compared with that received by an actual or hypothetical comparator, the relevant circumstances of the two cases must be the same or not materially different.

68.2 LESS FAVOURABLE TREATMENT

It is usually easier for a complainant to prove direct discrimination if he or she can point to an actual comparator. For example, a woman who has not been promoted will compare her case with that of a male colleague who *has* been promoted. The way in which such cases are approached by employment tribunals is considered under *Evidence of Discrimination*.

In cases under the *SDA 1975* or the *RRA 1976*, however (as distinct from cases under the *EPA 1970*) there is no need to point to an actual comparator. The comparison can be with, for example, a hypothetical fellow employee or job applicant – see *Comparator*.

68.3 Direct Discrimination

It should be noted that the treatment in respect of which a complaint can be made is 'less favourable treatment', not unfavourable or unfair treatment. Direct discrimination is not about unfairness. It is about differences in treatment which are for unacceptable reasons. This point was emphasised by the House of Lords in the leading case *of Zafar v Glasgow City Council [1998] IRLR 36*. The employment tribunal in that case had compared the treatment received by the complainant from the employer with the treatment which would have been received from a reasonable employer. That was the wrong comparison. The fact that an employer falls short of the standards of the reasonable employer is a key finding in a complaint of unfair dismissal but does not necessarily indicate direct discrimination. The proper comparison is not between the respondent employer and other employers, but with the way in which that same respondent employer has treated or would have treated other persons. Unreasonable treatment of, for example, a woman does not amount to direct sex discrimination if a man would have been treated equally unreasonably.

Although the above principle is clear, it should be added that a defence based on that principle will not be accepted uncritically. Any employment tribunal will scrutinise very carefully a claim that an employer who has treated a complainant in an outlandish manner would have treated anyone else equally badly.

The question whether there must be an intention to treat one person less favourably than another is or would be treated (as distinct from that of *Discriminatory Motive*) is considered under *Less Favourable Treatment*.

68.3 THE REASON FOR THE TREATMENT

The formula which was at one time commonly used was that there is direct discrimination where the less favourable treatment complained of is for a *Discriminatory Motive*. That formula is no longer applicable. A discriminatory motive is not a necessary ingredient of direct discrimination. The reason for the difference in treatment can be one which is not expressly formulated but which is subconscious or unconscious.

Where, for example, a woman is treated less favourably than a man is or would be treated, there are three cases in which the less favourable treatment can be found to be on the ground of her sex:

(*a*) The fact that she is a woman is the only reason for the difference in treatment.

(*b*) It is not the only reason, but it is a significant or important reason.

(*c*) The less-favourable treatment is *Gender Based*, usually for a reason relating to *Pregnancy*.

The question of *Gender Based Criteria* is considered under *Pregnancy*. The principle that there is direct discrimination when gender (or gender reassignment), marital status or race is the only reason, or a significant or important reason for the treatment complained of, has been established by three decisions of the House of Lords. None of these cases was a case of direct discrimination in employment.

(*a*) The case of *James v Eastleigh Borough Council [1990] ICR 554* is considered under *Age Discrimination*. This was in fact a case involving a gender based criterion (the use of pension age to determine eligibility for free access to a swimming pool), but the decision included a more general statement of the relevant principles, including the adoption of the *But For* test as a useful test of direct discrimination.

(*b*) *R v Birmingham City Council ex parte Equal Opportunities Commission [1989] IRLR 173* was a case involving sex discrimination in the access to grammar schools in Birmingham. The provision of more places for boys than for girls resulted in a finding of direct sex discrimination, even though the disparity was not intentional.

(*c*) *Nagarajan v London Regional Transport [1999] IRLR 572* is a case on *Victimisation*, but the House of Lords also gave a clear statement of the principles which apply to cases of direct discrimination.

68.4 THE RELEVANT CIRCUMSTANCES

The difference in treatment as between a complainant and a comparator of a different sex, marital status or race cannot lead to a finding of direct discrimination if there are material differences in the relevant circumstances of the two cases. This issue was considered by the Court of Appeal in the case of *Wakeman v Quick Corporation and another [1999] IRLR 424*. This case is considered in relation to *Pay*. It was suggested in the Court of Appeal judgments that the question was the first one to be considered in any complaint of direct discrimination based on a comparison between the treatment of the complainant, and the treatment of an identified comparator or comparators.

69 Directives

Under *Community Law*, a Council Directive requires Member States to legislate by a specified date in compliance with the Directive.

The most important Directive in the context of discrimination law is the *Equal Treatment Directive*. Other important Directives are those on:

(*a*) equal pay;

(*b*) safety and health at work of pregnant workers;

(*c*) posted workers;

(*d*) the burden of proof in sex discrimination cases; and

(*e*) part-time work.

On 29 June 2000 the Council of Ministers adopted a new Directive to implement the principle of equal treatment between persons irrespective of racial or ethnic origin. Member States will be required to implement this Directive by 19 July 2003.

The European Commission has also proposed a Framework Directive which would prohibit direct or indirect discrimination in relation to racial or ethnic origin, religion or belief, disability, age or *Sexual Orientation*.

The ECJ has jurisdiction to rule on questions whether a Member State has duly introduced the required legislation or in any way acted in breach of the requirements of the Directive.

There are two important principles in cases where an employment tribunal is applying domestic law in circumstances which are also covered by a Directive;

(*a*) the domestic legislation should if possible be construed in conformity with the Directive;

(*b*) the Directive can have direct effect (if the terms of it are sufficiently precise) as against a *Public Sector* employer.

Both these principles have had an important effect in cases covered by the *Equal Treatment Directive*. For example, in *Webb v EMO Air Cargo (UK) Limited (No 2)* [*1995*] *IRLR 645*, the House of Lords construed the definition of direct discrimination under the *SDA 1975* in conformity with the Directive in order to find that a dismissal of a woman recruited for an indefinite period because her pregnancy would make her unavailable during a critical period fell within the definition.

As an example of an important public sector case, the case of *Marshall and South-West Hampshire Area Health Authority* came before the ECJ twice. In the first case ([*1986*] *IRLR 140*) it was held that a policy of different compulsory retirement ages on grounds of sex (which was then lawful under domestic legislation) was contrary to the Directive. In the second case ([*1993*] *IRLR 445*) the limit on compensation which applied at that time under the *SDA 1975* was set aside as being contrary to the Directive.

70 Dirty Jobs

The question of discrimination in the assignment of employees to dirty or unpleasant work is considered under *Detriment*. All such decisions should be made according to consistent principles applied to individual circumstances. They must not be made on grounds of gender or on racial grounds.

The fact that a job is dirty and unpleasant can be a relevant factor in an *Equal Value* case. It can also be relevant to the *Material Factor* defence under the *EPA 1970*.

71 Disability

71.1 DEFINITION

Section 1(1) of the *DDA 1995* provides that a person has a disability 'if he has a physical or mental impairment which has a substantial and long-term adverse effect on his ability to carry out normal day-to-day activities'.

71.2 OBJECTIVE

In devising the definition of 'disability', the legislature intended to cover the vast majority of disabled person in Britain. In committee, the then Minister for Social Security and Disabled People stated that the aim was to achieve a common sense definition which fitted the generally accepted perception of what a disability is.

71.3 INTERPRETING THE DEFINITION

Early experience of cases brought under the *DDA 1995* has shown that tribunals often struggle to come to terms with the unfamiliar legal concepts which it has introduced. Moreover, the facts of specific cases are often difficult to judge. With this in mind, the EAT offered general guidance in *Goodwin v The Patent Office* [*1999*] *IRLR 4*:

(*a*) when faced with the disability issue, the tribunal should look carefully at what the parties have said in their originating application and response (the IT1 and IT3). The parties may not have identified the real questions at issue, and, generally, it will be unsatisfactory for the disability issue to remain unclear and unspecific until the hearing itself. In many, if not most, disability discrimination cases, it will be good practice either to make standard directions designed to clarify issues or to arrange a directions hearing. It may well be the parties will wish to present expert evidence to assist the tribunal, and it would be undesirable for any such evidence to be given without proper advance notice to the other party and the early provision of a copy of any expert report to be referred to;

(*b*) the role of the tribunal contains an inquisitorial element. The interventionist role which tribunals have in relation to equal value claims might be thought a suitable model for disability cases. According to the EAT, there is 'a risk of a genuine "catch 22" situation'. Some disabled persons may be unable or unwilling to accept that they suffer from any disability; indeed it may be symptomatic of their condition that they deny it. Without the direct assistance of the tribunal, there may be some cases where the claim has been drafted with outside assistance but which the applicant, for some reason related to his disability, is unwilling to support;

(*c*) the tribunal should bear in mind that with social legislation of this kind, a purposive approach to construction should be adopted. The language should be construed in a way which gives effect to the stated or presumed intention of Parliament, but with due regard to the ordinary and natural meaning of the words in question;

(*d*) at least during the early period of the *DDA 1995*'s operation, the tribunal should always make explicit reference to any relevant provision of the Guidance or Codes of Practice which has been taken into account in arriving at its decision;

(*e*) in many cases, the question whether the person has a disability under the *DDA*

1995 admits of only one answer. In such clear cases, it would be wrong to search the Guidance and use what it says as some kind of extra hurdle over which the applicant must jump;

(*f*) the Code of Practice gives practical guidance and will be found helpful and informative in almost every case under the *DDA 1995*;

(*g*) the definition of 'disability' requires a tribunal to look at the evidence by reference to four different conditions:

(i) *The impairment condition*

Does the applicant have an impairment which is either mental or physical?

(ii) *The adverse effect of the condition*

Does the impairment affect the applicant's ability to carry out normal day-to-day activities in one of the respects set out in *paragraph 4(1)* of *Schedule 1* to the Act and does it have an adverse effect?

(iii) *The substantial condition*

Is the adverse effect upon the applicant's ability substantial?

(iv) *The long-term condition*

Is the adverse effect upon the applicant's ability long-term?

Frequently, there will be a 'complete overlap' between conditions (iii) and (iv), but the EAT said that 'it will be as well to bear all four of them in mind. Tribunals may find it helpful to address each of the questions but at the same time beware of the risk that desegregation should not take one's eye off the whole picture'.

The EAT's comments in *Goodwin* are useful, but inevitably not comprehensive and there is no substitute for a thorough assessment of all relevant aspects of the definition of 'disability'. For ease of reference, in this Handbook, the three main components of the definition are each considered in distinct sections, but their inter-relationship must always be kept in mind. The three components are:

(*a*) What is a *Physical or Mental Impairment*?

(*b*) What is meant by a person's ability to carry out *Normal Day-to-Day Activities*?

(*c*) In what circumstances does an impairment have a *Substantial and Long-term Adverse Effect* upon the ability to carry out normal day-to-day activities?

72 Disability Discrimination Legislation

72.1 THE DEVELOPMENT OF THE STATUTORY REGIME

There has been legislation in the UK relating to employment discrimination against disabled people for over half a century. Until recently, however, the statutory regime was limited in both scope and practical impact. The *Disabled Persons (Employment) Act 1944* (*DPA 1944*), amended in 1958, required employers with more than 20 employees to maintain a quota of registered disabled persons, ensuring that at least three per cent of their workforce was registered disabled. These provisions were widely ignored and rarely enforced. As a result, they did little to improve employment levels amongst disabled people. Limited additional responsibilities were introduced in relation to companies employing over 250 people under *section 234(3)* and *Schedule 7, Part III* of the *Companies Act 1985*. The directors' report of a company employing, on average, more than 250 people must contain a statement describing the policy applied during the previous financial year:

(*a*) for giving full and fair consideration to disabled people applying for jobs;

(*b*) for continuing the employment of, and provision of training to, employees that become disabled; and

(*c*) otherwise for the training, career development and promotion of disabled employees.

Pressure for more effective legislation grew in the early 1990s. Research indicated that disabled people faced discrimination and barriers to equal opportunity and employment as well as in many other areas. The Government's original stance was that drafting legislation would be complex and that the result would be uncertainty and confusion. It was thought better to educate and encourage employers to treat disabled people fairly. Experience overseas, however, showed that legislation might be workable; for instance, substantial statutory reforms were introduced in the United States, Australia and New Zealand. More generally, the International Labour Organisation established minimum labour standards for persons with physical or mental disabilities, while the United Nations issued *Standard Rules on the Equalization of Opportunities for Persons with Disabilities*, setting a framework for nation states to introduce anti-discrimination legislation. Developments in the European Union were relatively limited, although *Article 26* of the *EC Charter of Fundamental Social Rights for Workers* expressed the right of disabled people to expect member states to take steps to improve their social and professional integration. The catalyst for reform in the UK, however, was domestic political pressure. This ultimately resulted in the *Disability Discrimination Act 1995* (*DDA 1995*). The employment provisions of the *DDA 1995* came into effect on 2 December 1996.

The then Minister for Social Security and Disabled People, Mr William Hague, stated that the Act would mark the UK out as 'the leader in Europe' in the move towards comprehensive anti-discrimination legislation for disabled people. He added that the Act: 'is a profound measure with significant implications for every part of the economy' and whatever the imperfections of the new law, few would disagree with that observation. Yet despite the change of heart amongst politicians, the complexity of the problem addressed by the law remains. In the first case under the *DDA 1995* to come before the Court of Appeal, Mummery LJ noted in *Clark v TDG Limited t/a Novacold* [*1999*] *IRLR 318*:

> 'It is without doubt an unusually complex piece of legislation which poses novel questions of interpretation. It is not surprising that different conclusions have been reached at different levels of decision.

This state of affairs should not be taken as a criticism of the Act or of its drafting or of judicial disagreements about its interpretation. The whole subject presents unique challenges to legislators and to tribunals and courts, as well as to those responsible for the day-to-day operation of the Act in the workplace. Anyone who thinks that there is an easy way of achieving a sensible, workable and fair balance between the different interests of disabled persons, of employers, and of able-bodied workers, in harmony with the wider public interests in an economically efficient workforce, in access to employment, in equal treatment of workers and in standards of fairness at work, has probably not given much serious thought to the problem.'

Again, the truth of these remarks cannot be doubted. It is notable, for instance, that although there are obvious similarities between disability discrimination law and the legislation on sex and race discrimination, there are also significant differences.

72.2 COMPARISON WITH OTHER DISCRIMINATION LEGISLATION

Those familiar with the law forbidding discrimination on the grounds of race and sex, should beware of assuming that concepts familiar from those areas of the law apply in precisely the same way in relation to discrimination on the ground of disability. The significance, or otherwise, of some of the points of difference will take time to become clear, but the following points are especially worthy of note:

(*a*) employers with fewer than 15 employees are not covered by the *DDA 1995*;

(*b*) operational staff in the police, armed services and prisons (but not their civilian staff) are not covered by the *DDA 1995*;

(*c*) the *DDA 1995*, like the *RRA 1976* but unlike the *SDA 1975*, does not derive from EU law and this may have a bearing on the interpretation of particular words, e.g. 'detriment', to be found in both the *SDA 1975* and the *DDA 1995*, as *Clark v TDG Limited t/a Novacold* [*1999*] *IRLR 318* indicates;

(*d*) the *DDA 1995* permits certain forms of direct discrimination to be legally justified;

(*e*) the *DDA 1995* does not utilise the concept of indirect discrimination. Rather, there is a duty to make reasonable adjustments which is relevant to the definition of discrimination on the ground of disability; and

(*f*) the test of less favourable treatment is based on the reason for the treatment of the disabled person and not on the fact of his disability. It does not turn on a like-for-like comparison of the treatment of the disabled person and of others in similar circumstances. Thus, it is not appropriate to make a comparison of the cases in the same way as in the *SDA 1975* and *RRA 1976*.

72.3 SCOPE OF THE DDA 1995

Part I and *Schedule 1–2* to the *DDA 1995* address the crucial definitions of 'disability' and 'disabled person'. *Part II* covers discrimination in employment and by *Trade Organisations*. The Act extends to discrimination in fields other than employment and which are *not* covered by this Handbook, i.e. discrimination in relation to goods, facilities and services; the disposal and management of premises; and education and transport.

When the employment provisions of the *DDA 1995* came into force on 2 December 1996, they effectively replaced the 1944 Act, but an individual who was registered as disabled on 12 January 1995 and remained so on 2 December 1996 was automatically deemed to be a disabled person for the purposes of the *DDA 1995* for a period of three years from 2 December 1996.

An act of discrimination on the ground of disability which took place before 2 December 1996 does not give a right of complaint in itself, but it may nevertheless be relevant to a complaint under the *DDA 1995*, since it may entitle a tribunal to draw inferences about an employer's acts or omissions after the *DDA 1995* came into force. An inference of disability discrimination was drawn on this basis in *British Sugar plc v Kirker* [*1998*] *IRLR 624*, where the employee was made redundant shortly after the *DDA 1995* came into force, having been marked down in the selection process because of subjective assessments influenced by his disability.

72.4 REGULATIONS, CODE OF PRACTICE, GUIDANCE AND THE DRC 1996

The *DDA 1995* is supplemented by various regulations. The *Disability Discrimination (Employment Regulations) 1996, SI 1996 No 1456* clarify the defence of *Justification* and related issues. The *Disability Discrimination (Meaning of Disability) Regulations 1996, SI 1996 No 1455* further address the meaning of *Disability*.

Pursuant to the *DDA 1995*, the Secretary of State has issued a Code of Practice which addresses the elimination of discrimination in the field of employment. The Code does not purport to set out a definitive statement of the detailed law, but offers general and practical guidance and is admissible in evidence in proceedings under the *DDA 1995*. If a provision of the Code itself (but not the Annexes to it, which contain information on associated matters) appears to be relevant, it must be taken into account by a tribunal.

The Secretary of State has also exercised his power under the *DDA 1995* to issue Guidance concerning matters to be taken into account in determining whether an impairment has a substantial adverse effect on a person's ability to carry out normal day-to-day activities, or whether such an impairment has a long-term effect. The Guidance has similar status to that of the Code of Practice.

The *Disability Rights Commission*, established by the *Disability Rights Commission Act 1999*, came into operation in April 2000 and has a role similar to those of the Equal Opportunities Commission and Commission for Racial Equality.

72.5 ELIGIBILITY FOR RIGHTS

Various classes of persons are excluded from protection by the *DDA 1995*:

(*a*) members of the armed forces, prison officers and fire fighters;

(*b*) certain overseas employees;

(*c*) employees who work on board ships, aircraft or hovercraft;

(*d*) members of certain special police forces and certain other police officers; and

(*e*) holders of statutory office.

'Employment' means 'employment under a contract of service or of apprenticeship or a contract personally to do any work': *section 68(1) DDA 1995*. This relatively wide definition means that a large number of self-employed people who perform their work personally are protected.

There is no qualifying threshold of hours that must be worked, or months or years for which employment must have lasted, for a person to be eligible for rights under the *DDA 1995*. In certain circumstances, the part-time nature of the job may be relevant to the extent of the duty to make *Reasonable Adjustments* under *section 6*.

Small employers are excluded from the coverage of the *DDA 1995* and thus their employees are not entitled to the statutory protection. Given the large number of small businesses in the UK, this is an important limitation on the value of the *DDA 1995*. The exemption currently applies to employers with fewer than 15 employees: *Disability Discrimination (Exemption for Small Employers) Order 1998, SI 1998 No 2618*. This figure is calculated without regard to the size of individual workplaces, branches or establishments. The cut-off point when the *DDA 1995* was first introduced was 20 employees, rather than 15, so the number of people protected is greater than it was originally. There is a continuing debate about whether a small employer exemption is justified at all and, if it is, at what point to draw the dividing line. The economic argument concerning burdens on business caused by the need to make adjustment for disabled people needs to be balanced against the desirability of protecting the rights of those disabled people.

The rigidity of the small employer exemption is illustrated by *Hardie v C D Northern Ltd [2000] IRLR 827*. An employee sought to bring a complaint of disability discrimination against a small employer. His employer had a wholly-owned subsidiary with two employees which, if taken into account, would have taken the employer outside the scope of the exemption. A tribunal rejected the claim, noting that there is no comparable provision in the *DDA 1995* relating to 'associated employers' to that found in other employment statutes such as the *SDA 1975*. On appeal, it was argued that the concept of 'employer' should be interpreted consistently as between the discrimination statutes; that the failure to include 'associated employers' in the *DDA 1995* was a legislative oversight; and that the tribunal should have lifted the corporate veil and found that the two employers formed a single economic unit. The EAT rejected those arguments. There is nothing in the *DDA 1995* which enlarges the meaning of 'employer' so as to include 'associated employers'. There was no presumption that Parliament did not intend to distinguish between disability discrimination and sex discrimination legislation. There is no reason to believe that Parliament had made any slip; having decided that there should be an exemption for small businesses, it had to draw a line somewhere. Finally, it was not legitimate in terms of legal principle to treat the employer and its subsidiaries as a single economic unit. Where a corporation has been interpolated so as to cloak the truth, the 'corporate veil' can be lifted so that the truth can be seen. But on the facts, there was nothing to justify lifting the veil. The EAT emphasised, as it has done in a similar subsequent case, that it is for Parliament and not the courts to extend the application of the *DDA 1995*'s employment provisions.

The *DDA 1995* contains special provisions relating to *Charities* for disabled people which in effect permit a limited form of *Positive Discrimination*. Nothing in *Part II* affects any charitable instrument conferring benefits on categories of persons determined by reference to any physical or mental capacity or makes unlawful any act done by a charity in pursuance of its charitable purposes, so far as these purposes are connected to such persons. Employers who provide 'supported employment' for the disabled are permitted to treat members of a particular group of disabled persons more favourably than other persons in providing such supported employment.

72.6 CONTRACTING OUT

Any term in a contract, which in relation to the employment provisions of the *DDA 1995*, purports to:

(*a*) require a person to contravene any such provision;

(*b*) exclude or limit the operation of any such provision; or

(*c*) prevent the presentation of a claim to an employment tribunal is void. But settlement of a complaint under the auspices of ACAS is legitimate: see below.

72.7 SUMMARY OF EMPLOYMENT DISCRIMINATION PROVISIONS IN THE DDA 1995

Section 4 of the *DDA 1995* outlaws discrimination (in a way defined in *section 5*) against disabled persons by employers in respect of employment opportunities generally: see *Discrimination Against Disabled Workers*. *Section 6* imposes a duty on employers to make *Reasonable Adjustments* where this will assist disabled persons to compete for such opportunities. The provisions on employment discrimination are extended to contract workers by *section 12*. Discrimination against disabled persons by trade organisations is covered in particular by *sections 13–15*. *Victimisation* is addressed by *section 55*. Matters of interpretation are covered in *section 68*.

72.8 TIME LIMIT FOR CLAIMS

A person complaining of breach of the employment provisions of the *DDA 1995*, whether by an employer, a 'principal' (in relation to a claim by a contract worker), or a trade organisation, may present a complaint to an employment tribunal. The basic time limit for bringing a complaint is three months, beginning when the act complained of was done. As in the case of claims under the *SDA 1975* and *RRA 1976*, the tribunal has a discretion to consider a claim that has been brought outside the time limit if, in all the circumstances of the case, the tribunal considers it 'just and equitable' to do so.

For time limit purposes, it is important to note that, where an unlawful act of discrimination is attributable to a term in a contract, that act is to be treated as extending throughout the duration of the contract. Any act extending over a period of time shall be treated as done at the end of that period. A deliberate omission is to be treated as done when the person decided upon it. In the absence of evidence establishing the contrary, an omission is decided upon when a person either does something inconsistent with doing the omitted act or (if he has done no such inconsistent act) the period expires within which he might reasonably have been expected to do the omitted act if it was to be done. The distinction between 'continuing' discrimination and 'one-off' acts or omissions of discrimination may be significant for time limit purposes. An analogy may be drawn with principles established in other areas of discrimination law. Thus employment policies, rules, regulations and custom and practice may, like contract terms, be classed as continuing over a period of time.

72.9 ACAS CONCILIATION

ACAS conciliation is available in respect of complaints to a tribunal under the *DDA 1995* in the same way as in relation to complaints of sex and race discrimination. It is a statute-based form of *Alternative Dispute Resolution*. Anything which is communicated to an ACAS conciliation officer is inadmissible in evidence in tribunal proceedings except with the consent of the person who communicated it. A settlement conciliated by ACAS, which will typically be recorded on Form COT3, will be binding on the parties. This is so notwithstanding the general principle that people protected by the *DDA 1995* cannot contract out of the rights which it affords them.

72.10 QUESTIONNAIRES

As in sex and race discrimination cases, there is provision for statutory questionnaires to assist a person complaining of discrimination under the *DDA 1995* to prove the case.

Replies to a questionnaire are admissible in evidence in proceedings before a tribunal and the tribunal may draw inferences from an employer's deliberate failure to respond within a reasonable period without reasonable excuse, or from evasive or equivocal replies.

72.11 RESTRICTING PUBLICITY

Where a tribunal hears a case under the *DDA 1995*, it may make an order restricting publicity where 'evidence of a personal nature' is likely to be heard. This covers any evidence of a medical or other intimate nature which might reasonably be assumed to be likely to cause significant embarrassment to the complainant if reported.

72.12 REMEDIES

If a complaint made under the *DDA 1995* succeeds, the tribunal must grant one or more of the following remedies:

(*a*) a declaration as to the rights of the complainant and the respondent in relation to the matters to which the complaint relates;

(*b*) an order that the respondent pays compensation to the complainant;

(*c*) a recommendation that the respondent take, within a specified period, action which appears to the tribunal to be reasonable in all the circumstances of the case, for the purpose of obviating or reducing the adverse effect on the complainant of any matters to which the complaint relates.

Crucially, there is no limit on the amount of compensation that a tribunal may award. The level of compensation is to be calculated by applying the principles applicable to the calculation of damages in claims in tort. Compensation may include an award for injury to feelings. It is almost inevitable that, in cases where discrimination results in the loss of a job, the typical award for compensation to a disabled person will tend to be higher than in cases of sex discrimination, simply because of the difficulties that many disabled persons encounter in seeking to obtain work. Compensation running into six figures was awarded even in one of the earliest cases brought under the *DDA 1995: British Sugar plc v Kirker [1998] IRLR 624*.

The need for care in making an award of compensation for disability discrimination was highlighted by the EAT in *Buxton v Equinox Design Limited [1999] IRLR 158*, which concerned the dismissal of a craftsman who had been diagnosed as having multiple sclerosis. The tribunal awarded compensation, including £500 for injury to feelings, on the basis that the period of future loss should be limited to one year from the date of the letter from a doctor advising on the employee's condition. The tribunal made its award without having heard oral evidence from any doctor called by either party. The EAT ruled that the tribunal was wrong to limit the period of future loss to one year without a sufficient evidential basis. More generally, the EAT said that the remedies hearing in a case of discrimination requires careful judicial management. In a case where compensation is unlimited, the relatively brief and informal hearing on remedy that has conventionally been regarded as appropriate in unfair dismissal cases may not be appropriate. It will often be the case that the remedies hearing should involve the parties in careful pre-preparation under the management of the tribunal. For this purpose, directions may be required involving an exchange of statements of case and any witness statements. Without proper directions by the tribunal, 'there is a real probability of trial by ambush leading to significant awards'. In disability cases, a medical expert may be required if the parties have been unable to agree the evidence. Where necessary, special consideration should be giving to fixing the hearing to accommodate a busy professional witness.

On the facts of the case, the crucial issue had been for the tribunal to decide, on a balance of probabilities and an assessment of the chances, what would have been the outcome of the risk assessment in relation to the employee if one had been carried out. The tribunal's finding that the period of loss should be one year could not be made on the evidence before it, since it involved making a finding as to the outcome of a risk assessment in the context of a disease which has variable effects. Without medical evidence, the tribunal was not in a position to say what the outcome would be. The case was therefore remitted back to the tribunal for further consideration. The employee argued that the award of £500 for injury to feelings was too low in a disability case, where the prospects of a disabled person getting another job might not be as good as those of a person dismissed for a race or gender reason. The EAT said that whilst this might be true, the tribunal was seeking to compensate a person for an injury to feelings, where such injury is proved. Each case will depend upon its own facts. This was a judgement which the tribunal was entitled to make and so there was no ground in law to interfere with the tribunal's decision in that particular respect.

73 Disability Discrimination and Unfair Dismissal

73.1 DISABILITY DISCRIMINATION MAY BE FAIR

An employer may, in dismissing a disabled employed, be guilty of discrimination contrary to the *DDA 1995*. If the employee is eligible for the right not to be unfairly dismissed, he or she may well bring a claim of unfair dismissal in addition to a claim of disability discrimination. Typically, the dismissal will be unfair if the reason for it was discriminatory contrary to the *DDA 1995*, but that is not necessarily the case. In *HJ Heinz Co Ltd v Kenrick (2000) IRLR 144*, for example, an employee with chronic fatigue syndrome was dismissed because of his lengthy sickness absence. The EAT upheld a tribunal's decision that the employer was in breach of the *DDA 1995* and had failed to justify the discrimination on the ground of disability. However, the tribunal's finding that the dismissal was unfair was set aside. The tribunal seemed to have proceeded on the basis that a disability-related dismissal which is not justified under the *DDA 1995* is *automatically* unfair. However, the EAT emphasised that that is not the case. There should have been separate consideration of the matters relevant to fairness which usually fall for consideration under *section 98(4)* of the *Employment Rights Act 1996*. Parliament has not provided that a dismissal that is discriminatory contrary to the *DDA 1995* is automatically unfair, in the way that, for example, certain dismissals are deemed to be automatically unfair pursuant to *section 99(1)* of the *Employment Rights Act 1996*, or *Reg 8(1)* of the *Transfer of Undertakings (Protection of Employment) Regulations 1981* (*SI 1981 No 1794*; amended by *SI 1987 No 442*).

74 Disability Policies

74.1 IS A SEPARATE DISABILITY POLICY NECESSARY?

Disability may be addressed in an organisation's general equal opportunities policy statement. This may help to avoid a proliferation of *Equal Opportunities Policies* as well as, from a presentational and perhaps substantive perspective, treating disabled people inappropriately as some form of 'special case'. There is, moreover, merit in having a single over-arching statement of policy in respect of equal opportunities. However, there may be attractions, perhaps especially in organisations which may not have addressed disability issues in detail previously, in having a separate disability policy statement, even if only as an interim measure while a comprehensive integrated policy is developed. It may for example be advantageous to have a separate policy on disability so as to raise awareness within the organisation of the key issues.

74.2 REVIEWING CURRENT PRACTICE

Whether there is to be a separate disability policy, or disability is covered by the organisation's general equal opportunities policy, it is sensible to assess current practice before drawing up the disability policy statement. The review process, sometimes called a 'disability audit', may range widely. Examples of subjects which may be considered include:

(*a*) Is there any current policy statement or associated documentation?

(*b*) If there is a current policy, who is responsible for implementing it?

(*c*) How are the needs of disabled employees in respect of matters such as premises and equipment met?

(*e*) How is disability dealt with in the recruitment process?

(*f*) Are any steps taken to help people with disabilities to develop their careers?

(*g*) How are *Employees Who Become Disabled* treated?

(*h*) How are the training needs of disabled people met?

(*i*) Does the organisation monitor its performance in respect of treating disabled employees equally?

74.3 IMPLEMENTATION

Because the *DDA 1995* is a much more recent enactment than either the *SDA 1975* or *RRA 1976* managers in an organisation may sometimes be slow to recognise both the importance and the implications of treating disabled people equally. The key elements of implementing an effective disability policy typically include:

(*a*) obtaining the commitment of the top managers to the policy;

(*b*) training staff responsible for recruitment, selection and promotion decisions to appreciate the impact of the *DDA 1995*, *Guidance and Code of Practice*;

(*c*) identifying the issues which need to be covered by the disability policy;

(*d*) drawing up the disability policy, consulting where appropriate with staff and with trade union representatives;

(*e*) keeping the policy up to date.

74.4 CONTENTS OF THE POLICY

The specific matters that may be covered in a disability policy are likely to vary from organisation to organisation. The following is a list of examples which is far from exhaustive:

(*a*) does recruitment literature and advertising welcome disabled people?

(*b*) are job advertisements placed in alternative media such as teletext?

(*c*) are questions asked at job interviews relating to disability concerned solely with the requirements of the job?

(*d*) are any particular needs that a disabled person may have as regards access to premises or equipment discussed with the individuals?

(*e*) are training courses accessible to disabled delegates?

(*f*) are disabled employees encouraged to give feedback on their particular needs?

74.5 STAFF TRAINING

Lack of familiarity with disability issues is still a widespread phenomenon. Managers dealing with disabled job applicants and employees, and front-line staff dealing with disabled customers, are obvious examples of staff who are likely to need appropriate training. There may also be a case for making training available to the whole workforce. Training may tackle both general awareness of disability issues and also more specific training implications of the legislation. It is often helpful for training to cover disability etiquette, i.e. courtesies with disabled people which may not be obvious to those who have had limited contact with people who have disabilities. For example:

(*a*) disabled adults (e.g. those with learning disabilities) should not be treated as if they are children;

(*b*) negative or intrusive questions should be avoided;

(*c*) jokes exploiting disabilities are unacceptable;

(*d*) if a disabled person appears to need assistance, one should offer it, but wait for the offer to be accepted before acting and not be offended if the offer is rejected;

(*e*) a wheelchair is part of the wheelchair user's body space and so one should not lean on it inappropriately;

(*f*) one should not shout at deaf people;

(*g*) one should talk directly to a deaf person rather than his or her interpreter;

(*h*) when a blind person enters an unfamiliar room, one should offer a brief explanation of the room, identifying possible hazards;

(*i*) one should tell a blind person when one is leaving the room;

(*j*) one should avoid language which may be perceived as belittling. Views on terminology vary, but commonly the following words and terms are regarded as inappropriate:

(i) 'handicapped';

(ii) 'the disabled';

(iii) 'wheelchair bound' or 'confined to a wheelchair';

(iv) 'spastic';

(*h*) one should avoid referring to a person simply by reference to their condition. For example, to refer to a 'person with epilepsy' is appropriate; an 'epileptic' is not.

75 Disability Rights Commission

75.1 NATIONAL DISABILITY COUNCIL

When the *Disability Discrimination Act 1995* was introduced, there was no provision for a rights agency along the same lines as the *Commission for Racial Equality* (CRE) or the *Equal Opportunities Commission* (EOC) to which individual complaints of discrimination might be submitted. Rather, the then government established the National Disability Council (NDC) an advisory body with a limited remit and no enforcement powers. The NDC lacked the power to provide assistance or advice to people complaining about disability discrimination, to conduct formal investigations or to bring proceedings. It also lacked the general power to monitor and review the operation of the new regime. The theory was that a Commission would not work, might create the risk of a backlash against disability rights and would be inappropriate to the prevailing social context. The NDC did not even have the power to issue codes of practice on its own initiative, although it did have the task of preparing or reviewing a code if and when asked to do so by the Secretary of State. The NDC also took over the majority of powers of the National Advisory Council for the Employment of People with Disabilities which had originally been established under the *Disabled Persons (Employment) Act 1944*.

It soon became apparent that, given the complexity of many aspects of the disability discrimination legislation, it would be desirable for there to be a Disability Rights Commission, which could make a more effective contribution than the NDC to the clarification of areas of difficulty. The present government accordingly legislated to achieve that aim.

75.2 DISABILITY RIGHTS COMMISSION ACT 1999

The Act established the Disability Rights Commission (DRC) which became operational in April 2000. The DRC replaces the NDC and comprises up to fifteen members, the majority of them disabled.

The role and functions of the DRC include the following:

(*a*) working towards the elimination of discrimination against disabled people;

(*b*) promoting the equalisation of opportunities for disabled people; with those of non-disabled people

(*c*) advising government on the law about discrimination against disabled people;

(*d*) assisting disabled people by offering information, advice and support in taking cases forward;

(*e*) providing information and advice to business and other stakeholders;

(*f*) investigating where the DRC has reason to believe that discrimination is taking place and to secure compliance with the law;

(*g*) preparing codes of practice and promoting good practice.

Thus the powers of the DRC are similar to those of the CRE and EOC.

76 Disability Rights Task Force

The Disability Rights Task Force was created in December 1997 to advise the government on how to progress civil rights for disabled people. The DRTF's final report on wider rights for disabled people was published in late 1999.

The main recommendations concerning employment were:

(*a*) the structure of the *DDA 1995* should be retained and built upon;

(*b*) where possible, the coverage of the *DDA 1995* and approach should be brought into line with the law on sex and race discrimination, taking into account proposals from the *Commission for Racial Equality* and *Equal Opportunities Commission* to reform those laws;

(*c*) the definition of disability should be clarified and extended;

(*d*) people with HIV should be covered from the point of diagnosis (rather than the development of symptoms as is now the case);

(*e*) people with cancer, in cases where it is unclear if recurrence of substantial effects is likely (e.g. as is the case with some cancers following medical treatment) should be protected;

(*f*) the public sector should take the lead in promoting equal opportunities, both in its own workforce and through encouraging good practice in its suppliers;

(*g*) disability-related enquiries before a job offer is made should be allowed only in limited circumstances.

Some of the recommendations are likely to gain more widespread acceptance than others. For instance the practical implications of the proposal to restrict disability-related questions needs to be considered with particular care. The government response to the proposals was awaited at the time of writing. Further consultation will take place before any legislation is introduced.

77 Disciplining and Dismissing Disabled Employees

77.1 ARE DISABLED EMPLOYEES SPECIALLY PROTECTED?

Even prior to the enactment of the *DDA 1995*, disabled employees had a measure of protection over and above the norm from unfair dismissal. In *Seymour v British Airways Board* [*1983*] *IRL.R 55*, decided when the *Disabled Persons (Employment) Act 1944* was still in force, the EAT ruled that a person who was registered disabled under the then statutory regime was entitled to special consideration, which included considering his personal circumstances, before dismissing him. The employers had a policy for assessing the effectiveness of disabled workers and for considering suitable alternative employment for them. On the facts, the EAT decided that the selection of the disabled employee for redundancy was fair.

While the *DDA 1995* (colloquially speaking) permits *Positive Discrimination*, this does not mean that employers cannot dismiss disabled employees in appropriate circumstances. Employers must, however, take care not to discriminate against disabled employees when taking disciplinary action or dismissal decisions. Thus the content of disciplinary policies and procedures needs to be properly accessible to, and understandable by, disabled employees. The duty to make *Reasonable Adjustments* may mean that the employer should operate the disciplinary procedure with particular flexibility in the case of a disabled employee. This might, for instance, entail permitting an adjournment of a disciplinary hearing to enable a disabled employee to take medication. It is essential that a disabled employee should understand fully the content and implications of any counselling, consultation or warning.

77.2 MISCONDUCT

A disabled employee may be dismissed for gross misconduct, or an instance of less serious misconduct following appropriate earlier warnings, in circumstances where another employee would have been dismissed. But, on occasion, for example in the case of an employee with a learning disability, an instance of apparent misconduct such as aggressive behaviour may be explicable by reference to the disability. In such a case, the employer may need to consider making a reasonable adjustment in terms (for instance) of establishing working conditions sufficiently flexible as to accommodate the behaviour of the employee in question without undue disruption to the business or to colleagues.

77.3 REDUNDANCY

Most employers now realise that, even where a genuine 'redundancy situation' (to use a non-legalistic term) exists, a decision to make an employee redundant must nevertheless be handled in a fair and reasonable manner. Typically, this involves ensuring that selection is fair and reasonable and based on objective and relevant criteria; undertaking meaningful consultation before a decision to dismiss is taken; and considering properly alternatives to redundancy, which for example may include short-time working, seeking volunteers, redeployment and revising employment terms.

By virtue of the *DDA 1995*, it is discriminatory to select for redundancy on the basis of disability. It is also necessary to ensure that the way in which the redundancy process is handled is non-discriminatory. This may give rise to tricky challenges for employers, especially if their method of selecting for redundancy involves the application of criteria such as attendance, productivity or (a common but often unsatisfactory catch-all) 'flexibility'. Attendance records, for instance, may appear to constitute a sound and objective factor to take into account when considering which employees to retain within a shrinking work force. But what if poor attendance results from a disability? In the light of the *DDA 1995*, a disability-related criterion will only be legitimate if the criterion has a demonstrably substantial and material effect on the organisation and it is not possible to make a reasonable adjustment to redress that effect. An illustration of the general principles arose in *Morse v Wiltshire County Council* [*1999*] *IRLR 352*. Following an accident, a road worker was left with a disability involving restrictions on movement and a susceptibility to black-outs. When a redundancy situation arose, management took the view that it was essential to retain only the most flexible workers, especially in order to ensure that a proper winter road surface was maintained. But it was necessary for many of the workers to be fully qualified drivers. The disabled employee's lack of driving ability (because of the black-outs) and the limitations on what he could do led to his selection for redundancy. There was no consultation directly with him as to his current state of health. A tribunal rejected his complaint of discrimination, even though it was undisputed that he had been dismissed for a reason relating to his disability. The tribunal concluded that the employers had shown that no reasonable adjustment to the working conditions or job description would have avoided the dismissal and the reason for his treatment was substantial and material within *section 5* of the *DDA 1995*. The EAT allowed the employee's appeal. The tribunal had failed to take the correct steps in considering the question of discrimination. It had not made any real enquiry into the steps which the employer might have taken to enable the employee to be kept on, or into the additional expense, if any, which was likely to be caused by any steps to enable his retention.

77.4 REDEPLOYMENT AND REDUNDANCY PROCEDURES

That the duty to make reasonable adjustments serves as a form of *Positive Discrimination* in favour of disabled employees is illustrated by *Kent County Council v Mingo* [*2000*] *IRLR 90*. A cook injured his back and received medical advice that it was almost inevitable that the back problem would recur if he returned to his cooking job, but that he would be fit for work that did not include heavy duties or lifting. He was found work as a supernumerary helper and, following a recommendation that he be redeployed, he was classified as a 'category B redeployee' under the employer's procedures. Category B covered staff to be redeployed on grounds of 'incapability/ill health'. In contrast, those at risk, or under notice of, redundancy were classified as category A employees and given priority consideration for suitable alternative employment. Following the introduction of the *DDA 1995*, the employers introduced a new category to cover staff with a disability where a reasonable adjustment could not be made to their present post to accommodate the disability. However, category A staff continued to be placed at a higher level. The disabled employee was turned down for an internal post for which he had applied and had been graded appointable. He was told that he would have been appointed if he had been a category A redeployee. He expressed interest in other vacancies but was told that they were reserved for category A redeployees. After his supernumerary post came to an end, he was dismissed. The EAT upheld a tribunal's decision that the employee had been unfairly dismissed and discriminated against unlawfully. The employer's redeployment procedures did not adequately reflect the requirements of the *DDA 1995*, since the policy of giving preferential treatment to redundant or potentially redundant employees meant that people with disabilities were relatively disadvantaged in the system of redeployment. Had the employer permitted the employee to be treated as a category A redeployee, he would have been redeployed and not dismissed. This justified a finding of disability discrimination.

77.5 LACK OF CAPABILITY

A reason relating to an employee's capability may constitute a potentially fair ground for dismissal. Lack of capability may take either of two forms: sub-standard performance or unsatisfactory attendance. Employers need to appreciate that a disability may lie behind both poor performance and poor attendance and take care to ensure that their procedures for dealing with such problems are not discriminatory.

Difficult cases may involve issues concerning *Knowledge of Disability* or *Employees Who Become Disabled*. The Court of Appeal's decision in *Clark v TDG Ltd t/a Novacold* [*1999*] *IRLR 318* is instructive. An employee who suffered a back injury was dismissed after an absence of about four months after his GP indicated that he was unlikely to be fit to return in the near future and an orthopaedic consultant said that, while the injury should improve over a period of a year, it was not possible to specify when the employee could resume his duties. A tribunal and the EAT considered that the employee had not suffered discrimination because he was treated no differently than a person who was off work for the same amount of time, but for a reason other than disability, would have been treated. The Court of Appeal said that this was the wrong approach. The test of less favourable treatment is based on the reason for the less favourable treatment of the disabled person and not on the fact of his disability. It does not turn on a like-for-like comparison of the disabled person and others in similar circumstances. So it is not appropriate to make a comparison of the cases in the same way as under the *SDA 1975* or *RRA 1976*. The statutory focus in the *DDA 1995* is narrower and the emphasis is on whether the less favourable treatment of the employee is shown to be justified. The employment tribunal had said that if there was less favourable treatment then it would not have been justified, but it was wrong to take that view without having regard to the relevant provision of the *Code of Practice* relating to termination of employment.

In particular, the Code states that:

> 'It would be justifiable to terminate the employment of an employee where disability makes it impossible for him any longer to perform the main functions of his job, if an adjustment such as a move to a vacant post elsewhere in the business is not practicable or otherwise not reasonable for the employer to make.'

The Court of Appeal noted that 'the critical question . . . is that of justification of the treatment. This will also probably be the case with many other complaints under the 1995 Act'. It follows that employers should pay particular heed to the matter of whether they can justify their actions in cases of lack of capacity.

78 Disciplinary Action

There must be no discrimination (as defined by the *SDA 1975*, *RRA 1976* and *DDA 1995*) in relation to disciplinary matters, even where the action taken falls short of dismissal. It is a clear *Detriment* for an employee to be given a warning. If, for example, the employee's gender was a significant factor in the decision to give a warning instead of taking no action at all, then the employee will have grounds for complaining of direct sex discrimination.

So far as *Reasonable Adjustments* in such cases are concerned, the principles stated in relation to *Capability Dismissals* and *Conduct Dismissals* also apply where action short of dismissal is taken.

79 Disciplinary Rules and Grievance Procedures

The *ACAS Code of Practice on Disciplinary & Grievance Procedures* (revised edition 2000) recommends that employers should prepare and issue written disciplinary rules. Management is encouraged to make every effort to ensure that all employees know and understand the rules, including those employees whose first language is not English or who have a visual impairment. Similarly, in order for grievance procedures to be effective, all employees need to be made aware of them and understand them. Special allowance should, the *Code of Practice* says, be made for employees whose first language is not English or who have a visual impairment. There was no comparable reference to equal opportunities considerations in the previous edition of the *Code of Practice* and, although brief, the points made in the new edition at least indicate growing awareness of the possible risk that the unthinking, even if superficially consistent, implementation of standard procedures may disadvantage certain minority groups in the workforce.

80 Discrimination Against Disabled Workers

80.1 PROHIBITED DISCRIMINATION

Section 4(1) of the *DDA 1995* renders it unlawful for an employer to discriminate against a disabled person:

(*a*) in the arrangements which he makes for the purpose of determining to whom he should offer employment;

(*b*) in the terms on which he offers that person employment; or

(*c*) by refusing to offer, or deliberately not offering, him employment.

Section 4(2) renders it unlawful for an employer to discriminate against a disabled person whom he employs:

(*a*) in the terms of employment which he affords him;

(*b*) in the opportunities which he affords him for promotion, a transfer, training or receiving any other benefits;

(*c*) by refusing to afford him, or deliberately not affording him, any such opportunity; or

(*d*) by dismissing him, or subjecting him to any other detriment.

Section 4(2) does not apply to benefits of any description if the employer is concerned with the provision of benefits of that description to the public, or to a section of the public which includes the employee in question, unless:

(*a*) that provision differs in a material respect from the provision of the benefits by the employer to his employee; or

(*b*) the provision of the benefits to the employee in question is regulated by his contract of employment; or

(*c*) the benefits relate to training.

'Benefits' for these purposes includes facilities and services.

80.2 MEANING OF 'DISCRIMINATION' AGAINST A DISABLED PERSON

An employer discriminates against a disabled person if:

(*a*) for a reason which relates to the disabled person's disability, he treats him less favourably than he treats or would treat others to whom that reason does not or would not apply; and

(*b*) he cannot show that the treatment in question is justified.

An employer also discriminates against a disabled person if:

(*a*) he fails to comply with a duty imposed on him by *section 6* (i.e. to make *Reasonable Adjustments* in relation to the disabled person); and

(*b*) he cannot show that his failure to comply with that duty is justified.

The concept of *Justification* needs to be understood since discriminatory treatment is justified if, but only if, the reason for it is both material to the circumstances of the particular case and substantial. If, in a case falling within *section 5(1)*, the employer is under a *section 6* duty in relation to the disabled person but fails without justification to comply with that duty, his treatment of that person cannot be justified under *section 5(3)* unless it would have been justified even if he had complied with the duty under *section 6*.

80.3 MEANING OF 'DISABLED PERSON'

Section 1(2) provides that 'disabled person' means a person who has a disability. The meaning of *Disability* is therefore of fundamental importance.

Interpreting the definition

Early experience of cases brought under the *DDA 1995* has shown that tribunals often struggle to come to terms with the unfamiliar legal concepts which it has introduced. Moreover, the facts of specific cases are often difficult to judge. With this in mind, the EAT offered general guidance in *Goodwin v The Patent Office* [*1999*] *IRLR 4*:

(*a*) when faced with a disability issue, the tribunal should look carefully at what the parties have said in their originating application and response (the IT1 and IT3). The parties may not have identified the real questions at issue, and generally, it will be unsatisfactory for the disability issue to remain unclear and unspecific until the hearing itself. In many, if not most, disability discrimination cases, it will be good practice either to make standard directions designed to clarify issues or to arrange a directions hearing. It may well be the parties will wish to present expert evidence to assist the tribunal, and it would be undesirable for any such evidence to be given without proper advance notice to the other party and the early provision of a copy of any expert report to be referred to;

(*b*) the role of the tribunal contains an inquisitorial element. The interventionist role which tribunals have in relation to equal value claims might be thought a suitable model for disability cases. According to the EAT, there is 'a risk of a genuine "catch 22" situation'. Some disabled persons may be unable or unwilling to accept that they suffer from any disability; indeed it may be symptomatic of their condition that they deny it. Without the direct assistance of the tribunal at the hearing, there may be some cases where the claim has been drafted with outside assistance but which the applicant, for some reason related to his disability, is unwilling to support. Tribunals should be alert to this and be prepared to intervene, should the need arise, to a proper and appropriate extent;

(*c*) the tribunal should bear in mind that with social legislation of this kind, a purposive approach to construction should be adopted. The language should be construed in a way which gives effect to the stated or presumed intention of Parliament, but with due regard to the ordinary and natural meaning of the words in question;

(*d*) at least during the early period of the *DDA 1995*'s operation, the tribunal should *always* make explicit reference to any relevant provision of the *Guidance or Code of Practice* which has been taken into account in arriving at its decision;

(*e*) in many cases, the question whether the person has a disability within the *DDA 1995* admits of only one answer. In such clear cases, it would be wrong to search the *Guidance* and use what it says as some kind of extra hurdle over which the applicant must jump;

(*f*) the *Code of Practice* gives practical guidance and will be found helpful and informative in almost every case under the *DDA 1995*, (*g*) the definition of 'disability' requires a tribunal to look at the evidence by reference to four different conditions:

(i) *The impairment condition*

Does the applicant have an impairment which is either mental or physical?

(ii) *The adverse effect condition*

Does the impairment affect the applicant's ability to carry out normal day-to-day activities in one of the respects set out in *paragraph 4(1)* of *Schedule 1* to the *Act*, and does it have an adverse effect?

(iii) *The substantial condition*

Is the adverse effect upon the applicant's ability substantial?

(iv) *The long-term condition*

Is the adverse effect upon the applicant's ability long-term?

Frequently, there will be a 'complete overlap' between conditions (iii) and (iv), but the EAT said that 'it will be as well to bear all four of them in mind. Tribunals may find it helpful to address each of the questions but at the same time beware of the risk that desegregation should not take one's eye off the whole picture'.

The EAT's comments in *Goodwin* are useful, but inevitably not comprehensive. There is no substitute for a thorough assessment of all relevant aspects of the definition of 'disability'. For ease of reference, in this *Handbook*, the three main components of the definition are each considered in distinct sections, but their inter-relationship must always be kept in mind. The three components are:

- What is a *Physical or Mental Impairment*?
- What is meant by a person's ability to carry out *Normal Day-to-Day Activities*?
- In what circumstances does an impairment have a *Substantial and Long-Term Adverse Effect* upon the ability to carry out normal day-to-day activities?

81 Discriminatory Motive

The definition of *Direct Discrimination* requires the consideration of two questions:

(*a*) Has a person been treated less favourably than another person has or would have been treated?

(*b*) If so, was this treatment for the reason specified in the legislation, e.g. on racial grounds or because she was a woman?

In some of the early authorities, this second question was sometimes expressed in terms of a discriminatory motive. Was there such a motive for the treatment complained of?

The expression 'discriminatory motive' should, however, no longer be used. A line of House of Lords authorities, ending with the case of *Nagarajan v London Regional Transport* [*1999*] *IRLR 572*, has clearly established that there can be direct discrimination or victimisation without a discriminatory motive or desire to victimise the complainant. The focus must be on the reason or reasons for the treatment complained of and not on any motive underlying those reasons. Proof of a discriminatory motive is not necessary, although it may be helpful in terms of indicating the probable reason for the treatment complained of.

82 Discriminatory Practice

Under *section 37* of the *SDA 1975* and *section 28* of the *RRA 1976*, it is unlawful for an employer (or any other person) to operate a discriminatory practice.

A discriminatory practice is the application of a requirement or condition which either:

(*a*) does result in an act of direct sex, marriage or racial discrimination; or

(*b*) would be likely to result in such an act if the persons to whom the requirement or condition is applied had not been all of one sex or (as the case may be) had included persons of a particular racial group.

An example of a discriminatory practice under the *RRA 1976* would be recruiting only relatives of existing employees, or by recommendations from existing employees, where all those existing employees are white. An example under the *SDA 1975* would be to operate a practice of refusing automatically all requests to transfer to part-time working.

It is only the relevant commission (the EOC or CRE as the case may be) which can take enforcement action in respect of a discriminatory practice. That enforcement action can take the form of:

(*a*) the service of a *Non-Discrimination Notice* as the result of a *Formal Investigation*;

(*b*) followed by an application to a county court (or sheriff court in Scotland) for an *Injunction* (or *Interdict* in Scotland), such application to be made within five years after the non-discrimination notice became final.

83 Dismissal

83.1 THE STATUTORY PROVISIONS

The *SDA 1975*, the *RRA 1976* and the *DDA 1995* all make it unlawful to discriminate against an employee by dismissing that employee. The reference to discrimination in the *SDA 1975* and the *RRA 1976* includes both direct and indirect discrimination; the definition in all three Acts includes victimisation.

83.2 EXAMPLES OF DISCRIMINATORY DISMISSALS

At first sight it may seem unlikely that discriminatory dismissals would often occur. An employer who is minded to discriminate against, say, black workers, by dismissing them, is unlikely to employ them in the first place.

A business can change hands and there can also be a change of management, but that is only a small part of the answer. The most common examples of discriminatory dismissals are:

(*a*) pregnancy-related dismissals;

(*b*) dismissals of disabled employees for poor attendance;

(*c*) selection for redundancy;

(*d*) inconsistency in conduct/capability dismissals;

(*e*) victimisation;

(*f*) constructive dismissals.

83.3 PREGNANCY RELATED DISMISSALS

It is a sad fact of life that all too many employers, when told that an employee is expecting a baby, congratulate her and then quickly find a pretext for dismissing her. The employer believes that she will disrupt the business by the amount of time which she has off during her pregnancy; or the employer does not wish to keep her job open during an extended maternity leave period which could last as long as 40 weeks. In one case, the owner of a high-class hairdressing salon felt that the presence of a heavily pregnant stylist would lower the tone of the establishment.

The law has been clear since the decision of the House of Lords in *Webb v EMO Air Cargo (UK) Limited (No 2)* [*1995*] *IRLR 645*. Pregnancy is a gender-based criterion and accordingly dismissing a woman because she is pregnant is direct sex discrimination. Furthermore, where a woman has been engaged for an indefinite period, she cannot lawfully be dismissed if her pregnancy makes her unavailable at the time when her services are particularly required.

It is also direct discrimination to dismiss a woman because of her long absence from work or poor attendance record, in a case where the absence from work during pregnancy has been caused by a pregnancy-related illness. This principle was established by the ECJ in *Brown v Rentokil Limited* [*1998*] *IRLR 445*.

There is no defence of justification in these cases. Justification is not available as a defence to direct discrimination.

83.4 DISABILITY

The dismissal of an employee for absences which are wholly or partly caused by a disability could lead to a complaint of disability discrimination. The employer must consider the following questions before dismissing or even giving a warning:

(*a*) Is this a case where the employee has or could have a disability?

(*b*) If the position is unclear, has it been thoroughly investigated by my medical adviser?

(*c*) Is it possible that at least part of the absence or absence record which I am reviewing is caused by the disability?

(*d*) If so, are there steps which I reasonably could and should have taken, under *section 6* of the *DDA 1995*, to enable the employee to improve his or her attendance?

(*e*) If not, can I justify a dismissal (or a warning if that is what I propose), for example by showing that the absence of the postholder is hitting profits or adversely affecting customer service?

It is particularly important that the issue of reasonable adjustments is fully explored before any decision to dismiss or give a warning is taken.

83.5 SELECTION FOR REDUNDANCY

If attendance is one of the selection criteria, no absence caused by pregnancy or a pregnancy-related illness must be taken into account. Otherwise the employee concerned will have a claim of direct sex discrimination.

There are several selection criteria, including timekeeping and job performance as well as attendance, under which an employee's score could be adversely affected by a disability. In such cases, the employer must ask the following questions:

(*a*) Could this employee's attendance, timekeeping or job performance have been improved if I had made a reasonable adjustment at the time?

(*b*) If so, what adjustments would it now be reasonable for me to make to the employee's scores under each of the criteria?

(*c*) Could I justify, within the meaning of the *DDA 1995*, relying on the adjusted scores to select the employee for redundancy?

One aspect of selection for alternative employment is considered under *Mobility*. There are also the following considerations:

(*a*) there is an express statutory obligation, under the *Employment Rights Act 1996*, to give priority to a woman returning from maternity leave;

(*b*) subject thereto, *section 6* of the *DDA 1995* may require that priority should be given to any disabled employee whose job is at risk;

(*c*) this duty to give priority to a disabled employee may arise where he or she is facing redundancy;

(*d*) it may also arise where there is a need for redeployment because a disability prevents the employee from continuing in his or her existing post.

This issue of redeployment for disabled employees is considered in the case of *Kent County Council v Mingo* [*2000*] *IRLR 90* (please see *Disciplining and Dismissing Disabled Employees*).

Employers must also, of course, apply redundancy selection criteria fairly and consistently in order to have a defence to complaints of direct discrimination under the *RRA 1976* and the *SDA 1975*. The days are, one hopes, long gone when employers could believe that it is legitimate to select women rather than men for redundancy because in most households the man is the main breadwinner.

Employers must also avoid selecting part-time workers for redundancy in priority to full-time workers, or using selection criteria which are loaded against part-time workers, unless the case is an exceptional one where this approach could be objectively justified. Otherwise, the employer could face complaints of:

(*a*) breach of the *Part-Time Workers (Prevention of Less Favourable Treatment) Regulations 2000 (SI 2000 No 1551)*;

(*b*) indirect sex discrimination;

(*c*) indirect marriage discrimination;

(*d*) unfair dismissal.

The issue of indirect discrimination was considered in the case of *Clarke v Eley (IMI) Kynoch Limited [1982] IRLR 482*. A complaint of indirect discrimination under the *SDA 1975* succeeded in the following circumstances:

(*a*) part-timers were selected for redundancy in priority to full-timers;

(*b*) a high proportion of the female employees and a very low proportion of the male employees worked part-time;

(*c*) there was no objective justification.

83.6 CONDUCT/CAPABILITY DISMISSALS

Some employers have a cavalier attitude towards dismissals for misconduct or poor attendance or performance, where the employee has not served the unfair dismissal qualifying period of one year. This is particularly so where employees are expressly excluded from the usual disciplinary procedures during that year.

Whatever the length of service, however, employers must act consistently. Otherwise they will be vulnerable to complaints of discrimination. Furthermore, no disabled employee must be dismissed until the employer has fully complied with the *section 6* duty to make reasonable adjustments.

The need to act consistently towards employees of different racial groups does not, however, mean that employers should ignore the context in which an offence takes place. An employer who has a rigid policy of treating all similar offences alike, disregarding racial provocation or any other mitigating circumstances, is likely to lose unfair dismissal cases.

This was one of the issues in the case of *Sidhu v Aerospace Composite Technology Limited [1999] IRLR 683*. The employers had organised a family day out, during which Mr Sidhu and his wife were subjected to violence and racial insults by another employee, who was white. Mr Sidhu received a cut head and broken glasses. During the incident, he picked up a plastic chair, which some witnesses said he had wielded in an aggressive manner, but he did not make contact with anyone. Both Mr Sidhu and the white employee were dismissed for gross misconduct, consisting of violent behaviour towards a fellow-employee (wielding the chair in Mr Sidhu's case) and using abusive language. The employer's disciplinary and appeal committees took a deliberate decision to exclude from the decision making process the fact that the assault on Mr Sidhu was a 'racial assault'.

83.7 Dismissal

The employment tribunal found that Mr Sidhu's dismissal was unfair, but not racially discriminatory. The EAT allowed an appeal and substituted a finding of racial discrimination, on the ground that the decision to disregard the racial provocation was a 'race-specific' decision. The Court of Appeal, *[2000] IRLR 602*, reversed this decision and restored the decision of the employment tribunal. Treating racial provocation like any other provocation was not race-specific and was not an act of racial discrimination. It should be noted, however, that the employment tribunal's finding of unfair dismissal was not challenged. It would be difficult to convince any employment tribunal that an employer had acted reasonably if, when considering whether to dismiss an employee for violence and abusive language, he deliberately disregards the fact that this conduct was provoked by serious acts of racial harassment.

83.7 VICTIMISATION

The definitions of discrimination, in the *SDA 1975*, the *RRA 1976* and the *DDA 1995*, include discrimination by way of *Victimisation*. The definition in the *SDA 1975* covers protected acts under the *Equal Pay Act 1970* as well as the *SDA 1975* itself.

The dismissal of an employee for having made allegations of discrimination, or done some other protected act, is generally unlawful under the relevant statutes. It will also generally be an unfair dismissal.

It is immaterial if the protected act is a discrimination or equal pay claim which has failed, so long as the claim was made in good faith. It would, for example, be unlawful for an employer to dismiss a female employee for having made an equal pay claim in the genuine but misplaced belief that a named male comparator was paid more than the complainant.

There is no victimisation, within the terms of the relevant legislation, if an employee is dismissed for having made a false allegation, if that allegation was not made in good faith. Where, for example, an employee has falsely accused a colleague of sexual harassment, it may be open to the employer to dismiss the complainant, after a thorough investigation and a fair disciplinary hearing, for gross misconduct. To have a good defence to a victimisation complaint, however, the employer would need to be able to show that the dismissed employee acted in bad faith in making a false and malicious allegation.

83.8 CONSTRUCTIVE DISMISSAL

The fact that an employee has been subjected to unlawful discrimination does not necessarily entitle the employee to resign and treat himself or herself as constructively dismissed. This principle is illustrated by the case of *Driskel v Peninsular Business Services Limited & Others* [2000] *IRLR 151*. In that case, Mrs Driskel complained of a number of remarks made to her by the head of her department. The final remark, the day before he was to interview her for promotion, was his suggestion that she should attend the interview in a short skirt and see-through blouse, showing plenty of cleavage. Mrs Driskel made a formal complaint of sexual harassment, which was rejected after a thorough and genuine internal investigation. She was dismissed after refusing to return to her job unless the manager against whom she had complained was moved elsewhere.

The employment tribunal dismissed Mrs Driskel's complaint of sexual harassment and also her complaint that her dismissal was both unfair and an act of victimisation. Mrs Driskel appealed successfully against the dismissal of her complaint of sexual harassment. The EAT rejected, however, the appeal against the dismissal of the unfair dismissal and victimisation claims. The employers had taken seriously her complaint of sexual harassment and had carried out a genuine investigation. She had not been dismissed for making that complaint. The employers had genuinely tried to accommodate her with acceptable employment, but she placed them in the position of having to dismiss the complainant or the manager about whom she had complained. There would have been no justification for the latter step, on the basis of the investigation which had been carried out.

There could well, however, be findings of constructive and discriminatory dismissal if an employee resigns in the following cases:

(*a*) the employer personally, or probably a senior fellow employee, such as the managing director, has subjected the employee to racial or sexual harassment;

(*b*) the management are aware that the employee is being bullied by her fellow employees for having made a complaint of racial discrimination, but they do nothing about this victimisation;

(*c*) an employee submits a grievance, complaining of discrimination, but the matter is not taken seriously.

In all these cases, it would be open to a tribunal to find that the employers are seriously in breach of their contractual obligations, that the employee's position has effectively been made untenable and that the employee is accordingly justified in treating himself or herself as constructively dismissed.

The case of *Reed and Bull Information Systems Limited v Stedman* [*1999*] *IRLR 299* is one in which there was a finding of a constructive and discriminatory dismissal. The employment tribunal found that Ms Stedman had been subjected to sexual harassment by her manager. The tribunal also found that, although she had made no formal complaint, the personnel department were aware of her deteriorating health and that she had made complaints to other members of staff. By failing to investigate the matter, the employer had failed to deal with the issue of sexual harassment adequately and was in breach of the duty of trust and confidence. Ms Stedman, who had resigned, was entitled to treat herself as constructively dismissed. That dismissal was an act of discrimination, contrary to *section 6(2)* of the *SDA 1975*.

83.9 DISCRIMINATORY DISMISSALS AND UNFAIR DISMISSALS

The above-mentioned case of *Sidhu* is an example of a case with a racial background where a dismissal was unfair but not discriminatory. Conversely, a discriminatory dismissal is not automatically unfair – *HJ Heinz Co Limited v Kenrick* [*2000*] *IRLR 144*. Discriminatory dismissals will, however, commonly also be unfair dismissals and both complaints should be pleaded.

A complaint of dismissal under the discrimination legislation has the following advantages from the complainant's point of view:

(*a*) there is no qualifying period (it was because the then qualifying period had not been completed that there was no unfair dismissal complaint in the above-mentioned case of *Reed and Bull Information Systems Limited v Stedman*);

(*b*) complaints can be presented by an employee who is above normal retiring age;

(*c*) the definition of 'employment' in each of the discrimination laws is broader than that contained in the *Employment Rights Act 1996* for unfair dismissal purposes;

(*d*) there is no limit on the amount of compensation;

(*e*) compensation for injury to feelings can be claimed.

83.9 Dismissal

The advantages of complaining of unfair dismissal as well as discriminatory dismissal are:

(*a*) the former may succeed while the latter fails, as in *Sidhu*;

(*b*) the compensation for unfair dismissal will include the basic award.

84 Disparate Impact

The expression 'disparate impact' is not used in the *SDA 1975* or the *RRA 1976*, but the concept is fundamental to *Indirect Discrimination*. It is not sufficient for a complainant to show that he or she cannot comply with an inflexible requirement or condition (or rule or policy). It is necessary also to show that the proportion of the members of a relevant group (such as women) who can comply is considerably smaller than the proportion of non-members of the group (such as men) who can comply. If this disparate impact can be proved, a complaint of indirect discrimination will succeed unless the employer (or other respondent) can show the requirement or condition to be justifiable irrespective of (if the complaint is one of indirect sex discrimination) the sex of the person to whom it is applied.

85 Diversity

A statement that diversity is valued is now included in many well developed equal opportunity policies in both the public and private sectors. The recent equal opportunities agreement in the *National Health Service* is a good example.

An effective equal opportunity policy will normally lead to a workforce which is diverse in a number of different ways, with:

(*a*) employees throughout the organisation from a variety of racial, cultural and religious backgrounds;

(*b*) men and women well represented at all levels;

(*c*) career opportunities for young and old;

(*d*) encouragement and practical support to enable employees to make an important contribution notwithstanding a wide range of disabilities;

(*e*) a culture in which a worker's sexual orientation is irrelevant to his or her career development.

The importance of making a policy statement that diversity is valued is that successful policies are more likely to result from a positive commitment of this kind than from a bland acceptance of the need to comply with the law.

Making senior management feel good about the policy is not (or should not) be the main benefit of valuing diversity. There can also be real commercial advantages. If managers and other employees come from the whole spectrum of personal, domestic, cultural and career backgrounds:

(*a*) the quality of decision making should be improved;

(*b*) new ideas and new and improved ways of working are more likely to be suggested;

(*c*) morale will be enhanced if all employees know that both they and their colleagues have been appointed or promoted on merit;

(*d*) the banishment of irrelevant factors such as race and sex encourages employees to focus on the needs of the team or organisation to which they belong.

Diversity comes at a price. Organisations need to:

(*a*) become adaptable in accepting the need for *Flexible Working*;

(*b*) accept the need for change and the management of change;

(*c*) invest substantially in *Training* and in the development of *Equal Opportunity Policies* and related practices and procedures.

86 Documents, disclosure of

When preparing for an employment tribunal hearing, the parties should each disclose to the other any documents on which they wish to rely and any other documents which are relevant to the proceedings. It is good practice (and it is sometimes expressly ordered by tribunals) for the parties to prepare a single bundle of documents (or, in Scotland, inventory of productions) for use at the hearing.

If one party (usually the complainant) asks for disclosure, or discovery, of documents which the other party (usually the respondent) is unwilling to give, then application can be made to the tribunal for an order. Sometimes disclosure is resisted on the ground of confidentiality. For example, in a complaint about discrimination in access to promotion, the complainant may ask for appraisals and other documents in relation to colleagues who have been promoted. The principles to be applied in such cases were established by the House of Lords in the case of *Science Research Council v Nassé [1979] IRLR 465*, as follows:

(*a*) An order should not be made automatically for the disclosure of a confidential document, simply because it is or could be relevant to the case.

(*b*) Disclosure should be ordered if it is necessary to dispose fairly of the proceedings or to save costs – these considerations override any confidentiality.

(*c*) The tribunal chairman should read the relevant documents in order to decide whether disclosure is necessary.

Disclosure is particularly important in recruitment cases, where the complainant has no information about other candidates for the post and comparisons can be made only if documents relating to successful or shortlisted candidates are produced.

Even if there is no issue of confidentiality, a request for disclosure of documents can be resisted on the ground that the request is oppressive because of the large number of documents involved. In *British Railways Board v Natarajan [1979] IRLR 45,* an employee complained of racial discrimination in an assessment of his performance and potential. He requested disclosure of the weekly work diaries and progress report sheets of himself and six colleagues for the whole of the year to which the complaint related. He also requested disclosure of the annual appraisals and assessment sheets relating to himself and these six colleagues for the whole of that year and for the three previous years. The EAT held that the documents were of doubtful relevance. Disclosure was ordered only of:

(*a*) the work diaries and progress report sheets for the four weeks prior to the date of the assessment complained of;

(*b*) the annual appraisals and assessments only for that year – not the previous three years.

It is good practice for a request for disclosure of documents to be made well in advance of the hearing, so that there is time to apply for an order if the request is refused.

87 Domestic employment

Under the *RRA 1976*, there is an exception for employment for the purposes of a *Private Household*, unless the complaint is one of *Victimisation*.

There was formerly a similar exception in the *SDA 1975*, but that general exception was removed by the *Sex Discrimination Act 1986*. The position now is that being a man (or being a woman) can be a *Genuine Occupational Qualification* in certain circumstances if the job is likely to involve the jobholder doing his work or living in a private home. Even where this GOQ exception applies in relation to recruitment and selection for the post, the *SDA 1975* applies once an appointment has been made. A domestic servant can complain of, for example, sexual harassment or sex discrimination in dismissing him or her.

There is no specific provision in the *DDA 1995* for jobs in private households, but most jobs in domestic employment would be covered by the exception for employers who have fewer than 15 employees. Domestic employment would be covered by the *DDA 1995* only if:

(*a*) the establishment is a particularly grand one, with 15 or more employees; or

(*b*) the employer also has a business in which he or she employs staff personally (and not through a company) so that the total number of household and business employees is 15 or more.

88 Dress and Appearance

Rules or instructions relating to dress and appearance could give rise to complaints of:

(*a*) direct sex discrimination, if there is one standard for employees of one sex and the employer has a lower standard, or no rules at all, for employees of the other sex;

(*b*) indirect racial discrimination, if there are inflexible rules relating to items such as trousers and *Turbans*;

(*c*) disability discrimination, if the employer refuses to make *Reasonable Adjustments* for disabled employees.

These issues are considered in more detail under *Physical Appearance*.

89 Employees – liability for

89.1 GENERAL PRINCIPLES

In most large organisations (and many medium sized and small organisations) whether in the public sector or the private sector, day to day decisions affecting employees are made by managers and other fellow employees. It also tends to be managers, interviewers and other employees who make decisions affecting job applicants. A key issue, therefore, is whether employers can be held accountable for acts of discrimination by their employees and, if so, in what circumstances.

The general principle, under the *SDA 1975* (*section 41*), the *RRA 1976* (*section 32*) and the *DDA 1995 (section 58)* is that anything done by a person in the course of that person's employment shall be treated for the purposes of the relevant Act as also done by that person's employer.

There is an exception for offences. An employer can be liable for any act of discrimination (including victimisation) done by an employee, but criminal liability for the handful of offences created by each Act rests with the person directly responsible for the offence, whether that person is an employer or an employee.

These provisions which make employers responsible for acts of discrimination by their employees are fundamental to the effective operation of the discrimination laws. The main employment provisions of the three Acts (such as *section 6* of the *SDA 1975*) make it unlawful for employers to discriminate in relation to offers of employment at any establishment in Great Britain or against existing employees at any such establishment. It is only employers, not their managers or other employees, who have this primary liability. If matters were left there, the discrimination laws would be of little effect. This consequence is avoided by treating the act of the manager or other employee as being also the act of the employer.

An employer cannot escape liability by showing that he did not and would not have authorised the act of discrimination complained of or even that the act was done without his knowledge. It is expressly provided in *section 41* of the *SDA 1975*, *section 32* of the *RRA 1976* and *section 58* of the *DDA 1995* that the act of the employee is treated as the act of the employer whether or not it was done with the employer's knowledge or approval. The employer does, however, have a defence if it can be shown that the employer took such steps as were reasonably practicable to prevent the employee from doing the particular act or doing acts of that description in the course of his employment.

There are three questions to be considered in any particular case:

(*a*) Was the act complained of done by a person in the course of his employment?

(*b*) Can the employer show that all *Reasonably Practicable Steps* were taken so as to establish the above-mentioned defence?

(*c*) Does any liability attach to the individual employee who did the act complained of?

89.2 COURSE OF EMPLOYMENT

There are two questions to be considered. The first is whether there is an employment relationship, within the meaning of the relevant Act, between the person who has done the act of discrimination complained of and the respondent who has been named by the complainant.

The *SDA 1975*, the *RRA 1976* and the *DDA 1995* each has an interpretation clause which contains a wide definition of *Employment*. That definition includes not only conventional employment contracts and apprenticeships but also employment under any other contract to do any work personally. This definition is relevant for the purpose of defining the employees who have rights under each of the three Acts (and the *EPA 1970*); it is also relevant for the purpose of defining the 'employees' for whose acts of discrimination the employer can be held liable.

Suppose, for example, that an employee is subjected to racial or sexual harassment by a person who is supervising his or her work but who is not employed in the ordinary sense by the complainant's employer. One possibility is that the supervisor will be an employee for the purposes of the *SDA 1975* or the *RRA 1976*, because of the extended definition of employment in those Acts. Another possibility is that the supervisor will not be an employee even in that sense, but will be acting as an *Agent* of the complainant's employer when supervising the work. It is important to establish the category into which the supervisor falls. If the supervisor is only an agent, the complainant's employer will be liable for the act complained of if the employer has authorised that act (whether expressly or by implication and whether before or after the event). If on the other hand the supervisor is deemed to be an employee of the complainant's employer, then no authority need be proved; it is instead up to the employer to make out if he can show the defence that all reasonably practicable steps have been taken.

The second key step, once the employment relationship has been established, is to show whether the act complained of was done in the course of that employment. The case law on *Course of Employment*, which is considered under *Harassment*, has established that the expression is a very broad one. The case law on employers' vicarious liability at common law for torts committed by their employees cannot be relied on.

89.3 REASONABLY PRACTICABLE STEPS

The question whether reasonably practicable steps have been taken to prevent the particular act of discrimination, or acts of that description, is one of fact in each case. It can be confidently stated, however, as a general principle, that no employer can expect to make out the defence if the only step taken has been the adoption of an equal opportunity policy, without effective measures to implement the policy. *Training* for managers, supervisors and interviewers is particularly important. For general guidance, see *Equal Opportunity Policies* and *Reasonably Practicable Steps*. For guidance on specific subjects see *Recruitment, Selection* and *Harassment*.

The acts by an employee which can also be treated as the acts of the employer are not limited to acts of unlawful discrimination. For example, when considering whether an employer has established the defence of having taken all reasonably practicable steps to prevent an act of discrimination, an employment tribunal can take into account, and impute to the employer, the failure of an employee to take appropriate action to prevent discrimination of which he has become aware. In particular, if a manager is aware that a fellow employee is being subjected to sexual and racial harassment, and does nothing about it, that omission is treated as an omission by the employer, and is likely to defeat any attempt to raise the statutory defence. This principle was referred to by the EAT in the case of *Canniffe v East Riding of Yorkshire Council* [*2000*] *IRLR 555*. The only way in which the employer could avoid being held responsible for the manager's omissions would be if the employer had taken all reasonably practicable steps to prevent such omissions. Accordingly, if, for example, there are three fellow employees, X, Y and Z, of whom X has sexually harassed Y to the knowledge of Z, who stood by and did nothing, the tribunal could be required to answer the following, somewhat complicated series of questions:

(*a*) Has X, in the course of his employment, subjected Y to a detriment?

(*b*) Has the employer, however, taken such steps as were reasonably practicable to prevent X from doing acts of that description?

(*c*) Have, however, the positive steps taken by the employer been undone by Z's omission, which is also treated as being the omission of the employer, to take appropriate action to prevent harassment of which he had become aware?

(*d*) Alternatively, is Z's omission not the omission of the employer, because the employer had taken such steps as were reasonably practicable (in particular by giving appropriate guidance and training) to inform him of and encourage him to perform his managerial duty to prevent sexual harassment?

89.4 THE EMPLOYEE'S LIABILITY

If an employee commits an act of discrimination outside the course of his employment, then both employer and employee escape liability for that act.

Where the act of discrimination is in the course of his employment, then the *SDA 1975*, the *RRA 1976* and the *DDA 1995* each adopt a circuitous route to make the employee liable as well as the employer. The employee is deemed to have 'aided' the employer to do the relevant act. Accordingly the law attaches liability to the employer by treating the employee's act as also the act of the employer; although liability then also falls on the employee himself because of what he has done, the law achieves this result by treating the employee as having aided the deemed act of discrimination by the employer.

The principle that an employee can be made liable for an unlawful act of discrimination against a fellow employee (or job applicant) is an elementary one, but it was affirmed in the case of *AM v WC and SPV* [*1999*] *IRLR 410*, a case under the *SDA 1975*.

Where the employer makes out the defence that all reasonably practicable steps were taken, that defence does not assist the individual employee who did the act complained of. It is expressly provided in each of the three Acts that the employee is treated as having knowingly aided the employer to do an unlawful act, even though the employer himself is regarded as not having acted unlawfully because the reasonably practicable steps defence has been established.

It is also possible for the employer to be liable for an unlawful act and for the employee who did the act not to be so liable. The employee has a defence if:

(*a*) he has acted in reliance on a statement by the employer that he would not be acting unlawfully because of some provision in the relevant Act; and

(*b*) it was reasonable for him to rely on the statement.

For example, this defence could be available to an employee involved in recruiting staff if his employer gives him false information which suggests that being a man is a *Genuine Occupational Qualification* for a particular job. If the employee, reasonably believing that information, discriminates against a female candidate for the post, then the employer but not the employee would be liable for that act of discrimination.

The employer who knowingly or recklessly makes a statement which is false or misleading in a material respect is guilty of an offence.

90 Employees Who Become Disabled

90.1 DOES THE EMPLOYER NEED TO KNOW?

The *Health and Safety at Work etc Act 1974* requires employees to take reasonable care for their health and safety and that of others who may be affected by their acts or omissions at work. If an employee's failure to disclose a disability jeopardises *Health and Safety*, the employee may be in breach of his or her statutory obligation.

There is, however, no general obligation to disclose a disability to an employer or a prospective employer and the *DDA 1995* is silent on the point. Views differ among disabled people as to whether disclosure is generally desirable. There is sometimes an understandable apprehension, perhaps based on past experience, that disclosure will lead to discrimination and that it is better to say nothing. The temptation to keep quiet may be stronger in cases where the disability is not readily apparent. The counter-argument is that employers need to have *Knowledge of Disability* in order to be able to comply with their legal obligations in respect of health and safety and the *DDA 1995*. However, it seems clear that the test of knowledge is objective, and not subjective (as originally suggested by the EAT in an early case which was subsequently disapproved by a different division of the EAT).

90.2 THE EMPLOYER'S RESPONSE

Often, the employer will be well aware of the disability. It may have arisen, for example, from an accident. Typically, it will be appropriate to allow the employee a reasonable period of time for treatment and rehabilitation. The disabled person may need specific training, e.g. in the use of appropriate technology.

The employer will also need to comply with the obligations concerning *Reasonable Adjustments*. Making required adjustments is not in itself necessarily enough. The disabled employee will often need time to adapt to new circumstances.

90.3 ADJUSTMENTS IN PRACTICE

The *DDA 1995* provides examples of types of adjustments which may be appropriate:

(*a*) making adjustments to the premises;

(*b*) allocating some of the disabled employee's tasks elsewhere;

(*c*) transferring the disabled employee to another job;

(*d*) agreeing a change to the disabled employee's hours of work;

(*e*) agreeing that the disabled employee can work at a different location;

(*f*) allowing the disabled employee time off for treatment and rehabilitation;

(*g*) acquiring or modifying equipment such as a Braille keyboard or a hearing loop;

(*h*) modifying instructions or reference manuals;

(*i*) providing a reader or interpreter;

(*j*) providing extra supervision.

But these are only illustrations of some possibilities and are not in any way exhaustive. That said, the employer is only required to do what is reasonable. Deciding what is and what is not reasonable is a matter for judgement, taking into account the *DDA 1995* and the *Code of Practice*.

In addition to discussing the position with the disabled employee, the employer may need to seek advice from outside. Disability Employment Advisers and Disability Service Teams run by the Employment Service are contactable via job centres. The guidance they may offer covers such matters as:

(*a*) assessment of suitability of work stations for disabled employees and recommendations as to how to make necessary improvements;

(*b*) guidance on the availability, cost and value of special equipment;

(*c*) assistance with funding;

(*d*) sources of further advice.

90.4 **MEDICAL EXAMINATIONS**

Medical advice is often essential. The more expert that advice is, the better. In some cases, typically including, but by no means limited to, cases of relatively uncommon disabilities, it will not be enough merely to consult a GP. The views of an occupational health doctor may be of considerable benefit. Usually, the employee will co-operate with a reasonable request to undergo a medical examination. In exceptional cases where the employee refuses to agree to be medically examined, he or she may be liable to disciplinary action, e.g. if the contract of employment records an employee's agreement to undergo such an examination and the request that it take place is legitimate and reasonable in the circumstances. Even where there is no contractual provision with regard to undergoing medical examinations, an employee who refuses to co-operate for no good reason runs the risk that the employer will take decisions based on inadequate and perhaps incorrect information.

In order to be able to provide a valuable opinion, the medical adviser should be given all relevant information including:

(*a*) a clear and accurate explanation of the employee's duties;

(*b*) an explanation of the reason why the report is required;

(*c*) a request for advice as to any difficulties that the employee will have in carrying out his or her job duties, together with a request for a prognosis concerning prospects for improvement and any further investigations that should be undertaken.

The employee's signed consent to the examination should be provided to the adviser. Where the medical adviser has been involved in the clinical care of the employee, then it will be necessary to comply with the *Access to Medical Reports Act 1988*, which provides amongst other matters that the employer must inform the employee that he or she has:

(*a*) the right to withhold consent to the employer seeking the report from the medical adviser;

(*b*) the right to state that he or she wishes to have access to the report;

(*c*) rights concerning access to the report before or after it is supplied;

(*d*) the right to withhold consent to the report being supplied to the employer;

(*e*) the right to request amendments to the report.

Where an employee expresses a wish to see the report, the employer must let the medical adviser know this when applying for the report and at the same time let the employee know that the report has been requested.

91 Employers

In most discrimination cases (and all equal pay cases), the respondent is an employer. Complaints of discrimination are brought against employers by employees, job applicants and contract workers. The extended definition of *Employment* (and all related terms, such as employer and employee) should be noted.

Complaints can also be brought by persons who are themselves employers, against *Qualifying Bodies* or *Employers' Associations*.

92 Employers' Associations

Section 12 of the *SDA 1975* and *section 11* of the *RRA 1976* impose obligations not only on trade unions, but also on any organisation of employers and also professional and trade organisations.

It is unlawful for any such organisation to discriminate against a non-member:

(*a*) in the terms on which it is prepared to admit him to membership; or

(*b*) by refusing, or deliberately omitting to accept, his application for membership.

It is also unlawful for any such organisation to discriminate against a member:

(*a*) in the way it affords him access to any benefits, facilities or services, or refusing or deliberately omitting to afford him access to them;

(*b*) by depriving him of membership, or varying the terms on which he is a member; or

(*c*) by subjecting him to any other detriment.

There are similar provisions in *section 15* of the *DDA 1995* in relation to any 'trade organisation'. The definition in *section 15* includes employers' associations and trade and professional associations as well as trade unions.

Section 15 of the *DDA 1995* also imposes on trade organisations the duty to make reasonable adjustments, corresponding to the *section 6* duty placed on employees. There is also under the *DDA 1995* a specific Code of Practice on the duties of trade organisations to their disabled members and their applicants.

93 Employment

The *EPA 1970*, *SDA 1975*, *RRA 1976* and *DDA 1995* each contains an extended definition of employment (and of related expressions such as employer and employee) to cover not only employment under a contract of service or apprenticeship, but also employment under a contract personally to execute any work or labour. This extended definition is relevant not only to the rights given to employees but also to the liability of employers for acts done by employees in the course of their employment (see *Employees – Liability for*).

In *Quinnen v Hovells* [*1984*] *IRLR 227*, it was held that a self-employed assistant taken on to sell fancy goods on commission over the Christmas season was covered by the extended definition. On the other hand, in *Mirror Group Newspapers Limited v Gunning* [*1986*] *IRLR 27*, a contract for the distribution of newspapers, employing staff for the purpose, was not covered. It was said that the extended definition contemplates 'a contract the dominant purpose of which is the execution of personal work or labour'. In *Sheehan v Post Office Counters Limited* [*1999*] *ICR 734*, it was said to be 'a rather brave argument' that what mattered was whether the work was in fact done personally rather than whether there was a contractual obligation to do it personally.

94 Employment Agencies

Both the *SDA 1975* and the *RRA 1976* contain specific provisions relating to employment agencies. Under *section 15* of the *SDA 1975* and *section 14* of the *RRA 1976*, it is unlawful for an employment agency to discriminate:

(*a*) in the terms on which it offers to provide any of its services;

(*b*) by refusing or deliberately omitting to provide any of its services; or

(*c*) in the way it provides any of its services.

Under the interpretation provisions in each Act, an employment agency is defined as a person who, for profit or not, provides services for the purpose of finding employment for workers or supplying employers with workers. Furthermore, the services in respect of which an employment agency must not discriminate include guidance on careers and any other services related to employment (no doubt including such matters as *Psychometric Testing*).

It is not unlawful for an employment agency to discriminate against a person by refusing or deliberately omitting to offer employment which the employer could lawfully refuse to offer the person in question. An obvious example is where the employment is covered by a *Genuine Occupational Qualification* exception.

The *DDA 1995* does not contain any provisions corresponding to *section 15* of the *SDA 1975* and *section 14* of the *RRA 1976* but an employment agency can be a provider of services for the purposes of *section 19*. This section is not in Part II of the Act and any complaint goes to a county court (or sheriff court in Scoland). Under all three Acts an employment agency can be liable jointly with an employer for discrimination when acting as an *Agent* with the express or implied authority of the employer.

95 English, as racial group

The *RRA 1976* almost certainly covers direct discrimination against a job applicant or employee because he or she is English and also indirect discrimination against English workers – see *Racial Grounds* and *Racial Group*.

Racial discrimination against English workers is no doubt most likely to occur (if at all) in those parts of Great Britain where the English are in the minority, Scotland and Wales. Direct discrimination could occur if a public or private sector employer discriminates in favour of a Scots or Welsh born candidate for a particular post; a Welsh language requirement could give rise to a complaint of indirect discrimination.

Language requirements are probably more likely to give rise to complaints of discrimination where it is English which is the required language. A job applicant for whom English is not his first language (for example a candidate from another European Union country or from Eastern Europe) could have a complaint of indirect racial discrimination if he is unable:

(*a*) to demonstrate a required command of the English language;

(*b*) to complete a written application form.

The employer may in either case may be unable to justify the requirement if it is unnecessary or excessive in relation to the work to be done.

96 Equal Opportunities Commission

The Equal Opportunities Commission (the EOC) is the statutory body which has been set up under the *SDA 1975*. It has powers and responsibilities in relation to both the *EPA 1970* and the *SDA 1975*.

Those powers and responsibilities are virtually identical to those given by the *RRA 1976* to the *Commission for Racial Equality*. They include the power to give *Assistance* to complainants and prospective complainants, whether under the *SDA 1975* or the *EPA 1970*.

The EOC has two additional functions which do not correspond to any of the CRE's functions:

(*a*) The EOC is required, in consultation with the Health and Safety Commission, to keep under review the provisions in health and safety legislation which require men and women to be treated differently. When necessary they must submit proposals for amendment to the Secretary of State.

(*b*) Since 1 May 1999, the EOC has also been required to promote equality of opportunity, in the field of employment and of vocational training, for persons who intend to undergo, are undergoing or have undergone *Gender Reassignment*.

There is one further obvious difference between the duties of the EOC and those of the CRE. Both Commissions are required to promote equality of opportunity, but the EOC does not have a duty corresponding to the CRE's more general duty to promote good race relations.

97 Equal Opportunity Policies

97.1 GENERAL PRINCIPLES

Employers are under no legal obligation to adopt equal opportunity policies, but organisations are unlikely to meet the standard which the law requires unless they have adopted suitable policies and carried out those policies successfully.

A clear policy statement is only a first step. A policy which is adopted and then left to gather dust is simply a monument to failure.

A well thought out and effectively implemented policy is an essential defensive mechanism. Many acts of discrimination, particularly *Harassment*, are committed without the knowledge of employers and senior management who would not have authorised those acts if they had known about them. Nevertheless, an employer cannot avoid legal liability for such acts unless all *Reasonably Practicable Steps* have been taken to prevent them.

An equal opportunity policy should not, however, be adopted only for negative reasons. It is good employment practice, which can make a positive contribution to the success of the organisation. The Code of Practice under the *SDA 1975* points out that an equal opportunities policy will ensure the effective use of human resources in the best interests of both the organisation and its employees. Similarly, the Code of Practice under the *RRA 1976* states that if a coherent and effective programme of equal opportunities is developed, it would help industry to make full use of the abilities of its entire workforce.

97.2 KEY STEPS

The key steps towards the adoption and implementation of an effective policy are:

(*a*) formulate the policy and adopt it;

(*b*) allocate overall responsibility for implementing it;

(*c*) tell people about it and put it into effect; and

(*d*) monitor it and review it.

97.3 POLICY FORMULATION AND ADOPTION

One of the first questions to be considered is who should contribute to the content of the policy. The Code of Practice under the CRE recommends that the policy's contents and implementation should be discussed and, where appropriate, agreed with trade union or employee representatives. This is sensible advice. A policy is more likely to be supported by the workforce if employee representatives have contributed to it than if it has simply been imposed by management.

The Code of Practice under the EOC recommends that where appropriate the policy should be included in a collective agreement. An example of such an agreement is considered under *National Health Service*. Employers need to be aware, however, of the implications of adopting policies which have contractual effect – see *Contractual Equal Opportunities Policies*.

It is also necessary to consider whether there should be a single policy or separate policies on different aspects of equal opportunities. The code of practice under the *RRA 1976* suggests that a concerted policy to eliminate both race and sex discrimination often provides the best approach. A strong argument in favour of a single, concerted policy is that the adoption of and insistence on best employment practice, such as the use of consistent and objective criteria for employment decisions, is the most effective way to eliminate unlawful discrimination and promote equality of opportunity.

On the other hand, there are particular issues, such as *Harassment*, which may need to be specifically addressed in a separate policy. Furthermore, the Code of Practice on the elimination of discrimination against disabled persons reminds employers that treating people equally will not always avoid a breach of the *DDA 1995*. An employer may be under a duty to make a *Reasonable Adjustment*. The implication of this advice is that a separate policy on disability may be appropriate.

Probably the best approach is to have an overall policy on equal opportunities, supported by additional, often more detailed, policies on specific issues, such as harassment and disability.

A further question to be considered is whether the policy documents should focus exclusively on preventing the discrimination which is prohibited by law and promoting equal opportunity only in those areas. The best practice is to draw up a policy which contains a general commitment to equal opportunities and which outlaws not only sex and marriage discrimination, racial discrimination and discrimination against the disabled, but also, for example:

(*a*) religious discrimination;

(*b*) age discrimination;

(*c*) discrimination on grounds of sexual orientation;

(*d*) political discrimination.

An additional advantage, in terms of the legislation, of a policy which goes beyond the bare minimum is that there can be an overlap between indirect racial and sex discrimination and direct discrimination on other grounds. For example direct religious discrimination can also be indirect racial discrimination.

In summary, therefore, the questions to be considered at the outset include:

(*a*) Who should be involved in drawing up the policy?

(*b*) Should the policy be contractual?

(*c*) Should there be a single policy or a whole series of policy documents?

(*d*) Should the policy be a comprehensive one, going further than the bare minimum required to achieve compliance with the law?

97.4 OVERALL RESPONSIBILITY

An important requirement, at the time when the policy is being drawn up, is to decide who should have overall responsibility for ensuring that it is properly carried out. The Codes of Practice under both the *SDA 1975* and the *RRA 1976* recommend that overall responsibility for implementing the policy should rest with senior management. There are obvious arguments in favour of this approach. The person or persons responsible for the policy need to be senior enough to ensure that it is taken seriously. At the same time, there is a risk that the implementation of the equal opportunity policy will not be given a sufficiently high priority if it is simply one of many responsibilities piled on to senior management. It is important, particularly in a large organisation, that any senior manager(s) with overall responsibility should receive all necessary support from individuals who have both the time and the expertise to make the policy work.

There is also no reason why employee involvement should end at the point when the policy has been drawn up and adopted. The appointment of a joint management and union or staff committee, to meet regularly and discuss the policy, could help to ensure both that the policy receives the necessary attention and that employee involvement and support are maintained.

97.5 COMMUNICATING AND IMPLEMENTING THE POLICY

It is obviously necessary that the employees and job applicants who are the potential beneficiaries of a policy should be told about the policy. The Code under the *SDA 1975* recommends that the policy should be made known to all employees and, where reasonably practicable, to all job applicants. The Code under the *RRA 1976* recommends that the policy should be clearly communicated to all employees, for example through a notice board, circular, contracts of employment or written notifications to individual employees. The Code also suggests that any literature sent to job applicants should include a statement that the employer is an equal opportunity employer. It is also good practice to include a similar statement in job advertisements. Steps taken to put the Code into effect could also usefully be explained in newsletters or bulletins or staff magazines.

All employees should be told about the procedure for complaining about discrimination or a failure to comply with the policy. They should also be reminded that they have obligations as well as rights under the policy. The disciplinary code should be amended where necessary to make it clear that discrimination is a disciplinary offence (amounting, in the most serious cases, to gross misconduct).

Perhaps the most important, and one of the most neglected, steps to be taken to eliminate discrimination is to give appropriate *Training* to employees, particularly managers and supervisors. The Code of Practice under the *RRA 1976* recommends that employers should provide training and guidance for supervisory staff and other relevant decision makers, such as personnel and line managers. The Code goes on to recommend that staff responsible for shortlisting, interviewing and selecting candidates should be given guidance or training on:

(*a*) selection criteria and the need for their consistent application;

(*b*) the effects which generalised assumptions and prejudices can have on selection decisions;

(*c*) the possible misunderstandings that can occur in interviews between persons of different cultural backgrounds.

The Code also recognises that junior employees may also need instruction and training. In many cases, the first person to speak to a job applicant is a receptionist, telephonist or gatekeeper. The Code under the *RRA 1976* recommends that gate, reception and personnel staff should be instructed not to treat casual or formal applicants from particular groups less favourably than other applicants. These instructions should be confirmed in writing. Instructions should also be given that the treatment of job applicants should not be affected by their sex or marital status.

The policy should also make it clear that senior management should take steps at regular intervals to ensure that they themselves are complying with the policy. For example senior management should look regularly at standard advertisements, application forms and various practices and procedures to ensure that they comply with the law and the policy.

97.6 MONITORING AND REVIEW

The Codes under both the *SDA 1975* and the *RRA 1976* stress the importance of effective *Monitoring*. The way in which monitoring should be carried out and the methods of analysing the information obtained are outlined in the section on monitoring. The importance of effective monitoring and analysis is to identify areas where the policy is not or may not be working, so that corrective action can then be taken. For example, if women, or racial minorities, are not being recruited for or promoted to particular jobs, or in particular departments, the possible explanations could be:

(*a*) The manager concerned is discriminating against them.

(*b*) Indirectly discriminatory requirements or practices are operating as a barrier.

(*c*) They are simply not coming forward.

Once a problem has been identified and analysed, then corrective action can be considered. For example, in the case where women or racial minorities are not applying for particular posts, then steps to encourage applications can be considered – this being one of the limited measures of *Positive Discrimination* which the law permits.

98 Equal Pay

98.1 REQUIREMENTS FOR A CLAIM

In a typical claim under the *EPA 1970*:

(*a*) The claim is made by a woman.

(*b*) She names one or more male workers – the *Comparator*(s).

(*c*) She claims the same pay, or rate of pay, as the comparator(s).

(*d*) The woman and any male comparator work for the same employer and at the same establishment.

(*e*) The grounds of the claim are that the woman's work and a male comparator's work are the same or broadly similar – *Like Work*.

Claims under the *EPA 1970* may, however, vary in each of the above respects, as follows:

(*a*) A claim under the *EPA 1970* may be made by a man.

(*b*) If the complainant is a man, then it follows that the comparator(s) must be female.

(*c*) An equal pay claim may be presented not only in order to come up to the comparator's level in terms of pay (which is very broadly defined) but also to obtain equality in relation to any other contract term in respect of which the comparator enjoys an advantage.

(*d*) A complainant and a comparator may be in the *Same Employment* for the purposes of a claim under the *EPA 1970* even if they have different employers and work at different establishments.

(*e*) The work which the complainant and the comparator do need not be the same or broadly similar; it suffices if it is work of *Equal Value* or work which has been rated as equivalent under a *Job Evaluation* study.

The way in which the *EPA 1970* operates is to introduce an *Equality Clause* into every contract under which a man or woman is employed at an establishment in Great Britain. The effect of an equality clause is that in certain circumstances an employee may rely on it in order to raise his or her pay or other contractual benefits up to the level enjoyed by a worker of the opposite sex. For example, where it is a woman who relies on an equality clause and who names a male comparator:

(*a*) If any term of her contract (whether concerned with pay or not) is less favourable to her than the corresponding term in the man's contract, then that term in her contract must be modified so that it ceases to be less favourable.

(*b*) If his contract includes a beneficial term which is not to be found in her contract, then that term must become part of her contract also.

Before an equality clause can operate in this way, it must first of all be shown that the woman and the man are in the *Same Employment*. This means that they must be employed:

(*a*) by the same employer or by *Associated Employers*;

(*b*) at the same establishment or at different establishments at which *Common Terms and Conditions* of employment are observed.

Decisions of the ECJ have resulted in some extension of the principle of *Same Employment*, so far as the *Public Sector* is concerned.

Once it has been established that the woman and the man are in the same employment, it is then necessary to compare the two jobs. Up to three questions need to be asked, in the following order:

(*a*) Have the two jobs been given the same rating under a *Job Evaluation* study?

(*b*) If not, are they *Like Work*?

(*c*) If not, are they of *Equal Value*?

Most equal pay cases are either like work or equal value claims. Both these expressions are considered below.

A case is not concluded by a finding that the complainant's job and the comparator's job are like work or of equal value. A claim can be defeated, and the equality clause can be prevented from operating, if the employer can prove that the variation between the two contracts is genuinely due to a material factor which is not the difference of sex.

98.2 LIKE WORK

A complainant is employed on like work with the comparator if:

(*a*) their work is of the same or a broadly similar nature; and

(*b*) any differences between the things they do are not of practical importance in relation to terms and conditions of employment.

The Act expressly states that it is relevant to have regard to the frequency or otherwise with which any differences occur in practice as well as to the nature and extent of the differences.

The Court of Appeal decision in the early case of *Shields v E Coomes (Holdings) Limited* [*1978*] *IRLR 263* emphasised the following important points:

(*a*) The focus is on the work which the woman and the man actually do in practice, not the work which they may theoretically be required to do.

(*b*) The fact that the two employees work at different times or for longer hours does not prevent the work from being like work. Night work or work for longer hours is to be dealt with by paying a night shift premium or overtime rate.

98.3 EQUAL VALUE

To ascertain whether two jobs are of equal value, it is necessary to measure the demands which each of the jobs makes on the person holding the job under various headings, such as effort, skill and decision making. For two jobs to be of equal value, there need be no similarity whatsoever between them in terms of the nature of the work being carried out. There are well established systems and processes for analysing jobs, allocating points under various headings and totting up the points in order to arrive at a value for the job.

There are two important differences between a like work claim and an equal value claim. The first is that any equal value claim must be dismissed by the tribunal if it is shown that the two jobs have been given different ratings under a *Job Evaluation* study, provided that the evaluation has been properly carried out on an analytical basis without any element of sex discrimination. Many employers commission job evaluation studies (even after an equal pay claim has been presented) with a view to having their pay structures reviewed objectively and comprehensively and under their own control, as opposed to having change forced on them as a result of successful equal value claims.

Secondly, there are special rules of procedure in equal value cases. In like work cases, as in other cases which come before employment tribunals, questions of fact are decided by the tribunal itself. In an equal value case, however, the tribunal may appoint an independent expert to consider whether the jobs are of equal value and to report back to the tribunal. Until 31 July 1996 a reference to an independent expert was mandatory, unless the tribunal was satisfied that there were no reasonable grounds for determining that the work was of equal value. Now the tribunal has discretion. Even where the question is referred to an independent expert, the tribunal is not obliged to accept the expert's report. Either party may, on giving reasonable notice to the tribunal and the other party, call one witness to give expert evidence supporting or challenging the independent expert's report.

98.4 THE MATERIAL FACTOR DEFENCE

The material factor defence is relied on in a great many equal pay cases. It should be raised at the outset, in the notice of appearance. In an equal value case, the tribunal may (and often does) decide to consider the defence at a preliminary hearing, before considering (or asking an independent expert to consider) the question whether the two jobs are of equal value.

A wide variety of factors may be relied on by employers to defend a claim under the *EPA 1970*. They include the following:

(*a*) the comparator's better qualifications, better experience or longer service;

(*b*) differences in grade under a genuine and non-discriminatory grading system;

(*c*) a desire to 'protect' the pay of a comparator who has been, for example, transferred to lighter work because of ill-health (the 'red circle' or 'red ringing' cases);

(*d*) the comparator's unpleasant working conditions.

So far as this last example is concerned, it seems illogical that a factor such as unpleasant working conditions, which is one of the demand factors which are relevant to the evaluation of the two jobs, can also be relied on as a material factor defence. It was, however, held by the EAT in the case of *Davies v McCartneys* [*1989*] *IRLR 439* that there is no limitation on the matters which may be relied upon. If an employer genuinely, and without any intention to discriminate on grounds of sex, places particular weight on one particular demand of the job, then the material factor defence can be made out.

An equal pay case in which a material factor defence is relied on can fall into one of three categories, as follows:

(*a*) The difference in pay or in some other contract term involves direct discrimination against the complainant, so that the material factor relied upon is the difference of sex – the defence cannot succeed.

(*b*) The difference involves indirect discrimination – objective justification is required.

(*c*) There is no evidence of either direct or indirect discrimination – the reason advanced for the difference in pay or otherwise need only be genuine – objective justification is not required.

The first category was considered by the *House of Lords in Ratcliffe v North Yorkshire County Council [1995] IRLR 439*. The dinner ladies employed by the council enjoyed the same rates of pay as male manual workers, the jobs having been given equal ratings under a job evaluation study. The rates for dinner ladies in the private sector were significantly lower because the work was done (as the colloquial job title suggests) by women. The council reduced the pay of its dinner ladies in order to be able to compete effectively with private sector employers in a compulsory competitive tendering exercise. The material factor defence failed. Although the council's only objective was to win the contract (and to continue employing the complainants), the pay of the complainants had been reduced because they were women, doing work traditionally regarded as women's work. This was direct discrimination and the material factor defence could not succeed.

The second category of case is where there is indirect discrimination because the proportion of women receiving, for example, lower pay is significantly greater than the proportion of men receiving lower pay. This was the issue in *Enderby v Frenchay Health Authority and Secretary of State for Health [1993] IRLR 591*. This was a case in which speech therapists, most of whom were women, claimed the same rate of pay as pharmacists and clinical psychologists, most of whom were men. It was held by the ECJ that because of this indirect sex discrimination the difference in pay required objective justification. The fact that the different pay structures were negotiated as a result of separate and distinct bargaining processes was not sufficient justification.

The remaining category of cases is where there is neither direct nor indirect sex discrimination. In *Strathclyde Regional Council v Wallace [1998] IRLR 146*, there was a difference in pay as between teachers and principal teachers. There were men and women in both groups and no significant disparity in the proportions. The teachers and principal teachers were employed on like work. There were genuine reasons for the difference in pay but the tribunal held that these reasons did not amount to objective justification. It was held by the House of Lords that there was no need for objective justification in the absence of any direct or indirect sex discrimination.

98.5 ARTICLE 141 (FORMERLY 119)

It is impossible to explain the law on equal pay without reference to *Article 141* (formerly *Article 119*) of the EU Treaty. The *EPA 1970* is detailed and technical; in contrast, *Article 141* states the following principle:

> *'Each Member State shall ensure that the principle of equal pay for male and female workers for equal work or work of equal value is applied.'*

The word 'pay' is broadly defined, to include any 'consideration whether in cash or in kind, which the worker receives directly or indirectly, in respect of his employment, from his employer'.

Council Directive No 75/117/EEC, the *Equal Pay Directive*, puts a little flesh on the bones, without in any way detracting from the above statement of principle. For example:

(*a*) Any job classification system which is used for determining pay must be based on the same criteria for both men and women and be so drawn up as to exclude any discrimination on grounds of sex.

(*b*) There must be no provisions which are contrary to the principle of equal pay in legislation, administrative rules, collective agreements, wage scales or individual contracts of employment.

(*c*) Employees must be protected against victimisation for taking steps aimed at enforcing compliance with the principle of equal pay.

The fundamental importance of *Article 141* arises from the following features of it:

(*a*) It prevails over any conflicting provision or omission in domestic legislation.

(*b*) Unlike Council Directives, it has direct effect, in the private sector as well as in the public sector.

Employment tribunals have jurisdiction to hear cases of the various kinds which have been assigned to them by Parliament. They have statutory jurisdiction to hear complaints under the *EPA 1970*, but not complaints under *Article 141*. This does not matter. It was held by the Court of Appeal in *Barber v Staffordshire County Council* [*1996*] *IRLR 209* that the effect of *Article 141* is to modify conflicting provisions in domestic legislation, for example by removing (or disapplying) from the *EPA 1970* (or the *SDA 1975*) exceptions which are incompatible with Community Law.

In the *EPA 1970* as originally enacted, there was an exception for provisions in relation to death or retirement. This meant that, for example, there could be no claim relating to pensions or redundancy payments. This exception was found to be incompatible with *Article 141* in the landmark pension case of *Barber v Guardian Royal Exchange Assurance Group* [*1990*] *IRLR 240*. Eventually (with effect from 1 January 1996) the *EPA 1970* and the *SDA 1975* were both amended to reflect the decision in *Barber*, but because of the direct effect of *Article 141* successful claims in relation to pensions and redundancy payments could be and were brought during the intervening period. A claim relating to a contractual redundancy or severance payment falls under the *EPA 1970*; the claim is probably under the *SDA 1975* if the payment is discretionary.

There was a much earlier modification to the *EPA 1970* which has still not been reflected in any amending legislation. The *EPA 1970* is so worded that the complainant and the comparator must be employed contemporaneously. That requirement of contemporaneous employment is inconsistent with *Article 141*. It was accordingly held by the ECJ in *Macarthys Limited v Smith* [*1980*] *IRLR 210* that a woman could claim the higher rate of pay enjoyed by the man who was employed in her post immediately before she was. The same principle applies (subject to any material factor defence) where an employee leaves and a person of the opposite sex is then appointed at a higher rate of pay.

98.6 REMEDIES

When an equal pay claim is successful, the complainant is entitled to an order declaring the rights of the complainant and the employee. The effect of an order in favour of the complainant is that (as the case may be):

(*a*) her (or his) pay is increased to the level of the comparator's pay; or

(*b*) her (or his) contract terms are improved to match those of the comparator.

Once the order has been made, the complainant has a contractual right to the increased pay or improved contractual terms, even if the comparator subsequently ceases to be employed by the employer. Indeed, as already mentioned, as a result of *Article 141* and the decision in *Macarthys v Smith*, an equal pay claim may be based on a comparison with someone who has already left the employment, being the complainant's predecessor in the post.

When the tribunal is considering the question of remedy, is it open to the employer to argue that the contracts of the complainant and the comparator should each be looked at as a complete package, so that no order should be made if contract terms which are more favourable to the comparator are matched by other terms which are more favourable to the complainant? This issue arose in the case of *Hayward v Cammell Laird Shipbuilders Limited [1988] IRLR 257.* This was an equal value case in which a canteen cook succeeded in claiming the same rate of pay as male welders and other craftsmen in the shipyard. It was argued by the employers, at the remedy stage, that although she had a lower rate of pay than her comparators did, she also enjoyed several benefits, such as paid meal breaks, which they did not. This argument was rejected by the House of Lords. It was held to be necessary to compare individual terms, such as the rate of pay, and not the employment package as a whole.

An order declaring the rights of the parties for the future is not the only remedy which may be claimed by a complainant. The tribunal may also award compensation, consisting of:

(*a*) arrears of remuneration, or *Back Pay*, if the complaint is about pay; or

(*b*) damages if the complaint is about some other contract term.

The *EPA 1970* provides that no payment by way of arrears of remuneration or damages may be awarded in respect of a time earlier than two years before the date on which the proceedings were instituted. As a result of a decision of the ECJ, and subsequent consideration of the matter by the EAT, this period has now been increased to six years (see *Back Pay*) in order to bring the *EPA 1970* into line with *Article 141*. The *EPA 1970* has not been formally amended, but as a result of the overriding effect of *Article 141* the Act now applies as if the two year limit had already been increased to six years by Parliament.

98.7 LIMITATIONS OF THE EPA 1970

The *EPA 1970* is about equal pay, not about fair pay. Because of the way in which the Act is structured, it is subject to serious limitations.

The first and most important limitation is that no complaint can succeed unless a suitable comparator of the opposite sex can be identified. It is not possible, for example, for a woman to claim the increased pay which she *would have* received if she had been a man. An actual male comparator is required. If her work is being done and has always been done only by women, and there are no men in the *Same Employment* who are employed on work of equal value, then she has no remedy.

Arguably the principle of equal pay for work of equal value is not being fully implemented if complaints on the basis of a hypothetical male comparator are ruled out. In practical terms, however, equal pay claims, particularly equal value cases, are already difficult and complicated for the parties to present and the tribunal to decide. There would be new difficulties if it became possible to base complaints on hypothetical comparisons.

The second limitation on the *EPA 1970* is that it is fairly crude in its operation. All that can be achieved is to bring the complainant's contractual terms up to the level of those of the comparator. There is no provision for a more sophisticated remedy, in order to reflect precisely any differences in value between the two jobs. The following examples illustrate the point:

(*a*) The evaluation of the two jobs in an equal value claim indicates that the value of the complainant's job is 95 per cent that of the value of the comparator's job, even though her pay is only half the comparator's pay. There is no provision for increasing her pay up to 95 per cent of the comparator's pay.

(*b*) A woman who is already paid as much as her comparator cannot bring an equal pay claim on the ground that she should be paid far more than he is because her work is of far greater value.

The *EPA 1970* offers workers a (often long and difficult) route to equality in pay and other contract terms as between men and women, where they are in the *Same Employment*, but it does not offer fair differentials in pay as between men and women.

99 Equal Treatment Directive

Article 2 of the *Equal Treatment Directive* begins with the uncompromising statement that 'the principle of equal treatment shall mean that there shall be no discrimination whatsoever on grounds of sex either directly or indirectly by reference in particular to marital or family status'. The Article then allows for exceptions in the following cases:

(*a*) occupational activities and related training where, by reason of the nature or context of the activities, the sex of the worker constitutes a determining factor;

(*b*) provisions concerning the protection of women, particularly as regards pregnancy and maternity;

(*c*) measures to promote equal opportunity for men and women, in particular by removing existing inequalities which affect women's opportunities.

The first of these exceptions authorises, for example, the *Genuine Occupational Qualification* provisions in the *SDA 1975*.

Later Articles require Member States to take the necessary steps to enable persons who consider themselves wronged to pursue their claims by judicial process and also measures to protect employees against victimisation.

The Directive, like other Directives, has direct effect in the *Public Sector*, overriding any inconsistent provisions in the *SDA 1975*, and courts and tribunals in Great Britain must also construe and apply domestic legislation consistently with the Directive wherever it is practicable to do so.

100 Equal Value

Proving that the work done by a complainant and that done by a comparator in the same employment are of equal value is one of the three ways of establishing the basis for an *Equal Pay* claim. The two jobs can be totally different provided that they are of equal value in terms of the demands made by them under various headings, such as the skill and effort required and the degree of responsibility and decision making involved. In one of the earliest successful cases, a canteen cook successfully compared her job with those of craftsmen in the same shipyard.

An equal pay claim will not necessarily succeed, however, even if the two jobs are of equal value. The employer can defeat the claim by showing that the difference in pay or other contract terms to which the claim relates is genuinely due to a *Material Factor* which is not the difference in sex between the complainant and the comparators.

101 Equality Clause

The equality clause is the mechanism by which the *EPA 1970* operates in order to enforce the principle of *Equal Pay*. The equality clause is introduced into every contract of employment, so as to give a complainant a contractual remedy where the necessary comparison can be established between the complainant's work and that of a comparator of the opposite sex in the *Same Employment* (unless the employer can make out the *Material Factor* defence).

102 Establishment

102.1 TERRITORIAL EXTENT

The employment provisions in the *EPA 1970*, the *SDA 1975*, the *RRA 1976* and the *DDA 1995* all apply to employment at an establishment in Great Britain.

This does not mean that only jobs which involve working *in* a factory, shop, office or other building are covered by the legislation. It is expressly provided for the purposes of each Act that if work is not done at an establishment it is to be treated as done at the establishment *from* which it is done or (if there is no such establishment) then at the establishment with which it has the closest connection. This means that, for example, a sales representative whose work consists of visiting customers will be regarded as being employed at the office to which he reports.

102.2 EQUAL PAY

It can be relevant for the purposes of an *Equal Pay* claim to ascertain whether two employees are employed at the same establishment – see *Same Employment*.

103 Ethnic Origins

The term 'ethnic origins' is relevant for the purposes of both direct and indirect racial discrimination. It is direct discrimination if on grounds of ethnic origins a person is treated less favourably than another person is or would be treated. A group of persons defined by reference to ethnic origins is also a *Racial Group* for the purposes of *Indirect Discrimination*.

Guidance on the meaning of 'ethnic origins' was given by the House of Lords in the non-employment case of *Mandla v Dowell Lee [1983] IRLR 209*. This was the case of the Sikh boy who was refused a place at a school because of his insistence on wearing a turban.

Lord Fraser said that there were two essential characteristics of an ethnic group:

(*a*) a long shared history, of which the group is conscious as distinguishing it from other groups;

(*b*) a cultural tradition of its own, including family and social customs and manners.

The essential cultural tradition is often but not necessarily associated with religious observance.

Lord Fraser also referred to other characteristics which are relevant but not essential:

(*a*) a common geographical origin or descent from a small number of common ancestors;

(*b*) a common language (not necessarily peculiar to the group);

(*c*) a common literature peculiar to the group;

(*d*) a common religion different from that of neighbouring groups or from the surrounding community;

(*e*) being a minority within a larger community.

An ethnic group can include converts, including those who marry into the group.

In the above case, it was held that *Sikhs* are an ethnic group for the purpose of the *RRA 1976*. It has also been held that *Gypsies* can be an ethnic group.

It should be noted, however, that the fact that a particular group can constitute an ethnic group does not necessarily mean that a particular complainant will be held to be a member of that group. The question is one of fact in each case, particularly in relation to groups such as gypsies, where by no means all those who have adopted a travelling way of life can thereby be regarded as being members of the relevant ethnic group.

In another case, it was held that Rastafarians were not an ethnic group. One reason was that they had insufficient shared history – *Crown Suppliers (PSA) Limited v Dawkins [1993] ICR 517*.

104 Evidence of Discrimination

104.1 DIRECT EVIDENCE RARELY AVAILABLE

The definitions of *Direct Discrimination* and *Victimisation* in employment have recently been clarified, as a result of the House of Lords decision in *Nagarajan v London Regional Transport* [*1999*] *IRLR 572*. There are two questions to be answered in each case. For example, if the complainant is a woman who alleges direct sex discrimination:

(*a*) Has she been treated less favourably than a man has been or would have been treated?

(*b*) If so, is her gender the reason or (if there is more than one reason) a significant or important reason for the less favourable treatment?

The questions are clear, but answering them is more difficult, particularly in *Recruitment*, *Promotion* and *Redundancy* cases. The main difficulty is usually presented by the second question, about the reason for the less favourable treatment. It is frequently no easy matter for a complainant in such a case to demonstrate that race or gender was the reason for the treatment complained of, or for the tribunal to decide this issue. The difficulty was explained in the following words in the leading case of *King v The Great Britain-China Centre* [*1991*] *IRLR 513* (a case which will be considered in more detail below):

> 'It is important to bear in mind that it is unusual to find direct evidence of racial discrimination. Few employers will be prepared to admit such discrimination even to themselves. In some cases the discrimination will not be ill-intentioned but merely based on an assumption that "he or she would not have fitted in"'.

The above comment that it is unusual to find direct evidence of racial discrimination also applies to complaints of direct sex discrimination and to complaints of victimisation (whether under the *SDA 1975*, the *RRA 1976* or the *DDA 1995*).

These evidential difficulties do not usually arise in cases of *Indirect Discrimination*. Generally, the requirement or condition complained of will have been openly stated, for example in an advertisement or job description. The main issues in cases of indirect discrimination are usually *Disparate Impact* and *Justification*.

Identifying the reason for the treatment complained of can be the main issue in cases of disability discrimination, particularly in *Recruitment* cases. It is more usual, however, for the main disputes of fact in cases under the *DDA 1995* to be whether the complainant is disabled, whether the treatment complained of has been justified or whether *Reasonable Adjustments* have been made.

104.2 COMPARATIVE TREATMENT

The starting point in many complaints of direct discrimination or victimisation is to show that the complainant has been treated less favourably than an actual *Comparator*. For example:

(*a*) White candidates for a job have been shortlisted and the complainant, who is black, has not, even though he has better qualifications.

(*b*) A man has been promoted over the head of the female complainant, even though she has more relevant experience.

(*c*) The complainant, who had previously made allegations of disability discrimination, has been dismissed for gross misconduct, while a fellow employee who had not made any such allegations was given a final written warning for an identical offence.

In the first of the above examples, it may be asked how the complainant would be able to prove that he is better qualified than the shortlisted white candidates. It is generally possible to obtain the relevant information by using the statutory *Questionnaire* and by requiring disclosure of relevant *Documents*.

Employment tribunals are required to follow the guidance given in the above-mentioned case of *King v the Great Britain-China Centre,* once the evidence shows a difference in race (if the complaint is one of direct racial discrimination) and a difference in treatment. In that case, the complainant had been born in China, of Chinese parents, but educated in Britain. She saw a newspaper advertisement for a post as deputy director of a government-sponsored organisation which had been set up to promote understanding between the peoples of the UK and China by fostering closer cultural and other contacts. She applied for the post, supporting her application with information about her relevant experience and her deep understanding of both cultures. Out of 30 candidates, she was one of five who were ethnic Chinese. Eight candidates were called for interview. They did not include the complainant or any of the other ethnic Chinese candidates.

The employment tribunal upheld the complaint of racial discrimination by a majority, with the chairman dissenting. The majority approached the case on the following basis:

(*a*) The complainant had clearly been treated less favourably than the shortlisted candidates.

(*b*) There was a difference in race – the shortlisted candidates were white and the complainant was not.

(*c*) The tribunal had to decide whether the employer had given a satisfactory and convincing explanation why the other candidates had been selected for interview and the complainant had not.

(*d*) If the employer was unable to give such an explanation, then it would be open to the tribunal to make a finding of discrimination.

Having adopted that approach, the majority then considered the explanation given by the employer for not shortlisting the complainant. They were not satisfied with the explanation and made a finding of racial discrimination. The matters which they took into account included the following:

(*a*) A comparison of the complainant's application for the post with those submitted by the shortlisted candidates indicated that she was entitled to anticipate selection for interview.

(*b*) The criteria for the post were changed during the selection process to her disadvantage and were not applied consistently.

(*c*) The employer had been inconsistent in complaining that she was simultaneously under-qualified and over-qualified.

(*d*) The employer had given an evasive or equivocal reply to a key question in the questionnaire.

(*e*) No ethnically Chinese person had ever been employed in the centre.

The EAT allowed an appeal against the finding of racial discrimination. The reason for that decision was that the majority in the employment tribunal had placed the burden of proof on the respondent and thereby erred in law.

The case then went to the Court of Appeal, which allowed an appeal against the EAT decision and restored the decision of the employment tribunal. The Court of Appeal, in a key passage which is set out below almost verbatim, endorsed the approach which had been adopted by the employment tribunal:

(*a*) There will be some cases where, for example, the non-selection of the applicant for a post or for promotion is clearly not on racial grounds.

(*b*) A finding of a difference in treatment and a finding of a difference in race will often, however, point to the possibility of racial discrimination.

(*c*) In such circumstances, the tribunal will look to the employer for an explanation.

(*d*) It will be legitimate for the tribunal to draw an inference of racial discrimination if no explanation is put forward or if the tribunal considers the explanation which is given to be inadequate or unsatisfactory.

(*e*) This is a matter of common sense rather than a matter of law.

The above approach involves the tribunal in drawing inferences from its primary findings of fact. This is a necessary approach because of the absence of direct evidence of discrimination in most cases. It was stated by the Court of Appeal that the outcome of the case will therefore usually depend on what inferences it is proper to draw from the primary facts found by the tribunal.

The Court of Appeal gave the following further guidance:

(*a*) It is unnecessary and unhelpful to introduce the concept of a shifting evidential burden of proof.

(*b*) At the conclusion of all the evidence, the tribunal should make findings as to the primary facts and draw such inferences as they consider proper from those facts.

(*c*) They should then reach a conclusion on the balance of probabilities.

(*d*) In doing so, they should bear in mind the difficulties which face a person who complains of unlawful discrimination.

(*e*) They should also bear in mind the fact that it is for the complainant to prove his or her case.

Considerable space has been devoted to the above case, because the guidance which the Court of Appeal gave in it is referred to and followed by employment tribunals in a great many complaints of direct discrimination and victimisation. The guidance was expressly approved by the House of Lords in the case of *Zafar v Glasgow City Council [1998] IRLR 36*. It was also stated by the House of Lords in that case that the guidance should be applied in cases of sex discrimination as well as cases of race discrimination (as had in fact been the practice). The guidance is also relevant to complaints of victimisation, whether under the *SDA 1975*, the *RRA 1976* or the *DDA 1995*. It is also relevant to some cases of disability discrimination, where for example the complainant alleges that it is because of a disability that she or he has not been shortlisted or selected.

In any such case, a finding of direct discrimination is likely if the respondent cannot give an adequate and satisfactory explanation for the difference in treatment. It should be noted, however, that an adequate and satisfactory explanation is not necessarily one which demonstrates a fair and reasonable approach. It is sufficient if the employer gives a reason which has nothing to do with the race, gender or disability (as the case may be) of the complainant and if the tribunal believes that explanation.

Although it was stated by the Court of Appeal in *King* that it is unnecessary and unhelpful to introduce the concept of a shifting evidential burden of proof, that concept will have to be introduced very shortly when the Directive on the *Burden of Proof* is implemented in Great Britain. In practical terms, however, the implementation of the Directive is likely to make very little difference. Whatever terminology is used, a respondent who is unable to give an adequate and satisfactory explanation for a difference in treatment is in practice likely to have a finding of discrimination made against him.

Although the relevant difference in treatment, in a recruitment or promotion case, is usually in relation to shortlisting or selection decisions, the principle is not limited to such cases. It could also apply in such cases as the following:

(*a*) A black candidate for a post is interviewed for only 20 minutes; the interviews of both the white candidates who have been shortlisted last for about an hour each. The black candidate is not appointed.

(*b*) An unsuccessful female candidate for a post is asked questions at the interview about her domestic circumstances and arrangements for looking after her children; questions of this kind are not put to the male interviewees.

In each of these cases, the difference in treatment at the interview, coupled with the difference in race or sex, would point to the possibility of racial discrimination (in the first case) or sex discrimination (in the second case). The Tribunal would look to the employer for an explanation. Suppose that in the first case the respondent's evidence was that after 20 minutes the black candidate answered a question in a way which showed that he was clearly unsuitable for the post, so that there was no point in continuing with the interview; and in the second case, it was the female candidate herself who raised the question of her childcare arrangements, inviting the interviewer to explore that question with her. These are explanations which, if believed by the tribunal, could be regarded as adequate and satisfactory.

104.3 OTHER EVIDENCE

It is not always possible, in a complaint of discrimination or victimisation, for the complainant to point to an actual comparator who has been treated more favourably. Sometimes, for example, in a sex discrimination case, a woman complains that she has been treated less favourably than a man *would have been* treated in similar circumstances, even though there is no actual male comparator. Furthermore, even where there is a relevant difference in treatment, with no adequate and satisfactory explanation, it is desirable to have other evidence to support the resulting inference of discrimination. Indeed there was further evidence in *King*.

Other evidence of discrimination could take the form of:

(*a*) revealing questions or statements;

(*b*) unsatisfactory replies to a questionnaire;

(*c*) false reasons for treatment complained of;

(*d*) previous or subsequent discrimination;

(*e*) statistical evidence;

(*f*) admissions of discrimination.

There are some cases where the issue is not the reason for the treatment complained of, but whether that treatment has occurred at all. The obvious examples are complaints of racial or sexual *Harassment*, where the respondent disputes that any acts of harassment have taken place. The question of evidence in such cases is considered under *Harassment*.

104.4 REVEALING QUESTIONS AND STATEMENTS

The second of the examples given in **104.2** above of a difference in treatment was that of an interviewer who asks a female candidate, but not male candidates, about her domestic circumstances and childcare arrangements. It does not follow that an interviewer is on safe ground putting questions about those matters in the same terms to all candidates, male and female. Discussion of childcare arrangements can arise naturally in the course of the interview; on the other hand, the way in which the issue is raised and pursued can indicate an inclination on the part of the interviewer to appoint a man, who will be less likely to need time off for childcare. The following examples illustrate the distinction:

(*a*) A job involves unsocial hours and travel. The interviewers speak to all the candidates about these requirements as well as other features of the job and ask each candidate if he or she will be able to meet the requirements. A female candidate is a single parent with care and custody of her children; a male candidate lives with and looks after his elderly mother. They each refer to their commitments but explain about the alternative arrangements which they will be able to make when the need arises.

(*b*) Candidates, who are nearly all female, are being interviewed for a clerical job, office based with conventional hours. All the candidates, male and female, are asked in detail about their childcare arrangements and whether they will need time off. The successful candidate is a childless woman; the complainant, who has had more relevant work experience, has young children.

In the first of these examples, the questioning was constructive and job related; in the second example, the fixation on childcare, coupled with the rejection of the best qualified candidate, points towards direct sex discrimination. The complainant has been treated less favourably than a man (or unmarried woman) with her work experience would have been treated.

Inappropriate questioning can also point towards racial or disability discrimination or victimisation. For example:

(*a*) The complainant has disclosed a disability, but it is one which will have no effect on job performance, because it is fully controlled by medication. The interviewer spends a good deal of the interview asking about the disability and does so in a negative way.

(*b*) A black candidate for a managerial post is asked at great length whether he believes that white employees will have any difficulty in taking orders from him and also whether he believes that he will fit in with the other members of the management team, who are all white.

(*c*) A female candidate is asked why she left her last job and explains that she did so because she had been subjected to serious acts of sexual harassment. The interviewer shows an obsessive interest in the details of the harassment and also in the way she complained about it.

In all these examples, the time spent on an issue which is not legitimately job related and the negative way in which that issue is approached would be evidence of an intention to discriminate unlawfully – disability discrimination in the first case, racial discrimination in the second and victimisation in the third. An intention to discriminate is not an essential ingredient of *Direct Discrimination* or *Victimisation*, but evidence of such an intention, coupled with evidence of less favourable treatment, could lead to a finding in the complainant's favour.

Interviewers can also give themselves away by what they write down as well as by the questions which they ask. Interview notes which contain personal or disparaging remarks about candidates can be important evidence of discrimination. The respondent can be required to produce the notes for the tribunal hearing – see *Documents*.

It is not only in the interview context that discriminatory attitudes are revealed. The wording of an *Advertisement* can lead to a finding of discrimination. Indeed there is a specific provision in the *DDA 1995* to that effect.

Furthermore, in cases where the complainant is an existing employee, such as a *Promotion* case, there is sometimes evidence of unguarded remarks made on a previous occasion by a manager who now has responsibility for shortlisting and selecting. For example:

(*a*) A woman applies for promotion to section head. The appointment is to be made by the manager of the department. The last time a similar post came up, he told her that the post was not a suitable job for a woman.

(*b*) A black employee applies for promotion to supervisor. The manager who will be making the appointment regularly makes racist remarks and tells racial jokes.

In both the above examples, if the employee seeking promotion were unsuccessful and complained of discrimination, the evidence would indicate that, respectively, their gender and race were likely to have been significant reasons for the decisions not to appoint them.

104.5 THE QUESTIONNAIRE

The *SDA 1975*, the *RRA 1976* and the *DDA 1995* each make provision for an aggrieved person to question the respondent, either before or after submitting a complaint. There is no statutory requirement for the respondent to answer the questions, but each Act states that the tribunal may draw an appropriate inference if:

(*a*) the respondent deliberately and without reasonable excuse, omits to reply within a reasonable period:

(*b*) the reply is evasive; or

(*c*) the reply is equivocal.

The inference which the tribunal may draw is any inference which the tribunal considers it just and equitable to draw, including an inference that the respondent has committed an unlawful act.

One of the matters which the tribunal took into account in *King* was that an evasive or equivocal reply had been given to a key question in the questionnaire. Part of the guidance given by the Court of Appeal in that case was that:

(*a*) the outcome of the case will usually depend on what inferences it is proper to draw from the primary facts found by the tribunal;

(*b*) these inferences can include, in appropriate cases, any inferences that it is just and equitable to draw from an evasive or equivocal reply to a questionnaire.

The following would be examples of evasive or equivocal (or false) replies to a questionnaire which could lead to an inference of unlawful discrimination or victimisation:

(*a*) A woman who has applied unsuccessfully for a post is told in the reply to the questionnaire that the successful male candidate had obtained a particular qualification which was relevant to the post. When the relevant documents, including the successful candidate's CV are disclosed, it turns out that he has not yet obtained that qualification.

(*b*) A candidate who was born overseas is interviewed for a post but not appointed. The reason given in the reply to the questionnaire was his inability to communicate effectively in English. Having heard him give his evidence, the tribunal find that the interviewers could not have genuinely believed that he had any difficulty in communicating.

(*c*) The reply to a questionnaire submitted by an unsuccessful disabled candidate for a post states that the manager who made the decision was not even aware of the disability. The tribunal, however, accept the complainant's evidence that the disability was mentioned by that manager at the interview.

(*d*) A questionnaire is submitted by an unsuccessful female candidate for promotion, who had previously complained of sexual harassment. The reply to the questionnaire states that the complaint of harassment was never even mentioned or considered. There is, however, a reference to the complaint in the interview notes which are disclosed.

104.6 **FALSE REASONS**

It is not only at the questionnaire stage that giving false information to a job applicant can subsequently lead to findings of discrimination.

There have been several cases along the following lines:

(*a*) A black worker applies for an advertised post.

(*b*) He or she is told that the vacancy has been filled.

(*c*) The employer continues to advertise the post.

(*d*) The black worker arranges for a white friend to enquire about the same post.

(*e*) The white friend is told that the post is still available and is invited for interview.

There could be a defence in such cases if the respondent gives credible and detailed evidence that a person who had been offered the job gave back word during the interval between the two enquiries. In the absence of a credible explanation of that kind, however, there have been findings of racial discrimination in such cases.

There can be no reasonable objection to the element of subterfuge in such cases. Asking a white friend to enquire about the same job is the obvious method for the unsuccessful candidate to test whether the reason given to him is a genuine one and it is surely a legitimate method for him to use.

There are, however, grounds for some reservations about those cases, of which several have been reported in the press, in which a candidate who submits a written application for a post also submits an identical application under a false name, purporting to be that of a candidate of the opposite sex or a different racial group. Sometimes the false application is submitted only after the candidate's genuine application has been rejected, but there have been cases where both applications have been submitted at the same time. If the candidate's own application is rejected but the false application leads to the offer of an interview then a complaint of direct discrimination is presented.

In such a case, if, for example, the complainant is black and the false application purported to be from a white candidate, the complaint is not that the complainant has been treated less favourably than a white candidate *has been* treated. That cannot be the basis of the complaint, because the white candidate mentioned in the false application did not exist. The complaint is instead that the complainant has been treated less favourably than a white candidate with the same relevant qualifications and experience *would have been* treated.

In principle, no doubt, where the false application is submitted only after the complainant's own application has been rejected, there is no distinction between that tactic and that of the tactic mentioned above of asking a friend to ring up to ask if an advertised post is still available. It is a different matter, however, if the genuine application and the false application are submitted at the same time. The complainant is starting off from the standpoint that discrimination is likely to occur. Before making any finding of discrimination, the tribunal would wish to be satisfied that he was genuinely seeking employment in the post and not simply trying to make a point or obtain an award of compensation.

104.7 PREVIOUS OR SUBSEQUENT ACTS

There are *Time Limits* of three months for complaints of sex, racial or disability discrimination (including victimisation). Unrelated things done or words spoken more than three months before the presentation of the complaint can, however, help to identify the reason for the treatment now complained of. So can things said or done after the presentation of the complaint but before the hearing.

This principle was affirmed by the EAT in the case of *Chattopadhyay v the Headmaster of Holloway School [1981] IRLR 487*. The issue in that case was whether it was relevant that a person involved in the act complained of had subsequently treated the complainant with hostility. It was held that such evidence was admissible but not conclusive. The relevant principles may be summarised as follows:

(*a*) An inference of racial discrimination may be drawn if a decision which is adverse to the complainant has been made by a person who is hostile to the complainant on racial grounds.

(*b*) If that person and the complainant are of different racial groups and his words or actions demonstrate hostility to the complainant, then that hostility calls for explanation.

(*c*) There may be a wholly non-racial explanation for the hostility, but in the absence of such explanation an inference of racial hostility may be drawn.

(*d*) It does not matter in principle whether the hostile words or actions are before or after the treatment about which the complaint is made.

The same principles would apply not only to a complaint of racial discrimination but also to one of sex or disability discrimination. For example:

(*a*) A woman has applied unsuccessfully for promotion. A year or so earlier, the manager who has turned down her application conducted an appraisal in which he scoffed at her ambitions. He told her during the appraisal interview that she should put her career on hold until her children are grown up.

(*b*) After a disabled employee had applied unsuccessfully for promotion, the manager who turned him down was heard to say to a colleague that with his disability he should think himself lucky to be employed at all.

In both the above examples, evidence about the remarks made before or after the treatment complained of would be relevant evidence about the reason for that decision.

104.8 STATISTICAL EVIDENCE

Statistics showing the racial composition of a workforce, or the proportion of women managers or the number of disabled employees cannot in themselves prove racial, sex or disability discrimination in recruitment. There could be wholly innocent explanations for an apparent 'under-representation' of, for example, black workers, women or disabled workers. Statistical evidence can be relevant, however, particularly where the organisation is large enough for the statistics to be significant.

The principle that statistical evidence can be relevant was established by the decision of the Court of Appeal in *West Midlands Passenger Transport Executive v Singh [1988] IRLR 186*. This was a complaint of racial discrimination in the rejection of an application by an inspector for promotion to senior inspector. The issue was whether the employers should be required to produce details of the ethnic origins of successful and unsuccessful candidates for comparable posts over a two year period. It was held by the Court of Appeal that the information should be provided.

Lord Justice Balcombe said:

> 'Statistical evidence may establish a discernible pattern in the treatment of a particular group; if that pattern demonstrates a regular failure of members of the group to obtain promotion to particular jobs and of under-representation in such jobs, it may give rise to an inference of discrimination against the group'.

He went on to say:

> 'If a practice is being operated against a group then, in the absence of a satisfactory explanation in a particular case, it is reasonable to infer that the complainant, as a member of the group, has himself been treated less favourably on grounds of race. Indeed, evidence of discriminatory treatment against the group in relation to promotion may be more persuasive of discrimination in the particular case than previous treatment of the applicant, which may be indicative of personal factors peculiar to the applicant and not necessarily racially motivated'.

This was an important judgment, but it is necessary to handle statistics with great care and to bear in mind that they may lead only to an inference, not a presumption, of discrimination. Whatever the statistics may indicate, a complaint of direct racial discrimination will fail if the employer gives, and the tribunal believes, evidence that race was not the reason or one of the reasons for the treatment complained of and that, for example, the complainant was turned down for the post because it was genuinely believed that he did not have the qualities required for the post.

The need for caution was underlined by the EAT in the case of *Carrington v Helix Lighting Limited [1990] IRLR 6*. This was a case in which the complainant was seeking an order requiring the employer to provide a schedule containing details of the ethnic composition of the workforce. It was held that the statistical evidence required could be relevant but 'on its own is unlikely to be sufficient'.

104.9 ADMISSIONS OF DISCRIMINATION

There are occasionally cases where discrimination is openly admitted. The most common examples are cases where the employer believes, rightly or wrongly, that an *Exception*, such as the *Genuine Occupational Qualification* exception, applies. The issue in such cases is not whether discrimination has occurred but whether the case is in fact covered by the exception relied upon.

There may also be cases where admissions or comments to third parties may be evidence of discrimination. The evidence could come, for example, from:

(*a*) a newspaper which has refused to take a discriminatory advertisement;

(*b*) a recruitment agency which has refused to comply with instructions to discriminate;

(*c*) an employee (or former employee) who has been party to or overheard a conversation in which unlawful discrimination was admitted;

(*d*) a former employee who has been dismissed because of a refusal to comply with an instruction to discriminate.

In the last of these examples the dismissed employee would also be able to complain of an act of *Victimisation* and also (if the instruction was to discriminate on *Racial Grounds*) of direct discrimination.

104.10 INDIRECT DISCRIMINATION

Although the main issues in cases of indirect discrimination are usually *Disparate Impact* and *Justification*, there are sometimes cases where it is necessary to subject the employer's actions to detailed analysis. In particular, there may be cases where it is argued by a complainant that a factor which has been described, in an advertisement or job description, as a mere preference, is in reality a *Requirement or Condition*. For example:

(*a*) An advertisement for a routine clerical post states that candidates with degrees are preferred.

(*b*) A candidate who has recently come to Great Britain as a refugee does not have a degree.

(*c*) The evidence shows that the proportion of workers of that candidate's national origin who have degrees is considerably smaller than the proportion of other workers who have degrees.

(*d*) The evidence shows that all the candidates with degrees have been shortlisted and that all candidates without degrees have been rejected at the shortlisting stage.

(*e*) This evidence suggests that the preference which was expressed for a degree was in fact a requirement.

104.11 ADVICE FOR COMPLAINANTS

It is evident from the above account of matters which can constitute relevant evidence that there are key steps which complainants should take in order to prepare a case for a tribunal hearing, as follows:

(*a*) Use the *Questionnaire* procedure. Information about your particular case, and also statistical information, can be relevant. Furthermore a failure by the respondent to reply to the questionnaire, or a response which is evasive or equivocal, could lead to an inference of unlawful discrimination.

(*b*) Ask for production of all relevant *Documents*. Ideally the request should be made at the questionnaire stage. In any event, the documents should be requested well in advance of the hearing and if necessary the tribunal should be asked to make an order. If you have not been shortlisted, the relevant documents will include the application forms and CVs of all the shortlisted candidates. If you have been shortlisted, they will include at least the application form and the CV of the successful candidate. If you have been interviewed, then the interview notes could be important documents.

(*c*) Evidence of what has been said to you, for example, when enquiring about the post or during an interview, can be relevant. A detailed note of any such discussion should be made as soon as possible after it has taken place. These notes should be included with any other relevant documents in the bundle of documents for the hearing.

(*d*) Witnesses whose evidence could be helpful should be asked to attend the hearing and if necessary a witness order should be obtained. Such witnesses could include, for example, a former employee who has witnessed a display of hostility or to whom an admission of discrimination has been made. The witness should be closely cross-questioned before the hearing, however, particularly where, as in the case of a dismissed former employee, there is a risk that the witness could be motivated by a desire to harm the employer.

104.12 ADVICE FOR RESPONDENTS

There are also key steps which employers and others should take in order to avoid unlawful discrimination and demonstrate that they have done so. In particular:

(*a*) The starting point is not to entrust decisions affecting employees or job applicants to managers or other employees who have shown that they cannot be relied upon to make decisions objectively and consistently. In particular, managers who display racist or sexist attitudes or who disparage the abilities of disabled workers should not be allowed to take decisions relating to recruitment, promotion or dismissal.

(*b*) Even when these obviously unreliable managers have been excluded, it is unsafe to rely simply on the good faith and good sense of managers, supervisors, interviewers and others who are called upon to make decisions about employees and job applicants. *Training* is essential.

(*c*) The reasons for shortlisting and selection decisions must be recorded, so that those decisions can if necessary be explained.

(*d*) Statistics should be monitored, so that any apparent patterns of discrimination can be addressed and corrected internally before they become part of the material for a tribunal hearing.

(*e*) It is essential that a *Questionnaire*, whether or not the statutory forms are used, should be answered promptly, carefully and accurately.

105 Exceptions

105.1 GENERAL COMMENTS

The circumstances in which discrimination is not unlawful fall broadly into two categories:

(*a*) cases which fall entirely outside the ambit of one or more of the discrimination laws; and

(*b*) cases which are within the area which is broadly covered but which are subject to exceptions in particular circumstances.

105.2 OUTSIDE THE AMBIT

None of the discrimination laws covers discrimination in relation to employment which is entirely *Overseas*, although publishing or causing the publication in Great Britain of an *Advertisement* relating to such employment can be unlawful under the *RRA 1976*.

Neither the *SDA 1975* nor the *RRA 1976* nor the *DDA 1995* covers discrimination in relation to employment in a *Statutory Office*, although a recent case suggests that that exclusion may be overridden by the Equal Treatment Directive.

The *DDA 1995* does not apply to employment:

(*a*) on a *Ship*;

(*b*) on an *Aircraft* or *Hovercraft*;

(*c*) in the *Armed Services*;

(*d*) as a *Prison Officer*;

(*e*) as a member of a fire brigade who is or may be required by the terms of service to engage in firefighting (there is a similar exclusion for posts in the service of the Crown where firefighting may be involved).

A *Police* officer is not an employee in the normal sense of the word. The *EPA 1970*, *SDA 1975* and *RRA 1976* expressly treat the holding of the office of constable as employment, but the *DDA 1995* does not. Furthermore the *DDA 1995* expressly excludes employment or service in various specialist police forces, such as the British Transport Police.

The most important exemption from the employment provisions of the *DDA 1995* is that for *Small Businesses*. Originally the exemption applied in relation to an employer who had fewer than 20 employees, but the figure of 20 was reduced to 15 with effect from 1 December 1998.

There is no corresponding exception in the *SDA 1975* or the *RRA 1976*, but the employment provisions of the *RRA 1976* (except in relation to *Advertisements* and *Victimisation*) do not apply to employment for the purposes of a *Private Household*. The latter exclusion was formerly also contained in the *SDA 1975*. There is now no blanket exclusion under the *SDA 1975* for employment in a private household, but such employment can in certain circumstances be covered by one of the *Genuine Occupational Qualification* exceptions.

In general, employment in the *Armed Services* is covered by the *EPA 1970*, the *SDA 1975* and the *RRA 1976* (subject to some limitations and special rules of procedure), but the *SDA 1975* does not cover discrimination in admission to any cadet training corps administered by the Ministry of Defence.

The *SDA 1975* also excludes employment as a *Minister of Religion* or any other employment for the purposes of an organised religion (where the employment is limited to one sex or to persons who are not undergoing and have not undergone *Gender Reassignment*), where that limitation is imposed so as to comply with the doctrines of the religion or to avoid offending the religious susceptibilities of a significant number of its followers. This means that, for example, a woman could not complain under the *SDA 1975* about the refusal of the Roman Catholic Church to consider her for ordination as a priest.

105.3 EXCEPTIONS TO THE GENERAL PROVISIONS

The *EPA 1970*, the *SDA 1975*, the *RRA 1976* and the *DDA 1995* all contain exceptions relating to:

(*a*) acts done under *Statutory Authority*;

(*b*) acts done for the purpose of safeguarding *National Security*;

(*c*) employment provided pursuant to the purposes of a *Charity*.

The *Statutory Authority* and *National Security* exceptions in the *SDA 1975* and the *EPA 1970* are more limited than those in the *RRA 1976* and the *DDA 1995*. Under the *DDA 1995*, there is an exception for *Supported Employment* even where such employment is not provided by a *Charity*.

The *SDA 1975* and the *RRA 1976* both contain provisions which permit discrimination in certain circumstances in relation to employment as a player or competitor in *Sport*. There is no corresponding exception in the *DDA 1995*, but a failure to employ a disabled person would clearly be justifiable in a case where the disability would prevent him or her from competing effectively.

The *SDA 1975* contains exceptions permitting discrimination in certain circumstances in relation to:

(*a*) Insurance;

(*b*) *Communal Accommodation*.

Both the *SDA 1975* and the *RRA 1976* permit very limited measures of *Positive Discrimination*. There are also provisions in the *RRA 1976* relating to:

(*a*) the *Special Needs* of persons of a particular racial group;

(*b*) education or training for *Workers from Overseas*.

Both the *SDA 1975* and the *RRA 1976* also provide for the GOQ exception in very limited circumstances.

106 Facility

The *SDA 1975*, the *RRA 1976* and the *DDA 1995* each covers discrimination in relation to the access of an employee to any benefit, facility or service. This issue is dealt with under *Benefits*. Where the right to a facility is contractual, then a claim will normally be brought under the *EPA 1970* rather than the *SDA 1975*, but it is prudent to specify both Acts in a complaint to tribunal.

Access to a grievance procedure would be an example of a facility, but it is unnecessary, when presenting a complaint, to state whether that complaint relates to a facility as opposed to a benefit or service.

107 Fair Employment

None of the discrimination laws contains an express requirement for employers or others to act fairly. The *DDA 1995* comes closest to such a requirement, with the obligation to make *Reasonable Adjustments*.

Employers and others who do not adopt fair employment practices, however, will find it difficult to comply with their statutory obligations. It is in practice a very difficult exercise to avoid disability discrimination or direct or indirect racial or sex discrimination and at the same time to be unfair, subjective and erratic in other respects. The organisations which are the most likely to comply with the law are those which have comprehensive *Equal Opportunity Policies* promising their employees and job applicants fair employment practices and which take effective measures to implement those policies.

108 Flexible Working

A rigid adherence to particular employment requirements and methods of working can make employers vulnerable to complaints of *Indirect Discrimination*. For example, indirect sex discrimination is likely to occur if an employer:

(*a*) automatically says no every time a full-time employee asks to go part-time because of her childcare commitments;

(*b*) rejects out of hand all job share requests;

(*c*) is unwilling to consider modifying start and finish times for employees who cannot work unsocial hours;

(*d*) insists that all employees should be prepared to relocate, even when the need hardly ever arises.

Furthermore, an organisation which is wedded to established practices and working arrangements and is resistant to change will have difficulty in making the *Reasonable Adjustments* which are required under the *DDA 1995*.

Conversely, employers are more likely to comply with the law if they adopt working arrangements which are as flexible as the needs of the business or organisation permits. Furthermore, employees are more likely to be loyal and enthusiastic if they can see that real efforts are being made to accommodate their personal and domestic circumstances.

The recent Whitley Council agreement on equal opportunities (see *National Health Service*) contains a good example of a comprehensive and imaginative policy on flexible working. There is a policy statement that employers should develop positive flexible working arrangements which allow people to balance work responsibilities with other aspects of their lives. Policies should be developed by agreement on a wide range of flexible working arrangements. These include arrangements which are already widely used, such as:

(*a*) part-time working;

(*b*) job sharing;

(*c*) flexi-time;

(*d*) flexible rostering;

(*e*) annual hours contracts.

The agreement also requires consideration to be given to more radical options, such as:

(*a*) working during the school term but not the school holidays;

(*b*) matching working time to school time;

(*c*) tele-working (working from home with a computer or telecommunication link to the office);

(*d*) voluntary reduced working time;

(*e*) work patterns under which, by agreement, days off can be irregular.

It is essential that employers who adopt and agree flexible working arrangements should do so for both men and women. It cannot and must not be assumed that it is only women who have responsibilities for childcare or for dependent relatives.

Employers may lawfully discriminate positively in favour of all disabled workers, but not in favour of one or more categories at the expense of other categories of disabled worker.

109 Formal Investigations

Each of the statutory Commissions has the power to carry out a formal investigation. The provisions relating to formal investigations are:

(*a*) *sections 57–61* of the *SDA 1975*;

(*b*) *sections 48–52* of the *RRA 1976*;

(*c*) *Schedule 3* to the *Disability Rights Commission Act 1999*.

Where the terms of reference of a formal investigation confine it to the activities of named persons (which expression includes companies and organisations) and the Commission propose to investigate whether a named person has acted unlawfully, the Commission must give that person the opportunity to make oral and written representations.

Each Commission, when carrying out a formal investigation, has extensive powers to demand information or documents.

A formal investigation may lead to the service of a *Non-Discrimination Notice*. There are provisions in *section 5* of the *Disability Rights Commission Act 1999* under which the DRC, if it believes that a person has committed or is committing an unlawful act, may (either following a formal investigation or as an alternative to an investigation) enter into an agreement with that person under which:

(*a*) the Commission undertakes not to take enforcement action; and

(*b*) the other party undertakes not to commit any further unlawful acts of the same kind and also to take any action which may be specified in the agreement.

The DRC may apply to a county court (or sheriff court in Scotland) for an order requiring the other party to comply with any such agreement.

110 Gender

The word ‘gender’ is commonly used in equal opportunity policies instead of the word ‘sex’, as one of the matters which must not be taken into account in selection and other employment decisions.

The word ‘gender’ does not appear in the *SDA 1975*, except in relation to *Gender Reassignment*, but generally the terms ‘sex discrimination’ and ‘discrimination on grounds of gender’ are interchangeable.

111 Gender Based Criteria

There are two clear cases where a particular act can be said to be one of *Direct Discrimination* by reason of the application of a gender related criterion.

The first case is where the reason for the act complained of is a factor or state of affairs which itself arises as a result of an act of direct discrimination, as in *James v Eastleigh Borough Council* [*1990*] *IRLR 288*. In that case, the difference in treatment was based on a difference in State retirement age which itself was discriminatory as between men and women.

The second case is where a woman is treated less favourably because of her pregnancy, which is a condition unique to women. It was said by Lord Keith of Kinkel in *Webb v EMO Air Cargo (UK) Limited* [*1993*] *IRLR 27* that:

> 'There can be no doubt that in general to dismiss a woman because she is pregnant or to refuse to employ a woman of childbearing age because she may become pregnant is unlawful direct discrimination. Childbearing and the capacity for childbearing are characteristics of the female sex. So to apply these characteristics as the criterion for dismissal or refusal to employ is to apply a gender-based criterion . . .'.

Case law does not, however, support the extension of the principle of gender based criteria to other cases where a person is treated less favourably because of a particular physical characteristic or medical condition, even if that characteristic or condition is unique either to men or to women. The case of *Webb v EMO Air Cargo (UK) Limited* was referred to the ECJ, [*1994*] *IRLR 482*. The judgment referred to the earlier case of *Handels* [*1991*] *IRLR 31*, in which 'the Court drew a clear distinction between pregnancy and illness, even where the illness is attributable to pregnancy but manifests itself after the maternity leave. . . . there is no reason to distinguish such an illness from any other illness'.

This principle was further developed by the ECJ in *Brown v Rentokil Limited* [*1998*] *IRLR 445*. On the one hand, if a woman is treated less favourably because of absences during her pregnancy, caused by the pregnancy itself or a pregnancy-related illness, then that is an act of direct sex discrimination; on the other hand, if she is ill after her return from maternity leave, and even if that illness is attributable to her pregnancy (and accordingly results from a condition which is unique to women), that absence through illness is to be treated in the same way as any other absence through illness.

112 Gender Reassignment

The *SDA 1975* was amended with effect from 1 May 1999 by the *Sex Discrimination (Gender Reassignment) Regulations 1999* (*SI 1999 No 1102*). Under the new *section 2A*, the definition of discrimination was extended to include direct discrimination (but not indirect discrimination) in relation to gender reassignment. There is discrimination for the purposes of the *SDA 1975* if a person is treated less favourably than other persons are or would be treated on the ground that he or she:

(*a*) intends to undergo gender reassignment;

(*b*) is undergoing gender reassignment; or

(*c*) has undergone gender reassignment.

For these and other provisions in relation to gender reassignment see *Transsexuals* and *Genuine Occupational Qualifications*.

113 Genetic Testing

113.1 WHAT IS GENETIC TESTING?

Advances in science bring challenges as well as benefits. The availability of genetic tests of individuals raises a variety of employment questions, including equal opportunities concerns. Genetic tests take several different forms, but commonly involve an examination designed to find out if there is an otherwise undetectable disease-related 'genotype' which may indicate an increased chance of an individual developing a specific disease in the future. Genetic testing has been the subject of a report issued in 1999 by the Human Genetics Advisory Commission (HGAC) and a Code of Practice, revised in 1999 and issued by the Association of British Insurers in connection with the use by insurers of results from genetic tests in deciding whether, and on what terms, to make insurance cover available. In May 2000, a Private Members' Bill was introduced into Parliament, albeit with little prospect of becoming law, requiring that genetic test results should only be used for medical and clinical purposes, and after the informal consent of the patient had been given. The worldwide publicity given in 2000 to the Human Genome Project illustrates that ethical debates about issues raised by advances in genetic science are here to stay. Clearly some of those debates impact on employment.

113.2 REASONS FOR GENETIC TESTING

Genetic testing offers a variety of possible benefits:

(*a*) diagnosis and treatment of a condition;

(*b*) provision of information about a person's future risk of contracting certain specific inherited diseases;

(*c*) ascertaining whether the person carries a gene for an inherited disorder;

(*d*) ascertaining whether the person may be susceptible to a condition (such as heart disease) which is technically described as 'multi-factorial', i.e. where the gene is not the only cause of the disorder but may, together with other factors such as living conditions and behaviour, lead to the person having the condition.

Employers and, perhaps especially, their insurers, see a variety of benefits from genetic testing. For instance, it may permit the identification of job applicants whose genetic make-up might render them a danger to themselves or other (e.g. drivers or pilots susceptible to heart attacks). Testing may also enable screening of individuals who might have a genetic sensitivity to a particular feature of the working environment (such as chemicals necessarily used in that environment). But opponents of genetic testing question its accuracy and its value. Testing also carries with it the potential for discriminatory treatment.

113.3 HGAC RECOMMENDATIONS

Amongst other matters, the HGAC report expressed the following views:

(*a*) it would be unacceptable for genetic testing to be used by employers specifically to screen out or dismiss individuals who may essentially have a shorter working life or increased propensity to be absent from work due to sickness;

(*b*) an employee should, as a general principle, have the right to know their genetic testing (although the need for exceptions to that general principle was acknowledged);

(*c*) a person should not be required to disclose past genetic test results unless there is clear evidence that this information is essential to assess his or her ability to do the job safely or susceptibility to harm from undertaking the job;

(*d*) genetic tests should only be used for employment purposes if subject to assured levels of accuracy and reliability;

(*e*) the results of the test should be communicated to the individual unless he or she has asked not to receive the results and professional advice should be made available;

(*f*) the interpretation of test results should be carefully considered;

(*g*) the Health and Safety Commission should be responsible for monitoring use of genetic tests at work and the issue should be reviewed in five years in the light of continuing developments.

113.4 LEGAL IMPLICATIONS

In the UK, unlike certain other jurisdictions including France and Austria, there is no legislation which specifically addresses the issue of genetic testing in the workplace and the *Genetic Testing (Consent and Confidentiality) Bill* introduced into Parliament in May 2000 had little chance of being enacted. However, genetic testing may have ramifications under a variety of current enactments.

It is, arguably, a curiosity (and perhaps a weakness in the drafting) of the *DDA 1995* that it does not protect an individual who is not disabled, but who is identified, as a result of a genetic test, as being at risk of having a disability at a future date.

In cases where the condition identified by genetic testing is gender or race-specific, the *SDA 1975* or *RRA 1976* may afford at least some safeguards. Haemophilia, for instance, is a condition found in men but not women. Thus to refuse to offer employment to a person because genetic testing reveals that he has haemophilia might constitute indirect discrimination on the ground of sex, although the employer might in an appropriate case be able to demonstrate an objective justification for the requirement that the employee should not have haemophilia. It may even be arguable that the requirement is *Gender Based*, so as to amount to *Direct Discrimination* and be incapable of justification. Members of ethnic groups which are particularly susceptible to certain medical conditions (an example might be the relatively high incidence of sickle cell disorder in Afro-Caribbean people in comparison to white people) may be able to complain under the *RRA 1976* if discriminated against in the context of genetic testing.

The *Data Protection Act 1998* may assist employees. The results of genetic testing would almost inevitably fall within the ambit of *section 2(e)* of the Act as 'sensitive personal data', i.e. personal data relating to the individual's 'physical or mental health or condition'. To comply with the regime established by the data protection law, a data controller must observe various conditions, such as obtaining express consent from the individual. At the time of writing, the government is reviewing whether to include the processing of genetic data in the categories of 'accessible processing' that appears particularly likely to cause substantial damage or stress to data subjects, or otherwise significantly prejudices their freedom. If genetic data processing were to be included, data controllers would need to notify the Data Protection Commissioner (formerly known as the Data Protection Registrar) of an intention to begin processing genetic data. Breach of the notification requirement is an offence. The Commissioner has already indicated an awareness that obtaining the consent of a person to the processing of their genetic data will not necessarily by itself mean that the personal data have been processed fairly and lawfully. If the employer unreasonably exploits his superior bargaining strength to obtain the consent, that will constitute a breach of the Act. To comply with the Act, a requirement that an applicant or employee undertakes a genetic test would have to be relevant to the job or workplace in question.

Human Rights issues may also be relevant. Requiring an applicant or employee to take a genetic test might constitute a breach of the right to privacy and family life and, in appropriate circumstances, an individual might be able to make a complaint under the *Human Rights Act 1998* or the *European Convention on Human Rights*. Similar issues have already arisen in respect of an AIDS screening test. In *X v Commission of the European Community* [*1995*] *IRLR 320*, the European Court ruled that *Article 8* of the European Convention includes in particular a person's right to keep his state of health secret, and although pre-recruitment medical examinations served a legitimate interest of the employer (the European Commission itself) that did not justify the carrying-out of a test against the will of the person concerned. This was so even though, if the individual concerned, after being properly informed, withholds his consent to a test which the medical officer appropriately considers necessary in order to evaluate the person's suitability for the post in question, the employer cannot be obliged to take the risk of recruiting him.

114 Genuine Occupational Qualifications (GOQs)

114.1 GENERAL PRINCIPLES

The law recognises that there are exceptional circumstances in which a person's gender or racial group is a genuine qualification for a particular job. Where this GOQ exception applies, the law permits discrimination in relation to:

(*a*) recruitment or selection;

(*b*) promoting or transferring an employee to the job;

(*c*) training an employee for the work involved;

(*d*) not allowing a *Contract Worker* to do the work or continue to do it.

The *SDA 1975* and the *RRA 1976* also permit discrimination relating to the offer of a partnership, where one of the GOQ exceptions would apply if employment were being offered.

Where a job is covered by the GOQ exception, the *SDA 1975* contains additional provisions relating to persons who intend to undergo, are undergoing or have undergone *Gender Reassignment*. Where, because of gender reassignment, the person is or will not be of the gender required, the Act permits discrimination not only in the respects mentioned above but also in dismissing the person from the relevant post.

The Code of Practice under the *SDA 1975* states that there are very few instances in which a job will qualify for a GOQ on the ground of sex. There are even fewer jobs where the GOQ exception under the *RRA 1976* applies. It is not safe for an employer to act on the assumption that a job of a particular kind is always covered by the exception. It is necessary to look closely at the circumstances of each individual case.

The GOQ exception can apply where only some of the duties of the job call for (as the case may be) a man or woman or member of a particular racial group. The employer must consider, however, whether there are existing employees of the required gender or racial group:

(*a*) who are capable of carrying out the relevant duties;

(*b*) whom it would be reasonable to employ on those duties; and

(*c*) whose numbers are sufficient to meet the employer's likely requirements in respect of those duties without undue inconvenience.

114.2 THE RRA 1976 – PERSONAL SERVICES

The most important GOQ exception in the *RRA 1976* is that relating to social and welfare work. The exception applies if:

(*a*) the holder of the job provides persons of a particular racial group with personal services promoting their welfare; and

(*b*) those services can most effectively be provided by a person of that same racial group.

The case of *Tottenham Green Under Fives' v Marshall* [*1989*] *IRLR 147* is an example of a case where the exception can apply. The centre ran a nursery for children aged between two and five, of whom 84 per cent were of Afro-Caribbean origin. When a nursery worker of Afro-Caribbean origin left, the advertisement for her replacement stipulated an Afro-Caribbean worker. The duties of the post included reading books in Afro-Caribbean dialect and talking to the children in the dialect. This was a genuine duty. It was a personal service which could most effectively be provided by a worker of Afro-Caribbean origin.

On the other hand, in *London Borough of Lambeth v CRE [1990] IRLR 230*, the Council advertised for Afro-Caribbean or Asian applicants for the post of assistant head and group manager in the housing benefits department. These racial groups were stipulated because over half of the tenants were of Afro-Caribbean or Asian ethnic origin. It was held by the Court of Appeal that the GOQ exception did not cover these jobs. For the exception to apply, there must generally be direct contact between the holder of the job and the person to whom personal services are to be given; in this case, the posts were management jobs involving minimal contact with the public.

114.3 THE RRA 1976 – AUTHENTICITY

The *RRA 1976* also states that the GOQ exception can apply if a person of a particular racial group is required for reasons of authenticity in a job involving:

(*a*) participation in a dramatic performance or other entertainment;

(*b*) specified work of various kinds as an artist's or photographic model; or

(*c*) working in a place where food or drink is provided and consumed (the need for authenticity being because of the particular setting).

114.4 THE SDA 1975 – PERSONAL SERVICES

The *SDA 1975* contains a similar but slightly broader exception to that contained in the *RRA 1976*, for jobs where personal services are to be provided. It is broader than that in the *RRA 1976* because it applies not only to personal services promoting the welfare of individuals, but also to personal services promoting their education and to similar personal services.

The White Paper which preceded the enactment of the *SDA 1975* gave the example of a team of probation officers, where it may be necessary to maintain a team including members of each sex. Another example would be women from particular minority racial groups who have had little contact with men outside their own families and who would be more likely to respond to a female social worker than to a male social worker.

There is a supplementary GOQ exception which applies where the job involves providing vulnerable individuals with personal services promoting their welfare or similar personal services. The GOQ exception applies if in the reasonable view of the employer the services cannot effectively be provided by a person whilst that person is undergoing gender reassignment. This exception permits discrimination, however, only against a person who intends to undergo or is undergoing gender reassignment; not one who has already undergone gender reassignment.

114.5 THE SDA 1975 – AUTHENTICITY

There are two cases under the *SDA 1975* where being of a particular gender can be a GOQ because the essential nature of the job calls for a person of that gender, so that the essential nature of the job would be materially different if carried out by a person not of that gender. The requirement can be:

(*a*) for reasons of physiology (excluding physical strength or stamina) – an obvious example would be certain modelling jobs; or (*b*) for reasons of authenticity, in dramatic performances or other entertainment.

114.6 THE SDA 1975 – DECENCY OR PRIVACY

There is a GOQ exception where a job needs to be held by (for example) a man to preserve decency or privacy because:

(*a*) it is likely to involve physical contact with men in circumstances where they might reasonably object to its being carried out by a woman; or

(*b*) the job holder is likely to do his work in circumstances where men might reasonably object to the presence of a woman because they are in a state of undress or are using sanitary facilities.

In *Lasertop Limited v Webster* [*1997*] *IRLR 498,* a salesperson's duties involved taking prospective members on a tour of a health club which was for women only. The duties included taking the prospective members into the changing room, sauna area, sunbed room and toilet. Women using these facilities would be likely to object if it was a man who came into these areas with the prospective members. The business was a new business, which had not yet recruited many female employees. The GOQ exception applied because the duties which involved going into the changing room and other areas could not be allocated to female employees without undue inconvenience.

There is a supplementary exception relating to gender reassignment where a job holder may be liable to be called upon to perform intimate physical searches pursuant to statutory powers. This exception permits discrimination against a person who intends to undergo, is undergoing or has undergone gender reassignment.

114.7 THE SDA 1975 – A PRIVATE HOME

The *SDA 1975* as originally enacted contained a general exception for employment for the purposes of a private household. The *RRA 1976* still contains a similar exception.

In the *SDA 1975*, that broad exception has now been replaced by a much more limited GOQ provision. Where, for example, the exception is relied upon in order to have a post filled by a woman, it applies if:

(*a*) the job is likely to involve the job holder doing her work or living in a private home;

(*b*) the job holder is likely to have a degree of physical or social contact with a person living in the home or knowledge of intimate details of that person's life;

(*c*) objection might reasonably be taken to allowing a man that degree of contact or that knowledge;

(*d*) accordingly the job needs to be held by a woman.

There is a supplementary provision where objection might reasonably be taken to allowing a person who is undergoing or has undergone gender reassignment the above mentioned degree of physical or social contact or knowledge of intimate details.

114.8 THE SDA 1975 – LIVING IN

The next exception under the *SDA 1975* applies where the nature or location of the establishment makes it impracticable for the job holder to live elsewhere than in premises provided by the employer. It applies if:

(*a*) the only available premises are lived in or normally lived in only by men (or only by women as the case may be); and

(*b*) those premises are not equipped with separate sleeping accommodation for both sexes and sanitary facilities which could be used by women in privacy from men.

There will be very few circumstances in which this GOQ exception could apply. It can be relied on by an employer only if it is not reasonable to expect the employer either:

(*a*) to equip the premises with accommodation and facilities for both sexes; or

(*b*) to provide other premises for persons of the gender not already catered for.

There is a supplementary GOQ exception relating to gender reassignment. This exception applies if reasonable objection could be taken, for the purpose of preserving decency and privacy, to the job holder sharing accommodation and facilities with either sex whilst undergoing gender reassignment. The exception can be relied on only to permit discrimination against a person who intends to undergo or is undergoing gender reassignment; not a person who has already undergone gender reassignment. Furthermore, this supplementary exception is also subject to the important proviso that an employer can rely on it only if it is not reasonable to expect the employer either to equip the premises with suitable accommodation or to make alternative arrangements.

114.9 THE SDA 1975 – SINGLE SEX ESTABLISHMENTS

The next GOQ exception applies to jobs in hospitals, prisons or other establishments for persons requiring special care, supervision or attention. The conditions are:

(*a*) those persons are all of one sex (disregarding any of the opposite sex whose presence is exceptional); and

(*b*) it is reasonable, having regard to the essential character of the establishment or the relevant part of the establishment, that the job should not be held by a person of the opposite sex to that of the inmates.

114.10 THE SDA 1975 – DUTIES OUTSIDE THE UK

The next GOQ exception is one of the rare cases where the law permits discrimination in deference to the prejudices of others. Sex discrimination (usually against women) is permitted if the job needs to be held by a man because it is likely to involve the performance of duties outside the UK in a country whose laws or customs are such that the duties could not, or could not effectively, be performed by a woman. There is no corresponding exception in the *RRA 1976*, even for a job which involves carrying out some duties in a country where members of a particular racial group would not be permitted to work (or even not allowed entry).

114.11 THE SDA 1975 – MARRIED COUPLES

The remaining GOQ exception under the *SDA 1975* is where a job is one of two to be held by a married couple, for example where a married couple are required for the management of a public house or a club. There will be a need to look again at this exception if and when the *SDA 1975* is amended to prohibit discrimination on grounds of sexual orientation. Under the exception as it stands, gay couples can lawfully be excluded from consideration for such posts.

114.12 PRACTICAL ADVICE

The legal annex to the Code of Practice under the *SDA 1975* states that a GOQ 'is not an automatic exception for general categories of jobs. In every case it will be necessary for an employer to show that the criteria detailed in the *SDA 1975* apply to the job or part of the job in question'.

Furthermore, if an employer has previously relied on a GOQ exception when filling a particular post, it cannot be assumed that the exception will apply next time the post has to be filled. The relevant circumstances may have changed. The EOC code expressly recommends that any such job should be re-examined whenever the post falls vacant to see whether the GOQ exception still applies.

These points apply equally to the GOQ exceptions under the *RRA 1976*.

115 Grading

For the purposes of the *EPA 1970*, the fact that the complainant and the comparator have different grades under a grading scheme can be a *Material Factor* defence, even though the two employees are employed on:

(*a*) *Like Work*;

(*b*) work of *Equal Value*; or

(*c*) work rated as equivalent under a *Job Evaluation* Scheme.

This principle was recognised by the Court of Appeal in the case of *National Vulcan Engineering Insurance Group Limited v Wade* [*1978*] *IRLR 225*. It was said in that case that a grading system according to skill, ability and experience is an integral part of good business management. A defence based on the different grades of the complainant and the comparator will not be upheld, however, if the way in which the grading scheme is applied includes any direct or indirect sex discrimination.

An employee can present a complaint under the *SDA 1975*, the *RRA 1976* or the *DDA 1995* if there is discrimination in relation to a grading decision. If because of the discrimination the employee has been given a lower grade than another person has or would have been given he or she can complain of having been subjected to a detriment or denied access to a benefit or facility.

116 Grievances

The law does not permit sex discrimination, racial discrimination or disability discrimination in access to the grievance procedure or in the handling of individual grievances.

The fact that a complainant has pursued an internal grievance before presenting a complaint to a tribunal may be a ground for extending the *Time Limit* where the complaint to a tribunal is out of time.

117 Gypsies

In the non-employment case of *Commission for Racial Equality v Dutton* [*1989*] *IRLR 8*, it was held by the Court of Appeal that gypsies could constitute a *Racial Group* for the purposes of the *RRA 1976* because they have a common race or *Ethnic Origin*.

If a gypsy were to apply for a job and be turned down for lack of a permanent address, that requirement could amount to indirect discrimination against him or her, unless the employer could show it to be justifiable in the particular circumstances. Turning a gypsy down because he or she is a gypsy would be direct discrimination, being less favourable treatment on racial grounds.

A person does not, however, become a member of a racial group, for the purposes of the *RRA 1976*, simply by adopting a travelling way of life. Far more than that is required – see *Ethnic Origin*.

118 Harassment

118.1 GENERAL PRINCIPLES

Neither the *SDA 1975* nor the *RRA 1976* nor the *DDA 1995* contains the word 'harassment'. Under *section 6(2)(b)* of the *SDA 1975*, however, it is unlawful to discriminate against a person employed at an establishment in Great Britain by subjecting that person to any *Detriment*. There are similar provisions in *section 4(2)(b)* of the *RRA 1976* and *section 4(2)(d)* of the *DDA 1995*. Harassment, in its various forms, is one of the most serious detriments to which employees can be subjected.

The European Union Code of Practice which is referred to below defines sexual harassment as: 'unwanted conduct of a sexual nature, or other conduct based on sex affecting the dignity of women and men at work'.

The Code goes on to say that sexual harassment pollutes the working environment and can have a devastating effect on the health, confidence, morale and performance of those affected by it.

Although the Code of Practice was drawn up specifically in relation to sexual harassment, the comments about the pollution of the working environment and the devastating effect upon individual victims apply equally to racial harassment and harassment of the disabled. These forms of harassment commonly involve verbal or physical aggression from a position of power by a person who has been placed in authority and abuses the trust placed in him, or by a vicious pack of employees who use their superior numbers to pick on an individual. *Sexual* harassment also commonly has these elements of aggression and of bullying or intimidation, but these are not necessary elements of the offence.

The key questions in any particular case are:

(*a*) Have all or some of the acts complained of been found to have occurred?

(*b*) On the basis of the acts which have been proved, has the complainant suffered a detriment?

(*c*) In a case where the words or acts complained of were not aimed directly at the complainant, has the necessary link been established?

(*d*) Does the treatment complained of amount to discrimination within the terms of the relevant Act?

(*e*) Subject to the defence mentioned below, is the employer liable for that act of discrimination?

(*f*) Can the employer establish the defence of having taken such steps as were reasonably practicable to prevent the act of discrimination or acts of that description?

118.2 PROVING THE ACTS COMPLAINED OF

Harassment, particularly sexual harassment, frequently takes place in the absence of witnesses. In many cases, the employment tribunal has only the evidence of the complainant and the alleged harasser(s).

Sometimes, in a case of sexual or racial harassment or harassment of a disabled person, the complainant may allege that several fellow employees have ganged up on him or her and participated in the alleged acts. At first sight, the complainant in such a case may appear to be at a serious disadvantage, because it will be one person's evidence, that of the complainant, against the evidence of the alleged harassers. It is, however, by no means unknown for the evidence of the one person to be believed, if that evidence carries credibility, particularly if the evidence of the alleged harassers contains inconsistencies and contradictions.

It is difficult for an alleged harasser to respond to, and for an employment tribunal to form a view on, allegations of harassment which are expressed in general terms. Before the hearing takes place, the complainant should state exactly what has been said or done to her (or him) and where and when each incident took place. If sufficient details are not given in the application to the tribunal, then further particulars should be requested and given.

It is also desirable to establish before the hearing whether there were witnesses to any of the alleged incidents. If there is a fellow employee who witnessed one or more incidents, but is unwilling to give evidence, and the complainant does not wish to take the risk of asking for a witness order to compel an unwilling witness to attend, the name of the fellow employee should nevertheless be disclosed to the respondent(s) so that the latter can then consider whether the witness should be called.

Employees who are being subjected to harassment are frequently advised to keep a diary, giving the date and details of each incident. Such a record can be relevant evidence in support of a complaint. Keeping the diary is also, however, an indication that the complainant is aware of the potential legal implications of the harassment and underlines the need for the complainant to be able to explain any failure to try to get the harassment stopped by making an internal complaint at the time.

Whether or not a written record is kept, a failure to speak up at the time is often relied on by respondents to challenge the credibility of the complainant. It can also be relevant to the question whether any real detriment was suffered, as mentioned in **118.3** below. If the complainant did speak about the harassment at the time, even to someone outside the workplace, such as a family member or close friend, the evidence of that person can be relevant at the hearing of the complaint. The evidence of a person who was not present, and whose only information has come from the complainant, cannot prove that the harassment did take place; that evidence can, however, help to explain why the complainant did not speak up at the time and it can also help to show how much distress was caused to the complainant.

From the employer's point of view, once a complaint of harassment has been received and particularised, it is important to carry out a rigorous internal investigation without delay. If harassment has in fact taken place, it is better to find out at the outset, discipline the offender(s) and offer redress to the complainant, rather than to incur the odium and unwelcome publicity of fighting a complaint which is well founded.

118.3 DETRIMENT

Important advice was given to tribunals by the EAT in the case of *Reed and Bull Information Systems Limited v Stedman [1999] IRLR 299*. The complainant was employed as a secretary for just over a year. She made a number of allegations against the manager to whom she reported. She alleged that he made remarks to her which had sexual connotations; that on one occasion he made an attempt to look up her skirt and laughed when she angrily left the room; that he frequently stood behind her when telling other colleagues dirty jokes (but ceased to do so after she complained). Her allegations were upheld by the tribunal, which also found that she had made complaints to her mother and to colleagues at work, but not to her own manager (apart from the complaint about the dirty jokes) or to other managers. There was also a finding that colleagues in the personnel department were aware of the complainant's deteriorating health, although not of the harassment which was causing that deterioration. Eventually she left because of the harassment and because of the effect of it on her health.

The tribunal found that the respondent had discriminated against the complainant, contrary to the *SDA 1975*, in subjecting her to a detriment and dismissing her. The finding of dismissal was because there had been a failure to investigate the cause of her illness and because the complaints which she had made to other members of staff (albeit not managers) had been dismissed by those members of staff. The employer was responsible for these omissions by its employees in the personnel department and elsewhere. There had been a breach of the implied term of trust and confidence and the complainant had been entitled to treat herself as constructively dismissed. Even though she had not completed the then qualifying period of two years for a complaint of unfair dismissal, she was entitled to be compensated for her dismissal under *section 6(2)(b)* of the *SDA 1975*.

The EAT dismissed an appeal against the findings and gave guidance which included the following matters:

(*a*) A characteristic of sexual harassment is that it undermines the victim's dignity at work. It creates an 'offensive' or 'hostile' environment for the victim and an arbitrary barrier to sexual equality in the workplace.

(*b*) The essential characteristic of sexual harassment is that it is words or conduct which are unwelcome to the recipient; it is for recipients to decide for themselves what is acceptable to them and what they regard as offensive.

(*c*) It is particularly important in cases of alleged sexual harassment that the fact-finding tribunal should not carve up the case into a series of specific incidents and try and measure the harm or detriment in relation to each.

The EAT illustrated this last point by reference to the facts of the case. A blatant act of a sexual nature, such as deliberately looking up the complainant's skirt, may well make other incidents, such as asking to be shown personal photographs which she was looking at, take on a different colour and significance. Once unwelcome sexual interest has been shown by a man in a female employee, she may well feel bothered about attentions which, in a different context, would appear quite unobjectionable.

Once the tribunal has assembled the totality of the matters complained of, and looked at the complaint as a whole, the tribunal must then decide whether the complainant was thereby subjected to a detriment. The EAT recognised that there may well be difficult factual issues to resolve in order to decide whether the conduct now complained of was unwelcome. The following guidance was given:

(*a*) Some conduct, if not expressly invited, could properly be described as unwelcome; a woman does not, for example, have to make it clear in advance that she does not want to be touched in a sexual manner.

(*b*) If the conduct about which a complainant now complains to the tribunal would normally be regarded as unexceptionable behaviour, the question is whether by words or conduct the complainant had made it clear that she found such conduct unwelcome.

(*c*) It is not necessary for a woman to make a public fuss to indicate her disapproval; walking out of the room might be sufficient. Tribunals will be sensitive to the problems that a victim may face in dealing with a man, perhaps in a senior position to herself, whose defence may be that she was being over-sensitive.

(*d*) Provided that any reasonable person would understand her to be rejecting the conduct of which she was complaining, continuation of that conduct would, generally, be regarded as harassment.

The need to look at the totality of relevant incidents, and at the context in which each incident occurs, was underlined by the decision of the EAT in the case of *Driskel v Peninsular Business Services Limited & Others* [*2000*] *IRLR 151*. In that case, Mrs Driskel complained of a number of remarks made to her by the head of her department. The final remark, the day before he was to interview her for promotion, was his suggestion that she should attend the interview in a short skirt and see-through blouse, showing plenty of cleavage. Mrs Driskel made a formal complaint of sexual harassment, which was rejected after a thorough and genuine internal investigation. She was dismissed after refusing to return to her job unless the manager against whom she had complained was moved elsewhere.

The employment tribunal dismissed Mrs Driskel's complaint of sexual harassment and also her complaint that her dismissal was both unfair and an act of victimisation. In relation to the complaint of sexual harassment, the tribunal carefully examined each incident complained of, accepted Mrs Driskel's evidence but, nevertheless, dismissed her complaint. The EAT upheld the tribunal's decision regarding her dismissal, in view of the genuine investigation which had been carried out by the employers – see DISMISSAL. The EAT upheld, however, Mrs Driskel's appeal in relation to the sexual harassment, finding that the tribunal had fallen into error in the following respects:

(*a*) The tribunal failed to give due weight to the fact that the remarks complained of on the final occasion were made the day before Mrs Driskel was to be interviewed by her manager for promotion. In those 'circumstances she was in receipt of remarks that in an appalling fashion sought to exploit the situation by reference to the sex of, respectively, interviewee and interviewer . . . that which was complained of was objectively prima facie discriminatory and it would need some exceptional findings to negate that inference . . .'.

(*b*) The tribunal looked at the incident in isolation and failed to put it in context 'as the latest in a line of incidents'.

(*c*) The tribunal placed excessive weight on Mrs Driskel's failure to complain immediately, disregarding the obvious risk that an immediate complaint would have damaged her chances of the promotion which she was seeking.

The EAT in *Reed and Bull Information Systems Limited v Stedman* also stated that a one-off act may be sufficient to damage a woman's working environment and constitute a barrier to sexual equality in the workplace, which would constitute a detriment. This principle was illustrated in the earlier case of *Bracebridge Engineering Limited v Darby* [*1990*] *IRLR 3*, in which the employee resigned after a serious assault by two managers. It is also illustrated by the case of *InSitu Cleaning Co Limited v Heads* [*1995*] *IRLR 4*, which is mentioned below.

In all the cases of sexual harassment which have been referred to, a female employee complained of sexual harassment by a male colleague (or in one case two male colleagues). It should be noted, however, that sexual harassment can take many forms. An employee could complain of having been subjected to a detriment contrary to the *SDA 1975* in any of the following cases:

(*a*) a female manager makes sexual advances to a junior subordinate and makes it clear that a positive response will be good for his career;

(*b*) a male secretary working in a typing pool which is otherwise exclusively female is repeatedly made to suffer suggestive remarks which he finds upsetting;

(*c*) a homosexual manager makes sexual advances to a male employee and finds fault with the employee's work when those advances are rejected;

(*d*) a lesbian employee continues to press her attentions on a female colleague after the latter has made it clear that those attentions are unwelcome.

118.4 'SUBJECTING' AND 'TREATMENT'

In most complaints of harassment, whether sexual or racial harassment or harassment of the disabled, the detriment which is alleged by the complainant takes the form of words spoken to the complainant or a physical action, such as an assault or threatened assault, which is directed at the complainant. Can there, however, be a successful complaint of discrimination relating to words or conduct which are not 'aimed' at the complainant? Can the complainant in such circumstances be said to have been subjected to a detriment or treated less favourably than other persons have been or would have been treated?

This issue arose in the case of *De Souza v The Automobile Association [1986] IRLR 103*. A manager made a racially insulting remark about the complainant to a fellow manager. He did not intend the complainant to overhear, but she did so.

It was held by the Court of Appeal that the complaint of racial discrimination failed. In the circumstances of the particular case, simply using a racially insulting word to describe the complainant did not amount to less favourable treatment of her. Because the manager who used the unpleasant word about her did not intend her to hear, and had no reason to believe that she would hear, what he was saying about her, his language was not in any sense 'aimed' at her. This issue is considered further under *Less Favourable Treatment* and *Unintentional Discrimination*.

It should be noted, however, that using a racially insulting term about a fellow employee could be, for example, an act of racial discrimination in the following circumstances:

(*a*) if use of the racial insult to describe the complainant reduces her standing in the eyes of the colleague to whom the remark is made – there would in such case be a clear detriment, and one which the maker of the remark must be taken to have intended, even though the claimant is not aware of it at the time;

(*b*) if the person making the remark knows or ought reasonably to anticipate that the complainant will be made aware of it.

The question of less favourable treatment has also arisen in relation to the display of calendars, posters or extracts from newspapers or magazines depicting nude women. It was held by the EAT in *Stewart v Cleveland Guest (Engineering) Limited [1994] IRLR 440* that it was open to an employment tribunal to decide that employers did not discriminate against a female employee by allowing male employees to display such pictures in the workplace even though they knew that the display was offensive to her. The basis of the tribunal's decision was that a man might have found the pictures as offensive as the complainant did, which meant that it had not been proved that she had been treated less favourably than a man was treated or would have been treated. Employers cannot rely upon similar findings in future cases. It would be open to an employment tribunal to find that:

(*a*) an employer subjects a woman to a detriment by requiring her to walk through parts of a factory or office or other establishment where such pictures are displayed;

(*b*) pictures of a naked female body are more likely to be offensive to a female employee than to a male employee, and a working environment in which men display such pictures in order to leer at them is likely to be hostile and intimidating to a female employee;

(*c*) any employer should be well aware that female employees are more likely than male employees to be upset or offended by such pictures, and must therefore be taken to intend that less favourable treatment.

Furthermore, an employer who allows such pictures to be displayed is at risk of undermining the objectives of any equal opportunity or sexual harassment or dignity at work policy. It is not consistent for an employer to adopt and enforce a policy under which employees of both sexes must be treated with respect at work and at the same time to allow employees to display posters in which women are shown as sex objects.

Arguably, an employee could succeed in a complaint of sexual harassment even if the conduct complained of is neither:

(*a*) conduct which by definition amounts to a detriment (such as an indecent assault);

(*b*) conduct which she has indicated is unwelcome.

Suppose, for example, that a male employee asks a female colleague for a date. They are of equal status and of a similar age and he has no reason at all to believe that his invitation will be unwelcome. She, however, is shy and sensitive and a very private person, determined to keep her working life separate from her personal life. She is very upset by the invitation. It is not an invitation which her male colleague would have made to a male employee, because he is heterosexual. Because of her sensitivity, she finds it very difficult to continue working side by side with her male colleague and in consequence her working environment becomes unpleasant to her.

Could a complaint of sex discrimination succeed in these circumstances, on the basis that:

(*a*) the invitation to her by her male colleague was on the ground of her sex – he would not have asked a male colleague for a date;

(*b*) she has been subjected to a detriment, because of the effect which the invitation has had on her;

(*c*) because of that detriment, she has also been treated less favourably than a man would have been?

This example is not a case of a woman being treated less favourably than a man would be treated, but without the *Discriminatory Motive* which has been held not to be a necessary feature of *Direct Discrimination*. In fact there is a discriminatory motive in this example; what is lacking is the intention to treat the woman less favourably than a man would be treated. Her male colleague neither knew nor had reasonable grounds for believing that his advances would be unwelcome to her. In these circumstances it is suggested that neither he nor his employer has acted unlawfully.

This issue is considered further under *Less Favourable Treatment* and *Unintentional Discrimination*. The suggestion that there is no unlawful discrimination where an alleged harasser does not know, and has no reason to know, that his words or conduct are unwelcome, is supported by the following extracts from the final paragraph of the decision in the above-mentioned case of *Reed and Bull Information Systems Limited v Stedman* [*1999*] *IRLR 299;*

> 'but because it is for each person to define their own levels of acceptance, the question would then be whether by words or conduct she had made it clear that she found such conduct unwelcome. ... Provided that any reasonable person would

understand her to be rejecting the conduct of which she was complaining, continuation of the conduct would, generally, be regarded as harassment'.

Similarly, in the European Union Code of Practice which is referred to below, it was stated:

'Sexual attention becomes sexual harassment if it is persisted in once it has been made clear that it is regarded by the recipient as offensive, although one incident of harassment may constitute sexual harassment if sufficiently serious'.

It is suggested that for a complaint of sexual harassment (or indeed racial harassment or harassment of a disabled person) to be based on a single incident, that incident would have to be so serious that any reasonable person would know that the words or conduct complained of would be offensive to the recipient.

118.5 THE REASON FOR THE TREATMENT

A complaint of harassment can succeed only if it is shown that the reason or an important reason for the treatment complained of was:

(*a*) the gender of the complainant (if the complaint is under the *SDA 1975*);

(*b*) the colour or ethnic origin etc. of the complainant (if the complaint is under the *RRA 1976*); or

(*c*) a reason relating to the employee's disability (if the complaint is under the *DDA 1995*).

It was stated by the EAT in the above-mentioned case *of Reed and Bull Information Systems Limited v Stedman* that, in a sexual harassment case, there are two questions:

(*a*) has the alleged victim been subjected to a detriment;

(*b*) if so, was it on the grounds of sex?

It was stated that the second question must always be asked, but in a sexual harassment case the answer will usually be quite clear without resort to a comparator, actual or hypothetical. It was also pointed out that:

(*a*) as in any other direct discrimination case, motive or intention on the part of the alleged discriminator is not an essential ingredient – although it will often be a relevant factor to take into account;

(*b*) lack of intent is not a defence.

There are broadly three kinds of case in which discrimination can be established, as follows:

(*a*) gender or race is the reason for the act complained of, as in the case of a racial assault;

(*b*) the motive for subjecting an employee to detrimental treatment is a personal dislike, but the weapon which is employed is one which takes advantage of the employee's gender, race or disability;

(*c*) gender, race or disability is the reason for the treatment complained of and also influences the nature of that treatment.

An example of the second category is the leading case of *Strathclyde Regional Council v Porcelli [1986] IRLR 134*. The complainant was subjected over a period of time to a series of detrimental acts by two male colleagues. Their personal dislike of the complainant, not her gender, was the reason for the treatment complained of; but a significant part of that treatment was conduct of a sexual nature to which a man would not be vulnerable, such as looking up the complainant's skirt when she was up a ladder.

The case of *Insitu Cleaning Co Limited v Heads [1995] IRLR 4* is another example of a case where the act complained of was intrinsically of a sexual nature, whatever the reason for that act may have been. This was a case in which a manager, the son of two directors of the company, addressed an employee twice his age using the expression 'Hiya, big tits'. It was held by the EAT that this single remark was sufficiently serious to constitute a detriment and that the nature of the remark was such that it was clearly on the ground of her sex that the complainant was being treated less favourably than a man would have been treated. For a manager to make a remark of this kind was a form of bullying which was not acceptable in the workplace in any circumstances. The conduct of the manager who made the remark was conduct likely to create an intimidating, hostile and humiliating work environment for the victim.

One of the grounds of appeal in the above case was that there was no sex discrimination because a similar remark could have been made to a man, for example in relation to a balding head or a beard. This ground of appeal was described by the EAT as absurd. The remark made to the complainant could not sensibly be equated to a remark about a man's bald head or beard. One is sexual, the other is not.

Similarly, in the above-mentioned case of *Driskel v Peninsula Business Services and Others*, the EAT said that the employment tribunal had seriously misdirected itself in putting weight on the manager's sexual vulgarity towards male employees. The EAT referred to the following passage in the judgment of the EAT in *Reed and Bull Information Systems v Stedman*:

> 'Sexual badinage of a heterosexual male by another such cannot be completely equated with like badinage by him of a woman. Prima facie the treatment is not equal: in the latter circumstance it is the sex of the alleged discriminator that potentially adds a material element absent as between two heterosexual men'.

118.6 THE EMPLOYER'S LIABILITY

In what circumstances is an employer liable to an employee who is subjected to harassment by a fellow employee?

It should first of all be noted that the interpretation section in each of the *SDA 1975*, *RRA 1976* and *DDA 1995* contains an extended definition of *Employment*. An employer can be liable for acts of harassment, and other acts of discrimination, not only by conventional employees but also by persons who are for the purposes of the relevant Act deemed to be employees under this extended definition.

Furthermore, an employer is also liable to his employees for acts of discrimination against them by the employer's 'agent' if the employer has authorised the acts of discrimination, whether expressly or by implication.

So far as discrimination by one employee against another is concerned, the key question is whether the act complained of was in the *Course of Employment*. Under *section 41* of the *SDA 1975*, anything done by a person in the course of that person's employment is treated as also done by that person's employer whether or not it was done with the employer's knowledge or approval. There are identical provisions in *section 32* of the *RRA 1976* and *section 58* of the *DDA 1995*.

Furthermore, the employee who has done the act of discrimination is also liable, for *Aiding* the deemed discrimination by the employer. That liability arises under *section 42* of the *SDA 1975*, *section 33* of the *RRA 1976* and *section 57* of the *DDA 1995*.

The employer, but not the employee who has done the act complained of, has a defence if the employer has taken such steps as were *Reasonably Practicable* to prevent the employee from doing the act complained of, or acts of that description.

Accordingly, the position can be summarised as follows:

(*a*) if an employee does an act of harassment or discrimination outside the course of his employment, then neither that employee nor his employer is liable for that act;

(*b*) if the act of harassment or other discrimination is in the course of the employee's employment, then the employee is liable for aiding an act of discrimination;

(*c*) in those circumstances the employer is also liable, unless he has taken all reasonably practicable steps to prevent the act of discrimination or acts of that description.

At one time a person complaining of particularly serious acts of racial or sexual harassment faced the argument that such acts were outside the course of employment, because the common law test of *Vicarious Liability* should be applied. In particular, under that test, indecent or other serious assaults could not be regarded as improper ways of doing what the employer had authorised; they fell entirely outside the course of the employment.

That approach was rejected by the Court of Appeal in the leading case of *Jones v Tower Boot Co Limited* [*1997*] *IRLR 168*. In that case, a 16 year old boy started work at a shoe factory. He was of mixed ethnic parentage. The workforce which he joined had never previously included anyone of ethnic minority origin. From the outset he was called by racially offensive names such as 'chimp' and 'monkey'. Two employees whipped him on the legs with a piece of welt and threw metal bolts at his head and one of them burned his arm with a hot screwdriver. The same two employees later tried to put his arm in a machine, causing the burn to bleed again. Understandably unable to endure this treatment, the boy left the job after four weeks. He complained of racial discrimination. His complaint was upheld by an employment tribunal which awarded him compensation of £5,000, but the EAT, by a majority, allowed the employer's appeal, on the ground that what had been done was not done in the course of the harassers' employment. There was then a further appeal to the Court of Appeal.

The Court of Appeal allowed the appeal and restored the decision of the employment tribunal. The judgment of Lord Justice Waite contained the following important passages:

(*a*) 'The legislation now represented by the Race and Sex Discrimination Acts currently in force broke new ground in seeking to work upon the minds of men and women and thus affect their attitude to the social consequences of difference between the sexes or distinction of skin colour. Its general thrust was educative, persuasive and (where necessary) coercive . . . consistently with the broad front on which it operates, the legislation has traditionally been given a wide interpretation . . .'

(*b*) 'A purposive construction accordingly requires section 32 of the Race Relations Act (and the corresponding section 41 of the Sex Discrimination Act) to be given a broad interpretation. It would be inconsistent with that requirement to allow the notion of the "course of employment" to be construed in any sense more limited than the natural meaning of those everyday words would allow'.

(*c*) 'It would be particularly wrong to allow racial harassment on the scale that was suffered by the complainant in this case at the hands of his workmates – treatment that was wounding both emotionally and physically – to slip through the

> net of employer responsibility by applying to it a common-law principle evolved in another area of the law to deal with vicarious responsibility for wrongdoing of a wholly different kind. To do so would seriously undermine the statutory scheme of the Discrimination Acts and flout the purposes which they were passed to achieve'.

Lord Justice Waite said that he would 'reject . . . entirely' a submission that 'the more heinous the act of discrimination, the less likely it will be that the employer would be liable'. He said that that submission:

> 'cuts across the whole legislative scheme and underlying policy of s 32 (and its counterpart in sex discrimination), which is to deter racial and sexual harassment in the workplace through a widening of the net of responsibility beyond the guilty employees themselves, by making all employers additionally liable for such harassment, and then supplying them with the reasonable steps defence under s 32(3) which will exonerate the conscientious employer who has used his best endeavours to prevent such harassment, and would encourage all employers who have not yet undertaken such endeavours to take the steps necessary to make the same defence available in their own workplace.'

The judgment has been quoted at length, because the decision was a landmark one which revolutionised the approach in racial and sexual harassment cases. The effect of that decision is that there is legal liability for every unlawful act of discrimination (whether harassment or otherwise) in the workplace. The employee who has done the act is liable; so also is the employer, unless the defence of having taken all reasonably practicable steps is made out.

There can also be liability for acts outside the workplace. In the case of *Chief Constable of the Lincolnshire Police v Stubbs [1999] IRLR 81,* the complainant was seconded to a Regional Crime Squad. She complained of sexual harassment by a detective sergeant. One incident was at a pub, when she met the detective sergeant and other officers. The other involved an offensive remark at a leaving party for a colleague. On each occasion the complainant and the detective sergeant were off duty.

The EAT held that the chief constable was liable for the acts complained of. Although these acts took place at social functions away from the police station, those social functions were work-related. There was an extension of the employment of the two officers.

On this basis, it is clearly open to employment tribunals to hold employers liable for acts of harassment which take place at (or in the aftermath of) office parties, sales and other conferences and away days. Employers must take the necessary steps to ensure that the appropriate standards of behaviour are maintained at such events. It could be difficult for an employer to make out the reasonably practicable steps defence in relation to an event which is awash with alcohol.

Can an employer be held accountable where the person who does an act of harassment (or some other discrimination) is neither an employee, in the extended sense, nor an agent? This question arose in the case *of Burton v De Vere Hotels [1996] IRLR 596.* This is the case in which two black waitresses at a hotel were subjected to racially offensive remarks by a well-known comedian who was the guest speaker at a social function. The speaker was not in any sense an employee or agent of the hotel. Nevertheless, the EAT held that the hotel company were directly liable for subjecting the two employees to racial harassment. The event was sufficiently under their control for them to have been able to prevent the harassment from taking place. It was predictable, in view of the speaker's reputation, that the two black employees would be the target of racist 'jokes'. In those circumstances the management could, and should, have ensured that the two employees were not required to be present during the speech.

118.7 REASONABLY PRACTICABLE STEPS

It was held in the case of *Canniffe v East Riding of Yorkshire Council* [*2000*] *IRLR 555* that a respondent cannot make out the above defence simply by persuading the tribunal that there was nothing they could have done to prevent the act complained of. This was a very serious complaint of sexual harassment, involving assaults or threats of assaults by a fellow employee on a woman who was also disabled, being profoundly deaf. The tribunal found that there was only one incident in respect of which a complaint had been made in time, but that incident was a particularly serious one. There was evidence that a personal harassment policy had been drawn to the attention of employees in a newsletter and at team meetings and the complainant herself gave evidence that the harasser had told her that he knew that he could lose his job as a result of what he was doing. The employment tribunal held that in these circumstances the employer had made out the defence under *section 41(3)* of the *SDA 1975* that all reasonably practicable steps to prevent acts of the type complained of had been taken. It was said by the tribunal that they failed to see that any better implementation of the adopted policies would have had any effect in relation to the criminal behaviour complained of.

It was held by the EAT that this was the wrong approach and that the case should be sent back to a freshly constituted tribunal. It is not appropriate for a tribunal to uphold the defence on the ground that nothing could have been done. The proper approach is:

(*a*) to identify whether the respondents took any steps at all;

(*b*) to consider whether there were any further steps which they could have taken and which were reasonably practicable.

The EAT added that:

(*a*) the question whether taking these further steps would have been successful in preventing the acts of discrimination may be worth addressing but is not determinative either way;

(*b*) the employer will not be exonerated if it has not taken reasonably practicable steps simply because those reasonable steps would not have led anywhere or achieved anything or prevented anything from occurring.

In the particular case, there was evidence that the complainant had spoken, albeit in confidence and without making a formal complaint, to three colleagues at work about the earlier incidents. One of these colleagues was also the harasser's line manager. It was held by the EAT that the employment tribunal had failed to consider whether there were steps which these three colleagues, for whose acts and omissions the employer was responsible, could have taken. The EAT also referred to the need to apply a purposive construction to the legislation, following the guidance given in the case of *Jones v Tower Boot Co Limited* [*1997*] *IRLR 168* which has already been referred to.

There was no reference in the decision in the above case to the 1991 European Union recommendation and Code of Practice on the protection of the dignity of women and men at work. An employer who fails to follow the guidance in that Code would have very little prospect, however, of satisfying a tribunal that all reasonably practicable steps had been taken. The Code is frequently referred to by tribunals and it was held by the ECJ in *Grimaldi v Fonds des Maladies Professionelles* [*1990*] *IRLR 400* that Recommendations of the kind under which the Code was adopted must be taken into consideration by national courts and tribunals.

The Code refers to the responsibilities of trade unions and individual employees as well as those of employers, but the main guidance is given to employers. The Code states that dealing with complaints is only one component of a strategy to deal with the problem. The prime objective should be to change behaviour and attitudes, to seek to ensure the prevention of sexual harassment. The key steps for employers are to:

(*a*) put the appropriate policies in place;

(*b*) communicate those policies to staff and job applicants;

(*c*) adopt and publicise mechanisms for assisting victims of harassment and enabling them to complain;

(*d*) provide training for managers and supervisors;

(*e*) monitor and review complaints of sexual harassment and how they have been resolved.

The *policy statement* should expressly state that:

(*a*) all employees have a right to be treated with dignity;

(*b*) sexual harassment at work will not be permitted or condoned;

(*c*) employees have a right to complain about it should it occur;

(*d*) allegations of sexual harassment will be dealt with seriously, expeditiously and confidentially;

(*e*) employees will be protected against victimisation or retaliation for bringing a complaint;

(*f*) appropriate disciplinary measures will be taken against employees found guilty of sexual harassment.

The policy statement should make clear what is considered inappropriate behaviour at work and explain that such behaviour may in certain circumstances be unlawful.

Disciplinary rules should also be amended where necessary to make it clear that both harassment itself and victimisation will be disciplinary offences. Indeed many employers have now adopted disciplinary rules under which sexual harassment or victimisation are treated as gross misconduct for which summary dismissal will be the normal penalty.

Effective *communication* of the policy is important. It is recommended in the code that managers should explain the policy to their staff and take steps to promote the policy positively. Effective communication of the policy will highlight management's commitment to eliminating sexual harassment, thus encouraging a climate in which it will not occur.

It is particularly important to tell employees where they can turn for *assistance* and to whom they can *complain* if they are subjected to sexual harassment. Many serious cases of harassment over a long period of time occur because the victim does not know where to turn or how to complain. The code recommends that employers should:

(*a*) designate a person or persons, such as confidential counsellors, to provide advice and assistance to employees;

(*b*) advise employees that if possible in the first instance they should attempt to resolve the problem informally;

(*c*) make employees aware that if this is too difficult or embarrassing then they may seek support from or ask for an initial approach to be made by a sympathetic friend or confidential counsellor;

(*d*) provide a formal procedure, in which employees can have confidence, for resolving complaints in those cases where informal resolution is inappropriate or unsuccessful.

The Code suggests that it may be helpful if confidential counsellors are designated with the agreement of the trade unions or employees, as this is likely to enhance their acceptability. They may be selected from, for example:

(*a*) the personnel department;

(*b*) the equal opportunities department;

(*c*) a trade union;

(*d*) women's support groups.

They must be given adequate resources to carry out their function and protection against victimisation for assisting any recipient of sexual harassment.

The complaints procedure should cater for the case where the normal grievance procedure is unsuitable, for example, because the alleged harasser is the employee's line manager. The code suggests that employees should also be able in the first instance to bring a complaint to someone of their own sex, should they so choose.

Training is a key step. Training should be given to managers and supervisors and any other employees with relevant responsibilities, such as the above-mentioned confidential counsellors and also those playing an official role in any formal complaints procedure. The training should cover:

(*a*) the factors which contribute to a working environment free of sexual harassment;

(*b*) the detail of the organisation's policy and procedures;

(*c*) knowledge and awareness of common signs that sexual harassment is occurring or has occurred (although the Code does not specifically mention this);

(*d*) the responsibilities under the policy of each of the individuals receiving training;

(*e*) how to deal with any problems they are likely to encounter.

It is necessary to *monitor* and *review* complaints of sexual harassment, and how they have been resolved, in order to ensure that the policy and procedures are working effectively. If several complaints are received, following the adoption and publication of the policy, this may be an indication that victims of harassment now have the confidence to complain; it could also mean, however, that the policy is not yet being successfully implemented and that attitudes are not being changed.

118.8 INVESTIGATIONS

A defence that all reasonably practicable steps to prevent harassment have been taken could be undermined if it is shown that complaints have not been properly investigated and dealt with. The Code of Practice gives the following advice:

(*a*) internal investigations of any complaints must be handled with sensitivity and with due respect for the rights of both the complainant and the alleged harasser;

(*b*) the investigation should be seen to be independent and objective;

(*c*) those carrying out the investigation should not be connected with the allegation in any way;

(*d*) every effort should be made to resolve complaints speedily;

(*e*) the investigation should focus on the facts of the complaint;

(*f*) a complete record should be kept of all meetings and investigations.

118.9 Harassment

The Code recommends that where a complaint is upheld and it is determined that it is necessary to relocate or transfer one party, consideration should be given, wherever practicable, to allowing the complainant to choose whether he or she wishes to remain in post or be transferred to another location. If anything, this advice in the Code is insufficiently forceful. There are often commercial objections to transferring the harasser to other work, particularly if he or she is in a senior position, but there may be no legally acceptable alternative, if the complainant finds it intolerable to continue working with the harasser.

The Code of Practice adds that:

(*a*) no element of penalty should be seen to attach to a complainant whose complaint is upheld;

(*b*) where a complaint is upheld, the employer should monitor the situation to ensure that the harassment has stopped;

(*c*) even where a complaint is not upheld, consideration should be given to transferring or re-scheduling the work of one of the employees concerned.

So far as the last of the above points is concerned, care must be taken not to victimise, for example by way of a compulsory transfer, an employee who has made a complaint which has not been upheld but which cannot be shown to have been made falsely and in bad faith.

118.9 **THE RRA 1976 AND THE DDA 1995**

The above-mentioned Code of Practice applies only to sexual harassment, but similar principles apply to racial harassment and the harassment of disabled employees. In particular:

(*a*) there should either be a single policy on harassment or dignity at work, or a separate policy on racial harassment and a section on harassment in the disability policy;

(*b*) there should be assistance for employees and informal and formal complaints procedures to deal with these kinds of harassment as well as sexual harassment;

(*c*) racial harassment and harassment of disabled employees should be disciplinary offences;

(*d*) training, particularly for managers and supervisors, is essential;

(*e*) complaints should be monitored and reviewed.

119 Health and Safety At Work

119.1 THE SCOPE OF HEALTH AND SAFETY LAW

Health and safety law is a subject of rapidly increasing importance. The detail of the extensive rules in this area lies outside the scope of this Handbook, but further information is available in *Tolley's Employment Handbook*. Briefly, an employer is under a common law duty to have regard to the safety of his employees. In addition, statutory obligations have been imposed upon employers in various circumstances e.g. by the *Health and Safety at Work etc. Act 1974*, and many regulations made pursuant to the legislation. The *Employment Rights Act 1996* protects employees from dismissal or victimisation by the employer in health and safety cases. An employer who breaks his common law duties in respect of health and safety may also face a claim of constructive unfair dismissal if the employee resigns because of an alleged breach of the employer's obligations. The rules are significant generally in respect of all employers and employees; some of them also have particular significance where equal opportunities issues arise.

119.2 THE LONG HOURS CULTURE

There has been growing recognition that the 'long hours culture' associated with many sectors of employment in the UK has implications not only for health and safety but also in respect of equal opportunities. *The Working Time Regulations 1998* (*SI 1998 No 1833*) implement in the UK the provisions of the European Directive on Working Time, which was introduced through qualified majority voting (so that the then UK government could not veto it) because it was classed as a health and safety measure. Hours of work have long been regarded as primarily a matter of concern, in the equal opportunities context, in relation to women, because of issues surrounding *Part-Time Work*. But it is now more widely recognised that the 'long hours culture' is apt to disadvantage men and result in discrimination against them. The debate about the proper 'work-life balance' is relevant, if sometimes in different ways, to both men and women. *The Working Time Regulations 1998* provide some protection, despite being complicated and selective in their coverage.

119.3 AIDS AND HIV

Acquired Immunity Deficiency Syndrome (AIDS) is caused by the HIV virus. Where an individual is HIV-positive, he or she may not develop an AIDS-related illness or the full-blown condition of AIDS for many years, if at all. Even those suffering from the full-blown condition may be able to work normally between periods of sickness. Medical screening of job applicants or existing employees for the HIV virus requires their specific consent to the test and also to disclosure of the result to the employer. The virus is apt to be transmitted when bodily fluids mix. This means that, in many jobs, the risk of contracting the disease from another person is minimal. Consequently, the employer will not be in breach of his duty of care to other employees if he allows an employee who is HIV positive or suffering from AIDS to continue to report for work. It may be unfair to dismiss a sufferer, even if the sufferer's colleagues, or the employer's clients, do not wish to work with him or her: the test of fairness to be applied is that set out in *section 98 of the Employment Rights Act 1996*. For an employer to disclose that an employee is HIV-positive or suffering from AIDS would be likely to amount to a breach of the implied duty of mutual trust and confidence in the contract of employment, entitling the employee to resign and claim constructive unfair dismissal. The *DDA 1995* classes HIV infection as a progressive condition. Accordingly, employers are under a duty to make reasonable adjustments to meet the needs of employees with that condition. In April 2000, it was reported in the press that a discount supermarket chain had agreed a settlement for suggesting an undisclosed sum which journalists suggested as being up to £250,000 of claims under the *SDA 1975* and *DDA 1995* brought by a store manager who was sent home on leave because he was HIV positive.

119.4 STRESS AT WORK

An employee who suffers from stress-related illness may contend that it was caused by conditions at work. This is a developing area of the law, but despite the publicity accorded to a few hefty settlements and compensation awards, proving cause and effect so as to justify a claim for compensation for personal injury is often difficult in practice. But where an employer exposes an employee to a reasonably foreseeable risk of illness as a result of work-induced stress, there may be a breach of the duty of care and liability for damages. Where a risk of stress is a feature of a particular job, a risk assessment ought to be made pursuant to the *Management of Health and Safety at Work Regulations 1992* (*SI 1992 No 2051*, as amended). An employee who is subjected to excessive stress at work may also be able to establish that the employer has broken the implied contractual obligation of mutual trust and confidence, entitling the employee to resign and claim to have been constructively unfairly dismissed. This may arise in the case of *Harassment* by fellow employees, customers or others. In extreme cases, the criminal law, e.g. the *Protection from Harassment Act 1997*, may become relevant in addition to the above principles. In practice, therefore, a prudent employer will investigate promptly and thoroughly any allegation from an employee that he or she is suffering from stress, whether as a result of discrimination or otherwise. Failure to take appropriate action will expose the employer to legal proceedings.

119.5 RISK ASSESSMENT AND PREGNANT WORKERS

Every employer, as well as each self-employed person, has to make a risk assessment relating to the premises, so as to identify the measures he must take to comply with the regulations applicable to him in respect of health and safety and fire precautions. The requirements are laid down by the *Management of Health and Safety at Work Regulations 1992*. The Regulations give effect to the *European Framework Directive and Temporary Workers Directive*. An amendment in 1994 gave effect to aspects of the *Pregnant Workers Directive*, while further amendments have covered, amongst other matters, the position in respect of children and young people under 18. In 1999, the Health and Safety Commission published a consultative document containing proposals to amend the Regulations, the related Code of Practice and various other health and safety provisions.

A risk assessment must be reviewed when necessary and (where there are more than five employees) recorded. Every employer must also make, and give effect to, adequate health and safety arrangements, including effective planning, organisation, control, monitoring and review of the measures to be taken. The employer must make sure that his employees are provided with appropriate health surveillance and appoint one or more competent people to assist him in implementing the measures to be taken. Specifically, each employer must, amongst other matters, establish (and where necessary give effect to) procedures to be followed in the event of serious and imminent danger to people working in his undertaking and nominate sufficient competent people to implement such procedures as regards the evacuation of the premises.

An assessment must be made of workplace risks to new and expectant mothers and measures taken to avoid any risk by altering working conditions or hours of work. Where it is not practicable to take those steps, the woman should be suspended from work (although she has the right to an offer of suitable alternative work, if the employer has it available, in accordance with *section 67* of the *Employment Rights Act 1996*). Where it is necessary for her health and safety, a new or expectant mother must be removed from night work: see also the *Suspension from Work (on Maternity Grounds) Order 1994 (SI 1994 No 2930)*. The decision of the EAT in *Day v T Pickles Farms Ltd* [*1999*] *IRLR 217*, shows that the employment of a woman of child-bearing age in itself suffices to trigger the need for risk assessment. That case concerned a sandwich shop assistant who became pregnant and told her manager that the smell of food made her feel nauseous. She became unfit for work and received statutory sick pay until a point when (mistakenly) the employers thought that her entitlement to it ceased. She claimed, amongst other matters, unfair constructive dismissal and sex discrimination. She argued that the employers were in breach of their obligations under the *Management of Health and Safety at Work Regulations 1992* to have carried out a risk assessment and that this would have led to her suspension on full pay. She also claimed to have suffered a detriment by not being allowed time off for ante-natal care. The EAT upheld a tribunal's ruling that she had not been constructively dismissed by reason of a failure to carry out the risk assessment when she was pregnant. This was because she had not given the employers an unequivocal communication that she was accepting some form of repudiation on the employer's part and treating the contract of employment as at an end. However, the tribunal had misdirected itself in finding that she had not suffered a detriment. The tribunal erred in finding that the obligation to carry out a risk assessment only applies when an employer has a pregnant employee. The employer should have carried out the assessment at the start of the employee's employment before she became pregnant. When the case returned to the tribunal, however, the tribunal concluded on the evidence that, despite its failure to carry out a risk assessment, the employer did not default in its obligations under *Reg 13A(2)* or *(3)* of the *Regulations*. The tribunal took into account the EAT's observation that 'the employer . . . cannot be expected to have in mind the most particular kind of conditions or objections or disabilities that some women might suffer from, for example being nauseous at handling fish or hard boiled eggs or something very much applicable only to the particular individual'.

120 Health-Related Benefits and Disability

120.1 TIME OFF FOR MEDICAL APPOINTMENTS AND TREATMENT

As a general principle, the effect of the *DDA 1995* is that an employer must allow disabled employees the same rights to time off for medical appointments as other employees. This is a matter which should be addressed in the contractual terms of employment. On occasion, *Reasonable Adjustments* may include agreement by the employer to allow the disabled employee extra time off for treatment. The cost and practicability of this may be relevant in deciding what is reasonable, e.g. in cases where extensive absence from work would create unacceptable difficulties for other members of the workforce and it is not cost-effective to engage others to cover the absences.

120.2 SICK PAY

In addition to Statutory Sick Pay, many employers operate schemes for occupational sick pay. This is a matter which ought to be covered in any adequately drafted contract of employment. To state the obvious, the effect of the *DDA 1995* is that employers should not discriminate in the matter of occupational sick pay between disabled employees and those who are not disabled. Some organisations even provide more generous terms to disabled employees than to other members of the workforce and this form of *Positive Discrimination* is not outlawed by the *DDA 1995*.

It may be unfair to dismiss an employee at a time when the employee's ongoing entitlement to sickness pay has not been exhausted, but this is not *automatically* the case. Once the contractual right to occupational sick pay has expired, an employee may be eligible for benefits under a permanent health insurance scheme. Failing that, the employer may be prepared to continue to make payments of sick pay (either in whole or in part) on a discretionary basis for a period of time, but it may be imprudent or inappropriate to offer an open-ended commitment at the outset. Allowing a period of unpaid leave is another possibility, especially if the duties of the absent employee can be adequately covered either by members of the existing workforce or by temporary replacements.

120.3 INSURED BENEFITS

While the *DDA 1995* applies generally to insurance schemes for employees, it permits insurers to discriminate in respect of disabled employees where actuarial or statistical data, or other evidence, indicate a higher risk. An employer can treat a disabled person less favourably than colleagues who are not disabled if there is medical evidence relating to the employee or general actuarial data, and providing the cover would entail substantial additional costs. What is 'substantial' would be a matter for judgment in each case.

Notwithstanding the *DDA 1995*, medical insurance cover for an employee with a disability may, if available at all, be restricted to cover in respect of conditions unrelated to the disability. If comprehensive cover is available, a higher premium may be required. Similarly, in the case of permanent health insurance, cover may be linked to long term ill health not related to the disability. Increased premiums may again be justifiable.

120.4 PENSION BENEFITS

The *DDA 1995* and regulations address discrimination in the context of occupational pension schemes. The rules apply to the following benefits, where they are provided by way of an occupational pension scheme:

(*a*) benefits arising in the event of accident, sickness, injury or invalidity;

(*b*) benefits arising on termination of employment;

(*c*) benefits arising on retirement, old age or death.

An unjustifiable act or omission by an employer or the trustees of the pension scheme is deemed to be contrary to the rules of the scheme. The employer and the trustees may, however, take into account an existing medical condition that increases the likelihood of a claim or of an earlier pension, provided so doing is based appropriately, on actuarial data. Where the cost of providing benefits is likely to be substantially greater by reason of the disability, it may be justifiable to revise the terms of membership of the scheme and contribution rate to be paid by the disabled scheme member. If all members pay the same rate, a disabled member who is excluded from certain benefits may nevertheless be obliged to pay at the standard rate of contribution.

121 Heavy Work

Even in an age of increasing mechanisation and computerisation, there are still many jobs which involve lifting, carrying or digging or are otherwise physically demanding. The avoidance of unlawful discrimination in recruitment for such work is considered under *Physical Requirements*.

There must also be no unlawful discrimination in deciding which employees should be given heavy work and which should be given lighter work. Clearly a manager can, and indeed should, take account of the strengths and skill of individual employees in deciding how the work should be allocated, but it would be a clear case of direct sex discrimination if the manager simply acted on an assumption that men would be able to do heavy work and women would not.

Indirect discrimination could arise if the heavy work is shared out equally, without regard to the ability of each individual to do the work. It would be an act of unlawful indirect sex discrimination to require a woman to do work of which she is physically incapable, unless the requirement could be objectively justified (which is unlikely). There should be no difficulty in proving *Disparate Impact* in such a case.

It would be a clear case of direct racial discrimination if the allocation of work (whether heavy work or dirty or difficult or otherwise unpleasant work) were to be influenced by any racial factor. For example, it would be direct racial discrimination if a manager were to adopt a policy of giving all the lighter jobs to employees of his own ethnic background.

When an employee is or becomes disabled, and is unable to do heavy work which forms a normal part of the job duties, consideration must be given to a *Reasonable Adjustment*, for example by changing the job duties or by offering the employee a transfer to other work.

122 Hours of Work

It can be difficult for employees with childcare or other family responsibilities to work long or unsocial hours. A requirement that a female or married employee should work unsocial hours (or a refusal to agree to part-time working) could amount to *Indirect Discrimination* unless the requirement (or refusal) can be objectively justified. As with other discrimination cases, it is no defence to a complaint that the employee has freely entered into a contract containing the requirement about which she now complains.

A reduction in the number of hours worked can also in certain circumstances be one of the *section 6 Reasonable Adjustments* which must be considered in relation to a disabled employee.

The number of hours worked can also be relevant as a *Material Factor* defence in an *Equal Pay* case, where the comparison which the complainant seeks to make is between the salaries (rather than the hourly rates) of the complainant and the comparator. The time at which work is done is not, however, a relevant factor. The fact that the complainant's work is done by day and the comparator's work is done by night does not prevent the jobs being like work or work of equal value and cannot be relied on as a material factor in relation to a difference in basic pay. The proper way to compensate an employee for working at night or at some other unsocial time is to pay a shift premium of a reasonable amount – *National Coal Board v Sherwin* [*1978*] *IRLR 122.*

Working hours may also raise questions relating to *Health and Safety at Work*.

123 Human Rights

123.1 BACKGROUND

The *European Convention on Human Rights* is a treaty of the Council of Europe adopted in 1950 and ratified by the UK in 1951. It was designed to give binding effect to the guarantee of various rights and freedoms in the United Nations Declaration on Human Rights, adopted in 1948. The immediate aim of the *Convention* was to protect Europe against totalitarianism and a repeat of the atrocities of the Second World War. However, its general purpose has been described as to protect human rights and fundamental freedoms and to maintain and promote the ideals and values of a democratic society. It is therefore not only of continuing relevance in the 21st century, but also capable of far-reaching interpretation, unforeseen at the time of original adoption.

While the *Convention* has had particular significance in the UK since 1966, when the government recognised the jurisdiction of the European Court of Human Rights and accepted the right of the individual in the UK to petition the Court, the *Convention's* impact on domestic employment law was for many years negligible. The landscape has been transformed by the *Human Rights Act 1998*. This came fully into force on 2 October 2000 and requires that the courts interpret UK law in accordance with the *Convention*. It will take time for the full significance of this measure to become widely appreciated. It is, however, foreseeable that it will have significant impact on the law of equal opportunities.

123.2 EUROPEAN CONVENTION

The *Convention* sets out, in broad terms, various fundamental rights and freedoms. It also established the European Commission of Human Rights and the European Court of Human Rights, both of which are based in Strasbourg. The *Convention* and its institutions should not be confused with the law and institutions of the European Union. The subscribing states are the Members of the Council of Europe. The *Convention* provides a right of direct complaint by an individual affected by an alleged breach of the *Convention*. A limiting factor in practice is that the aggrieved person must pursue every remedy available under domestic law. Only when these are exhausted without the complaint having been resolved to his satisfaction may he present a petition to the Commission. The Commission will then investigate and if it decides that there is, or may be, a breach of the *Convention* and that the complaint is admissible, it will endeavour to obtain a settlement between the parties. If no settlement can be achieved, the Commission will refer the case, together with its report, to the Court, which will decide on the complaint.

A leading case which had a direct connection with the law of equal opportunities was *Halford v United Kingdom* [*1997*] *IRLR 471*. The applicant was a senior police officer who was pursuing a complaint of sex discrimination against her employer. The employer recorded her telephone conversations with a view to gathering material to be used in defence of the claim. The court ruled that such recording, without her knowledge, was a breach of her right to privacy under *Article 8* of the *Convention* and she was awarded compensation of £10,000.

Even before its incorporation into domestic law, the *Convention* has had an influence on European Community law, as in a *Sexual Orientation* case, *Grant v South West Trains Ltd* [*1998*] *IRLR 206*, where the European Court of Justice took the *Convention* into account.

123.3 HUMAN RIGHTS ACT 1998

The *Human Rights Act 1998 (HRA 1998)* is one of the UK's most significant constitutional measures. Its immediate effect is to allow people to claim their rights under the *Convention* in UK courts and tribunals, instead of having to go to Strasbourg.

The *HRA 1998*:

(*a*) makes it unlawful for a public authority to act incompatibly with *Convention* rights, although an authority will not have acted unlawfully if as the result of primary legislation it could not have acted otherwise;

(*b*) requires all legislation to be interpreted and given effect so far as possible compatibly with *Convention* rights.

Article 14 of the *Convention* requires that its rights and freedoms shall be enjoyed 'without discrimination on any grounds such as sex, race, colour, language, religion, political or other opinion, national or social origin, association with a minority, property, birth or other status'. The application of this principle involves more than simply deciding whether a person has been discriminated against in the enjoyment of a *Convention* right. The question would also arise as to whether there is an objective and reasonable justification for treating different categories of people in a different way, and whether any such differential treatment was proportionate to the matter being pursued. It is not possible to pursue a case on *Article 14* grounds alone; there must be another *Convention* right at issue to which a claim of discrimination can be attached.

Perhaps the *Convention* rights which are most likely to impact on UK employment law are:

(*a*) the prohibition of slavery and forced labour (*Article 4*);

(*b*) the right to a fair trial (*Article 6*);

(*c*) the right to respect for private and family life (*Article 8*);

(*d*) the right to freedom of religion (*Article 9*);

(*e*) the right to freedom of expression (*Article 10*);

(*f*) the right to freedom of assembly and association (*Article 11*).

'Proportionality' is a crucial concept. Any interference with a *Convention* right must be proportionate to the intended objective. This means that even if a particular policy or action which interferes with a *Convention* right is aimed at a legitimate goal (for example, preventing crime), this will not justify the interference if the means used to achieve the aim are excessive in the circumstances. Interference with a *Convention* right must be appropriate, and neither arbitrary nor unfair. In any event, interference may be unjustified if the impact on an individual or group is too severe.

Only a person considered to be a victim can bring proceedings against a public authority under the Act. A victim is someone who is directly affected by the conduct in question. Victims can include companies as well as individuals and may also be relatives of the victim where a complaint is made about his death. A victim may also be a person who is at risk of being directly affected by a measure.

In relation to some *Convention* rights (particularly those requiring a balance to be struck between competing considerations), the European Court of Human Rights allows a 'margin of appreciation' to the domestic authorities, meaning that it is reluctant to substitute its own view of the merits of the case for those of the national authorities. It remains to be seen whether UK courts and tribunals will develop a doctrine analogous to that of 'the margin of appreciation'.

123.4 PRACTICAL IMPLICATIONS

The *Convention* has already had an impact in fields such as *Religious Discrimination* and *Sexual Orientation*. Remedies are available under the *HRA 1998* only against employers which are public authorities. The *HRA 1998* does not provide an exhaustive definition of 'public authorities' and borderline cases will need to be resolved by the courts. There is scope for the category of employers which carry out some functions of a 'public nature' to be defined quite broadly. In any event, incorporation of the *Convention* into domestic law will have a significant effect on private, as well as public, employment. For example, courts and tribunals, which are themselves public authorities, must act compatibly with *Convention* rights. Because of this, it may be expected that common law will develop in private employment disputes in a manner which gives effect to Convention rights. It may be argued, for instance, that the implied contractual duty of mutual trust and confidence embodies a duty to respect the *Convention* rights.

Dress Codes imposed by employers may give rise to issues under the *HRA 1998*. *Article 8* (right to respect for private and family life) and *Article 10* (freedom of expression) are both potentially relevant. The scope of protection from *Religious Discrimination*, currently very limited, is likely to be substantially expanded. Christians, Rastafarians and members of other religions are likely to be able to claim protection by virtue of *Article 9* and this may, for instance, curtail the right of employers to require employees to work on religious holidays.

123.5 FUNDAMENTAL RIGHTS

In June 1999, the European Council proposed that 'the fundamental rights applicable at [EU] level should be consolidated in a Charter and thereby made more evident'. This charter 'should contain the fundamental rights and freedoms' as well as basic procedural rights guaranteed by the *Convention*. The UK government says that it sees the charter as 'a showcase of existing rights . . . rather than a launch pad for a new set of rights and competences'. It is foreseeable that the charter and its implications will give rise to much political, as well as legal debate.

124 Illegality

Can a complaint of discrimination be defeated on the ground that the contract under which the complainant was employed was tainted with illegality?

This question arose in the case of *Hall v Woolston Hall Leisure Limited* [*2000*] *IRLR 578*. The complainant was employed as the head chef at a golf club. She was told that she was being dismissed on grounds of redundancy and incapability. She complained of sex discrimination and the employment tribunal found that she would not have been dismissed had she not been pregnant. The tribunal awarded her compensation for injury to feelings, but held that she was not entitled to compensation for loss of earnings. The reason was that her weekly pay was understated on her payslips. She had negotiated a pay rise on her promotion, asking for and being granted £250 per week net of deductions. The payslips, however, falsely showed £250 as her gross pay, not her net pay. When she queried this, she was told, 'It's the way we do business.' It was held by the employment tribunal that the contract of employment was tainted with illegality. The complainant knew that her employers were defrauding the Inland Revenue and turned a blind eye. She appealed unsuccessfully to the EAT against the decision not to award her any compensation for loss of earnings.

There was then a further appeal to the Court of Appeal, which allowed the appeal. In considering the relevant law, Lord Justice Peter Gibson started with the *Equal Treatment Directive*. He pointed out that although the complainant could not rely on it directly (the employer was a private sector employer), the tribunal must interpret the national law in the light of the wording and purpose of the Directive and, so far as possible, give effect to the Directive. He pointed out the Directive requires the United Kingdom to give real and effective judicial protection to victims of sex discrimination at work and to provide a sanction with a real deterrent effect on the employer. He said that a person in the complainant's position was clearly within the ambit of the Directive. Her dismissal because of her pregnancy contravened the purpose of the Directive, which also supported her not being denied an effective remedy under the *SDA 1975*.

It was also important to note that the complainant did not base her complaint on the terms of her contract. She had to establish that she was employed and was dismissed from her employment; to that extent reliance was placed on the contract of employment. She was, however, complaining not about breach of contract but about the statutory tort of sex discrimination. At most she had acquiesced in her employer's conduct; that acquiescence was in no way causally linked with her sex discrimination claim. Accordingly her claim should be allowed.

The Court of Appeal also approved the decision of the EAT in the earlier case of *Leighton v Michael* [*1996*] *IRLR 67*. In that case the employee worked in a fish and chip shop. After a change of ownership, her new employers, despite her complaint, refused to make proper deductions of tax and national insurance contributions. She presented complaints of sexual harassment and victimisation in dismissing her. The tribunal dismissed her complaint because the carrying out of her contract of employment involved a fraud on the Inland Revenue and she was a party to that illegality. Her appeal was allowed by the EAT.

In approving the decision of the EAT, Lord Justice Peter Gibson in *Hall* said that it was the sex discrimination that was the core of the complaint. In upholding that complaint, the court would not be seen to be condoning unlawful conduct by the employee. The complaint of sex discrimination was not based on the contract of employment. It was still less the case that the complaint of sex discrimination and the complainant's acquiescence in her employer's unlawful failure to make proper deductions were closely connected or inextricably linked.

If the claim had been based on the contract of employment, then illegality would have defeated the contract in any of the following circumstances:

(*a*) if the contract had been entered into for an illegal purpose;

(*b*) if the contract had been prohibited by statute;

(*c*) if the complainant had actively participated in the illegal performance of the contract.

These principles relating to claims based on contract would be relevant in *Equal Pay* cases. An employee would almost certainly not be permitted to pursue a claim under the *EPA 1970* if he or she had actively participated in a scheme for his or her pay to be under-declared so as to defraud the Inland Revenue. In such a case, the complaint would be based on the contract of employment and the illegality would go to the heart of the matter in respect of which a remedy was being claimed.

125 Immigration Control

Immigration control necessarily involves direct and indirect racial discrimination, because persons are admitted to the UK subject to conditions which prevent them from taking employment or restrict the work which they can do and those conditions are imposed on grounds of nationality or by reference to residential factors.

This discrimination is, however, authorised by *section 41* of the *RRA 1976* – see *Statutory Authority*. Measures taken pursuant to that authority can, however, be challenged if they are contrary to any provision of *Community Law*, such as *Article 39* (formerly *Article 48*) relating to the freedom of movement of nationals of Member States.

126 Independent Expert

Until 31 July 1996, no *Equal Value* claim could succeed unless the employment tribunal had appointed an independent expert to consider and report on the jobs of the complainant and the comparator(s). This did not mean that an independent expert was appointed in all cases. There are many *Equal Pay* cases which fail before the stage of appointing an independent expert is reached, for example because at some earlier stage the tribunal considers and upholds a *Material Factor* defence.

Now the position is that the tribunal may appoint an independent expert but is not obliged to do so. Where no independent expert is appointed, the usual practice is for the applicant and the respondent each to call their own expert witness. The tribunal then makes a decision after considering the expert and other evidence which it has heard.

Even where a report by an independent expert is commissioned and received by the tribunal, that report may be challenged and each party may, on giving reasonable notice to the tribunal and to the other party, call one expert witness. The directions made by the tribunal normally provide for the parties to exchange the reports of any expert witnesses before the hearing.

127 Indirect Discrimination

127.1 THE CONCEPT

The definitions of discrimination, in the *SDA 1975* and the *RRA 1976*, include indirect discrimination as well as *Direct Discrimination* and *Victimisation*. The *DDA 1995* does not contain a separate definition of indirect discrimination. The definition of *Disability Discrimination* is effectively a composite one which includes elements of both direct and indirect discrimination.

The reason for including indirect discrimination in the statutory definitions in the *SDA 1975* and the *RRA 1976* is to strike at employment decisions and practices which, while applied equally to all employees or job applicants, have a disproportionately adverse effect, or disparate impact, on members of a relevant group (such as women or ethnic minority workers).

127.2 THE STATUTORY APPROACH

A possible approach would have been to define indirect discrimination in general and flexible terms, leaving it to the Employment Tribunals to apply the definition to particular cases in the light of the relevant circumstances and the practical experience of the Members. That is the European approach. The Council Directive 76/207/EEC, the *Equal Treatment Directive*, states in *Article 2.1*:

> 'For the purposes of the following provisions, the principle of equal treatment shall mean that there shall be no discrimination whatsoever on grounds of sex either directly or indirectly by reference in particular to marital or family status'.

That one word, 'indirectly', is the Directive's only reference to indirect discrimination. It was left to national courts and, on receipt of a reference from a national court, the ECJ, to develop the principle.

The *SDA 1975* and the *RRA 1976* are based on a very different approach. Each of them contains a detailed definition or definitions of indirect discrimination. There are several words and phrases which are common to all these definitions and which have been argued over in numerous appeal cases. Because the actual wording of the definitions is so important, it is considered below in some detail.

127.3 THE STATUTORY DEFINITIONS

In order to establish whether an employer is indirectly discriminating against a woman, it is necessary to ask the following questions:

(*a*) Is the employer applying a requirement or condition to her (and if so what is it)?

(*b*) Is the employer applying, or would the employer apply, the requirement or condition equally to a man (if not the case is one of direct discrimination)?

(*c*) What proportion of women can comply with the requirement or condition?

(*d*) What proportion of men can comply with it?

(*e*) Is the proportion in (*c*) considerably smaller than that in (*d*)?

(*f*) Is the requirement or condition to the woman's detriment, because she cannot comply with it?

(*g*) Can the employer show the requirement or condition to be justifiable, irrespective of the sex of the person to whom it is applied?

There is indirect sex discrimination by the employer against the woman if the answer to questions (*a*), (*b*), (*e*) and (*f*) is yes and the answer to question (*g*) is no.

There is an identical definition of indirect discrimination against a man, but obviously with all references to men and women being reversed.

The *SDA 1975* also covers indirect discrimination against a married person, with 'unmarried person' substituted for 'man' in (*b*) and 'marital status' for 'sex' in (*g*). The relevant groups in (*c*) and (*d*) are married persons of the same sex and unmarried persons of the same sex as the Complainant.

A person is being subjected to indirect racial discrimination by an employer if he or she can show that the answer to questions (*a*), (*b*), (*e*) and (*f*) of the following questions is yes and the answer to (*g*) is no:

(*a*) Is the employer applying a requirement or condition to me (and if so what is it)?

(*b*) Is the employer applying, or would the employer apply, the requirement or condition equally to persons not of the same racial group as me?

(*c*) What proportion of persons of my racial group can comply with the requirement or condition?

(*d*) What proportion of persons not of my racial group can comply with it?

(*e*) Is the proportion in (*c*) considerably smaller than that in (*d*)?

(*f*) Is the requirement or condition to my detriment because I cannot comply with it?

(*g*) Can the employer show the requirement or condition to be justifiable irrespective of the colour, race, nationality or ethnic or national origin of the person to whom it is applied?

All the above definitions contain the following words or terms which have had to be considered in appeal decisions:

(*a*) requirement or condition;

(*b*) can comply;

(*c*) proportion;

(*d*) considerably smaller;

(*e*) justifiable.

127.4 **REQUIREMENT OR CONDITION**

Does the complainant, in a case of indirect discrimination, have to show that he or she has come up against a requirement or condition which operated as a must, so that inability to comply with it was an absolute bar, or is it sufficient if it was a factor to which weight was given, but not necessarily a conclusive factor?

The Court of Appeal gave the former answer in the early racial discrimination case of *Perera v Civil Service Commission* [*1983*] *IRLR 166*. In that case, Mr Perera was born in Sri Lanka. He applied for a post as a legal assistant in the Civil Service. He had a lack of relevant experience, which did not rule him out of consideration but was one of several factors taken into account. He presented a complaint of indirect racial discrimination, contending that the proportion of Sri Lankans who had the relevant experience was considerably smaller than the proportion of non-members of that racial group who had it. His claim failed, because relevant experience was not an absolute requirement.

As a general rule, appeal decisions on provisions which appear in the *RRA 1976* will be followed in cases on similar provisions in the *SDA 1975* (and vice versa), but the above decision was not followed by the EAT in the case *of Falkirk Council v Whyte [1997] IRLR 560*. In that case, the complainants were three women who had unsuccessfully applied for a managerial post at a prison in Scotland. Management training and supervisory experience were referred to in the specification for the post, but were stated to be 'desirable', not essential. It was found by the tribunal that in practice the absence of these qualifications was decisive against the complainants. The tribunal expressly decided to adopt a liberal interpretation of the legislation and found that a requirement had been applied to the complainants. Furthermore, women, who were mostly in basic grade posts, were disproportionately affected by the requirement, which had not been objectively justified. Accordingly the complaints were upheld.

On the facts, this decision may not have been inconsistent with *Perera*. The question whether a particular qualification is a requirement does not depend on the label attached to it by the employer. If in practice a stated preference is treated as an absolute bar, then the tribunal may properly treat the preference as being in fact a requirement.

The EAT, however, in upholding the tribunal's decision, made it clear that, in a sex discrimination case, they would not necessarily have regarded themselves as bound by *Perera*:

> 'if the case turned upon whether or not the relevant factors to become a requirement or condition had to be an absolute bar to qualification for the post in question, we would not be inclined to follow the race discrimination cases and, in particular, that of Perera'.

The submission in favour of the liberal approach which was made to and implicitly accepted by the EAT was based on the fact that the legislation (the *SDA 1975*) 'was based upon European Directive No 207/76 covering sex discrimination, which therefore fell to be treated differently from discrimination on grounds of race'.

There is, therefore, still some uncertainty in the interpretation of 'requirement or condition' in the *SDA 1975*. An employment tribunal, or division of the EAT, could regard itself as bound to follow *Perera*; alternatively, the Directive may be relied upon as the justification for adopting a more liberal and flexible approach. In practice, in both sex and race discrimination cases, employment tribunals will continue to examine stated criteria and their application very closely, in order to decide whether a stated preference is in practice a strict requirement.

127.5 CAN COMPLY

The expression 'can comply' is less strict than 'can physically comply' or 'can technically comply'. It is not sufficient, however, for a complainant to show that it would be inconvenient to comply. The test is whether the person can in practice can comply.

Under the *RRA 1976*, the issue has frequently arisen in relation to cultural or religious practices. The leading case is the non-employment case of *Mandla v Lee [1983] IRLR 209*. The complaint was about a school rule under which a Sikh schoolboy was required to wear a uniform, including a cap, and not permitted to wear a turban instead. It would of course have been physically possible for the boy to abandon the turban and wear a cap, but he would have had to break with the cultural traditions of the ethnic group to which he belonged. The House of Lords held that in these circumstances he could not comply with the school uniform requirement.

127.6 Indirect Discrimination

In the context of direct sex or marriage discrimination, the words 'can comply' most frequently arise in relation to the conflict between paid employment and childcare responsibilities. Many women, particularly (but by no means only) married women, try to resolve that conflict by working part-time while their children are young. In theory, they could insist on dividing the responsibility with their partners (or not seeking custody of children if they are single parents) but the law recognises the practical realities. When, for example, a full-time employee returning from maternity leave applies to go part-time, in order to spend part of the day with a small child, a tribunal would normally accept that for the time being she cannot comply with a requirement to work full time.

The circumstances in which the ability to comply must be considered are those prevailing at the time when the requirement or condition is applied. For example, in *Clarke v Eley (IMI) Kynoch [1982] IRLR 482,* the part-timers were selected for redundancy before full timers were considered. The requirement, in a case such as that, is that an employee must be full-time in order to avoid being at the head of the queue for compulsory redundancy. It is the fact of being a part-time worker at the time of redundancy selection that prevents compliance; the reasons why the complainant became a part-timer are immaterial.

127.6 DISPARATE IMPACT – PROPORTION

A key element in the statutory definitions is disparate or disproportionate impact (neither of these expressions is actually used in the legislation) on the members of the relevant group (such as women or black workers) to which the complainant belongs. It is also necessary to show disparate impact in order to prove indirect discrimination against women, men or married workers of either sex under the *Equal Treatment Directive*.

Before the Employment Tribunal can compare the proportion of members of the relevant group who can comply with the proportion of non-members who can comply, there are two important preliminary questions:

(*a*) who are the workers in the two groups – the 'pool'?

(*b*) is statistical evidence required?

127.7 THE POOL

The definition of the pool is a question of fact according to the circumstances of the case. There are at least five possible definitions:

(*a*) all the workers at a particular establishment;

(*b*) the whole workforce of a particular employer;

(*c*) all having a particular qualification;

(*d*) all economically active men and women in Great Britain;

(*e*) all workers in the catchment area of a particular factory.

The first or second of these cases will commonly apply when the complaint is made by an existing employee, as in the above-mentioned redundancy case of *Clarke v Eley (IMI) Kynoch Limited.* One of the other cases would normally apply in relation to a complaint made by a job applicant. For example, in *Jones v University of Manchester [1993] IRLR 218,* the complaint of indirect sex discrimination was about an upper age limit. An unchallenged requirement for the post was possession of a degree. It was held by the Court of Appeal that the pool consisted of the whole graduate population.

In the same case, it was held that it was impermissible to limit the pool artificially, to those on whom there is a potentially adverse impact, as happened in the 'rogue case' (the authors' expression, not the Court of Appeal's) of *Kidd v DRG (UK) Limited* [*1985*] *IRLR 190*.

127.8 STATISTICAL EVIDENCE

Relevant statistics are most likely to be available in the two extreme cases, that of a pool which covers all economically active men and women and that of a pool which is limited to the workers in a particular factory. National statistics relating to the former pool are published at regular intervals; even where the employer has not kept statistics, it is usually possible to count the men and women at a particular factory and (perhaps with more difficulty) the members of a particular ethnic group working at the factory.

Finding statistical evidence is likely to be more of a problem where the pool consists, for example, of all those with a particular qualification or of all the workers in an ill-defined catchment area. In such a case, an employment tribunal is likely to take a practical approach by, for example, using the statistics which relate to a larger group or by basing decisions on the knowledge and experience possessed by the members of the tribunal acting as an industrial jury. For example, it would not normally be difficult to persuade a tribunal that a considerably smaller percentage of women than of men can comply with a requirement of full-time working.

The Court of Appeal decision in *Perera v Civil Service Commission* has already been referred to. In the EAT [*1982*] *IRLR 147* it was said that elaborate statistical evidence should not be required unless it is clear that there is an issue as to whether disproportionate impact can be shown. A different approach was endorsed by the EAT in the above-mentioned case of *Kidd*, where in the absence of statistical evidence a tribunal was not prepared to accept that a requirement to work full-time had a disproportionate impact on women. That approach may occasionally still be adopted. It is prudent, therefore, if disproportionate impact cannot be agreed in advance between the parties, to apply for directions before the full tribunal hearing takes place.

127.9 CONSIDERABLY SMALLER

If statistics are available, then once the pool has been defined the following calculations must be carried out:

(*a*) How many members does the pool contain of the relevant group (e.g. women) to which the complainant belongs?

(*b*) What percentage of them are qualifiers (i.e. those who can comply with the requirement or condition complained of)?

(*c*) How many non-members (e.g. men) are there in the pool?

(*d*) What percentage of them are qualifiers?

It is then necessary to compare the two percentages. There is disproportionate impact if the percentage of qualifiers in the complainant's group (e.g. women) is considerably smaller than the percentage of qualifiers amongst the non-members of that group (e.g. men).

There is no simple arithmetical test to show whether any particular percentage difference is considerable. The exercise is not one of pure mathematics.

127.9 Indirect Discrimination

In *London Underground Limited v Edwards (No 2)* [*1998*] *IRLR 364*, a female train operator was unable to comply with new rostering arrangements. This was because she was a single parent with a young child.

The pool consisted of all the train operators to whom the new rostering arrangements applied. There were only 21 women in that pool and 20 of them (or 95.2 per cent) could comply with the new arrangements. There were more than 2000 men in the pool and all of them could comply with the new roster.

In terms of the bare statistics, 95.2 per cent (the female qualifiers) may not seem considerably smaller than 100 per cent (the male qualifiers). The difference is only 4.8 per cent, but a finding by the tribunal that 95.2 per cent was considerably smaller than 100 per cent was upheld by the Court of Appeal.

Potter LJ, accepted that a percentage difference of no more than 5 per cent or thereabouts is inherently likely to lead an employment tribunal to the conclusion that the case has not been made out, but he was not prepared to say that the conclusion must inevitably follow in every case (including this one). He made the following general observations:

(*a*) An employer should be required to justify a requirement or condition only if there is a substantial, and not merely marginal, discriminatory effect (or disparate impact) as between men and women.

(*b*) That disparate impact should be inherent in the application of the requirement or condition and not simply the product of unreliable statistics or fortuitous circumstances.

(*c*) There is an infinite number of employment situations and there is a need for an area of flexibility (or margin of appreciation).

In the present case, the tribunal was entitled to look behind the bare percentages. Even though the pool was a restricted one, the tribunal were entitled to take into account the fact, based on their own knowledge and experience, that nationally about ten female single parents for every male single parent have care of a child. This fact helped to show that the percentage difference in the present case was not fortuitous.

The tribunal was also entitled to have regard to the large discrepancy in numbers. Not one male operator out of more than 2000 was unable to comply with the rostering arrangements. If there had been one male non-qualifier, the percentage of male qualifiers would have been hardly at all affected; on the other hand, if there had been one extra woman who could not comply, then the percentage of female qualifiers would have been reduced by nearly 5 per cent.

Further guidance was given by both the ECJ and the House of Lords in *R v Secretary of State for Employment ex parte Seymour Smith and Perez*. As readers will recall, this case concerned the qualifying period for most complaints of unfair dismissal, which in 1985 was increased to two years and remained at two years until 1999. The question was whether the two year qualifying period was contrary to the *Equal Treatment Directive* because of an indirectly discriminatory effect on women.

The statistics showed that in 1985, when the qualifying period was increased, the percentage of men who had the two years' service was 77.4, as against 68.9 of women. The gap narrowed in most subsequent years, although with some fluctuations. The respective percentages were 74.5 and 67.4 in 1991, the year in which the applicants were dismissed, and 78.4 and 74.1 two years later.

The ECJ, [*1999*] *IRLR 253*, expressed the view that the 1985 statistics did not appear on the face of it to show that the percentage of women who could comply was considerably smaller than the percentage of men who could. In the House of Lords, *R v Secretary of State for the Employment ex parte Seymour Smith and Perez (No 2) [2000] IRLR 263*, Lord Nicholls pointed out that the relevant statistics were those for 1991, when the applicants were dismissed. The percentage difference was smaller then than it had been in 1985, but that was not the end of the matter. The ECJ had observed that 'statistical evidence revealing a lesser but persistent and relatively constant disparity over a long period could also be evidence of apparent sex discrimination'.

Lord Nicholls pointed out that over the period of seven years from 1985 up to and including 1991 the ratio of men and women who qualified was roughly 10:9. He said that these figures were 'in borderline country', but he found himself 'driven to the conclusion that a persistent and constant disparity of the order just mentioned in respect of the entire male and female labour forces of the country over a period of seven years cannot be brushed aside and dismissed as insignificant or inconsiderable ... I think these figures are adequate to demonstrate that the extension of the qualifying period had a considerably greater adverse impact on women than men'.

Lord Nicholls also suggested, in relation to disparate impact, that it may be appropriate to look at the respective percentages of non-qualifiers as well as those of qualifiers. He referred to several ECJ decisions where this has been done, but left the question open for another occasion. In *Barry v Midland Bank plc [1999] IRLR 581* he had taken a step further and suggested that a better guide will often be found in expressing the proportions of men and women in the disadvantaged group as a ratio of each other.

The following principles can be extracted from the above authorities:

(*a*) the starting point is to look at the percentage difference;

(*b*) a small percentage difference may be magnified somewhat if it is constant over a long period;

(*c*) the actual numbers of (if the case is one of indirect sex discrimination) women and men can also be relevant, if there is a big disparity;

(*d*) evidence which indicates that a disparity which is (on the one hand) fortuitous or (on the other hand) linked to the difference in sex can also be relevant.

127.10 DETRIMENT

There is no indirect discrimination unless the requirement or condition complained of is to the detriment of the complainant because he or she cannot comply with it.

There is usually no difficulty in showing detriment. If the complaint is about requirements or conditions for a new job or a promotion, the detriment is in not being eligible for the post. If the requirement or condition relates to selection criteria for redundancy, the detriment is in being dismissed on the ground of redundancy.

127.11 JUSTIFIABILITY

There will not necessarily be a finding of indirect discrimination, even if a requirement or condition has been applied to the complainant and the Tribunal is satisfied about inability to comply, detriment and disparate impact. The employer can defeat the complaint by showing the requirement or condition to be justifiable.

Both the *SDA 1975* and the *RRA 1976* contain an express proviso in relation to justification. In a complaint of indirect sex (or marriage) discrimination, the employer must be able to justify the requirement or condition irrespective of the sex (or marital status) of the person to whom it is applied. The *RRA 1976* requires justification irrespective of the colour, race, nationality or ethnic or national origins of the person to whom the requirement or condition is applied.

The case of *Mandla v Lee [1983] IRLR 209* has already been referred to. This was the case of the Sikh schoolboy who was required to wear a uniform, including a cap and not a turban. The justification claimed by the school was a policy of promoting good race relations. Pupils were to be encouraged to work and play together without regard to racial differences. It was felt that permitting a pupil to wear a turban would draw attention to such differences. It was held by the House of Lords that this reason for the requirement complained of, however well intentioned, could not amount to sufficient justification under the *RRA 1976*, because it was not a reason which had no regard to the ethnic origins of those to whom it was applied.

The circumstances of the above case were unusual, but the principle of the decision could on occasion could be relevant in the employment context. The following case would be an example:

(*a*) An organisation has a workforce which is predominantly white and male.

(*b*) The management has been encouraging job applications from black and female workers (with no discrimination at the point of selection).

(*c*) There is a need for redundancies.

(*d*) If length of service were the only or main criterion, most of the recently recruited black and female workers would go.

(*e*) So as not to prejudice the policy of diversity, the management and union agree criteria which target the workers over 50.

(*f*) This means that the organisation retains a considerably smaller percentage of white workers than of black workers and a considerably smaller percentage of men than of women.

It is difficult to see how the organisation could have a defence to complaints of indirect racial and sex discrimination. This is because the justification for the adopted criteria is based on the sex and colour of the workers to whom the criteria have been applied.

The question which more commonly arises is that of the standard by which the reason for a requirement or condition must be judged.

Is it enough for the employer to show that the requirement or condition is desirable or convenient or one which has traditionally been used? Or does the employer have to show that the requirement or condition is absolutely essential to the proper functioning of the organisation? The answer lies between the two extremes.

The leading case is that of *Hampson v Department of Education and Science.* The case concerned a refusal to recognise a teaching qualification obtained in Hong Kong, because the initial training course there was only two years, as opposed to the three years in England.

The Department of Education did not regard it as sufficient that Mrs Hampson had completed a further teaching course, lasting a full year, some years after the initial two years.

The case went to the House of Lords, but the meaning of 'justifiable' was dealt with by the Court of Appeal *[1989] IRLR 69.* An odd feature of the case was that Balcombe LJ gave a dissenting judgment, but the other members of the Court endorsed the guidance which he gave on the issue of justification. His judgment included the following key features:

(*a*) The test is objective.

(*b*) The standard is the reasonable need of the undertaking.

(*c*) That reasonable need may be, but is not confined to, economic or administrative efficiency.

(*d*) The Tribunal considering the matter must strike an objective balance between the discriminatory effect of the condition and the reasonable need of the undertaking.

This guidance was approved by the House of Lords, some years later, in *Webb v EMO Air Cargo (UK) Limited* [*1993*] *IRLR 27.*

Further guidance was given by the EAT in *Cobb and others v Secretary of State for Employment and Manpower Services Commission* [*1989*] *IRLR 464.* This case was about the eligibility criteria for entry to a programme to provide temporary work for unemployed young workers. These criteria were linked to receipt of unemployment or supplementary benefit in a way which, in spite of some adjustments, made it more difficult for married women to qualify for the programme. The EAT upheld a tribunal decision that the criteria were justifiable and gave the following guidance:

(*a*) The absence of a mass of statistics or sociological or expert evidence was not fatal to the defence.

(*b*) The justification put forward may be based on a broad view of the matter, provided that it is rational, based on logic and tenable.

(*c*) It is not essential to prove that there is no other possible way, however expensive and administratively complicated, of achieving the desired object.

(*d*) The defence may fail, however, if the tribunal find that there was an alternative method which ought reasonably to have been considered and adopted.

(*e*) A balancing exercise is appropriate, in that the tribunal might find that the detriment suffered by those excluded is too high a price to pay to achieve the object sought.

(*f*) There is no rule that a government department or publicly funded body cannot take into account financial considerations.

In both the above cases, there were references to the balancing exercise to be carried out by the tribunal, in weighing the reasonable needs of the undertaking against the discriminatory effect of the requirement or condition. It is important not to place too much weight on this factor when considering whether a requirement or condition has been shown to be justifiable. The question of justification only becomes relevant if the requirement or condition has *some* discriminatory effect; that discriminatory effect would normally be relevant to justification only if the case made out by the employer on justification is only a borderline one.

A cautionary note was struck by the Court of Appeal in the case of *Jones v University of Manchester* [*1993*] *IRLR 218,* a case which involved an upper age limit for a post as a careers advisor. It was claimed that the upper limit was indirectly discriminatory against female graduates. The tribunal referred to statistical evidence that there were thousands of women enrolled as mature students in English universities who would be affected by a requirement or condition of this kind. It was held by the Court of Appeal that the relevant discriminatory impact was not that on female graduates generally but on the small section affected by *this* requirement of *this* employer. The matters to which the tribunal were entitled to have regard were the quantitative and qualitative effect of the requirement or condition in the particular circumstances, i.e:

(*a*) how many will or are likely to suffer;

(*b*) how much damage or disappointment may be caused;

(*c*) how lasting or final is that damage?

The factors which employers should take into account, before deciding to apply a requirement or condition, can usefully be illustrated by considering two categories of case which frequently arise in practice, one under the *SDA 1975* and one under the *RRA 1976*.

Many women (and some men) who have childcare responsibilities apply to change from full-time working to part-time working. Such applications are commonly, but not exclusively, made when the employee returns or is about to return from maternity leave.

Employers who receive such requests face two main legal dangers. If they have a policy of granting the request if made by a woman but refusing it when made by a man, they are directly discriminating against male employees. If they have a policy of refusing all such requests, they will face indirect discrimination claims by female employees.

What the employer must do is have fair and consistent principles, but apply them on a case by case basis, always having regard to the requirements of the particular job and to the circumstances of the particular employee. The following are key principles:

(*a*) The employer must not have a blanket policy of refusing all requests for part-time working. Such a policy could never be justifiable.

(*b*) It is also unsafe to categorise particular jobs as permanently unsuitable for part-time working. Jobs and circumstances change.

(*c*) Where there are reasons for requiring full-time working in a particular job (such as the need for continuous staff supervision or customer care), those reasons must be questioned and ways of overcoming the objection to part-time working must be considered.

(*d*) Even if there are insuperable objections to having the work done part-time, that is not the end of the matter. Would job share be a possibility?

(*e*) If there are insuperable objections to part-time working in the current post, is there a suitable alternative part-time post which could be offered to the employee?

The issue of indirect racial discrimination can arise when requirements imposed by an employer conflict with the religious or cultural traditions of a particular ethnic group. For example, Sikh employees working in chocolate factories have on occasion been unable to comply with requirements that employees must be clean shaven.

Clearly in such cases product hygiene is a vital consideration to which an employer can, and indeed must, have regard. The matter does not, however, end there. No tribunal would be likely to uphold a total ban on beards in the chocolate factory unless the employer has carefully considered and been compelled to eliminate methods of reconciling the required objectives with the needs of the employee.

There have been cases in the past in which tribunals have upheld rules prohibiting beards in chocolate factories. It can certainly not be assumed that there would be the same outcome in a similar case today. Each case must be considered on its own facts. A tribunal today would almost certainly expect the employer to have given detailed consideration to the possibility of ensuring product hygiene by, for example, providing the employee with protective covering.

127.12 COMPENSATION

Compensation is usually awarded when a tribunal has made a finding of indirect discrimination, but an award of compensation is not inevitable.

Under the *RRA 1976*, the tribunal does not have the power to order payment of compensation if the respondent proves (on a balance of probability) that the requirement or condition complained of was not applied with the intention of treating the complainant unfavourably on racial grounds. The test is objective, in the sense that an employer will be taken to have intended the reasonably foreseeable consequences of his actions.

In practice, the only cases where this lack of intention is likely to be found proved are cases where the discriminatory effect of the requirement or condition has not occurred and should not have occurred to the respondent. For example:

An employer asks job applicants to fill in a written application form for a manual job, overlooking the possibility that this requirement will disadvantage (and could wholly exclude) job applicants for whom English is not their first language. He is not aware of the discriminatory effect until he receives notice of a tribunal complaint by a worker from another EU country who has settled in England and who has been deterred from applying for the job because of his inability to complete the application form.

In contrast, an employer in Wales insists that job applicants should have a good command of the Welsh language, even though they will not need to speak Welsh for the performance of their duties. The employer is well aware of the discriminatory effect of the requirement, but that factor is overridden by the employer's enthusiasm to promote the Welsh language.

In the latter case, compensation would almost certainly be awarded The employer would be taken to have intended the consequences which he foresaw his actions would have, even though his motive was a different one.

The position under the *SDA 1975* was initially identical to that under the *RRA 1976*, but the law was changed by regulations which came into effect on 25 March 1996. The position now under the *SDA 1975* is that the tribunal, having made a finding of indirect discrimination, has the power to make an award of compensation if it considers that it is just and equitable to do so. This is a very wide power. In practice, compensation is usually awarded in cases where indirect sex or marriage discrimination is found to have taken place. Cases of indirect sex and marriage discrimination are, however, comparatively few in number in relation to cases of direct discrimination.

Where compensation is awarded for indirect discrimination, whether under the *SDA 1975* or the *RRA 1976*, there is no limit on the amount of the compensation.

127.13 EXAMPLES OF INDIRECT SEX DISCRIMINATION

The main factor which places women at a disadvantage in relation to certain requirements and conditions is that women still have the primary responsibility in society for raising children, both in single parent and in two parent households. Women who have such responsibilities may be unable to comply with requirements to:

(*a*) work full-time;

(*b*) start early or finish late;

(*c*) work a rotating shift pattern;

(*d*) attend residential training courses;

(*e*) undertake overseas or overnight travel.

127.14 Indirect Discrimination

Contractual mobility requirements, or the implementation of such requirements, can also be indirectly discriminatory, because in the majority of two parent households the woman is not the primary earner and is unable to relocate at will.

127.14 EXAMPLES OF INDIRECT RACIAL DISCRIMINATION

Certain requirements and conditions are always likely to have an indirectly discriminatory effect under the *RRA 1976*, although there are over the years changes in the ethnic groups likely to be disadvantaged by them.

For example, complaints of indirect racial discrimination which in the 1970s would probably have been made by first generation immigrants from the Commonwealth could now well be made by recent immigrants from Eastern Europe relating to matters such as:

(*a*) educational qualifications which are excessive in relation to the work to be carried out;

(*b*) a requirement to have a command of written or spoken English in order to be given a manual job.

It is also important, in relation to educational qualifications, that employers (and *Qualifying Bodies*) should not insist exclusively on qualifications obtained in the UK. Equivalent qualifications obtained overseas should always be accepted.

Complaints of indirect racial discrimination can also arise where the employer's requirements conflict with religious or cultural practices or traditions. So far, the only part of the UK to have laws against *Religious Discrimination* is *Northern Ireland*, but there is a clear overlap between *Religious Discrimination* and *Racial Discrimination*. A group which is predominantly a religious group can also be an ethnic group, such as the Sikhs. Other religious groups, such as Muslims, draw their members predominantly, although not exclusively, from particular ethnic groups.

Complaints of indirect racial discrimination sometimes relate to requirements on dress or appearance, such as rules:

(*a*) prohibiting *Beards*;

(*b*) requiring headgear other than turbans;

(*c*) forbidding female employees from wearing trousers.

All these requirements could be indirectly discriminatory, the first two against Sikhs and the third against Muslim women who are also, for example, of Pakistani origin.

There is also a need for flexibility on the part of employers where an employee needs:

(*a*) short breaks for prayer;

(*b*) to take part of his or her annual leave on a feast or holy day;

(*c*) to carry leave forward in order to take extended leave for a pilgrimage.

128 Inferences

There is rarely an admission or other direct evidence of *Direct Discrimination*. Findings of discrimination are usually based on the inferences to be drawn by the tribunal from, in particular:

(*a*) a difference in treatment; or

(*b*) false or evasive answers to a *Questionnaire*.

An inference, however, is not as strong as a presumption. An inference to be drawn from, for example, a difference in treatment will not lead to a finding of discrimination if a non-discriminatory reason for the difference in treatment is given and believed by the tribunal. In every case, the tribunal is required, having drawn any appropriate inferences and considered the evidence as a whole, to decide whether discrimination has been proved on a balance of probability – see *Evidence of Discrimination*.

129 Injunctions and Interdicts

Most complaints heard by employment tribunals under the *SDA 1975*, the *RRA 1976* or the *DDA 1995* are complaints by individuals seeking compensation.

In addition, the three statutory Commissions, the EOC, the CRE and the DRC can apply to a county court (or sheriff court in Scotland) for an injunction (or interdict in Scotland):

(*a*) under the *SDA 1975*, *RRA 1976* or the *Disability Rights Commission Act 1999* to prevent *Persistent Discrimination*;

(*b*) under *section 72* of the *SDA 1975* or *section 63* of the *RRA 1976* to prevent a person from contravening any of the statutory provisions relating to discriminatory *Advertisements*, *Instructions to Discriminate* or *Pressure to Discriminate*.

It is, however, impossible for any of the Commissions to apply for an injunction or interdict against a person (or organisation) unless there has previously been a final finding by an employment tribunal against that person (or organisation) or unless a *Non-Discrimination Notice* has become final.

130 Injury to Feelings

It is expressly provided in the *SDA 1975*, the *RRA 1976* and the *DDA 1995* that the award of *Compensation* may include compensation for injury to feelings. This power is similar to the power of a court to award general damages in personal injury cases.

It is almost inevitable that an act of unlawful discrimination will cause distress, humiliation or some other hurt to the victim. Compensation for injury to feelings is normally awarded.

There is no provision in the *EPA 1970* for compensation for injury to feelings.

131 Instructions to Discriminate

A person complaining of sex discrimination, racial discrimination or disability discrimination may include as a respondent not only the person (such as an employer) on whom the law places primary liability but also any other person who has aided the discrimination complained of. The definition of *Aiding* discrimination covers *Employees* or *Agents* for whose acts their employer or principal respectively are liable.

The individual complainant may not, however, include as a respondent a person (other than the employer or principal) who gave instructions to discriminate without actually participating in that discrimination. A complaint about instructions to discriminate contrary to the *SDA 1975* or the *RRA 1976* can be presented only by:

(*a*) the EOC under *section 39* of the *SDA 1975*; or

(*b*) the CRE under *section 108* of the *RRA 1976*.

Under each of the two Acts, the person giving the instructions is acting unlawfully so long as:

(*a*) he has authority over the person to whom the instruction is given; or

(*b*) the person to whom the instruction is given is accustomed to act in accordance with his wishes.

There are no provisions in the *DDA 1995* (or the *Disability Rights Commission Act*) relating to instructions to discriminate unlawfully.

132 Internal Appeals

An employer can be liable for unintended discrimination, for example where:

(*a*) a discriminatory decision has resulted from an unrecognised prejudice;

(*b*) there has been unauthorised discrimination by a manager or other employee; or

(*c*) the discriminatory effect of a requirement or condition was not appreciated.

In all such cases, it is in the interests of both the employer and the employee who has been discriminated against for the matter to be resolved internally. The employee should pursue an internal appeal against a decision which he believes to have been discriminatory, for example, relating to a disciplinary matter, a grading decision or selection for redundancy; an employer considering such an appeal should give particularly careful consideration to, and investigate, any allegations of discrimination.

The fact that a complainant has tried to resolve the matter through an internal appeal can be a reason for extending the time limit for presenting a tribunal complaint. It is, however, prudent for a complainant to present a complaint to tribunal well within the prescribed time and if necessary ask for the hearing of the tribunal complaint to be stayed until the internal appeal has been dealt with. While there are sometimes advantages in delaying the making of a complaint to a tribunal, these are usually outweighed by serious disadvantages.

133 Internal Investigations

Employers and other respondents should carry out a thorough internal investigation into any allegation of harassment or other unlawful discrimination, whether the allegation is made before or after a complaint to tribunal is presented. Where an allegation is well founded, it is in the employer's interest to establish that fact and to take appropriate action without delay.

An issue which frequently arises where allegations of *Harassment* have been made is whether the alleged harasser should be suspended. In particular, what action should be taken where the complainant states that she (or occasionally he) would find it impossible to continue working with the alleged harasser?

Guidance on this issue cannot be found either in the legislation or in any of the Codes of Practice. The authors suggest the following general guidelines:

(*a*) The law does not require the *automatic* suspension of any employee against whom an allegation of harassment is made. Although suspension on pay need not be a disciplinary action, it can be detrimental to the employee concerned (and indeed to the employer if that employee has an important role in the organisation).

(*b*) It may be necessary to suspend the alleged harasser on full pay in order to carry out a thorough investigation.

(*c*) If the complainant objects strongly to continuing to work with the harasser, possible options, during the investigation, are to move the alleged harasser to other work (if this can be done within the terms of his or her contract), a voluntary transfer for either party or voluntary paid leave for either party.

(*d*) Compulsory transfer or suspension of the complainant is not an option – see *Victimisation*.

(*e*) If it proves to be unavoidable for the complainant and alleged harasser to continue to work together, appropriate safeguards, including instructions to managers and supervisors, should be given to prevent any (further) harassment and give reassurance to the complainant.

134 Interviews

The way in which *Job Interviews* are carried out can give rise to complaints of unlawful discrimination. It is particularly important that guidance and, if possible, training should be given to all persons who are required to carry out such interviews.

Job interviews are not the only interviews which lead to decisions which could be challenged under one of the discrimination laws. Other relevant interviews include disciplinary interviews, appraisal interviews and consultations with individual employees regarding sickness records or possible selection for redundancy. Guidance and (if possible) training should be given to all interviewers on conducting interviews and making relevant decisions in a way which both avoids unlawful discrimination and avoids giving a false impression of discrimination.

135 Irish – as racial group

Direct or indirect racial discrimination against an Irish worker is covered by the *RRA 1976* – see *Racial Grounds* and *Racial Group*.

A worker from Northern Ireland belongs to a racial group defined by national origin. A worker from the Republic of Ireland belongs to racial groups defined by reference to both national origin and nationality.

There have been cases in which employment tribunals have awarded compensation to Irish workers for direct racial discrimination. In one case, a job offer was withdrawn after the Birmingham pub bombings. In another, an employee complained that a regular diet of 'Irish jokes' amounted to racial harassment.

Religious discrimination against a Catholic worker could also be indirect racial discrimination where the victim is Irish, particularly from the Republic, because it is likely that the evidence would show a considerably lower percentage of non-Catholics in that worker's racial group than in the non-members of that group.

136 Job Applications

Many complaints of discrimination relate to the handling of job applications, whether made by external candidates or by employees seeking promotion or transfer. For guidance on the avoidance of discrimination see *Recruitment*, *Promotion*, *Selection* and *Job Interviews*.

Job applications and all related documents should be kept until at least six months after the job has been filled (longer if practicable). The time limit for a complaint of sex, racial or disability discrimination is three months, but the time limit can be extended. If a suitably qualified but unsuccessful candidate complains of discrimination, and the employer has destroyed the job applications and other relevant documents, the employment tribunal could draw an adverse inference.

It is also necessary to record information about job applications, and the reasons for shortlisting and selection decisions, as part of the *Monitoring* which should be carried out in order to ensure that an *Equal Opportunity Policy* is operating successfully.

137 Job Descriptions

Job descriptions should be prepared for all posts, whether they are to be filled externally or internally – see *Recruitment*, *Promotion* and *Selection*.

Without a job description (and also a person specification, showing the qualities required in the light of the job description) it is difficult to show that shortlisting and selection decisions have been made objectively, without any unlawful discrimination.

138 Job Duties

Whatever flexibility the contract of employment may give to the employer, in terms of the duties which employees can be required to carry out, there must be no sex, racial or disability discrimination in the way in which job duties are allocated – see *Benefits* and *Detriment*.

In considering whether a complainant's job and a comparator's job are *Like Work* or work of *Equal Value* for the purposes of a claim under the *EPA 1970*, it is necessary to focus on the duties which are actually performed in practice (and how frequently they are performed) and not on theoretical requirements.

Employers can be obliged to change or modify the job duties of disabled employees in order to comply with the *section 6* duty to make *Reasonable Adjustments*.

139 Job Evaluation

Job evaluation is the science (or art) of evaluating a job in terms of the demands made on the person doing that job under various headings. The process requires considerable expertise. It involves:

(*a*) identifying various demand factors, such as the skill, physical effort, mental effort, decision making and level of responsibility which a job demands;

(*b*) giving appropriate weightings to these factors, having regard to the nature of the particular job;

(*c*) allocating points under each heading.

This is a simplified account of a complicated process.

Job evaluation can be relevant in three respects in relation to *Equal Pay* cases, as follows:

(*a*) If the complainant's job and the comparator's job have been rated as equivalent under a job evaluation study, then the equal pay claim must succeed (assuming that the two workers are in the *Same Employment*), unless the *Material Factor* defence can be made out. A claim can be based on a job evaluation study which has been carried out, even if for some reason the study has not then been implemented – *O'Brien v Sim-Chem Limited* [*1980*] *IRLR 373.*

(*b*) In an *Equal Value* case, any experts appointed by the parties (and also the *Independent Expert* if the tribunal decide that one should be appointed) will carry out a job evaluation limited to the jobs of the complainant and the comparator(s).

(*c*) Under *section 2A* of the *EPA 1970* an *Equal Value* claim must fail if a job evaluation study has been carried out and has given a greater value to the work of the comparator (or all the comparators if there is more than one) than to the work of the complainant, so long as the study was a proper analytical study and did not involve any sex discrimination.

140 Job Interviews

Many employers still use the generally unscientific (and in some cases almost random) method of job interviews to make the final decision on the appointment of internal or external candidates to job vacancies. Many successful complaints of racial or sex discrimination in not appointing the complainant (or not offering the complainant a second interview) have been based on:

(*a*) questions or remarks which reveal discriminatory attitudes; or

(*b*) detailed and negative questioning about personal matters which are irrelevant to the job for which the candidate has applied.

In *Nagarajan v London Regional Transport [1999] IRLR 572* the House of Lords ruled (what some, but not the EAT or the Court of Appeal, would have thought to be self-evident) that discrimination or victimisation by interviewers is part of the arrangements for selection and is therefore covered by *section 4(1)(a)* of the *RRA 1976* (and also *section 6(1)(a)* of the *SDA 1975* and *section 4(1)(a)* of the *DDA 1995*).

In the early case of *Saunders v Richmond-upon-Thames Borough Council [1977] IRLR 362,* it was held by the EAT that it was not unlawful to ask offensive questions which are influenced by the candidate's gender; the importance of such questions was that in many cases they will be strong evidence that bias and prejudice were the reasons for not appointing the candidate. This was the case in which a well-known woman golfer, applying for the job of professional at a municipal golf course, was asked questions such as:

(*a*) do you think men respond as well to a woman golf professional as to a man?; and

(*b*) don't you think this type of job is rather unglamorous?

In principle, however, a finding of unlawful discrimination could be made if remarks made to a candidate are so offensive and insulting as to amount to a detriment in themselves, whatever the outcome of the interview. A complaint could also be made in respect of remarks which discourage and disadvantage the candidate, to the effect that the candidate is unable to make a good impression on the interview panel as a whole. In the case of *Simon v Brimham Associates [1987] IRLR 307,* Lord Justice Balcombe said that he was prepared to accept, as a proposition of law, that:

> 'in appropriate circumstances, words or acts of discouragement can amount to treatment of the person discouraged less favourable than that given to other persons'.

For general guidance on avoiding discrimination in filling job vacancies – see *Recruitment* and *Selection*.

Interviewers should prepare in advance for the interview by:

(*a*) agreeing the selection criteria and the scoring system, in the light of the job description and any person specification;

(*b*) deciding on standard questions, including situational questions relating to the particular job, and agreeing which interviewer should ask which questions;

(*c*) reading the candidates' application forms and CVs;

(*d*) ascertaining and meeting the special needs of any candidates who are known to be disabled (including, where necessary, allowing extra time).

During the interview itself, the focus should be on the requirements of the particular job for which the candidate has applied. The Codes of Practice make the following recommendations:

(*a*) questions should relate to the requirements of the job – where personal circumstances may affect job performance (for example because the job involves unsocial hours or extensive travel) the issues should be discussed objectively, without detailed questioning based on assumptions about marital status, childcare or domestic obligations (paragraph 23(c) of the Code of Practice under the *SDA 1975*);

(*b*) questions about marriage plans or family intentions should not be asked, if they could be construed as showing bias against women (paragraph 23(d));

(*c*) interviewers should be aware of the possible misunderstandings that can occur in interviews between persons of different cultural backgrounds (paragraph 1.14(b) of the Code under the *RRA 1976*).

If a candidate has a disability which could be relevant to the job, the issue should be discussed frankly but positively, with particular reference to any *Reasonable Adjustments* which may be required.

When making notes, interviewers should avoid flippant or derogatory comments, since the notes will be relevant documents for the purpose of any tribunal hearing. Scores, comments and reasons for decisions should be recorded and preserved.

141 Job Offers

Although most complaints of discrimination in *Recruitment* or *Promotion* are made by unsuccessful candidates, it should be noted that a complaint can also be made if there is discrimination in relation to the terms on which employment is offered. For example it is unlawful for an employer to offer a job to a disabled candidate but at a rate of pay which is lower than the rate which would have been offered if he had not been disabled, unless offering that pay can be justified – see *Justification and Disability Discrimination*.

Where a person wishes to complain under the *SDA 1975* about the salary which is offered or any other proposed contractual term for the payment of money, she can do so only if, on taking up the employment, she would have had a claim under the *EPA 1970* – see *Recruitment*.

142 Job Share

Many full-time employees who have childcare responsibilities need to reduce their working hours. This issue is frequently (but not exclusively) raised when a woman returns or is about to return from maternity leave.

The unjustifiable refusal of a request by a woman to go part-time because of her child-care responsibilities would generally be *Indirect Discrimination*. A refusal is normally justified if there is a real need for the particular work to be done on a full-time basis (for example because of the importance of regular customer contact). In such circumstances, however, the employer must also be willing to consider the possibility of jobshare. Any employer who rejects jobshare out of hand as a possible alternative to part-time working will be vulnerable to a complaint of indirect sex discrimination. Jobshare is not an easy option, because of the compatibility and commitment which it requires from the jobsharers, but it is one which must be explored as an alternative to the outright rejection of a request to work part-time.

Jobshare is not a facility which can lawfully be made available only for female employees. It would be direct sex discrimination to reject a request by a male employee to jobshare if a request by a female employee (the relevant circumstances being the same or not materially different) would have been accepted.

Jobshare should also be considered as a *Reasonable Adjustment* where a disabled employee seeks reduced working hours.

143 Joint Respondents

Most acts of discrimination are committed by managers and other employees acting in the course of their employment. In theory, in any such case, the employee responsible for the discrimination could be named as a joint respondent. In practice, it is mainly in cases where the complaint is one of harassment that the complainant names the alleged harassers as additional respondents. The importance of doing so, from the complainant's point of view, is that a finding can be made against the harassers, and they can be ordered to pay compensation, even if the employer establishes the defence that all *Reasonably Practicable Steps* to prevent the discrimination were taken.

Where a complaint is upheld against more than one respondent, then the tribunal decides how much compensation each respondent should be ordered to pay. The practice is to make a separate award against each respondent, rather than order payment of a sum for which each respondent is jointly and severally liable.

144 Justification

Complaints which would otherwise have succeeded can be defeated in the following cases:

(*a*) where a requirement or condition having an indirectly discriminatory effect under the *SDA 1975* or the *RRA 1976* is objectively justified by the respondent – see *Indirect Discrimination*;

(*b*) where less favourable treatment of a disabled person, for a reason relating to the disability, or a failure to make a reasonable adjustment, is justified – see *Justification and Disability Discrimination*;

(*c*) where a difference in pay or some other contract term as between a complainant and comparator involves indirect discrimination but that difference can be objectively justified – see *Equal Pay* and *Material Factor*.

Unless the case falls within one of the express exceptions contained in the *SDA 1975* or the *RRA 1976*, there are no circumstances in which direct sex or race discrimination can be justified.

145 Justification and Disability Discrimination

145.1 STATUTORY MEANING

Section 5(3) of the *DDA 1995* provides that less favourable treatment of a disabled person is justified if – but only if – the reason for it is both material to the circumstances of the particular case *and* substantial. Thus the reason must relate to the individual facts and not simply be trivial or minor.

Furthermore, *section 5(5)* provides that less favourable treatment cannot be justified where the employer is under a duty to make a reasonable adjustment but fails (without justification) to do so, *unless* the treatment would have been justified even after that adjustment.

Thus justification will be a crucial issue in many cases of alleged disability discrimination.

145.2 THE CODE OF PRACTICE

The Code of Practice for the elimination of discrimination in the field of employment against disabled persons or persons who have had a disability provides useful examples of what will, and what will not, be justified treatment. For instance:

(*a*) A factory worker with a mental illness is sometimes away from work due to his disability. Because of that, he is dismissed. However the amount of time off is very little more than the employer accepts as sick leave for other employees and so is very unlikely to be a substantial reason.

(*b*) Someone who has psoriasis is rejected for a job involving modelling cosmetics on a part of the body which in his case is severely disfigured by the condition, This will be lawful if his appearance would be incompatible with the purpose of the work. This is a substantial reason which is clearly material to the individual circumstances.

As regards adjustments, examples given by the Code include:

(*a*) An applicant for a typing job is not the best person on the face of it, but only because her typing speed is too slow due to arthritis in her hands. If a reasonable adjustment (e.g. an adapted keyboard) would overcome this, her typing speed would not in itself be a substantial reason for not employing. Therefore the employer would be unlawfully discriminating if on account of her typing speed he did not employ her and provide the adjustments.

(*b*) Someone who is blind applies for a job which requires a significant amount of driving. If it is not reasonable for the employer to adjust the job so that the driving duties are given to someone else, the employer's need for a driver might well be a substantial reason for not employing the blind person. It is clearly material to the particular circumstances. The non-appointment could therefore be justified.

145.3 INTERPRETATION

Experience to date has seen both employers and employment tribunals struggling, in some cases, to get to grips with the concept of justification in disability cases and the crucial related requirement of a duty to make *Reasonable Adjustments*. In *Clark v TDG*

Ltd t/a Novacold [1999] IRLR 318, the Court of Appeal ruled that whether treatment has been shown to be justified is a question of fact to be determined by an employment tribunal and on a proper self-direction on the relevant law. This includes taking into account those parts of the Code which a reasonable tribunal would regard as relevant to the determination of that question. In *Clark*, the tribunal had failed to have regard to relevant provisions in the Code relating to termination of employment. The question of justification of the dismissal therefore had to be remitted to the tribunal for re-hearing.

The EAT considered the statutory sequence for establishing justification in *Baynton v Saurus General Engineers Ltd [1999] IRLR 604*. The steps are as follows:

(*a*) the disabled applicant shows less favourable treatment, such as dismissal;

(*b*) the respondent shows that the treatment, the dismissal, is justified if:

  (i) the reason for the dismissal is both material to the circumstances of the particular case and substantial; unless

  (ii) the employer is under a duty to make reasonable adjustments in relation to the applicant but fails without justification to comply with that duty, subject to the treatment being justified even if he had complied with that duty.

Therefore, it is necessary for the employer to show that the reason for dismissal was material to the circumstances of the case and substantial and that he has not, without justification, failed to comply with any duty in respect of reasonable adjustment. In applying the test of justification under *section 5(3)*, the tribunal must carry out a balancing exercise between the interests of the disabled employee and the interests of the employer. The reason for the discriminatory treatment must be 'material to the circumstances of the case' and that must include the circumstances of both the employer and employee. On the facts of *Baynton*, in reaching a conclusion on the issue of justification, the tribunal mis-directed itself by failing to take into account relevant factors. Before finding that the applicant was dismissed because he could not do his job, the tribunal was bound to consider the effect of the failure by the employers to warn the applicant that he was at risk of dismissal, or to find out the up-to-date medical position before dismissing him. Had those steps been taken, the employers would have discovered that the applicant was due to see his consultant. Furthermore, the tribunal had apparently failed to balance the desirability of awaiting the outcome of that consultation with the employers' need to dismiss.

145.4 A LOW THRESHOLD OF JUSTIFICATION?

The threshold for justification of disability discrimination under *section 5(3)* is very low, according to the EAT in *H J Heinz & Co Ltd v Kenrick [2000] IRLR 144*. *Section 5(3)* provides that treatment 'is' justified if the reason for it is both material to the circumstances in the particular case and substantial, not that it 'can' or 'may' be justified. According to the EAT, the condition stipulated in *section 5(3)* is thus both necessary and sufficient. Taking account of what the Code of Practice says about the meaning of 'material to the circumstance of the particular case and substantial', if the reason for the treatment relates to the individual circumstance in question and is not just trivial or minor, then justification must be held to exist in a case in which the employer has no duty to make reasonable adjustment under *section 6*.

A balancing exercise between the interests of the disabled employee and the interests of the employer, as earlier suggested by the EAT in *Baynton* (above) is not precluded. However, the comparatively limited requirement of *section 5(3)* needs to be kept in mind when considering what is material. A wider survey of what is reasonable, along the lines of that found in *section 6*, is *not* required. On the facts of the case, however, the EAT declined to interfere with the tribunal's conclusion that less favourable treatment of an employee with chronic fatigue syndrome was subjected to discrimination on the ground of disability because of a failure to give sufficient consideration to part-time work, lighter duties or alternative work before dismissing him by reason of his long-term sickness absence.

146 Knowledge of Disability

146.1 DOES THE EMPLOYER NEED TO KNOW ABOUT THE DISABILITY?

Can an employer who is unaware that a job applicant or employee is disabled ever be liable for discrimination on the ground of the unknown disability? The short answer is yes. Knowledge by the employer is not, under the *DDA 1995*, an essential requirement for there to be liability. Thus it is sensible for employers to ask job applicants relevant (but not irrelevant) questions about disability in the recruitment process, for example by making an appropriate enquiry on application forms. Sometimes the question is asked as part of *equal opportunity monitoring*, but that may well be insufficient because such monitoring information is often detached from the application documents before short-listing. Yet an employer deciding which applicant to select needs to know about relevant disabilities because of the duty to make *Reasonable Adjustments*, e.g. in a case where the disability puts the applicant at a disadvantage in the recruitment process or affects ability to carry out the job duties. It is therefore appropriate to ask candidates to say whether they have any disability or health condition which may affect their ability to participate in the selection process or carry out the duties. It follows that the proposed selection process and the duties need to be explained so that candidates can answer appropriately. The employer should also explain that the reason for the inquiry is to ensure that any appropriate adjustments can be made. It is generally appropriate for employers to be proactive in discussing relevant disability issues with candidates.

In the case of *Employees Who Become Disabled* during the course of employment, sometimes the employer may be unaware of the disability, but reasonable and appropriate enquiries should be made about the possible existence of a relevant disability, for example in the context of proper absence management. Ignorance is not bliss, nor does it excuse employers from failure to comply with their obligations under the *DDA 1995*.

146.2 THE OBJECTIVE TEST

The law took a wrong turning in the early case of *O'Neill v Symm & Co Ltd [1998] IRLR 233*. An employee who had previously suffered from viral pneumonia recovered but was later off work again and self-certified her sickness as a viral illness. Following a further absence, she explained that she had been signed off work on the ground that she had a viral illness as a result of her earlier pneumonia. She was dismissed because of her absence whilst she was still away from work. She claimed to have been discriminated against because, during her employment, she had had several hospital appointments which had led to a diagnosis of chronic fatigue syndrome (CFS). A tribunal found that the employer understandably attributed the employee's hospital visits to viral illness and had not been put on notice that she had been diagnosed as having CFS. The EAT upheld that decision, ruling that knowledge of the disability, or at least the material features of it as set out in *Schedule 1* to the *DDA 1995*, is relevant as to whether the reason for the employer's action relates to the disabled person's disability. The word 'reason', the EAT said, as a matter of causation, involves knowledge of the matter that is material. What is material to discrimination on the ground of disability is disability and not merely one or other equivocal symptoms.

In a later case, again involving CFS, a different division of the EAT disagreed with the decision in *O'Neill. In H J Heinz Co Ltd v Kenrick [2000] IRLR 144*, an employee who had a lengthy absence from work told the employer's medical adviser that he thought that he was suffering from CFS. He was later dismissed because he was unfit to work, although he had asked the employer to wait until he had seen an immunologist before acting. After the dismissal, a diagnosis of CFS was confirmed. The EAT upheld a tribunal's view that, on the facts, the employer, through the medical adviser, knew that the employee was suffering from a disability. More importantly, the EAT held that *section 5(1)(a)* does not require the employer to have knowledge of the disability as such, or as to whether its material features fall within *Schedule 1*, in order to be said to have acted for a reason which relates to the disability. There is nothing in the statutory language that requires that the relationship between the disability and the treatment should be judged subjectively through the eyes of the employer. The correct test is the objective one of whether the relationship exists, not whether the employer knew about it. This requires employers to pause to consider whether the reason for a dismissal that they have in mind might relate to disability and, if it might, to reflect on the *DDA 1995* and the Code of Practice before dismissing. The EAT pointed out that, unless the test is objective, there will be difficulties with credible and honest yet ignorant or obtuse employers who fail to recognise or acknowledge the obvious. Furthermore, the reference in *section 5(1)(a)* to a reason 'which relates to' the disabled person's disability widens the description of the reasons which may be relevant so as to include a reason deriving from how the disability manifests itself, even where there is no knowledge of the disability as such.

146.3 IGNORANCE AND JUSTIFICATION

In *H J Heinz Co Ltd v Kenrick*, however, the EAT held that an employer's unawareness of the disability may be highly material *Justification* under *section 5(1)(b)* or *section 5(ii)(b)* or as to the steps to be considered or taken to make reasonable adjustments under *section 6*.

147 Language Requirements

The Code of Practice under the *RRA 1976* reminds employers that adopting excessive or otherwise unjustifiable language requirements could give rise to complaints of *Indirect Discrimination.* Where English is not the first language of a job applicant from a racial group defined by reference to nationality or national origin, it could be unlawful for an employer to insist on a standard of written or spoken English which is higher than that needed for the safe and effective performance of the job.

The Code states that in particular employers should not disqualify job applicants because they are unable to complete an application form unassisted, unless the requirement to complete the form personally is a valid test of the standard of English required for safe and effective performance of the particular job. There are also circumstances in which special arrangements in relation to application forms, and modification of language requirements generally, may be required as a *Reasonable Adjustment* for disabled job applicants.

The Code of Practice under the *RRA 1976* also refers to the responsibilities of individual employees. It states that employees from the racial minorities should recognise that in many occupations advancement is dependent on an appropriate standard of English.

It is lawful under *section 35* of the *RRA 1976* for employers and others to afford persons of a particular racial group access to facilities or services to meet their special needs in regard to education, training or welfare. This provision would cover special arrangements to provide language tuition.

148 Lawful Discrimination

An act of discrimination may be lawful in one of the following respects:

(*a*) if the discrimination is of a kind which has not yet been made unlawful, such as age discrimination or (except in Northern Ireland) religious discrimination;

(*b*) if the act complained of is outside the scope of the legislation, for example where work has been refused or withdrawn, but the complainant is not an employee even within the extended definition of *Employment*;

(*c*) where the case is covered by a specific exception, such as the *Genuine Occupational Qualification* exceptions.

It should never be assumed too readily, however, that a particular act can have no implications under discrimination legislation. For example:

(*a*) acts of age discrimination or religious discrimination can be acts of indirect sex and race discrimination respectively;

(*b*) the scope of the legislation can be extended in reliance on Articles of the EC Treaty (such as *Article 39* on the free movement of labour) or, in the public sector, in reliance on Directives;

(*c*) an Article of the Treaty or, in the public sector, a Directive can also require a provision containing an exception to be disapplied.

149 Leave

The Code of Practice under the *RRA 1976* points out (in paragraph 1.21) that employees may request extended leave from time to time in order to visit relations in their countries of origin or relations who have emigrated to other countries. The Code points out that employers should take care to apply consistently and without unlawful discrimination any policies under which:

(*a*) annual leave entitlement can be accumulated; or

(*b*) extra unpaid leave can be taken.

150 Less Favourable Treatment

Less favourable treatment is a key part of the definition of *Direct Discrimination.*

The *SDA 1975* and the *RRA 1976* do not prohibit unreasonable or unfair treatment (although most discriminatory treatment also satisfies both those descriptions). The essence of the definition is that the complainant has been treated less favourably than an actual or hypothetical comparator.

The definition of direct sex discrimination under *section 1(1)(a)* of the *SDA 1975* refers to the actual or hypothetical comparator in the singular. There is direct sex discrimination against a woman if on the ground of her sex a person treats her less favourably than he treats or would treat a man. In the *RRA 1976*, comparators are referred to in the plural. There is direct discrimination under *section 1(1)(a)* of the *RRA 1976* if on racial grounds a person is treated less favourably than other persons are or would be treated. Nothing turns on this distinction, having regard to the general principle of statutory interpretation that the singular includes the plural and vice versa.

Two more important questions are:

(*a*) Is it necessary to prove that there was an intention to treat the complainant in a particular way?

(*b*) If so, must there also be an intention to treat the complainant less favourably than another person is or would be treated?

The answer to the first question is clearly yes. If, for example, it is proved that a job application from a woman was overlooked by mistake, so that the failure to shortlist her was unintentional, the treatment which she has received is not on the grounds of her sex.

It is suggested that the answer to the second question is also yes, but only if intention is viewed in an objective sense. The following examples illustrate the point:

(*a*) A Ruritanian worker is told a grossly offensive joke about Ruritanians by his manager, who did not deliberately set out to offend him but simply did not stop to think.

(*b*) The same Ruritanian worker has a poor command of English. A different manager is aware that the *RRA 1976* permits the provision of facilities to meet the *Special Needs* of persons of a particular racial group in regard to education, training or welfare. He tactfully suggests to the worker that special language training would improve his promotion prospects and he offers to arrange such training for him. The worker is greatly offended and upset by the suggestion that he needs any language training.

In the second of these examples, there was not, in any sense, an intention to treat the worker, on racial grounds, less favourably than other workers were or would have been treated; on the contrary, there was an intention to treat him more favourably. The offer to arrange the special language training was made tactfully and no reasonable person could have expected it to cause offence. It would be surprising if the law required a finding of direct racial discrimination in those circumstances, even though the worker was genuinely offended and upset.

In the first example, however, even though there was no actual intention to be offensive, the manager must have realised, if he had thought about the matter, that offence would inevitably be caused. It would be open to an employment tribunal to find that there was an intention on the manager's part to cause the offence which he must or should have known was the likely consequence of his remarks.

In summary, therefore, it is suggested, the question whether A has treated B less favourably than other persons have been or would have been treated should be viewed objectively, not from the subjective viewpoint of either A or B. A's crassness or insensitivity should not enable him to escape responsibility for the consequence of his words or deeds where those consequences were reasonably foreseeable; at the same time, B's extreme sensitivity, of which he has given no intimation, should not make A responsible for the unforeseeable consequences of his actions. That approach to the meaning of less favourable treatment is consistent with the guidance given on *Detriment* in *Jeremiah v Ministry of Defence* [*1979*] *IRLR 436* and also with the more recent guidance in relation to sexual harassment (see *Harassment*).

151 Liability for Aiding Discrimination

The *SDA 1975*, *RRA 1976* and *DDA 1995* each provide that a person who knowingly aids another person to do an unlawful act must be treated as himself doing an unlawful act of the like description. The relevant provisions are *section 42* of the *SDA 1975*, *section 33* of the *RRA 1976* and *section 57* of the *DDA 1995*.

Liability for aiding discrimination arises most frequently in the context of complaints against agents or fellow-employees, because of the provisions under which they are deemed to have 'aided' discrimination by principals or employers – see *Agents* and *Employees – Liability For*.

In the case of *Anyanwu and Another v South Bank Students' Union and Another* [*2000*] *IRLR* 36, two students, both of black African origin, who had been elected as paid officers of the students' union, were expelled from the university on the basis of serious allegations against them. Their expulsion meant that it was inevitable that their contracts of employment with the students' union would be terminated. They had not been employed by the university and the issue in the case was whether the university had knowingly aided their dismissal by the students' union, so as to bring the case within *section 33* of the *RRA 1976*. The Court of Appeal held by a majority that the university could not be said to have done so. The verb 'aid' contemplates a state of affairs in which the prime mover is aided or helped by another party. In this case it was the university which was the prime mover and it could not be said to have aided or helped the union to dismiss the complainants.

Any employee or agent who is liable for knowingly having aided an act of racial discrimination by his or her employer is also normally a prime mover, but in those cases the employment tribunal is not concerned with the meaning of the verb 'to aid' because under the express provisions of *section 33(2)* of the *RRA 1976* the employee or agent is deemed to have aided the doing of the unlawful act.

152 Liability for Employees and Agents

The circumstances in which discrimination by an employee is treated as discrimination by the employer are considered in relation to *Employees – Liability For*. The circumstances in which discrimination by an agent is treated as discrimination by the principal are considered in relation to *Agents*.

There is an important distinction between the two cases. An employer is liable for discrimination by an employee in the course of his or her employment, whether or not that discrimination was authorised by the employer, subject only to the defence that the employer has taken all *Reasonably Practicable Steps* to prevent the act of discrimination or acts of that description. A principal is responsible for anything done by a person as his agent only if it was done with the principal's authority (whether express or implied and whether precedent or subsequent).

153 Licensing Authorities

The *SDA 1975* and the *RRA 1976*, but not the *DDA 1995*, contain provisions relating to *Qualifying Bodies*, which include any authority or body which can confer a licence or other authorisation or qualification which is needed for, or facilitates, engagement in a particular profession or trade.

154 Like Work

In an *Equal Pay* case, if the complainant's job and the comparator's job have not been given the same value in a *Job Evaluation* study, the next question to be considered is whether the complainant's work and the comparator's work are like work. There are two questions:

(*a*) is the work of the same or a broadly similar nature;

(*b*) are the differences (if any) between the things the complainant does and the things the comparator does not of practical importance in relation to terms and conditions of employment?

The *EPA 1970* expressly states that in comparing the work regard shall be had to the frequency or otherwise with which any differences occur in practice, as well as to the nature and extent of the differences.

The case of *Capper Pass v Lawton* [*1976*] *IRLR 366* illustrates that quite considerable differences between two jobs may nevertheless not be of practical importance in relation to terms and conditions of employment. In that case the complainant worked as a cook for the directors of a company, providing lunch for between 10 and 20 persons per day. The two male comparators were assistant chefs who provided 350 meals a day for six sittings in the factory canteen. It was held that the complainant and the comparators were employed on like work, so that she was entitled to the higher hourly rate which they enjoyed.

155 Local Authorities

Local authorities are major employers. They are also *Public Sector* employers, so that the *Equal Treatment Directive* and other *Directives* have direct effect and can be relied on in any proceedings if the relevant provisions are sufficiently precise.

Section 71 of the *RRA 1976* states that it is the duty of every local authority (including police authorities and joint authorities) to make appropriate arrangements to secure that their various functions are carried out with due regard to the need:

(*a*) to eliminate unlawful discrimination; and

(*b*) to promote equality of opportunity and good relations between persons of different racial groups.

This duty is strengthened, and applied to other public authorities, by the *Race Relations (Amendment) Act 2000*. The Act empowers the Home Secretary to make orders to impose specific duties on public authorities. These could include, for example, duties to produce and publish equality plans. There is also a power for the CRE to issue compliance notices and to bring enforcement proceedings in a county court or sheriff court.

156 Managers

In a small business, decisions relating to employees and job applicants are frequently taken by the owner or the partners. Large organisations act mainly through managers. Effective training for managers is an important part of any *Equal Opportunity Policy* if the policy is to be successful. It is also one of the essential *Reasonably Practicable Steps* which must be taken if liability for unauthorised discrimination by employees is to be avoided.

157 Market Forces

It was held by the House of Lords in *Rainey v Greater Glasgow Health Board [1987] IRLR 26* that a *Material Factor* defence in an *Equal Pay* case does not necessarily fail because it involves market forces. That, however, was a case where it was necessary to pay higher wages in order to recruit skilled persons from the private sector and there were significant numbers of both men and women in the existing employees on lower pay and the new employees on higher pay. Any material factor defence which involves reliance on market forces will be very carefully examined to ensure that it is genuinely unrelated to the sex of the employees concerned.

158 Marriage Discrimination

The definition of discrimination under the *SDA 1975* includes discrimination against a married person of either sex, but only for the purposes of Part II of the Act, which is the part relating to discrimination in the employment field.

Most complaints of marriage discrimination are of indirect discrimination, for example where requirements to work full-time or relocate or attend residential courses have a *Disparate Impact* on married women compared with unmarried women. In most such cases, however, there is also disparate impact on women compared with men.

159 Married Couples

Under the *SDA 1975* as it currently stands, the *Genuine Occupational Qualification* exception applies where a job is one of two to be held by a married couple. This means that, for example, if two employees are required to manage a club or public house, the employer can discriminate in favour of a married couple and against two men or two women who wish to live and work together.

There may well be a need to review this particular GOQ exception if and when the *SDA 1975* is amended to cover discrimination on grounds of *Sexual Orientation*.

160 Material Factor

Many *Equal Pay* cases fail, even though the complainant can establish that the complainant's work and the comparator's work are *Like Work* or work of *Equal Value*.

The reason is that an *Equality Clause* does not operate in relation to any difference in pay or other contract terms if the employer can show that that difference is genuinely due to a material factor which is not the difference of sex – see *Equal Pay*.

In a *Like Work* case, or one based on a *Job Evaluation*, the material factor to be relied on must be a material difference between the complainant's case and the comparator's case. In an *Equal Value* case, the material factor may be of a more general nature and need not be a material difference between the two individual cases.

A material factor defence should always be raised by a respondent at the outset, in the notice of appearance (or by way of a prompt application to amend if it does not come to light until later). In equal value cases, a material factor defence is generally considered before the tribunal decides whether the two jobs are of equal value (and before an independent expert is appointed to report on that question).

161 Maternity

The current rights to maternity leave are contained in *sections 71–75* of the *Employment Rights Act 1996* and in Part II of the *Maternity and Parental Leave etc. Regulations 1999 (SI 1999 No 3312)*. The provisions relating to statutory maternity pay are contained in *sections 164–171* of the *Social Security Contributions and Benefits Act 1992*.

The main provisions of the current statutory scheme for maternity leave are as follows:

(*a*) ordinary maternity leave is for 18 weeks, during which the employee continues to be entitled to contractual benefits (other than relating to remuneration);

(*b*) an employee is entitled to additional maternity leave if she has been continuously employed for at least a year at the beginning of the eleventh week before the expected week of childbirth;

(*c*) the additional maternity leave period continues until the end of the period of 29 weeks beginning with the week of childbirth, unless the employer brings it to an end by dismissal or the employee brings it to an end by returning to work (having given at least 21 days' of her intention to do so);

(*d*) certain contractual terms remain in force during additional maternity leave, including the employee's right to compensation in the event of redundancy and her implied obligation of good faith, but she is not entitled to contractual benefits (such as provision of a car) during this period unless the employer has expressly agreed to provide them;

(*e*) failure to return to work at the end of the additional maternity leave period does not lead to the automatic termination of the employment.

The provisions regarding the notices to be given by the employee have been simplified (but by no means removed).

Regulation 10 of the 1999 Regulations gives a woman on maternity leave an important right where she is at risk of dismissal on the ground of redundancy. If there is a suitable available vacancy, she must be offered that vacancy (on terms and conditions which are not substantially less favourable than those of her existing contract) in priority to any employee who is not on maternity leave.

There have been several cases in which it has been unsuccessfully argued that the terms of the statutory maternity scheme infringe the principles of Community law (particularly *Article 141*), for example because a woman on maternity leave is treated less favourably than a man on sick leave.

The main reason why such challenges have been unsuccessful was stated by the ECJ in the case of *Gillespie and Others v Northern Health and Social Services Board and Others [1996] IRLR 214*, a case in which the ECJ rejected a claim that women should continue to receive full pay during maternity leave. The judgment contained the following passage:

> 'It is well-settled that discrimination involves the application of different rules to comparable situations or the application of the same rule to different situations ... The present case is concerned with women taking maternity leave provided for by national legislation. They are in a special position which requires them to be afforded special protection, but which is not comparable either with that of a man or with that of a woman actually at work.'

It was, however, held in the above case that, insofar as maternity pay is based on the employee's average pay when she is at work, she must benefit from any relevant pay rise, even if backdated.

In the case of *Boyle v Equal Opportunities Commission [1998] IRLR 717,* the ECJ considered, amongst other things, a contractual term under which annual holiday entitlement accrued only during what is now the ordinary maternity leave period, not the additional maternity leave period. It was held that this term is not incompatible with Community law.

It is, however, contrary to the *Equal Treatment Directive* for a woman to be disadvantaged in her working conditions, on her return to work, by reason of having taken maternity leave. It was held in *CNAVTS v Thibault [1998] IRLR 399* that it was contrary to the Directive for a woman on maternity leave to be deprived of her right to an annual assessment of her performance and therefore of the opportunity to qualify for promotion to a higher pay grade.

162 Men – Discrimination Against

The *SDA 1975* covers discrimination against men as well as discrimination against women. The definitions of direct and indirect discrimination in *section 1* refer to discrimination against a woman, but *section 2* then states that *section 1*, and other provisions relating to sex discrimination against women, are to be read as applying equally to the treatment of men. The only proviso is that special treatment afforded to women in connection with pregnancy or childbirth is not treated as discrimination against men.

Although most complaints under the *EPA 1970* and the *SDA 1975* have been presented by women, there have also been many equal pay and sex discrimination complaints by men. For example there are still employers who discriminate against men when recruiting for secretarial work. There has also traditionally been discrimination against men in relation to *Pensions*, as in the leading case of *Barber v Guardian Royal Exchange Assurance Group* [*1990*] *IRLR 240.*

The *EPA 1970* adopts a similar approach to that in the *SDA 1975*. The *EPA 1970* refers to the operation of *Equality Clauses* in favour of women and to complaints by women, but *section 1(13)* states that provisions framed with reference to women and their treatment relative to men are to be read as applying equally in a converse case to men and their treatment relative to women.

163 Ministers of Religion

There have been several cases in which it has been held that ministers of various religions are not employees for the purpose of having unfair dismissal rights. Employment as a minister of religion could well, however, be covered by the *SDA 1975*, the *RRA 1976* and the *DDA 1995*, in view of the extended definition of *Employment*.

Section 19 of the *SDA 1975* authorises discrimination in relation to employment (and also any authorisation or qualification by a *Qualifying Body*) for purposes of an authorised religion by limiting the employment (or the authorisation or qualification) to:

(*a*) men;

(*b*) women; or

(*c*) persons who are not undergoing and have not undergone *Gender Reassignment*.

The discrimination in these cases is permitted if the limitation is imposed so as to:

(*a*) comply with the doctrines of the religion; or

(*b*) avoid offending the religious susceptibilities of a significant number of its followers.

There is no corresponding exception in the *RRA 1976*.

164 Mobility

164.1 MOBILITY REQUIREMENTS AND ASSUMPTIONS

The issue of mobility can arise in several contexts. For example:

(*a*) there is a business need to move an employee to a different establishment;

(*b*) alternative employment on redundancy involves relocation;

(*c*) a move is a condition of a promotion;

(*d*) a job involves considerable travel and overnight stays;

(*e*) contracts of employment contain a standard mobility clause;

(*f*) assumptions about mobility are made when selecting staff.

Sometimes it is the employee himself who wishes to move and is denied the opportunity. That issue is considered in the section on *Transfers*. This section is concerned with mobility requirements as a *Detriment* and also in the context of *Recruitment* and also with assumptions about mobility in the context of *Selection*.

164.2 MOBILITY CLAUSES

If a contract of employment gives the employer the right to require the employee to change working locations, either generally or on promotion, that contract term can be challenged if it has a discriminatory effect under the *RRA 1976* or the *SDA 1975*. The fact that the employee has willingly signed the contract does not bar a complaint about a term which is unlawful under the discrimination legislation. Furthermore, the employee does not have to wait until he or she is required to move.

The latter point was considered by the Court of Appeal in the case of *Meade-Hill and National Union of Civil and Public Servants v British Council* [*1995*] *IRLR 478*. This case concerned a mobility clause under which Officers at and above a specified grade were required to 'serve in such parts of the United Kingdom . . . as the Council may in its discretion require'. Mrs Meade-Hill, having agreed to the clause a year or two earlier, was faced with the prospect of a compulsory move to Manchester. That move would have caused difficulties because her husband, who earned substantially more than she did, would also have had to move. Accordingly she and her union issued proceedings in the County Court (which was the appropriate procedure at the time) under *section 77* of the *SDA 1975*.

The application was dismissed in the County Court on the ground that it was impossible to say in the abstract whether the mobility clause did discriminate; it would be necessary for Mrs Meade-Hill to wait until she was required to move and then consider that concrete factual situation.

The Court of Appeal, by a majority, allowed her appeal. The key elements of the decision were:

(*a*) The contract term itself could be challenged – it was not necessary to wait until the mobility requirement was implemented.

(*b*) The matter was to be judged as at the date when the contract was made.

(*c*) The proportion of women who were primary wage earners was considerably smaller than the proportion of men in that category.

(*d*) It followed that the clause was unlawful unless the British Council could justify it.

The case was remitted to the County Court to consider the question of justification. Millett LJ suggested that it was likely that justification could be proved. The British Council had only to show a need to be in a position if circumstances so required at any time in the future to direct an employee of the relevant grade to work elsewhere in the United Kingdom. Furthermore, even if the clause could not be justified in its present form, relatively minor adjustments could remove the questionable aspects of the clause.

Employers may also be required to consider *Reasonable Adjustments* to mobility clauses in order to comply with their *section 6* duties. If an employee who has signed a contract containing a mobility clause is or becomes subject to a disability which would prevent him or her from complying with the clause if so required, the employer must consider whether it is reasonably practicable to remove or modify the clause.

164.3 **RECRUITMENT, SELECTION AND PROMOTION**

The issues of indirect discrimination and reasonable adjustments can also arise before the contract is entered into, at the stage when the employer is advertising the post, preparing a job description or making a job offer. These issues can also arise when existing employees are being considered for promotion.

A woman may be able to make out a case of indirect sex discrimination if her inability, because of her domestic circumstances, to sign a mobility clause prevents her from:

(*a*) applying for a particular post;

(*b*) accepting an offer of a post;

(*c*) accepting a promotion.

In the first instance, her complaint would be about discrimination in the arrangements for determining who should be offered employment, contrary to *section 6(1)(a)* of the *SDA 1975*; in the second case it would be indirect discrimination in the terms on which employment is offered (*section 6(1)(b)*); and in the third case it would be indirect discrimination in the way in which she is afforded access to opportunities for promotion (*section 6(2)(a)*).

She would, of course, need to be able to show that the requirement to sign a mobility clause has a disproportionate impact on women. The assumption made in 1995, that the proportion of women who are primary earners is considerably smaller than the corresponding proportion of men, would probably (although not inevitably) still be made some years later. The employer may, however, be able to defeat her claim by showing a business need, and therefore objective justification, for the mobility clause.

Employers who are taking steps to fill a job vacancy, whether internally or externally, must also have regard to the impact of the clause on disabled employees or applicants. Consideration must always be given to the possibility of removing or modifying the clause where it operates as a bar to a disabled worker.

The question of reasonable adjustment must also be considered where the duties of the post involve travel and overnight stays. *Section 6* of the *DDA 1995* requires the employer to consider modifying the job description (particularly where the duties in question form only a small part of the job), in order to make the job available to a worker whose disability would limit his or her ability to travel or stay away overnight.

Direct Discrimination is most likely to arise where the employer makes selection or promotion decisions on the basis of unwarranted assumptions. It would be a clear case of direct discrimination if an employer assumed, without enquiry, that a female candidate would be less capable than a male candidate of complying with a mobility clause; a disabled candidate would have an unanswerable claim of disability discrimination if turned down for a post because the employer simply assumed that he would not be able to undertake job duties involving travel and overnight stays.

164.4 REDUNDANCY SELECTION

Where redundancies have been declared, but there are alternative jobs available, the employer has an absolute obligation, under *Regulation 10* of the *Maternity and Parental Leave etc. Regulations 1999 (SI 1999 No 3312)*, to give priority, in relation to any suitable vacancy, to a woman returning from maternity leave.

The employer must then have regard to the duties not to discriminate unlawfully and to make *section 6* adjustments under the *DDA 1995*. Suppose, for example, that a disabled employee is facing dismissal, whether for redundancy or inability to continue in his or her present post, and there are two vacancies, one of which involves a mobility requirement. If, because of the disability, the employee cannot comply with that requirement, then the *section 6* duty may require the employer to give the disabled employee priority in relation to the other vacant post, provided that he or she is a suitable candidate.

164.5 COMPULSORY MOVES

When an employer implements a mobility clause, and requires an employee to move (or be dismissed for refusing to do so), the fact that the employer is acting in pursuance of a contractual provision is not a defence to a complaint under the discrimination legislation. It is a common feature of discrimination claims that the employer has taken a step which he is contractually at liberty to take but which involves unlawful discrimination. Where there is more than one employee who could suitably be required to move, complaints of unlawful discrimination could arise in the following circumstances:

(*a*) a disabled employee is instructed to move, even though his disability prevents him from doing so;

(*b*) a female employee is told that she will have to relocate, even though her husband is unable or unwilling to do so and the employer could equally well have selected a male employee to whom relocation would be no problem;

(*c*) an employee who has made a complaint of racial discrimination (and done so in good faith) is required to move in order to defuse a difficult situation.

The last-mentioned case would be one of victimisation under the *RRA 1976*.

165 Models

One of the very few *Genuine Occupational Qualification* exceptions under *section 5* of the *RRA 1976* is where a job involves participation as an artist's or photographic model in the production of a work of art, visual image or sequence of visual images for which a person of a particular racial group is required for reasons of authenticity.

Such a case may also be covered by the more general GOQ exception under *section 7* of the *SDA 1975*, where the essential nature of the job calls for a woman (or man as the case may be) for reasons of physiology, so that the essential nature of the job would be materially different if carried out by a person not of the required gender.

166 Monitoring

Monitoring is an important part of any *Equal Opportunity Policy*, to ensure that the policy is working effectively. The way in which monitoring should be carried out depends on the size and nature of the organisation and (so far as the prevention of racial discrimination is concerned) the racial composition of the workforce and of the area(s) from which employees are recruited. General guidance is given in the *Codes of Practice* under the *SDA 1975* and the *RRA 1976*. Monitoring for the purposes of the *RRA 1976* can be a very sophisticated process; more detailed guidance can be obtained from the CRE.

The Code of Practice under the *RRA 1976* states (in paragraph 1.37) that the CRE recommends that analyses should be carried out of:

(*a*) the ethnic composition of the workforce of each plant, department, section, shift and job category;

(*b*) changes in distribution over periods of time;

(*c*) selection decisions for recruitment, promotion, transfer and training, according to the racial group of candidates;

(*d*) reasons for these decisions.

Similar analyses should be carried out by reference to the gender of employees and job applicants and also in relation to disabled employees and job applicants.

Regular analysis of the information obtained may indicate a need for investigation and possible corrective action if, for example, women, racial minorities or disabled workers:

(*a*) are not applying for particular posts;

(*b*) have a high failure rate when they do apply;

(*c*) are not well represented in senior positions; or

(*d*) are concentrated in certain jobs, shifts, sections or departments.

167 National Health Service

The National Health Service is part of the *Public Sector*, so that the *Equal Treatment Directive* and other *Directives* have direct effect. The leading case of *Marshall v Southampton and South-West Hampshire Area Health Authority* [*1986*] *IRLR 140* involved employment in the National Health Service.

Section 71 of the *RRA 1976* places on local authorities a duty to make appropriate arrangements to secure that their various functions are carried out with due regard to the need to eliminate unlawful racial discrimination and to promote equality of opportunity and good relations between persons of different racial groups. The *Race Relations (Amendment) Act 2000* strengthens that duty and extends it to other public authorities, including NHS bodies.

There is the possibility of *Equal Pay* claims by employees of one NHS body being made in relation to comparators in another NHS body, on the basis that employees in the two bodies are employed in the same service – see *Same Employment*.

The collective negotiating body in the National Health Service is the Whitley Council. Existing agreements on equal opportunities were in the year 2000 consolidated into a comprehensive new collective agreement, which has been approved by the Secretary of State. The stated aim of this agreement is to make equality and diversity part of everything that the NHS does.

168 National Origin

There is a distinction between national origin and *Nationality*. In particular:

(*a*) persons who and whose parents were born in England, Scotland, Wales and Northern Ireland could have four different national origins but the same British nationality;

(*b*) the great majority of men and women working in Great Britain are British citizens, sharing the same nationality, but racial minority workers have a wide variety of national origins because they (or more commonly their parents or remoter ancestors) were born overseas.

Under the earlier race relations legislation, the distinction between national origin and nationality was important; discrimination on grounds of national origin was covered but discrimination on grounds of nationality was not. Now, however:

(*a*) discrimination on grounds of nationality or national origin is discrimination on *Racial Grounds* and is, therefore, direct discrimination;

(*b*) a group of persons defined by reference to nationality or national origin is a *Racial Group* for the purposes of complaints of indirect racial discrimination.

169 National Security

The *SDA 1975 (section 52)*, the *RRA 1976* (*section 42*) and the *DDA 1995* (*section 59*) each contains a provision that an act done for the purpose of safeguarding national security is not unlawful.

The *SDA 1975* and the *RRA 1976* also contain provisions giving conclusive effect to a certificate purporting to be signed by or on behalf of a Minister of the Crown, that a particular act was done for the purpose of safeguarding national security. This provision regarding certificates ceased to apply, however, with effect from 25 February 1988 for the purpose of Part II of the *SDA 1975* (the part relating to discrimination in the employment field) and the provisions in the *SDA 1975* relating to vocational training. This amendment to the *SDA 1975*, which was made by the *Sex Discrimination (Amendment) Order 1998 (SI 1998 No 249)*, was necessary because of the decision of the ECJ in the case of *Johnston v Chief Constable of the Royal Ulster Constabulary* [*1986*] *IRLR 263*. This was a case in which a female officer in the RUC challenged a decision not to renew her contract of employment (because of a policy not to issue firearms to female officers). It was held by the ECJ that it would be contrary to the *Equal Treatment Directive* to give conclusive effect to a certificate by the Secretary of State that the decision was for the purpose of safeguarding national security.

A similar amendment to the *RRA 1976* will no doubt be required in due course when the new *Directive* on racial discrimination is implemented.

170 Nationality

Reference has already been made to the distinction between nationality and *National Origin*. Discrimination against a person on grounds of nationality is discrimination on *Racial Grounds* and is, therefore, direct racial discrimination; a group of persons defined by reference to nationality is a *Racial Group* for the purposes of a complaint of indirect racial discrimination.

There is statutory discrimination on grounds of nationality – see *Immigration Control* and *Work Permits*. No employer (or other person or organisation having a duty not to discriminate) may discriminate on grounds of nationality unless there is a statutory requirement to do so.

171 Night Work

Where an employer requires certain work to be carried out at night, for example on a night shift in a factory, complaints of discrimination could arise in the following circumstances:

(*a*) an unjustifiable refusal to allow a woman to transfer to the day shift, because of her childcare commitments, could be indirect sex and marriage discrimination;

(*b*) There may be a need to make *Reasonable Adjustments* (for example by a transfer to the day shift) if an employee has a disability which puts him at a substantial disadvantage when working at night.

The fact that one job is done at night and another by day does not prevent two jobs from being *Like Work* for the purposes of an *Equal Pay* claim. The appropriate way to compensate an employee for working at night is by paying a night shift premium of a reasonable amount.

172 Non-Discrimination Notices

A non-discrimination notice may be served:

(*a*) by the EOC under *section 67* of the *SDA 1975*;

(*b*) by the CRE under *section 58* of the *RRA 1976*; or

(*c*) by the DRC under *schedule 3* to the *Disability Rights Commission Act 1999.*

A non-discrimination notice may be served under the *SDA 1975* or the *RRA 1976* not only on the grounds that an unlawful discriminatory act has been committed, but also on the ground that there has been a contravention of the provisions relating to *Discriminatory Practices*, discriminatory *Advertisements*, *Instructions to Discriminate* or *Pressure to Discriminate*. Furthermore, a notice may be served under the *SDA 1975* on the ground that there has been a breach of a contractual term modified or included by virtue of an *Equality Clause*.

A non-discrimination notice may be served only as a result of a *Formal Investigation* by the relevant Commission. The person (or organisation) on whom the notice is or is to be served:

(*a*) must be given notice of the grounds on which the Commission proposes to issue the notice and must be given at least 28 days to make oral or written representations; and

(*b*) has a right of appeal within six weeks to an employment tribunal.

A non-discrimination notice may include requirements to change relevant practices or arrangements and provide information, as well as a requirement not to commit any further unlawful acts. The sanction for failure to comply with a non-discrimination notice is an application by the Commission for an *Injunction* (or *Interdict* in Scotland).

A non-discrimination notice under *section 4* of the *Disability Rights Commission Act 1999* may also require a person to propose an adequate action plan and to take any action specified in the plan once it has become final.

173 Normal Day-To-Day Activities

173.1 DEFINITION

Schedule 1, Paragraph 4 of the *DDA 1995*, provides that an impairment affects the ability of the person concerned to carry out normal day-to-day activities only if it affects one of the following:

(*a*) mobility;

(*b*) manual dexterity;

(*c*) physical co-ordination;

(*d*) continence;

(*e*) ability to lift, carry or otherwise move everyday objects;

(*f*) speech, hearing or eyesight;

(*g*) memory or ability to concentrate, learn or understand; or

(*h*) perception of the risk of physical danger.

173.2 GUIDANCE

Further assistance is provided by the 'Guidance on Matters to be taken into Account in Determining Questions Relating to the Definition of Disability'. The EAT noted, in *Goodwin v The Patent Office* [*1999*] *IRLR 4*, that judging what it described as 'the adverse effect condition' may be difficult to judge, and offered further general guidance:

> 'What the Act is concerned with is an impairment of the person's *ability* to carry out activities. The fact that a person can carry out such activities does not mean that his ability to carry them out has not been impaired. Thus, for example, a person may be able to cook, but only with the greatest difficulty. In order to constitute an adverse effect, it is not the doing of the acts which is the focus of attention but rather the ability to do (or not do) the act. Experience shows that disabled persons often adjust their lives and circumstances to enable them to cope for themselves. Thus a person whose capacity to communicate through normal speech was obviously impaired might well choose, more or less voluntarily, to live on their own. If one asked such a person whether they managed to carry on their daily lives without undue problems, the answer may well be "yes", yet their ability to lead a "normal" life had obviously been impaired. Such a person would be unable to communicate through speech and the ability to communicate through speech is obviously a capacity which is needed for carrying out normal day to day activities, whether at work or at home. If asked whether they could use the telephone, or ask for directions, or which bus to take, the answer would be "no". This might be regarded as day-to-day activities contemplated by the legislation, and that person's ability to carry them out would clearly be regarded as adversely affected.
>
> Furthermore, disabled persons are likely, habitually, to "play down" the effect that their disabilities have on their daily lives. If asked whether they are able to cope at home, the answer may well be "yes", even though, on analysis, many of the ordinary day-to-day tasks were done with great difficulty due to the person's impaired ability to carry them out . . .
>
> What is a day-to-day activity is best left unspecified: easily recognised, but defined with difficulty. What can be said is that the inquiry is not focused on a particular or

special set of circumstances. Thus, it is not directed to the person's own particular circumstances, either at work or home. The fact that a person cannot demonstrate a particular skill, such as playing the piano, is not an issue before the tribunal, even if it is considering a claim by a musician. Equally, the fact that a person had arranged their home to accommodate their disability would make inquiries as to how they managed at their particular home not determinative of the issue.

It will be borne in mind that the effect of a disability on a person's ability to conduct his daily life might have a cumulative effect, in the sense that more than one of the capacities had been impaired. It is not necessary for the tribunal to go further, if satisfied that one "capacity" has been impaired, which is sufficient for the adverse-effect condition to be fulfilled . . .

During the argument an example was given of a person whose hearing was exceptionally acute. One might say that this was not likely to be regarded as a handicap to the person's ability to carry out his normal day-to-day activities. Certainly, one might say that there was no adverse effect upon his hearing: quite the contrary. However, such a condition could well adversely affect other capacities, for example, such a person might find it impossible or difficult to cope with conversation in a group of people or to go to a busy shop or to concentrate. The condition from which he was suffering would not have a direct adverse effect on the particular capacity, but might well have an adverse effect on a different capacity.'

An illustration of misunderstandings that may arise is provided by *Vicary v British Telecommunications plc* [*1999*] *IRLR 680*. An Employment Tribunal, having made extensive reference to the Guidance, concluded that 'DIY tasks, filing of nails, tonging hair, ironing, shaking quilts, grooming animals, polishing furniture, knitting, sewing and cutting with scissors' were not 'normal day-to-day activities'. The EAT strongly disagreed: 'These are all activities which most people do on a frequent or fairly regular basis.'

174 Northern Ireland

The *EPA 1970*, *SDA 1975*, *RRA 1976* and *DDA 1995* do not apply in Northern Ireland, which has its own legislation. The important addition in Northern Ireland is that religious discrimination is unlawful. The laws of Northern Ireland fall outside the scope of this Handbook.

175 Objective Criteria

The most effective way to minimise the potential for unlawful discrimination in employment decisions, whether relating to selection, pay, redundancy or otherwise, is to adopt objective criteria and apply them consistently.

176 Offences

Discrimination itself is not a criminal offence. Unlawful discrimination is unlawful only in the sense of being a statutory tort, or wrong, which gives the aggrieved individual the right to present a complaint and seek compensation.

There are offences under the *SDA 1975* and the *RRA 1976* where a person knowingly or recklessly makes a false or misleading statement (that an unlawful act would in fact be lawful) to the publisher of an advertisement, an employment agency, an employee or an agent.

There are also, under the *SDA 1975*, the *RRA 1976* and the *Disability Rights Commission Act 1999*, offences relating to *Formal Investigations*, where:

(*a*) a person who has been required to give information knowingly or recklessly makes a false statement;

(*b*) a person who has been required to produce a document wilfully alters, suppresses, conceals or destroys the document; or

(*c*) information given to one of the Commissions in connection with a formal investigation is wrongfully disclosed.

177 Oil and Gas Platforms

The employment provisions of the *SDA 1975* and the *RRA 1976* cover employment at establishments not only in Great Britain and British territorial waters but also (for the purposes of employment in connection with oil or gas exploration) at establishments in parts of the continental shelf which are designated by order for that purpose.

178 Omissions

The general interpretation section in each of the *SDA 1975*, *RRA 1976* and *DDA 1995* provides that any reference to an act includes a deliberate omission. There is, for example, direct racial discrimination when on racial grounds an employer either gives a negative reply to a job application or deliberately omits to reply at all. For the purposes of *Time Limits* a deliberate omission is treated as done when it is decided upon. A person is taken to decide upon an omission:

(*a*) when he does an act inconsistent with doing the omitted act; or

(*b*) if he does no such inconsistent act, when the period expires within which he might reasonably have been expected to do the omitted act if it was to be done.

179 Overseas Qualifications

The Code of Practice under the *RRA 1976* recommends (in paragraph 1.13(c)) that overseas degrees, diplomas and other qualifications which are comparable with UK qualifications should be accepted as equivalents, and not simply be assumed to be of an inferior quality.

Where a job application is made by a foreign national, or a person of overseas national origin, the unjustifiable rejection or downgrading of any overseas qualifications obtained by that person would be an act of indirect racial discrimination.

180 Overseas Work

Section 4 of the *DDA 1995*, relating to discrimination against job applicants and employees, applies only in relation to employment at an establishment in Great Britain.

Under *section 10(1)* of the *SDA 1975* and *section 8(1)* of the *RRA 1976*, employment is to be regarded as being at an establishment in Great Britain unless the employee does his work wholly outside Great Britain. Formerly, neither Act applied where the work was done mainly outside Great Britain, but both Acts were amended with effect from 15 December 1999, to comply with the *Posted Workers Directive*.

Even in its amended form, *section 8(1)* may have to be disapplied in certain circumstances, to comply with *Article 39* (formerly *48*) of the EC Treaty. This is the Article which relates to the free movement of workers. In *Bossa v Nordstress Limited [1998] IRLR 284,* the complainant saw an advertisement in the national press for cabin crew to be based in Italy. He was interviewed and asked to produce his passport, which was Italian. He was told that he could not be interviewed because the Italian authorities would not allow the airline to take employees of Italian nationality back to Italy. A tribunal held that it did not have jurisdiction to hear a complaint of direct discrimination on the ground of nationality, because the employment would have been wholly or mainly outside Great Britain and accordingly was not deemed to be at an establishment in Great Britain.

An appeal was allowed by the EAT. The free movement of workers included the right for Mr Bossa to work anywhere within the EC. *Section 8(1)* of the *RRA 1976* prevented him from enforcing that right and had, therefore, to be disapplied.

Even in its amended form, *section 8(1)* of the *RRA 1976* must be disapplied in any case where it prevents a national of any European Union country complaining of discrimination on grounds of nationality or national origin in relation to employment anywhere within the European Union.

181 Overtime

The law does not permit sex, racial or disability discrimination in either the allocation of voluntary overtime (see *Benefits*) or in a requirement to work compulsory overtime (see *Detriment*). Payment of standard overtime rates during working hours which are additional to the normal full-time working week does not infringe the principle of *Equal Pay*. Furthermore, there is no requirement to pay overtime rates for *Part-Time Work* where the hours worked exceed the employee's normal part-time hours but fall short of the normal hours of full-time employees.

182 Parental Leave

The right to take unpaid parental leave is given to both men and women by the *Maternity and Parental Leave etc. Regulations 1999 (SI 1999 No 3312)*.

If an employer decides to give additional parental leave, or to pay employees for the whole or part of their parental leave, then in principle male or female employees should be treated the same. Otherwise there could be a claim under the *SDA 1975* (or the *EPA 1970* if the arrangements are contractual) in respect of the additional leave and under the *EPA 1970* in respect of the pay.

The conditions which must be satisfied before the employee can take parental leave are:

(*a*) the employee must have been continuously employed in the employment for at least a year;

(*b*) the employee must have or expect to have responsibility for a child; and

(*c*) the child must have been born on or after 15 December 1999 (or adopted by the employee or placed with the employee for adoption on or after that date).

The last-mentioned of these conditions has been challenged in the courts on the ground that it is not justified by the terms of the *Parental Leave Directive*. The outcome of that challenge was still awaited at the time of writing.

Where all the conditions are satisfied, an employee is entitled to 13 weeks' leave in respect of any individual child. Unless otherwise agreed (or unless the child is entitled to a disabled living allowance) the leave must be taken in segments of one or more weeks. Not more than four weeks' leave may be taken in any one year. For the purpose of the Regulations, a year runs from the date of the birth of the child (or adoption or placement for adoption) or, if later, the date of completion of the qualifying period of one year's continuous employment.

Parental leave must be taken:

(*a*) by the date of the child's fifth birthday;

(*b*) in adoption cases, by whichever is the earlier of the child's 18th birthday and the fifth anniversary of the date on which the placement for adoption began; or

(*c*) if the child is entitled to a disability living allowance, by the child's 18th birthday.

There are notice requirements and provisions enabling employers to postpone the date on which leave must be taken, but subject to the special provisions for expectant fathers (see *Paternity Leave*) and similar provisions at the time of a placement for adoption. Apart from these special cases, and unless otherwise agreed, the employee must give at leave 21 days' advance notice before taking any parental leave, specifying the dates on which the period of leave is to begin and end. The employer may, however, postpone the commencement of the period of parental leave for up to six months, subject to the following conditions:

(*a*) if the employer considers that the operation of his business would be unduly disrupted if the employee were to take the leave during the period identified in the employee's notice;

(*b*) the employer must consult the employee about the date to which the commencement of the period of leave is to be postponed;

(*c*) the employer's notice must be in writing;

(*d*) that notice must state the reason for the postponement and must also state the date to which the commencement of the period of leave is to be postponed; and

(*e*) the employer's notice must be given to the employee not more than seven days after the employee's notice was given to the employer.

There is an automatic extension if the effect of a written notice of postponement by the employer is to take the period of leave beyond the date by which it would normally have to be taken (e.g. beyond the child's fifth birthday).

183 Partnerships

183.1 THE SDA 1975 AND THE RRA 1976

Both the *SDA 1975* and the *RRA 1976* give rights not only to employees but also to partners and those who wish to become partners.

The only distinction between the two Acts is that the provisions in the *RRA 1976* apply only to firms consisting of six or more partners. There is no minimum number under the *SDA 1975*.

The rights given to partners and potential partners are similar to those given to employees and job applicants.

So far as a person who has not yet become a partner is concerned, it is unlawful for a firm to discriminate (within the definition contained in either Act):

(*a*) in the arrangements made for the purpose of determining who should be offered a position as a partner;

(*b*) in the terms on which a position is offered; or

(*c*) by refusing or deliberately omitting to offer a position as a partner.

It is unlawful for a firm to discriminate against an existing partner:

(*a*) in the way he or she is afforded access to any benefits, facilities or services;

(*b*) by a refusal or deliberate omission to afford him or her access to any of the above;

(*c*) by expelling him or her from the partnership; and

(*d*) by subjecting him or her to any other detriment.

The above provisions also, where applicable, cover a case where two or more persons or, under the *RRA 1976*, six or more persons, are proposing to form a partnership and, for example, exclude a woman or offer her less favourable terms, in either case because she is a woman.

There are provisions in both Acts to incorporate the *Genuine Occupational Qualification* exception which can occasionally arise in relation to employment.

The partnership provisions in the *SDA 1975* do not prohibit discrimination in relation to the financial provision made for partners on death or retirement.

183.2 THE DDA 1995

The *DDA 1995* does not have any provisions corresponding to those in the *SDA 1975* and the *RRA 1976* giving rights to partners or would-be partners.

184 Part-Time Work

184.1 THE EPA 1970, SDA 1975 AND RRA 1976

An employer's refusal on racial grounds or grounds of gender of an employee's request to transfer to (or from) part-time work would be discrimination in the way the employee is afforded access to opportunities for transfer, contrary to:

(*a*) *section 6(2)* of the *SDA 1975*; or

(*b*) *section 4(2)* of the *RRA 1976*.

Such complaints are not unknown. It would, for example, be direct sex discrimination to grant requests for part-time working when those requests are made by female employees but to refuse a request when made by a male employee, if:

(*a*) the relevant circumstances of the women's case and the man's case are the same or not materially different; and

(*b*) the refusal of the man's request is on the ground of his sex.

In practice, however, most complaints are of indirect sex discrimination in refusing a request by a female employee to transfer to part-time working. Such requests are commonly but not exclusively made when the employee returns or is about to return from maternity leave. It is usually not difficult to prove *Disparate Impact* because significantly more women than men have exclusive or primary responsibility for childcare – see *Indirect Discrimination*.

Complaints of indirect sex discrimination may also be made if part-timers are excluded from opportunities for *Promotion*, *Training* or other *Benefits* or if a redundancy procedure is weighted against part-timers.

Differences in the pay and other contract terms of part-time or full-time workers can also give rise to complaints of *Equal Pay*, so long as the part-timer can identify a suitable full-time *Comparator* of the opposite sex. The mere fact that the complainant's work is done on a part-time basis cannot be relied on as a *Material Factor* to explain or justify the difference in pay or other contract terms. Objective justification is required. The effect of the ECJ decision in the leading case of *Bilka-Kaufhaus GmbH v Weber von Hartz [1986] IRLR 317* is that the employer must be able to show that the measures taken are appropriate for the achievement of a necessary objective on the part of the undertaking.

This was a case on *Article 141* (formerly *Article 119*) of the European Treaty, which has direct effect. Any provisions in the *EPA 1970* which are inconsistent with *Article 141* must be disapplied. This principle has proved to be particularly important in relation to *Pensions*.

184.2 THE DDA 1995

A transfer from full-time work to part-time work must be looked at as a possible *Reasonable Adjustment* in cases where a disability places a disabled worker at a substantial disadvantage if he or she is required to work full-time. If a disabled employee is transferred to part-time work for a reason relating to a disability, it could then be *Disability Discrimination* to treat that employee less favourably than full-time employees in any respect by reason of his or her part-time status.

184.3 THE PART-TIME WORKERS REGULATIONS 2000

The *Part-time Workers (Prevention of Less Favourable Treatment) Regulations 2000 (SI 2000 No 1551)* came into force on 1 July 2000.

The Regulations give rights to part-time workers not to be treated less favourably than comparable full-time workers if:

(*a*) the treatment is on the ground that the worker is a part-time worker; and

(*b*) the treatment is not justified on objective grounds.

A complaint may be presented about less favourable treatment relating to:

(*a*) pay or other contract terms ; or

(*b*) subjection to any other detriment (whether caused by an act or a deliberate omission on the part of the employer).

It is clear, from the official guidance on the Regulations, that the above reference to 'detriment' is intended to include denial of a benefit, such as promotion, training and fringe benefits, as well as detriment in the conventional sense. A successful complainant under the Regulations may be awarded such amount of compensation as the Employment Tribunal deems to be just and equitable, with no limit on the amount. The compensation may not, however, include compensation for injury to feelings.

To a large extent the rights given by the Regulations overlap with existing rights under the *EPA 1970* and the *SDA 1975*, but they break new ground in the following respects:

(*a*) the full-time comparator can be of the same sex as the part-time complainant; and

(*b*) they give a right for the first time to men who suffer detriment (not relating to contract terms) by reason of their status as part-time workers.

The rights under the Regulations will not, however, replace existing rights under the *EPA 1970* and *SDA 1975*. Where there is an overlap, complaints will normally be presented under the *EPA 1970* or *SDA 1975* as well as under the Regulations. There will be some cases where a complainant will have to rely exclusively on the *EPA 1970* or the *SDA 1975*, because the Regulations are subject to certain limitations, relating in particular to the criteria for identifying a full-time comparator.

It is also important to note that the Regulations do not cover, or purport to cover, what tends to be the main issue under the *SDA 1975*, namely the refusal of requests to transfer from full-time to part-time working.

184.4 OVERTIME

The Regulations contain an important provision to bring them into line with case law on *Article 141*. It is not a breach of either the Regulations or *Article 141* or the *EPA 1970* for a part-time worker to be denied overtime rates until he or she has worked the number of hours above which overtime is paid to full-time workers. For example, it would not be unlawful to deny a part-time worker overtime pay (assuming that there is no contractual provision requiring overtime to be paid) in the following circumstances:

(*a*) the normal working week for full-timers in the organisation is 35 hours and they are paid overtime for any additional hours worked each week;

(*b*) a part-time worker normally works 15 hours per week; and

(*c*) in one particular week the part-timer works 30 hours.

185 Past Discrimination

There is a *Time Limit* of three months for presenting a complaint under the employment provisions of the *SDA 1975*, the *RRA 1976* or the *DDA 1995*.

Acts of discrimination which have occurred more than three months before the presentation of a complaint can, however, be relevant in one of the following ways:

(*a*) The case could be one of discrimination extending over a period – *Continuing Discrimination*.

(*b*) The earlier act or acts of discrimination could be relied on as *Evidence* that the more recent treatment now complained of was, for example, on racial grounds.

Allegations of or other steps in relation to earlier acts of discrimination are 'protected acts' for the purpose of a complaint of victimisation.

186 Paternity Leave

The nearest thing to a right to paternity leave in Great Britain, is the right for a father to take up to four weeks of *Parental Leave*, to start on the date on which the child is born. He must give his employer notice specifying the expected week of childbirth and the duration of the period of leave. That notice must be given at least 21 days before the beginning of the expected date of childbirth.

The parental leave to which employees are entitled is unpaid leave. Could there be legal complications if an employer gives male employees extended paternity leave, or pays them for the whole or part of the leave taken when the child is born? Could a female employee make a complaint under the *EPA 1970*, if male employees are given a contractual right to one or both of these benefits, or under the *SDA 1975* if the benefits are given on a discretionary basis in an individual case?

It is unlikely that any complaint would succeed, except perhaps in one of the following unlikely events:

(*a*) the paternity leave granted exceeds the minimum of 18 weeks' *Maternity* leave to which an expectant mother has a statutory entitlement; or

(*b*) the amount of paternity pay exceeds the total of the SMP to which the complainant would be entitled on taking maternity leave.

187 Pay

187.1 THE MEANING OF PAY

There are many contractual and non-contractual arrangements which affect the pay received by employees.

The terms which are normally contractual include:

(*a*) hourly rates of pay;

(*b*) salary, whether paid weekly or monthly;

(*c*) overtime rates;

(*d*) shift premia;

(*e*) commission on sales; and

(*f*) holiday pay.

The matters which may be either contractual or discretionary include:

(*a*) bonus arrangements;

(*b*) access to overtime; and

(*c*) sick pay (over and above SSP).

Redundancy payments are also treated as pay, whether they are statutory, contractual or discretionary.

Pensions are a form of deferred pay. For the purposes of the *RRA 1976* and the *DDA 1995*, it makes no difference whether the arrangements for pay to be earned and calculated are contractual or non-contractual. When it comes to the *SDA 1975* and the *EPA 1970*, however, the distinction is important.

187.2 THE RRA 1976

There is direct racial discrimination whenever an employee is, on racial grounds, paid less than another employee is or would be paid. The relevant principles are illustrated by the Court of Appeal decision in *Wakeman and others v Quick Corporation and Another* [*1999*] *IRLR 424*. Three English managers employed at the London office of a Japanese Company complained of direct racial discrimination. Their complaint was that they were paid substantially less than Japanese employees who had originally been employed in Japan and had been temporarily seconded to London. The picture was a complicated one. The company pointed out that they also had Japanese employees who had been hired in London and that these employees were paid on the same scale as non-Japanese employees who had been hired in London. It was argued by the complainants, however, that the locally hired Japanese employees were junior to them.

The complaints were rejected by the Employment Tribunal. This decision was upheld on appeal by both the EAT and the Court of Appeal. It was held by the Court of Appeal that the complainants could not claim the same pay as the managers who had been seconded from Japan, even if their work was identical or of equal value to that of the Japanese secondees. This was because the relevant circumstances of the complainants were materially different from those of the Japanese comparators. The latter were secondees and this was an important factor in the difference of pay. The complainants were not secondees; they had been recruited locally.

The locally recruited Japanese employees were not appropriate comparators either. This was because they were junior to the complainants in terms of the work which they carried out.

Accordingly, since there were no actual comparators, the tribunal had to consider how the employer would have treated Japanese employees whose relevant circumstances were the same as those of the complainants or at least not materially different from those of the complainants. This meant that the comparators had to be Japanese employees who were doing similar work, or work of equal value, to the work of the complainants and who were not secondees. There were no actual employees who fitted this description. The tribunal found that there was no evidence that hypothetical Japanese comparators fitting this description would have been paid more than the complainants.

187.3 THE SDA 1975 AND THE EPA 1970

The above-mentioned complaint was one of direct discrimination in relation to rates of pay and it was decided on the basis of a hypothetical comparison. There can be no similar case under the *SDA 1975*.

If an employee has a complaint about rates of pay on grounds of gender, that complaint relates to *Equal Pay* under the *EPA 1970* and it is necessary for the complainant to identify an appropriate comparator of the opposite sex. No complaint about rates of pay, or any other contractual term for the payment of money, may be brought under the *SDA 1975* and no complaint may be based on a hypothetical comparison.

The position is probably different in relation to discretionary payments. A claim in respect of such payments may be brought under the *SDA 1975* and the comparator may be actual or hypothetical. The following are examples of such complaints:

(*a*) A female manager is made redundant at the same time as a male manager. There is no contractual redundancy scheme, but the company makes discretionary payments which are decided individually. The man has a slightly higher grade than the woman, but his discretionary payment exceeds hers by a much greater amount than could be explained by that difference in grade. She could bring a complaint under the *SDA 1975*, relying on his case to argue that a hypothetical comparator at her grade would have received a higher payment than that which has been made to her.

(*b*) A company has sales teams which consist mainly of women but which are led mainly by men. There is a discretionary bonus scheme under which bonuses for good sales performance are paid to team leaders and not to the members of the teams. A female team member could present a complaint of indirect sex discrimination, even though her work is not of equal value to that of any of the team leaders who receive the bonuses.

If the redundancy and bonus schemes in the above examples had been contractual, any complaint would have had to be brought under the *EPA 1970* and would have failed for the lack of a suitable comparator.

187.4 THE DDA 1995

An employee would have a case for disability discrimination if his or her rate of pay were to be reduced, because of an assumption that job performance would be adversely affected by the disability.

Where a disability does in fact cause an employee to work more slowly or less efficiently, the starting point is the employer's duty to make *Reasonable Adjustments*. It may be possible, through the provision or adaptation of equipment, or by making other adjustments, to improve the employee's performance.

Once the duty to make *Reasonable Adjustments* has been fully complied with, there would probably be a defence of justification to any complaint of disability discrimination in relation to the pay received. That defence is likely to be available in whatever way the slow or inefficient work affects the pay received, whether in relation to:

(*a*) the amount of weekly pay;

(*b*) the amount of a productivity bonus; or

(*c*) the payment to the employee for piecework or measured work.

187.5 CONTRACTUAL OR DISCRETIONARY PAYMENTS

Many employers prefer to adopt discretionary rather than contractual arrangements in relation to such matters as sick pay (over and above SSP), bonus arrangements and extra redundancy payments, because of the flexibility which it gives them.

There are, however, two potential disadvantages. The first is the technical one that direct or indirect discrimination in relation to discretionary payments can lead to a complaint under the *SDA 1975*, which is a more flexible remedy than a complaint under the *EPA 1970*.

Secondly, unless discretionary payments are made on a consistent basis, there is a risk that there will be at least the appearance of discrimination and hence a risk of successful complaints under the *RRA 1976* or the *SDA 1975*.

187.6 EQUAL PAY – NOT FAIR PAY

The *EPA 1970* and the discrimination laws do not give employees the right to a fair day's pay for a fair day's work. The law is about equality, not about fairness. If an employer pays no more than the minimum wage, for work which is worth far more, an employee receiving that wage has a remedy only if a suitable comparator can be identified under the *EPA 1970* or if racial or disability discrimination can be proved.

188 Penalties

None of the discrimination laws provide for an employer or any other respondent to be fined or subjected to any other penalty for unlawful discrimination. Such discrimination can be costly to employers and others, but that is because the individual complainant can be awarded unlimited amounts of compensation. There are *Offences* under the *SDA 1975*, the *RRA 1976* and the *DDA 1995*, but they do not include unlawful discrimination.

All the statutory Commissions have enforcement powers, but the ultimate step is for the Commission to apply to a county court (or sheriff court in Scotland) for an *Injunction* (or *Interdict*) in Scotland. No application may be made for an injunction or interdict to prevent any unlawful act in the employment field until after:

(*a*) an Employment Tribunal has made a finding of unlawful discrimination;

(*b*) an Employment Tribunal has made a finding (on an application by the relevant Commission) of an unlawful act relating to discriminatory *Advertisements*, *Instructions to Discriminate* or *Pressure to Discriminate*; or

(*c*) a *Non-Discrimination Notice* has been served by the relevant Commission.

Furthermore, in each case, the application for an injunction or interdict cannot be made until the Employment Tribunal finding or non-discrimination notice has become final (i.e. an appeal has been unsuccessful or has been withdrawn or the time for appealing has expired).

189 Pensions

189.1 THE EPA 1970 AND THE SDA 1975 – ORIGINAL PROVISIONS

The *EPA 1970* and the *SDA 1975*, in their original form, permitted discrimination in access to occupational pension schemes and in benefits under such schemes, as well as other acts of discrimination in relation to death or retirement (including discrimination in relation to *Redundancy* payments). The most widespread forms of discrimination were:

(*a*) discrimination against women in relation to access to pension schemes (including the exclusion of most part-time workers);

(*b*) discrimination against female employees in relation to benefits for surviving spouses; and

(*c*) discrimination against men in relation to the age from which pensions could become payable.

The discriminatory structure of most occupational pension schemes began to collapse in 1990, with the decision of the ECJ in *Barber v Guardian Royal Exchange Assurance Group* [*1990*] *IRLR 240,* the case in which it was found to be incompatible with *Article 141* (then *Article 119*) to require a man to wait for his pension for five years longer than his female colleagues.

Following a series of further decisions of the ECJ, our domestic law was amended as mentioned below.

189.2 THE CURRENT LAW

The *Pensions Act 1995* and the *Occupational Pension Schemes (Equal Treatment) Regulations 1995 (SI 1995 No 3183)* both came into effect on 1 January 1996. With effect from that date, every occupational pension scheme is to be treated as including an equal treatment rule. This rule has the same effect in relation to pensions as an *Equality Clause* has in relation to other terms of employment. It applies to the right to join a scheme, the terms of membership and the terms on which members are treated.

These provisions are contained in *section 62* of the *Pensions Act 1995. Section 63* of that Act states that *section 62* shall be construed as one with *section 1* of the *EPA 1970.* The provisions of the *EPA 1970* with regard to disputes and enforcement are expressly incorporated. The structure of *section 62* is very similar to that of *section 1* of the *EPA 1970.* The equal treatment rule takes effect only where there is a *Comparator* of the opposite sex in the *Same Employment* employed on *Like Work*, work rated as equivalent or work of *Equal Value*. The *Material Factor* defence is available.

A special feature of discrimination in relation to benefits under a pension scheme is that discriminatory provisions which exist during a complainant's employment do not directly impinge on the complainant until he or she retires and becomes entitled to a lump sum payment and a pension. Accordingly the 1995 Regulations provide that it is only pensioner members who can be awarded arrears of benefits or damages. The remedy for an employee member is a declaration. In either case, although the proceedings have been brought against the trustees of the scheme, the employer can be ordered to provide additional resources and accordingly is treated as a party and is entitled to appear.

189.3 RETROSPECTIVE CLAIMS

A major issue is that of retrospective claims. Many pensioners and would-be pensioners spent most of their working lives under the discriminatory regimes which were permitted by domestic legislation until 1 January 1996.

The ECJ ruled in *Barber* that claims of discrimination in relation to pension benefits (apart from those already in the pipeline) could be based only on pensionable service after 17 May 1990 (the date of the decision in *Barber*). The position is different in relation to access to pension schemes. In *Preston and Others v Wolverhampton Healthcare NHS Trust and Others* [*2000*] *IRLR 506,* the ECJ considered a number of questions referred to it by the House of Lords. These were 22 test cases which were representative of some 60,000 claims by workers who had been excluded, because they were part-timers, from membership of various public and private sector occupational pension schemes. One of the questions referred to the ECJ was whether the respondents could rely on the provision in the *EPA 1970* under which no arrears of remuneration or damages could be awarded in respect of any time earlier than two years before the commencement of proceedings (see also *Back Pay*). It was held by the ECJ that this provision in the *EPA 1970* was precluded by Community law. The ECJ did not specify the period of service by reference to which claims for compensation can be based, but the logic of the decision is that compensation claims can be calculated by reference to any period of exclusion since 8 April 1976. This was the date of the decision of the ECJ in *Defrenne v Sabena* [*1976*] *ECR 455,* the first case in which the ECJ held that *Article 119* had direct effect. It was, however, pointed out by the ECJ in *Preston,* citing the case of *Fisscher* [*1994*] *IRLR 662,* an earlier decision of the ECJ, that the fact that a worker can claim retroactively to join an occupational pension scheme does not allow him or her to avoid paying the contributions relating to the period of membership concerned.

Other aspects of the decision in *Preston* are considered in relation to *Time Limits*.

190 Performance of Job Duties

The way in which an employee performs his or her job duties may lead either to a benefit, such as *Promotion*, or a *Detriment*, such as a warning (or ultimately *Dismissal*) for unsatisfactory performance.

It is important that all decisions based on an employee's performance at work, whether beneficial or detrimental, should be made objectively and consistently. Complaints of direct discrimination arise when double standards are applied.

Even a strictly objective and consistent approach will not always be sufficient. There could be complaints of *Indirect Discrimination* or *Disability Discrimination* in the following examples:

(*a*) where a manual worker's performance or the assessment of that performance is adversely affected by language difficulties which the employer has made no attempt to resolve;

(*b*) where the consideration of a female employee's performance by reference to output or sales ignores the fact that she has been on *Maternity* leave for part of the relevant period; or

(*c*) where a disabled employee's job performance is substantially affected by the *Disability* and no *Reasonable Adjustment* has been considered.

191 Persistent Discrimination

The relevant Commission may apply for an *Injunction* (or *Interdict* in Scotland) to prevent a person from discriminating unlawfully within five years after either of the following becoming final:

(*a*) a *Non-Discrimination Notice* served on that person; or

(*b*) a finding by an Employment Tribunal, on an individual complaint, of unlawful discrimination or breach of a contractual term modified or included by virtue of an *Equality Clause*.

If the EOC or the CRE wish to allege, when applying for an injunction against a person, that that person has done an unlawful act which has not already been the subject of a finding by an Employment Tribunal, then the Commission must first apply to an Employment Tribunal for a relevant finding, under *section 73* of the *SDA 1975* or *section 62* of the *RRA 1976*. There is no corresponding provision in the *Disability Rights Commission Act 1999*.

All references to a person include any organisation.

192 Personal Services

Most of the cases where gender or belonging to a particular racial group can be a *Genuine Occupational Qualification* are of very limited importance.

A GOQ which can be relevant to a wide range of jobs, under both the *SDA 1975* and the *RRA 1976*, is that relating to personal services. Whenever a person is to be recruited (or transferred) to a post as a carer, social worker, probation officer, housing officer or similar post dealing with a particularly vulnerable or disadvantaged group, it may be legitimate to consider whether the services which are required can most effectively be provided by a person of the same gender or racial group as that of the persons to whom the services are to be provided.

Any decision that such a post is covered by the GOQ exception should be made at a senior level, after careful consideration of the circumstances of the particular post. It can never be assumed that the exception will apply automatically to a post of a particular description. Furthermore, it would not be appropriate to apply the GOQ exception to a management post which does not involve any significant direct contact with the client group.

193 Physical Appearance

193.1 THE SDA 1975 – AN APPEARANCE CODE

In the early case of *Schmidt v Austicks Bookshops Limited [1977] IRLR 360*, a female employee complained about a requirement that she should wear a skirt and not trousers whilst serving the public. It was common ground that male employees would not be required to wear skirts. It was held by the EAT that there was no unlawful sex discrimination against the complainant. Both male and female employees were subject to rules relating to their apparel and appearance, although the rules which applied to the women were not the same as the rules which applied to the men.

The principle of this decision was approved by the Court of Appeal in *Smith v Safeway Plc [1996] IRLR 456*. In that case an assistant in a supermarket was dismissed because he was not prepared to comply with a code which required male employees to have tidy hair not below shirt-collar length.

The decision of the Court of Appeal established the following principles:

(*a*) where an employer adopts rules concerning appearance, those rules must be considered as a whole, not garment by garment or item by item;

(*b*) the rules will not be discriminatory because their content is different for men and for women, if taken as a whole they enforce a common principle of smartness or conventionality and neither gender is treated less favourably in enforcing that principle; and

(*c*) the principle is the same, whether the code relates to dress or to more permanent characteristics, such as hairstyle.

These two appeal decisions do not, however, mean that it is always lawful for an employer to prohibit female employees from coming to work in trousers or to require male employees to have short hair. The question whether a code on dress or appearance is directly discriminatory as between men and women in any particular case is one of fact for the Employment Tribunal. There could be a finding of direct discrimination if an employer has codes on dress or appearance which, taken as a whole, are more stringent for one sex than the other or which prohibit what have now become conventional standards.

193.2 THE RRA 1976

An inflexible code on dress or appearance could also give rise to complaints of indirect racial discrimination if, for example, a Sikh is forbidden to wear a turban at work or a Muslim woman of Pakistani origin is forbidden to wear trousers. It is unlikely that an Employment Tribunal would find these rules to be justifiable, if the only purpose was to maintain a particular standard of dress and appearance at work – see also *Indirect Discrimination*.

193.3 THE SDA 1975 – OTHER MATTERS

In theory, there is nothing in the *SDA 1975* to prevent employers from turning job applicants away on the ground that they are fat or ugly.

The reality is different, unless the same standards are applied to applicants of both sexes. The following would be a clear case of direct sex discrimination:

(*a*) two women apply for a secretarial post;

(*b*) one of them is superior in all relevant respects, such as qualifications and experience;

(*c*) the other is selected because she is younger and prettier and the employer finds her more attractive; and

(*d*) the employer would not have taken age or beauty or physical attraction into account if he had been considering two male candidates.

The unsuccessful female candidate has been treated less favourably than a male candidate would have been. *Her* age and appearance have been taken into account to her detriment; those factors would not have stood in the way of *his* appointment.

It may be thought unlikely that there would be sufficient evidence to prove direct discrimination in such a case. It is not unknown, however, for interviewers to write personal comments about candidates on the interview notes and for those comments to come to light as a result of the *Questionnaire* or disclosure of *Documents*. Furthermore, the employer would find it difficult in such a case to give a convincing and satisfactory explanation for his failure to appoint the better qualified candidate – see *Evidence of Discrimination*.

193.4 THE DDA 1995

The definition of *Disability* for the purpose of the *DDA 1995* expressly includes an impairment consisting of a severe disfigurement (other than one which has been deliberately acquired as a result of tattoos or non-medical body piercing). Accordingly rejecting a candidate for a job because he or she has a severe disfigurement would be an act of disability discrimination unless the decision could be justified.

Suppose that an employer turns down a job applicant with a severe facial disfigurement, on the ground that the job involves regular contact with members of the public who would suffer embarrassment. It is most unlikely that justification could be established in a case such as this. It is a fundamental principle of discrimination law that employers and others cannot use the real or assumed prejudice of customers or others as an excuse for discrimination. Once that principle is compromised, the next step could be to argue that employers are justified in rejecting candidates with severe disfigurement because fellow employees could be embarrassed.

194 Physical or Mental Impairment

194.1 MEANING

The term 'impairment' is fundamental to the definition of 'disability' in the *DDA 1995*. However, the *DDA 1995* does not contain a comprehensive definition of 'impairment'. A simplistic interpretation of the term 'impairment' may be inappropriate, since the term has medical significance; the World Health Organisation has defined it as 'any loss or abnormality of psychological, physiological, or anatomical structure or function'.

Certain conditions are not regarded as impairments pursuant to *paragraph 8* of the Guidance for the purposes of the *DDA 1995*:

(*a*) addiction to or dependency on alcohol, nicotine, or any other substance (other than in consequence of the substance being medically prescribed);

(*b*) hay fever, except where it aggravates the effect of another condition;

(*c*) pyromania, kleptomania, exhibitionism and voyeurism; or

(*d*) the tendency to physical or sexual abuse of others.

Paragraphs 10–15 of the Guidance make several practical points:

(*a*) often, there will be no dispute as to whether a person has an 'impairment'. A dispute is more likely to arise as to whether the effects of the impairment are sufficient to fall within the scope of the *DDA 1995*;

(*b*) how an impairment was caused is irrelevant (so, for instance, a disease caused by alcoholism constitutes an impairment);

(*c*) sensory impairments, such as those affecting sight or hearing, are included;

(*d*) 'mental impairment' includes a wide range of impairments, such as learning disabilities but not, pursuant to *Schedule 2, paragraph 2* of the *DDA 1995*, any impairment resulting from or consisting of a mental illness unless that illness is clinically well-recognised, i.e., by a respected body of medical opinion; and

(*e*) mental illness does not have the special meaning attributed to it in other legislation.

In *Goodwin v The Patent Office* [*1999*] *IRLR 4*, the EAT said that in cases of doubt, whether or not the impairment is mentioned in the World Health Organisation's International Classification of Diseases will 'very likely determine the issue one way or the other'.

194.2 DIFFICULT CASES

In some cases, tribunals may be called upon to choose between opposing expert medical evidence in order to determine whether or not a mental impairment is a 'clinically well-recognised illness'. An example may be chronic fatigue syndrome ('CFS'). Some doubt exists as to whether CFS is an illness. Even those who identify it as an illness disagree whether its origins are physical, viral or psychological. In the early case of *O'Neill v Symm & Co Limited* [*1998*] *IRLR 233*, a tribunal after hearing expert medical evidence, found that CFS can be a disability for the purposes of the *DDA 1995*. The EAT said, however, that this should not be taken 'as establishing that CFS is, generically, a category of disability that necessarily falls within the ambit of the Act', but despite that cautionary note, it has been treated as a disability in a number of later cases.

195 Physical Requirements

195.1 HEAVY WORK

There are physically demanding jobs both in construction and other industries and also in some jobs involving the care of the elderly and others – see also *Heavy Work*.

The following principles apply in recruitment for such jobs:

(*a*) It must never be assumed that a man is qualified and a woman is disqualified for such work on account of their respective genders. The assumption is unsound and acting on it would be a clear case of sex discrimination.

(*b*) It would also be an act of direct discrimination in the arrangements for recruitment for the job to require female candidates but not male candidates to undertake a test of strength or stamina.

(*c*) Direct discrimination can be avoided by asking candidates of both sexes to undergo the same tests, but there could be indirect discrimination against female candidates if the test requirements are excessive in relation to the demands of the job. There are many jobs which at first glance require considerable physical strength but which can be adapted by using equipment or skilled techniques.

195.2 MANUAL DEXTERITY

Similar principles apply to the many jobs for which employers regard female candidates as being generally more suitable. Many of these jobs require some degree of manual dexterity. They include traditional jobs operating machines, typing letters or assembling parts and also jobs in modern industries for which keyboard skills are required.

195.3 HEIGHT REQUIREMENTS

A requirement that candidates for the post should have at least a specified minimum height is indirectly discriminatory against women (and perhaps also candidates from some ethnic groups) unless it can be objectively justified; subject to that same proviso, a requirement that candidates should be below a specified height is indirectly discriminatory against men (and perhaps candidates from other ethnic groups).

It is difficult to envisage many circumstances in which requirements of either kind could be objectively justified. In particular, the notion that an imposing physical presence is a necessary (let alone sufficient) attribute for law enforcement or private security work is a somewhat unfashionable one.

The adoption of different height requirements for men and women (or candidates or employees of different racial groups) would be direct discrimination. There are statutory exceptions for *Prison Officers* and *Police* officers.

196 Physical Strength

The demands which different jobs make in terms of the physical effort required, is one of the relevant demand factors in evaluating the jobs for the purposes of an *Equal Value* claim.

In cases of *Selection* for jobs involving physical strength:

(*a*) there is direct sex discrimination if a decision is based on an untested assumption that a man is more suitable than a woman for such a job;

(*b*) there is also direct sex discrimination if a woman is required to demonstrate that she has the necessary strength and the man is not; and

(*c*) there is indirect sex discrimination if the physical strength required is excessive in relation to the needs of the job.

Under *section 7* of the *SDA 1975*, one of the cases where being a man can be a *Genuine Occupational Qualification* for a job is where the essential nature of the job calls for a man for reasons of physiology. It is expressly stated, however, that the reference to physiology excludes physical strength or stamina.

197 Psychometric Testing

Psychometric testing was originally conceived about a century ago, but its use in *Recruitment* has much increased over the past few years. Broadly speaking, psychometric tests are designed to assess either ability or personality and typically take one of the following forms:

(*a*) tests of specific ability, e.g. numeracy and verbal and spatial perception;

(*b*) tests of general mental ability, such as power of analytical reasoning; or

(*c*) tests for specific personality traits.

Alternatively, either tests may permit a comparison of the results of an individual with the average score for a population or the results may be descriptive instead of being scored.

Many different tests are now on the market, including tests which purport to identify specific characteristics such as 'leadership', 'honesty' and 'commercial acumen'. Tests vary in innumerable ways, not least in terms of cost and how time-consuming they are to operate. Even tests which are acknowledged as market leaders will not be 100 per cent accurate and therefore it is, as a practical matter, unwise for an employer not to utilise in addition other ways of assessing individual applicants or existing employees.

In any event, the use of psychometric tests, like *Genetic Testing*, may raise equal opportunities concerns. Some tests, especially those which were devised several years ago, are characterised by an element of bias. For instance, a test of a woman might suggest that she was by nature aggressive. An employer who refused to offer her employment because aggression was perceived as an unsuitable characteristic of a female employee, although regarded as acceptable in a male employee, would be vulnerable to a claim of direct discrimination on the ground of sex. Similarly, if a candidate for whom English is not the first language is rejected essentially because of a poor command of English in circumstances where adequate command of the English language is unnecessary to do the job, the employer may be vulnerable to a complaint of indirect discrimination under the *RRA 1976*.

Disabled employees may face particular difficulties with psychometric testing. For instance, the Royal National Institute for the Blind has expressed concern that such testing may have a negative effect on visually impaired people. The *DDA 1995* requires employers to make *Reasonable Adjustments* to tests which may discriminate against people with disabilities and particular problems unique to visually impaired people make this a complex task. A blind candidate tackling a numerical reasoning test in Braille, for instance, is said to need as much as seven times longer to complete the test comfortably as someone with no impairment. When a test takes a substantial amount of extra time, factors such as fatigue and boredom will affect performance. Similar problems occur when tests are taken in large print or on tape. Such issues make it even more essential that a thorough job analysis is carried out before a psychometric test is administered, and its contents regarded as valid. The RNIB has, in conjunction with the Employment Service, produced a guide for employers, *Psychometric Testing and Visual Impairment*, which includes useful practical tips. A companion guide for visually impaired individuals is also available.

198 Police

Police officers are not employees in the conventional sense. It is, however, expressly stated, in *section 17* of the *SDA 1975* and *section 16* of the *RRA 1976,* that the holding of the office of constable (which includes any rank) shall be treated as employment by:

(*a*) the chief officer of police as respects any act done by him; or

(*b*) by the police authority as respects any act done by them.

An appointment as a police cadet is treated as employment in the same way.

The *SDA 1975* provides that regulations under what is now the *Police Act 1996* may not treat men and women differently except in relation to:

(*a*) height requirements;

(*b*) uniform or equipment requirements or allowances;

(*c*) special treatment of women in connection with pregnancy or childbirth; or

(*d*) pensions to or in respect of special constables or police cadets.

The last-mentioned exception is subject to the principle of equal pay under *Article 141* and the *Equal Pay Directive*.

Police work falls within the *Public Sector* so that Directives can have direct effect. Furthermore, the police are included in the public authorities on whom new duties are placed by the extended provisions of *section 71* of the *RRA 1976* – see *Public Sector*.

199 Pools

Complaints of *Indirect Discrimination* require proof of *Disparate Impact* which may in turn involve consideration of *Statistics*.

The starting point in such cases is to identify the pool of workers in respect of whom the statistics are to be compiled – see *Indirect Discrimination, section 7*. If, for example, the case is one of indirect sex discrimination, it is necessary first of all to identify the pool and then to ascertain:

(*a*) the percentage of the men in the pool who can comply with the relevant requirement or condition; and

(*b*) the percentage of the women in the pool who can comply with it.

200 Positive Discrimination

200.1 THE SDA 1975

Sections 47 and *48* permit limited measures of sex discrimination by employers, *Training Bodies*, *Trade Unions* and other organisations.

An employer, for example, is permitted to take certain measures to discriminate in favour of women if, during the previous 12 months, there were no women doing some particular work or the number of women doing that work was comparatively small. The permitted measures are:

(*a*) encouraging women to take advantage of opportunities for doing that work; or

(*b*) affording only his female employees access to facilities for training which would help to fit them for that work.

Similar measures of discrimination in favour of men are permitted where it is men who have not been doing the work or doing it only in comparatively small numbers.

In either case, however, there must be no discrimination at the point of *Selection*.

Similar measures of encouragement or training are permitted to trade unions and other organisations. Training bodies may discriminate in favour of persons of one sex or the other where during the previous 12 months there have been no persons of that sex, or only a comparatively small number of persons of that sex, doing the work either in Great Britain as a whole or in the particular area where the persons given training are likely to take up work.

200.2 THE RRA 1976

Sections 38 and *39* of the *RRA 1976* contain similar provisions. Provided that a specified condition is satisfied, an employer may discriminate in favour of members of a particular racial group, in relation to particular work at a particular establishment, either by:

(*a*) encouraging only persons from that racial group to take advantage of opportunities for doing that work at that establishment; or

(*b*) by affording only to employees working at that establishment who belong to that racial group access to facilities for training which would help to fit them for that work.

The condition to be satisfied is one of the following, at any time within the previous 12 months:

(*a*) no persons of that racial group among those doing that work at that establishment;

(*b*) the proportion of employees doing the work at the establishment who belong to the racial group being small in comparison with the proportion of all the employees at the establishment who belong to the racial group; or

(*c*) the proportion of employees doing the work at the establishment who belong to the racial group being small in comparison with the proportion of the population of the normal recruitment area for the establishment who belong to the racial group.

For example, racial discrimination in encouraging job applicants or employees to apply for particular work, or discrimination in favour of employees in training them for that work, could be lawful if:

(*a*) only five per cent of the persons doing the particular work at the establishment are from the particular racial group; and

(*b*) 20 per cent of the employees at the establishment as a whole are from that racial group.

201 Post-Employment Discrimination

201.1 THE ISSUE

The *SDA 1975*, the *RRA 1976* and the *DDA 1995* all require any employer, 'in the case of a person employed by him at an establishment in Great Britain', not to discriminate against that employee (inter alia) in the way he affords the employee access to any benefits, facilities or services, or by refusing or deliberately omitting to afford the employee access to them or by subjecting the employee to a detriment.

Does the employer's duty not to discriminate in any of these ways continue after the employment has ended, so that the ex-employee can present a complaint of post-employment discrimination?

At the time of writing, there is the unedifying spectacle of authorities which give one answer for complaints under the *RRA 1976* and a different answer for complaints under the *SDA 1975*.

In *Adekeye v The Post Office (No 2)* [*1997*] *IRLR 105*, an employee was dismissed for misconduct. Her complaint of racial discrimination in dismissing her was out of time, but she submitted a new complaint of racial discrimination in relation to the conduct of her internal appeal against dismissal.

It was held by the Court of Appeal that the tribunal had had no jurisdiction to hear this second complaint. The words 'in the case of a person employed by him' in *section 4(2)* of the *RRA 1976* apply only to a person who is still employed at the time of the alleged discrimination; they cannot cover a person who has been previously so employed. Miss Adekeye was no longer an employee at the time of her internal appeal against dismissal and accordingly her complaint could not be entertained.

One of the arguments which was considered by the Court of Appeal in *Adekeye* was that the *SDA 1975* would have to be construed in accordance with the *Equal Treatment Directive*, so as to give a remedy to former employees, and that the *RRA 1976* should be construed in the same way. Two of the three members of the Court of Appeal doubted whether the *Equal Treatment Directive* required the *SDA 1975* to be construed in the way suggested, but in any event the Court decided unanimously, as a matter of principle, to reject the argument that, 'although the *Equal Treatment Directive* has no application whatsoever to the 1976 Act [the *RRA 1976*], nevertheless to achieve consistency with the 1975 Act [the *SDA 1975*] to which the Directive is relevant, the 1976 Act should be given a meaning which otherwise it cannot bear'.

The position under the *SDA 1975* was referred to the ECJ in the case of *Coote v Granada Hospitality Limited* [*1998*] *IRLR 656*. Ms Coote had brought a sex discrimination complaint, alleging that she had been dismissed because of pregnancy. This case had been settled without an admission of liability. She later had difficulty in obtaining new employment and she brought a further complaint alleging that her former employers had victimised her, within the definition contained in *section 4* of the *SDA 1975*, by failing to provide an employment agency with a reference. The tribunal, following *Adekeye*, held that there was no jurisdiction to hear her complaint, but on appeal the EAT referred the case to the ECJ.

Ms Coote's earlier pregnancy complaint fell within the definition of legal proceedings brought to enforce compliance with the principle of equal treatment within the meaning of the *Equal Treatment Directive*. The ECJ, referring to *Articles 6* and *7* of the Directive, ruled that there was a requirement for member states to take the measures necessary 'to ensure judicial protection for workers whose employer, after the employment relationship has ended, refuses to provide references as a reaction to "such proceedings" '.

The case then came back to the EAT as *Coote v Granada Hospitality Limited (No 2) [1999] IRLR 452*. Since the former employer was in the private sector, the issue to be considered by the EAT was whether the *SDA 1975* could be construed in conformity with the Directive.

The EAT took a different view from that taken by the Court of Appeal in *Adekeye*. As a matter of grammar, the word 'employed' in *section 6(2)* of the *SDA 1975* can mean 'who is employed' or 'who has been employed' or both. The latter construction should be adopted in order to construe the *SDA 1975* in conformity with the Directive.

It follows, that as the law currently stands, a former employee who wishes to complain of victimisation in withholding a reference, or giving a damaging reference, will be able to pursue the complaint if it is under the *SDA 1975* but not if it is under the *RRA 1976*. At the time of writing there are no appeal decisions on post-employment discrimination under the *DDA 1995*, but, since the *Equal Treatment Directive* does not apply to such cases, the doctrine of precedent may require tribunals to follow the decision in *Adekeye*. The only possible advice to employers, until the law has been clarified, is that they should not discriminate against or victimise (whether under the *SDA 1975*, the *RRA 1976* or the *DDA 1995*) either former employees or current employees.

201.2 EXAMPLES OF POST-EMPLOYMENT DISCRIMINATION

Three examples have already been given of circumstances in which a former employee may be able to present a complaint under the *SDA 1975*. These are cases of discrimination or victimisation in:

(*a*) withholding or refusing a reference;

(*b*) giving a damaging reference; and

(*c*) dealing with an internal appeal against dismissal.

The following further examples were given by the EAT in *Coote*:

(*a*) continued use of sports [or social] facilities;

(*b*) bonuses to former staff; and

(*c*) concessionary travel facilities.

201.3 POST-EMPLOYMENT BENEFITS – CONTRACTUAL TERMS

Consideration is given in the section on *Terms of Employment* to the possibility of presenting complaints during the employment, under the *RRA 1976* or *DDA 1995*, about terms and conditions or arrangements which will have a discriminatory effect in relation to post-employment benefits.

202 Pregnancy

202.1 STATUTORY RIGHTS

The relevant provisions are now contained in *section 99* of the *Employment Rights Act 1996* and *Regulation 20* of the *Maternity and Parental Leave etc Regulations 1999 (SI 1999 No 3312)*. A dismissal is automatically unfair if the reason or principal reason for the dismissal is a reason connected with the pregnancy of the employee or the fact that she has given birth to a child. The normal requirement that the employee must have been continuously employed for not less than one year does not apply and there is no upper age limit.

Further rights under the 1996 Act are the rights to paid time off for ante-natal care during pregnancy *(sections 55–57)* and the rights under *sections 66–71* relating to suspensions from work on maternity grounds. A suspension is on maternity grounds if:

(*a*) an employee is suspended from work on the ground that she is pregnant, has recently given birth or is breastfeeding a child; and

(*b*) the suspension is in consequence of one of several statutory provisions which have been specified by regulations.

Before the suspension takes place, the woman must be offered any suitable alternative work which is available (and which can be offered on terms and conditions which are not less favourable than her existing terms and conditions). If no such work is available, then she is entitled to remuneration during the period of suspension.

202.2 PREGNANCY AND SEX DISCRIMINATION

It is an act of direct sex discrimination to dismiss a woman because she is pregnant or because of an absence from work caused by a pregnancy-related illness – see *Dismissal*.

It was, however, held by the ECJ in *Brown v Rentokil Limited* [*1998*] *IRLR 445*, that under the *Equal Treatment Directive* there was a distinction between, on the one hand, a pregnancy related absence during pregnancy or maternity leave and, on the other hand, absence after maternity leave. The latter may be treated like any other absence, even though it is pregnancy related and is therefore caused by a condition which is unique to women.

It is also direct sex discrimination to refuse to employ a woman because she is or may become pregnant. That principle was established by the House of Lords in *Webb v EMO Air Cargo (UK) Limited* [*1993*] *IRLR 27*. Lord Keith said:

> 'There can be no doubt that in general to dismiss a woman because she is pregnant or to refuse to employ a woman of child-bearing age because she may become pregnant is unlawful direct discrimination. Child-bearing and the capacity for child-bearing are characteristics of the female sex. So to apply these characteristics as the criterion for dismissal or refusal is to apply a gender-based criterion . . .'

In that case, a firm with 16 employees had recruited the complainant after it became known that an import operations clerk was pregnant and would be taking maternity leave about six months later.

The complainant would need six months' training. She would then act as the temporary replacement for the import operations clerk during the period of maternity leave. It was anticipated that she would then probably be retained in employment when the permanent clerk returned. Some weeks after she started, however, while she was still being trained, she discovered that she was pregnant. She informed her employers who dismissed her.

The complainant had not been dismissed because she was pregnant, or because of any special feature of pregnancy, such as the statutory right to return to work. She had been dismissed because she would be unavailable for work at the very time when her services were required, to provide maternity cover. The House of Lords referred to the ECJ the question whether there was a breach of the *Equal Treatment Directive* in these circumstances.

The ECJ rather fudged the question by focusing on evidence that the complainant had been recruited not simply to provide maternity cover but for an unlimited term. The ECJ ruled that the Directive precluded dismissal in these circumstances. When the case came back to the House of Lords, [*1995*] *IRLR 645*, it was held that the *SDA 1975* could be construed in accordance with the ruling of the ECJ and accordingly the complaint succeeded. It was expressly stated by Lord Keith, however, that the outcome would not necessarily be the same in a case where a woman 'is denied employment for a fixed period in the future through the whole of which her pregnancy would make her unavailable for work, nor in the situation where after engagement for such a period the discovery of her pregnancy leads to cancellation of the engagement'.

In *Abbey National plc v Formoso* [*1999*] *IRLR 222*, it was held that there was direct sex discrimination in dismissing an employee for misconduct, in circumstances where she was unable to attend the disciplinary hearing because of a pregnancy-related condition and the hearing went ahead in her absence.

Health and Safety at Work issues also arise in relation to pregnant workers.

203 Pre-Hearing Discussion

It is very common for the Employment Tribunal to order a pre-hearing discussion in discrimination and equal pay cases. The purpose of the pre-hearing discussion is to clarify the issues in the case and for the tribunal to give directions for the future conduct of the case. Either party can also apply to the tribunal for the holding of a pre-hearing discussion. Such a discussion may well help to save both time and expense.

204 Pre-Hearing Review

A pre-hearing review may be arranged, under rule 7 of the Tribunal Rules, on the application of either party or by the tribunal of its own motion. The purpose of a pre-hearing review is for the tribunal to consider whether the contentions put forward by any party have no reasonable prospect of success, in which event that party may be ordered to pay a deposit of an amount not exceeding £150 as a condition of being permitted to continue to take part in the proceedings.

It is quite rare for a pre-hearing review to be conducted in a discrimination or equal pay case. One reason for this is that often the issues are too complex for it to be possible to form a fair view of the merits of the case without hearing all the evidence.

205 Prejudice

It is now well established law that conscious motivation is not required for a finding of *Direct Discrimination* or *Victimisation*. Unlawful acts can and do occur as a result of conscious or unconscious prejudices about racial minority workers, women (or men) or disabled workers.

The code of practice under the *RRA 1976* makes the important recommendation (in paragraph 1.14) that staff responsible for shortlisting, interviewing and selecting candidates should be given guidance or training on the effects which generalised assumptions and prejudices about race can have on selection decisions. The guidance or training should also extend to the effects which assumptions and prejudices about gender or disability can also have.

See also *Assumptions* and *Unintentional Discrimination*.

206 Preliminary Hearing

The purpose of a preliminary hearing is generally to deal with questions of jurisdiction, such as:

(*a*) *Time Limits*;

(*b*) whether the work which the complainant does or has applied for is *Employment* within the extended definition contained in the legislation; or

(*c*) *Territorial Extent*.

In some such cases, particularly where the issue is one of time limits, it is impossible for the tribunal to decide the question without hearing a significant amount of evidence and it may be more convenient for the issue to be decided at the full hearing.

A preliminary hearing is held in *Equal Value* cases, for the tribunal to consider whether to require an independent expert to prepare a report. It is also the common, but not invariable, practice at this stage for the tribunal to consider any *Material Factor Defence*.

207 Pressure to Discriminate

Under *section 40* of the *SDA 1975* and *section 31* of the *RRA 1976*, it is unlawful to induce, or attempt to induce, a person to discriminate unlawfully. The *SDA 1975*, but not the *RRA 1976*, defines what is meant in this context by an inducement, to cover:

(*a*) providing or offering to provide the person with any benefit; or

(*b*) subjecting or threatening to subject him to any detriment.

Under both Acts, the inducement need not be made directly to the person in question, if it is made in such a way that he is likely to hear of it.

A complaint about pressure to discriminate contrary to the *SDA 1975* or the *RRA 1976* can be presented only by the EOC or the CRE (as the case may be).

There are no provisions in the *DDA 1995* regarding pressure to discriminate unlawfully.

208 Principals

Employers and others who act through agents are liable for anything done by the agent with their authority (whether express or implied and whether precedent or subsequent). The liability of the principal in these circumstances is considered under *Agents*.

209 Prison Officers

Discrimination in relation to service as a prison officer is covered by both the *SDA 1975* and the *RRA 1976*.

There is a special provision in *section 18* of the *SDA 1975* relating to height requirements. It is lawful to specify different minimum height requirements for male and female officers. Without this special provision, it would have been direct sex discrimination against male officers to require a greater minimum height for them than for female officers.

Although the *DDA 1995* applies generally to Crown Servants, service as a prison officer is one of several categories expressly excluded (*section 64(5)*).

210 Private Households

The question of discrimination in employment for the purposes of a private household, is considered under *Domestic Employment.*

211 Professional Bodies

A professional body (as well as being an employer in its own right) can be:

(*a*) an *Employers' Association* for the purposes of the *SDA 1975* and the *RRA 1976*;

(*b*) a *Qualifying Body* for the purposes of those same Acts;

(*c*) a *Trade Organisation* for the purposes of the *DDA 1995*.

Under *section 77* of the *SDA 1975*, as extended by *section 6* of the *Sex Discrimination Act 1986*, an application may be made to a county court (or sheriff court in Scotland) for an order to remove or modify any rule made by a professional or trade organisation if that rule provides for the doing of an act which would be rendered unlawful by the *SDA 1975*.

There is also provision in *section 6* of the 1986 Act for a complaint to be presented by an interested party to an Employment Tribunal about a rule or term of an agreement which, for example, provides for the doing of something which would be unlawful under the *SDA 1975*. The interested parties who can make such a complaint include, in relation to rules made by employers' associations, a person who:

(*a*) is a member; or

(*b*) who is genuinely and actively seeking to become a member.

In relation to a qualifying body, an interested person is one:

(*a*) on whom the qualifying body has conferred an authorisation or qualification; or

(*b*) who is genuinely and actively seeking an authorisation or qualification.

212 Promotion

The *SDA 1975* (*section 6*), the *RRA 1976* (*section 4*) and the *DDA 1995* (*section 4*) each make it unlawful for an employer to discriminate in the way he affords an employee access to opportunities for promotion or by refusing or deliberately omitting to afford an employee access to such opportunities.

It is generally good practice for job vacancies to be advertised both internally and externally; it is particularly important that all vacancies should be advertised internally, so that any qualified employee can apply. There is an increased risk of complaints of discrimination if employees are *invited* to apply for posts, or simply *appointed* without any competition. Qualified employees could be overlooked because of (perhaps unstated) assumptions or prejudices based on gender, race or disability.

The general advice on *Selection* applies to promotion as well as to external *Recruitment*. It is particularly important, when considering an internal candidate, to ensure that the sources of information about the candidate are untainted by discrimination. If decisions are to be based partly on performance appraisals, they should where practicable be checked by a senior manager. The candidate should be given the opportunity to challenge negative comments and also to suggest the names of other managers who may be able to give a more favourable or balanced view.

213 Public Sector

An important distinction between public sector and private sector employment, is that in the public sector a *Directive* can have direct effect, where its terms are clear and specific, so as to be relied on by an employee or job applicant. Directives are addressed to Member States and the employers on whom a Directive can have direct effect are those employers who are emanations of the State. The ECJ, in *Foster and Others v British Gas Plc* [*1990*] *IRLR 353* gave the following definition:

> 'a body, whatever its legal form, which has been made responsible, pursuant to a measure adopted by the State, for providing a public service under the control of the State and has for that purpose special powers beyond those which result from the normal rules applicable in relations between individuals'.

Relevant bodies include local authorities, NHS Trusts and the police.

Certain public authorities are also now subject to a duty under the extended provisions of *section 71* of the *RRA 1976* to make appropriate arrangements to ensure that their various functions are carried out with due regard to the need to:

(*a*) eliminate unlawful racial discrimination; and

(*b*) promote equality of opportunity and good relations between persons of different racial groups.

The extended provisions are considered in more detail under *Local Authorities*.

214 Qualifying Bodies

Section 13 of the *SDA 1975* and *section 12* of the *RRA 1976* each contain provisions in almost identical terms relating to any authority or body which can confer an authorisation or qualification which is needed for, or facilitates, engagement in a particular profession or trade. These qualifying bodies must not discriminate:

(*a*) in the terms on which they are prepared to confer an authorisation or qualification;

(*b*) by refusing or deliberately omitting to grant an application for an authorisation or qualification; or

(*c*) by withdrawing an authorisation or qualification or varying the terms on which it is held.

The expressions 'authorisation or qualification' are broadly defined to include, for example, registration or approval; the reference to conferring an authorisation or qualification includes renewing or extending it.

The above section in the *SDA 1975* (but not that in the *RRA 1976*) also requires qualifying bodies to have regard to any evidence of unlawful discrimination in connection with any profession or trade whenever it is required to satisfy itself as to a person's good character before conferring any authorisation or qualification.

The *DDA 1995* does not contain any provisions relating to qualifying bodies.

215 Qualifying Periods

There is no qualifying period for rights under the *EPA 1970*, *SDA 1975*, *RRA 1976* or *DDA 1995*. Rights are granted from the commencement of the employment and rights are also granted to job applicants.

216 Questions at Interview

The ways in which the questions asked at interviews can constitute unlawful discrimination or, more commonly, provide evidence of discrimination (even when none was intended) are considered under *Job Interviews*. The key rules for interviewers are:

(*a*) prepare the questions, or at least the main areas to be covered, in advance, studying the job description and any person specification in order to identify the main topics to be explored;

(*b*) read the application forms and CVs submitted by the interviewees, to avoid asking for information which you have already been given;

(*c*) cover broadly the same ground with all the candidates – do *not* have one set of questions for men and a different set for women;

(*d*) do not ask candidates about private matters which are irrelevant to the job, such as plans to marry or start a family;

(*e*) if a candidate has a disability which could affect job performance, discuss it in a positive way, with particular reference to possible *Reasonable Adjustments*; and

(*f*) similarly, if a job involves mobility or unsocial hours, raise that issue positively with all the candidates – men as well as women.

217 Questionnaire

The statutory questionnaire is an important facility which is given to complainants in discrimination cases, but not to complainants in other employment cases. Persons who suspect unlawful discrimination against them, particularly job applicants, are frequently handicapped by a lack of information. The questionnaire is an important means of obtaining that information.

The relevant provisions are contained in *section 74* of the *SDA 1975*, *section 65* of the *RRA 1976* and *section 56* of the *DDA 1995*. Under each of these provisions, forms have been prescribed which may be used by persons who consider that they may have been discriminated against. The prescribed forms may be used by a complainant to question the respondent (the person suspected of unlawful discrimination) so long as the questionnaire is served:

(*a*) before a complaint has been presented to an Employment Tribunal and during the period of three months beginning when the act complained of was done;

(*b*) within the period of 21 days beginning with the day on which a complaint has been presented to an Employment Tribunal; or

(*c*) at a later date, if the tribunal gives leave, and in accordance with any directions made by the tribunal.

Under each of the three Acts, the questions and any replies are admissible in evidence in any Employment Tribunal proceedings. The tribunal may draw any inference which it considers just and equitable to draw, including an inference that the respondent has acted unlawfully, if it appears to the tribunal that:

(*a*) the respondent has deliberately, and without reasonable excuse, omitted to reply within a reasonable period; or

(*b*) the respondent's reply is evasive or equivocal.

An apparent difference between, on the one hand the *SDA 1975* and the *RRA 1976*, and on the other hand the *DDA 1995*, is that under the *DDA 1995* it appears that questions and replies are admissible, and inferences may be drawn, only if the prescribed forms are used. The wording of the provisions in the *SDA 1975* and the *RRA 1976* suggests that the prescribed forms need not be used, so that, for example, questions can be asked in correspondence.

It is, however, good practice to use the prescribed forms. Complainants who are not legally represented should generally seek advice (particularly from the relevant Commission) on the questions to be asked. It is particularly important to ask the reason for the treatment complained of and for information about persons who have been treated more favourably (for example all the shortlisted candidates in a case where the complainant is a job applicant who has not been shortlisted).

Respondents should reply to the questions with all reasonable speed. Above all, they must reply carefully, accurately and fully. The risk of an adverse inference being drawn is greatest when false or misleading information is given.

218 Quotas

The law does not permit race or sex discrimination in appointing persons to vacancies (whether by external recruitment or by internal promotion or transfer) in order to achieve a quota of employees defined by reference to gender or race.

Both the *SDA 1975* and the *RRA 1976* permit limited measures of encouragement or discrimination in the provision of training where there is 'under-representation' – see *Positive Discrimination*. These provisions do not, however, permit discrimination at the point of *Selection* for any post.

It would be lawful for an employer to discriminate in favour of disabled workers generally in order to achieve a minimum quota, but discrimination *against* disabled workers once that quota has been achieved is emphatically not permitted.

219 Racial Discrimination

Whenever the terms 'discriminate' and 'discrimination' are used in the *RRA 1976*, they are so used in the sense defined in *sections 1* and *2* of the Act.

Section 1 contains the definitions of direct and indirect racial discrimination. It also expressly incorporates, within the definition of direct discrimination, segregation on racial grounds.

Section 2 provides that references to discrimination include *Victimisation*, as defined in that section.

Part II of the *RRA 1976* then deals with discrimination in the employment field. It is *section 4* which makes it unlawful for employers to discriminate in various respects against job applicants or employees in relation to employment at an establishment in Great Britain.

220 Racial Grounds

There is direct racial discrimination where a person is, on racial grounds, treated less favourably than other persons are or would be treated. Treatment is on racial grounds if it is on grounds of colour, race, nationality or ethnic or national origins.

This is a much more flexible definition than that of direct sex and marriage discrimination. In particular:

(*a*) For the purposes of direct racial discrimination (as opposed to indirect racial discrimination) it is probably unnecessary to establish whether a group to which a complainant belongs is in fact a racial group. For example, less favourable treatment would arguably be on racial grounds if a Yorkshireman, regarding Lancastrians as an ethnic group and being hostile to that group, were to turn down a job application because the candidate comes from across the Pennines, or if a Cornishman, believing that he belongs to a Cornish race, turns down a job application because it is not from a fellow Cornishman.

(*b*) Similarly, a complaint of direct discrimination could succeed even though the discrimination is based on a mistaken belief about the relevant group to which the complainant belongs. Suppose that an English candidate for a job is married to a Frenchman and her married name is Jean Dubois. She is not shortlisted for the post, because the employer does not wish to employ a man or a French person. She could succeed in a complaint of direct racial discrimination but not in one of direct sex discrimination (unless, possibly, the job is in the *Public Sector* and she is able to base her complaint on the *Equal Treatment Directive*).

(*c*) Under the *RRA 1976*, a complaint could succeed if the less favourable treatment is on the ground of the race of the complainant's spouse or partner. There has been at least one case in which a white woman succeeded in a complaint of racial discrimination after being turned down for a job because her husband was black.

(*d*) It is direct racial discrimination (and also *Victimisation* in most cases) to dismiss an employee because he or she refuses to co-operate in a policy of racial discrimination. There have been several such cases, the most recent being the Court of Appeal decision in *Weathersfield Limited v Sargent* [*1999*] *IRLR 94*.

221 Racial Group

Under *section 3* of the *RRA 1976*, a racial group is a group of persons defined by reference to colour, race, nationality or ethnic or national origins. The Act contains that definition because *Disparate Impact*, for the purpose of the definition of indirect racial discrimination, is established by comparing:

(*a*) the proportion of members of the complainant's racial group who can comply with a particular requirement or condition; and

(*b*) the proportion of persons not of that racial group who can comply with it.

The terms 'racial minorities' and 'ethnic minorities' are commonly used to describe minority racial groups, even where those groups are defined by reference to one of the other factors mentioned above.

222 Racial Harassment

The law relating to both sexual and racial harassment is explained under *Harassment*. The legal principles and most of the case law are common to both kinds of harassment. The European Code of Practice was drawn up specifically in relation to sexual harassment, but most of the guidance is equally applicable to racial harassment.

The most extreme forms of racial harassment involve racial abuse or assaults, but racist jokes and nicknames can also amount to racial harassment. An employee is subjected to a detriment if he is made to hear racist remarks about himself or persons of his race generally which are intrinsically offensive or which he has indicated are unwelcome to him.

Managers and supervisors must be given clear instructions on the need for vigilance to prevent racial harassment, particularly where racial minority workers are employed for the first time or are isolated or unpopular for any reason. Guidance should be given on the signs to look out for and the action to be taken when racial harassment is reported, observed or suspected.

223 Racial Segregation

The definition of *Direct Discrimination* under *section 1* of the *RRA 1976* includes segregation on racial grounds. There is no need for a complainant to prove less favourable treatment. That is deemed to have occurred by reason of the segregation.

224 Reasonable Adjustments

224.1 THE CONCEPT

The *DDA 1995* is distinct from the *SDA 1975* and *RRA 1976* in imposing upon employers a duty to make reasonable adjustments to work arrangements and the working environment so as to avoid discrimination. It is a concept which is fundamental to the scheme of the legislation. If employers were not required to adjust working practices and policies, and to modify physical features of premises where appropriate, disabled people would face serious disadvantages. The reality is that working conditions in many organisations may make it difficult to achieve equal opportunity in practice.

224.2 THE STATUTORY DUTY

Section 6(1) of the *DDA 1995* provides that where any arrangements made by or on behalf of an employer, or any physical feature of premises occupied by the employer, place a disabled person at a substantial disadvantage in comparison with persons who are not disabled, the employer is under a duty to take such steps as it is reasonable, in all the circumstances, for him to take in order to prevent the arrangements or feature having that effect.

224.3 EXAMPLES OF STEPS TO BE TAKEN

Section 6(3) of the *DDA 1995*, sets out examples of steps which an employer may have to take in relation to a disabled person in order to comply with the duty to make adjustments, i.e:

(*a*) making adjustments to premises;

(*b*) allocating some of the disabled person's duties to another person;

(*c*) transferring him to fill an existing vacancy;

(*d*) altering his working hours;

(*e*) assigning him to a different place of work;

(*f*) allowing him to be absent during working hours for rehabilitation, assessment or treatment;

(*g*) giving him, or arranging for him to be given, training;

(*h*) acquiring or modifying equipment;

(*i*) modifying instructions or reference manuals;

(*j*) modifying procedures for testing or assessment;

(*k*) providing a reader or interpreter; and

(*l*) providing supervision.

224.4 ASSESSING REASONABLENESS

Section 6(4) of the *DDA 1995* provides that, in determining whether it is reasonable for an employer to have to take a particular step in order to comply with the duty to make reasonable adjustments, regard should be had in particular to:

(*a*) the extent to which taking the step would prevent the effect in question;

(*b*) the extent to which it is practicable for the employer to take the step;

(*c*) the financial and other costs which would be incurred by the employer in taking the step and the extent to which taking it would disrupt any of his activities;

(*d*) the extent of the employer's financial and other resources; and

(*e*) the availability to the employer of financial or other assistance with respect to taking the step.

224.5 TO WHOM IS THE DUTY OWED?

Section 6(5) of the *DDA 1995* provides that, for the purposes of the duty to make reasonable adjustments 'the disabled person concerned' means:

(*a*) in the case of arrangements for determining to whom employment should be offered, a disabled person who is, or who has notified the employer that he may be, an applicant for that employment;

(*b*) in any other case, a disabled person who is–

  (i) an applicant for the employment concerned;

  (ii) an employee of the employer concerned.

An employer is not subject to a duty to make reasonable adjustments in relation to a disabled person if the employer does not know, and could not reasonably be expected to know:

(*a*) in the case of an applicant, or potential applicant, that the disabled person concerned is, or may be, an applicant for the employment;

(*b*) in any case, that the person has a disability and is likely to be placed at a substantial disadvantage in comparison with persons who are not disabled.

Further, the general principle is that, subject to the provisions of *section 6*, an employer is not required to treat a disabled person more favourably than he treats or would treat others.

224.6 THE EMPLOYER'S KNOWLEDGE

An employer has to decide whether his employment arrangements or premises are causing a disabled job applicant or employee a substantial disadvantage. If the employer is unsure about this, the solution is to ask the disabled person. There will be no duty to make a reasonable adjustment if the employer does not know, or could not reasonably be expected to have known, that the person is disabled. But that raises important issues relating to *Knowledge of Disability*. The case of *Ridout v TC Group [1999] IRLR 628*, is illustrative. A woman applied for a job and stated on her CV that she had 'photosensitive epilepsy controlled by Epilin'. In a confidential medical questionnaire she added that her epilepsy had been diagnosed 20 years ago and that this was controlled by daily medication. The employer did not discuss the interview arrangements with her. The interview room had bright fluorescent lighting without diffusers or baffles. The woman was wearing sunglasses around her neck. When she came into the room, she made comments to the effect that she might be disadvantaged by the lighting. The employers thought that this was an explanation relating to her sunglasses. In the event, she never used the sunglasses and did not tell the employers that she was in any way unwell or felt disadvantaged. A tribunal said that, although the employers knew that she had a disability, whether they had discriminated against her by failing to make a reasonable adjustment in respect of the physical arrangements for the interview centred on what they could reasonably be expected to know about the candidate's requirement for particular lighting arrangements. The EAT concluded that the tribunal had been entitled to find that the employer was not in breach of the duty to make a reasonable adjustment to the physical features of the place where the interview was conducted. The duty is to be construed in the light of *section 6(6)(b)* which provides that: 'nothing in this section imposes any duty on an employer in relation to a disabled person if the employer does not know, and could not reasonably be expected to know . . . that that person has a disability' and is likely to be placed at a substantial disadvantage in comparison with persons who are not disabled. This requires a tribunal to measure the extent of the duty, if any, against the actual or assumed knowledge of the employer both as to the disability and the likelihood of causing the individual substantial disadvantage in comparison with people who are not disabled. Tribunals should be careful not to impose upon disabled people a duty to give a long detailed explanation as to the effects of their disability, merely to cause the employer to make adjustments which he should probably have made in the first place. On the other hand, it is equally undesirable that an employer should be required to ask a number of questions as to whether a person with a disability feels disadvantaged merely to protect himself from liability. On the facts of the case, the applicant had a very rare form of epilepsy and the tribunal was entitled to conclude that no reasonable employer could be expected to know, without being told specifically by the individual, that the arrangements made for the interview might disadvantage her.

The extent of knowledge that it is reasonable for an employer to have will inevitably depend upon the circumstances. For instance, typically, an employer can reasonably be expected to have more knowledge of a long serving employee's long-standing disability than the employer in *Ridout* was expected to have of the unusual disability in that case.

224.7 LIMITS ON THE DUTY

An employer is not required to make an adjustment:

(*a*) if the advantage to the disabled person would be minor and trivial;

(*b*) to make employment more practicable for disabled people generally. The duty is confined to individual disabled people, as and when the circumstances arise;

(*c*) where the employer does not have, and could not reasonably be expected to have, knowledge of the disability; or

(*d*) where, although the employer is aware that the person has a disability, he does not know and could not reasonably be expected to know, that it is likely to cause a substantial disadvantage.

Generally, the duty will not require the employer to:

(*a*) make the best possible adjustment;

(*b*) reallocate crucial job duties; or

(*c*) provide materials that the disabled person could reasonably be expected to have already for his or her personal use.

Failure to comply with a duty to make reasonable adjustment may also be justified in appropriate circumstances, such as:

(*a*) where the employer can show that the failure arose because of reliance upon advice which appeared to be reputable and informed;

(*b*) where the employer made a reasonable effort to inform himself about adjustments which might be appropriate but nevertheless remained unaware of certain other possibilities; or

(*c*) if the employee refuses to co-operate with a proposed adjustment, because he or she prefers an alternative which would cost the employer more.

Kenny v Hampshire Constabulary [*1999*] *IRLR 76*, illustrates the limits on the scope of the duty imposed on employers. An employer offered a job to a man with cerebral palsy who needed assistance in urinating. The employer sought volunteers within the department he was to join, but was unable to find the necessary staff able to help him. The employer considered that it was impracticable, for security reasons, for the disabled person to work at home via a modem link. An application for a support worker was made under the Access to Work Scheme and a meeting was held with a member of PACT, which deals with applications under the Scheme. However, the funding required for outside care support would have exceeded the authority of the local manager and the application was referred to the Scheme's head office. In the absence of a definite immediate response to the application, the employers withdrew the job offer because they had an urgent need to fill the vacancy. A tribunal dismissed a complaint of disability discrimination, finding that the withdrawal of the offer was for a reason relating to the applicant's disability, but that the employers were justified in rejecting possible options for providing him with the necessary personal care. The EAT upheld the tribunal's ruling. An employer's duty under *section 6* is restricted to 'job-related' matters. Not every failure to make an arrangement which deprives an employee of a chance to be employed is unlawful. The definition in *section 6(2)*, which refers to 'any term, condition or arrangements on which employment, promotion, a transfer, training, or any other benefit is offered or afforded', directs employers to make adjustments to the way the job is structured and organised so as to accommodate those who cannot fit into existing arrangements. Employers are not under a statutory duty to provide carers to attend to the employee's personal needs, such as assistance in going to the toilet. A line has to be drawn on the extent of the employer's responsibilities in providing adjustments to accommodate a disabled person. Although an employer is required to consider making physical arrangements for a disabled person to use the toilet and physical adjustments to accommodate the presence of a personal carer, had Parliament intended to impose on employers the duty to cater for an employee's personal needs in the toilet, it would have said so and the Code of Practice would have laid out the criteria to be applied. However, as the tribunal had not fully considered the question of *Justification*, in relation to whether the employers were justified in not waiting for the result of the application for a support worker before withdrawing the job offer, the case was remitted to a different tribunal for consideration of that issue. In other words, even once an employer has concluded that it is not reasonable to make an adjustment, the duty may require the employer to consider whether the adjustment can be made by a third party or with financial assistance from a third party.

224.8 THE APPROACH TRIBUNALS SHOULD TAKE

In *Morse v Wiltshire County Council* [*1999*] *IRLR 352*, the EAT offered guidance as to the steps that an Employment Tribunal must go through in considering a disability discrimination case. First, the tribunal must decide whether the employer is under a duty to make reasonable adjustments in the circumstance of the particular case. If such a duty is imposed, the tribunal must next decide whether the employer has taken such steps as it is reasonable, in all the circumstances, for him to have to take in order to prevent the arrangements or feature having the effect of placing the disabled person concerned at a substantial disadvantage in comparison with person who are not disabled. This, in turn, involves the tribunal inquiring whether the employer could reasonably have taken any of the steps set out in paragraph (a) to (l) of *section 6(3)*. The purpose of this sub-section is to focus the employer's mind on possible steps which it might take in compliance with its duty and to focus the tribunal's mind when considering whether the employer has failed to comply with its obligations. At the same time, the tribunal must take into account the factors set out in *section 6(4)(a)* to *(e)*.

If, but only if, the tribunal (having followed these steps) find that the employer has failed to comply with a duty, in respect of the disabled person, to make a reasonable adjustment, the tribunal finally has to decide whether the employer has shown that its failure to comply with the duty is justified. This means deciding whether it is shown that the reason for the failure to comply is both material to the circumstance of a particular case and substantial. In taking these steps, the tribunal must apply an objective test, asking for instance whether the employer has taken such steps as were reasonable and whether any of the steps in *section 6(3)* were reasonably available in the light of the actual situation so far as the factors in *section 6(4)* were concerned. It must also ask whether the employer's failure to comply with this duty was in fact objectively justified, and whether the reason for failure to comply was in fact material to the circumstance of the particular case and in fact substantial. It is not the case that a tribunal can only consider whether the employer's explanation for its conduct is reasonably capable of being material and substantial. There is nothing in the wording of *section 5* or *section 6* which indicates that the tribunal should not substitute its own judgement for that of the employer. The tribunal must scrutinise the employer's explanation and reach its own decision on what, if any, steps were reasonable and what was objectively justified, and material and substantial.

The EAT confirmed that a duty under *section 6(1)* to make adjustments arises where a disabled person is dismissed, even though that section only applies in the circumstances set out in *section 6(2)*, which makes no express mention of dismissal. Taking a purposive view, the words 'any . . . arrangements on which employment . . . is . . . afforded' in *section 6(2)(b)* are wide enough to cover arrangements in relation to which employment continues or is terminated. The valuable and specific protection which *section 6* offers would be lost to many vulnerable employees at the time of greatest need if it did not apply to dismissal.

225 Reasonably Practicable Steps

A key principle of discrimination law is that employers are liable for the acts and omissions of their employees in the course of their employment. There is an extended definition of *Employment* (and hence of employee).

Course of Employment is also broadly defined – see *Harassment*.

The employer is given a statutory defence, however, if he has taken such steps as were reasonably practicable to prevent the act complained of or acts of that description. The question whether such steps have been taken most commonly arises in the context of *Harassment* and the matter is dealt with under that heading. It should be noted that:

(*a*) an employer cannot establish the defence by showing that there was nothing to be done and therefore he did nothing; and

(*b*) the adoption of comprehensive and well-written policies is only a first step, which should be followed up by other steps, including training.

226 Recommendations

Where an Employment Tribunal finds a complaint under the *SDA 1975*, *RRA 1976* or *DDA 1995* to be well-founded, it has the power to recommend that the respondent should take action appearing to the tribunal to be reasonable, in all the circumstances of the case. The purpose is to obviate or reduce the adverse effect on the complainant of any matter to which the complaint relates. The recommendation should specify the period within which the action is to be taken.

There is no power to compel the respondent to take the recommended action. If, however, the respondent does not comply with a recommendation, the complainant can then bring the matter back before the tribunal. Compensation, or increased compensation, can then be ordered by the tribunal if:

(*a*) the respondent has failed, without reasonable justification, to comply with the recommendation; and

(*b*) the tribunal thinks it just and equitable to order the payment.

In practice, recommendations are most likely to be necessary or desirable where there has been harassment or other discrimination against a person who continues to be employed by the respondent. If a complaint of discrimination in recruitment is upheld, a possible recommendation would be that the complainant should be guaranteed an interview if he or she makes a further application for a particular kind of post, within a specified period.

227 Recruitment

227.1 GENERAL PRINCIPLES

One of the fundamental objectives of the discrimination laws is to promote equality of opportunity in access to employment. It is a great social and economic evil if workers are unfairly denied suitable employment for reasons relating to colour etc, disability or gender or marital status.

The law forbids discrimination both in the arrangements for deciding who should be offered employment and in the actual selection for the post. The arrangements can involve several stages prior to the *Selection* of the successful candidate, including drawing up the job description, advertising the post, shortlisting, first interviews and second interviews.

There must be no discrimination, as defined by the *SDA 1975*, the *RRA 1976* and the *DDA 1995*, at any stage of the recruitment process. An employer's obligation not to discriminate in the arrangements for deciding who should be offered employment covers both the setting up of those arrangements and their implementation. This principle was confirmed by the House of Lords in *Nagarajan v London Regional Transport* [*1999*] *IRLR 572.*

Although most complaints are by unsuccessful job applicants, a person who is actually offered a job can also bring a complaint if there is discrimination in the terms on which employment has been offered.

227.2 TERMS OF THE OFFER

Complaints about the terms on which employment is offered are rare in practice, but can occur. For example:

(*a*) Offers of employment are made both to a female candidate and a male candidate, but the woman is required to serve a longer probationary period.

(*b*) The rate of pay offered to a black candidate is lower than the rate which would have been offered if he had been white.

(*c*) A disabled candidate receives a job offer, but the employer is not prepared to modify the job duties by removing a small and non-essential duty which, because of his disability, would cause the candidate considerable difficulties.

A candidate who wishes to complain under the *SDA 1975* about the rate of pay which has been offered, or any other financial term, can do so only if he or she would, on taking the job, have had a claim under the *EPA 1970*. For example, a woman who wishes to complain that she has been offered lower pay than a man has been offered, will be unable to present a complaint if the previous holder of the post is also a woman and if the employer does not have any male employees employed on *Like Work*, work of *Equal Value* or work which has been given an equivalent rating under a *Job Evaluation Scheme*.

227.3 DIRECT DISCRIMINATION AND VICTIMISATION

Most complaints of direct discrimination or victimisation are presented by complainants who:

(*a*) have enquired about a job, or applied informally, and been rejected at that stage, perhaps even by a receptionist;

(*b*) have been falsely told that a vacancy no longer exists;

(*c*) have applied for a post but not been shortlisted or offered an interview; or

(*d*) have been interviewed but not offered the job.

The question of direct discrimination in all these cases is covered under *Selection*.

227.4 INDIRECT DISCRIMINATION AND REASONABLE ADJUSTMENTS

Employers must consider the risk of indirect discrimination and also the need to make *Reasonable Adjustments* under the *DDA 1995*, in relation to:

(*a*) job advertisements and vacancy notices;

(*b*) job descriptions;

(*c*) person specifications; and

(*d*) application forms.

Employers must also have regard to the same risk and the same need, in relation to the various methods used for whittling down the number of candidates and making an appointment, including:

(*a*) aptitude tests;

(*b*) psychometric testing;

(*c*) IQ tests;

(*d*) other tests and assessments; and

(*e*) shortlisting and selection criteria.

Employers, when drawing up or using any of the above, should:

(*a*) ensure that they are focused on the needs of the job;

(*b*) avoid using language that could be seen as indicating an intention to discriminate, for example in favour of a man or against a disabled candidate;

(*c*) carefully scrutinise any method of assessment, to ensure that it is not 'loaded', for example against members of any particular ethnic group; and

(*d*) be prepared at all times to modify the requirements and conditions of the job, or the method of assessment, to overcome disadvantages faced by a disabled candidate.

The advice regarding shortlisting and selection criteria applies whether the criteria are written or unwritten. In one case a retailer automatically excluded job applicants from a particular district in a city. That district had a high proportion of black workers. There was indirect racial discrimination against candidates from the district, even though the requirement being applied to them was neither written down in any job advertisement nor communicated to them in any other way.

227.5 TRAWLING FOR CANDIDATES

In the majority of complaints about recruitment arrangements, the complainant has applied for the post but been unsuccessful either at the shortlisting stage or when the ultimate selection is made. There can be circumstances, however, in which a complaint is made by a person who never actually applied for the job.

This principle at least, whatever the final outcome of the case, is illustrated by *Coker and Osamor v Lord Chancellor and Lord Chancellor's Department* [*1999*] *IRLR 396*. This was the widely reported tribunal case which related to the arrangements made by the Lord Chancellor for the appointment of a special adviser. The complainants had not been invited to apply for the post. Indeed they were not aware that an appointment was being made. Their contention was that they would have been suitable candidates, and would have had a chance of being appointed, if selection had not been limited to eligible candidates who were known personally to the Lord Chancellor.

The Codes of Practice under both the *SDA 1975* and the *RRA 1976* make it clear that complaints of discrimination can arise where eligible candidates are excluded from consideration without even being aware at the time that a job vacancy exists. For example, it has been known for employers to recruit, particularly for unskilled jobs, by inviting existing employees to put forward their relatives for a vacancy. If these informal methods are used, and the existing workforce is exclusively white, then it is likely that all new employees will also be white. Employment arrangements of this kind involve indirect racial discrimination. Employers who use them could face enforcement action by the CRE (see *Discriminatory Practices*). Furthermore, a complaint could be brought by a black worker who lives in the catchment area for the factory where vacancies are being filled without being advertised.

There would also be the risk of enforcement action or of individual complaints if an employer operated an arrangement under which the head of a local single sex school was asked to send along a few girls for interview whenever a secretarial vacancy arose. Indeed that could be a case of direct rather than indirect sex discrimination, because the employer would be using a gender related requirement (attendance at a school which is exclusively for girls).

The above examples relate to junior posts. At the opposite end of the spectrum candidates for very senior posts are frequently selected informally, or headhunted, without the post being advertised. Great care is needed in such cases to ensure that the recruitment and selection arrangements are not directly or indirectly discriminatory – see *Search and Selection*.

Another major issue is that of restricting posts to internal candidates – particularly at managerial level so that posts are advertised externally only if there is no suitable internal candidate. Such practices could be indirectly discriminatory, where the existing workforce is, for example, predominantly white or contains a large majority of men. Employers may seek to justify such practices on the ground of the need to offer career development to existing employees. The better practice is to advertise posts externally and internally but to guarantee an interview to internal candidates.

Whatever the general practice, the employer must also cater for the following special circumstances:

(*a*) Where a woman returning from maternity leave cannot go back to her old job, because of redundancy, she must be offered a suitable alternative post, if one is vacant and available.

(*b*) Where there is a need to redeploy a worker, because of his or her disability, consideration should be given to offering any suitable alternative post as a *Reasonable Adjustment*.

(*c*) It would normally be justifiable for an employer to suspend any policy of advertising posts externally during any redundancy period, so that priority can be given to finding suitable alternative employment for the employees who are facing redundancy.

It can be a difficult exercise for employers to comply with sometimes conflicting legal obligations in a way which:

(*a*) promotes equal opportunity;

(*b*) gives the employer the widest possible choice;

(*c*) encourages diversity; and

(*d*) motivates existing staff.

227.6 PRACTICAL ADVICE ON RECRUITMENT

Some suggestions have been made in *section 4* above about avoiding indirect or disability discrimination in methods of testing. Further advice is given in relation to *Advertisements*, *Job Interviews* and *Selection*. The following are guidelines on the recruitment process as a whole:

(*a*) The general practice should be to prepare at the outset a job description and also a person specification, listing both the essential and the desirable qualities for the post. It helps to avoid both the fact and the appearance of discrimination at any stage if candidates can be measured against specified criteria.

(*b*) The general practice should be to advertise jobs, always internally and usually externally as well. Simply picking a person out, or using other informal recruitment methods, invites complaints from potential candidates, particularly internal candidates who have been overlooked.

(*c*) Many organisations have a large number of employees who are involved in recruitment in some way and who have the power to reject or eliminate candidates. Sometimes the employee can be quite junior, such as a receptionist or telephonist who deals with enquiries about unskilled jobs which have been advertised. Appropriate guidance and preferably *Training* should be given to all these employees.

(*d*) It is good practice to include a short statement of the equal opportunity policy and the 'disability symbol' in all advertisements and application forms, both to encourage candidates and to help focus the minds of employees involved in selection.

Even where guidance and training have been given, there are some decisions which should always be made at a senior level and based on specialist advice, for example from the HR department. These include decisions relating to:

(*a*) any decision in exceptional circumstances to recruit for a post without advertising that post, even internally;

(*b*) the adoption of requirements or conditions which will exclude candidates who cannot comply with them;

(*c*) the design and content of application forms;

(*d*) adoption of the limited measures of *Positive Discrimination* which the law permits;

(*e*) reliance on the *Genuine Occupational Qualification*; and

(*f*) the use of *Psychometric Testing* or other tests.

228 Redundancy

The question of discrimination in relation to selection for redundancy is considered under *Dismissal*.

Access to voluntary redundancy is potentially a *Benefit*. There must be no sex, racial or disability discrimination when inviting or dealing with applications.

Complaints may also be made about the amount of a redundancy payment, whether the redundancy is voluntary or compulsory and whether the scheme under which the payment is made is statutory, contractual or discretionary. Where the complaint is one of sex discrimination, it should be under both the *SDA 1975* and the *EPA 1970*. A redundancy payment is pay for the purposes of *Article 141*, but the *SDA 1975* may be the appropriate Act if the scheme is discretionary.

The statutory scheme is vulnerable to complaints of indirect sex discrimination, relating to the qualifying period of two years or the upper age limit of 65.

229 References

Great care must be taken by employers in considering applications for references by or in respect of former employees. A refusal to grant a reference, or giving an unfavourable reference, could lead to a complaint of discrimination or victimisation – see *Post-Employment Discrimination*.

230 Relationships At Work

Many people marry or have long-term relationships with people whom they meet at work. But in some employments, it is potentially inappropriate and a breach of trust for certain workers to form relationships with those whom they meet through the job. This includes teachers and their pupils, social workers and their clients, foster parents and their charges, and probation officers and those on probation. The *Sexual Offences (Amendment) Act 2000* outlaws sexual activity between those caring for young people or vulnerable adults and their clients. It also includes volunteers, regardless of whether they are in the public, private or voluntary sectors.

Some employers lay down policies about forming relationships at work. These may set out, for example, what the parties should do in terms of reporting the relationship to management. In some cases, it may be appropriate for the parties to agree to appropriate redeployment, so that they are not working directly together. But it is important that any such provision should not discriminate unlawfully, e.g. between male and female partners, and that there should be a clear objective justification for it.

Employers may have a legitimate concern that if a relationship at work breaks down, then personal animosity may spill over into the workplace. For instance, if one party tries to rekindle the relationship when the other party is unwilling to do so, there may be a risk of *Harassment*. In the United States of America, some businesses have asked employees who form personal relationships to sign legally binding agreements, by which typically they undertake not to sue the company if the relationship breaks down. These 'consensual relationship agreements' are sometimes colloquially referred to as 'love contracts'. They may range from letters countersigned by the employees, indicating that they have entered voluntarily into the relationship (and, therefore, not as a result of improper pressure, perhaps from one partner who occupies a more senior role than the other) to more formal documents setting out explicit examples of appropriate behaviour. The agreement may require the couples to use the organisation's grievance procedure if the relationship breaks down or to agree to use *Alternative Dispute Resolution* in preference to issuing court proceedings to resolve any disputes.

It seems unlikely that such agreements will find widespread favour in the UK. Quite apart from differences in workplace culture, the statutory prohibition on contracting-out of employment protection rights operates as a major constraint on the value of any such agreement. Furthermore, it may be that the *Human Rights Act 1998* will be relevant in some cases, since a public employer's attempt to control personal relationships may fall foul of the right to respect for private life.

231 Religious Discrimination

The *RRA 1976* does not expressly prohibit religious discrimination in relation to employment at an establishment in Great Britain, although the position is different in *Northern Ireland*.

New legislation, or the amendment of the *RRA 1976*, will be necessary in due course, if the proposed new Framework Directive is adopted – see *Directives*.

Many acts of direct or indirect religious discrimination are also, however, acts of indirect racial discrimination – see *Indirect Discrimination*. This is because most of the workers who subscribe to some of the major religions (including Muslim, Hindu, Buddhist and Sikh) are also members of particular racial minorities.

Discrimination against an *Irish* Catholic could also be indirect racial discrimination.

232 Remedies

Remedies for discrimination in the employment field are dealt with in *section 65* of the *SDA 1975*, *section 56* of the *RRA 1976* and *section 8* of the *DDA 1995*.

Under each of these sections, an Employment Tribunal which has found a complaint to be well-founded must then consider which of the following remedies it is just and equitable to grant:

(*a*) a declaration as to the rights of the complainant and the respondent in relation to the matters to which the complaint relates;

(*b*) an order for the respondent to pay *Compensation* to the complainant; or

(*c*) a *Recommendation*.

There is no limit on the amount of compensation which may be awarded under the *SDA 1975*, the *RRA 1976* or the *DDA 1995*, although an award of compensation is not automatic where the complaint is one of *Indirect Discrimination*.

Where a complaint under the *EPA 1970* is upheld, the Employment Tribunal makes an order declaring the rights of the parties. The Employment Tribunal may also award damages or arrears of remuneration. *Section 2(5)* of the *EPA 1970* provides that no payment by way of arrears of remuneration or damages may be awarded in respect of a time earlier than two years before the date of commencement of the proceedings. That limitation has now been disapplied because it was inconsistent with *Article 141* – see *Back Pay*.

233 Requirements and Conditions

Requirements and conditions form part of the definition of *Indirect Discrimination* contained in *section 1(1)(b)* of the *SDA 1975* and *section 1(1)(b)* of the *RRA 1976*. In each case, there is indirect discrimination if:

(*a*) the requirement or condition is to the complainant's detriment because he or she cannot comply with it;

(*b*) the requirement or condition has a *Disparate Impact* (not the expression used in the legislation) on a relevant group defined by reference to gender or race; and

(*c*) it cannot be shown to be justifiable irrespective of the sex (or race etc) of the person to whom it is applied.

In certain respects, the expression 'requirement or condition' is a flexible one. It can include rules, policies and practices. A requirement or condition need not be written down or even articulated.

An important limitation, however, is that a requirement or condition must operate as an absolute bar, not merely a factor which has an adverse impact – see *Indirect Discrimination*. This limitation could be challenged, in a case where the employer is an emanation of the State (see *Public Sector*), as being inconsistent with the *Equal Treatment Directive*.

234 Residential Requirements

The issue of residential requirements is more likely to arise outside the employment field, but *Indirect Discrimination* in employment can occur where there are requirements or conditions relating to the place of residence or length of residence in a particular area.

An obvious example is a requirement or condition relating to length of residence in the UK.

A policy of not employing workers from a particular district could also be indirect racial discrimination, if that district contains a high proportion of racial minority workers. *Hussein v Saints Complete House Furnisher* [*1979*] *IRLR 337* is an example of such a case. The owner of the business had found in the past that, when he recruited staff from the central districts of Liverpool, their unemployed friends tended to loiter outside the shop and discourage customers. Accordingly he stipulated that he would not consider job applicants from those districts. Approximately half of the population of the districts in question were black. The Employment Tribunal decided that the requirement was not justifiable. Accordingly a complaint of indirect racial discrimination was upheld.

235 Respondent

The respondent to a tribunal case is the party against whom the case is brought.

Most complaints about discrimination in employment are by job applicants or employees against employers and most of the examples given in this book relate to such cases.

Where the alleged act of discrimination is by an agent or by a manager or other employee acting in the course of his employment, that agent or manager or other employee can also be made a respondent to the complaint – see *Joint Respondents*.

Respondents can also include:

(*a*) *Qualifying Bodies*;

(*b*) *Employers', Trade and Professional Associations*;

(*c*) *Trade Unions*;

(*d*) *Training Bodies*; and

(*e*) *Employment Agencies*.

Partnerships, like any other employer, can be respondents to complaints by job applicants and employees. In addition, under the *SDA 1975* and the *RRA 1976*, they can be respondents to complaints by partners in the firm or by a person who wishes to become a partner. Under the *RRA 1976*, however, the firm must have six or more partners for a complaint to be brought against it by a partner or would-be partner.

236 Restricted Reporting Orders

Under rule 14 of the Tribunal Rules, an Employment Tribunal may make a restricted reporting order in two circumstances:

(*a*) if the case involves allegations of sexual misconduct; or

(*b*) if the complaint is under the *DDA 1995* and evidence of a personal nature is likely to be heard by the tribunal.

Either party may apply for a restricted reporting order. Alternatively the tribunal may make an order of its own motion. An order may not be made until each party has been given the opportunity to oppose the making of the order at a hearing.

Where a restricted reporting order is made, it specifies the persons who may not be identified in any report of the proceedings. The order is, however, of limited value to any party or witness who is protected by it, because it remains in force only until the promulgation of the decision (or earlier if revoked by the tribunal).

In *Chief Constable of the West Yorkshire Police v A* [*2000*] *IRLR 465*, an Employment Tribunal made a restricted reporting order to protect the identity of a transsexual complainant, having heard unchallenged evidence of the abuse which she was likely to suffer if her identity were to be revealed. The tribunal purported to make the order under rule 13 and also under an inherent jurisdiction deriving from the *Equal Treatment Directive*, the respondent in the case, the *Police*, being an emanation of the State (see *Public Sector*). The EAT held that the case was not covered by rule 13, but there was no appeal against the making of the order under the Directive and the President of the EAT said that he was not in a position to rule the tribunal to have been wrong in law. Furthermore, the EAT exercised its own jurisdiction under the Directive to grant a restricted reporting order in perpetual terms.

237 Review

As with other tribunal cases, an unsuccessful party can apply under rule 11 for the tribunal to review its decision, for example because new evidence has become available or because the interests of justice require a review.

An application for a review must be made at the hearing or in writing, supported by full grounds, not later than 14 days after the date on which the decision is sent to the parties. Although a chairman may extend the time under the general power contained in rule 15(1), extensions are not lightly granted.

Where review hearings are granted, they do not always take place within 42 days after the date on which the decision is sent to the parties. In such circumstances any appeal should be lodged within the 42 day period (and withdrawn if the review is successful and there is no longer any need for the appeal).

238 Same Employment

The *EPA1970* requires that any comparator must be in the same employment as the complainant. There are two ingredients of 'same employment', as follows:

(*a*) the complainant and the comparator must be employed by the same employer or by *Associated Employers*;

(*b*) they must also be employed at the same establishment or at two establishments, at which *Common Terms and Conditions* are observed.

It was, however, held by the EAT in *Scullard v (1) Knowles and (2) Southern Regional Council for Education and Training* [*1996*] *IRLR 344* that *Article 141*, which has 'paramount force', permits a wider class of comparators. Under the wider test, a complainant may name a comparator carrying out work 'in the same establishment or service'. The EAT remitted the case to a different Employment Tribunal to consider whether unit managers employed by two different regional advisory councils were part of the same service for the purpose of *Article 141*.

In *Lawrence and Others v Regent Office Care and Others* [*2000*] *IRLR 608*, the Court of Appeal has referred to the ECJ the question whether catering assistants and school cleaners, all now employed by private contractors but some being former employees of North Yorkshire County Council, are entitled to bring an equal pay claim naming as comparators current employees of the county council whose work had been rated as of equal value to their own work.

239 Scotland

The *EPA 1970*, *SDA 1975*, *RRA 1976* and *DDA 1995* all apply to Scotland as well as to England and Wales. There are some differences in terminology and in references to other legislation, but in substance the same discrimination laws apply in each part of Great Britain.

Employment Tribunals sit in Scotland as well as in England and Wales, but with their separate (albeit similar) rules of procedure – see *Tribunal Procedure*.

In England and Wales, the EOC, CRE or DRC can apply to the county court for an injunction to prevent *Persistent Discrimination*. In Scotland, the application is made to the sheriff court for an interdict.

240 Scots, as racial group

Direct or indirect racial discrimination against Scots job applicants or employees will be covered by the *RRA 1976* – see *Racial Grounds* and *Racial Group*.

241 Search and Selection

Not all posts filled with the assistance of recruitment consultants are advertised. In some cases, particularly where the post is a senior one, potentially suitable candidates are approached and invited to apply, or even 'head-hunted' and offered the post without having to compete for it.

There is a danger that any such process, if it tends to exclude, for example, women or racial minorities, may be vulnerable to an individual complaint of *Indirect Discrimination* or to a complaint by the relevant Commission that a *Discriminatory Practice* is being operated. Such methods of recruitment may be justifiable, however, particularly in circumstances where suitable candidates who already occupy senior positions in other organisations would not be likely to answer an advertisement and would respond only to a direct approach.

242 Secondment

Consideration has already been given to the status of *Agency Workers* and *Contract Workers*, with particular reference to the case where there is a commercial relationship between the agency which supplies the workers and the organisation which needs to have the work carried out.

Arrangements for employees to do work for other organisations also commonly take the form of secondments, for example by one group company to another. In any such case, it is necessary to look closely at the circumstances in order to ascertain what obligations either or both of the organisations have under the discrimination laws. Where one group company seconds or assigns a worker to another group company, the most likely consequences are:

(*a*) the second company becomes the employer for the duration of the secondment; or

(*b*) the first company continues to be the employer, and has obligations in that capacity, but the worker also, as a contract worker, has rights against the second company.

The case of *Chief Constable of the Lincolnshire Police v Stubbs [1999] IRLR 81* has already been referred to under *Harassment*. In that case, both the complainant and the harasser were seconded by their own force to the Regional Crime Squad. It was held that the Chief Constable of their own force continued to be the employer and was therefore liable for the acts of harassment complained of.

243 Segregation

It is only the *RRA 1976* which expressly includes segregation (on racial grounds) within the definition of direct discrimination.

Even though segregation is not expressly referred to in the *SDA 1975* or the *DDA 1995*, however, there are circumstances in which segregation by reference to gender or disability could be unlawful – see *Detriment*.

244 Selection

Under *section 6* of the *SDA 1975*, *section 4* of the *RRA 1976* and *section 4* of the *DDA 1995*, it is unlawful for an employer to discriminate:

(*a*) against a job applicant by refusing or deliberately omitting to offer employment; and

(*b*) against an employee, by refusing or deliberately omitting to afford the employee access to opportunities for promotion.

The issue in many discrimination cases, whether brought by a job applicant or by an employee, is whether there has been discrimination or victimisation against the complainant because he or she has not been:

(*a*) shortlisted and offered an interview;

(*b*) offered a second interview; or

(*c*) offered the job applied for.

There are a handful of jobs covered by *Genuine Occupational Qualification*, but apart from those exceptional cases there are no circumstances in which the law permits sex, racial or disability discrimination or victimisation at the point of selection.

Guidance is given elsewhere in this book on avoiding discrimination in *Recruitment*, *Shortlisting* or *Job Interviews*. The following general guidance applies at all stages, from shortlisting to the selection of the candidate to be appointed:

(*a*) An objective, structured and consistent approach will help to ensure that selection decisions are demonstrably free from the taint of discrimination or victimisation. Accordingly, job descriptions, a person specification and a scoring system should be used.

(*b*) Great care should be taken in the preparation of these documents. Essential requirements should be specified, so as to eliminate unqualified candidates at an early stage. At the same time, standards must not be set too high and unnecessary requirements must be avoided. Otherwise there is a risk of both indirect discrimination and disability discrimination.

(*c*) Training should be given to all interviewers and other persons involved in the selection process. Unlawful discrimination will not necessarily be avoided by individuals who rely only on untutored good intentions.

(*d*) The reasons for all decisions, whether in shortlisting or at later stages, should be recorded. A person who has made a decision to reject a particular candidate could have great difficulty in explaining the decision to a tribunal many months later if the reasons were not written down at the time.

(*e*) The Code of Practice under the *RRA 1976* recommends that, wherever possible, shortlisting and interviewing should not be done by one person alone but should at least be checked at a more senior level. That is good advice. Decisions are more likely to be made objectively and consistently (albeit more slowly) if they are discussed by two or more decision-makers acting together rather than being made by one person acting alone. It is also good practice for a member of the personnel department to be a party to all decisions and to be present at all interviews.

(*f*) Candidates should at all times be treated with courtesy and consideration, whether at interviews or in correspondence or on the telephone. If the treatment which they receive is off-hand, inconsiderate or rude, they are more likely to suspect discrimination even when none has occurred.

(*g*) All documents, including the notes made by those involved in shortlisting and selection and interview notes, should be preserved for at least six months, and longer if possible, in case any aspect of the selection process leads to a tribunal complaint. Indeed it may be necessary to keep statistical information, and summary reasons for decisions, indefinitely, as part of the *Monitoring* of the equal opportunity policy.

The training given to interviewers and others involved in the selection process should cover:

(*a*) relevant provisions of the discrimination legislation and the codes of practice;

(*b*) recognition and avoidance of the common prejudices and assumptions which can lead to direct discrimination;

(*c*) the preparation and use of job descriptions, person specifications and scoring systems;

(*d*) the importance of not adopting new requirements and conditions, particularly at the shortlisting stage (with a consequent risk of indirect discrimination), in order to reduce the number of candidates;

(*e*) the preparation and conduct of interviews;

(*f*) information about the disabilities which are most likely to be encountered and the positive steps which should be taken; and

(*g*) handling applications from candidates who have previously complained of discrimination and the ways in which such candidates should be reassured that there will be no victimisation against them.

245 Self-Employed Workers

The *EPA 1970, SDA 1975, RRA 1976*, and *DDA 1995* all give rights to workers who are not conventional employees and who may be self-employed for the purposes of tax, national insurance and/or unfair dismissal – see *Employment*.

246 Seniority

It is suggested in the Code of Practice under the *SDA 1975* (paragraph 25(c)) that in some circumstances promotion on the basis of length of service could amount to unlawful indirect discrimination, as it may unjustifiably affect more women than men. The above guidance is given in the context of a recommendation that promotion and career development patterns should be reviewed to ensure that the traditional qualifications are justifiable requirements for the job to be done.

The Code of Practice does not give examples. It is unlikely that Employment Tribunals would expect employers to place no weight at all on seniority when considering promotion decisions. So far as redundancy is concerned, while many employers have moved away from LIFO (last in first out) as the sole criterion for redundancy selection in recent years, some weight is usually given to the length of service. Indeed, failure to give it any weight may in some cases be unfair.

On the other hand, in any organisation where proportions of women, racial minority and disabled employees have increased, as a result of effective equal opportunity policies, basing promotion and redundancy decisions exclusively on length of service would be a move in the opposite direction and could, as the Code of Practice suggests, be unlawful unless justifiable in the particular circumstances. Furthermore, promotion on merit rather than seniority is more likely to serve the needs of the organisation.

247 Sex Discrimination

Whenever the terms 'discriminate' and 'discrimination' are used in the *SDA 1975*, they are so used in the sense defined in *sections 1*, *2*, *2A*, *3* and *4* of the Act.

Section 1 contains the definitions of direct and indirect sex discrimination against women. *Section 2* then provides that *section 1*, and later provisions of the Act, are to be read as applying equally to the treatment of men (but with no account to be taken of special treatment afforded to women in connection with pregnancy or childbirth).

The further definitions are contained in:

(*a*) *Section 2A – Gender Reassignment*;

(*b*) *Section 3 – Marriage Discrimination*;

(*c*) *Section 4 – Victimisation.*

Part II of the *SDA 1975* then deals with discrimination in the employment field. It is *section 6* which makes it unlawful for employers to discriminate in various respects against job applicants or employees in relation to employment at an establishment in Great Britain.

248 Sexual Harassment

The law relating to sexual harassment is considered in some detail under *Harassment*.

There are superficial differences between, on the one hand, some of the forms which sexual harassment can take and, on the other hand, the most common examples of racial harassment and harassment of disabled workers. In the latter cases, harassment usually takes the form of openly offensive or insulting language or even violence or threats of violence. Sexual harassment, however, frequently takes the form of words or actions which are intended, or apparently intended, to be friendly – indeed too friendly.

The differences are, however, only superficial. The essential characteristic of any harassment, whether sexual, racial or otherwise, is that it is conduct which is unwelcome to the recipient. The Code of Practice issued with the European Commission's Recommendation on the protection of the dignity of women and men at work contains the following passage:

> 'The essential characteristic of sexual harassment is that it is unwanted by the recipient, that it is for each individual to determine what behaviour is acceptable to them and what they regard as offensive. Sexual attention becomes sexual harassment if it is persisted in once it has been made clear that it is regarded by the recipient as offensive, although one incident of harassment may constitute sexual harassment if sufficiently serious. It is the unwanted nature of the conduct which distinguishes sexual harassment from friendly behaviour, which is welcome and mutual.'

The Code of Practice points out that sexual harassment covers a range of behaviour, including both words and actions and including:

(*a*) conduct which is unwanted, unreasonable and offensive to the recipient;

(*b*) the use of a person's rejection of or submission to such conduct as a basis for a decision affecting that person's access to vocational training or to employment, continued employment, promotion, salary or any other employment decisions;

(*c*) conduct which creates an intimidating, hostile or humiliating working environment for the recipient.

The Code of Practice also refers to research in Member States which suggests that some specific groups are particularly vulnerable to sexual harassment, including:

(*a*) divorced and separated women;

(*b*) young women and young men;

(*c*) new entrants to the labour market;

(*d*) those with irregular or precarious employment contracts;

(*e*) women in non-traditional jobs;

(*f*) women with disabilities;

(*g*) lesbians and gay men; and

(*h*) women from racial minorities.

249 Sexual Orientation

249.1 UNFAIR DISMISSAL

The leading case on the fairness of an employee's dismissal on the ground of sexual orientation dates back a generation: *Saunders v Scottish National Camps Association Ltd [1980] IRLR 174*. A maintenance handyman was employed to work at a children's camp. His job did not require him to be in contact with the children. However, the camp manager received complaints that the employee had been found at night in the company of boy residents, although the explanations which the employee gave were accepted. A senior manager was told that the employee was homosexual and that he 'had recently been involved in a homosexual incident'. The matter was investigated and the employee did not deny that he was homosexual. He was dismissed and given a letter stating: 'The reason is that information was received that you indulge in homosexuality. At a camp accommodating large numbers of school children and teenagers, it is totally unsuitable to employ any person with such tendencies'. The employee claimed that his dismissal was unfair. He contended that he was able to keep his private life separate from his work, and was not, in any event, interested in young persons. A psychiatrist who gave evidence on his behalf expressed the view that the employee's sexual orientation did not create a danger to young people. However, a tribunal found that the dismissal was for a 'substantial reason' and that it was fair. The EAT sitting in Glasgow upheld that ruling. The employer had shown that the reason for dismissal was considered to be substantial and of a kind such as to justify dismissal. Moreover, the employers had acted reasonably. The employee argued that the tribunal's decision was contrary to the evidence, but the EAT said that did 'less than justice to their finding, which is that a considerable portion of employers would take the view that the employment of a homosexual should be restricted, particularly when required to work in proximity and contact with children. Whether that view is scientifically sound may be open to question, but there was clear evidence from the psychiatrist that it exists as a fact'. Whether, in the light of changing attitudes and experience, a tribunal nowadays would be so ready to dismiss a psychiatrist's opinion that 'heterosexuals were as likely to interfere with children as homosexuals' is surely open to question.

To bully someone on the ground of their sexual orientation may found a claim of constructive unfair dismissal; see *Harassment*.

249.2 SEXUAL ORIENTATION AND HARASSMENT

Where, for example, a male employee has been harassed and has suffered less favourable treatment by reason of his homosexual orientation, in order to compare like with like in deciding whether the harassment constitutes discrimination on the ground of sex, the treatment of him must be compared with the treatment of a female homosexual: *Smith v Gardner Merchant Ltd [1998] IRLR 520*. This is so notwithstanding the European Court's decision in *Grant v South-West Trains Ltd* (see below). A tribunal's task is to ascertain:

(*a*) what, as a matter of fact, was the treatment received by the employee;

(*b*) was he treated less favourably than the one with whom he fell to be compared; and

(*c*) would he have been so treated but for his sex?

It is not enough for an applicant to show that, by reason of sexual harassment, he or she has been subjected to a 'detriment' within the meaning of *section 6(2)(b)* of the *SDA*

1975. It must also be shown that this constituted discrimination within the meaning of *section 1(1)(a)*. If the applicant was subjected to sexual harassment, for instance, in the form of homophobic abuse by his colleague, it is for the tribunal to determine whether the treatment was less favourable than would have been meted out to a homosexual woman in a similar position to him. If a female homosexual would have been subjected to similar harassment, no discrimination under *section 1(1)(a)* would have been established. The applicant would also have to establish that it was the fact of his being male that caused his colleague to treat him in a way which was less favourable than the way the colleague would have treated a female with the same personal characteristic of homosexual preference. Where the applicant had been dismissed, the tribunal would also have to find whether the employer treated the applicant less favourably than his female colleague in dismissing him and not her, and, if so, whether they effectively decided against him because he was a man whereas she was a woman.

Pearce v Governing Body of Mayfield School [*2000*] *IRLR 548* concerned a lesbian teacher who suffered from regular homophobic taunts by pupils at her school. Following *Smith*, the EAT confirmed that the use of gender-specific words such as 'lesbian' or 'dyke' was not sufficient to constitute automatically unlawful discrimination. If to call someone a lesbian was automatically discriminatory, that elevated lesbianism into a unique feminine condition, like pregnancy, not available to a man. But such an argument had been expressly rejected in *Smith*.

249.3 SEXUAL ORIENTATION AND SEX DISCRIMINATION

Discrimination based on sexual orientation is not sex discrimination prohibited by European Community law. This was the unequivocal ruling of the European Court in *Grant v South West Trains Ltd* [*1998*] *IRLR 206*. An employee was refused a travel pass for her female partner. She claimed that this was discrimination, since the pass would have been provided if her partner had been male. However, the condition that no concession was to be offered to a same-sex partner applied equally to male and female employees and that did not constitute discrimination based on sex.

The contrary view is that a different analysis of the meaning of 'sex' is appropriate. It is possible to argue that sex is not merely a matter of anatomical qualities that determine whether one is male or female. Sex discrimination is normally based on gender characteristics and the stereotypes which flow from them. If a purposive and liberal approach to the concept of equal treatment is adopted, discrimination based on stereotyping may give rise to sex discrimination without the need for considering the actual (or hypothetical) treatment of someone of the opposite sex. Stereotyping of this kind typically takes the form of prejudice connected with characteristics associated with sex (as in the case of pregnancy-related discrimination). An approach along these lines may be discerned in the law on *Transsexuals*. But the European Court was not prepared to adopt such reasoning. The focus of gay rights campaigners therefore shifted to the law on *Human Rights*.

249.4 SEXUAL ORIENTATION AND HUMAN RIGHTS

Smith & Grady v United Kingdom [*1999*] *IRLR 734*, concerned claims brought by men and women discharged from the UK armed forces by reason of their homosexual orientation. Under domestic law, their claims failed. They lodged complaints with the European Commission on Human Rights, which were successful. It was held that the employees' right to respect for their private lives under *Article 8* of the *European Convention on Human Rights* was violated by the investigations conducted into their homosexuality and by their discharge from the armed forces pursuant to the policy of the Ministry of Defence. The investigations and the employees' discharge on the sole ground of their sexual orientation constituted a direct interference with their right to respect for their private lives. Although the interferences were in pursuant of legitimate aims within the meaning of *Article 8(2)*, the interests of national security and the prevention of disorder, it had not been shown that the interferences were 'necessary in a democratic society' to attain those aims. When the relevant restrictions concern a most intimate aspect of an individual's private life, particularly serious reasons by way of justification are required to satisfy *Article 8(2)*. In the present case, convincing and weighty reasons were not offered by the UK Government to justify the policy against homosexuals in the armed forces. The core argument in support of the policy was that the presence of homosexuals in the armed forces would have a substantial negative effect on morale and, consequently, on the fighting power and operational effectiveness of the armed forces. These perceived problems were founded solely upon the negative attitudes of heterosexual personnel to those of homosexual orientation. To the extent that they represented a predisposed bias on the part of the heterosexual majority against a homosexual minority, these negative attitudes could not, of themselves, be considered by the Court to amount to sufficient justification for the interferences with the applicant's rights, any more than could similar negative attitudes towards those of a different race, origin or colour. Furthermore, there had been a violation of *Article 13* of the Convention in that the employees had no effective remedy before a national authority in relation to the violation of their right to respect for their private lives. The employees had not, however, established a violation of their rights under *Article 3* of the Convention not to be subjected to 'degrading treatment or punishment' and it was unnecessary to examine their complaints under *Article 10* of the Convention that their right to freedom of expression had been infringed. The freedom of expression element of the case was subsidiary to the employee's right to respect for their private lives.

As a result of this ruling and the need to comply with it, policy in the UK in relation to 'gays in the military' has been relaxed significantly. *The Armed Forces Code of Social Conduct: Policy Statement* explains the new approach. Sexual orientation is acknowledged to be 'essentially a private matter for the individual'.

The coming into force of the *Human Rights Act 1998* extends protection against dismissal or detriment on the ground of sexual orientation to all individuals employed by 'public authorities'. This means that public sector employees enjoy greater protection than those who work in the private sector.

249.5 THE FUTURE

At present those in same sex relationships enjoy no general right, under either domestic or European law, to equal treatment in law. Case law development corresponding to that in relation to *Transsexuals* may occur. The Treaty of Amsterdam, which came into force on 1 May 1999, contains provisions to enable European legislation to cover discrimination based on sexual orientation and the proposed new *Framework Directive* (see *Age Discrimination*) encompasses discrimination on the ground of sexual orientation. In the meantime, the Code of Conduct on sexual equality produced by the Government and the EOC may influence employers to adopt a culture that treats homosexual employees in the same way as heterosexual employees.

250 Shift Work

The fact that two jobs are done at different times, one during the day and the other at night, does not prevent them from being *Like Work*. It does not, however, infringe the principle of *Equal Pay* for the employer to pay a shift premium of a reasonable amount for night shifts and weekend shifts.

There must be no direct or indirect discrimination or disability discrimination in allocating employees to different shifts, whether dealing with a request to transfer to a popular shift or in transferring an employee against his wishes.

A requirement for a woman with childcare commitments to work unsocial hours or on a rotating shift pattern could be an act of indirect sex discrimination; on the other hand, one would expect a tribunal to find such a requirement to be justifiable where there is a business need for a rotating shift pattern and there is no other suitable work available for the employee.

Consideration must be given to transferring a disabled employee away from shift work, as a *Reasonable Adjustment*, if having to work at night or on an irregular pattern places the disabled employee at a substantial disadvantage (for example because of the effect on the diet which must be followed).

251 Ships

251.1 **THE SDA 1975**

Although generally the *SDA 1975* and the *EPA 1970* apply only to employment at an establishment in Great Britain, both Acts also cover employment on a ship (the ship being treated as the establishment) subject to the following conditions:

(*a*) the ship must be registered at a port of registry in Great Britain; and

(*b*) the employee must not work wholly outside Great Britain (and outside British territorial waters).

251.2 **THE RRA 1976**

Where the employee works on a ship which is registered at a port of registry in Great Britain, the position is exactly the same as under the *SDA 1975*.

The *RRA 1976* can also, however, cover cases where the ship is not so registered, provided that the following conditions are satisfied:

(*a*) the employee does not work wholly outside Great Britain (and British territorial waters);

(*b*) there is an establishment in Great Britain (such as the office where the employee was recruited or to which he reports after each voyage) which can properly be regarded as the establishment from which his work is done or the establishment with which his work has the closest connection.

The employment provisions of the *RRA 1976* do not apply where an employee or contract worker has applied or been engaged outside Great Britain for the employment. This exception itself does not apply, however, where the employment is for exploration or exploitation of the continental shelf for oil or gas.

251.3 **THE DDA 1995**

Employment on board a ship is expressly excluded.

252 Shortlisting

Where discrimination in not shortlisting a complainant is proved, compensation can be awarded for injury to feelings and loss of opportunity, even if the evidence shows that candidates who *were* shortlisted were better qualified than the complainant.

All the documents on the basis of which shortlisting takes place, such as application forms and CVs, must be disclosed to the tribunal hearing the complaint. Where the complainant is on paper better qualified than shortlisted candidates of a different race or gender (or non-disabled candidates in a case under the *DDA 1995*) tribunals will look closely at the credibility of any explanation which is given for this difference in treatment.

For general advice on avoiding discrimination when filling vacancies see *Recruitment* and *Selection*. In addition:

(*a*) the Code of Practice under the *SDA 1975* recommends (in paragraph 23(b)) that applications from men and women should be processed in exactly the same way and that there should not be separate lists of male and female or married and single candidates;

(*b*) a candidate should never be excluded from the shortlist by reason of a disability, unless it is clear beyond all possible doubt that the disability disqualifies the candidate, no matter what *Reasonable Adjustments* may be made – where a disability is not an obvious disqualification, its relevance or otherwise and possible adjustments should be discussed positively at the interview; and

(*c*) reasons for shortlisting or not shortlisting candidates should be recorded, if necessary simply by noting them on the application forms or CVs.

253 Sikhs

Sikhs have been held to be a *Racial Group*, defined by reference to *Ethnic Origin* – see *Indirect Discrimination*.

Sikhs are the one racial group to be specifically referred to in the *RRA 1976* – see *Turbans*.

254 Single Sex Establishments

Being a man (or being a woman) can be a *Genuine Occupational Qualification* for certain jobs in hospitals, prisons or other establishments which are for persons who are all (or nearly all) of the same sex (see G*enuine Occupational Qualifications*).

255 Small Businesses

The general principle is that small businesses have the same obligations under the discrimination laws (and are equally subject to the *EPA 1970*) as Government departments, local authorities and major companies. There is only one exception. An employer who has fewer than 15 employees is not subject to the employment provisions of the *DDA 1995*. The original figure was 20; it could well be further reduced.

Under the *RRA 1976* (but not now the *SDA 1975*), the duties which partnerships owe to partners and would-be partners apply only if the partnership has six or more partners.

256 Special Needs

Under *section 35* of the *RRA 1976*, it is lawful to provide facilities or services to meet the special needs of persons of a particular racial group in regard to their education, training or welfare, or any ancillary benefits.

An obvious example is language training for racial minority employees who, because they were born overseas or because their education has been disrupted, are unable to communicate effectively.

257 Sport

257.1 THE SDA 1975

Section 44 of the *SDA 1975* authorises sex discrimination in relation to any sport, game or other activity of a competitive nature where:

(*a*) the discrimination is in relation to the participation of a person as a competitor in events which are confined to competitors of one sex; and

(*b*) the activity is one where the physical strength, stamina or physique of the average woman puts her at a disadvantage to the average man.

Accordingly, where, for example, there is a football league in which all the teams are exclusively male, a football club playing in that league is permitted to discriminate against women in the recruitment of playing staff and the governing body of the sport is permitted to discriminate in refusing to permit women to play in the league.

The exception applies only to competitors, however, and not for example to administrators, referees or other officials – *British Judo Association v Petty [1981] IRLR 484.*

257.2 THE RRA 1976

Section 39 of the *RRA 1976* permits direct discrimination on the ground of nationality and indirect discrimination on the basis of residential requirements in:

(*a*) selection to represent a country, place or area, or any related association, in any sport or game; or

(*b*) in pursuance of the rules of any competition so far as they relate to eligibility to compete in any sport or game.

257.3 THE DDA 1995

There are no provisions in the *DDA 1995* expressly relating to sport, but clearly physical (and sometimes mental) fitness is a justifiable requirement for most sports professionals.

258 Statistics

Statistics are commonly produced to Employment Tribunals (and in some cases are essential) to show whether there has been *Disparate Impact* in a case of *Indirect Discrimination*. There are, however, some cases where a tribunal may be prepared to make a finding without statistical evidence. For example a tribunal could take the view that it is a matter of common knowledge that because of childcare commitments a considerably smaller percentage of women than of men are able to comply with a requirement of full-time working.

In any case of *Indirect Discrimination* where relevant statistics are unavailable, or available only with considerable difficulty or at great expense, it may be appropriate for one or both of the parties to ask the tribunal for a *Pre-hearing Discussion*, so that appropriate directions can be considered.

Complainants also commonly ask for relevant statistics when submitting a *Questionnaire* (for example the numbers of men and the numbers of women at each grade in the respondent organisation). Statistics may indicate a pattern of discrimination – see *Evidence of Discrimination*.

259 Statutory Authority

259.1 THE RRA 1976 AND THE DDA 1995

Section 41 of the *RRA 1976* and *section 59* of the *DDA 1995* both authorise, in similar terms, any act done:

(*a*) in pursuance of a statute or statutory instrument; or

(*b*) to comply with any condition or requirement imposed by a Minister of the Crown by virtue of any statute.

It was held by the House of Lords in *Hampson v Department of Education and Science* [*1990*] *IRLR 302* that these provisions must be narrowly construed; the exception will apply only where an act of discrimination is *required* by the terms of the relevant statute etc, not where a discretion is given. There is also a more specific provision in *section 41* of the *RRA 1976* under which a Minister of the Crown may make or approve arrangements or impose conditions requiring discrimination on the basis of:

(*a*) nationality;

(*b*) place of ordinary residence; and

(*c*) duration of presence or residence in or outside the UK or an area within the UK.

These provisions are particularly relevant to *Immigration Control.*

259.2 THE SDA 1970

The corresponding exception in *section 51* of the *SDA 1975* is in much narrower terms. At the time when the *SDA 1975* became law, there were statutory provisions for the protection of women against risks specifically affecting either women in general or women who are pregnant or have recently given birth. Some of those provisions have been re-enacted since the *SDA 1975* became law. There are also provisions contained in Regulations made after 12 November 1975 under either pre-existing or re-enacted legislation.

Section 51 of the *SDA 1975* authorises any discrimination which is *necessary* to comply with any such provisions, whether contained in the original legislation, the re-enacted legislation or the regulations. Relevant enactments and statutory instruments (relating, for example, to the manufacture of red or orange lead and merchant shipping) are listed in Schedule 1 to the *Employment Act 1989.*

The defence of *necessity* is also available where an employer or other person discriminates:

(*a*) in order to comply with a requirement of a relevant statutory provision (within the meaning of *Part I* of the *Health and Safety at Work etc Act 1974)*; and

(*b*) for the purpose of the protection of the woman in question (or that woman and other women).

Until 16 January 1990 (the date from which it was amended by the *Employment Act 1989*) the exception under *section 51* of the *SDA 1975* was in much wider terms, similar to those contained in the *RRA 1976* and the *DDA 1995*. The case of *Page v Freight Hire (Tank Haulage) Limited* [*1981*] *IRLR 13* was a case under *section 51* before it was amended, but the outcome would probably be the same under the current provisions. In that case, the complainant was refused permission to drive a tanker carrying a particular chemical which was known to be dangerous to women of childbearing age. The complainant said that she knew the risks and did not want any children, but her employers still refused. It was held by the EAT that the employers had a good defence because of their duties under health and safety legislation.

260 Statutory Bodies

It is expressly provided in the *EPA 1970*, the *SDA 1975*, the *RRA 1976* and the *DDA 1995* that service on behalf of the Crown for the purposes of a statutory body is treated in the same way as ordinary employment. Complaints may be presented to an Employment Tribunal both by persons working for statutory bodies and by persons who have applied to work for a statutory body.

A statutory body is defined in each Act as a body set up by or in pursuance of an enactment. The EOC, CRE and DRC are all examples of statutory bodies.

261 Statutory Officers

The *EPA 1970*, the *SDA 1975*, the *RRA 1976* and the *DDA 1995* each contain exceptions relating to service in a statutory office, which is defined as an office set up by or in pursuance of an enactment.

It was held in *Knight v Attorney-General* [*1979*] *ICR 194* that this exception prevented a woman from complaining under the *SDA 1975* about a failure to appoint her to the position of justice of the peace.

It has, however, been held by the Northern Ireland Court of Appeal, in the case of *Perceval-Price and Others v Department of Economic Development and Others* [*2000*] *IRLR 380*, that provisions containing a similar exception were incompatible with *Article 141*, the *Equal Treatment Directive* and the *Equal Pay Directive* and must therefore be disapplied. This was a case brought by tribunal chairmen in Northern Ireland concerning the continuing effects of past discrimination in the judicial pension scheme.

Decisions of the Northern Ireland Court of Appeal are not technically binding in cases heard in England, Wales or Scotland but are of strongly persuasive authority. It is possible that Employment Tribunals will entertain equal pay cases brought by the holders of statutory offices and also complaints of sex discrimination in relation to statutory offices (because the *Equal Treatment Directive* has direct effect in the *Public Sector*).

262 Stereotypes

Not all acts of discrimination are committed by employers or others who have gone out of their way to discriminate – see *Unintentional Discrimination*. Many employers, mangers and interviewers have mental pictures of the kind of person they expect to see or are accustomed to see in a particular occupation and reject almost automatically any candidate for *Recruitment* or *Promotion* who does not fit the stereotype. In doing so they are acting unlawfully if gender, race or disability (or absence of disability) is one of the factors contributing to the stereotype.

Employers have a duty to ensure that both they and their employees are properly informed, so that *Selection* and other employment decisions can be made objectively and rationally, not subjectively and instinctively.

263 Subconscious Discrimination

The judgment of Lord Nicholls of Birkenhead, in *Nagarajan v London Regional Transport* [*1999*] *IRLR 572* (see *Direct Discrimination* and *Victimisation*) contains the following important passage:

> 'I turn to the question of subconscious motivation. All human beings have preconceptions, beliefs, attitudes and prejudices on many subjects. It is part of our make-up. Moreover, we do not always recognise our own prejudices. Many people are unable, or unwilling, to admit even to themselves that actions of theirs may be racially motivated. An employer may genuinely believe that the reason why he rejected an applicant had nothing to do with the applicant's race. After careful and thorough investigation of a claim, members of an Employment Tribunal may decide that the proper inference to be drawn from the evidence is that, whether the employer realised it at the time or not, race was the reason why he acted as he did. It goes without saying that in order to justify such an inference the tribunal must first make findings of primary fact from which the inference may properly be drawn. Conduct of this nature by an employer, when the inference is legitimately drawn, falls squarely within the language of s 1(1)(a). The employer treated the complainant less favourably on racial grounds. Such conduct also falls within the purpose of the legislation. Members of racial groups need protection from conduct driven by unrecognised prejudice as much as from conscious and deliberate discrimination.'

Lord Nicholls added that the same approach should be adopted in relation to complaints of *Victimisation*. A complaint is made out if it is shown that the complainant was treated less favourably by reason of having done a 'protected act', even if that person 'did not consciously realise, for example, that he was prejudiced because the job applicant had previously brought claims against him under the Act'.

264 Subjectivity

It is not unlawful for an employer or anyone else to make *Selection* or other employment decisions which are subjective, irrational or eccentric, so long as no racial or sex or disability discrimination is involved.

Where, however, there is a difference in the treatment of persons of different race or gender, an Employment Tribunal will expect to hear a genuine and non-discriminatory reason for that difference in treatment – see *Evidence of Discrimination*. Where decisions are made objectively, and reasons are recorded, the decision-maker should be able to explain to the tribunal the process of reasoning which was followed. Where no rational explanation can be given for a decision, however, a tribunal is unlikely to believe a bare assertion that no discrimination was involved.

265 Substantial and Long Term Adverse Effects

265.1 RELEVANCE TO DEFINITION OF 'DISABILITY'

Section 1(1) of the *DDA 1995* provides that, for there to be a 'disability', the effect which a physical or mental impairment has on a person's ability to carry out normal day-to-day activities must be 'a substantial and long-term adverse effect'.

265.2 SUBSTANTIAL

The Guidance on Matters to be taken into Account in Determining Questions relating to the Definition of Disability provides useful clarification of the meaning of 'substantial' in this context. As the EAT pointed out in *Goodwin v The Patent Office [1999] IRLR 4*, the word 'is potentially ambiguous' since it might mean 'very large' or 'more than minor or trivial'. The Guidance shows that the word is used in the latter sense. Factors which may need to be considered include:

(*a*) the time taken by a person with an impairment to carry out a normal day-to-day activity in comparison with the time that might be expected if the person did not have the impairment; and

(*b*) the way in which the person with the impairment carries out a normal day-to-day activity in comparison to the way the person may be expected to carry it out if he or she did not have the impairment.

The EAT said in *Goodwin* that 'the tribunal may where the applicant still claims to be suffering from the same degree of impairment as at the time of the events complained of, take into account how the applicant appears to the tribunal to "manage", although tribunals will be slow to regard a person's capabilities in the relatively strange adversarial environment as an entirely reliable guide to the level of ability to perform normal day-to-day activities', as *Kapadia v London Borough of Lambeth [2000] IRLR 14* (below) illustrates.

265.3 CUMULATIVE EFFECT

Schedule 1, paragraph 4 of the DDA 1995 provides that an impairment is to be taken to affect the ability of a person to carry out normal day-to-day activities only if it affects:

(*a*) mobility;

(*b*) manual dexterity;

(*c*) physical co-ordination;

(*d*) continence;

(*e*) ability to lift, carry or otherwise move everyday objects;

(*f*) speech, hearing or eyesight;

(*g*) memory or ability to concentrate, learn or understand; or

(*h*) perception of the risk of physical danger.

However, an impairment might not have a *substantial* adverse effect on a person in any one of these respects, but its effects in more than one of these respects taken together could result in a substantial adverse effect on the person's ability to carry out normal day-to-day activities. Moreover, a person may have more than one impairment, any one of which alone would not have a substantial effect. It is necessary to consider whether the impairments together have a substantial effect overall on the person's ability to carry out normal day-to-day activities.

265.4 EFFECTS OF BEHAVIOUR

A relevant issue is how far a person can reasonably be expected to modify behaviour to prevent or reduce the effects of an impairment on normal day-to-day activities. If a person can behave so that the impairment ceases to have a substantial adverse effect on his or her ability to carry out normal day-to-day activities, the definition of 'disability' under the *DDA 1995* would no longer be satisfied. Some people, however, have 'coping' strategies which cease to work in certain circumstances (e.g. when subjected to stress). If the management of the effects of an impairment may break down so that the effects will sometimes still occur, that must be taken into account when making the overall judgement. If a disabled person is advised by a medical practitioner to behave in a particular way so as to reduce the impact of the disability, that may count as treatment to be disregarded (see below).

265.5 EFFECTS OF ENVIRONMENT

Variable environmental conditions may be relevant to the question of whether adverse effects are 'substantial'. These include temperature and the hour of the day. When assessing whether adverse effects are 'substantial', the extent to which environmental factors are likely to have an impact should be taken into account.

265.6 EFFECTS OF TREATMENT

Schedule 1, paragraph 6(1) of the *DDA 1995* provides that where an impairment has been treated or corrected, it is to be treated as having the effect it would have without the measures in question. The measures to be so disregarded include medical treatment and the use of a prosthesis or other aid. This is the case even if the measures result in the effect being completely under control or not at all apparent. Thus, if a person with a hearing impairment wears a hearing aid, whether the impairment has a substantial adverse effect is to be decided by reference to what the hearing level would be without the hearing aid. However, this principle does not apply to sight impairments to the extent that they are capable of correction by spectacles or contact lenses. The EAT acknowledged in *Goodwin* that this question of 'deduced effects' is a difficult one for a tribunal to address.

Kapadia v London Borough of Lambeth [2000] *IRLR 14*, is a case in point. An accountant was diagnosed as having reactive depression and received counselling. Following promotion, he started taking more time off work for illness, attributed in part to pressure of work. Following consultation with a medical specialist who advised that he was 'permanently unfit for his duties' he was retired on medical grounds. A tribunal rejected his complaint under the *DDA 1995* on the ground that his depression, although a clinically well-recognised illness, had no more than a trivial effect on his normal day-to-day activities. On appeal, he argued that the tribunal erred by not considering the 'deduced effects' of the impairment on his day-to-day activities in the absence of medical treatment, and that without the counselling sessions there would have been a very strong likelihood that he would have had a total mental breakdown. The employers argued that the counselling sessions did not constitute 'treatment' within the meaning of *Schedule 1, paragraph 6*. The EAT held that the tribunal had been wrong to find that there was no evidence that the employee's mental impairment had a substantial adverse effect, notwithstanding that there was uncontested medical opinion evidence from his GP and consultant clinical psychologist that he was disabled within the meaning of the *DDA 1995*. The possibility that a tribunal may, for good reason, reject uncontradicted medical evidence cannot be precluded. On the facts, however, the tribunal had simply disregarded the medical evidence in favour of a judgement made on the basis of how the employee appeared when giving his evidence and – not least bearing in mind the comments of the EAT in *Goodwin* – that was wholly impermissible. The tribunal also erred by disregarding the 'deduced effects' of the impairment. Counselling sessions with a consultant clinical psychologist do constitute 'medical treatment' for these purposes, even though they consist of talking to the patient, or are directed to reducing the patient's symptoms, rather than to correcting the impairment. The employers seemed to be suggesting that a series of counselling sessions which prevent the patient from needing drug treatment for his condition does not amount to 'treatment' and the EAT could not accept that. The employers appealed to the Court of Appeal, but without success: the medical evidence showed that the case clearly fell within the *DDA 1995* and the EAT had been entitled to substitute its own decision for that of the tribunal.

265.7 PROGRESSIVE CONDITIONS

Schedule 1, paragraph 8 of the *DDA 1995*, provides that where:

(*a*) a person has a progressive condition (such as cancer, multiple sclerosis or muscular dystrophy or infection by HIV); and

(*b*) as a result of that condition, he has an impairment which has (or had) an effect on his ability to carry out normal day-to-day activities; but

(*c*) that effect is not (or was not) a substantial adverse effect,

he shall be taken to have an impairment which has such a substantial adverse effect if the condition is likely to result in his having such an impairment.

The Guidance amplifies this. Where a person has a progressive condition, he or she will be treated as having an impairment which has a substantial adverse effect from the time when an impairment resulting from the condition first has some effect on ability to carry out normal day-to-day activities. The effect need not be continuous and need not be substantial. For this principle to operate, medical diagnosis of the condition is not by itself enough.

265.8 SEVERE DISFIGUREMENT

Schedule 1, paragraph 3 of the *DDA 1995*, provides that an impairment which consists of a severe disfigurement is to be treated as having a substantial adverse effect on the person's ability to carry out normal day-to-day activities. There is no need to demonstrate such an effect. However, severe disfigurements resulting from tattoos and body-piercing are excluded by the *Disability Discrimination (Meaning of Disability) Regulations 1996 (SI 1996 No 1455)* (although disfigurements resulting from the removal of such self-inflicted disfigurements appear not to be excluded). Disfigurements include: scars, birth marks, limb or postural deformation or diseases of the skin. Assessing severity is mainly a matter of degree, although it may be necessary to take account of whereabouts on the body the disfigurement is (e.g. on the back as opposed to the face).

265.9 LONG TERM EFFECTS

Schedule 1, paragraph 2 of the *DDA 1995*, provides that the effect of an impairment is long-term if:

(*a*) it has lasted at least twelve months;

(*b*) the period for which it lasts is likely to be at least twelve months; or

(*c*) it is likely to last for the rest of the life of the person affected.

Schedule 2, paragraph 5 of the *DDA 1995* provides that, for the purpose of deciding whether a person has had a disability in the past, a long-term effect of the impairment is one which lasts at least twelve months.

It is not necessary for the effect to be the same throughout the relevant period. The main adverse effect might disappear permanently or temporarily while one or other effects on ability to carry out normal day-to-day activities continue or develop. The Guidance makes it clear that, provided the impairment continues to have, or is likely to have, such an effect throughout the period, there is a long-term effect.

265.10 RECURRING EFFECTS

Schedule 2, paragraph 2 of the *DDA 1995* provides that where an impairment ceases to have a substantial effect on a person's ability to carry out normal day-to-day activities, it is to be treated as continuing to have that effect if that effect is likely to recur. Conditions which recur sporadically, or only for short periods of time (such as epilepsy) may be covered, but seasonal allergic rhinitis is specifically excluded, except where it aggravates the effects of an existing condition.

The Guidance states that the likelihood of recurrence should be considered, taking all the circumstances into account. But the possibility that 'coping strategies' may legitimately break down should be taken into account, if relevant, when assessing the likelihood of a recurrence.

265.11 EFFECTS OF TREATMENT

If medical or other treatment is likely to cure an impairment so that the recurrence of its effects would then be unlikely even if there were no further treatment, this should be taken into account when looking at the likelihood of recurrence of those effects. But if the treatment simply delays or prevents a recurrence, and a recurrence would be likely if the treatment stops, then the treatment is to be ignored and the effect is to be regarded as likely to recur.

265.12 LIKELIHOOD

The Guidance states that an event is likely to happen if it is more probable than not that it will happen. In assessing the likelihood of an effect lasting for any period, account should be taken of the total period for which the effect exists. This includes any time before the point when the discriminatory behaviour occurred as well as time afterwards. Account should also be taken of the typical length of such an effect on an individual, and any relevant factors specific to the individual in question, such as the general state of health and age.

265.13 PAST DISABILITY

Section 2 and *Schedule 2, paragraph 5* of the *DDA 1995* provide that a person who has had a disability within the statutory definition is protected from discrimination even if he or she has since recovered or the effects have become less substantial. In deciding whether a past condition was a disability, its effects count as long-term if they lasted twelve months or more after the first occurrence, or if a recurrence happened or continued until more than twelve months after the first occurrence.

In *Greenwood v British Airways plc [1999] IRLR 600*, the EAT held that an Employment Tribunal erred in finding that the applicant was not protected by the *DDA 1995* because, at the time the alleged discriminatory act took place, his condition had ceased and was not likely to recur. The tribunal wrongly took the view that events which occur after the date of the alleged discriminatory act are irrelevant for the purposes of determining whether the complainant has a disability. In deciding that the applicant's impairment did not have a long-term substantial adverse effect, the tribunal erred by focusing solely on the state of the applicant's medical condition at the date of the alleged discriminatory act. In determining whether the effect of an impairment is likely to last at least twelve months, as the Guidance makes clear, the tribunal should consider the adverse effects of the person's condition up to and including the tribunal hearing. By disregarding its own finding that the adverse effects of the condition recurred and led to him being off work until the date of the tribunal hearing, the tribunal adopted an approach which was fatally flawed. In any event, even if he was not disabled within the meaning of *section 1*, he had had a disability within the meaning of *section 2*. The EAT said that *Schedule 2, paragraph 5(2)* may be contrasted with *Schedule 1, paragraph 2(2)* which deals with the likelihood of the effect recurring. The tribunal's failure to take into account the fact that the adverse effect recurred meant that, on the facts as found, the employee made out his case that he had a past disability under *section 2*.

266 Supported Workshops

In addition to the special provisions for *Charities*, there is a provision in *section 10(2)* of the *DDA 1995* under which it is lawful for a person who provides *'supported employment'* to treat members of a particular group of disabled persons more favourably than other disabled persons in providing such employment.

'Supported employment' means facilities provided, or in respect of which payments are made, under *section 15* of the *Disabled Persons (Employment) Act 1944*.

If, under the terms of the 1944 Act, a workshop is established to provide employment for workers with a particular disability, the exclusion of disabled workers who do not have that disability would be an act of disability discrimination, unless it could be justified under *section 5(1)* of the *DDA 1995*. There is, however, no need for justification, because reliance can be placed on the above exception in *section 10(2)*.

267 Surveillance of Employees at Work

Although employment protection rights have become increasingly well established in recent years, over the same period technological changes have given rise to new challenges, notably the availability of means for employers to conduct covert surveillance on employees' activities in the workplace. This trend raises a variety of general concerns, including concerns about *Human Rights* and on occasion issues connected with equal opportunities, as a leading case demonstrates. *Halford v United Kingdom [1997] IRLR 471*, concerned a senior police officer who unsuccessfully applied for promotion in her own force and others on numerous occasions. She alleged that she had been subjected to a campaign which included interception of her telephone calls at work and at home for the purpose of obtaining information to use against her in sex discrimination proceedings which she had brought. Her claim to an Employment Tribunal was settled, but the European Court of Human Rights ruled that interception of calls she made on her office telephone was a violation of *Article 8* of the *European Convention on Human Rights*. The UK Government argued that an employer should in principle, without the employee's prior knowledge, be able to monitor calls made to the employee on telephones provided by the employer, but the court rejected that view. Since no warning had been given to the employee that calls made on her office telephone would be liable to interception, she would have had a reasonable expectation of privacy for such calls. In 1999, the Government responded to *Halford* with a consultation paper proposing to implement that ruling, but at the time of writing legislation had not been enacted. OFTEL has also published recommendations alerting employers which provide telephone services to their employees to their legal obligations. OFTEL recommends, amongst other matters, that employers should develop guidelines about their policy on telephone monitoring at work.

268 Targets

Some employers, as part of their equal opportunity policies, have set targets to be achieved over a period. The targets set commonly include one or more of the following:

(*a*) an increased number or percentage of women at senior levels;

(*b*) a minimum percentage of black or ethnic minority employees; and

(*c*) a minimum percentage of disabled employees.

The third of these targets should give rise to no legal difficulty, because the *DDA 1995* does not prohibit discrimination *in favour of disabled employees generally*. It is a different matter if there is discrimination in favour of certain categories of disabled workers and against other categories (unless the case is covered by the exceptions relating to *Charities* and *Supported Workshops*).

There is, however, a need for great care in setting targets which are based on gender or on racial factors. The law does permit certain measures in relation to encouragement and training for 'under-represented' groups (see *Positive Discrimination*), but there must be no discrimination in *Selection* for any particular post. Targets are legitimate if (but only if) they are used in the following ways:

(*a*) to discriminate in favour of disabled workers generally;

(*b*) to identify apparent 'under-representation' of other groups, defined by reference to gender or a racial factor;

(*c*) to underline the need for vigilance in avoiding direct or indirect discrimination against members of those groups; and

(*d*) to take advantage of the modest measures of *Positive Discrimination* which the law permits.

269 Temps

The expression 'temp' is traditionally used to describe office workers who provide secretarial services, usually on a short-term basis, to clients of an agency. Usually the temp is employed by the agency but sometimes he or she is self-employed. In either case, there is no contractual relationship between the temp and the client.

The client is, however, under a duty not to discriminate against the temp, for example by subjecting him or her to racial or sexual harassment – see *Contract Workers*.

270 Terms of Employment

Section 4(2) of the *RRA 1976*, and also *section 4(2)* of the *DDA 1995*, apply to complaints of discrimination relating to *Pay* or other *Benefits*, whether the complaint relates to a contractual term or to discretionary pay or benefits. The question is whether there has been racial discrimination (direct or indirect), disability discrimination or victimisation (under either Act) in relation to the particular matter complained of.

The position under the *EPA 1970* and the *SDA 1975* is more complicated. In summary:

(*a*) a complaint about a contractual term for the payment of money must be brought under the *EPA 1970*;

(*b*) a complaint about any other contractual term must be brought under the *EPA 1970* if there is an available *Comparator*, but otherwise may be brought under the *SDA 1975*;

(*c*) a complaint about a non-contractual benefit must be brought under the *SDA 1975*.

It is not always clear which is the appropriate Act and it is usual to plead alternative complaints under the *EPA 1970* and the *SDA 1975*.

The effect of these provisions is that a person who wishes to complain about a contractual term for the payment of money has no remedy if a suitable comparator cannot be identified, but it may be possible to rely on *Article 141* to extend the ambit of search for a comparator beyond the strict confines of the *EPA 1970* – see *Same Employment*.

271 Territorial Extent

The general rule is that the provisions relating to employment in the *EPA 1970*, the *SDA 1975*, the *RRA 1976* and the *DDA 1995* all apply to employment at an *Establishment* in Great Britain. These Acts do not apply to employment in Northern Ireland, which has its own legislation.

A key provision is that employment is deemed to be at an establishment in Great Britain unless the employee works wholly overseas. Accordingly all four Acts will apply in a case where an employee spends only a few days each year working at an establishment in Great Britain and spends the rest of the time working overseas.

There are special rules relating to *Ships* and *Aircraft* (including hovercraft). It is also relevant, particularly in relation to ships, that the references to Great Britain include the UK territorial waters adjacent to Great Britain.

272 Tests

Employers use a wide variety of tests in *Recruitment* and also in selecting candidates for *Promotion*. They include:

(*a*) *Aptitude Tests*;

(*b*) Intelligence Tests; and

(*c*) *Psychometric Testing*.

Whatever kind of test is used, there is a risk of:

(*a*) direct discrimination, if all candidates are not tested in the same way;

(*b*) indirect discrimination, if tests are biased or 'loaded' against women (or men) or against members of particular racial groups; and

(*c*) disability discrimination if *Reasonable Adjustments* are not made.

273 Theatre

Under the *SDA 1975*, being of a particular gender can be a *Genuine Occupational Qualification* for reasons of authenticity, in recruiting or casting for dramatic performances of other entertainment. There is a similar GOQ exception under the *RRA 1976*.

It should not be assumed, however, that these GOQ exceptions automatically authorise discrimination where, for example, a part has traditionally been played by a white actor. It is now commonplace for theatrical roles to be taken by black or white actors and actresses without distinction. It would be unusual for a dramatic performance to lack authenticity simply because a character was not played by a person from a particular racial group.

The authenticity GOQ in the *SDA 1975* is more firmly rooted, although there have been some notable successes in crossing boundaries of gender, recently as well as historically.

274 Time Limits

274.1 THE SDA 1975, THE RRA 1976 AND THE DDA 1995

Under *section 76* of the *SDA 1975*, *section 68* of the *RRA 1976* and *Schedule 3* of the *DDA 1995*, a complaint must be presented before the end of the period of three months beginning when the act complained of was done. There are special provisions in the *SDA 1975* and the *RRA 1976* relating to complaints of discrimination in the *Armed Forces*.

The starting point in any case is to ascertain the date on which the period of three months starts to run. Each Act contains the following provisions:

(*a*) any act extending over a period shall be treated as done at the end of that period – see *Continuing Discrimination*;

(*b*) where the inclusion of any term in a contract renders the making of the contract an unlawful act, that act shall be treated as extending throughout the duration of the contract; and

(*c*) a deliberate omission shall be treated as done when the person in question decided upon it.

It is also provided that, in the absence of evidence establishing the contrary, an omission is decided upon by a person:

(*a*) if the person does an act inconsistent with doing the omitted act, at the time of doing the inconsistent act; or

(*b*) otherwise, when the period expires within which the person might reasonably have been expected to do the omitted act, if it was to be done at all.

The case of *Cast v Croydon College [1998] IRLR 318* has already been referred to, under *Continuing Discrimination*. It was also held in that case, where the complainant had twice asked if she could work part-time or job share, and been twice refused, that each refusal was a separate act of discrimination. This was because the matter had been reconsidered in response to the further request. The employer had not simply referred back to the earlier decision.

Each of the three Acts provides that a tribunal may consider a complaint which is out of time if, in all the circumstances, the tribunal considers that it is just and equitable to do so. The tribunal has a very wide discretion. Factors which should be taken into account were identified by the EAT in *British Coal Corporation v Keeble and Others [1997] IRLR 336*. Consideration must be given to the prejudice which each party would suffer as the result of the decision to be made, the respondent if the time is extended and the complainant if it is not. The relevant circumstances of the case could also include:

(*a*) the length of and reasons for the delay;

(*b*) the extent to which the cogency of the evidence is likely to be affected by that delay;

(*c*) the extent to which the respondent had co-operated with any request for information;

(*d*) the promptness with which the complainant acted once he or she knew of the facts giving rise to the action; and

(*e*) the steps taken by the complainant to obtain appropriate professional advice once he or she knew of the possibility of taking action.

274.2 THE EPA 1970

Under *section 2* of the *EPA 1970*, a complaint must be presented either during the employment or within six months after the end of the employment. There is no provision in the *EPA 1970* for the time to be extended.

The question of time limits was considered by the ECJ, on a reference from the House of Lords, in the case of *Preston and Others v Wolverhampton Healthcare NHS Trust and Others* [*2000*] *IRLR 506*. This case has already been referred to under *Pensions*.

Some of the complainants in the case were teachers or lecturers who worked regularly but were employed under successive and legally separate contracts. Under one of the questions which was referred, the ECJ was asked whether it was compatible with *Community Law* (and in particular with *Article 141*) if time starts to run at the end of each separate contract and not at the end of the employment relationship. If so, the employees concerned would be able to pursue their complaints only in relation to the final contract in each case, because they would have been out of time as regards the earlier contracts.

It was held by the ECJ that time should not start to run so long as there is a stable relationship resulting in a succession of short-term contracts concluded at regular intervals in respect of the same employment to which the same pension scheme applies.

The more general question which was referred to the ECJ on time limits was whether the six month time limit under the *EPA 1970* was compatible with Community Law. The answer given by the ECJ was that the time limit is not precluded provided that the limitation period is not less favourable for actions based on Community law than for those based on domestic law.

The way in which direct effect is given to equal pay claims in Great Britain is by modifying the *EPA 1970* to make it compatible with *Article 141*. Accordingly, the question which, at the time of writing, has still to be considered by the House of Lords, is whether the six month time limit under the *EPA 1970* is at least as favourable to complainants as the time limit under other domestic proceedings which the House of Lords decide are relevant for purposes of comparison. If, for example, complaints relating to unfair dismissal or statutory redundancy payments were used for purposes of comparison, the following factors could be relevant:

(*a*) on the one hand, the limitation periods in such cases are three months and six months respectively; and

(*b*) on the other hand, the time for presenting those complaints can be extended, while there is no provision for extending the time limit under the *EPA 1970*.

275 Time Off

Employees have numerous statutory rights to take paid or unpaid time off (such as the right under *section 57A* of the *Employment Rights Act 1996* to have a reasonable amount of unpaid time off to take necessary action relating to dependants). In addition, employers operate a wide variety of contractual and discretionary arrangements under which employees are given time off, for example, to care for children or for study, or continue to receive full pay during sickness and other absences.

There must be no unlawful discrimination in the adoption or implementation of any such arrangements. It would be direct sex discrimination (as well as a breach of the employee's rights under *section 57A* of the 1996 Act in the first example) for an employer:

(*a*) to refuse a male employee time off to look after a child who has been sent home sick from school, on the ground that his wife should take time off from her employment; and

(*b*) to grant a male employee time off for study, but refuse a request from his female colleague because she is pregnant and may not return after her maternity leave.

Permitting an employee to take time off, for example for medical treatment, may also be a *Reasonable Adjustment* under the *DDA 1995*.

276 Trade Organisations and Disability Discrimination

Discrimination by trade organisations is covered in *sections 13–15* of the *DDA 1995*. A 'trade organisation' is an organisation of workers, an organisation of employers or any other organisation whose members carry on a particular profession or trade for the purposes of which the organisation exists.

It is unlawful for a trade organisation to discriminate against a disabled person:

(*a*) in the terms on which it is prepared to admit him to membership of the organisation; or

(*b*) by refusing to accept, or deliberately not accepting, his application for membership.

It is unlawful for a trade organisation to discriminate against a disabled person who is one of its members:

(*a*) in the way it affords him access to any benefits or by refusing or deliberately omitting to afford him access to them;

(*b*) by depriving him of membership, or varying the terms on which he is a member; or

(*c*) by subjecting him to any other detriment.

The rules are similar to those governing employers and it may be possible for the organisation to justify treating a disabled person less favourably than someone who is not disabled.

A duty to make *Reasonable Adjustments* came into force on 1 October 1999 and at the same time a Code of Practice in respect of the duties of trade organisations to their disabled members and applicants came into force.

277 Trade Unions

Section 12 of the *SDA 1975*, *section 11* of the *RRA 1976* and *sections 13–15* of the *DDA 1995* impose duties on various organisations (defined in the *DDA 1995* as *Trade Organisations*), including organisations of workers.

There must be no discrimination against applicants for membership:

(*a*) in the terms on which the organisation is prepared to admit the applicant to membership; or

(*b*) by refusing, or deliberately omitting to accept, the application for membership.

It is unlawful for an organisation of workers to discriminate against a member:

(*a*) in the way it affords the member access to any benefits, facilities or services, or by refusing or deliberately omitting to afford access to them;

(*b*) by depriving the member of membership, or varying the terms of membership; or

(*c*) by subjecting the member to any other detriment.

There are provisions in the *SDA 1975*, as amended by *section 6* of the *Sex Discrimination Act 1986*, under which a union member can apply to an employment tribunal for an order that a term in a collective agreement is void if, for example, that term provides for the doing of an act of unlawful discrimination – see *Collective Bargaining*. A complaint may also be made, on similar grounds, in relation to a union rule.

The Codes of Practice under the *SDA 1975* and the *RRA 1976* refer to the statutory responsibilities of trade unions and also refer to the important part which unions can play in promoting equal opportunities, for example by:

(*a*) co-operating in the introduction and implementation of *Equal Opportunity Policies*;

(*b*) negotiating the adoption or extension of such policies; and

(*c*) co-operating with measures to monitor the progress of such policies.

278 Training

It is expressly provided in *section 6* of the *SDA 1975*, *section 4* of the *RRA 1976* and *section 4* of the *DDA 1995* that there must be no discrimination against an employee in the way the employer affords him or her access to opportunities for training or by refusing or deliberately omitting to afford the employee access to such opportunities.

It would, for example, be a clear case of *Direct Discrimination* if an employer failed to send a female employee on a suitable training course because she was pregnant and he was concerned that the cost of the course would be wasted if she failed to return to work after her maternity leave. An example of indirect sex discrimination would be an employer's refusal to consider alternative arrangements for a female employee who is unable to attend a residential training course because of her childcare commitments.

Residential training could also be an issue in relation to certain *Disabilities*. If a disabled worker is placed at a substantial disadvantage in relation to any residential or other training which is provided by the employer, then consideration must be given to providing the training in some other way, as a *Reasonable Adjustment*.

The law permits a measure of *Positive Discrimination* in favour of employees who are in a minority by reason of their gender or employees who belong to a racial group which is 'under-represented'. See also *Special Needs*.

Training is a vital component of any effective *Equal Opportunity Policy*. In a small business *Selection* and other employment decisions may be made personally by the owners, partners or directors. In many such cases, they themselves need training. In larger organisations, where decisions are made by managers, the employer has little or no prospect of persuading a tribunal that *Reasonably Practicable Steps* have been taken to prevent discrimination unless appropriate training has been given at least to managers. In many organisations, an effective policy will also require training for other employees as well as managers. The Codes of Practice under both the *SDA 1975* (paragraph 23(a)) and the *RRA 1976* (paragraph 1.4(d)) recommend provision of training or guidance for personnel staff, line managers, supervisors and other decision makers. The *SDA 1975* Code also refers to training for other employees who come into contact with job applicants. Training and guidance for interviewers should also be provided. The *RRA 1976* Code also refers to comparatively junior staff, such as gatekeepers and receptionists, who may in some organisations be called on to deal with job applicants.

279 Training Bodies

279.1 **THE SDA 1975 AND THE RRA 1976**

Section 14 of the *SDA 1975* and *section 13* of the *RRA 1976* are in virtually identical terms. Under both sections, it is unlawful for any person or organisation providing or arranging vocational training to discriminate:

(*a*) in the terms on which access to training (or related facilities) is afforded;

(*b*) by refusing or deliberately omitting to afford access to the training or facility;

(*c*) by terminating a person's training; or

(*d*) by subjecting a person to any detriment during the course of his or her training.

Where it is the employer who provides the training, then any complaint is under *section 6* of the *SDA 1975* or *section 4* of the *RRA 1976*, not under the above provisions.

Vocational training bodies are permitted to discriminate in circumstances covered by a relevant exception, for example where the work for which a person is to be trained is covered by a *Genuine Occupational Qualification*.

279.2 **THE DDA 1995**

Discrimination in relation to vocational training is dealt with by *section 19* of the *DDA 1995* as one example of discrimination in relation to goods, facilities and services. This section is in *Part III* of the *DDA 1995*, which means that any complaint has to be presented to a county court (or sheriff court in Scotland), not to an Employment Tribunal.

280 Transfers

A transfer may be from one place to another, from one kind of work to another or from full-time work to part-time work (or vice versa). For the latter case, please see *Indirect Discrimination* and *Part-Time Work*.

Section 6 of the *SDA 1975*, *section 4* of the *RRA 1976* and *section 4* of the *DDA 1995* each make it unlawful for an employer to discriminate in the way an employee is afforded access to opportunities for transfer or by refusing or deliberately omitting to afford an employee access to a transfer.

A compulsory transfer, for example from one job to another or from one place of work to another, will normally be a *Detriment* and accordingly any discrimination in relation to any such transfer will also be covered by the above provisions. It is immaterial, for the purposes of the discrimination laws, whether the compulsory transfer is in pursuance of an express or implied contract term.

A transfer involving a change of duties, a change of location or a reduction in hours may also be a *Reasonable Adjustment* under the *DDA 1995*.

281 Transsexuals

281.1 BACKGROUND

A small but significant minority of people, estimated at about 5000 in the UK, is affected by transsexualism. Medical treatment to enable transsexuals to alter their bodies to match their gender identity is known as 'gender reassignment'.

The *Sex Discrimination Act 1975* did not, on its face, cover discrimination in employment on the ground of transsexualism or gender reassignment. The picture altered as a result of a ruling of the European Court which has led to an amendment of the Act. The position under European Community law therefore contrasts, perhaps surprisingly, with the position as regards *Sexual Orientation.*

The cost of discrimination in this area, as in others, can be high. In late 1999, it was reported that a former employee of the DHSS had agreed to accept £10,000 in settlement of her claim that she was sexually harassed by work colleagues because she is a transsexual.

281.2 CASE LAW

In *P v S and Cornwall County Council* [*1996*] *IRLR 347*, the European Court held that the scope of the *Equal Treatment Directive* cannot be confined simply to discrimination based on the fact that a person is of one or other sex. The Directive is the expression of the principle of equality, a fundamental principle of Community law. In view of its purpose and the fundamental nature of the rights which it seeks to safeguard, the scope of the Directive also applies to discrimination based essentially, if not exclusively, on the sex of the person concerned. Where such discrimination arises from the gender reassignment of the person concerned, he or she is treated unfavourably by comparison with persons of the sex to which he or she was deemed to belong before undergoing gender reassignment. To tolerate such discrimination would, the European Court held, be tantamount as regards such person to a failure to respect the dignity and freedom to which he or she is entitled and which the Court has a duty to safeguard. Thus dismissal of a transsexual for a reason related to a gender reassignment is contrary to *Article 5(1)* of the Directive.

Following that decision, the EAT upheld a tribunal's decision to construe the *Sex Discrimination Act 1975* to accord with the European Court's decision: *Chessington World of Adventures Ltd v Reed* [*1997*] *IRLR 556*. The EAT held that discrimination arising from a declared intention to undergo gender reassignment is based on the person's sex. Where the reason for unfavourable treatment is sex based, in accordance with the reasoning of the House of Lords in *Webb v EMO Air Cargo (UK) Ltd* [*1993*] *IRLR 627*, there is no requirement for a male/female comparison to be made. Accordingly, the *Sex Discrimination Act 1975* can be interpreted consistently with the purpose of the *Equal Treatment Directive* as interpreted in *P v S*. The employee in question had been subjected to concerted harassment by male colleagues following her announcement of a change of gender identity from male to female. The EAT upheld the tribunal's decision that the employers were directly liable for sex discrimination by failing to act on knowledge that the employee was being subjected to harassment, which constituted a continuing detriment.

However, this measure of legal protection is based on discrimination, which requires an appropriate comparison and worse treatment. *Bavin v NHS Trust Pensions Agency & another* [*1999*] *ICR 1192*, is a reminder of the limits of the protection. Under the NHS pension scheme, a widow or widower could benefit on a member's death, but unmarried partners of scheme members could not. The employee was in a long-term relationship with a transsexual, who had been registered as female at birth, but who had undergone gender reassignment and was accepted as a male. The employee claimed that the pension scheme was discriminatory and in breach of *Article 119*, but a tribunal found that it was not, since it applied equally to men and women and depended entirely on whether the survivor had been married in accordance with English law. The EAT upheld that ruling: the terms 'widow' and 'widower' in the pension scheme could only mean surviving spouse, so that unmarried partners of members could never obtain benefits whatever the reason for their not being married. Accordingly, the scheme discriminated between members who were married and members who were not, and the employee was not discriminated against because her partner was a transsexual, but rather because they were unmarried. The EAT did, however, say:

> '. . . we can and do invite those who are responsible for such matters to consider whether it is sensible in modern times for eligibility to any concession or benefit to depend on the marital status of the people concerned. It is the experience of the members of this court that many if not most pension schemes give trustees a discretion to make payments where relationships outside marriage are stable. We can think of no good social reason why travel facilities or derived pension benefits should not be available where there is a stable long-term relationship between two unmarried people, whatever the reasons for not being married. Such a change would not have to address the more complicated and difficult question as to whether persons of the same sex should be permitted to marry or transsexuals be permitted formally to change their birth certificate.'

281.3 GENDER REASSIGNMENT REGULATIONS

The *Sex Discrimination (Gender Reassignment) Regulations 1999 (SI 1999 No 1102)* came into force on 1 May 1999. They extend the *SDA 1975* to cover discrimination in employment and vocational training on the ground of gender reassignment. They bring domestic law into line with the decision of the European Court in *P v S and Cornwall County Council* (above) by making discrimination on the basis of gender reassignment discrimination on the ground of sex contrary to the *SDA 1975*. The regulations:

(*a*) define 'gender reassignment' broadly so as provide protection against discrimination by employers at all stages of the process of gender reassignment, including the sometimes critical phase where the individual indicates an intention to embark upon gender reassignment;

(*b*) define discrimination in terms of the comparative treatment of a transsexual and the treatment of 'other persons';

(*c*) equate the absence allowed to a person undergoing gender reassignment with absence due to sickness or injury in order to determine whether there has been less favourable treatment; and

(*d*) establish genuine occupational qualification exceptions to the core principle of non-discrimination.

The regulations do not, however, define the time when sex actually changes or the time when the process of gender reassignment is deemed to be complete.

The Department for Education and Employment has published *A Guide to the Sex Discrimination (Gender Reassignment) Regulations 1999* to provide guidance and suggest good practice. But the guide is not a Code of Practice and has no special legal status. Moreover, although the recommendations it makes are likely to be found useful by tribunals as well as by employers and employees, they must be treated with some caution. For instance, the Guide suggests that it may be discriminatory to dismiss a person because of the impending gender reassignment treatment, in the same way as it is unlawful to dismiss a woman for pregnancy – but the Regulations do not give gender reassignment protected status equal to that afforded by legislation to pregnancy. The Guide recognises that medical treatment for transsexualism 'could result in a prolonged incapacity for work. If incapacity continues beyond the normal expectations for the process undergone, a transsexual employee could be retired on medical grounds in the same way as any other person who becomes unfit for duty'. It remains to be seen whether this caveat to the principle of non-discrimination survives legal challenge.

282 Tribunal Procedure

282.1 THE SDA 1975, THE RRA 1976 AND THE DDA 1995

Complaints of discrimination relating to employment are heard by Employment Tribunals. The rules of procedure are the same as those which apply in other Employment Tribunal cases. They are the *Employment Tribunals (Constitution and Rules of Procedure) Regulations 1993 (SI 1993 No 2687)* and the corresponding regulations for Scotland (referred to in this Handbook as the Tribunal Rules).

The usual procedure is for the complainant and the complainant's witnesses to give evidence first. It follows that in cases in England and Wales (but not in Scotland) the complainant's representative (or the complainant himself if he is unrepresented) will have the last word in making submissions to the tribunal.

A special feature in certain complaints under the *DDA 1995* and in cases involving allegations of sexual misconduct (usually complaints of *Sexual Harassment* under the *SDA 1975*) is the tribunal's power to make a *Restricted Reporting Order.*

Where a case appears to involve allegations that a sexual offence has been committed, the tribunal and tribunal staff must take steps to protect the identity of the person making the allegation and the person against whom it is made. This means omitting names and other identifying material from the decision and any other document which is available to the press or public. Where the persons whose identities are to be protected are parties to the proceedings, their names will be omitted from the case details which are displayed at the tribunal offices throughout each day's hearing. Allegations of sexual offences are unlikely to be made except in cases of *Sexual Harassment* (and are not a normal feature even of these cases).

282.2 THE EPA 1970

The Regulations include separate rules of evidence for *Equal Value* cases. The main special feature is the power of the tribunal to appoint an *Independent Expert.*

283 Turbans

283.1 SIKHS ON CONSTRUCTION SITES

There are express provisions in relation to *Sikhs* and turbans under *sections 11* and *12* of the *Employment Act 1989.*

Normal requirements to wear a safety helmet do not apply when a Sikh:

(*a*) is on a construction site (whether as an employee or as a contract worker or otherwise); and

(*b*) is wearing a turban.

The Act defines:

(*a*) 'construction site' as any place where any building operations or works of engineering construction are being undertaken;

(*b*) 'safety helmets' as any form of protective headgear; and

(*c*) 'Sikh' as a follower of the Sikh religion.

This last definition distinguishes the case from the normal one in which a Sikh must be defined as a member of an ethnic group in order to bring a complaint of indirect racial discrimination, but the Act goes on to ensure that a Sikh would succeed in a complaint of indirect racial discrimination if he were to be penalised in any way for refusing to wear a safety helmet on a construction site. The Act does this by expressly providing that the requirement could not be shown to be justifiable in such circumstances. The Act also provides that a person who is not a Sikh cannot present a complaint of racial discrimination on the ground that he has been required to wear a safety helmet and denied the special treatment which is given to Sikhs on construction sites.

283.2 OTHER CASES

Away from construction sites, the normal principles in cases of *Indirect Discrimination* apply. If a Sikh (or a member of any other relevant ethnic group) is unable to comply with a requirement relating to protective headgear (or a requirement not to wear a turban) then the question for consideration will be whether the requirement is 'justifiable'. It may well be justifiable if it is on safety grounds and there is no satisfactory way of reconciling the safety requirements with the needs of the individual concerned – see also *Beards.*

284 Unconscious Discrimination

As a result of the decision of the House of Lords in *Nagarajan v London Regional Transport [1999] IRLR 572,* it has been clearly established that there can be *Direct Discrimination* or *Victimisation* without conscious motivation. Lord Nicholls of Birkenhead said in that case:

> 'Members of racial groups need protection from conduct driven by unrecognised prejudice as much as from conscious and deliberate discrimination.'

He referred also to the comment by Lord Justice Balcombe in *West Midlands Passenger Transport Executive v Singh [1988] IRLR 186,* that a high rate of failure to achieve promotion by members of a particular racial group may indicate that 'the real reason for refusal is a conscious or unconscious racial attitude which involves stereotyped assumptions' about members of the group.

These comments apply equally to cases under the *SDA 1975* and the *DDA 1995.*

285 Unfair Dismissal

Where an Employment Tribunal makes a finding that there has been a discriminatory dismissal, contrary to the *SDA 1975*, the *RRA 1976* or the *DDA 1995*, a finding of unfair dismissal does not automatically follow – *HJ Heinz Co Ltd v Kenrick* [*2000*] *IRLR 144*. The tribunal must give separate consideration to the question of unfair dismissal under *section 98* of the *Employment Rights Act 1996*.

Furthermore there are cases where a tribunal has jurisdiction to hear a complaint of discrimination but not a complaint of unfair dismissal, for example where:

(*a*) the employee does not have the necessary period of continuous employment for the purpose of presenting a complaint of unfair dismissal; or

(*b*) the complainant is an employee within the extended definition of *Employment* contained in the discrimination laws but not for the purposes of a complaint of unfair dismissal.

An employee who has been subjected to unlawful discrimination is not necessarily entitled to resign and treat himself or herself as constructively dismissed, so as to bring a complaint of discriminatory dismissal and/or unfair dismissal – see *Dismissal (section 8)* and *Constructive Dismissal*.

286 Uniforms

Under the *SDA 1975*, it is lawful for an employer to require employees to wear uniforms and to insist on different uniforms for male and female employees, so long as, looking at uniform requirements as a whole, employees of one gender are not being treated less favourably than employees of the other gender – see *Physical Appearance*.

It could be indirect racial discrimination for an employer to refuse to modify a uniform which a racial minority employee cannot wear because of the customs or conventions of the *Racial Group* to which he or she belongs – see *Indirect Discrimination*.

If, because of a disability, a disabled employee cannot wear a particular uniform, or cannot do so without discomfort, then a *Reasonable Adjustment* may be called for.

287 Unintentional Discrimination

Nouns like 'intention' and 'motive' can be misleading when used imprecisely.

There are several questions to be considered in relation to any complaint of *Direct Discrimination* or *Victimisation*. Some of those questions are factual questions which do not involve any consideration of the intention, motivation or mental processes of the person who is alleged to be responsible for the act complained of. In particular:

(*a*) has the complainant been treated in the way complained of;

(*b*) is that treatment less favourable than the treatment afforded to some other relevant person or persons (such as persons of a different gender or racial group or who have not done a protected act);

(*c*) are the relevant circumstances of the complainant's case, and of those other cases, the same or not materially different; and

(*d*) if the relevant act has not been done by the respondent personally, has the act been done by a person (such as an employee or agent) for whose actions the respondent is responsible?

Where there is no actual comparator, it may be necessary to consider the mental processes of the person who has done the act complained of in order to ascertain how a hypothetical comparator would have been treated.

Establishing whether there has been less favourable treatment is only the first question. Lord Nicholls of Birkenhead pointed out in *Nagarajan v London Regional Transport [1999] IRLR 572* that:

> 'in every case it is necessary to enquire why the complainant received less favourable treatment. This is the crucial question ... save in obvious cases, answering the crucial question will call for some consideration of the mental processes of the alleged discriminator. Treatment, favourable or unfavourable, is a consequence which follows from a decision.'

If a person has treated the complainant less favourably than an actual or hypothetical comparator has been treated, it is relevant, in order to ascertain the reason for the less favourable treatment, to look at that person's state of mind or mental processes in the following respects:

(*a*) knowledge of (or, in cases under the *RRA 1976*, belief about – see *Racial Grounds*) the complainant's race (or, as the case may be the complainant's gender or marital status or the fact that the complainant has done a protected act); it is difficult to see how a particular factor can be the reason for a particular act unless the person doing that act is aware of that factor;

(*b*) intention – in the sense of deliberately doing the relevant act or omission; and

(*c*) probably also intention, in the sense that less favourable treatment of the complainant than of an actual or hypothetical comparator was intended or at least foreseen.

Evidence of conscious motivation (for example the use of language which indicates an intention to treat the complainant less favourably because she is a woman) can assist a tribunal to decide the reason for the treatment complained of but such evidence is usually not available and is not essential. As Lord Nicholls of Birkenhead said in *Nagarajan*:

> 'Direct evidence of a decision to discriminate on racial grounds will seldom be forthcoming. Usually the grounds of the decision will have to be deduced, or inferred, from the surrounding circumstances.'

In deciding what the grounds of the decision were, it is not necessary to find that there was conscious motivation connected with, for example, the race or gender of the complainant. Lord Nicholls said:

> 'Members of racial groups need protection from conduct driven by unrecognised prejudice as much as from conscious and deliberate discrimination.'

Lord Nicholls also said that the crucial question of the reason for the treatment complained of:

> 'is to be distinguished sharply from a second and different question: if the discriminator treated the complainant less favourably on racial grounds, why did he do so? The latter question is strictly beside the point when deciding whether an act of racial discrimination occurred . . . racial discrimination is not negatived by the discriminator's motive or intention or reason or purpose (the words are interchangeable in this context) in treating another person less favourably on racial grounds.'

Accordingly, there are two respects in which it can be said that there are cases of unlawful discrimination which do not necessarily involve a hostile intention towards the complainants:

(*a*) there can be a finding that, for example, the race or gender of the complainant was the reason for the treatment complained of, even though the discriminator did not articulate this reason even to himself and acted on the basis of an unconscious or subconscious prejudice; and

(*b*) once it is established that, for example, the race or gender of the complainant was the reason, or an important reason, for the act complained of, it is irrelevant to consider why that factor played a part in the decision-making.

288 Unmarried Persons

The definition of discrimination under the *SDA 1975* includes direct and indirect discrimination against married workers; it does not include discrimination against unmarried workers.

It would, however, be *Direct Discrimination* to discriminate against, say, a man because of his single status, if there would have been no discrimination against an unmarried woman in similar circumstances. The unlawful discrimination in such a case would be treating the man, on the ground of his sex, less favourably than a woman would have been treated in similar circumstances.

289 Variation of Contracts

There is a provision in both the *SDA 1975* and the *RRA 1976* under which application may be made to a county court (or sheriff court in Scotland) for the removal or modification of a term which is inconsistent with the legislation – see *Agreements*. An application may be made for the amendment of a collective agreement (see *Collective Bargaining*) as well as an individual contract. Under the *Sex Discrimination Act 1986*, the application may be made to an Employment Tribunal.

A provision in the *DDA 1995* for the variation of contracts applies only to non-employment contracts.

290 Vicarious Liability

Vicarious liability is the expression commonly used in other areas of the law, particularly in relation to accidents at work, where employers are made legally responsible for the negligent actions of their employees.

The same expression is also frequently used to describe the liability of employers under the *SDA 1975*, the *RRA 1976* and the *DDA 1995* for acts and omissions by their employees in the course of their employment. The expression is misleading in this context, however, because of the broader and more robust approach adopted in discrimination cases following the decision of the Court of Appeal in *Jones v Tower Boot Co Limited* [*1997*] *IRLR 168* – see *Harassment*.

291 Victimisation

291.1 THE STATUTORY PROVISIONS

The definition of discrimination, under the *SDA 1975*, the *RRA 1976* and the *DDA 1995*, includes treating a person less favourably than other persons would be treated in the same circumstances, by reason that the person victimised has done what is commonly (although not in the legislation itself) referred to as a 'protected act'. The acts covered by this term are:

(*a*) bringing proceedings under the relevant legislation;

(*b*) giving evidence or information in connection with any proceedings under the relevant legislation (whether the proceedings are brought by the person victimised or any other person and whether they are brought against the discriminator or against any other person);

(*c*) doing anything else under or by reference to the relevant legislation (in relation to the discriminator or any other person); and

(*d*) alleging that the discriminator or any other person has committed an act which would amount to a contravention of the relevant legislation (whether or not the allegation expressly states that the act committed contravenes the legislation).

The relevant legislation for the purpose of these definitions is:

(*a*) under the *SDA 1975*, the *SDA 1975* itself, the *EPA 1970* and the relevant provisions of the *Pensions Act 1995* (see *Pensions*);

(*b*) under the *RRA 1976*, the *RRA 1976* itself; and

(*c*) under the *DDA 1995*, the *DDA 1995* itself.

There is also discrimination by way of victimisation if the discriminator:

(*a*) knows that the person victimised intends to do any of the above things;

(*b*) suspects that the person victimised has done any of them; or

(*c*) suspects that the person victimised intends to do any of them.

Less favourable treatment does not, however, amount to discrimination by way of victimisation if it is by reason of an allegation which was false and not made in good faith.

291.2 THE CASE LAW

In early appeal decisions relating to victimisation, the EAT and then the Court of Appeal extended the ambit of protected acts very widely, so that something was done under or by reference to the relevant legislation even where it was an unconventional and discreditable action. In *Kirby v Manpower Services Commission [1980] IRLR 229*, making a report containing allegations of discrimination was treated as a protected act even though the report was made in breach of an obligation of confidentiality. In *Aziz v Trinity Street Taxis Limited [1988] IRLR 204*, secretly tape recording conversations with fellow taxi drivers, in order to obtain evidence of discrimination, was also treated as a protected act.

No remedy was given in these cases, however, because it was held, notably by the Court of Appeal in *Aziz*, that in making a complaint of discrimination by way of victimisation the complainant had to be able to prove that the respondent had a motive which was consciously connected with the relevant discrimination legislation. Unfortunately, this also meant that a discriminatory motive of this kind also had to be proved even where the protected act was of a wholly conventional and legitimate nature. In theory, at least, the effect of the decision in *Aziz* was that a complaint that, for example, the respondent had dismissed the complainant for bringing proceedings under the *EPA 1970* was at risk of failing if the respondent could show that he would have dismissed an employee for bringing any other proceedings (unrelated to the relevant legislation) against him.

There is no longer, however, a requirement for conscious motivation, following the decision of the House of Lords in *Nagarajan v London Regional Transport* [*1999*] *IRLR 572*. In that case, the complainant applied to the respondent for a post as a travel information assistant. He was interviewed and was subsequently told that his application had been unsuccessful. The two interviewers, and an equal opportunities adviser who was also present, were aware at the time of the interview that he was a former employee of the respondent who had previously brought racial discrimination cases against the respondent.

The industrial tribunal upheld a complaint of victimisation. The tribunal found that the score which one of the interviewers had given to the complainant for articulacy was ridiculous and unrealistically low. The tribunal found that a view formed by the same interviewer that the complainant was very anti-management was derived from the interviewer's knowledge of his previous complaint. The tribunal reached the conclusion that the interviewers, particularly the one who had given the above score and formed the above view, were 'consciously or subconsciously influenced' by the fact that the complainant had brought the previous proceedings.

The EAT, later supported by the Court of Appeal, set aside the decision of the tribunal on two grounds, the first of which was that *section 2(1)* of the *RRA 1976* 'contemplates a motive which is consciously connected with the race relations legislation'. There was no scope for subconscious influence.

The House of Lords, by a majority, allowed a further appeal and restored the decision of the tribunal. No conscious motivation need be proved, whether the complaint is one of *Direct Discrimination* or one of *Victimisation*.

In the words of Lord Nicholls:

> 'If racial grounds or protected acts had a significant influence on the outcome, discrimination is made out.'

A side effect of this decision may be, however, that a complaint of victimisation must be upheld even where the protected act is unconventional and discreditable, such as wrongly disclosing confidential information or secretly tape recording conversations.

A further important decision on victimisation is that of the Court of Appeal in *Chief Constable of West Yorkshire Police v Khan* [*2000*] *IRLR 324*. In that case a sergeant, who had applied unsuccessfully for promotion to inspector, presented an Employment Tribunal complaint of racial discrimination. Before the case was heard, he applied to another force for an inspector's post. The West Yorkshire Police refused to give the other force an opinion about his suitability, giving the pending tribunal case as the reason.

A complaint of victimisation was upheld by the tribunal. The complainant was awarded compensation of £1,500 for injury to feelings. The issue on appeal was whether the complainant's case should be compared with that of any other officer who had a pending case against the force. If that was the appropriate test, then the appeal should be upheld. The refusal to express an opinion about the complainant's suitability was not because it was racial discrimination that he had complained about. There would have been the same refusal if his pending case against West Yorkshire Police had been entirely unrelated to racial discrimination.

The Court of Appeal held that this was not the correct test. The judgment of the Master of the Rolls (Lord Woolf) referred to the *Nagarajan* case and to the earlier House of Lords decisions *(R v Birmingham City Council ex parte Equal Opportunities Commission* [*1989*] *IRLR 173* and *James v Eastleigh Borough Council* [*1990*] *IRLR 288*) in which the 'but for' test had been adopted. The test embraces both the application of a gender based criterion and also selection on grounds of sex or race. It avoids complicated terms such as intention, motive or purpose.

The appropriate comparator in a victimisation case is to be identified not by looking at the reason why the reference was not provided, but by considering what was requested. A reference on the complainant had been requested. The appropriate comparators were other employees in relation to whom a reference had been or might have been requested. How would such requests normally be treated? The answer was that they would normally have been granted. The request in this case was not granted because the complainant had presented a complaint to tribunal of racial discrimination. Accordingly his complaint of victimisation succeeded. It was immaterial that the reason or motive for withholding the reference was not to victimise him for having complained of discrimination, but a concern that giving the reference could be prejudicial in the context of the forthcoming proceedings.

291.3 PRACTICAL ADVICE

Guidance and training must be given:

(*a*) to interviewers and others involved in the selection process, where a person who has done a protected act applies for employment; and

(*b*) to managers and supervisors, where a person continues in employment after having done a protected act.

Where a complaint of harassment or other discrimination has been made against an individual manager (and particularly if the complaint has been upheld), it is not good practice to give that manager responsibility for future decisions relating to the complainant, unless the employer:

(*a*) is fully satisfied that the manager understands and will comply with the obligation not to victimise the complainant; and

(*b*) has given appropriate reassurance to the complainant.

The following steps should also be taken (or at least considered) in all cases where an employee has done a protected act:

(*a*) a clear explanation to that employee of the procedure for making an internal complaint if any victimisation does take place;

(*b*) the involvement of an independent person, such as a personnel manager from another department, in all future decisions relating to the employee;

(*c*) the appointment of a senior person to monitor any such decisions to ensure that they are made fairly and objectively; and

(*d*) appropriate disciplinary action against the persons concerned, if the allegations made by the employee have been upheld.

292 Voluntary Bodies

A voluntary body is subject to obligations under the *EPA 1970* and the discrimination laws in the same way as any other employer.

293 Voluntary Workers

It is unlikely that a voluntary worker would be treated as an employee for the purposes of the *EPA 1970*, the *SDA 1975*, the *RRA 1976* or the *DDA 1995*. Where a person works entirely without any payment or other reward, that work is not normally done under a contract, whether a conventional contract of service or a contract personally to execute any work or labour.

294 Wales

The *EPA 1970*, the *SDA 1975*, the *RRA 1976* and the *DDA 1995* all apply in Wales. Both the substantive law and the procedure are identical, whether the employment is at an establishment in Wales or at one in England.

295 Welsh, as a Racial Group

Direct or indirect racial discrimination against a Welsh job applicant or employee would be covered by the *RRA 1976* – see *Racial Grounds* and *Racial Group* – although the authors are not aware of any such case.

There is a danger of indirect racial discrimination against workers who are not of Welsh origin if Welsh language requirements are adopted in cases where the job duties do not justify them.

296 Word of Mouth Recruitment

Employers should not use word of mouth or similar informal methods to recruit employees. Such methods could involve *Indirect Discrimination* where, for example, a considerably smaller proportion of women than of men or a considerably smaller proportion of black workers than of white workers are made aware of a particular vacancy.

An employer adopting such methods could face complaints of indirect discrimination by individuals or action by the EOC or the CRE (as the case may be) in relation to the *Discriminatory Practice* which is being operated.

297 Work Permits

Employers have statutory obligations to satisfy themselves that new employees are entitled to work in the United Kingdom. Employers must, however, have standard procedures and requirements for all cases. It would be entirely unacceptable, and unlawful, to ask black appointees but not white appointees to produce work permits or other satisfactory evidence.

298 Workers From Overseas

Section 6 of the *RRA 1976* permits an employer to discriminate in favour of a person not ordinarily resident in Great Britain:

(*a*) where the purpose of the employment is to provide that person with training in certain skills; and

(*b*) it appears to the employer that the person intends to exercise those skills wholly outside Great Britain.

There is a more general provision to a similar effect in *section 36* of the *RRA 1976*, under which either an employer or a *Training Body* or any other person or body can discriminate for the benefit of persons not ordinarily resident in Great Britain in affording them access to facilities for education or training or any ancillary benefits. Such discrimination is permitted where it appears to the discriminator that the persons in question do not intend to remain in Great Britain after their period of education or training there.

299 Working Conditions

The fact that work is to be carried out in dangerous, difficult, dirty or otherwise unpleasant working conditions can be relevant in the following respects:

(*a*) There must be no direct discrimination in the allocation of such work, and in particular the person deciding who should do what work must not act on the basis that dangerous or difficult work is more suitable for men than for women – see *Detriment*.

(*b*) Similarly, an employer must not make recruitment or selection decisions on the basis that dangerous or unpleasant working conditions make a job 'men's work' rather than 'women's work'.

(*c*) An employer must consider *Reasonable Adjustments*, where the nature of the work places a disabled employee at a substantial disadvantage.

The fact that the work of a comparator named by the complainant in an *Equal Pay* case has to be done in unpleasant conditions can be relevant to the following questions:

(*a*) Is the comparator's work and that of the complainant *Like Work*?

(*b*) Are the two jobs of *Equal Value*?

(*c*) If a difference in pay or other contract terms is attributable to the unpleasant working conditions, has a *Material Factor* defence been made out?

Issues relating to *Health and Safety at Work* may also arise.

300 Works Rules

Most employers make rules to be obeyed by their employees and set them out in a handbook or in notices which are displayed or issued to the workforce.

If a works rule provides for something to be done which would be unlawful under the *SDA 1975* or which would be a breach of an *Equality Clause* under the *EPA 1970*, any employee who is or may in the future be affected may apply to the county court (or the sheriff court in Scotland) or to an Employment Tribunal for the rule in question to be removed or modified. Any such application is made under *section 77* of the *SDA 1975* as extended by *section 6* of the *Sex Discrimination Act 1986*.

An example would be a works rule stating that a particularly hazardous machine may be operated by a woman only if she is supervised.

CHECKLISTS

INTRODUCTORY NOTE

These checklists indicate matters which commonly arise or should usually be considered. They do not purport to be comprchensive or to cover all possible eventualities.

1. ADOPTING AND IMPLEMENTING AN EQUAL OPPORTUNITY POLICY

- Involve staff and unions in policy formulation.
- Consider more detailed policies, e.g. on harassment and disability.
- Appoint a suitable person or team to take responsibility for policy implementation.
- Set up effective mechanisms for informal and formal complaints.
- Identify new disciplinary offences where necessary, both for managers and for other employees (e.g. racial, sex or disability discrimination as misconduct and harassment, victimisation or, for managers, condoning harassment or victimisation as gross misconduct).
- Revise other policies, procedures and practices, e.g. those on recruitment, selection and redundancy, in the light of the equal opportunity policy.
- Communicate the policy effectively to all employees and to job applicants.
- Provide effective training for managers and for other persons involved in recruitment and selection, redundancy selection and other employment decisions.

2. MONITORING AND REVIEWING EQUAL OPPORTUNITY POLICIES

- Decide on a system of classification.
- Obtain the starting information about the racial composition of the workforce and numbers of men and women and of disabled workers at various levels.
- Set up systems for recording changes to this initial information.
- Set up systems for classifying job applications at various levels and successful and unsuccessful applicants by reference to racial origin, gender and disability.
- Adopt a system for recording and classifying all complaints and how they are dealt with.
- Set up arrangements to analyse and review all the information at regular intervals.
- Consider, at each review, whether the policy needs to be changed or whether implementation needs to be improved in any respect.
- Adopt a system of regular reporting on the success or otherwise of the policy, including reports to senior management at least once a year.

3. REASONABLY PRACTICABLE STEPS TO PREVENT DISCRIMINATION

- Adopt a suitably worded policy which clearly describes the kind of conduct which is unacceptable in the organisation.

- Ensure that the policy is communicated effectively to employees and in particular that all employees are aware that they must not discriminate unlawfully themselves and that they must report any discrimination of which they become aware.
- Provide detailed training and guidance where necessary, particularly for managers, supervisors, interviewers and any other persons responsible for dealing with, or making decisions about, job applicants or employees.
- Give any necessary instructions and guidance to recruitment and other agents used by the organisation.
- Provide further training when necessary, e.g. refresher courses and updates, training for new managers and training for new eventualities.
- Consider at regular intervals whether further measures are required.
- Investigate thoroughly and promptly any cases which come to light, whether through the complaints procedure or otherwise, and take appropriate action.

4. RECRUITMENT AND SELECTION

- Appoint a senior person or team to oversee and be responsible for the policies and procedures and their implementation.
- As a general policy, advertise all job vacancies, both internally and externally (but with special provision for cases where there is a need to redeploy, if possible, potentially redundant employees, particularly women returning from maternity leave, or disabled employees).
- Set up objective procedures, involving the use of job descriptions, person specifications, structured interviews and scoring systems.
- Scrutinise and review, in the light of legal requirements and the equal opportunity policy, all documents which are used in recruitment or selection, including job advertisements and application forms.
- Review any tests which are used, such as intelligence tests, aptitude tests or psychometric tests, to ensure that they are not indirectly discriminatory in their operation.
- Set up a system for asking all candidates invited for interview to indicate in advance whether arrangements are needed to accommodate any disability.
- Provide effective training for all selectors, interviewers and other persons involved in recruitment or selection.
- Set up a system under which the consent of a suitably qualified person is required before treating a post as one to which a GOQ or other exception applies.
- Review all procedures and standard documentation at regular intervals and consider whether any changes are needed.
- Ensure that all shortlisting and selection decisions and the reasons for them are recorded and that the records are kept.

5. COMMON EXAMPLES OF INDIRECT RACIAL DISCRIMINATION

- Many acts of religious discrimination are also examples of indirect racial discrimination.

- Inflexible rules on dress and appearance, which fail to take account of the customs or religious practices of particular ethnic groups.
- Refusal to give reasonable consideration to requests for short prayer breaks, for accumulation of annual leave or to take annual leave on a feast or holy day.
- Recruitment arrangements which artificially restrict the pool of candidates, with a disproportionate impact on particular racial groups.
- Failing to give due weight to qualifications or relevant experience obtained overseas.
- Requiring qualifications which are excessive in relation to the duties to be performed.
- The use of intelligence or psychometric or other tests which have the effect of disadvantaging candidates not brought up in Great Britain.
- Requiring a standard of written or spoken English which is excessive in relation to the duties to be performed (including a requirement to complete a written application form for a manual job).

Note: the three last-mentioned requirements are likely to disadvantage racial minority workers who have recently settled in Great Britain. At one time these would have been predominantly Afro-Caribbean and Asian workers; they are now increasingly members of other racial minorities.

6. COMMON EXAMPLES OF INDIRECT SEX DISCRIMINATION

- Recruitment arrangements which artificially restrict the pool of candidates to one consisting mainly of men (or women).
- Intelligence or psychometric or other tests which are biased in their operation against women (or men).
- A refusal to agree to part-time working or job sharing.
- Inflexibility in relation to starting and finishing times.
- Insistence on a rotating shift pattern.
- A requirement to attend residential training courses.
- Obligations to undertake overseas or overnight travel.
- Contractual mobility requirements or the implementation of such requirements.

Note: all but the first two of the above-mentioned requirements and conditions are potentially indirectly discriminatory against women because a much greater proportion of women than of men have childcare and other family responsibilities which limit their freedom of action. These requirements and conditions are, however, unlawful only if not objectively justified.

7. PRELIMINARY ACTION FOR COMPLAINANTS

- Check on the time limit for presenting the complaint to the tribunal – this is vital.
- Enquire about the possibility of assistance, e.g. from the relevant Commission and apply in good time.
- If still employed, consider using the grievance procedure.

- Use the statutory questionnaires – taking advice if possible on the questions to be asked.
- Keep the time limits in mind throughout – if out of time, present a complaint without any further delay.
- Ensure that the complaint to tribunal specifies all your grounds of complaint (e.g. unfair dismissal as well as discrimination).
- Consider whether you have correctly identified the respondent and whether there is any further respondent to be added (e.g. a fellow employee against whom you have made allegations of harassment).

8. PRELIMINARY ACTION FOR RESPONDENTS

- Comply with the 21 day time limit for entering appearance.
- If it is impossible to comply, apply promptly for an extension, giving reasons.
- Investigate the complaint as thoroughly as possible before entering appearance, but subject to the time limits.
- Deal promptly and fairly with any grievance submitted by the complainant, whether before or after the commencement of proceedings.
- Respond promptly, carefully, thoroughly and accurately if a questionnaire is submitted.
- If the complainant is still employed by you, take effective measures to prevent any victimisation.
- If further particulars are required, ask for them promptly.
- Consider whether you can take any points on jurisdiction, such as a failure to present the complaint in time, and bring any such point to the attention of the tribunal.
- Consider whether the case is one of the exceptional cases where it is appropriate to apply for a pre-hearing review, at which the complainant could be ordered to pay a deposit.
- In a discrimination case, consider whether to plead the defence that all reasonably practicable steps have been taken to prevent the act complained of or acts of that description.
- In an equal pay case, consider whether there is any material factor defence to be pleaded.
- Consider the possibility of trying to settle the case through ACAS.

9. PREPARING A CASE FOR HEARING

- Has the case been fully pleaded, so that all the issues have been clearly identified?
- Have the parties been correctly identified and are there any further parties to be joined in?
- Have you disclosed all relevant documents to the other party?
- Have all relevant documents been disclosed to you – or do you need to apply for an order for discovery?

- Have steps been taken to agree a joint bundle of documents for the hearing – and which party is to prepare the necessary copies for the hearing?
- Have all the witnesses whom you wish to call been interviewed and statements obtained?
- Is a witness order required?
- Is there any need to apply for a postponement (in which case an application must be made promptly, supported by full reasons)?
- Have all the legal issues in the case been fully researched?
- Has the possibility of a negotiated settlement through ACAS been fully explored?

10. INDIRECT DISCRIMINATION – KEY ISSUES

- What is the precise definition of the requirement or condition complained of?
- Has that requirement or condition been applied to the complainant?
- Was the complainant unable to comply with the requirement or condition?
- If so, was the inability to comply with the requirement or condition to the complainant's detriment?
- If the case is one of indirect racial discrimination, what is the relevant racial group to which the complainant belongs?
- Is disparate impact admitted or self evident (in which case it is appropriate to proceed to the final question)?
- If not, what is the relevant 'pool' of workers?
- Within that pool, what are the respective percentages (in a case of indirect sex discrimination, the percentage of women and the percentage of men) who can comply with the requirement or condition?
- Is the difference between these percentages a considerable one, having regard to the case law on how this question should be approached?
- If the indirectly discriminatory effect of the requirement or condition is established, can the respondent defeat the complaint by showing that the requirement or condition is objectively justified?

11. EQUAL PAY – KEY ISSUES

- To what contract term(s) (e.g. rate of pay) does the complaint relate?
- Has the complainant identified one or more comparators of the opposite sex?
- Are the complainant and the comparator(s) in the same employment – bearing in mind the case law on the extended definition of 'same employment' under *Article 141*?
- Have the jobs of the complainant and one or more comparator(s) been given the same rating under a job evaluation scheme (in which case proceed to the final question)?
- If not, are they like work (in which case proceed to the final question)?

- If the claim is that the jobs of the complainant and the comparator(s) are of equal value, can the respondent defeat the complaint by showing that the jobs have been given different values under a non-discriminatory and analytical job evaluation scheme?
- If not, should the question of whether the jobs are of equal value be referred to an independent expert?
- In any event, has the respondent made out the material factor defence so as to defeat the complaint?

12. RECRUITING PEOPLE WITH DISABILITIES

- Ensure that staff involved in the recruitment process are familiar with the legal rules.
- Consider the post and what could be done to encourage applications from people with disabilities, e.g. by ensuring that the 'disability symbol' is displayed on all advertising outlets.
- Check that the job description is framed in a way which enables a disabled applicant to apply.
- Check that the essential requirements in the person specification (qualifications, experience etc.) are genuinely necessary, so as not unjustifiably to exclude certain applicants, perhaps including disabled applicants.
- Check the wording of any advertisement and make any appropriate reference to the organisation's equal opportunities policy, providing a copy to the disability employment adviser.
- Where a disabled person attends for interview, ensure that the venue is accessible and any additional facilities that are provided are identified in the response to the interview invitation or subsequently in discussion.
- Consider providing an induction loop to assist hearing-aid users or where sign language interpreters might be obtained if necessary. It may also be appropriate to allow an applicant with learning disabilities to be accompanied in the interview by a friend or support worker.
- Check with the disabled applicant whether they have any special needs at the interview stage and if there are any special requirements for this interview. For example, if there is a typing aptitude test, adaptation may be required.
- Check that staff who may be escorting or directing candidates to interview are aware of any special needs and facilities and that any appropriate aids are provided.
- Make sure that, at the interview, the disability is not the main item of discussion.
- Respond in a positive and appropriate manner to any reasonable adjustments suggested by the disabled applicant.
- If a disabled person is appointed, check what reasonable adjustments, if any, need to be made.

Appendix 1

CODE OF PRACTICE ON EQUAL PAY

Editorial note: This Code was issued by the Equal Opportunities Commission under the Sex Discrimination Act 1975, and was brought into force on 26 March 1997.

INTRODUCTION

This Code of Practice on Equal Pay aims to provide practical guidance and to recommend good practice to those with responsibility for or interest in the pay arrangements within a particular organisation. It is grounded in the concept that a right to equal pay free of sex bias is conferred under both domestic and European legislation. The guidance contained in the Code is based on decisions from the United Kingdom (the UK) courts and the European Court of Justice (the ECJ) and on good practice known to the Equal Opportunities Commission.

In addition to the need to meet the legal requirements, there are sound business reasons for implementing equal pay. Pay systems which are transparent and value the entire workforce send positive messages about an organisation's values and ways of working. Fair and non-discriminatory systems represent good management practice and contribute to the efficient achievement of business objectives by encouraging maximum productivity from all employees.

Moreover, equal pay cases are extremely time consuming and expensive for employers, so it is in their own interest to attempt to avoid litigation by having in place systems which do not discriminate and are seen not to discriminate.

The Equal Opportunities Commission is a statutory body established under the Sex Discrimination Act 1975 and charged with the duty to work towards the elimination of sex discrimination, to promote equality of opportunity between men and women generally and to keep under review the working of the Sex Discrimination Act 1975 and the Equal Pay Act 1970, (each as amended).

The Commission fulfils its duties in various ways, including providing advice and assistance to employers, employees, trade unions and other interested parties, about rights and obligations under the law.

The law is complex and pay systems are increasing in complexity. There is therefore a need for guidance on the law and on good practice to minimise uncertainty and to enable firms and other organisations to establish policies and procedures to ensure that all employees receive equal pay free of sex bias under the law.

Once in effect the Code shall be admissible in evidence in any proceedings under the Sex Discrimination Act 1975 or the Equal Pay Act 1970, (each as amended), before an Industrial Tribunal, and any provisions of the Code which appear to the Tribunal to be relevant to any question arising in the proceedings shall be taken into account in determining that question.

The Code contains chapters on the following: the requirements of the law; the implications of the law for employers; the process of a pay review and the identification of discriminatory elements in pay systems. In addition, there is a chapter which briefly addresses the basis of sex discrimination in payment systems. The Code also provides guidance on drawing up an equal pay policy and a suggested equal pay policy.

There is no legal obligation on employers to carry out a pay systems review or to adopt an equal pay policy. These are included in the Code as good practice which is recommended by the Equal Opportunities Commission.

Appendix 1

Much of the detail and formalised procedures of the Code will not apply to small firms. What is important is that pay is not influenced by sex.

When reviewing pay systems for sex bias and developing non-discriminatory systems, consultation is likely to increase understanding and acceptance of any changes required. A consultation process could include trade unions and other groups representing staff where this is felt to be appropriate.

This Code refers to all aspects of pay. Sex discrimination in matters of recruitment, selection, promotion and training is dealt with in the Code of Practice: Equal Opportunity Policies, Procedures and Practices in Employment (available from the EOC).

Research by the Equal Opportunities Commission suggests that women from ethnic minorities may be particularly disadvantaged in their terms and conditions of employment. Employers should therefore be aware that, while this particular Code relates only to pay between men and women, payment systems may be open to challenge under the Race Relations Act 1976.

EQUAL PAY LEGISLATION

1. This chapter provides a basic outline of current equal pay legislation. Subsequent chapters expand on the main legal concepts and explain their implications for pay practices.

   a) The law relating to sex discrimination in pay is contained in both UK statute and European Community law. The former is required to conform with the latter and UK legislation is interpreted by domestic courts in the light of European law. Claims should be taken under domestic law where possible, but in some circumstances claims can be made directly under European law.

   b) The law applies to both men and women but to avoid repetition throughout this Code it is assumed that the claimant is a woman comparing herself with a man, as in practice most claimants are women.

Domestic Law

2. The relevant law is contained in the Equal Pay Act 1970, the Sex Discrimination Act 1975, (each as amended), and the Pensions Act 1995. Despite its name, the Equal Pay Act covers all contractual terms and not simply those relating to pay. The Sex Discrimination Act covers claims which do not relate to contractual issues. Claims under both Acts are taken initially to an Industrial Tribunal. Those under the Sex Discrimination Act must be taken within 3 months of the act complained of. Those under the Equal Pay Act can be taken at any time up to 6 months after leaving the employment to which the claim relates. The Pensions Act allows claims in relation to the terms of, and access to, occupational pension schemes.

3. The Equal Pay Act 1970, as amended by the Equal Pay (Amendment) Regulations 1983, provides for equal pay between women and men in the same employment by giving a woman the right to equality in the terms of her contract of employment where she is employed on:

   - like work to that of a man or
   - work rated as equivalent to that of a man or
   - work of equal value to that of a man,

   hereafter referred to as equal work.

4. The employer can defeat a claim under the Equal Pay Act by proving that the difference between the woman's contractual terms and those of the man is genuinely due to a material factor other than sex.

5. Where a claim under the Equal Pay Act is successful at Tribunal, equal pay is achieved by raising the pay of the woman to that of the man. This means that any beneficial term which is in the man's contract but missing from the woman's is to be treated as if it is in her contract, and/or any term in the woman's contract which is less favourable to her than the same term in the man's contract is improved so that it is as good.

6. This legislation applies to:

   - All employees, (including apprentices and those working from home) whether on full-time, part-time, casual or temporary contracts, regardless of length of service.
   - Other workers (e.g. self-employed) whose contracts require personal performance of the work.
   - Employment carried out wholly or mainly in Great Britain.
   - Employment carried out on British registered ships or UK registered aircraft operated by someone based in Great Britain unless the employee works wholly outside Great Britain.

   Great Britain includes such of the territorial waters of the UK as are adjacent to Great Britain and certain areas designated in relation to employment in the off-shore oil and gas industry.

7. The employment provisions of the Sex Discrimination Act 1975 prohibit sex discrimination in, among other things, access to non-contractual benefits and in grading schemes.

8. Employees victimised for taking an equal pay claim or giving information or acting as a witness or comparator in the course of a claim can make a claim under the Sex Discrimination Act.

9. Also, if a woman considers that a term in a collective agreement or an employer's rule provides for the doing of an unlawful discriminatory act, and that the term or rule may at some time have effect in relation to her, she can challenge that term or rule under the Sex Discrimination Act 1986 as amended by section 32 of the Trade Union Reform and Employment Rights Act 1993.

European Community Law

10. The relevant principles of European equal pay law are contained in Article 119 of the Treaty of Rome and the Equal Pay Directive 75/117.

    a) Article 119 of the Treaty of Rome establishes the principle that men and women should receive equal pay for equal work.

       It defines pay as:

       - the ordinary basic or minimum wage or salary and
       - any other consideration, in cash or in kind, which the employee receives directly or indirectly from her employer in respect of her employment.

    b) The Equal Pay Directive 75/117 states that the principle of equal pay outlined in Article 119 means that, for the same work or for work to which equal value is attributed, all discrimination on grounds of sex must be eliminated in all aspects and conditions of remuneration. It also states that where a job classification system is used for determining pay, it must be based on the same criteria for men and women and exclude any discrimination on grounds of sex.

Meaning of Pay

11. The courts have established that a woman may bring a complaint under the Equal Pay Act in relation to any term or condition contained in her contract whether or not it relates to money. This Act excludes non-contractual benefits, even if they relate to money. Claims concerning non-contractual benefits may be taken under the Sex Discrimination Act.

12. The definition of pay under Article 119 as interpreted by the ECJ is very broad and not limited to contractual terms.

IMPLICATIONS OF THE LAW FOR EMPLOYERS

13. Sex discrimination in pay is unlawful. The law provides a procedure by which an individual can take a claim for equal pay to an Industrial Tribunal. In the course of an equal pay claim employers may be called upon to explain and justify their pay practices and arrangements. Variations in pay practices are dealt with in pages 11–18. This section looks at the grounds on which an employer can defend a claim.

Burden of Proof

14. The burden of proof is initially on the employee to show on the balance of probabilities that her male comparator is doing the same or broadly similar work, or that her work has been rated as equivalent to his, or that her work is of equal value; and that his contract contains a more favourable term. If the employee succeeds in this, equal pay will be awarded unless the employer can prove that the difference between the contracts is genuinely due to a material factor which is not the difference of sex.

Material Factor Defence

15. The material factor defence is the reason put forward by the employer to explain why the comparator, although doing equal work, is paid more than the applicant. To be successful this factor must be significant and relevant; that is, it must be an important cause of the difference and apply to the jobs in question. The difference in pay must be genuinely due to the material factor which must not be tainted by sex discrimination. For example, if the reason given for paying the comparator more is that he has certain skills which the applicant does not have, then the employer would have to demonstrate that these skills are necessary for the job. and genuinely applied during the performance of the job, and are not simply rewarded because past pay agreements recognised and rewarded skills which are no longer applicable.

16. To succeed in a defence the employer needs to show that the material factor accounts for the whole of the difference in pay Where it accounts for only part of the difference equal pay can be awarded for the rest. For example, if the material factor defence relates to rates of pay determined by skill shortages, but on examination it is found that these shortages can only justify part of the higher pay of the comparator, then the Tribunal may award the applicant the difference.

Objective Justification

17. In circumstances where a particular pay practice results in an adverse impact on substantially more members of one or other sex, the ECJ has introduced a test of objective justification. This means that the employer must be able to justify the pay practice in question objectively in terms unrelated to sex. In practice he or she must show that the practice which causes the difference in pay corresponds to a business need on the part of the organisation, is appropriate with a view to achieving the objective pursued and is necessary to that end. For example, where a firm excludes part-time workers from an occupational pension scheme and this exclusion affects a far greater proportion of women than men, the employer would need to show that the exclusion is based on objectively justified factors unrelated to any discrimination on grounds of sex. If the ground for the exclusion is that the firm seeks to employ as few part-time workers as possible then the exclusion must be shown to correspond to a real need on the part of the undertaking and be appropriate and necessary to achieving that need.

18. Both the material factor defence and the objective justification test are essentially explanations for how the difference in pay arises and are closely related.

Transparency

19. It is important that the pay system is clear and easy to understand; this has become known as transparency. A transparent pay system is one where employees understand not only their rate of pay but also the components of their individual pay packets and how each component contributes to total earnings in any pay period. Transparency is an advantage to the employer as it will avoid uncertainty and perceptions of unfairness and reduce the possibility of individual claims.

20. The ECJ has held that where the organisation concerned applies a system of pay which is wholly lacking in transparency and which appears to operate to the substantial disadvantage of one sex, then the onus is on the employer to show that the pay differential is not in fact discriminatory. An employer should therefore ensure that any elements of a pay system which could contribute to pay differences between employees are readily understood and free of sex bias.

SEX DISCRIMINATION IN PAY SYSTEMS

21. Sex discrimination in pay now occurs primarily because women and men tend to do different jobs or to have different work patterns. As a result it is easy to undervalue the demands of work performed by one sex compared with the demands associated with jobs typically done by the other. Such differences can be reinforced by discriminatory recruitment, training, selection and promotion procedures which may restrict the range of work each sex performs; for example, by allocating the full-time, higher paid, bonus-earning jobs mainly to men.

Different Jobs

22.a) There is some degree of job segregation in most employing organisations. Frequently the jobs done mainly by men have a higher status and are more highly rewarded than those done by women. Commonly men and women do different types of work within an organisation. It is also common for men to be in the majority at managerial level and women to occupy lower graded jobs. In certain occupations there is further segregation to the extent that there is an even greater concentration of ethnic minority women in lower status, lower paid jobs.

b) Gender segregation in employment is often historical. Consequently it may be difficult to recognise the discriminatory effects of past pay and grading decisions based on traditional values ascribed to 'male' and 'female' work. In addition, the pay and conditions of 'male' and 'female' jobs within a firm might have been bargained separately by different unions, It is not sufficient to explain how the difference in pay came about. Arguments based on 'tradition' or separate bargaining would not justify paying women less than men when their work is of equal value.

c) The fact that certain jobs are associated with one sex can affect the level of wages for those jobs which in turn can result in discrimination.

d) Past discriminatory assumptions about the value of what has been regarded as men's or women's work may be reflected in current grading schemes. For example, men and women may be doing the same or very similar work but have different job titles and consequently be in separate grades, with the women's jobs being graded lower. They may, on the other hand, be doing quite different jobs which are actually of equal value though the women are in lower grades. In both examples the grading scheme could result in discrimination and fail to value the actual work done.

Different Work Patterns

23.a) Many women take time out of work for pregnancy and maternity. Women also tend to carry the main responsibility for family care. As a result women in general have shorter periods of service than men and more women than men work part-time. This difference in work patterns has contributed to the gender segregation of jobs.

b) There has been a tendency for payment systems to be designed to reward work patterns traditionally associated with men's employment and fail to recognise the different pattern of 'female' work. For example, a performance pay scheme which relies on an annual appraisal could mean that a woman who begins maternity leave before the appraisal, but has performed well for part of the year, will be denied a performance pay increase altogether. Another example is where pay benefits, such as occupational pensions or sick pay, are available only to full-time employees. This rule may mean that a group of female employees, i.e. those who work part-time, are denied access to important benefits.

24. Most of the discrimination in pay systems takes the form of indirect or hidden discrimination. This occurs where pay rules and agreements appear to be neutral between men and women but the effect of their application is to disadvantage substantially more of one sex than the other. Whatever the cause of the discrimination and regardless of whether it was intentional or not, once an applicant has established that someone of the opposite sex is paid more for equal work, the employer will be required to show that the difference is not based on sex, using the criteria set out on pages 4–5 under 'Material Factor Defence' and 'Objective Justification'.

REVIEW OF PAY SYSTEMS FOR SEX BIAS

25.a) Pay arrangements are frequently complicated and the features which can give rise to sex discrimination are not always obvious. Although pay systems reviews are not required by law, they are recommended as the most appropriate method of ensuring that a pay system delivers equal pay free from sex bias.

b) A pay systems review also provides an opportunity to investigate the amount of information employees receive about their pay. Pay systems should be clear and easy to understand. Where they are not and where pay differentials exist, these may be inferred to be due to sex discrimination (see page 5). It is therefore in an employer's interest to have transparent pay systems to prevent unnecessary equal pay claims.

c) The Equal Opportunities Commission recommends that a pay systems review should involve the following stages:

Stage One
Undertake a thorough analysis of the pay system to produce a breakdown of all employees, which covers for example, sex, job title, grade, whether part-time or full-time, with basic pay performance ratings and all other elements of remuneration.

Stage Two
Examine each element of the pay system against the data obtained in stage one (see paragraph 27).

Stage Three
Identify any elements of the pay system which the review indicates may be the source of any discrimination.

Stage Four
Change any rules or practices, including those in collective agreements, which stages 1 to 3 have identified as likely to give rise to discrimination in pay. It is recommended that this should be done in consultation with employees, trade unions or staff representatives where appropriate. Stages 1 to 3 may reveal that practices and procedures in relation to recruitment, selection and access to training have contributed to discrimination in pay; in that event, these matters should also be addressed.

Stage Five
Analyse the likely effects of any proposed changes in practice to the pay system before implementation, to identify and rectify any discrimination which could be caused.

Stage Six
Give equal pay to current employees. Where the review shows that some employees are not receiving equal pay for equal work and the reasons cannot be shown to be free of sex bias, then a plan must be developed for dealing with this.

Stage Seven
Set up a system of regular monitoring to allow checks to be made to pay practices.

Stage Eight
Draw up and publish an equal pay policy with provision for assessing the new pay system or modification to a system in terms of sex discrimination. Also, in the interests of transparency provide pay information as described on page 5 where this is not already usual practice.

THE PAY REVIEW PROCESS

The following section provides guidance on carrying out stages 1 to 3 of the review process.

Initial Analysis

26. Undertake a thorough analysis of pay systems. This will require a breakdown of all employees to include for example, sex, job title, and grade, whether part-time or full-time, with performance ratings and the distribution of basic pay and all other elements of the remuneration package, to identify potential vulnerability to claims of pay discrimination. This will reveal whether there are any vulnerabilities, and what their extent is, and enable a plan to be developed to correct any problems.

Appendix 1

Identification of Discriminatory Elements

27.a) Pay systems vary in complexity. Some have more elements than others. In the process of a review, each element will require examination against the statistical data generated at the initial analysis stage. Investigation may show discrimination in written rules and agreements, for example, limiting profit-related pay to employees who work above a minimum number of hours; or in the way processes are interpreted and applied, for example, failure to obtain adequate job descriptions during a job evaluation exercise.

b) Some of the more common pay elements are set out below, with examples of facts which could indicate problems of discrimination in pay and suggestions of further questions to be asked to reveal the cause of the pay difference and whether it can be shown to be free of sex bias in the terms explained under 'Material Factor Defence' and 'Objective Justification' on pages 4–5.

Basic Pay

28.a) *Problem:*
Women are consistently appointed at lower points on the pay scale than men.

Recommended Action:
Check the criteria which determine promotion or recruitment starting pay. Are these spelt out clearly?

Examine recruitment and promotion records for evidence of criteria which appear to be disadvantaging women. Can these criteria, e.g. qualification requirements, be justified objectively in terms of the demands of the job?

Check the records for evidence of sex bias in the application of managerial discretion.

b) *Problem:*
Women are paid less per hour than men for doing virtually the same job, but with different job and grade titles.

Recommended Action:
Check whether there are any reasons other than custom and practice for the difference; if so, are these reasons justified objectively?

c) *Problem:*
Women progress more slowly through incremental salary scales and seldom reach higher points.

Recommended Action:
Investigate the criteria applied for progression through the scale. Are these clearly understood? Does any particular criterion, e.g. length of service, work to the detriment of women more than men? If so, can the use of that criterion, or the extent to which it is relied on, be justified objectively?

Review the length of the incremental scale. Is the scale longer than it need be? Are there good practical reasons for a scale of that length?

d) *Problem:*
Women progress more slowly through non-incremental salary ranges and seldom reach higher points.

Recommended Action:
Check the criteria that applied when the structure was introduced and the current criteria for new recruits/promotees to each salary.

Check whether there is a clear, well-understood mechanism for progressing through the salary range.

Investigate the criteria for progression through the salary range and whether there are performance, qualification or other bars to upward movement. Can these be justified?

Review the length of the salary range. Can this be justified by real need?

Bonus/Premium Rates/Plus Elements

29.a) *Problem:*
Female and male manual workers receive the same basic pay but only jobs mainly done by men have access to bonus earnings and those mainly done by women do not.

Recommended Action:
Check the reason why. Does this reflect real differences, for example, in the value of the work or in productivity? Can it be justified objectively on grounds unrelated to sex?

b) *Problem:*
Where shift and overtime work is available and paid at a premium rate, fewer full-time women employees have access to this higher rated work.

Recommended Action:
Check that women and men employees have equal access to this work and, if not, that the reasons can be justified objectively.

c) *Problem:*
A smaller percentage of women employees receive enhanced rates for weekend and unsocial hours work.

Recommended Action:
Check the eligibility requirements for this work. Do any of these, for example, requiring that employees must be working full-time, work to the disadvantage of women? Can these requirements be objectively justified?

d) *Problem:*
Average female earnings under a variable payment system are lower than average male earnings (even where some women may have higher earnings than most men).

Recommended Action:
Review the design and operation of the variable payment system. Do these genuinely reflect the demands of the jobs and the productivity needs of the organisation?

In particular, check how factors such as down-time and personal needs breaks are dealt with in a variable payment system covering men and women.

Performance Pay

30.a) *Problem:*
The performance pay system is applied largely to employees of one sex only and results in a pay discrepancy to the advantage of that group.

Recommended Action:
Investigate the reasons why employees of the other sex are largely excluded from performance pay awards. Are these justified objectively for reasons unrelated to sex?

b) *Problem:*
Women receive lower performance ratings on average than men.

Recommended Action:
Investigate the performance rating system. Is it really likely that women would on average perform less well than men?
What are the possible reasons for this?

Review the criteria for performance rating. Do employees and managers know what these are? Do any of these disadvantage women? Do any of these disadvantage ethnic minority women in particular? If so, are these criteria justified objectively?

Monitor the ratings of individual managers. Do the results of the monitoring suggest a stereotypical interpretation of criteria? Are there appropriate controls on managerial discretion?

c) *Problem:*
Although women and men receive similar ratings, men achieve higher performance pay awards.

Recommended Action:
Investigate the reasons for this. Is it linked to managerial discretion? Are potentially discriminatory criteria being applied in the linking of ratings to pay? Can these be justified objectively?

Pay Based on Additional Skills or Training

31. *Problem:*
In practice only or mainly male employees receive this supplement.

Recommended Action:
Investigate the reasons for this. Are 'female' skills not recognised? Do women have the same access to any skills or training modules offered?

Review the training/skills/qualifications criteria. Do they genuinely reflect enhanced ability to carry out the job duties?

Review the procedures for implementing the supplement. Are managers and employees aware of the procedure? Are they operated fairly between men and women?

Pay Based on an Assessment of Individual Competencies

32. *Problem:*
There is a pay gap between the male and female employees who are assessed in this way

Recommended Action:
Review the competencies assessed. Are women and men assessed for the same set of competencies? Are the competencies being interpreted in a consistent way?

Are potentially discriminatory criteria being applied? If so, are these justified objectively?

Monitor the assessment of individual managers.

Pay Benefits

33.a) *Problem:*
A smaller percentage of women employees than men are covered by the organisation's sick pay pensions, low interest loans, share option schemes.

Recommended Action:
Check eligibility requirements. Are there restrictions which impact negatively on women? For example, are any of these limited to employees working over a minimum number of hours?

Can these requirements be justified objectively?

b) *Problem:*
Proportionately fewer women than men are in receipt of contractual benefits, for example, cars, telephone rentals and bills, rent and rates on tied accommodation, reimbursement of council tax in residential occupations.

Recommended Action:
Review the criteria for such benefits and any differences in treatment between male and female dominated groups. Can these differences be justified in terms of the needs of the work?

Review policies for the payment of such benefits between departments within the organisation. Are they consistent and can any differences be justified?

Grading

34.a) *Problem:*
Jobs predominantly occupied by women are graded lower than jobs predominantly occupied by men.

Recommended Action:
Review the method of grading. Was it devised for the current jobs? Is it adapted from a scheme used in a different organisation? What was the method used to determine job size? Some methods, e.g. felt-fair or whole job comparison, are potentially more discriminatory than others, e.g. analytical job evaluation. Are separate grading schemes used for jobs predominantly done by women and those predominantly done by men? If so, why and is this difference objectively justified?

b) *Problem:*
Some jobs held mainly by men are in higher grades because of 'recruitment and retention' problems.

Recommended Action:
Check that there is genuine evidence of a current 'recruitment and retention' problem.

Check that the whole of the difference in pay is attributable to market pressure. If not, investigate the reasons for the rest of the difference.

Consider amending the grading/pay structure so that the 'labour market' element of pay is 'transparent'.

c) *Problem:*
Red-circling, for example, where salary is protected when a job has been downgraded, is mainly applied to male employees.

Recommended Action:
Check the criteria for red-circling. Why do they favour male jobs? Can this be justified objectively?

Investigate whether other criteria which are more equitable could be used.

Ensure the difference in pay is phased out as soon as possible so that unequal pay is not unnecessarily perpetuated.

Appendix 1

Job Evaluation Method of Grading

35.a) *Problem:*
An analytical job evaluation scheme has resulted in jobs predominantly done by women being graded lower than those predominantly done by men.

Recommended Action:
Check that all features of the scheme's design and implementation took full account of the need to avoid sex bias. Was the job information collected consistently and accurately? Do the factors and weighting favour characteristics typical of jobs dominated by one sex? If so, is this justified objectively? Was training in the avoidance of sex bias given to those responsible for implementing the scheme?

b) *Problem:*
Jobs which have been evaluated as the same have widely differing salaries to the detriment of jobs largely held by women.

Recommended Action:
Investigate the possible causes, for example, how were the jobs assimilated to the evaluated structure?

Are different pay scales in use?

Could elements like additional skills payments or performance pay awards be responsible? What part do market rate or productivity considerations play? Can the cause of the difference be justified objectively?

Monitoring

36. Once the current pay systems have been reviewed it is important that periodic checks are made to ensure that discrimination does not creep in. This is best done by incorporating statistics on pay broken down by sex into the existing management information package, so that the necessary information can be checked regularly.

A POLICY ON EQUAL PAY

37. Good equal opportunities practice in employment not only helps to avoid unlawful or unfair discrimination but is also good for business and the right and fair thing to do. Many employers have adopted Equal Opportunities Policies in order to signal to employees and clients or customers that the organisation takes equality issues seriously. Equal pay is an important part of equality at work because pay is the most direct way an organisation values the contribution made by employees and should be covered in any Equal Opportunities Policy.

38. An Equal Pay Policy is an important way of showing commitment to achieving equal pay free of sex bias. The Policy should set out clear objectives which enable priorities for action to be identified and an effective programme to achieve them to be implemented. The internal pay review described on pages 9–10 would allow the identification of priorities.

39. It is good employment practice for employees to understand how their rate of pay is determined. Information about priorities and proposed action could be communicated to employees as part of the process of informing them about how the pay systems affect them individually. This will serve to assure employees that any sex bias in the payment system is being addressed.

40. Experience shows that the effectiveness of any Equal Pay Policy depends on the following:

A commitment to the policy by senior management.

A recognition by all staff involved in decisions about pay that they share responsibility for the proper implementation of the policy.

Effective training in identifying sex discrimination in pay for all staff who take decisions about the pay and grading of other employees.

Moving beyond a statement of intent to include a provision for a review of the payment system and periodic monitoring to ensure continuing effectiveness.

Information given to employees about the review and any plan of action drawn up as a result.

A suggested Equal Pay Policy is to be found at Annex A.

ANNEX A:
SUGGESTED EQUAL PAY POLICY

Equal Pay Statement

This organisation supports the principle of equal opportunities in employment and believes as part of that principle that male and female staff should receive equal pay for the same or broadly similar work, for work rated as equivalent and for work of equal value.

We understand that a right to equal pay between men and women free of sex bias is a fundamental principle of European Community law and is conferred by United Kingdom legislation.

We believe it is in our company's interest and good business practice that pay is awarded fairly and equitably.

We recognise that in order to achieve equal pay for employees doing equal work we should operate a pay system which is transparent, based on objective criteria and free from sex bias.

Action to implement policy

In order to put our commitment to equal pay into practice we will:

- Examine our existing and future pay practices for all our employees including those in non-standard employment and those who are absent on pregnancy and maternity leave.
- Carry out regular monitoring of the impact of our practices.
- Inform employees of how these practices work and how their own pay is arrived at.
- Provide training and guidance for managers and supervisory staff involved in decisions about pay and benefits.
- Discuss and agree the equal pay policy with employees, trade unions or staff representatives where appropriate.

We intend through the above action to avoid unfair discrimination, to reward fairly the skills, experience and potential of all staff and thereby to increase efficiency, productivity and competitiveness and enhance the organisation's reputation and image.

Appendix 2

CODE OF PRACTICE FOR THE ELIMINATION OF DISCRIMINATION ON THE GROUNDS OF SEX AND MARRIAGE AND THE PROMOTION OF EQUALITY OF OPPORTUNITY IN EMPLOYMENT

Editiorial note: This Code of Practice was issued by the Equal Opportunities Commission under the Sex Discrimination Act 1975 and was brought into effect on 30 April 1985 by the Sex Discrimination Code of Practice Order 1985, SI 1985/387.

INTRODUCTION

1. The EOC issues this Code of Practice for the following purposes:
   (a) for the elimination of discrimination in employment;
   (b) to give guidance as to what steps it is reasonably practicable for employers to take to ensure that their employees do not in the course of their employment act unlawfully contrary to the Sex Discrimination Act (SDA);
   (c) for the promotion of equality of opportunity between men and women in employment. The SDA prohibits discrimination against men, as well as against women. It also requires that married people should not be treated less favourably than single people of the same sex. It should be noted that the provisions of the SDA – and therefore this Code – apply to the UK-based subsidiaries of foreign companies.

PURPOSE OF THE CODE

2. The Code gives guidance to employers, trade unions and employment agencies on measures which can be taken to achieve equality. The chances of success of any organisation will clearly be improved if it seeks to develop the abilities of all employees, and the Code shows the close link which exists between equal opportunity and good employment practice. In some cases, an initial cost may be involved, but this should be more than compensated for by better relationships and better use of human resources.

SMALL BUSINESSES

3. The Code has to deal in general terms and it will be necessary for employers to adapt it in a way appropriate to the size and structure of their organisations. Small businesses, for example, will require much simpler procedures than organisations with complex structures and it may not always be reasonable for them to carry out all the Code's detailed recommendations. In adapting the Code's recommendations, small firms should, however, ensure that their practices comply with the Sex Discrimination Act.

EMPLOYERS' RESPONSIBILITY

4. **The primary responsibility at law rests with each employer to ensure that there is no unlawful discrimination.** It is important, however, that measures to eliminate

discrimination or promote equality of opportunity should be understood and supported by all employees. Employers are therefore recommended to involve their employees in equal opportunity policies.

INDIVIDUAL EMPLOYEES' RESPONSIBILITY

5. While the main responsibility for eliminating discrimination and providing equal opportunity is that of the employer, individual employees at all levels have responsibilities too. They must not discriminate or knowingly aid their employer to do so.

TRADE UNION RESPONSIBILITY

6. The full commitment of trade unions is essential for the elimination of discrimination and for the successful operation of an equal opportunities policy. Much can be achieved by collective bargaining and throughout the Code it is assumed that all the normal procedures will be followed.

7. It is recommended that unions should co-operate in the introduction and implementation of equal opportunities policies where employers have decided to introduce them, and should urge that such policies be adopted where they have not yet been introduced.

8. Trade Unions have a responsibility to ensure that their representatives and members do not unlawfully discriminate on grounds of sex or marriage in the admission or treatment of members. The guidance in this Code also applies to trade unions in their role as employers.

EMPLOYMENT AGENCIES

9. Employment agencies have a responsibility as suppliers of job applicants to avoid unlawful discrimination on the grounds of sex or marriage in providing services to clients.

   The guidance in this Code also applies to employment agencies in their role as employers.

DEFINITIONS

10. For case of reference, the main employment provisions of the Sex Discrimination Act, including definitions of direct and indirect sex and marriage discrimination, are provided in a Legal Annex to this Code.

PART 1: THE ROLE OF GOOD EMPLOYMENT PRACTICES IN ELIMINATING SEX AND MARRIAGE DISCRIMINATION

11. This section of the Code describes those good employment practices which will help to eliminate unlawful discrimination. It recommends the establishment and use of consistent criteria for selection, training, promotion, redundancy and dismissal which are made known to all employees. Without this consistency, decisions can be subjective and leave the way open for unlawful discrimination to occur.

Appendix 2

RECRUITMENT

12. It is unlawful: UNLESS THE JOB IS COVERED BY AN EXCEPTION*: TO DISCRIMINATE DIRECTLY OR INDIRECTLY ON THE GROUNDS OF SEX OR MARRIAGE – IN THE ARRANGEMENTS MADE FOR DECIDING WHO SHOULD BE OFFERED A JOB – IN ANY TERMS OF EMPLOYMENT – BY REFUSING OR OMITTING TO OFFER A PERSON EMPLOYMENT. [*Section 6(1)(a); 6(1)(b); 6(1)(c)*]†

13. It is therefore recommended that:

    (a) each individual should be assessed according to his or her personal capability to carry out a given job. It should not be assumed that men only or women only will be able to perform certain kinds of work;

    (b) any qualifications or requirements applied to a job which effectively inhibit applications from one sex or from married people should be retained only if they are justifiable in terms of the job to be done; [*Section 6(1)(a), together with section 1 (1)(b) or 3(1)(b)*]

    (c) any age limits should be retained only if they are necessary for the job. An unjustifiable age limit could constitute unlawful indirect discrimination, for example, against women who have taken time out of employment for child-rearing;

    (d) where trade unions uphold such qualifications or requirements as union policy, they should amend that policy in the light of any potentially unlawful effect.

GENUINE OCCUPATIONAL QUALIFICATIONS (GOQs)

14. It is unlawful: EXCEPT FOR CERTAIN JOBS WHEN A PERSON'S SEX IS A GENUINE OCCUPATIONAL QUALIFICATION (GOQ) FOR THAT JOB to select candidates on the ground of sex. [*Section 7(2); 7(3) and 7(4)*]

15. There are very few instances in which a job will qualify for a GOQ on the ground of sex. However, exceptions may arise, for example, where considerations of privacy and decency or authenticity are involved. The SDA expressly states that the need of the job for strength and stamina does not justify restricting it to men.

    When a GOQ exists for a job, it applies also to promotion, transfer, or training for that job, but cannot be used to justify a dismissal.

16. In some instances, the GOQ will apply to some of the duties only. A GOQ will not be valid, however, where members of the appropriate sex are already employed in sufficient numbers to meet the employer's likely requirements without undue inconvenience. For example, in a job where sales assistants may be required to undertake changing room duties, it might not be lawful to claim a GOQ in respect of all the assistants on the grounds that any of them might be required to undertake changing room duties from time to time.

17. It is therefore recommended that:

    – A job for which a GOQ was used in the past should be re-examined if the post falls vacant to see whether the GOQ still applies. Circumstances may well have changed, rendering the GOQ inapplicable.

* There are a number of exceptions to the requirements of the SDA, that employers must not discriminate against their employees or against potential employees.

† For the full text of section 6 or other sections of the Sex Discrimination Act referred to in this code, readers are advised to consult a copy of the Act which is available from Her Majesty's Stationery Office.

SOURCES OF RECRUITMENT

18. It is unlawful: UNLESS THE JOB IS COVERED BY AN EXCEPTION:

- TO DISCRIMINATE ON GROUNDS OF SEX OR MARRIAGE IN THE ARRANGEMENTS MADE FOR DETERMINING WHO SHOULD BE OFFERED EMPLOYMENT WHETHER RECRUITING BY ADVERTISEMENTS, THROUGH EMPLOYMENT AGENCIES, JOB CENTRES, OR CAREER OFFICES.
- TO IMPLY THAT APPLICATIONS FROM ONE SEX OR FROM MARRIED PEOPLE WILL NOT BE CONSIDERED. [*Section 6(1)(a))*]
- TO INSTRUCT OR PUT PRESSURE ON OTHERS TO OMIT TO REFER FOR EMPLOYMENT PEOPLE OF ONE SEX OR MARRIED PEOPLE UNLESS THE JOB IS COVERED BY AN EXCEPTION. [*Sections 39 and 40*]

It is also unlawful WHEN ADVERTISING JOB VACANCIES,

- TO PUBLISH OR CAUSE TO BE PUBLISHED AN ADVERTISEMENT WHICH INDICATES OR MIGHT REASONABLY BE UNDERSTOOD AS INDICATING AN INTENTION TO DISCRIMINATE UNLAWFULLY ON GROUNDS OF SEX OR MARRIAGE. [*Section 38*]

19. It is therefore recommended that:

Advertising

(a) job advertising should be carried out in such a way as to encourage applications from suitable candidates of both sexes. This can be achieved both by wording of the advertisements and, for example, by placing advertisements in publications likely to reach both sexes. All advertising material and accompanying literature relating to employment or training issues should be reviewed to ensure that it avoids presenting men and women in stereotyped roles. Such stereotyping tends to perpetuate sex segregation in jobs and can also lead people of the opposite sex to believe that they would be unsuccessful in applying for particular jobs;

(b) where vacancies are filled by promotion or transfer, they should be published to all eligible employees in such a way that they do not restrict applications from either sex;

(c) recruitment solely or primarily by word of mouth may unnecessarily restrict the choice of applicants available. The method should be avoided in a workforce predominantly of one sex, if in practice it prevents members of the opposite sex from applying;

(d) where applicants are supplied through trade unions and members of one sex only come forward, this should be discussed with the unions and an alternative approach adopted.

Careers Service Schools

20. When notifying vacancies to the Careers Service, employers should specify that these are open to both boys and girls. This is especially important when a job has traditionally been done exclusively or mainly by one sex. If dealing with single sex schools, they should ensure, where possible, that both boys' and girls' schools are approached: it is also a good idea to remind mixed schools that jobs are open to boys and girls.

Appendix 2

SELECTION METHODS

Tests

21. (a) If selection tests are used, they should be specifically related to job and or career requirements and should measure an individual's actual or inherent ability to do or train for the work or career;

    (b) Tests should be reviewed regularly to ensure that they remain relevant and free from any unjustifiable bias, either in content or in scoring mechanism.

Applications and Interviewing

22. It is unlawful: UNLESS THE JOB IS COVERED BY AN EXCEPTION: TO DISCRIMINATE ON GROUNDS OF SEX OR MARRIAGE BY REFUSING OR DELIBERATELY OMITTING TO OFFER EMPLOYMENT. [*Section 6(1)(c)*]

23. It is therefore recommended that:

    (a) employers should ensure that personnel staff line managers and all other employees who may come into contact with job applicants, should be trained in the provisions of the SDA, including the fact that it is unlawful to instruct or put pressure on others to discriminate;

    (b) applications from men and women should he processed in exactly the same way. For example, there should not be separate lists of male and female or married and single applicants. All those handling applications and conducting interviews should be trained in the avoidance of unlawful discrimination and records of interviews kept where practicable, showing why applicants were or were not appointed;

    (c) questions should relate to the requirements of the job. Where it is necessary to assess whether personal circumstances will affect performance of the job (for example, where it involves unsocial hours or extensive travel) this should be discussed objectively without detailed questions based on assumptions about marital status, children and domestic obligations. Questions about marriage plans or family intentions should not be asked, as they could be construed as showing bias against women. Information necessary for personnel records can be collected after a job offer has been made.

PROMOTION, TRANSFER AND TRAINING

24. It is unlawful: UNLESS THE JOB IS COVERED BY AN EXCEPTION, FOR EMPLOYERS TO DISCRIMINATE DIRECTLY OR INDIRECTLY ON THE GROUNDS OF SEX OR MARRIAGE IN THE WAY THEY AFFORD ACCESS TO OPPORTUNITIES FOR PROMOTION, TRANSFER OR TRAINING. [*Section 6(2)(a)*].

25. It is therefore recommended that:

    (a) where an appraisal system is in operation, the assessment criteria should be examined to ensure that they are not unlawfully discriminatory and the scheme monitored to assess how it is working in practice;

    (b) when a group of workers predominantly of one sex is excluded from an appraisal scheme, access to promotion, transfer and training and to other benefits should be reviewed, to ensure that there is no unlawful indirect discrimination;

(c) promotion and career development patterns are reviewed to ensure that the traditional qualifications are justifiable requirements for the job to be done. In some circumstances, for example, promotion on the basis of length of service could amount to unlawful indirect discrimination, as it may unjustifiably affect more women than men;

(d) when general ability and personal qualifies are the main requirements for promotion to a post, care should be taken to consider favourably candidates of both sexes with differing career patterns and general experience;

(e) rules which restrict or preclude transfer between certain jobs should be questioned and changed if they are found to be unlawfully discriminatory. Employees of one sex may be concentrated in sections from which transfers are traditionally restricted without real justification;

(f) policies and practices regarding selection for training, day release and personal development should be examined for unlawful direct and indirect discrimination. Where there is found to be an imbalance in training as between sexes, the cause should be identified to ensure that it is not discriminatory;

(g) age limits for access to training and promotion should be questioned.

HEALTH AND SAFETY LEGISLATION

26. Equal treatment of men and women may be limited by statutory provisions which require men and women to be treated differently. For example, the Factories Act 1961 places restrictions on the hours of work of female manual employees, although the Health and Safety Executive can exempt employers from these restrictions, subject to certain conditions. The Mines and Quarries Act 1954 imposes limitations on women's work and there are restrictions where there is special concern for the unborn child (e.g. lead and ionising radiation). However the broad duties placed on employers by the Health and Safety at Work, etc. Act 1974 makes no distinctions between men and women. Section 2(1) requires employers to ensure, so far as is reasonably practicable, the health and safety and welfare at work of all employees. SPECIFIC HEALTH AND SAFETY REQUIREMENTS UNDER EARLIER LEGISLATION ARE UNAFFECTED BY THE ACT. It is therefore recommended that: company policy should be reviewed and serious consideration given to any significant differences in treatment between men and women, and there should be well-founded reasons if such differences are maintained or introduced.

Note. Some statutory restrictions placed on adult women's hours of work were repealed in February 1987 and others in February 1988.

They now no longer apply. Paragraph 26 of the code is still relevant, however, to other health and safety legislation which requires men and women to be treated differently, and which has not been repealed.

TERMS OF EMPLOYMENT, BENEFITS, FACILITIES AND SERVICES

27. It is unlawful: UNLESS THE JOB IS COVERED BY AN EXCEPTION: TO DISCRIMINATE ON THE GROUNDS OF SEX OR MARRIAGE, DIRECTLY OR INDIRECTLY, IN THE TERMS ON WHICH EMPLOYMENT IS OFFERED OR IN AFFORDING ACCESS TO ANY BENEFITS*, FACILITIES OR SERVICES. [*Sections 6(1)(b); 6(2)(a);29*].

*Certain provisions relating to death and retirement are exempt from the Act.

28. It is therefore recommended that:

(a) all terms of employment, benefits, facilities and services are reviewed to ensure that there is no unlawful discrimination on grounds of sex or marriage. For example, part-time work, domestic leave, company cars and benefits for dependants should be available to both male and female employees in the same or not materially different circumstances.

29. In an establishment where part-timers are solely or mainly women, unlawful indirect discrimination may arise if, as a group, they are treated less favourably than other employees without justification. It is therefore recommended that:

(b) where part-time workers do not enjoy pro-rata pay or benefits with full-time workers, the arrangements should be reviewed to ensure that they are justified without regard to sex.

GRIEVANCES, DISCIPLINARY PROCEDURES AND VICTIMISATION

30. It is unlawful: TO VICTIMISE AN INDIVIDUAL FOR A COMPLAINT MADE IN GOOD FAITH ABOUT SEX OR MARRIAGE DISCRIMINATION OR FOR GIVING EVIDENCE ABOUT SUCH A COMPLAINT. [*Section 4(1); 4(2): and 4(3)*].

31. It is therefore recommended that:

(a) particular care is taken to ensure that an employee who has in good faith taken action under the Sex Discrimination Act or the Equal Pay Act does not receive less favourable treatment than other employees, for example by being disciplined or dismissed;

(b) employees should be advised to use the internal procedures, where appropriate, but this is without prejudice to the individual's right to apply to an employment tribunal within the statutory time limit i.e. before the end of the period of three months beginning when the act complained of was done. (There is no time limit if the victimisation is continuing);

(c) particular care is taken to deal effectively with all complaints of discrimination, victimisation or harassment. It should not be assumed that they are made by those who are over-sensitive.

DISMISSALS, REDUNDANCIES AND OTHER UNFAVOURABLE TREATMENT OF EMPLOYEES

32. It is unlawful: TO DISCRIMINATE DIRECTLY OR INDIRECTLY ON GROUNDS OF SEX OR MARRIAGE IN DISMISSALS OR BY TREATING AN EMPLOYEE UNFAVOURABLY IN ANY OTHER WAY. [*Section 6(2)(b)*]. It is therefore recommended that:

(a) care is taken that members of one sex are not disciplined or dismissed for performance or behaviour which would be overlooked or condoned in the other sex;

(b) redundancy procedures affecting a group of employees predominantly of one sex should be reviewed, so as to remove any effects which could be disproportionate and unjustifiable;

(c) conditions of access to voluntary redundancy benefit* should be made available on equal terms to male and female employees in the same or not materially different circumstances;

(d) where there is down-grading or short-time working (for example, owing to a change in the nature or volume of an employer's business) the arrangements should not unlawfully discriminate on the ground of sex;

(e) all reasonably practical steps should be taken to ensure that a standard of conduct or behaviour is observed which prevents members of either sex from being intimidated, harassed or otherwise subjected to unfavourable treatment on the ground of their sex.

PART 2: THE ROLE OF GOOD EMPLOYMENT PRACTICES IN PROMOTING EQUALITY OF OPPORTUNITY

33. This section of the Code describes those employment practices which help to promote equality of opportunity. It gives information about the formulation and implementation of equal opportunities policies. While such policies are not required by law, their value has been recognised by a number of employers who have voluntarily adopted them. Others may wish to follow this example.

FORMULATING AN EQUAL OPPORTUNITIES POLICY

34. An equal opportunities policy will ensure the effective use of human resources in the best interests of both the organisation and its employees. It is a commitment by an employer to the development and use of employment procedures and practices which do not discriminate on grounds of sex or marriage and which provide genuine equality of opportunity for all employees. The detail of the policy will vary according to size of the organisation.

IMPLEMENTING THE POLICY

35. An equal opportunities policy must be seen to have the active support of management at the highest level. To ensure that the policy is fully effective, the following procedure is recommended:

(a) the policy should be clearly stated and where appropriate, included in a collective agreement;

(b) overall responsibility for implementing the policy should rest with senior management;

(c) the policy should be made known to all employees and, where reasonably practicable, to all job applicants.

36. Trade unions have a very important part to play in implementing genuine equality of opportunity and they will obviously be involved in the review of established procedures to ensure that these are consistent with the law.

MONITORING

37. It is recommended that the policy is monitored regularly to ensure that it is working in practice. Consideration could be given to setting up a joint Management/Trade Union Review Committee.

*Certain provisions relating to death and retirement are exempt from the Act.

38. In a small firm with a simple structure it may be quite adequate to assess the distribution and payment of employees from personal knowledge.

39. In a large and complex organisation a more formal analysis will be necessary, for example, by sex, grade and payment in each unit. This may need to be introduced by stages as resources permit. Any formal analysis should be regularly updated and available to Management and Trade Unions to enable any necessary action to be taken.

40. Sensible monitoring will show, for example, whether members of one sex:

 (a) do not apply for employment or promotion, or that fewer apply than might be expected;

 (b) are not recruited, promoted or selected for training and development or are appointed/selected in a significantly lower proportion than their rate of application;

 (c) are concentrated in certain jobs, sections or departments.

POSITIVE ACTION

Recruitment, Training and Promotion

41. Selection for recruitment or promotion must be on merit irrespective of sex. However, the Sex Discrimination Act does allow certain steps to redress the effects of previous unequal opportunities. Where there have been few or no members of one sex in particular work in their employment for the previous 12 months, the Act allows employers to give special encouragement to, and provide specific training for, the minority sex. Such measures are usually described as Positive Action. [*Section 48*].

42. Employers may wish to consider positive measures such as:

 (a) training their own employees (male or female) for work which is traditionally the preserve of the other sex, for example, training women for skilled manual or technical work;*

 (b) positive encouragement to women to apply for management posts – special courses may be needed;

 (c) advertisements which encourage applications from the minority sex, but make it clear that selection will be on merit without reference to sex;

 (d) notifying job agencies, as part of a Positive Action Programme that they wish to encourage members of one sex to apply for vacancies, where few or no members of that sex are doing the work in question.

 In these circumstances, job agencies should tell both men and women about the posts and, in addition, let the under-represented sex know that applications from them are particularly welcome. Withholding information from one sex in an attempt to encourage applications from the opposite sex would be unlawful.

* *Note.* Section 47 of the SDA 1975 allowed training bodies to run single-sex courses. Since November 1986, this has applied also to other persons including employers. Single-sex training need therefore no longer be confined to an organisation's own employees, as indicated in paragraph 42(a) of the Code, but may be extended to other groups – for example, job applicants or school leavers. Positive Action in recruitment for employment however, is still not allowed.

Other Working Arrangements

43. There are other forms of action which could assist both employer and employee by helping to provide continuity of employment to working parents, many of whom will have valuable experience or skills. Employers may wish to consider with their employees whether:

(a) certain jobs can be carried out on a part-time or flexi-time basis;

(b) personal leave arrangements are adequate and available to both sexes. It should not be assumed that men may not need to undertake domestic responsibilities on occasion, especially at the time of childbirth;

(c) child-care facilities are available locally or whether it would be feasible to establish nursery facilities on the premises or combine with other employers to provide them;

(d) residential training could be facilitated for employees with young children. For example, where this type of training is necessary, by informing staff who are selected well in advance to enable them to make childcare and other personal arrangements; employers with their own residential training centres could also consider whether childcare facilities might he provided;

(e) the statutory maternity leave provisions could be enhanced, for example, by reducing the qualifying service period, extending the leave period, or giving access to part-time arrangements on return.

These arrangements, and others, are helpful to both sexes but are of particular benefit to women in helping them to remain in gainful employment during the years of child-rearing.

Appendix 3

EU RECOMMENDATION ON SEXUAL HARRASSMENT

EQUAL TREATMENT FOR WOMEN AND MEN

Protection of the dignity of women and men at work

Editorial note: These recommendations were issued by the European Union.

1) OBJECTIVE
To promote greater awareness of the problem of sexual harrassment at work and its consequences: to draw attention to the code of conduct and recommend application of the same.

2) COMMUNITY MEASURES
Commission Recommendation 92/131/EEC of 27 November 1991 on the protection of the dignity of women and men at work.

3) CONTENTS
1. The Member States are recommended to take action to promote awareness that conduct of a sexual nature, or other conduct based on sex and affecting dignity, is unacceptable.

2. Sexual harassment is defined as:

conduct which is unwanted, unreasonable and offensive to the recipient; the fact that a person's rejection of, or submission to, such conduct on the part of employers or workers (including superiors or colleagues) is used explicitly or implicitly as a basis for a decision which affects that person's access to vocational training, access to employment, continued employment or salary; any conduct which creates an intimidating, hostile or humiliating work environment for the recipient.

3. Such conduct may, in certain circumstances, be contrary to the principle of equal treatment within the meaning of Articles 3, 4 and 5 of Council Directive 76/207/EEC on equal treatment.

4. Member States are called on to take action in the public sector to implement the Commission's code of conduct, with such action serving as an example to the private sector. Member States should also encourage employers and employee representatives to develop measures to implement the code of conduct.

5. The Commission is to draw up a report based on the information forwarded by the Member States concerning the measures taken, with the Commission having to be notified of these within three years of the date on which the Recommendation is adopted.

4) DEADLINE FOR IMPLEMENTATION OF THE LEGISLATION IN THE MEMBER STATES
Not applicable.

5) DATE OF ENTRY INTO FORCE (if different from the above)

6) REFERENCES
Official Journal L 49, 24.02.1992

7) FOLLOW-UP WORK
Declaration on the implementation of the Recommendation adopted by the Council on 19 December 1991.

8) COMMISSION IMPLEMENTING MEASURES

EQUAL TREATMENT FOR MEN AND WOMEN
Preventing sexual harassment at work

---

1) OBJECTIVE
To seek the opinion of the social partners on the question of protecting the dignity of men and women at work (referred to as "sexual harassment").

2) COMMUNITY MEASURE
Commission communication of 24 July 1996 concerning the consultation of management and labour on the prevention of sexual harassment at work.

3) CONTENTS
1. In accordance with Article 4 of the Recommendation of 27 November 1991 (see summary, 9.14a), the Member States informed the Commission in 1994 and in 1995 of measures taken to promote awareness of the fact that sexual harassment is unacceptable. These are the elements used in drawing up the "Evaluation report concerning the Commission Recommendation on the protection of the dignity of men and women at work" which is attached to the communication.

2. As sexual harassment is an affront to the dignity of the individual and a hindrance to productivity within the European Union, it constitutes an obstacle to an efficient labour market in which men and women work together.

3. Some specific groups are particularly vulnerable: divorced or separated women, new entrants to the labour market, those with irregular or precarious employment, women with disabilities, women from racial minorities, homosexuals and young men.

4. Given the growing trend towards men and women working together at similar levels, many cases of sexual harassment now take place between persons at the same level in the hierarchy, not always between employees and their superiors.

5. Sexual harassment has adverse consequences for all:

- workers subject to it, in terms of health, confidence, morale, performance and career prospects;
- workers not themselves the object thereof but who are witness to it or have knowledge of it, in terms of working environment, etc;
- employers, in terms of economic efficiency, negative publicity and possible legal implications.

6. The problem of sexual harassment has in recent years been acknowledged in a majority of the Member States and has resulted in the enactment or preparation of legislative acts in Belgium, France, Germany, Italy, Ireland, the Netherlands and Spain and in collective agreements in some sectors in Spain, the United Kingdom, the Netherlands and Denmark.

7. The evaluation report concludes, however, that the Recommendation and the code of practice have not led to the adoption of sufficient measures to ensure a working environment where sexual harassment can be effectively prevented and combated. Since it deals with an affront to

the dignity of the individual and an obstacle to productivity, the problem deserves to be tackled at European level.

8. The evaluation report underlines the need for a global approach:

- to highlight points of agreement and differences between different national policies;
- to enable the social partners to play a part in elaborating any form of future action;
- to work towards the adoption of a binding instrument setting out a common plan to be adapted to each country's achievements, needs and preferences.

9. The practical knowledge and experience of the social partners in implementing measures to combat sexual harassment are widely recognised. Their action could take the form of a collective agreement at European level. In the light of their reaction to this communication, the Commission will consider what further action is required.

4) DEADLINE FOR IMPLEMENTATION OF THE LEGISLATION IN THE MEMBER STATES
Not applicable.

5) DATE OF ENTRY INTO FORCE (if different from the above)

6) REFERENCES
Commission communication COM(96) 373 final
Not published in the Official Journal.

7) FOLLOW-UP WORK
On 19 March 1997, the Commission adopted a communication initiating the second-stage consultation of management and labour on the prevention of sexual harassment at work [SEC(97) 568 final, not published in the Official Journal].

In the first round of consultations, which began in July 1996, replies were received from 17 of the 39 employer and trade union organisations consulted. A majority recognised that sexual harassment is a widespread problem which must be prevented in the workplace for the sake of both the individual and the company.

However, opinions differed on the best ways of dealing with the problem:

- the employers' organisations regarded the steps taken at national level as a good basis for further action, in line with the principle of subsidiarity;
- the trade union organisations considered that very little had been done at national level and that this would also be the case in future if a binding Community instrument was not adopted.

In the consultation document, the Commission presents evidence of the occurrence of sexual harassment and highlights the ineffectiveness of the national legislation, which is primarily repressive and thus provides remedies, by either civil or penal procedures, only for severe isolated cases of sexual harassment. The Commission favours a comprehensive prevention policy, with rules and procedures that are specifically applicable to the context of the workplace.

The proposal on which the Commission seeks the opinions of the social partners covers three points:

- a legal definition of sexual harassment;
- a framework of minimum standards setting out the main steps to be taken to prevent harassment;
- a system of help and advice for victims (with the appointment of counsellors at the workplace).

The Commission has already stated its commitment, should the social partners be unable to conclude an agreement at European level, to seeking other ways of preventing sexual harassment (possibly involving the adoption of a binding legal instrument). However, it will not take a final decision until it has considered the comments received during the consultation procedure.

8) COMMISSION IMPLEMENTING MEASURES

EQUAL TREATMENT FOR WOMEN AND MEN
Code of practice – dignity of women and men at work

---

1) OBJECTIVE
To provide practical guidance to employers, trade unions and employees with a view to clamping down on sexual harassment, and to ensure that adequate procedures are readily available to deal with the problem and prevent its recurrence. To encourage men and women to respect one another's human integrity.

2) COMMUNITY MEASURES
Commission code of practice on sexual harassment.

3) CONTENTS
1. The Commission restates the general definition of sexual harassment contained in its Recommendation. National judges will still have to decide whether cases brought to their attention fall within this category and are to be regarded as a criminal offence, an infringement of statutory obligations (especially in health and safety matters) or a contravention of obligations imposed on employers by contract or otherwise. It calls on employers in the public and private sectors, trade unions and employees to follow the guidelines of the code and to include appropriate clauses in collective bargaining agreements.

2. Recommendations to employers

a) Prevention

Employers should issue a policy statement which expressly states that sexual harassment will not be permitted or condoned and that employees have a right to complain about it should it occur. The policy statement should leave no doubt as to what is considered inappropriate behaviour which may, in certain circumstances, be unlawful. It should also explain the procedure to be followed for making a complaint or obtaining assistance, and should specify the disciplinary measures applicable. It should provide assurance that complaints will be dealt with seriously, expeditiously and confidentially, and that complainants will be protected against victimization. Once it has been drawn up, the statement must be communicated to everyone concerned, so as to ensure the widest possible awareness. Managers are to explain the organization's policy to their staff, and are expected to take appropriate measures, act supportively towards victims and provide any information required. The provision of training for managers and supervisors is an important means of combating sexual harassment.

b) Procedures

Clear and precise procedures must be developed, giving practical guidance on how to deal with this problem. Such guidance must draw the employees' attention to their legal rights and to any time limits within which they must be exercised. Employees should be advised to try first of all to resolve the problem informally by explaining, either themselves or through a third party, that the behaviour in question is not welcome, offends them and interferes with their work. If the unwelcome conduct persists, there will be grounds for making a complaint. To this end, it is recommended that a formal procedure for dealing with complaints be set up, in which employees can place their trust and which specifies the person to whom the complaint should be brought. It is also recommended that someone be designated to provide advice and assistance. The complainant and the alleged harasser have the right to be represented by a trade union representative, a friend or a colleague. Employers should monitor and review these procedures in order to ensure that they are working effectively. Investigations of complaints are to be carried out with sensitivity by independent persons, with due respect for the rights of the complainant and the alleged harasser. Complaints must be resolved speedily and confidentially at the end of an investigation focusing on the facts. Any violation of the organization's policy should be treated as a disciplinary offence. Disciplinary rules should make clear what is regarded as inappropriate behaviour and should indicate the range of penalties. Any victimization or retaliation against an employee bringing a complaint in good faith is to be considered as a disciplinary offence.

3. Recommendations to trade unions

Sexual harassment is a trade union issue which must be treated seriously and sympathetically when complaints arise. Trade unions are expected to formulate and issue clear policy statements on sexual harassment and to take steps to raise awareness of the problem, in order to help create a climate in which sexual harassment is neither condoned nor ignored. They should declare that sexual harassment is inappropriate behaviour and should inform staff about its consequences. It is also a good idea to ensure that there are sufficient female representatives to support women subjected to sexual harassment.

4. Employees' responsibilities

Employees have a clear role to play in discouraging any form of reprehensible behaviour and making it unacceptable. They can contribute to preventing sexual harassment through awareness and sensitivity towards the issue and by ensuring that standards of conduct for themselves and for colleagues do not cause offence. Employees should lend support to victims of harassment and should inform management and/or their staff representative through the appropriate channels.

4) DEADLINE FOR IMPLEMENTATION OF THE LEGISLATION IN THE MEMBER STATES
Not applicable.

5) DATE OF ENTRY INTO FORCE (if different from the above).

6) REFERENCES
Official Journal L 49, 24.02.1992.

7) FOLLOW-UP WORK
Declaration on the implementation of the code adopted by the Council on 19 December 1991.

8) COMMISSION IMPLEMENTING MEASURES

Appendix 4

CODE OF PRACTICE FOR THE ELIMINATION OF RACIAL DISCRIMINATION AND THE PROMOTION OF EQUALITY OF OPPORTUNITY IN EMPLOYMENT

Editorial note: The Code was issued by and is reproduced here with the kind permission of the Commission for Racial Equality. This Code is currently being revised. An additional new Code is being prepared to accompany the Race Relations (Amendment) Bill when it comes into force in 2001.

INTRODUCTION

1. THE PURPOSE AND STATUS OF THE CODE

This Code aims to give practical guidance which will help employers, trade unions, employment agencies and employees to understand not only the provisions of the Race Relations Act and their implications, but also how best they can implement policies to eliminate racial discrimination and to enhance equality of opportunity.

The Code does not impose any legal obligations itself, nor is it an authoritative statement of the law – that can only be provided by the courts and tribunals. If, however, if its recommendations are not observed, this may result in breaches of the law where the act or omission falls within any of the specific prohibitions of the Act. Moreover, its provisions are admissible in evidence in any proceedings under the Race Relations Act before an industrial tribunal and if any provision appears to the tribunal to be relevant to a question arising in the proceedings it must be taken into account in determining that question. If employers take the steps that are set out in the Code to prevent their employees from doing acts of unlawful discrimination they may avoid liability for such acts in any legal proceedings brought against them.

Employees of all racial groups have a right to equal opportunity. Employers ought to provide it. To do so is likely to involve some expenditure, at least in staff time and effort. But if a coherent and effective programme of equal opportunity is developed it will help industry to make full use of the abilities if its entire workforce. It is therefore particularly important for all those concerned – employers, trade unions and employees alike – to cooperate with good will in adopting and giving effect to measures for securing such equality. We welcome the commitment already made by the CBI and TUC to the principle of equal opportunity. The TUC has recommended a model equal opportunity clause for inclusion in collective agreements and the CBI has published a statement favouring the application by companies of constructive equal opportunity policies.

A concerted policy to eliminate both race and sex discrimination often provides the best approach. Guidance on equal opportunities between men and women is the responsibility of the Equal Opportunities Commission.

2. APPLICATION OF THE CODE

The Race Relations Act applies to all employers. The Code itself is not restricted to what is required by law, but contains recommendations as well. Some of its detailed provisions may need to be adapted to suit particular circumstances. Any adaptations that are made, however, should be fully consistent with the Code's general intentions.

2.2 SMALL FIRMS

In many small firms employers have close contact with their staff and there will therefore be less need of formality in assessing whether equal opportunity is being achieved, for example, in such matters as arrangements for monitoring. Moreover, it may not be reasonable to expect small firms to have the resources and administrative systems to carry out the Code's detailed recommendations. In complying with the Race Relations Act, small firms should, however, ensure that their practices are consistent with the Code' general intentions.

3. UNLAWFUL DISCRIMINATION

The Race Relations Act 1976 makes it unlawful to discriminate against a person, directly or indirectly, in the field of employment.

Direct discrimination consists of treating a person, on racial grounds*, less favourably than others are or would be treated in the same or similar circumstances.

Segregating a person from others on racial grounds constitutes less favourable treatment.

Indirect discrimination consists of applying in any circumstances covered by the Act a requirement or condition which, although applied equally to persons of all racial groups, is such that a considerably smaller proportion of a particular racial group can comply with it and it cannot be shown to be justifiable on other than racial grounds. Possible examples are:

- A rule about clothing or uniforms which disproportionately disadvantages a racial group cannot be justified;
- An employer who requires higher language standards than are needed for safe and effective performance of the job.

The definition of indirect discrimination is complex, and it will not be spelt out in full in every relevant section of the Code. Reference will be only to the terms 'indirect discrimination' or 'discriminate indirectly'.

Discrimination by victimisation is also unlawful under the Act. For example, a person is victimised if he or she is given less favourable treatment than others in the same circumstances because it is suspected or known that he or she has brought proceeding under the Act, or given evidence or information relating to such proceedings, or alleged that discrimination has occurred.

4. THE CODE AND GOOD EMPLOYMENT PRACTICE

Many of the Code's provisions show the closed links between equal opportunity and good employment practice. For example, selection criteria which are relevant to job requirements and carefully observed selection procedures not only help to ensure that individuals are appointed according to their suitability for the job and without regard to racial group; they are also part of good employment practice. In the absence of consistent selection procedures and criteria, decisions are often too subjective and racial discrimination can easily occur.

5. POSITIVE ACTION

Opportunities for employees to develop their potential through encouragement, training and careful assessments are also part of good employment practice. Many employees from the racial minorities have potential which, perhaps because of previous discrimination and other causes of disadvantage, they have not been able to realise, and which is not reflected in their qualifications and experience. Where members of particular racial groups have been under-represented over the previous twelve months in particular work, employers and specific training bodies† are allowed under the Act to encourage them to take advantage of opportuni-

* Racial grounds are the grounds of race, colour, nationality, – including citizenship – or ethnic or national origins, and groups defined by reference to these grounds are referred to as racial groups.

† Section 7(3) of the Employment Act 1989 has amended section 37 of the Race Relations Act with effect from 16/01/90. Section 7(3) now allows any person including employers (not just training bodies) to provide positive action training without the need for any designation as long as the criteria on underrepresentation are met.

ties for doing that work and to provide training to enable them to attain the skills needed for it. In the case of employers, such training can be provided for persons currently in their employment (as defined by the Act) and in certain circumstances for others too, for example if they have been designated as training bodies. This Code encourages employers to make use of these provisions.

6. GUIDANCE PAPERS

The guidance papers referred to in the footnotes contain additional guidance on specific issues but do not form part of the statutory Code.

PART ONE
THE RESPONSIBILITIES OF EMPLOYERS

Responsibility for providing equal opportunity for all job applicants and employees rests primarily with employers. To this end it is recommended that they should adopt, implement and monitor an equal opportunity policy to ensure that there is no unlawful discrimination and that equal opportunity is genuinely available*.

This policy should be clearly communicated to all employees – e.g. through notice boards, circulars, contracts of employment or written notifications to individual employees.

EQUAL OPPORTUNITY POLICIES

An equal opportunity policy aims to ensure that:

(a) No job applicant or employee receives less favourable treatment than another on racial grounds.
(b) No applicant or employee is placed at a disadvantage by requirements or conditions which have a disproportionately adverse effect on his or her racial group and which cannot be shown to be justifiable on other than racial grounds.
(c) Where appropriate, and where permissible under the Race Relations Act, employees of underrepresented racial groups are given training and encouragement to achieve equal opportunity within the organisation.

In order to ensure that an equal opportunity policy is fully effective, the following action by employers is recommended:

(a) Allocating overall responsibility of the policy to a member of senior management.
(b) Discussing and, where appropriate, agreeing with trade union or employee representatives the policy's contents and implementation.
(c) Ensuring that the policy is known to all employees and if possible, to all job applicants.
(d) Providing training and guidance for supervisory staff and other relevant decision makers (such as personnel and line managers, foremen, gatekeepers and receptionists), to ensure that they understand their position in law and under company policy.
(e) Examining and regularly reviewing existing procedures and criteria and changing them where they find that they are actually or potentially unlawfully discriminatory.
(f) Making an initial analysis of the workforce and regularly monitoring the application of the policy with the aid of analyses of the ethnic origins of the workforce and of job applicants in accordance with the guidance.

* The CRE has issued guidance papers on equal opportunity policies: 'Equal Opportunity in Employment' and 'Monitoring an Equal Opportunity Policy'.

Appendix 4

RECRUITMENT, PROMOTION, TRANSFER, TRAINING & DISMISSAL

SOURCES OF RECRUITMENT

ADVERTISEMENTS

When advertising job vacancies, it is unlawful for employers to publish an advertisement which indicates, or could reasonably be understood as indicating, an intention to discriminate against applicants from a particular racial group. (For exceptions see the Race Relations Act.)

It is therefore recommended that:

(a) Employers should not confine advertisements unjustifiably to those areas or publications which would exclude or disproportionately reduce the numbers of applicants of a particular racial group.
(b) Employers should avoid prescribing requirements such as length of residence or experience in the UK and where a particular qualification is required it should be made clear that a fully comparable qualification obtained overseas is as acceptable as a UK qualification.

In order to demonstrate their commitment to equality of opportunity it is recommended that where employers send literature to applicants, this should include a statement that they are equal opportunity employers.

EMPLOYMENT AGENCIES

When recruiting through employment agencies, job centres, career offices and schools, it is unlawful for employers:

(a) To give instructions to discriminate, for example by indicating that certain groups will or will not be preferred. (For exceptions see the Race Relations Act.)
(b) To bring pressure on them to discriminate against members of a particular racial group. (For exceptions see the Race Relations Act.)

In order to avoid indirect discrimination it is recommended that employers should not confine recruitment unjustifiably to those agencies, job centres, careers offices and schools which, because of their particular source of applicants, provide only or mainly applicants of a particular racial group.

OTHER SOURCES

It is unlawful to use recruitment methods which exclude or disproportionately reduce the numbers of applicants of a particular racial group and which cannot be shown to be justifiable. It is therefore recommended that employers should not recruit through the following methods:

(a) Recruitment, solely or in the first instance, through the recommendations of existing employees where the workforce concerned is wholly or predominately white or black and the labour market is multi-racial.
(b) Procedures by which applicants are mainly or wholly supplied through trade unions where this means that only members of particular racial group, or a disproportionately high number of them, come foreword.

SOURCES FOR PROMOTION AND TRAINING

It is unlawful for employers to restrict access to opportunities for promotion or training in such a way which is discriminatory. It is therefore recommended that:

(a) Job and training vacancies and the application procedure should be made known to all eligible employees, and not in such a way as to exclude or disproportionately reduce the numbers of applicants from a particular racial group.

SELECTION PROCESS

It is unlawful to discriminate*, not only in recruitment, promotion, transfer and training, but also in the arrangements made for recruitment and in the ways of affording access to opportunities for promotion, transfer and training.

SELECTION CRITERIA AND TESTS

In order to avoid direct or indirect discrimination, it is recommended that selection criteria and tests are examined to ensure that they are related to job requirements and are not unlawfully discriminatory. For example:

(a) A standard of English higher than that needed for the safe and effective performance of the job or clearly demonstrable career pattern should not be required, or a higher level of education qualification than is needed.

(b) In particular, employers should not disqualify applicants because they are unable to complete an application form unassisted unless personal completion of the form is a valid test of the standard of English required for safe and effective performance of the job.

(c) Overseas degrees, diplomas and other qualifications which are comparable with UK qualifications should be acceptable as equivalents, and not simply be assumed to be of an inferior quality.

(d) Selection tests which contain irrelevant questions or exercises on matter which may be unfamiliar to racial minority applicants should not be used (for example, general knowledge questions on matters more likely to be familiar to indigenous applicants).

(e) Selection tests should be checked to ensure that they are related to the job's requirements, i.e. an individual's test markings should measure ability to do or train for the job in question.

TREATMENT OF APPLICANTS, SHORTLISTING, INTERVIEWING AND SELECTION

In order to avoid direct or indirect discrimination it is recommended that:

(a) Gate, reception and personnel staff should be instructed not to treat casual or formal applicants from particular racial groups less favourably than others. These instructions should be confirmed in writing.

(b) In addition, staff responsible for shortlisting, interviewing an selection candidates should be:

- clearly informed of selection criteria and of the need for their consistent application;
- given guidance or training to he effects which generalised assumptions and prejudices about race can have on selection decisions;
- made aware of the possible misunderstandings that can occur in interviews between persons of different cultural background.

(c) Wherever possible, shortlisting and interviewing should not be done by one person alone but should at least be checked at a more senior level.

GENUINE OCCUPATIONAL QUALIFICATION

Selection on racial grounds is allowed in certain jobs where being of a particular racial group is a genuine occupational qualification for that job. An example is where the holder of a particular job provides persons of a racial group with personal services promoting their welfare, and those services can most effectively be provided by a person of that group.

* It should be noted that discrimination in selection to achieve 'racial balance' is not allowed. The clause in the 1968 Race Relations Act which allowed such discrimination for the purpose of securing or preserving a reasonable balance of persons of different racial groups in the establishment is not included in the 1976 Race Relations Act.

Appendix 4

TRANSFERS AND TRAINING

In order to avoid direct or indirect discrimination it is recommended that:

(a) Staff responsible for selecting employees for transfer to other jobs should be instructed to apply selection criteria without unlawful discrimination.
(b) Industry or company agreements and arrangements of custom and practice on job transfers should be examined and amended if they are found to contain requirements or conditions which appear to be indiscriminatory. For example, if employees of particular racial groups are concentrated in particular sections, the transfer arrangements should be examined to see if they are unjustifiably and unlawfully restrictive and amended if necessary.
(c) Staff responsible for selecting employees for training, whether induction, promotion or skill training should be instructed not to discriminate on racial grounds.
(d) Selection criteria for training opportunities should be examined to ensure that they are not indirectly discriminatory.

DISMISSAL (INCLUDING REDUNDANCY) AND OTHER DETRIMENT

It is unlawful to discriminate on racial grounds in dismissal, or other detriment to an employee.

It is therefore recommended that:

(a) Staff responsible for selecting employees for dismissal, including redundancy, should be instructed not to discriminate on racial grounds.
(b) Selection criteria for redundancies should be examined to ensure that they are not indirectly discriminatory.

PERFORMANCE APPRAISALS

It is unlawful to discriminate on racial grounds in appraisals of employee performance.

It is recommended that:

(a) Staff responsible for performance appraisals should be instructed not to discriminate on racial grounds.
(b) Assessment criteria should be examined to ensure that they are not unlawfully discriminatory.

TERMS OF EMPLOYMENT, BENEFITS, FACILITIES AND SERVICES

It is unlawful to discriminate on racial grounds in affording terms of employment and providing benefits, facilities and services for employees. It is therefore recommended that:

(a) All staff concerned with these aspects of employment should be instructed accordingly.
(b) The criteria governing eligibility should be examined to ensure that they are not unlawfully discriminatory.

In addition, employees may request extended leave from time to time in order to visit relations in their country of origin or who have emigrated to other countries. Many employers have policies which allow annual leave entitlement to be accumulated, or extra unpaid leave to be taken to meet these circumstances. Employers should take care to apply such policies consistently and without unlawful discrimination.

GRIEVANCE, DISPUTES AND DISCIPLINARY PROCEDURES

It is unlawful to discriminate in the operation of grievance, disputes and disciplinary procedures, for example by victimising an individual through disciplinary measures because he or she has complained about racial discrimination, or given evidence about such a complaint.

Employers should not ignore or treat lightly grievances from members of particular racial groups on the assumption that they are over-sensitive about discrimination.

It is recommended that in applying disciplinary procedures consideration should be given to the possible effect on an employee's behaviour of the following:

— Racial abuse or other racial provocation.
— Communication and comprehension difficulties.
— Differences in cultural background or behaviour.

CULTURAL AND RELIGIOUS NEEDS

Where employees have particular cultural and religious needs which conflict with existing work requirements, it is recommended that employers should consider whether it is reasonably practicable to vary or adapt these requirements to enable such needs to be met. For example, it is recommended that they should not refuse employment to a turbanned Sikh because he could not comply with unjustifiable uniform requirements.

Other examples of such needs are:

(a) Observance of prayer times and religious holidays*.
(b) Wearing of dress such as sarees and the trousers worn by Asian women.

Although the Act does not specifically cover religious discrimination, work requirements would generally be unlawful if they have a disproportionately adverse effect on particular racial groups and cannot be shown to be justifiable†.

COMMUNICATIONS AND LANGUAGE TRAINING FOR EMPLOYEES

Although there is no legal requirement to provide language training, difficulties in communication can endanger equal opportunity in the workforce. In addition, good communications can improve efficiency, promotion prospects and safety and health and create a better understanding between employers, employees and unions. Where the workforce includes current employees whose English is limited it is recommended that steps are taken to ensure that communications are as effective as possible.

These should include, where reasonably practicable:

(a) Provision of interpretation and translation facilities, for example, in the communication of grievance and other procedures, and of terms of employment.
(b) Training in English language and in communication skills.‡
(c) Training for managers and supervisors in the background and culture of racial minority groups.
(d) The use of alternative or additional methods of communication, where employees find it difficult to understand heath and safely requirements, for example:

    — Safety signs; translations of safety notices.
    — Instructions through interpreters.
    — Instruction combined with industrial language training.

* The CRE has issued a guidance paper entitled 'Religious Observance by Muslim Employees'.

† Genuinely necessary safety requirements may not constitute unlawful discrimination.

‡ Industrial language training is provided by a network of local education authority units throughout the country. Full details of the courses and the comprehensive services offered by these units are available from the National Centre for Industrial Language Training, The Havelock Centre, Havelock Road, Southall, Middlesex.

Appendix 4

INSTRUCTIONS AND PRESSURE TO DISCRIMINATE

It is unlawful to instruct or put pressure on others to discriminate on racial grounds.

(a) An example of unlawful instruction is:

— An instruction from a personnel or line manger to junior staff to restrict the number of employees from a particular racial group in any particular work.

(b) An example of pressure to discriminate is:

— An attempt by a shop steward or group of workers to induce an employer not to recruit members of particular racial groups, for example by threatening industrial action.

It is also unlawful to discriminate in response to such instructions or pressure.

The following recommendations are made to avoid unlawful instructions and pressure to discriminate:

(a) Guidance should be given to all employees, and particularly those in positions of authority or influence, on the relevant provisions of the law.
(b) Decision-makers should be instructed not to give way to pressure to discriminate.
(c) Giving instructions or bringing pressure to discriminate should be treated as a disciplinary offence.

VICTIMISATION

It is unlawful to victimise individuals who have made allegations or complaints of racial discrimination or provided information about such discrimination, for example by disciplining them or dismissing them.

It is recommended that guidance on this aspect of the law should be given to all employees and particularly to those in positions of influence or authority.

MONITORING EQUAL OPPORTUNITY*

It is recommended that employers should regularly monitor the effects of selection decisions and personnel practices and procedures in order to asses whether equal opportunity is being achieved.

The information needed for effective monitoring may be obtained in a number of ways. It will best be provided by records showing the ethnic origins of existing employees and job applicants. It is recognised that the need for detailed information and the methods of collecting it will vary according to the circumstances of individual establishments. For example, in small firms or in firms in areas with little or no racial minority settlement it will often be adequate to assess the distribution of employees from personal knowledge and visual identification.

It is open to employers to adopt the method of monitoring which is best suited to their needs and circumstances, but whichever method is adopted, they should be able to show that it is effective. In order to achieve the full commitment of all concerned the chosen method should be discussed and agreed, where appropriate, with trade union or employee representatives.

Employers should ensure that information on individual's ethnic origins is collected for the purpose of monitoring equal opportunity alone and is protected from misuse.

The following is the comprehensive method recommended by the CRE†.

* See the CRE's guide on 'Monitoring an Equal Opportunity Policy'.

† This is outlined in detail in 'Monitoring of Equal Opportunity Policy'.

Analyses should be carried out of:

(a) The ethnic composition of the workforce of each plant, department, section, shift and job category, and changes in distribution over periods of time.
(b) Selection decisions for recruitment, promotion, transfer and training, according to the racial group of candidates, and reasons for these decisions.

Except in cases where there are large numbers of applicants and the burden on resources would be excessive, reasons for selection and rejection should be recorded at each stage of the selection process, e.g. initial shortlisting and final decisions. Simple categories of reason for rejection should be adequate for the early sifting stages.

Selection criteria and personnel procedures should be reviewed to ensure that they do not include requirements or conditions which constitute or may lead to unlawful indirect discrimination.

This information should be carefully and regularly analysed and, in order to identify areas which may need particular attention, a number of key questions should be asked.

Is there evidence that individuals from any particular racial group:

(a) Do not apply for employment or promotion, or that fewer apply than might be expected?
(b) Are not recruited or promoted at all, or are appointed in a significantly lower proportion than their rate of application?
(c) Are under-represented in training or in jobs carrying higher pay, status or authority?
(d) Are concentrated in certain shifts, sections or departments?

If the answer to any of these questions is yes, the reason for this should be investigated. If direct or indirect discrimination is found action must be taken to end it immediately.

It is recommended that deliberate acts of unlawful discrimination by employees are treated as disciplinary offences.

POSITIVE ACTION*

Although they are not legally required, positive measures are allowed by the law to encourage employees and potential employees and provide training for employees who are members of particular racial groups which have been underrepresented† in particular work. Discrimination at the point of selection for work, however, is not permissible in these circumstances.

Such measures are important for the development of equal opportunity. It is therefore recommended that, where there is under-representation of particular work, the following measures should be taken wherever appropriate and reasonably practicable:

(a) Job advertisements designed to reach members of these groups and to encourage their applications: for example, through the use of the ethnic minority press, as well as other newspapers.
(b) Use of the employment agencies and careers offices in areas where these groups are concentrated.
(c) Recruitment and training schemes for school leavers designed to reach members of these groups.

* The CRE has issued a guidance paper on positive action, entitled, 'Equal Opportunity in Employment: Why positive action?'

† A racial group is underrepresented if, at any time during the previous twelve months, either there was no-one of that group doing the work in question, or there were disproportionately few in comparison with the group's proportion in the workforce at that establishment, or in the population from which the employer normally recruits for work at that establishment.

(d) Encouragement to employees from these groups to apply for promotion or transfer opportunities.
(e) Training for promotion or skill training for employees of these groups who lack particular expertise but show potential: supervisory training may include language training.

PART 2
THE RESPONSIBILITIES OF INDIVIDUAL EMPLOYEES

While the primary responsibility for providing equal opportunity rests with the employer, individual employees at all levels and of all racial groups have responsibilities too. Good race relations depend on them as much as on management, and so their attitudes and activities are very important.

The following actions by individual employees would be unlawful:

(a) Discrimination in the course of their employment against fellow employees or job applicants on racial grounds, for example, in selection decisions for recruitment, promotion, transfer and training.
(b) Inducing, or attempting to induce other employees, unions or management to practise unlawful discrimination. For example, they should not refuse to accept other employees from particular racial groups or refuse to work with a supervisor of a particular racial group.
(c) Victimising individuals who have made allegations or complaints of racial discrimination or provided information about such discrimination.

To assist in preventing racial discrimination and promoting equal opportunity it is recommended that individual employees should:

(a) Co-operate in measures introduced by management designed to ensure equal opportunity and non-discrimination.
(b) Where such measures have not been introduced, press for their introduction (through their trade union where appropriate).
(c) Draw attention of management and, where appropriate, their trade unions to suspected discriminatory acts or practices.
(d) Refrain from harassment or intimidation of other employees on racial grounds, for example, by attempting to discourage them from continuing employment. Such action may be unlawful if it is taken by employees against those subject to their authority.

In addition to the responsibilities set out above individual employees from the racial minorities should recognise that in many occupations advancement is dependent on an appropriate standard of English. Similarly an understanding of the industrial relations procedures which apply is often essential for good working relationships.

They should therefore:

(a) Where appropriate, seek means to improve their standards of English.
(b) Co-operate in industrial language training schemes introduced by employers and/or unions.
(c) Co-operate in training or other schemes designed to inform them of industrial relations procedures, company agreements, work rules, etc.
(d) Where appropriate, participate in discussions with employers and unions, to find solutions to conflicts between cultural or religious needs and production needs.

PART 3
THE RESPONSIBILITIES OF TRADE UNIONS

Trade unions, in common with a number of other organisations, have a dual role as employers and providers of services specifically covered by the Race Relations Act.

In their role as employer, unions have the responsibilities set out in Part 1 of the Code. They also have a responsibility to ensure that their representatives and members do not discriminate against any particular racial groups in the admission or treatment of members, or as colleagues, supervisors, or subordinates.

In addition, trade union officials at national and local level and shop floor representatives at plant level have an important part to play on behalf of their members in preventing unlawful discrimination and in promoting equal opportunity an good race relations. Trade unions should encourage and press for equal opportunity policies so that measures to prevent discrimination at the workplace can be introduced with the clear commitment of both management and unions.

ADMISSION OF MEMBERS

It is unlawful for trade unions to discriminate on racial grounds:

(a) By refusing membership.
(b) By offering less favourable terms of membership.

TREATMENT OF MEMBERS

It is unlawful for trade unions to discriminate on racial grounds against existing members:

(a) By varying their terms of membership, depriving them of membership or subjecting them to any other detriment.
(b) By treating them less favourably in the benefits, facilities or services provided. These may include:

- Training facilities.
- Welfare and insurance schemes.
- Entertainment and social events.
- Processing of grievances.
- Negotiations.
- Assistance in disciplinary or dismissal procedures.

In addition, it is recommended that unions ensure that in cases where members of particular racial groups believe that they are suffering racial discrimination, whether by the employer or the union itself, serious attention is paid to the reasons for this belief and that any discrimination which may be occurring is stopped.

DISCIPLINING MEMBERS WHO DISCRIMINATE

It is recommended that deliberate acts of unlawful discrimination by union members are treated as disciplinary offences.

POSITIVE ACTION

Although they are not legally required, positive measures are allowed by the law to encourage and provide training for members of particular racial groups which have been under-represented* in trade union membership or in trade union posts. (Discrimination at the point of selection, however, is not permissible in these circumstances.)

* A racial group is underrepresented in trade union membership, if at any time during the previous twelve months no person of that group were in membership, or disproportionately few in comparison with the proportion of persons of that group among those eligible for membership. Under-representation in trade union posts applies under the same twelve month criteria, where there were no persons of a particular racial group on those posts or disproportionately few in comparison with the proportion of that group in the organisation.

Appendix 4

It is recommended that, wherever appropriate and reasonably practicable, trade unions should:

(a) Encourage individuals from these groups to join the union. Where appropriate, recruitment material should be translated into other languages.
(b) Encourage individuals from these groups to apply for union posts and provide training to help fit them for such posts.

TRAINING AND INFORMATION

Training and information play a major part in the avoidance of discrimination and the promotion of equal opportunity. It is recommended that trade unions should:

(a) Provide training and information for officers, shop stewards and representatives on their responsibilities for equal opportunity. This training and information should cover:

— The Race Relations Act and the nature and causes of discrimination.
— The backgrounds of racial minority groups and communication needs.
— The effects of prejudice.
— Equal opportunity policies.
— Avoiding discrimination when representing members.

(b) Ensure that members and representatives, whatever their racial groups, are informed of their role in the union, and of industrial relations and union procedures and structures. This may be done, for example:

— Through translation of material.
— Through encouragement to participate in industrial relations courses and industrial language training.

PRESSURE TO DISCRIMINATE

It is unlawful for trade union members or representatives to induce or attempt to induce those responsible for employment decisions to discriminate:

(a) In the recruitment, promotion, transfer, training or dismissal of employees.
(b) In terms of employment, benefits, facilities or services.

For example, they should not:

(a) Restrict the numbers of a particular racial group in a section, grade or department.
(b) Resist changes designed to remove indirect discrimination, such as those in craft apprentice schemes, or in agreements concerning seniority rights or mobility between departments.

VICTIMISATION

It is unlawful to victimise individuals who have made allegations or complaints of racial discrimination or provided information about such discrimination.

AVOIDANCE OF DISCRIMINATION

Where unions are involved in selection decisions for recruitment, promotion, training or transfer, for example, through recommendation or veto, it is unlawful for them to discriminate on racial grounds.

It is recommended that they should instruct their members accordingly and examine their procedures and joint agreements to ensure that they do not contain indirectly discriminatory conditions, such as:

(a) Unjustifiable restrictions on transfers between departments.

(b) Irrelevant and unjustifiable selection criteria which have a disproportionately adverse effect on particular racial groups.

UNION INVOLVEMENT IN EQUAL OPPORTUNITY POLICIES

It is recommended that:

(a) Unions should co-operate in the introduction and implementation of all equal opportunity policies.
(b) Unions should negotiate the adoption of such policies where they have not been introduced or the extension of existing policies where these are too narrow.
(c) Unions should co-operate with measures to monitor the progress of equal opportunity polices, or encourage management to introduce them where they do not already exist. Where appropriate this may be done through analysis of the distribution of employees and job applicants according to ethnic origin.
(d) Where monitoring shows that discrimination has occurred or is occurring, unions should co-operate in measures to eliminate it.

Although positive action is not legally required, unions should encourage management to take such action where there is underrepresentation of particular racial groups in particular jobs, and where management itself introduces positive action, representatives should support it.

Similarly, where there are communication difficulties, management should be asked to take whatever action is appropriate to overcome them.

PART 4
THE RESPONSIBILITIES OF EMPLOYMENT AGENCIES

Employment agencies, in their role as employers, have the responsibilities outlined in Part 1 of the Code. In addition, they have responsibilities as suppliers of job applicants to other employers.

It is unlawful for employment agencies (for exceptions see Race Relations Act):

(a) To discriminate on racial grounds in providing services to clients.
(b) To publish job advertisements indicating, or which might be understood to indicate, that applications from any particular group will not be considered or will be treated more favourably or less favourably than others.
(c) To act on directly discriminatory instructions from employers to the effect that applicants from a particular racial group will be rejected or preferred or that their numbers should be restricted.
(d) To act on indirectly discriminatory instructions from employers i.e. that requirements or conditions should be applied that would have a disproportionately adverse effect on applicants of a particular racial group and which cannot be shown to be justifiable.

It is recommended that agencies should also avoid indicating such conditions or requirements in job advertisements unless they can be shown to be justifiable. Examples in each case may be those relating to educational qualifications or residence.

It is recommended that staff should be given guidance on their duty not to discriminate and on the effect which generalised assumptions and prejudices can have on their treatment of members of particular racial groups.

In particular staff should be instructed:

(a) Not to ask employers for racial preferences.
(b) Not to draw attention to racial origin when recommending applicants unless the employer is trying to attract applicants of a particular racial group under the exceptions in the Race Relations Act.

(c) To report a client's refusal to interview an applicant for reasons that are directly or indirectly indiscriminatory to a supervisor who should inform the client that discrimination is unlawful. If the client maintains this refusal the agency should inform the applicant of his or her right to complain to an industrial tribunal and to apply to the CRE for assistance. An internal procedure for receding such cases should be operated.

(d) To inform their supervisor if they believe that an applicant, though interviewed, has been rejected on racial grounds. It the supervisor is satisfied that there are grounds for this belief, he or she should arrange for the applicant to be informed of the right to complain to an industrial tribunal and to apply to the CRE for assistance. An internal procedure for recording such cases should be operated.

(e) To treat job applicants without discrimination. For example, they should not send applicants from particular racial groups to only those employers who are believed to be willing to accept them, or restrict the range of job opportunities for such applicants because of assumptions about their abilities based on race or colour.

It is recommended that employment agencies should discontinue their services to employers who give unlawful discriminatory instructions and who refuse to withdraw them.

It is recommended that employment agencies should monitor the effectiveness of the measures they take for ensuring that no unlawful discrimination occurs. For example, where reasonably practicable they should make periodic checks to ensure that applicants from particular racial groups are being referred for suitable jobs for which they are qualified at a similar rate to that for other comparable applicants.

Appendix 5

CODE OF PRACTICE FOR THE ELIMINATION OF DISCRIMINATION IN THE FIELD OF EMPLOYMENT AGAINST DISABLED PERSONS OR PERSONS WHO HAVE HAD A DISABILITY

Editorial note: This Code was issued by the Department for Education and Employment under the Disability Discrimination Act 1995 s 53. It came into force on 2 December 1996. The provisions applying to trade organisations have effectively been superseded by a separate Code relating to trade organisations.

1 INTRODUCTION

Purpose and status of the Code

1.1 Pages 3 to 58 are a Code of Practice issued by the Secretary of State for Education and Employment under section 53(1)(*a*) of the Disability Discrimination Act 1995 ('the Act'). The Code comes into effect on 2 December 1996.

1.2 The employment provisions of the Act and the Disability Discrimination (Employment) Regulations 1996 protect disabled people, and people who have been disabled, from discrimination in the field of employment. Although the Code is written in terms of 'disabled' people, it also applies to people who no longer have a disability but have had one in the past. The date from which the employment provisions take effect is 2 December 1996 (but see paragraph 7.12). The Code of Practice gives practical guidance to help employers and others—including trade organisations and people who hire staff from employment businesses—in eliminating discrimination and should assist in avoiding complaints to industrial tribunals.

1.3 The Code applies in England, Scotland and Wales. It does not itself impose legal obligations and is not an authoritative statement of the law. Authoritative interpretation of the Act and regulations is for the tribunals and courts. However, the Code is admissible in evidence in any proceedings under the Act before an industrial tribunal or court. If any provision in the Code appears to the tribunal or court to be relevant to a question arising in the proceedings, it must be taken into account in determining that question.

Using the Code

1.4 The Code describes—and gives general guidance on—the main employment provisions of the Act in paragraphs 4.1 to 4.66. More specific guidance on how these provisions operate in different situations is in later paragraphs but it may be necessary to refer back to the general guidance occasionally. For example, someone thinking of recruiting new staff will need to read paragraphs 5.1 to 5.29 and also, unless already familiar with it, the general guidance on the provisions in paragraphs 4.1 to 4.66. Someone dealing with a new or existing employee should read paragraphs 6.1 to 6.23, again with reference to the general guidance as necessary. Examples of how the Act is likely to work in practice are given in boxes (see also paragraph 3.1). Annexes 1–3 are not part of the Code but include information on related subjects. There is a detailed index at the end of the Code [*not reproduced*].

1.5 References to the legal provisions relevant to the guidance in the Code are generally just on the first, or only, main mention of a provision. For example,'s 5(1)' means section 5, sub-s (1) of the Act.'Sch 1 para 1(1)' means Schedule 1 paragraph 1 sub-para (1) of the Act.

1.6 References in footnotes to 'Employment Regulations' mean The Disability Discrimination (Employment) Regulations 1996 and to 'Definition Regulations' mean The Disability Discrimination (Meaning of Disability) Regulations 1996.

1.7 In the examples, references to male and female individual disabled people are given for realism. All other references are masculine for simplicity but could, of course, apply to either sex.

2 WHO IS, AND WHO IS NOT, COVERED BY THE EMPLOYMENT PROVISIONS

What is the main purpose of the employment provisions of the Act?

2.1 The Act protects disabled people from discrimination in the field of employment. As part of this protection employers may have to make 'reasonable adjustments' if their employment arrangements or premises place disabled people at a substantial disadvantage compared with non-disabled people. These provisions replace the quota scheme, the designated employment scheme and registration as a disabled person (s 61(7)).

2.2 The Act does not prohibit an employer from appointing the best person for the job. Nor does it prevent employers from treating disabled people more favourably than those without a disability.

Who has rights or obligations under the Act?

2.3 Disabled people have rights under the Act, as do people who have had disabilities but have fully or largely recovered. The Act defines a disabled person as someone with a physical or mental impairment which has a substantial and long-term adverse effect on his ability to carry out normal day-to-day activities (s 1 and Sch 1).(See Annex 1.)

2.4 The following people and organisations may have obligations under the Act:

- employers;
- the Crown (including Government Departments and Agencies)(s 64);
- employees and agents of an employer;
- landlords of premises occupied by employers;
- people who hire contract workers;
- trustees or managers of occupational pension schemes;
- people who provide group insurance schemes for an employer's employees;
- trade organisations.

2.5 This Act does not confer rights on people who do not have—and have not had—a disability, with the exception of the provisions covering victimisation (see paragraphs 4.53 and 4.54).

Who does not have obligations or rights under the Act?

2.6 The employment provisions do not apply to employers with fewer than 20 employees (s 7). The Act applies when an employer has 20 or more employees in total, regardless of the size of individual workplaces or branches. However, if the number of employees falls below 20 the employer will be exempted for as long as there are fewer than 20 employees. Independent franchise holders are exempt if they employ fewer than 20 people even if the franchise network has 20 or more employees. The Government must carry out a review of the threshold for the exclusion of small firms within 5 years of the employment provisions coming into force.

2.7 The employment provisions do not apply to:

- members of the Armed Forces (s 64(7));
- prison officers (s 64(5)(*b*));
- firefighters (s 64(5)(*c*) and (6));
- employees who work wholly or mainly outside Great Britain (s 68(2));
- employees who work on board ships, aircraft or hovercraft (s 68(3));
- members of the Ministry of Defence Police, the British Transport Police, the Royal Parks Constabulary and the United Kingdom Atomic Energy Authority Constabulary (s 64(5)(*a*)); and
- other police officers who are in any event not employees as defined in s 68(1).

Who counts as an employee under the Act?

2.8 'Employment' means employment under a contract of service or of apprenticeship, or a contract personally to do any work (s 68). The last category covers persons who are self-employed and agree to perform the work personally.'Employee' means anyone whose contract is within that definition of employment, whether or not, for example, he works full-time.

3 GENERAL GUIDANCE TO HELP AVOID DISCRIMINATION

Be flexible

3.1 There may be several ways to avoid discrimination in any one situation. Examples in this Code are *illustrative only*, to indicate what should or should not be done in those and other broadly similar types of situations. They cannot cover every possibility, so it is important to consider carefully how the guidance applies in any specific circumstances. **Many ways of avoiding discrimination will cost little or nothing**. The Code should not be read narrowly; for instance, its guidance on recruitment might help avoid discrimination when promoting employees.

Do not make assumptions

3.2 It will probably be helpful to talk to each disabled person about what the real effects of the disability might be or what might help. There is less chance of a dispute where the person is involved from the start. Such discussions should not, of course, be conducted in a way which would itself give the disabled person any reason to believe that he was being discriminated against.

Consider whether expert advice is needed

3.3 It is possible to avoid discrimination using personal, or in-house, knowledge and expertise, particularly if the views of the disabled person are sought. The Act does not oblige anyone to get expert advice but it could help in some circumstances to seek independent advice on the extent of a disabled person's capabilities. This might be particularly appropriate where a person is newly disabled or the effects of someone's disability become more marked. It may also help to get advice on what might be done to change premises or working arrangements, especially if discussions with the disabled person do not lead to a satisfactory solution. Annex 2 gives information about getting advice or help.

Plan ahead

3.4 Although the Act does not require an employer to make changes in anticipation of ever having a disabled applicant or employee, nevertheless when planning for change it could be cost-effective to consider the needs of a range of possible future disabled employees and applicants. There may be helpful improvements that could be built into plans. For example, a new telecommunications system might be made accessible to deaf people even if there are currently no deaf employees.

Promote equal opportunities

3.5 If an employer has an equal opportunities policy or is thinking of introducing one, it would probably help to avoid a breach of the Act if that policy covered disability issues. Employers who have, and follow, a good policy—including monitoring its effectiveness—are likely to have that counted in their favour by a tribunal if a complaint is made. But employers should remember that treating people equally will not always avoid a breach of the Act. An employer may be under a duty to make a reasonable adjustment. This could apply at any time in the recruitment process or in the course of a disabled person's employment.

4 THE MAIN EMPLOYMENT PROVISIONS OF THE ACT

Discrimination

What does the Act say about discrimination?

4.1 The Act makes it unlawful for an employer to discriminate against a disabled person in the field of employment (s 4). The Act says 'discrimination' occurs in two ways.

4.2 One way in which discrimination occurs is when:

- for a reason which relates to a disabled person's disability, the employer treats that disabled person less favourably than the employer treats or would treat others to whom the reason does not or would not apply; *and*
- the employer cannot show that this treatment is justified (s 5(1)).

> A woman with a disability which requires use of a wheelchair applies for a job. She can do the job but the employer thinks the wheelchair will get in the way in the office. He gives the job to a person who is no more suitable for the job but who does not use a wheelchair. The employer has therefore treated the woman less favourably than the other person because he did not give her the job. The treatment was for a reason related to the disability—the fact that she used a wheelchair. And the reason for treating her less favourably did not apply to the other person because that person did not use a wheelchair.
>
> If the employer could not justify his treatment of the disabled woman then he would have unlawfully discriminated against her.
>
> An employer decides to close down a factory and makes all the employees redundant, including a disabled person who works there. This is not discrimination as the disabled employee is not being dismissed for a reason which relates to the disability.

4.3 A disabled person may not be able to point to other people who were actually treated more favourable. However, it is still 'less favourable treatment' if the employer would give better treatment to someone else to whom the reason for the treatment of the disabled person did not apply. This comparison can also be made with other disabled people, not just non-disabled people. For example, an employer might be discriminating by treating a person with a mental illness less favourably than he treats or would treat a physically disabled person.

4.4 The other way the Act says that discrimination occurs is when:

- an employer fails to comply with a duty of reasonable adjustment imposed on him by section 6 in relation to the disabled person; *and*
- he cannot show that this failure is justified (s 5(2)).

4.5 The relationship between the duty of reasonable adjustment and the need to justify less favourable treatment is described in paragraphs 4.7–4.9. The duty itself is described from paragraph 4.12 onwards and the need to justify a failure to comply with it is described in paragraph 4.34.

What will, and what will not, be justified treatment?

4.6 The Act says that less favourable treatment of a disabled person will be justified only if the reason for it is both material to the circumstances of the particular case *and* substantial (s 5(3)). This means that the reason has to relate to the individual circumstances in question and not just be trivial or minor.

> Someone who is blind is not shortlisted for a job involving computers because the employer thinks blind people cannot use them. The employer makes no effort to look at the individual circumstances. A general assumption that blind people cannot use computers would not in itself be a material reason—it is not related to the particular circumstances.

> A factory worker with a mental illness is sometimes away from work due to his disability. Because of that he is dismissed. However, the amount of time off is very little more than the employer accepts as sick leave for other employees and so is very unlikely to be a substantial reason.

> A clerical worker with a learning disability cannot sort papers quite as quickly as some of his colleagues. There is very little difference in productivity but he is dismissed. That is very unlikely to be a substantial reason.

> An employer seeking a clerical worker turns down an applicant with a severe facial disfigurement solely on the ground that other employees would be uncomfortable working alongside him. This will be unlawful because such a reaction by other employees will not in itself justify less favourable treatment of this sort—it is not substantial. The same would apply if it were thought that a customer would feel uncomfortable.

> An employer moves someone with a mental illness to a different workplace solely because he mutters to himself while he works. If the employer accepts similar levels of noise from other people, the treatment of the disabled person would probably be unjustified—that level of noise is unlikely to be a substantial reason.

> Someone who has psoriasis (a skin condition) is rejected for a job involving modelling cosmetics on a part of the body which in his case is severely disfigured by the condition. That would be lawful if his appearance would be incompatible with the purpose of the work. This is a substantial reason which is clearly related—material—to the individual circumstance.

4.7 The Act says that less favourable treatment cannot be justified where the employer is under a duty to make a reasonable adjustment but fails (without justification) to do so, *unless* the treatment would have been justified even after that adjustment (s 5(5)).

> An employee who uses a wheelchair is not promoted, solely because the work station for the higher post is inaccessible to wheelchairs—though it could readily be made so by rearrangement of the furniture. If the furniture had been rearranged, the

reason for refusing promotion would not have applied. The refusal of promotion would therefore not be justified.

An applicant for a typing job is not the best person on the face of it, but only because her typing speed is too slow due to arthritis in her hands. If a reasonable adjustment—perhaps an adapted keyboard—would overcome this, her typing speed would not in itself be a substantial reason for not employing her. Therefore the employer would be unlawfully discriminating if on account of her typing speed he did not employ her and provide the adjustment.

An employer refuses a training course for an employee with an illness which is very likely to be terminal within a year because, even with a reasonable adjustment to help in the job after the course, the benefits of the course could not be adequately realised. This is very likely to be a substantial reason. It is clearly material to the circumstances. The refusal of training would therefore very likely be justified.

Someone who is blind applies for a job which requires a significant amount of driving. If it is not reasonable for the employer to adjust the job so that the driving duties are given to someone else, the employer's need for a driver might well be a substantial reason for not employing the blind person. It is clearly material to the particular circumstances. The non-appointment could therefore be justified.

How does an employer avoid unlawful discrimination?

4.8 An employer should not treat a disabled employee or disabled job applicant less favourably, for a reason relating to the disability, than others to whom that reason does not apply, unless that reason is material to the particular circumstances and substantial. If the reason is material and substantial, the employer may have to make a reasonable adjustment to remove it or make it less than substantial (s 5(3) and (5)).

4.9 Less favourable treatment is therefore justified if the disabled person cannot do the job concerned, and no adjustment which would enable the person to do the job (or another vacant job) is practicable (s 5(3) and (5)).(See paragraph 4.20 for examples of adjustments which employers may have to make.)

4.10 The Act says that some charities (and Government-funded supported employment) are allowed to treat some groups of disabled people more favourably than others. But they can do this only if the group being treated more favourably is one with whom the charitable purposes of the charity are connected and the more favourable treatment is in pursuance of those purposes (or, in the case of supported employment, those treated more favourably are severely disabled people whom the programme aims to help)(s 10).

What does the act say about helping others to discriminate?

4.11 The Act says that a person who knowingly helps another to do something made unlawful by the Act will also be treated as having done the same kind of unlawful act (s 57(1)).

A recruitment consultant engaged by an engineering company refuses to consider a disabled applicant for a vacancy, because the employer has told the consultant that he does not want the post filled by someone who is 'handicapped'. Under the Act the consultant could be liable for aiding the company.

Reasonable adjustment

What does the act say about the duty of 'reasonable adjustment'?

4.12 The Act says that the duty applies where any physical feature of premises occupied by the employer, or any arrangements made by or on behalf of the employer, cause a substantial disadvantage to a disabled person compared with non-disabled people. An employer has to take such steps as it is reasonable for him to have to take in all the circumstances to prevent that disadvantage—in other words the employer has to make a 'reasonable adjustment' (s 6(1)).

> A man who is disabled by dyslexia applies for a job which involves writing letters within fairly long deadlines. The employer gives all applicants a test of their letter-writing ability. The man can generally write letters very well but finds it difficult to do so in stressful situations. The *employer's arrangements* would mean he had to begin his test immediately on arrival and to do it in a short time. He would be *substantially disadvantaged compared to non-disabled people* who would not find such arrangements stressful or, if they did, would not be so affected by them. The employer therefore gives him a little time to settle in and longer to write the letter. These new arrangements do not inconvenience the employer very much and only briefly delay the decision on an appointment. These are *steps that it is reasonable for the employer to have to take in the circumstances to prevent the disadvantage*—a 'reasonable adjustment'.

4.13 If a disabled person cannot point to an existing non-disabled person compared with whom he is at a substantial disadvantage, then the comparison should be made with how the employer would have treated a non-disabled person.

4.14 How to comply with this duty in recruitment and during employment is explained in paragraphs 5.1–5.29 and 6.1–6.21. The following paragraphs explain how to satisfy this duty more generally.

What 'physical features' and 'arrangements' are covered by the duty?

4.15 Regulations define the term 'physical features' to include anything on the premises arising from a building's design or construction or from an approach to, exit from or access to such a building; fixtures, fittings, furnishings, equipment or materials; and any other physical element or quality of land in the premises. All of these are covered whether temporary or permanent[1].

1 Employment Regulations (see paragraph 1.6).

4.16 The Act says that the duty applies to 'arrangements' for determining to whom employment should be offered and any term, condition or arrangement on which employment, promotion, transfer, training or any other benefit is offered or afforded (s 6(2)). The duty applies in recruitment and during employment; for example, selection and interview procedures and the arrangements for using premises for such procedures as well as job offers, contractual arrangements, and working conditions.

> The design of a particular workplace makes it difficult for someone with a hearing impairment to hear. That is a disadvantage caused by the *physical features*. There may be nothing that can reasonably be done in the circumstances to change these features. However, requiring someone to work in such a workplace is an *arrangement made by the employer* and it might be reasonable to overcome the disadvantage by a transfer to another workplace or by ensuring that the supervisor gives instructions in an office rather than in the working area.

What 'disadvantages' give rise to the duty?

4.17 The Act says that only substantial disadvantages give rise to the duty (s 6(1)). Substantial disadvantages are those which are not minor or trivial.

> An employer is unlikely to be required to widen a particular doorway to enable passage by an employee using a wheelchair if there is an easy alternative route to the same destination.

4.18 An employer cannot be required to prevent a disadvantage caused by premises or by non-pay arrangements by increasing the disabled person's pay.(See paragraph 5.29.)

4.19 The duty of reasonable adjustment does not apply in relation to benefits under occupational pension schemes or certain benefits under other employment-related benefit schemes although there is a duty not to discriminate in relation to such benefits (see paragraphs 6.9–6.16).

What adjustments might an employer have to make?

4.20 The Act gives a number of examples of 'steps' which employers may have to take, if it is reasonable for them to have to do so in all the circumstances of the case (s 6(3)). Steps other than those listed here, or a combination of steps, will sometimes have to be taken. The steps in the Act are:

- making adjustments to premises

  An employer might have to make structural or other physical changes such as: widening a doorway, providing a ramp or moving furniture for a wheelchair user; relocating light switches, door handles or shelves for someone who has difficulty in reaching; providing appropriate contrast in decor to help the safe mobility of a visually impaired person.

- allocating some of the disabled person's duties to another person

  Minor or subsidiary duties might be reallocated to another employee if the disabled person has difficulty in doing them because of the disability. For example, if a job occasionally involves going onto the open roof of a building an employer might have to transfer this work away from an employee whose disability involves severe vertigo.

- transferring the person to fill an existing vacancy

  If an employee becomes disabled, or has a disability which worsens so she cannot work in the same place or under the same arrangements and there is no reasonable adjustment which would enable the employee to continue doing the current job, then she might have to be considered for any suitable alternative posts which are available.(Such a case might also involve reasonable retraining.)

- altering the person's working hours

  This could include allowing the disabled person to work flexible hours to enable additional breaks to overcome fatigue arising from the disability, or changing the disabled person's hours to fit with the availability of a carer.

- assigning the person to a different place of work

  This could mean transferring a wheelchair user's work station from an inaccessible third floor office to an accessible one on the ground floor. It could mean moving the person to other premises of the same employer if the first building is inaccessible.

- allowing the person to be absent during working hours for rehabilitation, assessment or treatment

  For example, if a person were to become disabled, the employer might have to allow the person more time off during work, than would be allowed to non-disabled employees, to receive physiotherapy or psychoanalysis or undertake employment rehabilitation. A similar adjustment might be appropriate if a disability worsens or if a disabled person needs occasional treatment anyway.

- giving the person, or arranging for him to be given, training

This could be training in the use of particular pieces of equipment unique to the disabled person, or training appropriate for all employees but which needs altering for the disabled person because of the disability. For example, all employees might need to be trained in the use of a particular machine but an employer might have to provide slightly different or longer training for an employee with restricted hand or arm movements, or training in additional software for a visually impaired person so that he can use a computer with speech output.

- acquiring or modifying equipment

  An employer might have to provide special equipment (such as an adapted keyboard for a visually impaired person or someone with arthritis), or an adapted telephone for someone with a hearing impairment or modified equipment (such as longer handles on a machine). There is no requirement to provide or modify equipment for personal purposes unconnected with work, such as providing a wheelchair if a person needs one in any event but does not have one: the disadvantage in such a case does not flow from the employer's arrangements or premises.

- modifying instructions or reference manuals

  The way instruction is normally given to employees might need to be revised when telling a disabled person how to do a task. The format of instructions or manuals may need to be modified (eg produced in braille or on audio tape) and instructions for people with learning disabilities may need to be conveyed orally with individual demonstration.

- modifying procedures for testing or assessment

  This could involve ensuring that particular tests do not adversely affect people with particular types of disability. For example, a person with restricted manual dexterity might be disadvantaged by a written test, so an employer might have to give that person an oral test.

- providing a reader or interpreter

  This could involve a colleague reading mail to a person with a visual impairment at particular times during the working day or, in appropriate circumstances, the hiring of a reader or sign language interpreter.

- providing supervision

  This could involve the provision of a support worker, or help from a colleague, in appropriate circumstances, for someone whose disability leads to uncertainty or lack of confidence.

When is it 'reasonable' for an employer to have to make an adjustment?

4.21 Effective and practicable adjustments for disabled people often involve little or no cost or disruption and are therefore very likely to be reasonable for an employer to have to make. The Act lists a number of factors which may, in particular, have a bearing on whether it will be reasonable for the employer to have to make a particular adjustment (s 6(4)). These factors make a useful checklist, particularly when considering more substantial adjustments. The effectiveness and practicability of a particular adjustment might be considered first. If it is practicable and effective, the financial aspects might be looked at as a whole—cost of the adjustment and resources available to fund it. Other factors might also have a bearing. The factors in the Act are listed below.

The effectiveness of the step in preventing the disadvantage

4.22 It is unlikely to be reasonable for an employer to have to make an adjustment involving little benefit to the disabled employee.

> A disabled person is significantly less productive than his colleagues and so is paid less. A particular adjustment would improve his output and thus his pay. It is more likely to be reasonable for the employer to have to make that adjustment if it would significantly improve his pay, than if the adjustment would make only a relatively small improvement.

The practicability of the step

4.23 It is more likely to be reasonable for an employer to have to take a step which is easy to take than one which is difficult.

> It might be impracticable for an employer who needs to appoint an employee urgently to have to wait for an adjustment to be made to an entrance. How long it might be reasonable for the employer to have to wait would depend on the circumstances. However, it might be possible to make a temporary adjustment in the meantime, such as using another, less convenient entrance.

The financial and other costs of the adjustment and the extent of any disruption caused

4.24 If an adjustment costs little or nothing and is not disruptive, it would be reasonable unless some other factor (such as practicability or effectiveness) made it unreasonable. The costs to be taken into account include staff and other resource costs. The significance of the cost of a step may depend in part on what the employer might otherwise spend in the circumstances.

> It would be reasonable for an employer to have to spend at least as much on an adjustment to enable the retention of a disabled person—including any retraining—as might be spent on recruiting and training a replacement.

4.25 The significance of the cost of a step may also depend in part on the value of the employee's experience and expertise to the employer.

Examples of the factors that might be considered as relating to the value of an employee would include:

- the amount of resources (such as training) invested in the individual by the employer;
- the employee's length of service;
- the employee's level of skill and knowledge;
- the employee's quality of relationships with clients;
- the level of the employee's pay.

4.26 It is more likely to be reasonable for an employer to have to make an adjustment with significant costs for an employee who is likely to be in the job for some time than for a temporary employee.

4.27 An employer is more likely to have to make an adjustment which might cause only minor inconvenience to other employees or the employer than one which might unavoidably prevent other employees from doing their job, or cause other significant disruption.

The extent of the employer's financial or other resources

4.28 It is more likely to be reasonable for an employer with substantial financial resources to have to make an adjustment with a significant cost, than for an employer with fewer resources. The resources in practice available to the employer as a whole should be taken into account as well as other calls on those resources. The reasonableness of an adjustment will depend, however, not only on the resources in practice available for the adjustment but also on all other relevant factors (such as effectiveness and practicability).

4.29 Where the resources of the employer are spread across more than one 'business unit' or 'profit centre' the calls on them should also be taken into account in assessing reasonableness.

> A large retailer probably could not show that the limited resources for which an individual shop manager is responsible meant it was not reasonable for the retailer to have to make an adjustment at that shop. Such an employer may, however, have a number—perhaps a large number—of other disabled employees in other shops. The employer's expenditure on other adjustments, or his potential expenditure on similar adjustments for other existing disabled employees, might then be taken into account in assessing the reasonableness of having to make a new adjustment for the disabled employee in question.

4.30 It is more likely to be reasonable for an employer with a substantial number of staff to have to make certain adjustments, than for a smaller employer.

> It would generally be reasonable for an employer with many staff to have to make significant efforts to reallocate duties, identify a suitable alternative post or provide supervision from existing staff. It could also be reasonable for a small company covered by the Act to have to make any of these adjustments but not if it involved disproportionate effort.

The availability to the employer of financial or other assistance to help make an adjustment

4.31 The availability of outside help may well be a relevant factor.

> An employer, in recruiting a disabled person, finds that the only feasible adjustment is too costly for him alone. However, if assistance is available eg from a Government programme or voluntary body, it may well be reasonable for him to have to make the adjustment after all.

A disabled person is not required to contribute to the cost of a reasonable adjustment. However, if a disabled person has a particular piece of special or adapted equipment which he is prepared to use for work, this might make it reasonable for the employer to have to take some other step (as well as allowing use of the equipment).

> An employer requires his employees to use company cars for all business travel. One employee's disability means she would have to use an adapted car or an alternative form of transport. If she has an adapted car of her own which she is willing to use on business, it might well be reasonable for the employer to have to allow this and pay her an allowance to cover the cost of doing so, even if it would not have been reasonable for him to have to provide an adapted company car, or to pay an allowance to cover alternative travel arrangements in the absence of an adapted car.

Other factors

4.32 Although the Act does not mention any further factors, others might be relevant depending on the circumstances. For example:

- effect on other employees
  Employees' adverse reaction to an adjustment being made for the disabled employee which involves something they too would like (such as a special working arrangement) is unlikely to be significant.
- adjustments made for other disabled employees
  An employer may choose to give a particular disabled employee, or group of disabled employees, an adjustment which goes beyond the duty—that is, which is more than it is

reasonable for him to have to do. This would not mean he necessarily had to provide a similar adjustment for other employees with a similar disability.

- the extent to which the disabled person is willing to cooperate
  An employee with a mobility impairment works in a team located on an upper floor, to which there is no access by lift. Getting there is very tiring for the employee, and the employer could easily make a more accessible location available for him (though the whole team could not be relocated). If that was the only adjustment which it would be reasonable for the employer to have to make but the employee refused to work there then the employer would not have to make any adjustment at all.

Could an employer have to make more than one adjustment?

4.33 Yes, if it is reasonable for the employer to have to make more than one.

A woman who is deafblind is given a new job with her employer in an unfamiliar part of the building. The employer (i) arranges facilities for her guide dog in the new area,(ii) arranges for her new instructions to be in Braille and (iii) suggests to visitors ways in which they can communicate with her.

Does an employer have to justify not making an adjustment?

4.34 The Act says that it is discrimination if an employer fails to take a step which it is reasonable for him to have to take, and he cannot justify that failure (s 5(2)). However, if it is unreasonable (under s 6) for an employer to have to make any, or a particular, adjustment, he would not then also have to justify (under s 5) not doing so. Failure to comply with the duty of reasonable adjustment can only be justified if the reason for the failure is material to the circumstances of the particular case and substantial (s 5(4)).

An employer might not make an adjustment which it was reasonable for him to have to make because of ignorance or wrong information about appropriate adjustments or about the availability of help with making an adjustment. He would then need to justify failing in his duty. It is unlikely that he could do so unless he had made a reasonable effort to obtain good information from a reputable source such as the local Placing Assessment and Counselling Team or an appropriate disability organisation.

If either of two possible adjustments would remove a disadvantage, but the employer has cost or operational reasons for preferring one rather than the other, it is unlikely to be reasonable for him to have to make the one that is not preferred. If, however, the employee refuses to cooperate with the proposed adjustment the employer is likely to be justified in not providing it.

A disabled employee refuses to follow specific occupational medical advice provided on behalf of an employer about methods of working or managing his condition at work. If he has no good reason for this and his condition deteriorates as a result, the refusal may justify the employer's subsequent failure to make an adjustment for the worsened condition.

Building regulations, listed buildings, leases

How do building regulations affect reasonable adjustments?

4.35 A building or extension to a building may have been constructed in accordance with Part M of the building regulations (or the Scottish parallel, Part T of the Technical standards) which is concerned with access and facilities for disabled people. Regulations provide in these circumstances that the employer does not have to alter any physical characteristic of the building or extension which still complies with the building regulations in force at the time the building works were carried out[1].

> Where the building regulations in force at the time of a building's construction required that a door should be a particular width, the employer would not have to alter the width of the door later. However, he might have to alter other aspects of the door (eg the type of handle).

1 Employment Regulations (see paragraph 1.6).

4.36 Employers can only rely upon this defence if the feature still satisfies the requirement of the building regulations that applied when the building or extension was constructed.

What about the need to obtain statutory consent for some building changes?

4.37 Employers might have to obtain statutory consent before making adjustments involving changes to premises. Such consents include planning permission, listed building consent, scheduled monument consent and fire regulations approval. The Act does not override the need to obtain such consents (s 59). Therefore an employer does not have to make an adjustment if it requires a statutory consent which has not been given.

4.38 The time it would take to obtain consent may make a particular adjustment impracticable and therefore one which it is not reasonable for the employer to have to make. However, the employer would then also need to consider whether it was reasonable to have to make a temporary adjustment—one that does not require consent—in the meantime.

4.39 Employers should explore ways of making reasonable adjustments which either do not require statutory consent or are likely to receive it. They may well find it useful to consult their local planning authority (in England and Wales) or planning authority (in Scotland).

> An employer needs statutory consent to widen an internal doorway in a listed building for a woman disabled in an accident who returned to work in a wheelchair. The employer considers using a different office but this is not practicable. In the circumstances the widening would be a reasonable adjustment. The employer knows from the local planning authority that consent is likely to be given in a few weeks. In the meantime the employer arranges for the woman to share an accessible office which is inconvenient for both employees, but does not prevent them doing their jobs and is tolerable for that limited period.

What happens where a lease says that certain changes to premises cannot be made?

4.40 Special provisions apply where a lease would otherwise prevent a reasonable adjustment involving an alteration to premises. The Act modifies the effect of the lease so far as necessary to enable the employer to make the alteration if the landlord consents, and to provide that the landlord must not withhold consent unreasonably but may attach reasonable conditions to the consent (s 16).

How will arrangements for getting the landlord's consent work?

4.41 The Act says that the employer must write to the landlord (called the 'lessor' in the Act) asking for consent to make the alteration. If an employer fails to apply to the landlord for consent, anything in the lease which would prevent that alteration must be ignored in deciding whether it was reasonable for the employer to have to make that alteration (Sch 4 para 1). If the landlord consents, the employer can then carry out the alteration. If the landlord refuses consent the employer must notify the disabled person, but then has no further obligation[1].

Where the landlord fails to reply within 21 days or a reasonable period after that he is deemed to have withheld his consent. In those circumstances the withholding of the consent will be unreasonable (see paragraph 4.44)[1].

1 Employment Regulations (see paragraph 1.6).

4.42 If the landlord attaches a condition to the consent and it is reasonable for the employer to have to carry out the alteration on that basis, the employer must then carry out the alteration. If it would not be reasonable for the employer to have to carry out the alteration on that basis, the employer must notify the disabled person, but then has no further obligation.

When is it unreasonable for a landlord to withhold consent?

4.43 This will depend on the circumstances but a trivial or arbitrary reason would almost certainly be unreasonable. Many reasonable adjustments to premises will not harm a landlord's interests and so it would generally be unreasonable to withhold consent for them.

> A particular adjustment helps make a public building more accessible generally and is therefore likely to benefit the landlord. It would very probably be unreasonable for consent to be withheld in these circumstances.

4.44 Regulations provide that withholding consent will be unreasonable where:

- a landlord has failed to act within the time limits referred to in paragraph 4.41 above (ie 21 days of receipt of the employer's application or a reasonable period after that);
- the lease says that consent will be given to alterations of that type or says that such consent will be given if it is sought in a particular way and it has been sought in that way[1].

1 Employment Regulations (see paragraph 1.6).

When is it reasonable for a landlord to withhold consent?

4.45 This will depend on the particular circumstances.

> A particular adjustment is likely to result in a substantial permanent reduction in the value of the landlord's interest in the premises. The landlord would almost certainly be acting reasonably in withholding consent.
>
> A particular adjustment would cause significant disruption or inconvenience to other tenants (for example, where the premises consist of multiple adjoining units). The landlord would be likely to be acting reasonably in withholding consent.

What conditions would it be reasonable for a landlord to make when giving consent?

4.46 This will depend on the particular circumstances. However, Regulations provide that it would be reasonable for the landlord to require the employer to meet any of the following conditions:

- obtain planning permission and other statutory consents;
- submit any plans to the landlord for approval (provided that the landlord then confirms that approval will not be withheld unreasonably);
- allow the landlord a reasonable opportunity to inspect the work when completed;
- reimburse the landlord's reasonable costs incurred in connection with the giving of his consent;
- reinstate the altered part of the premises to its former state when the lease expires but

only if it would have been reasonable for the landlord to have refused consent in the first place[1].

1 Employment Regulations (see paragraph 1.6).

What happens if the landlord has a 'superior' landlord?

4.47 The employer's landlord may also hold a lease which prevents him from consenting to the alteration without the consent of the 'superior' landlord. The statutory provisions have been modified by regulations to cover this. The employer's landlord will be acting reasonably by notifying the employer that consent will be given if the superior landlord agrees. The employer's landlord must then apply to the superior landlord to ask for agreement. The provisions in paragraphs 4.41–4.46, including the requirements not to withhold consent unreasonably and not to attach unreasonable conditions, then apply to the superior landlord[1].

1 The Disability Discrimination (Sub-leases and Sub-tenancies) Regulations 1996.

What if some agreement other than a lease prevents the premises being altered?

4.48 An employer or landlord may be bound by the terms of an agreement or other legally binding obligation (for example, a mortgage or charge or restrictive covenant or, in Scotland, or feu disposition) under which the employer or landlord cannot alter the premises without someone else's consent. In these circumstances regulations provide that it is always reasonable for the employer or landlord to have to take steps to obtain the necessary consent so that a reasonable adjustment can be made. Unless or until that consent is obtained the employer or landlord is not required to make the alteration in question. The step of seeking consent which it is always reasonable to have to take does not extend to having to apply to a court or tribunal[1]. Whether it is reasonable for the employer or landlord to have to apply to a court or tribunal would depend on the circumstances of the case.

1 Employment Regulations (see paragraph 1.6).

Agreements which breach the Act's provisions

Can a disabled person waive rights, or an employer's duties, under the act?

4.49 The Act says that any term in a contract of employment or other agreement is 'void'(ie not valid) to the extent that it would require a person to do anything that would breach any of the Act's employment provisions, or exclude or limit the operation of those provisions (s 9).

4.50 An employer should not include in an agreement any provision intended to avoid obligations under the Act, or to prevent someone from fulfilling obligations. An agreement should not, therefore, be used to try to justify less favourable treatment or deem an adjustment unreasonable. Moreover, even parts of agreements which have such an effect (even though unintended) are made void if they would restrict the working of the employment provisions in the Act. However, special arrangements cover leases and other agreements which might prevent a change to premises which could be an adjustment under the Act but where the possible restrictions to the Act's working were unintentional. These are described in paragraphs 4.40–4.48.

4.51 The Act also says that a contract term is void if it would prevent anyone from making a claim under the employment provisions in an industrial tribunal (s 9). Further information is given in Annex 3 about such agreements.

What about permits issued in accordance with the agricultural wages acts?

4.52 Under the Agricultural Wages Act 1948 and the Agricultural Wages (Scotland) Act minimum wages, and terms and conditions, can be set for agricultural workers. Permits can be issued to individuals who are 'incapacitated' for the purposes of those Acts and they can then be paid such lower minimum rates or be subject to such revised terms and conditions of employment that the permit specifies. Regulations provide that the treatment of a disabled person in accordance with such a permit would be taken to be justified[1]. This would not prevent the employer from having to comply with the duty not to discriminate, including the duty of reasonable adjustment, for matters other than those covered by the permit.

1 Employment Regulations (see paragraph 1.6).

Victimisation

What does the act say about victimisation?

4.53 Victimisation is a special form of discrimination covered by the Act. The Act makes it unlawful for one person to treat another (the victim) less favourably than he would treat other people in the same circumstances because the 'victim' has:

- brought, or given evidence or information in connection with, proceedings under the Act (whether or not proceedings are later withdrawn);
- done anything else under the Act; or
- alleged someone has contravened the Act (whether or not the allegation is later dropped);

or because the person believes or suspects that the victim has done or intends to do any of these things (s 55).

It is unlawful for an employer to victimise either disabled or non-disabled people.

> A disabled employee complains of discrimination. It would be unlawful for the employer to subject non-disabled colleagues to any detriment (eg suspension) for telling the truth about the alleged discrimination at an industrial tribunal hearing or in any internal grievance procedures.

4.54 It is not victimisation to treat a person less favourably because that person has made an allegation which was false and not made in good faith (s 55(*b*)).

(Harassment is covered in paragraphs 6.22–6.23.)

Setting up management systems to help avoid discrimination

What management systems might be set up to help avoid discrimination?

4.55 The Act says that employers are responsible for the actions done by their employees in the course of their employment. In legal proceedings against an employer based on actions of an employee, it is a defence that the employer took such steps as were reasonably practicable to prevent such actions. It is not a defence for the employer simply to show the action took place without his knowledge or approval. Employers who act through agents will also be liable for the actions of their agents done with the employer's express or implied authority (s 58).

> An employer makes it clear to a recruitment agency that the company will not take kindly to recruits with learning disabilities being put forward by the agency. The agency complies by not putting such candidates forward. Both the employer and the agency will be liable if such treatment cannot be justified in an individual case.

4.56 Employers should communicate to their employees and agents any policy they may have on disability matters, and any other policies which have elements relevant to disabled employees (such as health, absenteeism or equal opportunities). All staff should be made aware that it is unlawful to discriminate against disabled people, and be familiar with the policies and practices adopted by their employer to ensure compliance with the law. Employers should provide guidance on non-discriminatory practices for all employees, so they will be aware what they should do and how to deal with disabled colleagues and disabled applicants for vacancies in the organisation, and should ensure so far as possible that these policies and practices are implemented. Employers should also make it clear to their agents what is required of them with regard to their duties under the Act, and the extent of their authority.

4.57 The Act says that an employer is not under an obligation to make an adjustment if he does not know, and could not reasonably be expected to know, that a person has a disability which is likely to place the person at a substantial disadvantage (s 6(6)). An employer must therefore do all he could reasonably be expected to do to find out whether this is the case.

> An employee has a disability which sometimes causes him to cry at work although the cause of this behaviour is not known to the employer. The employer's general approach on such matters is to tell staff to leave their personal problems at home and to make no allowance for such problems in the work arrangements. The employer disciplines the employee without giving him any opportunity to explain that the problem in fact arises from a disability. The employer would be unlikely to succeed in a claim that he could not reasonably be expected to have known of the disability or that it led to the behaviour for which the employee was disciplined.

> An employer has an annual appraisal system which specifically provides an opportunity to notify the employer in confidence if any employees are disabled and are put at a substantial disadvantage by the work arrangements or premises. This practice enables the employer to show that he could not reasonably be expected to know that an employee was put at such a disadvantage as a result of disability, if this was not obvious and was not brought to the employer's attention through the appraisal system.

4.58 In some cases a reasonable adjustment will not work without the co-operation of other employees. Employees may therefore have an important role in helping to ensure that a reasonable adjustment is carried out in practice.

> It is a reasonable adjustment for an employer to communicate in a particular way to an employee with autism (a disability which can make it difficult for someone to understand normal social interaction among people). As part of the reasonable adjustment it is the responsibility of that employer to seek the co-operation of other employees in communicating in that way.

4.59 It may be necessary to tell one or more of a disabled person's colleagues (in confidence) about a disability which is not obvious and/or whether any special assistance is required. This may be limited to the person's supervisor, or it may be necessary to involve other colleagues, depending on the nature of the disability and the reason they need to know about it.

> In order for a person with epilepsy to work safely in a particular factory, it may be necessary to advise fellow workers about the effects of the condition, and the methods for assisting with them.

> An office worker with cancer says that he does not want colleagues to know of his condition. As an adjustment he needs extra time away from work to receive treatment and to rest. Neither his colleagues nor the line manager needs to be told the precise reasons for the extra leave but the latter will need to know that the adjustment is required in order to carry it out effectively.

4.60 The extent to which an employer is entitled to let other staff know about an employee's disability will depend at least in part on the terms of employment. An employer could be held to be discriminating in revealing such information about a disabled employee if the employer would not reveal similar information about another person for an equally legitimate management purpose; or if the employer revealed such information without consulting the individual, whereas the employer's usual practice would be to talk to an employee before revealing personal information about him.

4.61 The Act does not prevent a disabled person keeping a disability confidential from an employer. But this is likely to mean that unless the employer could reasonably be expected to know about the person's disability anyway, the employer will not be under a duty to make a reasonable adjustment. If a disabled person expects an employer to make a reasonable adjustment, he will need to provide the employer—or, as the case may be, someone acting on the employer's behalf—with sufficient information to carry out that adjustment.

> An employee has symptomatic HIV. He prefers not to tell his employer of the condition. However, as the condition progresses, he finds it increasingly difficult to work the required number of hours in a week. Until he tells his employer of his condition—or the employer becomes or could reasonably be expected to be aware of it—he cannot require the employer to change his working hours to overcome the difficulty. However, once the employer is informed he may then have to make a reasonable adjustment.

4.62 If an employer's agent or employee (for example, an occupational health officer, a personnel officer or line manager) knows in that capacity of an employee's disability, then the employer cannot claim that he does not know of that person's disability, and that he is therefore excluded from the obligation to make a reasonable adjustment. This will be the case even if the disabled person specifically asked for such information to be kept confidential. Employers will therefore need to ensure that where information about disabled people may come through different channels, there is a means—suitably confidential—for bringing the information together, so the employer's duties under the Act are fulfilled.

> In a large company an occupational health officer is engaged by the employer to provide him with information about his employees' health. The officer becomes aware of an employee's disability, which the employee's line manager does not know about. The employer's working arrangements put the employee at a substantial disadvantage because of the effects of her disability and she claims that a reasonable adjustment should have been made. It will not be a defence for the employer to claim that he did not know of her disability. This is because the information gained by the officer on the employer's behalf is imputed to the employer. Even if the person did not want the line manager to know that she had a disability, the occupational health officer's knowledge means that the employer's duty under the Act applies. It might even be necessary for the line manager to implement reasonable adjustments without knowing precisely why he has to do so.

4.63 Information will not be imputed to the employer if it is gained by a person providing services to employees independently of the employer. This is the case even if the employer has arranged for those services to be provided.

> An employer contracts with an agency to provide an independent counselling service to employees. The contract says that the counsellors are not acting on the employer's behalf while in the counselling role. Any information about a person's disability obtained by a counsellor during such counselling would not be imputed to the employer and so could not itself place a duty of reasonable adjustment on the employer.

What if someone says they have a disability and the employer is not convinced?

4.64 If a candidate asks for an adjustment to be made because of an impairment whose effects are not obvious, nothing in the Act or Regulations would prohibit the employer from asking for evidence that the impairment is one which gives rise to a disability as defined in the Act.

An applicant says she has a mental illness whose effects require her to take time off work on a frequent, but irregular, basis. If not satisfied that this is true, the employer would be entitled to ask for evidence that the woman has a mental illness which was likely to have the effects claimed and that it is clinically well recognised (as required by the Act).

Effects of other legislation

What about the effects of other legislation?

4.65 An employer is not required to make an adjustment—or do anything under the Act—that would result in a breach of statutory obligations (s 59).

If a particular adjustment would breach health and safety or fire legislation then an employer would not have to make it. However, the employer would still have to consider whether he was required to make any other adjustment which would not breach any legislation. For instance, if someone in a wheelchair could not use emergency evacuation arrangements such as a fire escape on a particular floor, it might be reasonable for the employer to have to relocate that person's job to an office where that problem did not arise.

An employer shortlisting applicants to fill a junior post is considering whether to include a blind applicant who the employer believes might present a safety risk moving around the crowded office. A reasonable adjustment might be to provide mobility training to familiarise the applicant with the work area, so removing any risk there might otherwise be.

What about legislation which places restrictions on what employers can do to recruit disabled people?

4.66 The Disability Discrimination Act does not prevent posts being advertised as open only to disabled candidates. However, the requirement, for example, under section 7 of the Local Government and Housing Act 1989 that every appointment to local authorities must be made on merit means that a post cannot be so advertised. Applications from disabled people can nevertheless be encouraged. However, this requirement to appoint 'on merit' does not exclude the duty under the 1995 Act to make adjustments so a disabled person's 'merit' must be assessed taking into account any such adjustments which would have to be made.

5 RECRUITMENT

Discrimination against applicants

How does the act affect recruitment?

5.1 The Act says that it is unlawful for an employer to discriminate against a disabled person:

- in the arrangements made for determining who should be offered employment;
- in the terms on which the disabled person is offered employment; or
- by refusing to offer, or deliberately not offering, the disabled person employment (s 4(1)).

5.2 The word 'arrangements' has a wide meaning. Employers should avoid discrimination in, for example, specifying the job, advertising the job, and the processes of selection, including the location and timing of interviews, assessment techniques, interviewing, and selection criteria.

Specifying the job

Does the act affect how an employer should draw up a job specification?

5.3 Yes. The inclusion of unnecessary or marginal requirements in a job specification can lead to discrimination.

> An employer stipulates that employees must be 'energetic', when in fact the job in question is largely sedentary in nature. This requirement could unjustifiably exclude some people whose disabilities result in them getting tired more easily than others.
>
> An employer specifies that a driving licence is required for a job which involves limited travelling. An applicant for the job has no driving licence because of the particular effects in his case of cerebral palsy. He is otherwise the best candidate for that job, he could easily and cheaply do the travelling involved other than by driving and it would be a reasonable adjustment for the employer to let him do so. It would be discriminatory to insist on the specification and reject his application solely because he had no driving licence.

5.4 Blanket exclusions (ie exclusions which do not take account of individual circumstances) may lead to discrimination.

> An employer excludes people with epilepsy from all driving jobs. One of the jobs, in practice, only requires a standard licence and normal insurance cover. If, as a result, someone with epilepsy, who has such a licence and can obtain such cover, is turned down for the job then the employer will probably have discriminated unlawfully in excluding her from consideration.
>
> An employer stipulates that candidates for a job must not have a history of mental illness, believing that such candidates will have poor attendance. The employer rejects an applicant solely because he has had a mental illness without checking the individual's probable attendance. Even if good attendance is genuinely essential for the job, this is not likely to be justified and is therefore very likely to be unlawful discrimination.

Can an employer stipulate essential health requirements?

5.5 Yes, but the employer may need to justify doing so, and to show that it would not be reasonable for him to have to waive them, in any individual case.

Can employers simply prefer a certain type of person?

5.6 Stating that a certain personal, medical or health-related characteristic is desirable may also lead to discrimination if the characteristic is not necessary for the performance of the job. Like a requirement, a preference may be decisive against an otherwise well-qualified disabled candidate and may have to be justified in an individual case.

> An employer prefers all employees to have a certain level of educational qualification. A woman with a learning disability, which has prevented her from obtaining the preferred qualification, is turned down for a job because she does not have that qualification. If the qualification is not necessary in order to do the job and she is otherwise the best candidate, then the employer will have discriminated unlawfully against her.

Publicising the vacancy

What does the act say about how an employer can advertise vacancies?

5.7 Where a job is advertised, and a disabled person who applies is refused or deliberately not offered it and complains to an industrial tribunal about disability discrimination, the Act requires the tribunal to assume (unless the employer can prove otherwise) that the reason the person did not get the job was related to his disability if the advertisement could reasonably be taken to indicate:

- that the success of a person's application for the job might depend to any extent on the absence of a disability such as the applicant's; or
- that the employer is unwilling to make an adjustment for a disabled person (s 11).

> An employer puts in an advertisement for an office worker,'Sorry, but gaining access to our building can be difficult for some people'. A man, who as a result of an accident some years previously can only walk with the aid of crutches but can do office work, applies for the job and is turned down. He complains to an industrial tribunal. Because of the wording of the advertisement, the tribunal would have to assume that he did not get the job for a reason relating to his disability unless the employer could prove otherwise.

What is an 'advertisement' for the purposes of the act?

5.8 According to the Act 'advertisement' includes every form of advertisement or notice, whether to the public or not (s 11(3)). This would include advertisements internal to a company or office.

Does an employer have to provide information about jobs in alternative formats?

5.9 In particular cases, this may be a reasonable adjustment.

> A person whom the employer knows to be disabled asks to be given information about a job in a medium that is accessible to her (in large print, in braille, on tape or on computer disk). It is often likely to be a reasonable adjustment for the employer to comply, particularly if the employer's information systems, and the time available before the new employee is needed, mean it can easily be done.

Can an employer say that he would welcome applications from disabled people?

5.10 Yes. The Act does not prevent this and it would be a positive and public statement of the employer's policy.

Can an employer include a question on an application form asking whether someone is disabled?

5.11 Yes. The Act does not prevent employers including such a question on application forms. Employers can also ask whether the individual might need an adjustment and what it might be.

Selection

Does the duty of reasonable adjustment apply to applicants?

5.12 The Act says that the duty to make a reasonable adjustment does not apply where the employer does not know, and could not reasonably be expected to know, that the disabled person in question is or may be an applicant for the post, or, that a particular applicant has a disability which is likely to place him at a disadvantage (s 6(*a*)).

Does an employer have to take special care when considering applications?

5.13 Yes. Employers and their staff or agents must not discriminate against disabled people in the way in which they deal with applications. They may also have to make reasonable adjustments.

> Because of his disability, a candidate asks to submit an application in a particular medium, different from that specified for candidates in general (eg typewritten, by telephone, or on tape). It would normally be a reasonable adjustment for the employer to allow this.

Whom can an employer shortlist for interview?

5.14 If an employer knows that an applicant has a disability and is likely to be at a substantial disadvantage because of the employer's arrangements or premises, the employer should consider whether there is any reasonable adjustment which would bring the disabled person within the field of applicants to be considered even though he would not otherwise be within that field because of that disadvantage. If the employer could only make this judgment with more information it would be discriminatory for him not to put the disabled person on the shortlist for interview if that is how he would normally seek additional information about candidates.

What should an employer do when arranging interviews?

5.15 Employers should think ahead for interviews. Giving applicants the opportunity to indicate any relevant effects of a disability and to suggest adjustments to help overcome any disadvantage the disability may cause, could help the employer avoid discrimination in the interview and in considering the applicant, by clarifying whether any reasonable adjustments may be required.

5.16 Nevertheless, if a person, whom the employer previously did not know, and could not have known, to be disabled, arrives for interview and is placed at a substantial disadvantage because of the arrangements, the employer may still be under a duty to make a reasonable adjustment from the time that he first learns of the disability and the disadvantage. However, what the employer has to do in such circumstances might be less extensive than if advance notice had been given.

What changes might an employer have to make to arrangements for interviews?

5.17 There are many possible reasonable adjustments, depending on the circumstances.

> A person has difficulty attending at a particular time because of a disability. It will very likely be reasonable for the employer to have to rearrange the time.
>
> A hearing impaired candidate has substantial difficulties with the interview arrangements. The interviewer may simply need to ensure he faces the applicant and speaks clearly or is prepared to repeat questions. The interviewer should make sure that his face is well lit when talking to someone with a hearing or visual impairment. It will almost always be reasonable for an employer to have to provide such help with communication support if the interviewee would otherwise be at a substantial disadvantage.
>
> An employer who pays expenses to candidates who come for interview could well have to pay additional expenses to meet any special requirements of a disabled

person arising from any substantial disadvantage to which she would otherwise be put by the interview arrangements. This might include paying travelling expenses for a support worker or reasonable cost of travel by taxi, rather than by bus or train, if this is necessary because of the disability.

A job applicant does not tell an employer (who has no knowledge of her disability) in advance that she uses a wheelchair. On arriving for the interview she discovers that the room is not accessible. The employer did not know of the disability and so could not have been expected to make changes in advance. However, it would still be a reasonable adjustment for the employer to hold the interview in an alternative accessible room, if a suitable one was easily available at the time with no, or only an acceptable level of, disruption or additional cost.

Should an employer consider making changes to the way the interview is carried out?

5.18 Yes, although whether any change is needed—and, if so, what change—will depend on the circumstances.

It would almost always be reasonable to allow an applicant with a learning disability to bring a supportive person such as a friend or relative to assist when answering questions that are not part of tests.

It would normally be reasonable to allow a longer time for an interview to someone with a hearing impairment using a sign language interpreter to communicate.

Does an employer have to make changes to anticipate any disabled person applying for a job?

5.19 No. An employer is not required to make changes in anticipation of applications from disabled people in general. It is only if the employer knows or could be reasonably expected to know that a particular disabled person is, or may be, applying and is likely to be substantially disadvantaged by the employer's premises or arrangements, that the employer may have to make changes.

Should an employer ask about a disability?

5.20 The Act does not prohibit an employer from seeking information about a disability but an employer must not use it to discriminate against a disabled person. An employer should ask only about a disability if it is, or may be, relevant to the person's ability to do the job—after a reasonable adjustment, if necessary. Asking about the effects of a disability might be important in deciding what adjustments ought to be made. The employer should avoid discriminatory questions.

An applicant whose disability has left him using a wheelchair but healthy, is asked by an employer whether any extra leave might be required because of the condition. This is unlikely to be discriminatory because a need for extra time off work may be a substantial factor relevant to the person's ability to do the job. Therefore such a question would normally be justified. Similarly, a reasonable question about whether any changes may need to be made to the workplace to accommodate the use of the wheelchair would probably not be discriminatory.

Does the act prevent employers carrying out aptitude or other tests in the recruitment process?

5.21 No, but routine testing of all candidates may still discriminate against particular individuals or substantially disadvantage them. If so, the employer would need to revise the tests—or the way the results of such tests are assessed—to take account of specific disabled candidates, except where the nature and form of the test were necessary to assess a matter relevant to the job. It may, for instance, be a reasonable adjustment to accept a lower 'pass rate' for a person whose disability inhibits performance in such a test. The extent to which this is required would depend on how closely the test is related to the job in question and what adjustments the employer might have to make if the applicant were given the job.

> An employer sets a numeracy test for prospective employees. A person with a learning disability takes the test and does not achieve the level the employer normally stipulates. If the job in fact entails very little numerical work and the candidate is otherwise well suited for the job it is likely to be a reasonable adjustment for the employer to waive the requirement.

> An employer sets candidates a short oral test. An applicant is disabled by a bad stammer, but only under stress. It may be a reasonable adjustment to allow her more time to complete the test, or to give the test in written form instead, though not if oral communication is relevant to the job and assessing this was the purpose of the test.

Can an employer specify qualifications?

5.22 An employer is entitled to specify that applicants for a job must have certain qualifications. However, if a disabled person is rejected for the job because he lacks a qualification, the employer will have to justify that rejection if the reason why the person is rejected (ie the lack of a qualification) is connected with his disability. Justification will involve showing that the qualification is relevant and significant in terms of the particular job and the particular applicant, and that there is no reasonable adjustment which would change this. In some circumstances it might be feasible to reassign those duties to which the qualification relates, or to waive the requirement for the qualification if this particular applicant has alternative evidence of the necessary level of competence.

> An employer seeking someone to work in an administrative post specifies that candidates must have the relevant NVQ Level 4 qualification. If Level 4 fairly reflects the complex and varied nature and substantial personal responsibility of the work, and these aspects of the job cannot reasonably be altered, the employer will be able to justify rejecting a disabled applicant who has only been able to reach Level 3 because of his disability and who cannot show the relevant level of competence by other means.

> An employer specifies that two GCSEs are required for a certain post. This is to show that a candidate has the general level of ability required. No particular subjects are specified. An applicant whose dyslexia prevented her from passing written examinations cannot meet this requirement, but the employer would be unable to justify rejecting her on this account alone if she could show she nevertheless had the skill and intelligence called for in the post.

Can an employer insist on a disabled person having a medical examination?

5.23 Yes. However, if an employer insists on a medical check for a disabled person and not others, without justification, he will probably be discriminating unlawfully. The fact that a person has a disability is unlikely in itself to justify singling out that person to have a health check, although such action might be justified in relation to some jobs.

> An employer requires all candidates for employment to have a medical examination. That employer would normally be entitled to include a disabled person.

An applicant for a job has a disabling heart condition. The employer routinely issues a health questionnaire to job applicants, and requires all applicants who state they have a disability to undergo a medical examination. Under the Act, the employer would not be justified in requiring a medical examination whenever an applicant states he has a disability—for example, this would not normally be justified if the disability is clearly relevant neither to the job nor to the environment in which the job is done. However, the employer would probably be justified in asking the applicant with the disabling heart condition to have a medical examination restricted to assessing its implications for the particular job in its context. If, for example, the job required lifting and carrying but these abilities were limited by the condition, the employer would also have to consider whether it would be reasonable for him to have to make a change such as providing a mechanical means of lifting and/or carrying, or arranging for the few items above the person's limit to be dealt with by another person, whilst ensuring that any health and safety provisions were not breached.

How can an employer take account of medical evidence?

5.24 In most cases, having a disability does not adversely affect a person's general health. Medical evidence about a disability can justify an adverse employment decision (such as dismissing or not promoting). It will not generally do so if there is no effect on the person's ability to do the work (or any effect is less than substantial), however great the effects of the disability are in other ways. The condition or effects must be relevant to the employer's decision.

An applicant for a post on a short-term contract has a progressive condition which has some effects, but is likely to have substantial adverse effects only in the long term. The likelihood of these long-term effects would not itself be a justifiable reason for the employer to reject him.

An employer requires all candidates for a certain job to be able to work for at least two years to complete a particular work project. Medical evidence shows that a particular candidate is unlikely to be able to continue working for that long. It would be lawful to reject that candidate if the two-year requirement was justified in terms of the work, and if it would not be reasonable for the employer to have to waive it in the particular circumstances.

Advice from an occupational health expert simply that an employee was 'unfit for work' would not mean that the employer's duty to make a reasonable adjustment was waived.

What will help an employer decide to select a particular disabled person?

5.25 The employer must take into account any adjustments that it is reasonable for him to have to make. Suggestions made by the candidate at any stage may assist in identifying these.

What if a disabled person just isn't the right person for the job?

5.26 An employer must not discriminate against a disabled candidate, but there is no requirement (aside from reasonable adjustment) to treat a disabled person more favourably than he treats or would treat others. An employer will have to assess an applicant's merits as they would be if any reasonable adjustments required under the Act had been made. If, after allowing for those adjustments, a disabled person would not be the best person for the job the employer would not have to recruit that person.

Terms and conditions of service

Are there restrictions on the terms and conditions an employer can offer a disabled person?

5.27 Terms and conditions of service should not discriminate against a disabled person. The employer should consider whether any reasonable adjustments need to be made to the terms and conditions which would otherwise apply.

> An employer's terms and conditions state the hours an employee has to be in work. It might be a reasonable adjustment to change these hours for someone whose disability means that she has difficulty using public transport during rush hours.

Does that mean that an employer can never offer a disabled person a less favourable contract?

5.28 No. Such a contract may be justified if there is a material and substantial reason and there is no reasonable adjustment which can be made to remove that reason.

> A person's disability means she has significantly lower output than other employees doing similar work, even after an adjustment. Her work is of neither lower nor higher quality than theirs. The employer would be justified in paying her less in proportion to the lower output if it affected the value of her work to the business.

Can employers still operate performance-related pay?

5.29 Regulations provide that this is justified so long as the scheme applies equally to all employees, or all of a particular class of employees. There would be no requirement to make a reasonable adjustment to an arrangement of this kind to ensure (for example) that a person's pay was topped up if a deteriorating condition happened to lead to lower performance[1]. However, there would still be a duty to make a reasonable adjustment to any aspect of the premises or work arrangements if that would prevent the disability reducing the employee's performance.

1 Employment Regulations (see paragraph 1.6).

6 EMPLOYMENT

Discrimination against employees

Does the act cover all areas of employment?

6.1 Yes. The Act says that it is unlawful for an employer to discriminate against a disabled person whom he employs:

- in the terms of employment which he affords him;
- in the opportunities which he affords him for promotion, a transfer, training or receiving any other benefit;
- by refusing to afford him, or deliberately not affording him, any such opportunity; or
- by dismissing him, or subjecting him to any other detriment (s 4(2)).

6.2 Therefore, an employer should not discriminate in relation to, for example: terms and conditions of service, arrangements made for induction, arrangements made for employees who become disabled (or who have a disability which worsens), opportunities for promotion, transfer, training or receiving any other benefit, or refusal of such opportunities, pensions, dismissal or any detriment.

Induction

What is the effect on induction procedures?

6.3 Employers must not discriminate in their induction procedures. The employer may have to make adjustments to ensure a disabled person is introduced into a new working environment in a clearly structured and supported way with, if necessary, an individually tailored induction programme (s 4(2) and s 6(1)).

> An employer runs a one day induction course for new recruits. A recruit with a learning disability is put at a substantial disadvantage by the way the course is normally run. The employer might have to make an alternative arrangement: for example running a separate, longer course for the person, or permitting someone to sit in on the normal course to provide support, assistance or encouragement.

Promotion and transfer

What are an employer's duties as far as promotion and transfer are concerned?

6.4 Employers must not discriminate in assessing a disabled person's suitability for promotion or transfer, in the practical arrangements necessary to enable the promotion or transfer to take place, in the operation of the appraisal, selection and promotion or transfer process, or in the new job itself—and may have to make a reasonable adjustment (s 4(2)(*b*) and (*c*) and s 6(1)).

> A garage owner does not consider for promotion to assistant manager a clerk who has lost the use of her right arm, because he wrongly and unreasonably believes that her disability might prevent her performing competently in a managerial post. The reason used by the employer to deny the clerk promotion has meant that she was discriminated against.
>
> An employer considering a number of people for a job on promotion is aware that one of the candidates for interview has a hearing impairment, but does not find out whether the person needs any special arrangements for the interview, for example a sign language interpreter. If the candidate requires such an adjustment, and it would be reasonable for the employer to have to make it, the employer would fail in his duty if he did not make that adjustment.
>
> A civil engineer whose disability involves kidney dialysis treatment, is based in London and regularly visits hospital for the treatment. She wishes to transfer to a vacant post in her company's Scottish office. She meets all the requirements for the post, but her transfer is turned down on the ground that her need for treatment would mean that, away from the facilities in London, she would be absent from work for longer. The employer had made no attempt to discuss this with her or get medical advice. If the employer had done so, it would have been clear that similar treatment would be equally available in Belfast. In these circumstances, the employer probably could not show that relying on this reason was justified.
>
> Someone disabled by a back injury is seeking promotion to supervisor. A minor duty involves assisting with the unloading of the weekly delivery van, which the person's back injury would prevent. In assessing her suitability for promotion, the employer should consider whether reallocating this duty to another person would be a reasonable adjustment.

What should an employer do to check that promotion and transfer arrangements do not discriminate?

6.5 The employer should review the arrangements to check that qualifications required are justified for the job to be done. He should also check that other arrangements, for example systems which determine other criteria for a particular job, do not exclude disabled people who may have been unable to meet those criteria because of their disability but would be capable of performing well in the job.

Training and other benefits provided by the employer

Does the act apply to the provision of training?

6.6 Yes. Employers must not discriminate in selection for training and must make any necessary reasonable adjustments (s 4(2)(*b*) and (*c*) and s 6(1)).

> An employer wrongly assumes that a disabled person will be unwilling or unable to undertake demanding training or attend a residential training course, instead of taking an informed decision. He may well not be able to justify a decision based on that assumption.
>
> An employer may need to alter the time or the location of the training for someone with a mobility problem, make training manuals, slides or other visual media accessible to a visually impaired employee, perhaps by providing braille versions or having them read out, or ensure that an induction loop is available for someone with a hearing impairment.
>
> An employer refuses to allow a disabled employee to be coached for a theory examination relating to practical work which the disability prevented the employee from doing. The employer would almost always be justified in refusing to allow the coaching because it was designed to equip employees for an area of work for which, because of the disability, the person could not be suited even by a reasonable adjustment.

What about other benefits provided by employers?

6.7 An employer must not discriminate in providing disabled people with opportunities for receiving benefits (which include 'facilities' and 'services') which are available to other employees (s 4(2)(*b*) and (*c*)). The employer must make any necessary reasonable adjustment to the way the benefits are provided (s 6(1)) although this does not apply to benefits under occupational pension schemes or certain other employment related benefit schemes (paragraph 6.16).

> Benefits might include canteens, meal vouchers, social clubs and other recreational activities, dedicated car parking spaces, discounts on products, bonuses, share options, hairdressing, clothes allowances, financial services, healthcare, medical assistance/insurance, transport to work, company car, education assistance, workplace nurseries, and rights to special leave.
>
> If physical features of a company's social club would inhibit a disabled person's access it might be a reasonable adjustment for the employer to make suitable modifications.
>
> An employer provides dedicated car parking spaces near to the workplace. It is likely to be reasonable for the employer to have to allocate one of these spaces to a disabled employee who has significant difficulty getting from the public car parks further away that he would otherwise have to use.

6.8 If an employer provides benefits to the public, or to a section of the public which includes the disabled employee, provision of those benefits will normally fall outside the duty not to discriminate in employment. Instead, the duty in the Act not to discriminate in providing goods, facilities and services will apply. However, the employment duty will apply if the benefit to employees is materially different (eg at a discount), is governed by the contract of employment, or relates to training (s 4(2) and (3)).

> A disabled employee of a supermarket chain who believes he has been discriminated against when buying goods as a customer at any branch of the supermarket would have no claim under the employment provisions. However, if that employee were using a discount card provided only to employees, then the employment provisions would apply if any less favourable treatment related to his use of the card.

Occupational pension schemes and insurance

What does the act say about occupational pension schemes?

6.9 The Act inserts into every scheme a 'non-discrimination' rule. The trustees or managers of the scheme are prohibited by that rule from doing—or omitting to do—anything to members or non-members of schemes that would be unlawful discrimination if done by an employer (s 17). References to employers in paragraphs 6.11–6.15 should therefore be read as if they also apply to trustees or managers when appropriate.

When is less favourable treatment justified?

6.10 Less favourable treatment for a reason relating to a disability can be justified only if the reason is material and substantial.

> Trustees of a pension scheme would not be justified in excluding a woman simply because she had a visual impairment. That fact, in itself, would be no reason why she should not receive the same pension benefits as any other employee.

6.11 There are circumstances when a disabled person's health or health prognosis is such that the cost of providing benefits under a pension scheme is substantially greater than it would be for a person without the disability. In these circumstances regulations provide that an employer is regarded as justified in treating a disabled person less favourably in applying the eligibility conditions for receiving the benefit. Employers should satisfy themselves, if necessary with actuarial advice and/or medical evidence, of the likelihood of there being a substantially greater cost[1].

1 Employment Regulations (see paragraph 1.6).

When could the justification be used?

6.12 The justification would be available whenever the disabled person is considered for admission to the scheme. However, the justification cannot be applied to a disabled member, unless a term was imposed at the time of admission which allowed this.

Which benefits does this justification apply to?

6.13 The justification can apply to the following types of benefits provided by an occupational pension scheme: termination of service, retirement, old age or death, accident, injury, sickness or invalidity[1].

1 Employment Regulations (see paragraph 1.6).

Would a minor degree of extra cost amount to a justification for less favourable treatment?

6.14 No. Only the likelihood of a substantial additional cost should be taken to be a justification. Substantial means something more than minor or trivial[1].

An employer receives medical advice that an individual with multiple sclerosis is likely to retire early on health grounds. The employer obtains actuarial advice that the cost of providing that early retirement benefit would be substantially greater than an employee without MS and so the individual is refused access to the scheme. This is justified.

1 Employment Regulations (see paragraph 1.6).

What happens to an employee's rate of contributions if the employer is justified in refusing the employee access to some benefits but not others?

6.15 Regulations provide that if the employer sets a uniform rate of contribution the employer would be justified in applying it to a disabled person. A disabled person could therefore be required to pay the same rate of contributions as other employees, even if not eligible for some of the benefits[1].

1 Employment Regulations (see paragraph 1.6).

Does the duty to make a reasonable adjustment apply?

6.16 No. The duty of reasonable adjustment does not apply to the provision of benefits under an occupational pension scheme or any other benefit payable in money or money's worth under a scheme or arrangement for the benefit of employees in respect of:

- termination of service;
- retirement, old age or death; or
- accident, injury, sickness or invalidity (s 6(11)).(Although there is power to add other matters to this list by regulations, none have been added at the date of this Code).

Therefore, neither the employer nor the scheme's trustees or managers need to make any adjustment for a disabled person who, without that adjustment, will be justifiably denied access either to such a scheme or to a benefit under the scheme. Nor will they have to make an adjustment for someone receiving less benefit because they justifiably receive a lower rate of pay.

Does the act cover the provision of insurance schemes for individual employees?

6.17 The Act also applies to provision of group insurance, such as permanent health insurance or life insurance, by an insurance company for employees under an arrangement with their employer. A disabled person in, or who applies or is considering applying to join, a group of employees covered by such an arrangement is protected from discrimination in the provision of the insurance services in the same way as if he were a member of the public seeking the services of that insurance company under the part of the Act relating to the provision of goods, facilities and services. However, the right of redress in this case would be exercised through an industrial tribunal (and not the courts)(s 18).

Does the act cover the provision of insurance to an employer?

6.18 The employer may have to make reasonable adjustments to remove any disadvantage caused to a disabled person which arose from the arrangements made by the employer to provide himself with insurance cover. Such adjustments could include measures which would reduce any risk otherwise posed by the disabled person so that the insurer would then provide cover, or seeking alternative cover. If cover could not be obtained at all at realistic cost it is most unlikely that the employer would have to bear the risk himself.

> It comes to an employer's attention that someone who works for his antiques business has epilepsy. The employer is obliged to notify his insurance company who refuse to cover the employer against damage caused by the disabled person. To avoid dismissing the employee, it might be reasonable for the employer to have to bar the person from contact with valuable items, if this would mean the insurance company then provided cover.

Retention of disabled employees

6.19 An employer must not discriminate against an employee who becomes disabled, or has a disability which worsens (s 4(2)). The issue of retention might also arise when an employee has a stable impairment but the nature of his employment changes.

6.20 If as a result of the disability an employer's arrangements or a physical feature of the employer's premises place the employee at a substantial disadvantage in doing his existing job, the employer must first consider any reasonable adjustment that would resolve the difficulty. The employer may also need to consult the disabled person at appropriate stages about what his needs are and what effect the disability might have on future employment, for example, where the employee has a progressive condition. The nature of the reasonable adjustments which an employer may have to consider will depend on the circumstances of the case.

> It may be possible to modify a job to accommodate an employee's changed needs. This might be by rearranging working methods or giving another employee certain minor tasks the newly disabled person can no longer do, providing practical aids or adaptations to premises or equipment, or allowing the disabled person to work at different times or places from those with equivalent jobs (for instance, it may be that a change to part-time work might be appropriate for someone who needed to spend some time each week having medical treatment).
>
> A newly disabled employee is likely to need time to readjust. For example, an employer might allow: a trial period to assess whether the employee is able to cope with the current job, or a new one; the employee initially to work from home; a gradual build-up to full time hours; or additional training for a person with learning disabilities who moves to another workplace.
>
> It may be a reasonable adjustment for an employer to move a newly disabled person to a different post within the organisation if a suitable vacancy exists or is expected shortly.
>
> Additional job coaching may be necessary to enable a disabled person to take on a new job.
>
> In many cases where no reasonable adjustment would overcome a particular disability so as to enable the disabled person to continue with similar terms or conditions, it might be reasonable for the employer to have to offer a disabled employee a lower-paying job, applying the rate of pay that would apply to such a position under his usual pay practices.
>
> If new technology (for instance a telephone or information technology system) puts a disabled person at a substantial disadvantage compared with non-disabled people, then the employer would be under a duty to make a reasonable adjustment. For example, some telephone systems may interfere with hearing aids for people with hearing impairments and the quality of the inductive coupler may need to be improved.

Termination of employment

6.21 Dismissal—including compulsory early retirement—of a disabled person for a reason relating to the disability would need to be justified and the reason for it would have to be one which could not be removed by any reasonable adjustment.

> It would be justifiable to terminate the employment of an employee whose disability makes it impossible for him any longer to perform the main functions of his job, if an adjustment such as a move to a vacant post elsewhere in the business is not practicable or otherwise not reasonable for the employer to have to make.
>
> It would be justifiable to terminate the employment of an employee with a worsening progressive condition if the increasing degree of adjustment necessary to accommodate the effects of the condition (shorter hours of work or falling productivity, say) became unreasonable for the employer to have to make.
>
> An employer who needs to reduce the workforce would have to ensure that any scheme which was introduced for choosing candidates for redundancy did not discriminate against disabled people. Therefore, if a criterion for redundancy would apply to a disabled person for a reason relating to the disability, that criterion would have to be 'material' and 'substantial' and the employer would have to consider whether a reasonable adjustment would prevent the criterion applying to the disabled person after all.

Harassment

What does the act say about harassment?

6.22 The Act does not refer to harassment as a separate issue. However, harassing a disabled person on account of a disability will almost always amount to a 'detriment' under the Act.(Victimisation is covered in paragraphs 4.53–4.54.)

Are employers liable for harassment by their employees?

6.23 An employer is responsible for acts of harassment by employees in the course of their employment unless the employer took such steps as were reasonably practicable to prevent it. As a minimum first step harassment because of disability should be made a disciplinary matter and staff should be made aware that it will be taken seriously.

7 PARTICULAR PROVISIONS

Discrimination against contract workers

7.1 The Act deals specifically with work which is carried out by individuals ('contract workers') for a person (a 'principal') who hires them under contract from their employer (generally an employment business)—referred to below as the 'sending' employer.

What does the act say about contract workers?

7.2 The Act says that it is unlawful for a principal to discriminate against a disabled person:

- in the terms on which the person is allowed to do the contract work;
- by not allowing the person to do, or continue to do, the contract work;
- in the way he affords the person access to, or by failing to afford him access to, benefits in relation to contract work; or

- by subjecting the person to any other detriment in relation to contract work (s 12(1)).

7.2 The Act and Regulations apply, generally speaking, as if the principal were, or would be, the actual employer of the contract worker. Therefore, the same definition of 'discrimination'—including the need to justify less favourable treatment—applies as for employers (s 12(3)).

> The employer of a labourer, who some years ago was disabled by clinical depression but has since recovered, proposes to supply him to a contractor to work on a building site. Although his past disability is covered by the Act, the site manager refuses to accept him because of his medical history. Unless the contractor can show that the manager's action is justified, the contractor would be acting unlawfully.

What will be the effect of the duty to make adjustments for principals?

7.4 The duty to make a reasonable adjustment applies to a principal as to an employer (s 12(3)).

7.5 In deciding whether any, and if so, what, adjustment would be reasonable for a principle to have to make, the period for which the contract worker will work for the principal is important. It might well be unreasonable for a principle to have to make certain adjustments if the worker will be with the principal for only a short time.

> An employment business enters into a contract with a firm of accountants to provide an assistant for two weeks to cover an unexpected absence. The employment business wishes to put forward a person who, because of his disability, finds it difficult to travel during the rush hour and would like his working hours to be modified accordingly. It might not be reasonable for the firm to have to agree given the short time in which to negotiate and implement the new hours.

Will the principal and the 'sending' employer both have duties to make reasonable adjustments?

7.6 Both the 'sending' employer and the principal may separately be under a duty of reasonable adjustment in the case of a contract worker who is disabled. If the 'sending' employer's own premises or arrangements place the contract worker at a substantial disadvantage, then the 'sending' employer may have a duty to make a reasonable adjustment (s 6(1)). The 'sending' employer may also have a duty to make a reasonable adjustment where a similar substantial disadvantage is likely to affect a contract worker as a result of the arrangements or premises of all or most of the principals to whom he might be supplied. The employer would not have to take separate steps in relation to each principal, but would have to make any reasonable adjustment within his power which would overcome the disadvantage wherever it might arise. The principal would not have to make any adjustment which the employer should make[1]. However, subject to that the principal would be responsible only for any additional reasonable adjustment which is necessary solely because of the principal's own arrangements or premises (s 6(1) applied by s 12(3)). It would also usually be reasonable for a principal and a 'sending' employer to have to cooperate with any steps taken by the other to assist a disabled contract worker.

> A travel agency hires a clerical worker from an employment business to fulfil a three month contract to file travel invoices during the busy summer holiday period. The contract worker is a wheelchair user, and is quite capable of doing the job if a few minor, temporary changes are made to the arrangement of furniture in the office. It would be reasonable for the travel agency to make this adjustment.
>
> A bank hires a blind word processor operator as a contract worker from an employment business. The employment business provides her with a specially adapted

portable computer because she would otherwise be at a similar substantial disadvantage in doing the work wherever she does it.(In such circumstances the bank would not have to provide a specially adapted computer if the employment business did not.) The bank would have to cooperate by letting the contract worker use her computer whilst working for the bank if it is compatible with the bank's systems. If not, it could be a reasonable adjustment for the bank to make the computer compatible and for the employment business to allow that change to be made.

1 Employment Regulations (see paragraph 1.6).

What about contract workers in small firms?

7.7 The Act applies to any employment business which has 20 or more employees (including people currently employed by it but hired out to principals). It also applies to any principal who has 20 or more workers (counting both the principal's own employees and any contract workers currently working for the principal). It does not apply to employment businesses or principals with fewer than 20 employees. Note the extended definition of 'employment' in the Act (see paragraph 2.8).

An employment business has 15 employees (including people currently hired out to others) and enters a contract to provide a worker in a shop. The shop employs 29 people. Neither the duty not to discriminate nor the duty to make a reasonable adjustment applies to the employment business, but both duties apply to the owner of the shop. However, the length of time the worker was contracted to work at the shop would be an important factor in assessing whether the shop-owner had to make any significant adjustment.

A deaf individual is employed by an employment business that has 100 employees (including people currently hired out to others). He is hired regularly to do contract work and, as a reasonable adjustment, the business provides a portable induction loop for assignments. If he works for a principal with, say, 17 workers (counting both employees and contract workers), that principal would not be required to cooperate with use of the induction loop. However, if the principal has 20 or more such workers the principal would be obliged to cooperate.

What about the supported placement scheme (sps)?

7.8 These arrangements also apply to the Employment Service's Supported Placement Scheme (SPS) for severely disabled people. The 'contractor' under the scheme (usually a local authority or voluntary body) is the equivalent of the 'sending' employer, and the 'host employer' is the equivalent of the principal. A local authority can even be both the contractor and the host employer at the same time (as can a voluntary body) in which case the duty not to discriminate and the duty of reasonable adjustment would apply to it as to an employer.

Provisions applying to trade organisations

What does the act say about trade organisations?

7.9 A trade organisation is defined as an organisation of workers or of employers, or any other organisation whose members carry on a particular profession or trade for the purposes of which the organisation exists (s 13(4)). Therefore trade unions, employers' associations, and similar bodies like the Law Society and chartered professional institutions, for example, must comply with the legislation.

7.10 The Act says that it is unlawful for a trade organisation to discriminate against a disabled person:

- in the terms on which it is prepared to admit the person to membership; or
- by refusing to accept, or deliberately not accepting, an application for membership.

It is also unlawful for a trade organisation to discriminate against a disabled member of the organisation:

- in the way it affords the person access to any benefits or by refusing or deliberately omitting to afford access to them;
- by depriving the person of membership, or varying the terms of membership; or
- by subjecting the person to any other detriment (s 13).

Trade organisations should therefore check that they do not discriminate as regards, for example, training facilities, welfare or insurance schemes, invitations to attend events, processing of grievances, assistance to members in their employers' disciplinary or dismissal procedures.

7.11 The Act defines discrimination by a trade organisation in similar terms to the definition relating to discrimination by an employer. Therefore, the need to justify less favourable treatment for a reason relating to disability applies as in the case of an employer (s 14(3)).

> A trade organisation is arranging a trip to some of its members' workplaces but it decides to exclude a member in a wheelchair because too many of the sites are inaccessible to make participation worthwhile. This could well be justified.(Note, however, paragraph 7.12)

Do trade organisations have a duty to make adjustments?

7.12 The Act includes a requirement on trade organisations to make reasonable adjustments (s 15). However, this duty will not be brought into force until after the other employment provisions, at a date which will be subject to consultation.

What about the actions of employees or representatives of trade organisations?

7.13 Individual employees or agents of trade organisations who have dealings with members or applicants are treated in the same way as individual employees or agents of employers who deal with job applicants or employees: the trade organisation is responsible for their actions (s 58).

8 RESOLVING DISAGREEMENTS WITHIN THE EMPLOYING ORGANISATION

What does the Act say about resolving disagreements?

8.1 The Act does not require employers to resolve disputes within their organisations. However, it is in an employer's interests to resolve problems as they arise where possible. This should be in a non-discriminatory way to comply with the Act's general provisions.

8.2 One method might be the use of a grievance procedure. Grievance procedures provide an open and fair way for employees to make known their concerns and enable grievances to be resolved quickly before they become major difficulties. Use of the procedures can highlight areas where the employer's duty of reasonable adjustment may not have been observed, and can prevent misunderstandings in this area leading to tribunal complaints.

Do existing grievance and disciplinary procedures need changing?

8.3 Where grievance or disciplinary procedures are in place, the employer might wish to review, and where necessary adapt, them to ensure that they are flexible enough to be used by disabled employees. Where a formal grievance (or disciplinary) procedure operates, it must be open, or applied, to disabled employees on the same basis as to others. Employers will have to ensure that grievance (or disciplinary) procedures do not, in themselves, discriminate against disabled employees and may have to make reasonable adjustments to enable some disabled employees to use grievance procedures effectively or to ensure disciplinary procedures have the same impact on disabled employees as on others.

> An employee with a learning disability has to attend an interview under the employer's disciplinary procedures. The employee would like his guardian or a friend to be present. The employer agrees to this but refuses to rearrange the interview to a time which is more convenient to the guardian or friend. The employer may be in breach of the duty to make a reasonable adjustment.

(See Annex 3 for information about industrial tribunals.)

ANNEX 1 WHAT IS MEANT BY DISABILITY

1 This Annex is included to aid understanding about who is covered by the Act and should provide sufficient information on the definition of disability to cover the large majority of cases. The definition of disability in the Act is designed to cover only people who would generally be considered to be disabled. A Government publication *Guidance on matters to be taken into account in determining questions relating to the definition of disability*, is also available.

When is a person disabled?

2 A person has a disability if he has a physical or mental impairment which has a substantial and long-term adverse effect on his ability to carry out normal day-to-day activities.

What about people who have recovered from a disability?

3 People who have had a disability within the definition are protected from discrimination even if they have since recovered.

What does 'impairment' cover?

4 It covers physical or mental impairments; this includes sensory impairments, such as those affecting sight or hearing.

Are all mental impairments covered?

5 The term 'mental impairment' is intended to cover a wide range of impairments relating to mental functioning, including what are often known as learning disabilities. However, the Act states that it does not include any impairment resulting from or consisting of a mental illness, unless that illness is a clinically well-recognised illness. A clinically well-recognised illness is one that is recognised by a respected body of medical opinion.

What is a 'substantial' adverse effect?

6 A substantial adverse effect is something which is more than a minor or trivial effect. The requirement that an effect must be substantial reflects the general understanding of disability as a limitation going beyond the normal differences in ability which might exist among people.

What is a 'long-term' effect?

7 A long-term effect of an impairment is one:

- which has lasted at least 12 months; or
- where the total period for which it lasts is likely to be at least 12 months; or
- which is likely to last for the rest of the life of the person affected.

8 Effects which are not long-term would therefore include loss of mobility due to a broken limb which is likely to heal within 12 months and the effects of temporary infections, from which a person would be likely to recover within 12 months.

What if the effects come and go over a period of time?

9 If an impairment has had a substantial adverse effect on normal day-to-day activities but that effect ceases, the substantial effect is treated as continuing if it is likely to recur; that is if it is more probable than not that the effect will recur. To take the example of a person with rheumatoid arthritis whose impairment has a substantial adverse effect, which then ceases to be substantial (ie the person has a period of remission). The effects are to be treated as if they are continuing, and are likely to continue beyond 12 months, *if*:

- the impairment remains; and
- at least one recurrence of the substantial effect is likely to take place 12 months or more after the initial occurrence.

This would then be a long-term effect.

What are 'normal day-to-day activities'?

10 They are activities which are carried out by most people on a fairly regular and frequent basis. The term is not intended to include activities which are normal only for a particular person or group of people, such as playing a musical instrument, or a sport, to a professional standard or performing a skilled or specialised task at work. However, someone who is affected in such a specialised way but is also affected in normal day-to-day activities, would be covered by this part of the definition. The test of whether an impairment affects normal day-to-day activities is whether it affects one of the broad categories of capacity listed in Schedule 1 to the Act. They are:

- mobility;
- manual dexterity;
- physical co-ordination;
- continence;
- ability to lift, carry or otherwise move everyday objects;
- speech, hearing or eyesight;
- memory or ability to concentrate, learn or understand; or
- perception of the risk of physical danger.

What about treatment?

11 Someone with an impairment may be receiving medical or other treatment which alleviates or removes the effects (though not the impairment). In such cases, the treatment is ignored and the impairment is taken to have the effect it would have had without such treatment. This

does not apply if substantial adverse effects are not likely to recur even if the treatment stops (ie the impairment has been cured).

Does this include people who wear spectacles?

12 No. The sole exception to the rule about ignoring the effects of treatment is the wearing of spectacles or contact lenses. In this case, the effect while the person is wearing spectacles or contact lenses should be considered.

Are people who have disfigurements covered?

13 People with severe disfigurements are covered by the Act. They do not need to demonstrate that the impairment has a substantial adverse effect on their ability to carry out normal day-to-day activities.

What about people who know their condition is going to get worse over time?

14 Progressive conditions are conditions which are likely to change and develop over time. Examples given in the Act are cancer, multiple sclerosis, muscular dystrophy and HIV infection. Where a person has a progressive condition he will be covered by the Act from the moment the condition leads to an impairment which has *some* effect on ability to carry out normal day-to-day activities, even though not a *substantial* effect, if that impairment is likely eventually to have a substantial adverse effect on such ability.

What about people who are registered disabled?

15 Those registered as disabled under the Disabled Persons (Employment) Act 1944 both on 12 January 1995 and 2 December 1996 will be treated as being disabled under the Disability Discrimination Act 1995 for three years from the latter date. At all times from 2 December 1996 onwards they will be covered by the Act as people who have had a disability. This does not preclude them from being covered as having a current disability any time after the three year period has finished. Whether they are or not will depend on whether they—like anyone else—meet the definition of disability in the Act.

Are people with genetic conditions covered?

16 If a genetic condition has no effect on ability to carry out normal day-to-day activities, the person is not covered. Diagnosis does not in itself bring someone within the definition. If the condition is progressive, then the rule about progressive conditions applies.

Are any conditions specifically excluded from the coverage of the Act?

17 Yes. Certain conditions are to be regarded as not amounting to impairments for the purposes of the Act. These are:

- addiction to or dependency on alcohol, nicotine, or any other substance (other than as a result of the substance being medically prescribed);
- seasonal allergic rhinitis (eg hayfever), except where it aggravates the effect of another impairment;
- tendency to set fires;
- tendency to steal;
- tendency to physical or sexual abuse of other persons;

- exhibitionism;
- voyeurism.

Also, disfigurements which consist of a tattoo (which has not been removed), non-medical body piercing, or something attached through such piercing, are to be treated as not having a substantial adverse effect on the person's ability to carry out normal day-to-day activities[1].

1 Definition Regulations (see paragraph 1.6).

ANNEX 2 HOW TO GET FURTHER INFORMATION, HELP AND ADVICE

1 A range of leaflets about various aspects of the Act is available. To obtain copies, call 0345 622 633 (local rate), or textphone 0345 622 644. Copies of the leaflets are also available in braille and audio cassette.

2 Statutory Guidance on the definition of disability is produced separately. This can be obtained from HMSO bookshops . . .[1]. This Guidance should prove helpful where it is not clear whether or not a person has or has had a disability.

1 The Guidance is set out at para **[1351]**.

3 There is a wide range of practical help and advice available to assist employers in the recruitment and employment of people, including disabled people, for example from Jobcentres, Careers Service offices, Training and Enterprise Councils (in England and Wales) and Local Enterprise Companies (in Scotland). Addresses and telephone numbers are available in local telephone directories.

4 Where necessary, specialist help and advice for disabled people and for employers who might, or do, employ disabled people is available from the Employment Service through its local Placing, Assessment and Counselling Teams (PACTs). PACTs can help with issues related to employing disabled people, but cannot advise on an employer's specific legal obligations.

5 PACTs may also be able to provide help with special aids, equipment and other measures to overcome the effects of disability in the working environment.

6 The addresses and telephone numbers of PACTs are listed in local telephone directories under 'Employment Service', or can be obtained from the nearest Jobcentre.

7 Many specialist organisations for disabled people also offer a range of employment help and advice. The Employment Service publish a booklet called *Sources of Information and Advice (Ref PGP6)* which lists many of the specialist organisations offering help to employers on employment and disability issues. The booklet can be obtained from PACTs.

8 The Advisory, Conciliation and Arbitration Service (ACAS) can help employers and individuals with factual information on the legislation and assistance related to its effects on industrial relations practices and procedures. The address and telephone numbers of ACAS offices are listed in local telephone directories under 'ACAS'.

9 Employers working in historic buildings, or other heritage properties, may also wish to obtain a copy of *Easy Access to Historic Properties* from English Heritage at 23 Savile Row, London W1X 1AB. Telephone 0171 973 3434.

10 Disability can take a very large number of forms and the action an employer may be required to take will depend to a very large extent on the particular circumstances of the case. Any advice and information employers receive should be considered in that light. In some circumstances employers may wish to consider whether they should seek legal advice.

ANNEX 3 COMPLAINTS UNDER THE EMPLOYMENT PROVISIONS

What does the Act say about making complaints?

1 The Act says that a person who believes that an employer has unlawfully discriminated or failed to make a reasonable adjustment, or that a person has aided an employer to do such an act, may present a complaint to an industrial tribunal (s 8(1)).

What does the Act say about conciliation?

2 When a formal complaint has been made to an industrial tribunal the Act places a duty on the Advice, Conciliation and Arbitration Service's (ACAS) conciliation officers to try to promote settlement of the dispute without a tribunal hearing (Sch 3 para 1). ACAS can also assist in this way without a formal application to a tribunal being made.

What does the Act say about obtaining a remedy for unlawful discrimination?

3 The Act says that a disabled person who believes someone has unlawfully discriminated against him or failed to make a reasonable adjustment, in breach of the employment provisions of the Act or Regulations, may present a complaint to an industrial tribunal (s 8(1)).

4 If the tribunal upholds the complaint it may:

- declare the rights of the disabled person (the complainant), and the other person (the respondent) in relation to the complaint;
- order the other person to pay the complainant compensation; and
- recommend that, within a specified time, the other person take reasonable action to prevent or reduce the adverse effect in question (s 8(2)).

5 The Act allows compensation for injury to feelings to be awarded whether or not other compensation is awarded (s 8(4)).

6 The Act says that if a respondent fails, without reasonable justification, to comply with an industrial tribunal's recommendation, the tribunal may:

- increase the amount of compensation to be paid; or
- order the respondent to pay compensation if it did not make such an order earlier (s 8(5)).

Who can be taken to an industrial tribunal?

7 The tribunal complaints procedure applies to anyone who, it is claimed, has discriminated in the employment field—employers (and their employees and agents for whose acts they are responsible), trade organisations, people who hire contract workers and people who aid any of these to discriminate.

Complaints involving landlords

8 If a reasonable adjustment requiring the consent of the employer's landlord (or a superior landlord) is not made, for whatever reason, the disabled person may bring a complaint against the employer in an industrial tribunal. Either the disabled person or the employer may ask the tribunal to make the landlord a party to the proceedings. If the industrial tribunal finds that the landlord acted unreasonably in withholding consent, or gave consent but attached an unreasonable condition, it can make any appropriate declaration, order that the alteration may be made, or award compensation against the landlord (s 27 and Sch 4 para 2).

Complaining about pension schemes

9 A disabled person who considers that the trustees or managers of a pension scheme have discriminated against him, may complain through the pensions dispute resolution mechanism. Information about the scheme should give details about this. If necessary, a complaint may be made to the Pensions Ombudsman.

10 From April 1997, all occupational pension schemes will be required to set up and operate procedures for resolving disputes between individual pension scheme members and the trustees or managers.

11 The Occupational Pensions Advisory Service (OPAS) can provide an advice and conciliation service for members of the public who have problems with their occupational pension. OPAS can be contacted at 11 Belgrave Road, London SW1U 1RB. Tel: 0171 233 8080.

12 A disabled person who considers that an employer has discriminated against him in providing access to a pension scheme can complain to an industrial tribunal following the same process for other complaints against employers.

What is the 'questionnaire procedure'?

13 The Act provides for a procedure (the questionnaire procedure) to assist a person who believes that discrimination has occurred, to decide whether or not to start proceedings and, if the person does, to formulate and present a case in the most effective manner (s 56). Questionnaire forms will be obtainable from Jobcentres.

Can compromise agreements be an alternative to making tribunal complaints?

14 The Act says that, in general, the terms of an agreement (such as a contract of employment) cannot prevent a disabled person from complaining to an industrial tribunal, or force a complaint to be stopped (s 9). However, the Act also says that in some circumstances a disabled person can make an agreement not to make a complaint or to stop one (s 9).

15 These circumstances are if:

- an ACAS conciliation officer has acted under the Act on the matter; *or* the following conditions apply:
- the disabled person must have received independent legal advice from a qualified lawyer about the terms and effects of the agreement, particularly its effect on his ability to complain to a tribunal;
- the adviser must have an insurance policy covering any loss arising from the advice; and
- the agreement must be in writing, relate to the complaint, identify the adviser and say that these conditions are satisfied.

16 It may be in the interests of some disabled people to make such 'compromise' agreements instead of pursuing complaints to industrial tribunal hearings, but care should be taken to ensure that the above conditions are met.

How is a complaint made to an industrial tribunal?

17 Complaints to an industrial tribunal can be made on an application form (IT1). Forms are obtainable from Jobcentres. Completed applications should be returned to the Industrial Tribunals Central Office. The address is on the form.

18 Applications to an industrial tribunal must be made within three months of the time when the incident being complained of occurred. The time limit will not normally be extended to

allow for the time it might take to try to settle the dispute within the organisation eg by way of internal grievance procedures (see paragraphs 8.1–8.3). A tribunal may, however, consider a complaint which is out of time, if it considers, in all the circumstances of the case, that it is just and equitable to do so (Sch 3 para 3).

What does the Act say about reporting restrictions?

19 The Act empowers a tribunal to make 'restricted reporting orders' if it considers that evidence of a personal nature is likely to be heard by the tribunal. Such orders prohibit the publication, for example in a newspaper, of any matter likely to lead members of the public to identify the complainant or any other person mentioned in the order, until the tribunal's decision is promulgated.

Appendix 6

GUIDANCE ON MATTERS TO BE TAKEN INTO ACCOUNT IN DETERMINING QUESTIONS RELATING TO THE DEFINITION OF DISABILITY

Editorial note: This Guidance was issued by the Department for Education and Employment under the Disability Discrimination Act 1995. Its legal status is explained in the preamble. It came into force on 31 July 1996.

STATUS AND PURPOSE OF THE GUIDANCE

This guidance is issued by the Secretary of State under section 3 of the Disability Discrimination Act 1995. It concerns the definition of disability in the Act. Section 3 of the Act enables the Secretary of State to issue guidance about matters to be taken into account in determining whether an impairment has a substantial adverse effect on a person's ability to carry out normal day-to-day activities and/or whether an impairment has a long-term effect. The guidance may give examples.

This guidance does not impose any legal obligations in itself, nor is it an authoritative statement of the law. However, section 3(3) of the Act requires that an industrial tribunal or a court, which is determining for any purpose of the Act whether a person's impairment has a substantial and long-term adverse effect on his or her ability to carry out normal day-to-day activities, must take into account any of this guidance which appears to it to be relevant.

PART I INTRODUCTION

Using the guidance

1 Although this guidance is primarily designed for courts and tribunals, it is likely to be of value to a range of people and organisations. In the vast majority of cases there is unlikely to be any doubt whether or not a person has or has had a disability, but this guidance should prove helpful in cases where it is not clear.

2 The definition of disability has a number of elements. The guidance covers each of these elements in turn. Each section contains an explanation of the relevant provisions of the Act which supplement the basic definition; guidance and examples are provided where relevant. Those using this guidance for the first time may wish to read it all, as each part of the guidance builds upon the part(s) preceding it.

3 Part II of this guidance relates to matters to be taken into account when considering whether an effect is substantial and/or long term. Most of the examples are to be found here, and particularly in Section C. Because the purpose of this guidance is to help in the cases where there is doubt, examples of cases where there will not be any doubt are not included.

4 Throughout the guidance descriptions of the provisions in the legislation are immediately preceded by bold italic text. They are immediately followed by a reference to the relevant provision of the Act or Regulations. References to sections of the Act are marked 's'; references to schedules are marked 'Sch'; and references to paragraphs in schedules are marked 'para'. References in footnotes to 'Definition Regulations' mean The Disability Discrimination (Meaning of Disability) Regulations 1996.

Main elements of the definition of disability

5 The Act defines 'disabled person' as a person with 'a physical or mental impairment which has a substantial and long-term adverse effect on his ability to carry out normal day-to-day activities'(s 1).

6 This means that:

- the person must have an impairment, that is either physical or mental (see paragraphs 10–15 below);
- the impairment must have adverse effects which are substantial (see Section A);
- the substantial effects must be long-term (see Section B); and
- the long-term substantial effects must be adverse effects on *normal day-to-day activities* (see Section C).

This definition is subject to the provisions in Schedule 1 (Sch 1).

Inclusion of people who have had a disability in the past

7 The Act says that Part I of the Act (definition), Part II (employment) and Part III (goods, facilities, services and premises) also apply in relation to a person who has had a disability as defined in paragraphs 5 and 6 above. For this purpose, those Parts of the Act are subject to the provisions in Schedule 2 to the Act (s 2, Sch 2).

Exclusions from the definition

8 Certain conditions are not to be regarded as impairments for the purposes of the Act. These are:

- addiction to or dependency on alcohol, nicotine, or any other substance (other than in consequence of the substance being medically prescribed);
- the condition known as seasonal allergic rhinitis (eg hayfever), except where it aggravates the effect of another condition;
- tendency to set fires;
- tendency to steal;
- tendency to physical or sexual abuse of other persons;
- exhibitionism;
- voyeurism.

Also, disfigurements which consist of a tattoo (which has not been removed), non-medical body piercing, or something attached through such piercing, are to be treated as not having a substantial adverse effect on the person's ability to carry-out normal day-to-day activities[1].

1 Definition Regulations.

Registered disabled people

9 The introduction of the employment provisions in the Act coincides with the abolition of the Quota scheme which operated under the Disabled Persons (Employment) Act 1944. The Disability Discrimination Act says that anyone who was registered as a disabled person under the Disabled Persons (Employment) Act 1944 and whose name appeared on the register both on 12 January 1995 and on 2 December 1996 (the date the employment provisions come into force) is to be treated as having a disability for the purposes of the Disability Discrimination

Act during the period of three years starting on 2 December 1996. This applies regardless of whether the person otherwise meets the definition of 'disabled person' during that period. Those who are treated by this provision as being disabled for the three-year period are also to be treated after this period has ended as having had a disability in the past (Sch 1 para 7).

Impairment

10 The definition requires that the effects which a person may experience arise from a physical or mental impairment. In many cases there will be no dispute whether a person has an impairment. Any disagreement is more likely to be about whether the effects of the impairment are sufficient to fall within the definition. Even so, it may sometimes be necessary to decide whether a person has an impairment so as to be able to deal with the issues about its effects.

11 It is not necessary to consider how an impairment was caused, even if the cause is a consequence of a condition which is excluded. For example, liver disease as a result of alcohol dependency would count as an impairment.

12 Physical or mental impairment includes sensory impairments, such as those affecting sight or hearing.

13 Mental impairment includes a wide range of impairments relating to mental functioning, including what are often known as learning disabilities (formerly known as 'mental handicap'). However, the Act states that it does not include any impairment resulting from or consisting of a mental illness unless that illness is a clinically well-recognised illness (Sch 1, para 1).

14 A clinically well-recognised illness is a mental illness which is recognised by a respected body of medical opinion. It is very likely that this would include those specifically mentioned in publications such as the World Health Organisation's International Classification of Diseases.

15 The Act states that mental impairment does not have the special meaning used in the Mental Health Act 1983 or the Mental Health (Scotland) Act 1984, although this does not preclude a mental impairment within the meaning of that legislation from coming within the definition in the Disability Discrimination Act (s 68).

PART II GUIDANCE ON MATTERS TO BE TAKEN INTO ACCOUNT IN DETERMINING QUESTIONS RELATING TO THE DEFINITION OF DISABILITY

A Substantial

Meaning of 'substantial' adverse effect

A1 The requirement that an adverse effect be substantial reflects the general understanding of 'disability' as a limitation going beyond the normal differences in ability which may exist among people. A 'substantial' effect is more than would be produced by the sort of physical or mental conditions experienced by many people which have only minor effects. A 'substantial' effect is one which is more than 'minor' or 'trivial'.

The time taken to carry out an activity

A2 The time taken by a person with an impairment to carry out a normal day-to-day activity should be considered when assessing whether the effect of that impairment is substantial. It should be compared with the time that might be expected if the person did not have the impairment.

The way in which an activity is carried out

A3 Another factor to be considered when assessing whether the effect of an impairment is substantial is the way in which a person with that impairment carries out a normal day-to-day activity. The comparison should be with the way the person might be expected to carry out the activity if he or she did not have the impairment.

Cumulative effects of an impairment

A4 The Act provides that an impairment is to be taken to affect the ability of a person to carry out normal day-to-day activities only if it affects that person in one (or more) of the respects listed in paragraph C4 (Sch 1 para 4). An impairment might not have a substantial adverse effect on a person in any one of these respects, but its effects in more than one of these respects taken together could result in a substantial adverse effect on the person's ability to carry out normal day-to-day activities.

A5 For example, although the great majority of people with cerebral palsy will experience a number of substantial effects, someone with mild cerebral palsy may experience minor effects in a number of the respects listed in paragraph C4 which together could create substantial adverse effects on a range of normal day-to-day activities: fatigue may hinder walking, visual perception may be poor, co-ordination and balance may cause some difficulties. Similarly, a person whose impairment causes breathing difficulties may experience minor effects in a number of respects but which overall have a substantial adverse effect on their ability to carry out normal day-to-day activities. For some people, mental illness may have a clear effect in one of the respects in C4. However, for others, depending on the extent of the condition, there may be effects in a number of different respects which, taken together, substantially adversely affect their ability to carry out normal day-to-day activities.

A6 A person may have more than one impairment, any one of which alone would not have a substantial effect. In such a case, account should be taken of whether the impairments together have a substantial effect overall on the person's ability to carry out normal day-to-day activities. For example a minor impairment which affects physical co-ordination and an irreversible but minor injury to a leg which affects mobility, taken together, might have a substantial effect on the person's ability to carry out certain normal day-to-day activities.

Effects of behaviour

A7 Account should be taken of how far a person can reasonably be expected to modify behaviour to prevent or reduce the effects of an impairment on normal day-to-day activities. If a person can behave in such a way that the impairment ceases to have a substantial adverse effect on his or her ability to carry out normal day-to-day activities the person would no longer meet the definition of disability.

A8 In some cases people have such 'coping' strategies which cease to work in certain circumstances (for example, where someone who stutters or has dyslexia is placed under stress). If it is possible that a person's ability to manage the effects of an impairment will break down so that effects will sometimes still occur, this possibility must be taken into account when assessing the effects of the impairment.

A9 If a disabled person is advised by a medical practitioner to behave in a certain way in order to reduce the impact of the disability, that might count as treatment to be disregarded (see paragraph A11 below).

Effects of environment

A10 Whether adverse effects are substantial may depend on environmental conditions which may vary; for example, the temperature, humidity, the time of day or night, how tired the person is or how much stress he or she is under may have an impact on the effects. When assessing whether adverse effects are substantial, the extent to which such environmental factors are likely to have an impact should also therefore be considered.

Effects of treatment

A11 The Act provides that where an impairment is being treated or corrected the impairment is to be treated as having the effect it would have without the measures in question (Sch 1 para 6(1)). The Act states that the treatment or correction measures to be disregarded for these purposes include medical treatment and the use of a prosthesis or other aid (Sch 1 para 6(2)).

A12 This applies even if the measures result in the effects being completely under control or not at all apparent.

A13 For example, if a person with a hearing impairment wears a hearing aid the question whether his or her impairment has a substantial adverse effect is to be decided by reference to what the hearing level would be without the hearing aid. And in the case of someone with diabetes, whether or not the effect is substantial should be decided by reference to what the condition would be if he or she was not taking medication.

A14 However, the Act states that this provision does not apply to sight impairments to the extent that they are capable of correction by spectacles or contact lenses. In other words the only effects on ability to carry out normal day-to-day activities to be considered are those which remain when spectacles or contact lenses are used (or would remain if they were used). This does not include the use of devices to correct sight which are not spectacles or contact lenses (Sch 1 para 6(3)).

Progressive conditions

A15 A progressive condition is one which is likely to change and develop over time. The Act gives the following examples of progressive conditions: cancer, multiple sclerosis, muscular dystrophy, HIV infection. The Act provides for a person with such a condition to be regarded as having an impairment which has a substantial adverse effect on his or her ability to carry out normal day-to-day activities before it actually does so. Where a person has a progressive condition, he or she will be treated as having an impairment which has a substantial adverse effect from the moment any impairment resulting from that condition first has some effect on ability to carry out normal day-to-day activities. The effect need not be continuous and need not be substantial. For this rule to operate medical diagnosis of the condition is not by itself enough (Sch 1 para 8).

Severe disfigurements

A16 The Act provides that where an impairment consists of a severe disfigurement, it is to be treated as having a substantial adverse effect on the person's ability to carry out normal day-to-day activities. There is no need to demonstrate such an effect (Sch 1 para 3). Regulations provide that a disfigurement which consists of a tattoo (which has not been removed) is not to be considered as a severe disfigurement. Also excluded is a piercing of a body for decorative purposes including anything attached through the piercing[1].

1 Definition Regulations.

A17 Examples of disfigurements include scars, birthmarks, limb or postural deformation or diseases of the skin. Assessing severity will be mainly a matter of the degree of the disfigurement. However, it may be necessary to take account of where the feature in question is (eg on the back as opposed to the face).

B Long term

Meaning of long-term effects

B1 The Act states that, for the purpose of deciding whether a person is disabled, a long-term effect of an impairment is one:

- which has lasted at least twelve months; or
- where the total period for which it lasts, from the time of the first onset, is likely to be at least twelve months; or
- which is likely to last for the rest of the life of the person affected (Sch 1 para 2).

For the purpose of deciding whether a person has had a disability in the past, a long-term effect of an impairment is one which lasted at least 12 months (Sch 2 para 5).

B2 It is not necessary for the effect to be the same throughout the relevant period. It may change, as where activities which are initially very difficult become possible to a much greater extent. The main adverse effect might even disappear—or it might disappear temporarily—while one or other effects on ability to carry out normal day-to-day activities continue or develop. Provided the impairment continues to have, or is likely to have, such an effect throughout the period, there is a long-term effect.

Recurring effects

B3 The Act states that if an impairment has had a substantial adverse effect on a person's ability to carry out normal day-to-day activities but that effect ceases, the substantial effect is treated as continuing if it is likely to recur; that is, it is more likely than not that the effect will recur.(In deciding whether a person has had a disability in the past, the question is whether a substantial adverse effect has in fact recurred.) Conditions which recur only sporadically or for short periods (eg epilepsy) can still qualify.(Sch 1 para 2(2), Sch 2 para 5). Regulations specifically exclude seasonal allergic rhinitis (eg hayfever) from this category, except where it aggravates the effects of an existing condition[1].

1 Definition Regulations.

B4 For example, a person with rheumatoid arthritis may experience effects from the first occurrence for a few weeks and then have a period of remission. But, if the effects are likely to recur, they are to be treated as if they were continuing. If the effects are likely to recur beyond twelve months after the first occurrence, they are to be treated as long-term.

B5 Likelihood of recurrence should be considered taking all the circumstances of the case into account. This should include what the person could reasonably be expected to do to prevent the recurrence; for example, the person might reasonably be expected to take action which prevents the impairment from having such effects (eg avoiding substances to which he or she is allergic). This may be unreasonably difficult with some substances. In addition, it is possible that the way in which a person can control or cope with the effects of a condition may not always be successful because, for example, a routine is not followed or the person is in an unfamiliar environment. If there is an increased likelihood that the control will break down, it will be more likely that there will be a recurrence. That possibility should be taken into account when assessing the likelihood of a recurrence.

Effects of treatment

B6 If medical or other treatment is likely to cure an impairment, so that recurrence of its effects would then be unlikely even if there were no further treatment, this should be taken into consideration when looking at the likelihood of recurrence of those effects. However, as Section A describes, if the treatment simply delays or prevents a recurrence, and a recurrence would be likely if the treatment stopped, then the treatment is to be ignored and the effect is to be regarded as likely to recur.

Meaning of 'likely'

B7 It is *likely* that an event will happen if it is more probable than not that it will happen.

B8 In assessing the likelihood of an effect lasting for any period, account should be taken of the total period for which the effect exists. This includes any time before the point when the discriminatory behaviour occurred as well as the time afterwards. Account should also be taken of both the typical length of such an effect on an individual, and any relevant factors specific to this individual (for example, general state of health, age).

Assessing whether a past disability was long-term

B9 The Act provides that a person who has had a disability within the definition is protected from discrimination even if he or she has since recovered or the effects have become less than substantial. In deciding whether a past condition was a disability, its effects count as long-term if they lasted twelve months or more after the first occurrence, or if a recurrence happened or continued until more than twelve months after the first occurrence (s 2, Sch 2 para 5).

C Normal day-to-day activities

Meaning of 'normal day-to-day activities'

C1 The Act states that an impairment must have a long-term substantial adverse effect on normal day-to-day activities (s 1).

C2 The term 'normal day-to-day activities' is not intended to include activities which are normal only for a particular person or group of people. Therefore in deciding whether an activity is a 'normal day-to-day activity' account should be taken of how far it is normal for most people and carried out by most people on a daily or frequent and fairly regular basis.

C3 The term 'normal day-to-day activities' does not, for example, include work of any particular form, because no particular form of work is 'normal' for most people. In any individual case, the activities carried out might be highly specialised. The same is true of playing a particular game, taking part in a particular hobby, playing a musical instrument, playing sport, or performing a highly skilled task. Impairments which affect only such an activity and have no effect on 'normal day-to-day activities' are not covered. The examples included in this section give an indication of what are to be taken as normal day-to-day activities.

C4 The Act states that an impairment is only to be treated as affecting the person's ability to carry out *normal day-to-day activities* if it affects one of the following:

- mobility;
- manual dexterity;
- physical co-ordination;
- continence;
- ability to lift, carry or otherwise move everyday objects;
- speech, hearing or eyesight;
- memory or ability to concentrate, learn or understand; or
- perception of the risk of physical danger (Sch 1 para 4).

C5 In many cases an impairment will adversely affect the person's ability to carry out a range of normal day-to-day activities and it will be obvious that the overall adverse effect is substantial or the effect on at least one normal day-to-day activity is substantial. In such a case it is unnecessary to consider precisely how the person is affected in each of the respects listed in paragraph C4. For example, a person with a clinically well-recognised mental illness may experience an adverse effect on concentration which prevents the person from remembering why he or she is going somewhere; the person would not also have to demonstrate that there was an effect on, say, speech. A person with an impairment which has an adverse effect on sight might be unable to go shopping unassisted; he or she would not also have to demonstrate that there was an effect on, say mobility.

C6 Many impairments will, by their nature, adversely affect a person directly in one of the respects listed in C4. An impairment may also indirectly affect a person in one or more of these respects, and this should be taken into account when assessing whether the impairment falls within the definition. For example:

- medical advice: where a person has been professionally advised to change, limit or refrain from a normal day-to-day activity on account of an impairment or only do it in a certain way or under certain conditions;
- pain or fatigue: where an impairment causes pain or fatigue in performing normal day-to-day activities, so the person may have the capacity to do something but suffer pain in doing so; or the impairment might make the activity more than usually fatiguing so that the person might not be able to repeat the task over a sustained period of time.

C7 Where a person has a mental illness such as depression account should be taken of whether, although that person has the physical ability to perform a task, he or she is, in practice, unable to sustain an activity over a reasonable period.

C8 Effects of impairments may not be apparent in babies and young children because they are too young to have developed the ability to act in the respects listed in C4. Regulations provide that where an impairment to a child under six years old does not have an effect in any of the respects in C4, it is to be treated as having a substantial and long-term adverse effect on the ability of that child to carry out normal day-to-day activities where it would normally have a substantial and long-term adverse effect on the ability of a person aged six years or over to carry out normal day-to-day activities[1].

1 Definition Regulations.

C9 In deciding whether an effect on the ability to carry out a normal day-to-day activity is a substantial adverse effect, account should be taken of factors such as those mentioned under each heading below. The headings are exhaustive—the person must be affected in one of these respects. The lists of examples are not exhaustive; they are only meant to be illustrative. The assumption is made in each example that there is an adverse effect on the person's ability to carry out normal day-to-day activities. A person only counts as disabled if the substantial effect is adverse.

C10 The examples below of what it would, and what it would not, be reasonable to regard as substantial adverse effects are indicators and not tests. They do not mean that if a person can do an activity listed then he or she does not experience any substantial adverse effects; the person may be inhibited in other activities, and this instead may indicate a substantial effect.

C11 In reading examples of effects which it would not be reasonable to regard as substantial, the effect described should be thought of as if it were the only effect of the impairment. That is, if the effect listed in the example were the only effect it would not be reasonable to regard it as substantial in itself.

C12 Examples of effects which are obviously within the definition are not included below. So for example, inability to dress oneself, inability to stand up, severe dyslexia or a severe speech impairment would clearly be covered by the definition and are not included among the examples below. The purpose of these lists is to provide help in cases where there may be doubt as to whether the effects on normal day-to-day activities are substantial.

C13 The examples below describe the effect which would occur when the various factors described in Parts A and B above have been allowed for. This includes, for example the effects of a person making such modifications of behaviour as might reasonably be expected, or of disregarding the impact of medical or other treatment.

Mobility

C14 This covers moving or changing position in a wide sense. Account should be taken of the extent to which, because of either a physical or a mental condition, a person is inhibited in getting around unaided or using a normal means of transport, in leaving home with or without assistance, in walking a short distance, climbing stairs, travelling in a car or completing a journey on public transport, sitting, standing, bending, or reaching, or getting around in an unfamiliar place.

Examples

It *would be reasonable* to regard as having a substantial adverse effect:

- inability to travel a short journey as a passenger in a vehicle;
- inability to walk other than at a slow pace or with unsteady or jerky movements;
- difficulty in going up or down steps, stairs or gradients;
- inability to use one or more forms of public transport;
- inability to go out of doors unaccompanied.

It *would not be reasonable* to regard as having a substantial adverse effect:

- difficulty walking unaided a distance of about 1.5 kilometres or a mile without discomfort or having to stop—the distance in question would obviously vary according to the age of the person concerned and the type of terrain;
- inability to travel in a car for a journey lasting more than two hours without discomfort.

Manual dexterity

C15 This covers the ability to use hands and fingers with precision. Account should be taken of the extent to which a person can manipulate the fingers on each hand or co-ordinate the use of both hands together to do a task. This includes the ability to do things like pick up or manipulate small objects, operate a range of equipment manually, or communicate through writing or typing on standard machinery. Loss of function in the dominant hand would be expected to have a greater effect than equivalent loss in the non-dominant hand.

Examples

It *would be reasonable* to regard as having a substantial adverse effect:

- loss of function in one or both hands such that the person cannot use the hand or hands;
- inability to handle a knife and fork at the same time;
- ability to press the buttons on keyboards or keypads but only much more slowly than is normal for most people.

It *would not be reasonable* to regard as having a substantial adverse effect:

- inability to undertake activities requiring delicate hand movements, such as threading a small needle;
- inability to reach typing speeds standardised for secretarial work;
- inability to pick up a single small item, such as a pin.

Physical co-ordination

C16 This covers balanced and effective interaction of body movement, including hand and eye co-ordination. In the case of a child, it is necessary to take account of the level of achievement which would be normal for a person of the particular age. In any case, account should be taken of the ability to carry out 'composite' activities such as walking and using hands at the same time.

Examples

It *would be reasonable* to regard as having a substantial adverse effect:

- ability to pour liquid into another vessel only with unusual slowness or concentration;
- inability to place food into one's own mouth with fork/spoon without unusual concentration or assistance.

It *would not be reasonable* to regard as having a substantial adverse effect:

- mere clumsiness;
- inability to catch a tennis ball.

Continence

C17 This covers the ability to control urination and/or defecation. Account should be taken of the frequency and extent of the loss of control and the age of the individual.

Examples

It *would be reasonable* to regard as having a substantial adverse effect:

- even infrequent loss of control of the bowels;
- loss of control of the bladder while asleep at least once a month;
- frequent minor faecal incontinence or frequent minor leakage from the bladder.

It *would not be reasonable* to regard as having a substantial adverse effect:

- infrequent loss of control of the bladder while asleep;
- infrequent minor leakage from the bladder.

Ability to lift, carry or otherwise move everyday objects

C18 Account should be taken of a person's ability to repeat such functions or, for example, to bear weights over a reasonable period of time. Everyday objects might include such items as books, a kettle of water, bags of shopping, a briefcase, an overnight bag, a chair or other piece of light furniture.

Examples

It *would be reasonable* to regard as having a substantial adverse effect:

- inability to pick up objects of moderate weight with one hand;
- inability to carry a moderately loaded tray steadily.

It *would not be reasonable* to regard as having a substantial adverse effect:

- inability to carry heavy luggage without assistance;
- inability to move heavy objects without a mechanical aid.

Speech, hearing or eyesight

C19 This covers the ability to speak, hear or see and includes face-to-face, telephone and written communication.

(i) Speech

Account should be taken of how far a person is able to speak clearly at a normal pace and rhythm and to understand someone else speaking normally in the person's native language. It is necessary to consider any effects on speech patterns or which impede the acquisition or processing of one's native language, for example by someone who has had a stroke.

Examples

It *would be reasonable* to regard as having a substantial adverse effect:

- inability to give clear basic instructions orally to colleagues or providers of a service;
- inability to ask specific questions to clarify instructions;
- taking significantly longer than average to say things.

It *would not be reasonable* to regard as having a substantial adverse effect:

- inability to articulate fluently due to a minor stutter, lisp or speech impediment;
- inability to speak in front of an audience;
- having a strong regional or foreign accent;
- inability to converse in a language which is not the speaker's native language.

(ii) Hearing

If a person uses a hearing aid or similar device, what needs to be considered is the effect that would be experienced if the person were not using the hearing aid or device. Account should be taken of effects where the level of background noise is within such a range and of such a type that most people would be able to hear adequately.

Examples

It *would be reasonable* to regard as having a substantial adverse effect:

- inability to hold a conversation with someone talking in a normal voice in a moderately noisy environment;
- inability to hear and understand another person speaking clearly over the voice telephone.

It *would not be reasonable* to regard as having a substantial adverse effect:

- inability to hold a conversation in a very noisy place, such as a factory floor;
- inability to sing in tune.

(iii) Eyesight

If a person's sight is corrected by spectacles or contact lenses, or could be corrected by them, what needs to be considered is the effect remaining while they are wearing such spectacles or lenses, in light of a level and type normally acceptable to most people for normal day-to-day activities.

Examples

It *would be reasonable* to regard as having a substantial adverse effect:

- inability to see to pass the eyesight test for a standard driving test;
- inability to recognise by sight a known person across a moderately-sized room;
- total inability to distinguish colours;

- inability to read ordinary newsprint;
- inability to walk safely without bumping into things.

It *would not be reasonable* to regard as having a substantial adverse effect:

- inability to read very small or indistinct print without the aid of a magnifying glass;
- inability to distinguish a known person across a substantial distance (eg playing field);
- inability to distinguish between red and green.

Memory or ability to concentrate, learn or understand

C20 Account should be taken of the person's ability to remember, organise his or her thoughts, plan a course of action and carry it out, take in new knowledge, or understand spoken or written instructions. This includes considering whether the person learns to do things significantly more slowly than is normal. Account should be taken of whether the person has persistent and significant difficulty in reading text in standard English or straightforward numbers.

Examples

It *would be reasonable* to regard as having a substantial adverse effect:

- intermittent loss of consciousness and associated confused behaviour;
- persistent inability to remember the names of familiar people such as family or friends;
- inability to adapt after a reasonable period to minor change in work routine;
- inability to write a cheque without assistance;
- considerable difficulty in following a short sequence such as a simple recipe or a brief list of domestic tasks.

It *would not be reasonable* to regard as having a substantial adverse effect:

- occasionally forgetting the name of a familiar person, such as a colleague;
- inability to concentrate on a task requiring application over several hours;
- inability to fill in a long, detailed, technical document without assistance;
- inability to read at faster than normal speed;
- minor problems with writing or spelling.

Perception of the risk of physical danger

C21 This includes both the underestimation and overestimation of physical danger, including danger to well-being. Account should be taken, for example, of whether the person is inclined to neglect basic functions such as eating, drinking, sleeping, keeping warm or personal hygiene; reckless behaviour which puts the person or others at risk; or excessive avoidance behaviour without a good cause.

Examples

It *would be reasonable* to regard as having a substantial adverse effect:

- inability to operate safely properly-maintained equipment;
- persistent inability to cross a road safely;
- inability to nourish oneself (assuming nourishment is available);

- inability to tell by touch that an object is very hot or cold.

It *would not be reasonable* to regard as having a substantial adverse effect:

- fear of significant heights;
- underestimating the risk associated with dangerous hobbies, such as mountain climbing;
- underestimating risks—other than obvious ones—in unfamiliar workplaces.

Index

Index

Index

Index

Index

Index